Lecture Notes in Computer Science 9721

Commenced Publication in 1973
Founding and Former Series Editors:
Gerhard Goos, Juris Hartmanis, and Jan van Leeuwen

Editorial Board

David Hutchison
  Lancaster University, Lancaster, UK
Takeo Kanade
  Carnegie Mellon University, Pittsburgh, PA, USA
Josef Kittler
  University of Surrey, Guildford, UK
Jon M. Kleinberg
  Cornell University, Ithaca, NY, USA
Friedemann Mattern
  ETH Zurich, Zürich, Switzerland
John C. Mitchell
  Stanford University, Stanford, CA, USA
Moni Naor
  Weizmann Institute of Science, Rehovot, Israel
C. Pandu Rangan
  Indian Institute of Technology, Madras, India
Bernhard Steffen
  TU Dortmund University, Dortmund, Germany
Demetri Terzopoulos
  University of California, Los Angeles, CA, USA
Doug Tygar
  University of California, Berkeley, CA, USA
Gerhard Weikum
  Max Planck Institute for Informatics, Saarbrücken, Germany

More information about this series at http://www.springer.com/series/7410

Juan Caballero · Urko Zurutuza
Ricardo J. Rodríguez (Eds.)

Detection of Intrusions and Malware, and Vulnerability Assessment

13th International Conference, DIMVA 2016
San Sebastián, Spain, July 7–8, 2016
Proceedings

 Springer

Editors
Juan Caballero
IMDEA Software Institute
Pozuelo de Alarcón, Madrid
Spain

Ricardo J. Rodríguez
Universidad de Zaragoza
Zaragoza
Spain

Urko Zurutuza
Mondragon University
Arrasate, Guipúzcoa
Spain

ISSN 0302-9743 ISSN 1611-3349 (electronic)
Lecture Notes in Computer Science
ISBN 978-3-319-40666-4 ISBN 978-3-319-40667-1 (eBook)
DOI 10.1007/978-3-319-40667-1

Library of Congress Control Number: 2016941320

LNCS Sublibrary: SL4 – Security and Cryptology

Printed on acid-free paper

This Springer imprint is published by Springer Nature
The registered company is Springer International Publishing AG Switzerland

Preface

It is our pleasure to welcome you to the proceedings of the 13th International Conference on Detection of Intrusions and Malware and Vulnerability Assessment (DIMVA 2016), which took place in Donostia-San Sebastián, Spain, during July 7–8, 2016. DIMVA is an international conference advancing the state of the art in intrusion detection, malware analysis, and vulnerability assessment. It brings together members of academia, industry, and governmental institutions to discuss novel ideas as well as mature research results.

This year, DIMVA received 66 submissions, which were carefully reviewed by the Program Committee. Each submission had at least three independent reviews. In the end, 21 papers were accepted to be presented at the conference and included in this proceedings. Of these, 19 are full papers presenting mature research results and two are extended abstracts presenting new ideas in the early stages of research. Overall, the acceptance rate was 31.8 %. The accepted papers present novel ideas, techniques, and applications in important areas of computer security including vulnerability detection, attack prevention, Web security, malware detection and classification, authentication, data leakage prevention, and countering evasive techniques such as obfuscation. Beyond the research papers, the program also included insightful keynote talks by Prof. Christopher Kruegel (University of California at Santa Barbara) and by David Barroso (CounterCraft).

Many individuals and organizations contributed to the success of DIMVA 2016. First of all, we would like to express our appreciation to the Program Committee members and external reviewers for the time spent reviewing, discussing papers, and attending the Program Committee meeting in Madrid. We are also deeply grateful to all members of the Organizing Committee for their tremendous work and for excelling in their respective tasks. The conference was also made possible thanks to the support of our sponsors Huawei and Inycom, and thanks to the collaboration of the Basque Business Development Agency (SPRI) and the Department of Education, Linguistic Policy and Culture of the Basque Government. We also thank Springer for publishing these proceedings in their LNCS series, and the DIMVA Steering Committee for continuing to bring together the conference.

Finally, the success of DIMVA hinges on the authors who contribute their work and on the attendees who come to the conference. We would like to thank them and we look forward to thier next contribution to DIMVA.

July 2016

Juan Caballero
Urko Zurutuza
Ricardo J. Rodríguez

Organization

DIMVA was organized by the special interest group Security – Intrusion Detection and Response (SIDAR) of the German Informatics Society (GI).

Organizing Committee

General Chair

Urko Zurutuza   Mondragon University, Spain

Program Chair

Juan Caballero   IMDEA Software Institute, Spain

Financial Chair

Iñaki Hurtado   Mondragon University, Spain

Publication Chair

Ricardo J. Rodríguez   University of Zaragoza, Spain

Steering Committee (Chairs)

Ulrich Flegel   Infineon Technologies, Germany
Michael Meier   University of Bonn, Germany

Steering Committee (Members)

Magnus Almgren   Chalmers University of Technology, Sweden
Herbert Bos   Vrije Universiteit Amsterdam, The Netherlands
Danilo M. Bruschi   Università degli Studi di Milano, Italy
Roland Bueschkes   RWE AG, Germany
Lorenzo Cavallaro   Royal Holloway, University of London, UK
Herve Debar   Telecom SudParis, France
Sven Dietrich   City University of New York, USA – John Jay College
                              of Criminal Justice, USA
Bernhard Haemmerli   Acris GmbH & HSLU Lucerne, Switzerland
Thorsten Holz   Ruhr-Universität Bochum, Germany
Marko Jahnke   Federal Office for Information Security, Germany
Klaus Julisch   Deloitte, Switzerland
Christian Kreibich   ICSI, USA
Christopher Kruegel   UC Santa Barbara, USA
Pavel Laskov   University of Tüebingen, Germany
Federico Maggi   Politecnico di Milano, Italy

Konrad Rieck   University of Göttingen, Germany
Robin Sommer   ICSI/LBNL, USA

Program Committee

Manos Antonakakis   Georgia Institute of Technology, USA
Marco Balduzzi   Trend Micro Research, USA
Leyla Bilge   Symantec Research Labs, France
Herbert Bos   Vrije Universiteit, The Netherlands
Levente Buttyan   Budapest University of Technology and Economics,
                             Hungary
Mauro Conti   University of Padua, Italy
Baris Coskun   Yahoo! Labs, USA
Lucas Davi   TU Darmstadt, Germany
Sven Dietrich   John Jay College of Criminal Justice, City University
                             of New York, USA
Brendan Dolan-Gavitt   New York University, USA
Zakir Durumeric   University of Michigan, USA
Nigel Edwards   Hewlett Packard Laboratories, UK
Manuel Egele   Boston University, USA
Ulrich Flegel   Infineon Technologies AG, Germany
Vincenzo Gulisano   Chalmers University of Technology, Sweden
Bernhard Haemmerli   Acris GmbH, Switzerland
Sotiris Ioannidis   FORTH, Greece
Somesh Jha   University of Wisconsin-Madison, USA
Tim Kornau   Google, Switzerland
Andrea Lanzi   University of Milan, Italy
Pavel Laskov   Huawei European Research Center, Germany
Corrado Leita   Lastline, UK
Zhiqiang Lin   University of Texas at Dallas, USA
Martina Lindorfer   SBA Research, Austria
Federico Maggi   Politecnico di Milano, Italy
Jean-Yves Marion   Lorraine University, France
Michael Meier   University of Bonn and Fraunhofer FKIE, Germany
Simin Nadjm-Tehrani   Linköping University, Sweden
Nick Nikiforakis   Stony Brook University, USA
Roberto Perdisci   University of Georgia and Georgia Tech, USA
Jason Polakis   Columbia University, USA
Konrad Rieck   University of Göttingen, Germany
Christian Rossow   Saarland University, Germany
Stelios   MIT, USA
  Sidiroglou-Douskos
Gianluca Stringhini   University College London, UK
Juan Tapiador   Carlos III University of Madrid, Spain
Yves Younan   Cisco Systems, USA
Stefano Zanero   Politecnico di Milano, Italy

Additional Reviewers

Daniel Arp	Lorenzo De Carli	Mizuhito Ogawa
Sebastien Bardin	Parvez Faruki	Raphael Otto
Guillaume Bonfante	Dario Fiore	Davide Quarta
Michele Carminati	Máté Horváth	Vaibhav Rastogi
Jean-Luc Danger	Kaitai Liang	Sanjay Rawat
Drew Davidson	Srdan Moraca	Valentin Tudor

Sponsoring Institutions (Gold)

Sponsoring Institutions (Silver)

Collaborators

Contents

Evasion

Web Security

Data Leaks

Authentication

Malware Classification

Attacks

Subverting Operating System Properties Through Evolutionary DKOM Attacks

Mariano Graziano[1,3]($\boxtimes$), Lorenzo Flore[2], Andrea Lanzi[2],
and Davide Balzarotti[1]

[1] Eurecom, Biot, France
magrazia@cisco.com
[2] Università degli Studi di Milano, Milan, Italy
[3] Cisco Systems, Inc., San Jose, CA, USA

Abstract. Modern rootkits have moved their focus on the exploitation of dynamic memory structures, which allows them to tamper with the behavior of the system without modifying or injecting any additional code.

In this paper we discuss a new class of Direct Kernel Object Manipulation (DKOM) attacks that we call *Evolutionary* DKOM (E-DKOM). The goal of this attack is to alter the way some data structures "evolve" over time. As case study, we designed and implemented an instance of *Evolutionary* DKOM attack that targets the OS scheduler for both userspace programs and kernel threads. Moreover, we discuss the implementation of a hypervisor-based data protection system that mimics the behavior of an OS component (in our case the scheduling system) and detect any unauthorized modification. We finally discuss the challenges related to the design of a general detection system for this class of attacks.

1 Introduction

Rootkits are a particular type of malicious software designed to maintain a hidden access to a compromised machine by targeting the running kernel. To mitigate this severe threat, several defense techniques for code protection and attestation have been proposed in the literature [27,37,39,46]. These mechanisms try to protect the applications and the kernel code against any illicit modification of its instructions. This also prevents hooking techniques that attempt to divert the control flow to a routine controlled by the attacker.

However, while the code of the kernel is easy to protect, its dynamic data structures often remain outside the boundaries of traditional defenses. Left unprotected, they quickly became one of the main targets of modern *rootkits*, that manipulates their values to tamper with the behavior of the system without the need to modify the existing code. Even though these attacks are simple to understand and relatively easy to perform, protecting the dynamic memory structures of an operating system is a very difficult task. For instance, the classic example of Direct Kernel Object Manipulation (or DKOM) attack consists of hiding a running process by simply removing its corresponding element from the

© Springer International Publishing Switzerland 2016
J. Caballero et al. (Eds.): DIMVA 2016, LNCS 9721, pp. 3–24, 2016.
DOI: 10.1007/978-3-319-40667-1_1

processes list (e.g., the EPROCESS structure in Microsoft Windows). Detecting DKOM attacks often rely on the assumption that even though some information can be modified, the original value can still be present in other OS context. For example, even if an element is deleted from the EPROCESS linked-list, in order to be executed the process still needs to be present in the scheduling queue. Consequently, a common technique to detect DKOM attacks consists in cross-checking different sources of information to verify if their values are consistent. For instance, this is the approach adopted by the psxview Volatility plugin [45] to detect hidden processes. Researchers also proposed more sophisticated monitoring techniques that maintain a reference model of the running system to compare with the actual data structures. For example, Rhee et al. [36] proposed to use an *allocation driven mapping* to identify dynamic kernel objects by intercepting their allocations/deallocation operations, and use this information to maintain a precise model of the running kernel. This approach also included a hidden kernel object detector that uses this un-tampered view of kernel memory to detect DKOM data hiding attacks.

Despite the recent efforts in detecting DKOM attacks, all the proposed techniques are based on the assumption that during an attack there is always something *anomalous* in the *state* of the kernel dynamic data structures, typically in the form of a missing or modified element. However, a closer look at DKOM techniques reveals that there are two different ways to manipulate data to influence the behavior of the system. More precisely, from an attacker point of view, we can identify a *discrete* attack that only tampers with a dynamic structure at an isolated point in time, and an *evolutionary* attack that works by continuously tampering with the internal state of the system. In the first case, the objective of the attack is reached by changing some information stored in a data structure, by adding or removing elements, or by changing the pointer relationship between data structures. As we described above, this may leave the system in an inconsistent state, which can often be detected. In the second case, presented in this paper, the goal of the attack is instead obtained by influencing the behavior of the system by *continuously* modifying its memory and thus by affecting the evolution of its dynamic data structures.

Due to the nature of this attack, it is possible that every single snapshot of the system is indistinguishable from a clean state. Therefore, the attack only manifests itself in an anomalous *evolution in time* of a given *property* of the operating system. While this may seem just a minor variation of the original DKOM technique, in this paper we show that it has very severe consequences from a detection point of view. In fact, the only way to detect an evolutionary attack is to implement a detector that can verify if a certain behavioral property of the kernel is satisfied over time. This requires a very complex tool that continuously monitor the system, and replicates (or emulates) part of its behavior inside the detector.

The goal of this paper is twofold. First, we present the design and implementation of an *Evolutionary* DKOM (E-DKOM) attack, and show that it cannot be detected by any of the existing techniques. As a case study, we describe a novel attack against the OS scheduling algorithm. This attack can be used to silently block the execution of any critical security application, both in user- and kernel-space. The second contribution of the paper is to discuss the possible countermeasures. It is important to note that our goal is to detect the tampering of the operating system, and not the code of the rootkit itself.

At the moment, the only generic defense solution would be to use a reference monitor to trace all memory operations and enforce that only the authorized code can modify a given critical structure. Unfortunately, this technique has two big limitations. First, it is likely to introduce a large computational overhead. Second, any memory access needs to be properly identified and attributed to the piece of code responsible for that operation. Unfortunately, a precise attribution in a compromised system is still an open problem – known as "confused deputy attack" [16].

As an alternative, we discuss a custom defense technique based on a monitor (implemented as a thin hypervisor) that can duplicate part of the behavior of the OS that needs to be protected (the scheduler's properties in our case), and guarantee that this behavior is respected by the running system. Unfortunately, this is not a general solution, as it would require a different monitor for every property that needs to be enforced.

The rest of the paper is organized as follows. In Sects. 2 and 3 we describe our attack and its own threat model, discuss its properties, and emphasize the differences with respect to traditional DKOM attacks. We then focus on a prac- tical example in Sect. 4, in which we present the details of an attack against the Linux operating system scheduler. Section 5 shows the results of our attack tests, and Sect. 6 introduces our prototype hypervisor-based defense mechanism. Finally, Sect. 7 discusses the generality of the attack, its limitations and future work, Sect. 8 describes related work and Sect. 9 concludes the paper.

2   Evolutionary DKOM Attacks

There is a subtle difference between a traditional DKOM attack and its evolu- tionary counterpart that we present in this paper: in the evolutionary attack, the goal of the attacker is to affect the **evolution** of a data structure in memory, and not just its values. For instance, the two classic DKOM examples of privilege escalation and process hiding require the attacker to directly modify a number of kernel data structures to achieve the *desired state* (respectively remove an element from a linked list, or modify the UID of a process). In the more sophis- ticated version of DKOM attack we present in this paper, the *"desired state"* is replaced by a *"desired property"*. More in detail, the attack we present in the next sections affects the normal evolution of the red-black tree containing vital information for the scheduling algorithm. On the other hand, the traditional DKOM attacks change individual fields in data structures of interest, like the `task_struct` to unlink a task. The latter operation is discrete and does not affect the evolution of the `task_struct` list in any way.

This difference has a number of important consequences. First of all, while a traditional DKOM can be performed in one single shot, an evolutionary attack needs to continuously modify the kernel memory to maintain the target condition. Moreover, when the attacker stops his manipulation, the system naturally resumes its original operation. This fundamental difference seems to be in favor of traditional DKOMs, since a single memory change should be harder to detect that a continuous polling process. However, in this paper we show that in practice the result is the opposite of what suggested by common sense. In fact, from a defense point of view, it is easier to detect an *altered state* than to detect an *altered property*. To detect the latter, a monitor needs to record the evolution of the affected data structures over time, and also needs to replicate the logic of the kernel property that it wants to enforce.

While it is possible to implement such a detector (as we discuss in Sect. 6 for our attack), this needs to be necessarily customized for each property. As a result, it is difficult to propose a general solution for evolutionary attacks.

3   Threat Model

In this paper we assume a powerful attacker who is able to execute malicious code both at the kernel and at the user level, and who can modify any critical kernel data structures. Kernel-level access can be achieved via kernel-level exploits or social engineering the user to install a malicious kernel module. The attacker can also use sophisticated ROP rootkit techniques [20,44] or other stealthy techniques [41,42] in order to overcome existing code protection mechanisms. The attacker has the ability to make its malicious code undetected to any current state of the art anti-malware software.

However, since our defense solution is based on a custom hypervisor, we include both the hypervisor and the security VM as part of the trusted computing base (TCB). To focus only on the detection of E-DKOM attacks without replicating previous works, we also assume that the core kernel code of the user VM is protected and cannot be subverted by any malicious code. This can be achieved by making the kernel's code pages read-only [18,38] or by using others code protection systems proposed in the past [10,27,39]. Existing protection techniques also ensure that the attacker cannot tamper or hook code of the OS, and cannot shutdown processes or kernel threads without the system notice [23,27].

To summarize, our threat model covers an attacker that can run arbitrary code in the OS kernel and tamper with dynamic data structures, but that cannot modify the existing code or attack the hypervisor.

4   Subverting the Scheduler

In this section we first introduce the Completely Fair Scheduler (CFS) algorithm adopted by Linux-based OS. We then describe the principles of our attack to subvert the scheduling algorithm and present two different scenarios where our attack can be applied.

4.1   Goal

The goal of the attacker is to silently and temporarily stop the execution of a process without leaving direct evidences. This means the target process is no more able to run on the CPU but it is still visible and listed as a normal running application.

In a post-exploitation phase, this feature is a really valuable asset. Miscreants may disable security monitors and detectors so that system administrators or final victims do not notice any suspicious activity. A perfect target in this scenario is either an antivirus software or a network/host intrusion detection system. The desired result is to reach this goal without raising any warning or visible alarms. This can be achieved in several ways in a modern operating system like Linux or Windows. The first idea that comes to mind is to kill the target application. However, this technique is easily detectable by the victim because the process (or processes) is no more listed in the list of the running applications. Several security applications have a watchdog specifically designed to detect these circumstances to restart the application. Another simple approach would be to suspend the process or turn it into a zombie. Unfortunately also this technique is not stealthy, and in a post-exploitation phase this cannot be tolerated. For example, it would be fairly easy to spot the anomaly by inspecting the output of a program like ps. Finally, another possible option could be to directly modify the code of the target application, for instance to inject an infinite loop or an attempt to acquire a lock on some unavailable resource. While this would be definitely more difficult to detect, security-critical applications often have kernel components to protect the integrity of their code.

Therefore, in order to reach our objective in a completely transparent way, a good target for the attacker would be to tamper with the scheduler implementation in the OS. This is a complex task and the implementation details may vary between different systems. For instance, a desktop machine has to be more reactive than a server. Indeed, it is clear the scheduling load may differ in a server spawning several tasks for all the incoming connections compared to a desktop machine used by an average secretary. All these differences affect the scheduler implementation. To perform the attack on the scheduler implementation the rootkit's author has to study in detail the inner mechanisms of the targeted component. We implemented this idea in a proof of concept attack against the current implementation of the Linux scheduler on a Debian "jessie" GNU/Linux distribution for both x86-32 and x86-64 systems. It is worth noting that our scheduler attack is able to stop the defensive mechanisms for an arbitrary amount of time. For example during an attack the intrusion detection system can be disabled, and then enabled again when the attack is terminated. We call such attack evolutionary transient attacks.

4.2   An Overview of the CFS Algorithm

As the name says, the main goal of the CFS algorithm used by the Linux kernel is to maintain a *fair execution* by balancing the processor time assigned to the different tasks of the system. The objective is to prevent one or more tasks from not receiving enough CPU time compared with the others. For this purpose, the CFS algorithm maintains the total amount of time assigned so far to a given task in a field called *the virtual runtime*. The smaller a task virtual runtime is in terms of execution, the higher the probability is to be the next being scheduled on the system. The CFS also includes the concept of *sleeper fairness*. This concept is used for the tasks that are not at the moment ready to run (e.g., those waiting for I/O) and it ensures that such tasks will eventually receive a comparable share of the processor when they are ready to execute. The CFS algorithm is implemented using a time-ordered red-black tree. A red-black tree is a tree with some interesting properties. First of all, it is self-balancing, which means that no path in the tree will ever be more than twice as long as the others. Second, any operation on the tree occurs in $O(logn)$ time – where n is the number of nodes in the tree.

4.3   CFS Internals

All tasks in Linux are represented by a memory structure called `task_struct` that contains all the task information. In particular, it includes information about the task's current state, the task stack, the process flags, the priority (both static and dynamic), and other additional fields defined by the Linux OS kernel in the `sched.h` file. It is important to note that since not all the tasks are runnable, the CFS scheduling fields are not included in the `task_struct`. Instead, the Linux OS defined a new memory structures called `sched_entity` to track all the scheduling information.

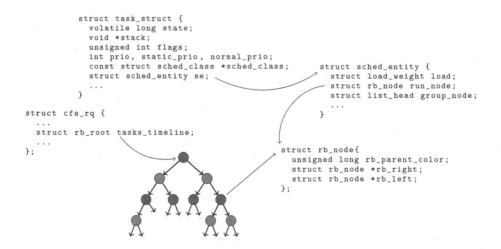

Fig. 1. CFS black tree structures

The relationships between the various memory structures and the scheduling algorithm are summarized in Fig. 1. At the root of the tree we have the `rb_root` element from the cfs_rq structure. Leaves in a red-black tree do not have any useful information; instead the internal nodes represent one or more tasks that can be executed. Each node in the red-black tree is represented by a rb_node. Such a node only contains the reference to the child and the color of the parent. The rb_node is defined into the sched_entity structure, which includes the rb_node reference, the load weight, and some data statistics. The most important field inside the sched_entity memory structures is the vruntime, which represents the amount of time the task has been running on the system. Such field is also used as the index for the red-black tree. The task_struct is at the top, and is responsible for describing the task and including the sched_entity structure.

The scheduling algorithm is quite simple and it is implemented inside the function schedule(). The first action of the function is to preempt the currently running task. Since for each task the CFS only knows the virtual running time, the algorithm does not have a real notion of time slices for preemption, and therefore the preemption time is variable. After the scheduler interrupts the current running task, the task is put back into the red-black tree by calling the put_prev_task function. After that the scheduling function invokes the pick_next_task function that is in charge of selecting the next task to execute. This function simply takes the left-most task from the red-black tree and returns the associated sched_entity. By using the sched_entity and invoking the task_of() function the system returns the reference to the relative task_struct. At the end of this procedure the scheduler passes the task to the processor to execute it.

4.4   Scheduler E-DKOM Attack

In this Section we describe how an attacker can target the OS scheduler to suspend the execution of one or more of the processes running in a Linux system. Such an attack can be used in order to stop security applications such as antivirus software or Network Intrusion Detection System. Consequently, by using this technique the attacker is able to elude the system protection mechanisms without tampering with any OS code or modifying the control-flow of the running system.

Attack Principles. From an architectural point of view, the attack requires a kernel module that executes code at regular time intervals (e.g., by registering a timer). The module walks the process list and identifies the process it wants to stop. It then collects the process descriptor and uses it to locate the corresponding node in the CFS *red-black* tree. Afterward, the attack alters the scheduling list by changing the *virtual runtime*'s value of the target process. In this way the attacker forces the scheduling algorithm to push the process at the end of the list and postpone its execution. By using this technique the attacker can stop any processes, thread, and kernel thread that are running on the system.

Implementation Details. Our prototype first initializes a global kernel timer registering a call-back function to be executed at regular intervals. Then, the malicious module spawns two CPU-bound kernel threads to populate the scheduling list in case the queue is empty. This can be useful in cases when most of the processes are waiting for I/O operations, and the target process is the only one that requires to be executed. It is important to note that the kernel threads represent a normal task for the scheduling system, consequently the scheduler puts them in the same scheduling queue with the others user space processes and threads. Two is the minimum number to assure at least one predecessor and one successor of the target process.

After these two initial operations, the attack algorithm identifies the reference of the target process into the CFS red-black tree and queue it at the end of the scheduling list. This can be done by walking the `task_struct` looking for the element representing the target process. From there, the code can extract the `sched_entity` struct and use the `struct_rb_node` field to identify the corresponding element in the CFS red-black tree. In Fig. 1 we show the link among the memory structures described so far. At this point the attack algorithm locates the rightmost element in the tree, which correspond to the last task that will be scheduled for execution. Afterwards the kernel module changes the *virtual runtime* of the target process to a value higher than the value of the rightmost element. After this change, the scheduling algorithm, following the CFS policies, will move the target process at the end of the scheduling list. This operation is repeated every time the global kernel timer expires.

5   Attack Evaluation

In order to evaluate the real impact of our attack, we used it to stop two common security mechanism: a popular IDS, and the Inotify notification mechanisms [28] that is used by many programs to identify any modification on the files that occurs in the system. For instance, Inotify is used by several security applications, including Tripwire [1,24] and by most of the antivirus systems.

Case Study I: Blocking an IDS. In this experiment, a possible attack scenario is represented by a Linux router machine used to protect an intranet network. The router machine is equipped with an IDS and a system that verifies the code integrity of the kernel and user-space applications [27]. By using such defensive mechanisms, the attacker cannot modify any code running on the router and she cannot shutdown any user-space applications without the system noticing it. For our test we set up the IDS with a simple signature to detect a remote buffer overflow attack by looking at the presence of the shellcode pattern in the network packets.

Our experiment is divided in two parts. We first launched a simple buffer overflow attack over the network protected by the IDS, and we verified that the alert was correctly raised.

In the second test, we simulated that an attacker was able to install our rootkit into the router, using the IDS application as a target. While the IDS application was stopped by our rootkit, we run the network attack and double-checked that no alerts were generated. Meanwhile, Linux was reporting the targeted process as a running process. It is important to note that the kernel uses a circular memory buffer to store the network packets copied from the network card into the OS system before delivering them to the right application. Therefore, before resuming the execution of the IDS the attacker needs to generate benign traffic to force the queue to rotate and overwrite the network packets related to the attack.

Case Study II: Blocking Inotify. *Inotify* is an inode monitoring system introduced in Linux 2.6.13. This API provides mechanisms to monitor filesystem events involving both files or entire directories. Most of the security applications, such as integrity checker (Tripwire) or antivirus software use such mechanism in order to detect any modification of the filesystem. For example, antivirus detectors re-scan any modified file in order to check whether a malicious infection occurred.

Inotify provides its own set of system calls: `inotify_init()` to create a new monitoring instance with its own file descriptor, `inotify_add_watch()` to add a file to the monitored group, and `inotify_rm_watch()` to remove the monitor. After the registration of the files and directories that the application wants to monitor, the code needs to invoke the `poll()` API to be notified when the registered events happen. It is important to note that the inotify events are reported through a user-space device created as a communication channel between the user-space application and the kernel. This device is associated to a kernel buffer used to collect and temporarily store the filesystem events. By using the `read()` function, the application can retrieve information about which event have occurred.

For our evaluation we created a user space application that monitors a chosen group of files on our system. The goal of the attack is twofold. First, the attacker should be able to modify a file without the inotify-based application noticing the change. Second, the attack needs also to guarantee that after the attack phase, the inotify events should resume and correctly reach the application as if nothing has happened.

To this end our evaluation is composed by three steps. In the first step we run the inotify-based application and use our rootkit to temporarily stop its execution. In the second step, the attacker modifies one of the monitored file, and then forces a number of events (at least 1024*16) on other files with the goal to saturate the kernel buffer associated to the device. This way the event associated to the target file is overwritten by the new benign modifications. Finally, the rootkit wakes up the inotify application, and we verified that it did not receive any event about the attacker modification.

This can be quite severe in a number of scenarios. For instance, the Android system uses a similar inotify mechanism that is mainly adopted to build security monitors and detectors [12]. Our attack can temporarily disable them without leaving any trace in the system.

Attack Discussion: One may argue that a malicious kernel module could be detected by a simple detector that is able to find out in memory a footprint of the malicious code or detect any suspicious activities by monitoring the frequency of the interrupt timer issued at the kernel level (e.g., timing traces). Even if those techniques could be effective against our attack, the kernel module can hide its own timing activities and code in several sophisticated ways.

First of all it can hide the presence of the code just diverting the control flow of a benign timer kernel module by using dynamic hooking that targets transient control data as described in [43] and then perform a ROP attack for changing the time scheduling activity. By using these attack techniques the detector cannot see any suspicious kernel modules among the list of the registered kernel modules timer and the malicious code is reduced to a few ROP gadgets resulting in minimal memory footprint. A more resilient approach is called Address Translation Redirection Attack (ATRA) and is presented in [21]. By using such a technique the attacker can relocate important kernel objects (e.g., malicious kernel module) and makes the entire system refer to the copy by attacking the page table data structures of the OS kernel. Finally, as shown in [25], our malicious kernel module could be completely implemented in GPU space. A GPU-assisted malware binary contains code destined to run on different processors. When executing it, the malware loads the device-specific code on the GPU, allocates a memory area accessible by both the CPU and the GPU, initializes it with any shared data, and schedules the execution of the GPU code. Depending on the design, the flow of control can either switch back and forth between the CPU and the GPU, or separate tasks can run in parallel on both processors.

Other defense solutions to this attack could rely on a remote code attestation mechanism [7], a method to remotely check whether some security proprieties of the running application are preserved. In this case it is important to note that the attacker, as we can show in the previous section, can stop the defensive mechanism to be scheduled for the duration of the attack, and then restored it. By using code attestation method or any other watchdog mechanisms that check the status of the process (e.g., stack, registers, etc.) it is difficult to set up the right time to check since we do not know when the attack will happen. Remote attestation could be set to run constantly for the entire life of the process. Deploying this solution on real-time systems could be prohibitive in terms of performance overhead, and it could be difficult to use to monitor more than one precess at a time.

6   Mitigation

In this section we describe the design and implementation of a detection system that can be used to protect against the scheduler attack presented in Sect. 4. We start by presenting the idea behind our solution, we then describe our system architecture, and we finally evaluate our approach against some scheduling attack samples.

6.1   Defense Mechanism Principles

Our approach for the detection of scheduling attacks is to observe and mimic the behavior of the OS scheduler by intercepting events that occur in the OS context. More in details, in case of the scheduling subsystem, the idea is to monitor the execution time of all processes and check if the fairness property is preserved. In order to obtain the real execution time for each process/task we need to intercept some fundamental operations about the process activities such as the process creation and termination, the process execution, and the process I/O waiting. By using those operations our system can carefully estimate the execution time for each process and, by mimicking the behavior of a real scheduler, detect whether any anomaly (i.e., a process starvation) occurs in the system.

6.2   Defense Framework Architecture

Our defense mechanism is implemented as a custom hypervisor. This is required in order to obtain a resilient and robust reference monitor in presence of kernel-level attacks. Our anomaly detection mechanism is based on the assumption that the system should give the same amount of execution time to each process (fairness scheduling property). Consequently, if one process that is not blocked in I/O operations is not scheduled at least once for each quantum of time, the system raises an alarm. From an architectural point of view, our system consists of two main software components: (1) the *Task Tracer* and (2) the *Periodic Monitor*. Both components work together to simulate the fairness property and to reveal any anomaly on the system.

The main goal of the Task Tracer is to replicate the tasks information at the hypervisor level, storing them in a list of `task_struct` data structures. To this end, the *Task Tracer* needs to intercept a number of process events. In particular it needs to detect four main events:

- **Process Creation:** This event happens when the *create process* system call is invoked.
- **Process Exit:** This event occurs when an exit system call or any process error exception is invoked by the system.
- **Process Execution:** This event occurs when a process is assigned to a given processor for its execution.
- **Queue Insertion and Removing:** These events happen when a task is inserted or removed from the scheduling queue (CFS red-black tree).

When a new process is created, the *Task Tracer* component allocates a new `task_struct` element to keep track of its information: name, process description etc. Moreover, for each new process, the system adds a life timestamp field named `last_seen`. This value represents the starting time of the process life, that will later be used to check the time spent by the process waiting on the scheduling queue. The queue insertion and removing operations are at the core of our detection mechanism. In fact they allow the system to set the starting and ending time for each process. The starting time begins when the process is inserted into the scheduling queue. In particular when a process will be inserted in the scheduling queue (CFS red-black tree), the hypervisor detects it and it sets the timestamp field for this particular task. In case the process is not scheduled for execution after a certain time (defined by a configurable scheduling threshold) the system reports an anomaly. The effect of the remove operation from the scheduling queue is to reset the timer associated to a particular process. It is important to note that intercepting the insert and remove operations is sufficient to monitor the execution time for all the processes of the system, since one of the main assumption of the Linux scheduling algorithm is that every process needs to be added to the scheduling list before it can be executed.

The goal of the other software component, the *Periodic Monitor*, is to periodically check the status of the execution time for each process and update their timestamps (`last_seen` fields). More in details, every time the timeout occurs, the *Periodic Monitor* goes through all the elements of the *task_list* created by the *Task Tracer* software component and checks among all the monitored processes the timestamp field reported in the `task_struct` element. If the difference between this timestamp field and the current timestamp is greater than the scheduling threshold the system reports an anomaly, otherwise it just update its value with the new timestamp.

6.3   Implementation Details

Our current prototype is implemented as an extension of HyperDbg, an open-source hardware-assisted hypervisor framework [11]. Typically, by monitoring low-level interactions between the guest operating system and the memory management structures on which the OS depends, a hypervisor can infer when a guest operating system creates processes, destroys them, or triggers a context-switch between them. These techniques can be performed without any explicit information about the guest operating system vendor, version, or implementation details [23]. Unfortunately, our detector needs some information that cannot be inferred only by observing the interactions between the guest OS and the memory management structures. For example, insert and remove operations on the scheduling queue or the creation and destruction of userspace and kernel threads are fine-grained operations that cannot be identified by observing from outside the OS. Therefore, our framework needs to rely on a hooking mechanism that is specific for a particular operating system (Linux in our current prototype). In order to intercept each task creation event, we inserted a hook on the `wake_up_new_task` function. Such function is invoked the first time a new task is inserted into the scheduling queue after the system invokes `do_fork`. This is used to create a process on the system. We chose this function since the argument of the `wake_up_new_task` function is the `task_struct_element` that already contains all the process information that will be stored into the hypervisor memory. The system also needs to intercept a process or task termination for two reasons: (1) when a process explicitly call the `exit` function and (2) when it receives a signal or exception for its own termination. In both cases the function that is invoked is the `do_exit`. When such a function is called, by using the kernel macro `current` the system obtains the pointer to the `task_struct` related to the process to terminate. Consequently our hypervisor puts an hook on the `do_exit` function to intercept this information. Finally the system needs to intercept the queue operations: insert and remove. In particular when a process is inserted in the scheduler running queue (CFS black-red tree) a function called `enqueque_task` is invoked. This function is in charge for inserting the `task_struct` structures inside the CFS tree, and any information about the inserted process can be retrieved starting from `ecx` register. For removing elements from the scheduler queue, the operating system provides a function called `dequeue_task`. This function is called when the scheduler removes a task from the CFS tree and the reference to the task in this case is stored into `edx` register.

To implement the *Periodic Monitor* component inside the hypervisor we extended the core of HyperDbg. In particular, we created a time simulator inside the hypervisor by using the Timestamp Counter `TSC` register provided by the `x86` architecture. This register counts the clock cycle and it is independent from the processor frequency. In particular, the hypervisor core reads the value of TSC each time a `VMexit` occurs in the system. If the elapsed time reach the timeout set by the *Periodic Monitor*, the hypervisor invokes the periodic monitor component. It is important to note that the `VMexit` are very frequent in the system, consequently our timer simulator does not suffer from any considerable delay.

6.4   Evaluation

In this section we describe the experiments that we performed in order to test our defensive mechanism. The main goal of the experiments is to test the efficacy and the efficiency of the detection system.

Overhead. In the first experiment we measure the overhead produced by our system. To this end we performed two main tests. In the first test we measured the execution time with our detection framework enabled, while the user performs a number of normal operations – like browsing the web (e.g., Facebook, Google, etc.), reading PDF documents, and editing files for a total of 60 min. To compute the overhead we use the TSC timer provided inside the hypervisor. We compute the ratio between the time spent inside the hypervisor with respect to the time spent for the OS execution. We report the result in Fig. 2. As we can see from the Figure, the gray area represents the window time where the detector is active. The line in the graph shows instead the ratio between the execution time spent into the hypervisor and the execution time spent into the OS. We can observe that overhead never goes above 5 %.

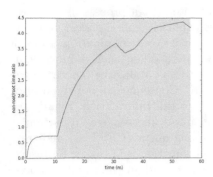

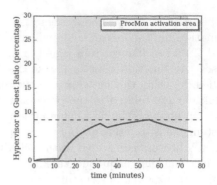

Fig. 2. Detection system overhead during normal operation

Fig. 3. Detection system overhead under an artificial stress

Since during the normal operation the system overhead is low, we performed a second test where we stress the allocation/dis-allocation of the processes in order to measure the worst case scenario. For this test we used the stress suite to simulate a huge allocation/deallocation of the processes on a Linux system. The overhead we observed in this case was at most 9 %. The test was run for 80 min and the final result is reported in Fig. 3. Again, it is important to note the experiments performed in these tests produced a very intensive process allocation/deallocation and therefore it is not representative of the behavior during the normal process activities of the system.

Detection Accuracy. In order to measure the detection accuracy of our system we tested the system while running some scheduler attacks. Since we have never observed such attacks in the wild, we used our artificial dataset to test the application. More in details, we again performed the experimental evaluation with a popular IDS and with *Inotify* (as explained in Sect. 4) but this time with our defensive mechanism enabled. In this test, our system was able to detect both attacks and correctly recognize the anomalous process that was under attack. We also performed an artificial experiment on kernel threads. In this case we first created some artificial kernel threads and we then blocked their execution by using our attack. Also in this experiment, our system was able to detect all the attacks performed against the OS kernel.

6.5   False Positives and False Negatives

It is important to note that both false positives and false negatives can occur depending on the value of the detection threshold set by the system. In particular, if such a threshold is too low, and therefore close to the real waiting time for scheduled tasks, the system can raise false alarms. On the other hand, if the threshold is too large, the system can miss short attacks that fits into the time window. Therefore, the threshold should be tuned on the values of scheduler waiting times observed on the monitored OS. After a short training period, we set the threshold to 40ms. We then run our defensive system on our work computers for one week without observing any false alarm.

7 Discussion

In this section we discuss the generality of the proposed attack, the limitation of the defense solutions and possible future work.

7.1 Generality

In this paper we presented a new class of attacks. For the sake of simplicity we only described a single instance of E-DKOMs. In particular we chose to investigate the scheduler attack because it perfectly summarizes all the important key points of the evolutionary DKOMs attacks and it was relatively easy to implement.

The scheduler subsystem is a good candidate but it is not the only possible target. In fact, the operating system offers other interesting functional components to investigate such as the memory management, the network subsystem, and the I/O subsystem. A requirement for E-DKOM attacks is to tamper with dynamic data structures that contain fundamental information for controlling the OS behavior. The targeted data structure needs to contain information that defines an OS *property* along with an OS specific behavior. In the scheduler attack example the OS *property* to subvert was the execution fairness, every process defined into the run-queue structure need to be scheduled for running after a certain time window. The goal of the attacker was to create starvation for a select set of processes (e.g. AVs, IDSs). Another possible target for E-DKOM attacks can be the virtual memory subsystem. In this case the *property* is related to the memory pages replacement algorithm and the way the algorithm chooses the page to swap to disk (e.g., LRU or FIFO). The attacker can alter this *property* by changing the memory structure that contains the numbers of accesses received by the page. By altering this number an attacker can decide which page should be stored on disk and also on which disk location (e.g., filesystem inode), creating a potential data leakage among the applications.

We believe that the OS contains a significant number of sensitive memory structures that can be tampered by an attacker to consequently tamper a certain OS behavior without being detected. Automatically discovering such memory structures along with the analysis of attack impact will be the task of our future research.

7.2 Limitations

The defensive solution described in the previous sections is based on a custom hypervisor that plays the role of an external agent able to monitor the execution of the guest operating system. Unfortunately, collecting information from outside the OS is not a trivial task, and requires to overcome the well-known problem of the *semantic gap* [6,9,22]. The Intel hardware support for virtualization simplifies only in part this issue, allowing the hypervisor to catch only low level events (e.g., writing attempts to control registers). Unfortunately, all the abstractions introduced by the operating system are lost and need to be reconstructed by the hypervisor code.

In the literature, several solutions have been proposed to detect hidden processes from a virtual machine monitor. These techniques typically intercept all the writing attempts to the CR3 register by leveraging the Intel hardware support. This control register contains the base address of the *page directory*, a fundamental data structure to translate virtual to physical addresses. At every *context-switch*, the OS loads the right value of the CR3 register to access the process's virtual address space. In this way, systems like *Antfarm* [23] are able to discover all the running processes by observing this low level event. Other systems, like *Patagonix* [27], achieve the same goal by setting the process's pages as non-executable (using the NX flag). In this way, every execution attempt is intercepted, allowing the hypervisor to discover all running processes.

Our scheduler attack introduces a new challenge: the hypervisor needs to identify the processes that are in the scheduled queue but are not executed in the system. If a process is not executed, then there is no access to its CR3, nor to its NX pages. In fact, the attack introduced in this paper may stop the process during its creation, so that the monitoring system would never observe the CR3 associated to the program.

To make the problem worse, the granularity of this instance of E-DKOM is at the thread level, but the address space is shared among all threads of the same process – making an approach based on the monitoring of the CR3 register too imprecise. For this reason, to implement a successful defense technique, the hypervisor needs to set breakpoints in the kernel code to extract threads information and to inspect the state of each tasks, (e.g. if it is in the running or waiting queue).

Moreover, the hypervisor has to mimic the OS scheduler component to guarantee the scheduling property and detect deviations from the expected behavior. In our example, this requires to follow over time the evolution of the scheduler data structures, in particular the evolution of the runqueue to spot any anomaly.

For all these reasons, we believe this instance of E-DKOM attack sheds light on several limitations of current solutions to address the *semantic gap*. Moreover, since each solution would need to be specifically tailored for the property tampered by the attack, this example also shows the challenge of developing a general solution for the detection of E-DKOM attacks.

8   Related Work

Over the years, operating systems have introduced several countermeasures to hinder the exploitation of userland applications. These protections have significantly raised the bar for the attackers, making it increasingly difficult to gain full control of a remote machine. As a consequence, it is now fundamental for criminals to gain a persistent and stealth access on a compromised target immediately after the breach. This is often achieved by installing a rootkit in the OS kernel. The role of a rootkit is to hide resources in the compromised machine, and this can be achieved either by using hooking techniques or by tampering with dynamic kernel data structures.

In the literature, several approaches have been proposed to protect the kernel from the malicious modifications introduced by rootkits. A first set of countermeasures was designed to guarantee the integrity of the kernel, in order to prevent attackers from modifying its code and introducing hooks [46]. There are two ways to achieve this objective: i) by introducing a self-defense mechanism in the kernel, such as PatchGuard [29] for Windows x86-64 or ii) by adopting an external monitor, such as a VMM-based system [14,37,38,46] or a dedicated hardware coprocessor [26,30,32,48]. For instance, SecVisor [38] and Nickle [37] are two hypervisor solutions that protect the integrity of the kernel code from unintended modifications. Unfortunately, this class of protections have been bypassed by DKOM attacks [19,31] which target dynamic kernel data without the need to modify the kernel code.

A more complex and comprehensive defensive solution is to enforce the control flow integrity (CFI) of the kernel. CFI was initially proposed by Abadi et al. [2] for userland applications and then extended and ported to the kernel by Petroni et al. [33]. The state-based CFI (*SBCFI*) proposed by Petroni is enforced by a hypervisor and periodically scans the kernel memory to detect deviations from the allowed control flow. *SBCFI* can detect persistent control flow changes but fails to prevent DKOM attacks.

To protect against DKOM, it was necessary to introduce new solutions to enforce the kernel *data* integrity. The most interesting approaches in this direction are based on invariants or on data partitioning. The first class can be split into two subgroups: external systems [3,18,36] and memory analysis [5,8] techniques. External systems are implemented as either a virtual machine monitor [18,36] or by using a separate machine [3]. The rationale behind these defensive techniques is to take an untampered view of the objects running in the target kernel and then compare this list with the invariants derived by walking the kernel data structures. Similarly, memory analysis solutions [5,8] leverage memory snapshots to isolate kernel objects and then compare with a list retrieved directly from the live system. Unfortunately, invariants may not exist for some kernel data structures, thus a different approach has been proposed around the concept of object partitioning. For instance, Srivastava et al. [40] proposed *Sentry*, a hypervisor solution able to divide kernel objects fields in different memory regions depending on their security impact. Writes on these sensitive fields are then monitored and a strict access control policy is enforced to detect if the writer is legitimated. This approach has two main drawbacks: a large performance overhead and the complexity of the writer's identification process.

More formal architectures have been proposed to verify dynamic kernel structures as proposed by Petroni et al. [34]. These rule-based systems may be effective to detect advanced threats but they are error prone and depend on the astuteness of the rules writer. E-DKOM attacks are able to bypass these protections given the huge new attack surface exposed by this generic technique.

The solution we propose in this paper belongs to the class of mimic defensive solutions. Researchers have often proposed approaches to isolate a single OS component and emulate it outside the system to provide a ground truth to the analyst [15,17]. In our case, a custom hypervisor reproduces the same scheduling algorithm (CFS) in a faithful step by step emulation. The drawback of these approaches is that they only solve a particular instance of the problem. In fact, we show how to protect the scheduler but an attacker can still exploit a different property of the kernel. Moreover, these defensive solutions are not ideal, as discussed by Garfinkel [13]. Specifically, the developers have to carefully think and manage all possible corner cases in order to avoid possible bypasses, making this process highly prone to errors.

To the best of our knowledge, E-DKOM attacks – as formalized in this paper – have never been discussed in the literature. The most complete overview of the DKOM's problem has been provided by Baliga et al. [4] as well as Rhee et al. [35]. They proposed a DKOM's taxonomy and investigated a novel data kernel attacks and possible POC solutions. Although they mention the huge attack surface exposed by modern kernels and the failing approach adopted by current detectors, they did not address our attack. In light of the current state of the art, it is clear that all the existing defense mechanisms are not able to detect this new class of attack and new comprehensive solutions are required to address this new and complex threat.

In our example of E-DKOM attack, we use soft timer interrupt requests (STIR) in order to perform polling tasks and modify the targeted dynamic memory structures. Even if the detection of malicious soft timer interrupt has been addressed in the literature [47], an attacker can use several stealthy techniques to hide the execution of malicious kernel code. For example, by using Address Translation Redirection Attacks (ATRA) [21], an attacker can hide memory pages along with kernel interrupt routines (e.g. code memory page). This would trick an integrity code checker to analyze the code of a benign timer routine. Finally, it is worth noting that in our threat model we consider an attacker equipped with state of the art offensive tools, that are not always detectable by the current defensive solutions.

9 Conclusion and Future Work

In this paper we discuss a new type of DKOM attack that targets the evolution of a data structure in memory, with the goal of tampering with a particular property of the operating system. Since at every single point in time the internal state of the OS is not anomalous, the detection of this type of attack, which we call evolutionary kernel object manipulation, requires a completely new approach as well.

We conducted a number of experiments to show the feasibility of an evolutionary attack against the Linux scheduler. Our attack is able to temporarily block any process or kernel thread, without leaving any trace that could be identified by existing DKOM detection and protection systems. Moving to the defense side, we then presented the design and implementation of a hypervisor-based detector that can verify the fairness of the OS scheduler. While our prototype is able to detect all the attacks with zero false positives, the implementation needs to be customized on a case-by-case basis, and it also requires the hooking of a number of internal functions of the operating systems (making the technique harder to maintain and port to other systems). This shows that evolutionary attacks are very hard to deal with, and more research is needed to mitigate this threat.

As a future work we are now investigating other possible E-DKOM attacks that can be executed on some specific kernel subsystems. As we already discussed in the Generality Section, one example could be related to the virtual memory subsystem and in particular to the selection of the candidate memory page to swap. It would also be interesting to work on an automated analysis system that can autonomously inspect the OS kernel and identify possible candidate data structures that have an interesting time-evolutionary behavior – and that therefore could be targeted by future E-DKOM attacks.

References

1. Tripwire. http://www.tripwire.com/
2. Abadi, M., Budiu, M., Erlingsson, U., Ligatti, J.: Control-flow integrity. In: Proceedings of the 12th ACM Conference on Computer and Communications Security, CCS 2005, pp. 340–353 (2005)
3. Baliga, A., Ganapathy, V., Iftode, L.: Automatic inference and enforcement of kernel data structure invariants. In: Proceedings of the 2008 Annual Computer Security Applications Conference, ACSAC 2008, pp. 77–86 (2008)
4. Baliga, A., Kamat, P., Iftode, L.: Lurking in the shadows: identifying systemic threats to kernel data. In: Proceedings of the 2007 IEEE Symposium on Security and Privacy, SP 2007, pp. 246–251(2007)
5. Carbone, M., Cui, W., Lu, L., Lee, W., Peinado, M., Jiang, X.: Mapping kernel objects to enable systematic integrity checking. In: Proceedings of the 16th ACM Conference on Computer and Communications Security, CCS 2009, pp. 555–565. ACM, New York (2009)
6. Chen, P.M., Noble, B.D.: When virtual is better than real. In: Proceedings of the Eighth Workshop on Hot Topics in Operating Systems, HOTOS (2001)
7. Coker, G., et al.: Principles of remote attestation. Int. J. Inf. Secur. **10**(2), 63–81 (2011)
8. Cui, W., Peinado, M., Xu, Z., and Chan, E. Tracking rootkit footprints with a practical memory analysis system. In: Presented as Part of the 21st USENIX Security Symposium (USENIX Security 2012), pp. 601–615. USENIX, Bellevue (2012)
9. Dolan-Gavitt, B., Leek, T., Zhivich, M., Giffin, J., Lee, W.: Virtuoso: narrowing the semantic gap in virtual machine introspection. In: Proceedings of the IEEE Symposium on Security and Privacy (Oakland), May 2011
10. Fattori, A., Lanzi, A., Balzarotti, D., Kirda, E.: Hypervisor-based malware protection with accessminer. Comput. Secur. **52**, 33–50 (2015)

11. Fattori, A., Paleari, R., Martignoni, L., Monga, M.: Dynamic and transparent analysis of commodity production systems. In: Proceedings of the 25th International Conference on Automated Software Engineering (ASE), Antwerp, Belgium, September 2010. https://code.google.com/p/hyperdbg/
12. Fedler, R., Kulicke, M., Schtte, J.: An antivirus api for android malware recognition. In: MALWARE (2013)
13. Garfinkel, T.: Traps and pitfalls: practical problems in in system call interposition based security tools. In: Proceedings of the Network and Distributed Systems Security Symposium, February 2003
14. Garfinkel, T., Rosenblum, M.: A virtual machine introspection based architecture for intrusion detection. In: Proceedings of the Network and Distributed Systems Security Symposium, pp. 191–206 (2003)
15. Grill, B., Platzer, C., Eckel, J.: A practical approach for generic bootkit detection and prevention. In: EuroSec (2014)
16. Hardy, N.: The confused deputy: (or why capabilities might have been invented). SIGOPS Oper. Syst. Rev. **22**(4), 36–38 (1988)
17. Haukli, L.: Exposing bootkits with bios emulation. In: Blackhat US, August 2014
18. Hofmann, O., Dunn, A.M., Kim, S., Roy, I., Witchel, E.: Ensuring operating system kernel integrity with OSck. In: ASPLOS (2011)
19. Hoglund, G., Butler, J.: Rootkits: Subverting the Windows Kernel. Addison-Wesley Professional, Boston (2005)
20. Hund, R., Holz, T., Freiling, F.C.: Return-oriented rootkits: bypassing kernel code integrity protection mechanisms. In: Presented as Part of the 18th USENIX Security Symposium (USENIX Security 2009). USENIX, Montreal (2009)
21. Jang, D., Lee, H., Kim, M., Kim, D., Kim, D., Kang, B.B.: Atra: address translation redirection attack against hardware-based external monitors. In: Proceedings of the 2014 ACM SIGSAC Conference on Computer and Communications Security, CCS 2014, pp. 167–178. ACM, New York (2014)
22. Jiang, X., Wang, X., Xu, D.: Stealthy malware detection through vmm-based out-of-the-box semantic view reconstruction. In: Proceedings of the ACM Conference on Computer and Communications Security (CCS) (2007)
23. Jones, S.T., Arpaci-Dusseau, A.C., Arpaci-Dusseau, R.H.: Antfarm: tracking processes in a virtual machine environment. In: Proceedings of the USENIX 2006 Annual Technical Conference, USENIX 2006, Boston, MA, June 2006
24. Kim, G.H., Spafford, E.H.: The design, implementation of tripwire: a file system integrity checker. In: Proceedings of the 2nd ACM Conference on Computer and Communications Security, CCS 1994, pp. 18–29 (1994)
25. Ladakis, E., Koromilas, L., Vasiliadis, G., Polychronakis, M., Ioannidis, S.: You can type, but you can't hide: a stealthy GPU-based keylogger. In: Proceedings of the 6th European Workshop on System Security, EuroSec, Prague, Czech Republic, April 2013
26. Lee, H., Moon, H., Jang, D., Kim, K., Lee, J., Paek, Y., Kang, B.B.: Ki-mon: a hardware-assisted event-triggered monitoring platform for mutable kernel object. In: Presented as Part of the 22nd USENIX Security Symposium, pp. 511–526. USENIX, Washington, D.C. (2013)
27. Litty, L., Lagar-Cavilla, H.A., Lie, D.: Hypervisor support for identifying covertly executing binaries. In: Proceedings of the 17th Usenix Security Symposium, San Jose, CA, July 2008
28. Love, R.: intro to inotify. http://www.linuxjournal.com/article/8478
29. Microsoft. PatchGuard - Kernel Patch Protection. https://technet.microsoft.com/en-us/library/cc759759

30. Moon, H., Lee, H., Lee, J., Kim, K., Paek, Y., Kang, B.B.: Vigilare: toward snoop-based kernel integrity monitor. In: Proceedings of the 2012 ACM Conference on Computer and Communications Security, CCS 2012, pp. 28–37. ACM, New York (2012)
31. Peter Silberman and C.H.A.O.S. FUTo. http://uninformed.org/index.cgi?v=3& a=7&p=7
32. Petroni, J., Fraser, T., Molina, J., Arbaugh, W. A.: Copilot - a coprocessor-based kernel runtime integrity monitor. In: Proceedings of the 13th Conference on USENIX Security Symposium - vol. 13, SSYM 2004, p. 13. USENIX Association, San Diego (2004)
33. Petroni, Jr., N.L., Hicks, M.: Automated detection of persistent kernel control-flow attacks. In: Proceedings of the ACM Conference on Computer and Communications Security (CCS), pp. 103–115, October 2007
34. Petroni Jr., N.L., Fraser, T., Walters, A.A., Arbaugh, W.A.: An architecture for specification-based detection of semantic integrity violations in kernel dynamic data. In: Proceedings of the 15th Conference on USENIX Security Symposium, p. 20 (2006)
35. Rhee, J., Riley, R., Xu, D., Jiang, X.: Defeating dynamic data kernel rootkit attacks via vmm-based guest-transparent monitoring. In: Proceedings of the International Conference on Availability, Reliability and Security (ARES 2009), Fukuoka, Japan, March 2009
36. Rhee, J., Riley, R., Xu, D., Jiang, X.: Kernel malware analysis with un-tampered and temporal views of dynamic kernel memory. In: Jha, S., Sommer, R., Kreibich, C. (eds.) RAID 2010. LNCS, vol. 6307, pp. 178–197. Springer, Heidelberg (2010)
37. Riley, R., Jiang, X., Xu, D.: Guest-transparent prevention of kernel rootkits with VMM-based memory shadowing. In: Lippmann, R., Kirda, E., Trachtenberg, A. (eds.) RAID 2008. LNCS, vol. 5230, pp. 1–20. Springer, Heidelberg (2008)
38. Seshadri, A., Luk, M., Qu, N., Perrig, A.: SecVisor: a tiny hypervisor to guarantee lifetime kernel code integrity for commodity oses. In: Proceedings of the ACM Symposium on Operating Systems Principles (SOSP), October 2007
39. Seshadri, A., Perrig, A., Doorn, L.V., Khosla, P.: Swatt: software-based attestation for embedded devices. In: Proceedings of the IEEE Symposium on Security and Privacy (2004)
40. Srivastava, A., Giffin, J.: Efficient protection of kernel data structures via object partitioning. In: Proceedings of the 28th Annual Computer Security Applications Conference, ACSAC 2012, pp. 429–438 (2012)
41. Srivastava, A., Lanzi, A., Giffin, J.T.: System call API obfuscation (extended abstract). In: Lippmann, R., Kirda, E., Trachtenberg, A. (eds.) RAID 2008. LNCS, vol. 5230, pp. 421–422. Springer, Heidelberg (2008)
42. Srivastava, A., Lanzi, A., Giffin, J., Balzarotti, D.: Operating system interface obfuscation and the revealing of hidden operations. In: Holz, T., Bos, H. (eds.) DIMVA 2011. LNCS, vol. 6739, pp. 214–233. Springer, Heidelberg (2011)
43. Vogl, S., Gawlik, R., Garmany, B., Kittel, T., Pfoh, J., Eckert, C., Holz, T.: Dynamic hooks: hiding control flow changes within non-control data. In: 23rd USENIX Security Symposium (USENIX Security 2014), pp. 813–328. USENIX Association, San Diego, August 2014
44. Vogl, S., Pfoh, J., Kittel, T., Eckert, C.: Persistent data-only malware: function hooks without code. In: Proceedings of the 21th Annual Network and Distributed System Security Symposium (NDSS), February 2014
45. Volatility Foundation. psxview Volatility command. https://github.com/ volatilityfoundation/volatility/wiki/Command

46. Wang, Z., Jiang, X., Cui, W., Ning, P.: Countering kernel rootkits with lightweight hook protection. In: Proceedings of the 16th ACM Conference on Computer and Communications Security, CCS 2009, pp. 545–554 (2009)
47. Wei, J., Payne, B. D., Giffin, J., Pu, C.: Soft-timer driven transient kernel control flow attacks and defense. In: ACSAC (2008)
48. Zhang, X., van Doorn, L., Jaeger, T., Perez, R., Sailer, R.: Secure coprocessor-based intrusion detection. In: Proceedings of the Tenth ACM SIGOPS European Workshop, September 2002

DeepFuzz: Triggering Vulnerabilities Deeply Hidden in Binaries

(Extended Abstract)

Konstantin Böttinger$^{(\boxtimes)}$ and Claudia Eckert

Fraunhofer Institute for Applied and Integrated Security,
85748 Garching (near Munich), Germany
konstantin.boettinger@aisec.fraunhofer.de

Abstract. We introduce a new method for triggering vulnerabilities in deep layers of binary executables and facilitate their exploitation. In our approach we combine dynamic symbolic execution with fuzzing techniques. To maximize both the execution path depth and the degree of freedom in input parameters for exploitation, we define a novel method to assign probabilities to program paths. Based on this probability distribution we apply new path exploration strategies. This facilitates payload generation and therefore vulnerability exploitation.

Keywords: Concolic execution · Fuzzing · Random testing

1 Introduction

As ubiquitous software is ever increasing in size and complexity, we face the severe challenge to validate and maintain the systems that surround us. Software testing has come a long way from its origins to the recent developments of sophisticated validation techniques. In this paper we introduce a new method combining symbolic execution and random testing. Our goals are (1) code coverage in deep layers of targeted binaries which are unreachable by current technologies and (2) maximal degree of freedom in the input variables when discovering a program error.

Before we present the main idea of our approach and the summary of our contributions, we give some background on concolic execution and fuzzing. We especially highlight limitations of concolic execution and fuzzing when applied isolated and motivate a combination of both as a promising new strategy.

Concolic Execution. The main idea of symbolic execution is to assign symbolic representations to input variables of a program and generate formulas over the symbols according to the transformations in the program execution. Reasoning about a program on the bases of such symbolic representations of execution paths can provide new insight into the behavior of the program. Besides program

© Springer International Publishing Switzerland 2016
J. Caballero et al. (Eds.): DIMVA 2016, LNCS 9721, pp. 25–34, 2016.
DOI: 10.1007/978-3-319-40667-1_2

verification, symbolic execution nowadays has its biggest impact in program testing. The original idea was extended over the years and developed into concrete symbolic (concolic) execution. The program is initially executed with arbitrary concrete input values and symbolic constraints over the symbols are generated along the program execution path. Next, one of the collected branch conditions is negated and together with the remaining constraints given to an SMT solver. The solution (also called *model*) generated by the SMT solver is injected as new input into the program, which now takes the branch alternative when executed. This is because the SMT solver just calculated the solution of the negation of the former branch constraint so that the newly generated input follows the alternative path. This procedure is iteratively repeated until a halt condition is reached. In the best case the reached halt condition resembles full path coverage of all alternative paths of the program, in the worst case the halt condition is caused by an overloaded SMT solver. The latter is a natural consequence of the exponential growth of the number of paths we have to deal with, which we refer to as the *path explosion* problem. Concolic execution is advantageous in code regions where pure symbolic reasoning is ineffective or even infeasible. This is often the case for complex arithmetic operations, pointer manipulations, calls to external library functions, or system calls.

Pure concolic execution, however, has strong limitations. Current SMT solvers are very limited in the number of variables and constraints they can handle efficiently so that concolic execution gets stuck in very early stages of the program. Despite huge advances in the field of SMT solvers, concolic execution of large programs is infeasible and in practice will only cover limited parts of the execution graph. The major part of graph coverage must therefore be done with fuzzing.

Fuzzing. Existing fuzzing tools generate random input values for the targeted program in order to drive it to an unexpected state. Fuzzing has generated a long list of vulnerabilities over the years and is by now the most successful approach when it comes to program testing. However, it has severe limitations even in very simple situations. To illustrate this, consider the following code snippet:

```
#include <stdint.h>
...
int check( uint64_t num ){
        if( num == UINT64_C(0) )
                assert( false );
}
```

If we want to reach the assertion in the check function with a random choice of the integer num, we have a probability of 2^{-64} for each try to pass the if statement. The situation gets even worse if there are multiple such checks, e.g. in the calculation of a checksum or character match during input parsing. Such code areas are very hard to be passed by pure random input generation and code regions beyond such examples are most likely not covered by fuzzing. In the following we will refer to such cases as *fuzzing walls*. However, the false assertion in the above code listing can easily be reached with concolic execution, as the comparison to zero directly translates to a simple expression for the SMT solver.

The Hybrid Approach. As we just showed, critical limitations of fuzzing can be overcome with concolic execution, and in turn fuzzing scales much better to path explosion than SMT solvers do. As a natural next step we combine both methods. The idea is to apply concolic execution whenever fuzzing saturates (i.e. stops exploration at a fuzzing wall), and in turn switch back to fuzzing whenever the fuzzing walls are passed by concolic execution.

However, we still have to deal with the problem of path explosion and therefore still may end up covering only the first execution layers of a program. In the following, we refer to *path depth* as the number of branches along that path, which directly corresponds to the number of basic blocks. Even in the combined approach we are confronted with two challenges. First, if we want to fuzz deep areas of a program, we have to find a way to construct execution paths into such areas and somehow delay path explosion until we have found such a tunnel. Second, to generate a payload and exploit a detected vulnerability in the program under test, we not only have to reach the bug with a single suitable input, but we have to reach it with maximal degree of freedom in the input values. To be more precise, if we reach a vulnerability with exactly one constellation of the input variables, we most probably would not be able to exploit it in a meaningful way because any attempt to generate a payload (and thereby change the input variables) would lead the input to take a different path in the execution graph. Therefore, we propose a way to maximize the degree of freedom regarding input variables. This yields both alleviation of vulnerability exploitation and execution paths that reach into deep layers of the program.

In summary, we make the following contributions:

– We propose a new search heuristic that delays path explosion effectively into deeper layers of the tested binary.
– We define a novel technique to assign probabilities to execution paths.
– We introduce DeepFuzz, an algorithm combining initial seed generation, concolic execution, distribution of path probabilities, path selection, and constrained fuzzing.

2   Related Work

Symbolic execution has experienced significant development since its beginnings in the seventies to the advanced modern variants invented for program testing in recent years. Especially the last decade has seen a renewed research interest due to powerful Satisfiability Modulo Theory (SMT) solvers and computation capabilities that have led to advanced tools for dynamic software testing. Cadar et al. [2] give an overview of the current status of dynamic symbolic execution. In concolic execution [5,10] symbolic constraints are generated along program execution paths of concrete input values.

Research in random test generation established powerful fuzzing tools such as AFL, Radamsa, the Peach Fuzzer, and many more. We refer to [12] for a comprehensive account.

Both concolic execution and fuzzing have severe limitations when aiming for code coverage (see Sect. 1). Since those limitations are partly complementary to each other, a fusion of concolic execution and fuzzing emerges as natural approach. Majumdar et al. [8] made a first inspiring step into this direction by proposing hybrid concolic testing: by interleaving random testing with concolic execution the authors of [8] increase code coverage significantly. However, it is still an open question how to efficiently generate restricted inputs for random testing. We propose a solution for high frequency test case generation that scales to large sets of constraints. Further, we specify the rather general test goals of [8] by focusing on maximization of the degree of freedom regarding input variables to achieve both, alleviation of vulnerability exploitation and execution paths that reach into deep layers of the program.

Closely related to our approach is Driller by Stephens et al. [11] who also combine fuzzing with selective concolic execution in order to reach deep execution paths. Driller switches from pure fuzzing to concolic execution whenever random testing saturates, i.e. gets stuck at a fuzzing wall. To keep the load for symbolic execution low while simultaneously maximizing the chance to pass fuzzing walls with concolic execution, Driller also selects inputs. This selection privileges paths that first trigger state transitions or first reach loops which are similarly iterated by other paths. In contrast, we systematically assign probabilities to paths based on SMT solving performance and select paths according to this probability distribution. This assignment of probabilities to execution paths has no direct counterpart in related work. Although the authors of [4] also propose assertion of probability weights to paths in the execution graph, they differ significantly in their proposed methods which are based on path condition slicing and computing volumes of convex polytopes.

3   The DeepFuzz Algorithm

In this section we present the DeepFuzz algorithm in detail. The main idea is interleaving concolic execution with constrained fuzzing in a way that allows us to explore paths providing maximal input generation frequency. We achieve this by assigning weights (corresponding to fuzzing performance) to the explored paths after each concolic execution step in order to select the ones with highest probability. In the following, we first describe the individual building blocks, namely initial seed generation, concolic execution, distribution of path probabilities, path selection, and constrained fuzzing. Next, we combine these parts in the overall DeepFuzz algorithm.

3.1   Initial Seed Generation

Initially we start with a short period of concrete input generation for the subsequent concolic execution. If the inputs belong to a predefined data format, we generate inputs according to the format definition (as in generational fuzzing). If there is no format specified or available we just generate random input seeds. We denote the set of all possible concrete input values as X and the initial seeds generated in this initial step as $X_0 \subset X$.

3.2 Concolic Execution

The concolic execution step receives a set of concrete program inputs $X_{seed} \subset X$ and outputs a set of symbolic constraints collected along the paths belonging to these inputs. At the beginning, directly after the initial seed generation step, we set $X_{seed} = X_0$. The symbolic expressions are basically generated as described in Sect. 1. However, we adapt the path search heuristics to our approach in a similar way as introduced in [6]. We conduct concolic execution of the program with each input $x_i \in X_{seed}$ until one of the following two halt conditions occur: either the program reaches the predefined goal, which in our case is basically an unexpected error condition, or the number of newly discovered branches taken exceeds a fixed maximum $b_{max} \in \mathbb{N}$.

To keep the notation as clear as possible, in the following we assume without loss of generality that the halting conditions are reached after exactly b_{max} branches. Let c_i' denote the execution path belonging to input x_i and $n' = |X_{seed}|$ denote the number of inputs in X_{seed}. For each branch $j \in \{1, ..., b_{max}\}$ there is a sub-path c_{ij}' which equals c_i' until branch number j is reached. Clearly, the c_{ij}' are sub-paths of c_i'. For each $i = 1, ..., n'$ and $j = 1, ..., b_{max}$ we store the logical conjunction of the negated branch condition λ_{ij} (corresponding to branch number j of execution path c_i') and the path condition ρ_{ij} of the sub-path c_{ij}' leading to this branch, which yields the $n' * b_{max}$ expression sets $\phi_{ij} := \neg\lambda_{ij} \wedge \rho_{ij}$. With this notation, concolic execution of the input set X_{seed} yields the total set of constraints $\Phi := \{\phi_{ij} \mid i = 1, ..., n', \ j = 1, ..., b_{max}\}$. For each element in Φ the SMT solver checks if the the symbolic constraints are satisfiable and in that case computes a new input x_{ij} for each element $\phi_{ij} \in \Phi$. These newly generated inputs x_{ij} drive the program execution along the original paths c_i' until branch number j is reached and then takes the alternative. We denote these new explored paths as c_{ij}. In the next step we assign probabilities to these paths. To maintain a clear notation and avoid too many indices we work with the union set

$$C := \{c_1, ..., c_n\} := \bigcup_{i,j} c_{ij}'. \tag{1}$$

3.3 Distribution of Path Probabilities

Next, we describe our approach to assign probabilities to program paths. This step takes as input a set of paths C and outputs a probability distribution on this set.

One possible strategy is to calculate the cardinality $|I_i|$ of the set of solutions I_i for the path constraint $\phi_i \in \Phi$ corresponding to c_i and then define weights on the paths according to number of inputs that travel through it. This strategy is chosen and comprehensively described in [4], where the purpose of assigning probabilities to paths is to provide estimates of likelihood of executing portions of a program in the setting of general software evaluation. In contrast to this we are interested in deep fuzzing and therefore must guarantee maximal possible sample generation in a fixed amount of time. To illustrate this more clearly, consider two sets of constraints Φ_A and Φ_B with (non-empty) solution sets A and B. If we are given only the constraints Φ_A and Φ_B and are interested in *some* solutions in A or B, we simply feed an SMT solver with the constraints and receive solutions. However, computing the cardinality $|A|$ and $|B|$ of *all* solutions corresponding to Φ_A and Φ_B (also called the model counting problem) can be significantly more expensive than the decision problem (asking if there is a single solution of the constraints at all). The authors of [4] rely on expensive algorithms for computing volumes of convex polytopes and integrating functions defined upon them. This would yield a theoretical sound distribution of path probabilities, with the disadvantage of extremely low fuzzing performance in our setting. Further, even if cardinality $|A|$ is significantly greater than $|B|$, meaning that Φ_A has much more solutions than Φ_B, computation of B may take much longer than computation of A. In other words $\big(|A| > |B|\big) \nRightarrow \big(T(\Phi_A) > T(\Phi_B)\big)$, where $T(\Phi_i)$ is the time it takes an SMT solver to compute *all* solutions corresponding to the constraints Φ_i. To guarantee high frequency of model generation for effective deep fuzzing we have to build our strategy around a time constraint. Therefore, in order to assign probabilities to the paths $c_1, ..., c_n$ we apply another strategy.

For a fixed time interval T_0 let $k_i(\phi_i, T_0)$ denote the number of solutions for constraints ϕ_i that the applied SMT solver finds in the amount of time T_0. Among the paths $c_1, ..., c_n$ we choose the one whose constraints yield - when given to the SMT solver - the maximal number of satisfying solutions in the fixed amount of time T_0. Therefore, we distribute the probabilities $p(c_i)$ belonging to path c_i according to

$$p(c_i) := k_i\,(\phi_i, T_0) \left(\sum_{j=1}^{n} k_j(\phi_j, T_0) \right)^{-1} \tag{2}$$

for $i = 1, ..., n$. With $\sum_{i=1}^{n} p(c_i) = 1$ this probability distribution is well defined.

3.4   Path Selection

Now that we have n explored paths $C = \{c_1, ..., c_n\}$ weighted with probabilities according to Eq. (2) in the execution graph, our goal in this step is to select the paths that provide us maximal model generation frequency. Such a set of paths will guarantee us efficient fuzzing and maximal degree of freedom for subsequent payload generation in case we detect a vulnerability.

The defined probabilities $p(c_i)$ in Eq. (2) directly correspond to the performance in computing inputs for subsequent fuzzing. Practical calculation of those probabilities is efficient: we simply let the SMT solver compute solutions for the path constraints $\Phi_i (i = 1, ..., n)$ in a round-robin schedule and count the number of solutions for each path, which directly yields the probabilities $p(c_i)$. A sufficiently small choice of the computing time T_0 will result in fast path selection. To gain maximal input generation frequency, we could simply choose the single path whose assigned probability is maximal. However, some paths are dead ends and if we would restrict the algorithm to select only a single path for subsequent fuzzing, path exploration might stop too early in some binaries.

Therefore, we select the $m < n$ different paths $\tilde{c}_j$ ($j = 1, ..., m$) with highest probability. In order to make sure that the following path choice is well defined, we prepend a short side note first: it almost never happens in practice that there are two paths assigned with exactly the same probability. If this unlikely situation occurs in practice, we could just randomly choose one among these equiprobable paths and proceed without much changes in the subsequent algorithm. For simplicity of notation we assume without loss of generality that the set $\{p(c_i) \mid i = 1, ..., n\}$ is strictly ordered. We initially choose the path with highest probability

$$\tilde{c}_1 = \arg\max_{c_i \in C} p(c_i) \tag{3}$$

and then proceed in the same way

$$\tilde{c}_j = \arg\max_{c_i \in C \setminus \{\tilde{c}_1, ..., \tilde{c}_{j-1}\}} p(c_i) \tag{4}$$

until we obtain the path set $C_{high} = \{\tilde{c}_j \mid j = 1, ..., m\}$ including the m paths with hightest probability. On the one hand, setting the parameter m close to n will result in fast path explosion. On the other hand, setting $m = 1$ might be too restrictive for some binaries. Therefore, we initially set m to a small integer and then run parameter optimization to adapt to the specific binaries in testing experiments.

3.5 Constrained Fuzzing

Now that we have selected the paths C_{high} with highest probability, we continue with fuzzing deeper layers of the program. Remember we denoted the set of all possible concrete input values as X and the set of inputs belonging to path c_i as $I_i \subset X$ ($i = 1, ..., n$). To start fuzzing into the program from an endpoint of a selected path $c_i \in C_{high}$, the generated fuzzing inputs have to fulfill the respective path constraints ϕ_i, otherwise they would result in a different execution path. There are basically three possible strategies to generate inputs (i.e. subsets of I_i) that satisfy the respective constraints:

Random Generation of Inputs with Successive Constraint Filtering. This strategy would initially generate a random input set $X_{rand} \subset X$, which would be given to an SMT solver in order to check if a concrete input $x \in X_{rand}$ satisfies the constraint ϕ_i and therefore belongs to I_i. However, filtering the generated inputs in X_{rand} by checking for satisfiability of respective path constraints would most unlikely leave any input over, i.e. $X_{rand} \cap I_i = \emptyset$ with high probability. This is obvious due to the fact that the path constraints in ϕ_i symbolically represent all branch conditions along the path c_i, in particular fuzz-walls (as introduced in Sect. 1). Randomly generating input values that satisfy such a fuzz-wall constraint in ϕ_i is therefore clearly as unlikely as passing such a wall with pure fuzzing.

Pure SMT Solver-Based Input Generation. With this strategy we would inject all the constraints in ϕ_i into an SMT solver, that in turn computes a set of possible solutions. The problem with this strategy is that an SMT solver is sometimes slow and inefficient in computing solutions and the fuzzing input generation rate would drop significantly. This is due to the fact that an SMT solver cannot effectively handle large amounts of variables constrained in large amounts of equations. For example, consider a situation where the input consists of a large file F and the targeted program only checks a small part F' of it during initial parsing. Using an SMT solver to generate both the constrained part F' *and* the unconstrained part of F would be inefficient. This motivates the third strategy.

Random Generation of Independent Input Variables with Subsequent Constraint Solving. Here, we randomly generate input values for all variables that are independent (also called *free*) in ϕ_i. An SMT solver subsequently generates a model for the remaining dependent variable constraints.

In summary, the first strategy is infeasible, whereas strategies two and three are more similar to each other for small input sizes. However, if we deal with larger inputs where only a small minority of input variables are constrained by the current path constraint ϕ_i there is no need to feed a huge amount of path constraints for independent input variables into an SMT solver. We proceed with the third approach as it guarantees us maximal input generation frequency and scales better to large inputs.

In the following, we refer to the frequency of input generation for path c_i as $f(\phi_i)$. The above reasoning yields

$$f(\phi_i) \geq \frac{k_i(\phi_i, T_0)}{T_0}, \tag{5}$$

i.e. the number of models for ϕ_i found by the SMT solver in time T_0 is less or equal than the number of inputs generated with strategy three in time T_0.

3.6   Joining the Pieces

Now that we have described all individual parts we can combine them for the overall DeepFuzz algorithm, as depicted in Fig. 1. After the initial seed generation (SG) is completed we run concolic execution (CE), distribution of path probabilities (DP), path selection (PS), and constrained fuzzing (CF) in a loop, where CF is run for a fixed amount of time T_1. This loop is executed until a halt condition is reached. A halt condition is given either if a predefined goal (e.g. a

Input: Program P, Parameters m, k_{min}, T_0, T_1, T_2, b_{max}

$X_{seed} \leftarrow$ SG (P)
do:
  $\Phi = \emptyset$
  $C = \emptyset$
  for each x in X_{seed} **do:**
      c, ϕ $\leftarrow$ CE (x, b_{max})
      append ϕ to Φ
      append c to C
  $Prob \leftarrow$ DP (Φ, C, T_0)
  $C_{high} \leftarrow$ PS $(Prob, C)$
  $X_{seed} \leftarrow$ CF (C_{high}, Φ, T_1)

  while $\neg$ condition (11)   ; i.e. $\left(\sum_{i=1}^{m} k_i(\phi_i, T_0) \geq k_{min} \right)$

CF(C_{high}, Φ, T_2)

Fig. 1. DeepFuzz main algorithm.

program crash) is reached, or if the constrained fuzzing performance collapses. In the latter case the total number of solutions that the applied SMT solver finds in the fixed amount of time $m * T_0$ drops below a predefined bound k_{min}

$$\sum_{i=1}^{m} k_i(\phi_i, T_0) < k_{min} \tag{6}$$

and we leave the loop to procede with solely constrained fuzzing for a long testing time T_2.

4   Conclusion

We present an approach to trigger vulnerabilities in deep layers of binary executables. DeepFuzz constructs a tunnel into the program by applying concolic execution, distribution of path probabilities, path selection, and constrained fuzzing in a way that allows fuzzing deep areas of the program.

Instead of source code instrumentation, we only need compiled binaries for program testing. This is an advantage for the same reasons as stated in [7]. First, we are independent on the high level language and build processes. Second, we avoid any problems caused by compiler transformation after the build process, realized for example by obfuscation. Third, DeepFuzz is suited to fuzz closed source targets. Another important aspect of DeepFuzz is the ability to highly parallelize the proposed algorithm in Sect. 3. All intermediate steps can be modularized and distributed for parallel computing with a suitable framework. One disadvantage of DeepFuzz is that it is not directed towards a tagged point in the execution graph. It builds paths as deep as possible into the program, however with no preferably direction. In order to address this issue we are currently considering how to combine our approach with previous work on driving execution of the input space towards a selected region. Such a directed exploration can be achieved by using fitness functions as described in [13]. For example, we could integrate fitness functions in the path selection step.

First tests targeting OpenSSL-based parsers of Base64-encoded X.509 certificates promise well. Here, we adapted the concolic execution framework Triton [9], which itself uses the Z3 SMT solver [3]. A comprehensive evaluation of our approach on a broad range of targets is subject to future work.

Finally, DeepFuzz may help to circumvent current bottlenecks related to automatic exploit generation as described by Avgerinos et al. in [1]. We expect that our proposed algorithm can be deployed for automatic exploitation of vulnerabilities deeply hidden in binaries.

References

1. Avgerinos, T., Cha, S.K., Rebert, A., Schwartz, E.J., Woo, M., Brumley, D.: Automatic exploit generation. Commun. ACM **57**(2), 74–84 (2014)
2. Cadar, C., Sen, K.: Symbolic execution for software testing: three decades later. Commun. ACM **56**(2), 82–90 (2013)
3. de Moura, L., Bjørner, N.S.: Z3: an efficient SMT solver. In: Ramakrishnan, C.R., Rehof, J. (eds.) TACAS 2008. LNCS, vol. 4963, pp. 337–340. Springer, Heidelberg (2008)
4. Geldenhuys, J., Dwyer, M.B., Visser, W.: Probabilistic symbolic execution. In: Proceedings of the 2012 International Symposium on Software Testing and Analysis, pp. 166–176. ACM (2012)
5. Godefroid, P., Klarlund, N., Sen, K.: DART: directed automated random testing. In: ACM SIGPLAN Notices, vol. 40, pp. 213–223. ACM (2005)
6. Godefroid, P., Levin, M.Y., Molnar, D.: SAGE: whitebox fuzzing for security testing. Commun. ACM **55**(3), 40–44 (2012)
7. Godefroid, P., Levin, M.Y., Molnar, D.A.: Automated whitebox fuzz testing. In: NDSS, vol. 8, pp. 151–166 (2008)
8. Majumdar, R., Sen, K.: Hybrid concolic testing. In: 29th International Conference on Software Engineering, 2007, ICSE 2007, pp. 416–426. IEEE (2007)
9. Saudel, F., Salwan, J.: Triton: a dynamic symbolic execution framework. In: Symposium sur la sécurité des technologies de l'information et des communications, SSTIC, France, Rennes, 3–5 June 2015, pp. 31–54. SSTIC (2015)
10. Sen, K., Marinov, D., Agha, G.: CUTE: a concolic unit testing engine for C. In: European Software Engineering Conference, pp. 263–272 (2005)
11. Stephens, N., Grosen, J., Salls, C., Dutcher, A., Wang, R., Corbetta, J., Shoshitaishvili, Y., Kruegel, C., Vigna, G.: Driller: augmenting fuzzing through selective symbolic execution. In: Proceedings of the Network and Distributed System Security Symposium (NDSS) (2016)
12. Takanen, A., Demott, J.D., Miller, C.: Fuzzing for Software Security Testing and Quality Assurance. Artech House, Norwood (2008)
13. Xie, T., Tillmann, N., De Halleux, J., Schulte, W.: Fitness-guided path exploration in dynamic symbolic execution. In: IEEE/IFIP International Conference on Dependable Systems and Networks DSN 2009, pp. 359–368. IEEE (2009)

Defenses

AutoRand: Automatic Keyword Randomization to Prevent Injection Attacks

Jeff Perkins[1(✉)], Jordan Eikenberry[1], Alessandro Coglio[2], Daniel Willenson[1],
Stelios Sidiroglou-Douskos[1], and Martin Rinard[1]

[1] MIT/CSAIL, Cambridge, MA, USA
{jhp,jeikenberry,dwillenson,stelios,rinard}@csail.mit.edu
[2] Kestrel Institute, Palo Alto, CA, USA
coglio@kestrel.edu

Abstract. AutoRand automatically transforms Java applications to use
SQL keyword randomization to defend against SQL injection vulnerabilities. AutoRand is completely automatic. Unlike previous approaches it
requires *no* manual modifications to existing code and does not require
source (it works directly on Java bytecode). It can thus easily be applied
to the large numbers of existing potentially insecure applications without
developer assistance. Our key technical innovation is *augmented strings*.
Augmented strings allow extra information (such as random keys) to
be embedded within a string. AutoRand transforms string operations so
that the extra information is transparent to the program, but is always
propagated with each string operation. AutoRand checks each keyword
at SQL statements for the random key. Experimental results on large,
production Java applications and malicious inputs provided by an independent evaluation team hired by an agency of the United States government showed that AutoRand successfully blocked all SQL injection
attacks and preserved transparent execution for benign inputs, all with
low overhead.

1 Introduction

SQL injection attacks are a critical vector of security exploits in deployed applications. SQL Injection [1] is the first entry in the CWE/SANS list of the top
25 most dangerous software errors [2]. Injection errors are also the first entry
in OWASP's top 10 web application security problems [3]. Given the demonstrated ability of attackers to exploit such vulnerabilities [4] and the exploitable
opportunities that this class of vulnerabilities presents to attackers on an ongoing basis [5], techniques that eliminate SQL injection vulnerabilities and prevent
SQL injection attacks are of primary importance to the future security of our
information technology infrastructure.

On the surface it would seem that SQL attacks could be prevented by following good coding practices (such as using prepared statements and/or sanitizing
inputs) that have been available for many years. Unfortunately, these practices
have to be followed 100 % of the time or an attack may be enabled. The con-
tinued prevalence of SQL injection attacks [5] bears evidence to the fact that a

© Springer International Publishing Switzerland 2016
J. Caballero et al. (Eds.): DIMVA 2016, LNCS 9721, pp. 37–57, 2016.
DOI: 10.1007/978-3-319-40667-1_3

different approach that doesn't rely on error-free development is required. Furthermore there is a large amount of existing SQL code that needs protection. It is unrealistic to expect this code to be retrofitted. The developer resources are often not available and in many cases the source code may not be accessible.

1.1 SQL Keyword Randomization

Instruction set randomization [6] protects systems against code-injection attacks by creating randomized instruction sets. An attacker that does not know the instruction set in use will inject invalid code which will not execute correctly.

SQL keyword randomization applies the same technique to SQL injection attacks. Conceptually the SQL grammar is changed to use randomized SQL keywords that are not known to possible attackers. Any code that is injected will not contain valid keywords and will thus yield an error when parsed thwarting any attack.

Existing randomization systems [7] require the developer to *manually* modify the program to randomize the SQL keywords that appear in constant strings. This requires program source and possibly significant developer time (see Sect. 6.2). In many cases, neither of these may be available. An automatic system is needed to address the large numbers of existing potentially insecure applications.

Building an automatic system, however, is challenging. A working solution must randomize all SQL keywords that can reach an SQL statement (by any path) while ensuring that those modifications do not change the semantics of the program or are made visible outside of the program (because that would leak the random key). Operations on strings containing random keys must preserve the keys and the original semantics of the operation. Since the keys change both the length and contents of the string, many operations (e.g., `substring`, `charAt`, `replace`) must be automatically converted.

1.2 AutoRand

We present a new system, AutoRand, that automatically transforms Java applications to use randomized SQL keywords[1].

The resulting transformed Java application is protected against SQL injection attacks that rely on using SQL keywords in the malicious input to change the structure of the SQL command passed to the SQL execution engine.

AutoRand automatically translates the Java bytecodes of the application to randomize any SQL keywords that appear in program constants or in trusted inputs. It transparently propagates the randomized versions of the keywords across string operations. Any use of randomized SQL keywords in other operations (e.g., file/socket writes, string comparisons, etc.) are automatically derandomized to ensure that the program's semantics are maintained.

---

[1] We use the term *keyword* to include keywords, operators and comment tokens.

AutoRand also inserts code that checks each SQL command to ensure that all keywords have the correct random value. If any keywords (such as those inserted by an attacker) are not correct, an exception is thrown. If all of the keywords are correct, the query is de-randomized and passed to the normal SQL routine.

AutoRand operates directly on byte-code and does not require source or manual modifications. It can easily be applied to existing applications without developer assistance. To our knowledge it is the first system to automatically apply SQL keyword randomization to existing programs.

Experimental results on large, production Java applications and malicious inputs provided by an independent evaluation team hired by an agency of the United States government showed that AutoRand successfully blocked all SQL injection attacks with no false positives and negligible overhead.

1.3 Augmented Strings

Our key technical innovation is *augmented strings*. Augmented strings allow additional information to be added to strings. This additional information is handled *transparently* with respect to the application. Augmented strings are designed to ensure that, with the exception of augmented checks (such as SQL query checks), the application exhibits the same behavior with augmented strings as without. The additional information is accounted for in all string operations to ensure that it is propagated across the operation without changing the semantics of the program. To accomplish this transparency, AutoRand automatically modifies string operations to ensure that the presence of the additional information is not visible to the program itself (e.g., conditionals over string values, reflection, etc.) or externally (e.g., network writes, environment variables access, etc.).

The additional information in an augmented string is identified by a random key. The key is complex enough to ensure that it will not occur (within some arbitrarily small probability) by happenstance in the program's input or constants. This allows the additional information to be precisely identified.

In the case of AutoRand, the random key is placed immediately after each SQL keyword to create a randomized version of the keyword in the augmented string. To our knowledge the augmented strings approach is novel and could be used in broader contexts than SQL injection, such as tracking the detailed provenance (filename, URL) of each token in a string, randomization for other injection issues (such as command injection) or carrying debug information.

1.4 Experimental Evaluation

We evaluate the AutoRand implementation on a set of benchmarks and associated inputs developed by an independent evaluation team hired by the sponsor of this research (an agency of the United States government). The evaluation team started with a set of existing large, production Java applications, inserted SQL injection vulnerabilities into the applications, and developed inputs that exploit the vulnerabilities. The evaluation team was given complete information about the AutoRand implementation. The results of the evaluation show that

AutoRand successfully blocked all SQL injection attacks. To test transparency and preservation of functionality, the evaluation also exercised the applications on benign inputs. The results showed identical behavior for each benign input. We note that this evaluation worked with applications that are over an order of magnitude larger than any previous evaluation of SQL injection attack defenses for Java programs of which we are aware [8–10]. AutoRand's ability to successfully block SQL injection attacks in these applications highlights the effectiveness of AutoRand's techniques and the robustness of the AutoRand implementation.

1.5 Contributions

This paper makes the following contributions:

- **AutoRand:** It presents a system for automatic and transparent SQL keyword randomization to *automatically* eliminate SQL injection vulnerabilities.
- **Augmented Strings:** It presents a technique that transparently adds information (in this case a random key) to strings and propagates that information across string operations. The original semantics of the application are preserved except where explicit checks utilizing the additional information are added (in this case for SQL injection attacks).
- **Experimental Evaluation:** It presents results from applications and inputs developed by an independent evaluation team. These results show that AutoRand successfully blocked all of the developed SQL injection attacks and correctly preserved transparent execution for all of the benign inputs.

2   Example

We next present an example that illustrates how AutoRand nullifies SQL injection attacks.

2.1 Vulnerable Code

Consider the Java fragment

```
String query = "select * from users where"
    "username='" + username + "' and password='" + password + "'";
ResultSet results =  databaseConnection.
    createStatement().executeQuery(query);
```
(1)

which looks up, in the users table of a database, the user whose name and password are in the string variables **username** and **password**. The query is constructed by combining a constant SQL code template with variable fragments that should only specify data. If **username** is jqd and **password** is xB34qy5s, the query sent to the database is

```
select * from users where username='jqd' and password='xB34qy5s'
```
(2)

and the application operates normally. However, if **username** is "' or 1=1 --" and **password** is the empty string, the query sent to the database is

```
select * from users where username='' or 1=1 --' and password=''     (3)
```

which always returns all records from the users table, since the password check has been commented out by the comment marker --. The latter input is crafted to subvert normal operation by executing SQL code that is part of the input data. This kind of subversion may cause loss of confidentiality and/or integrity. E.g., if username is "'; drop table users --" and password is the empty string, the query sent to the database is

```
select * from users where username=''; drop table users
    --' and password=''                                               (4)
```

where the semicolon separates the (now irrelevant) query from an injected drop statement that deletes the users table from the database.

If username and password are set from application inputs, the execution of the SQL query in (1) should be preceded by input validation, i.e., checks that username and password do not contain characters that may alter the structure of the SQL query (e.g., that they only contain letters and numbers). If the check fails, the inputs should be rejected or sanitized (e.g., by removing any character that is not a letter or a number). If the developer fails to include these checks, the code in (1) is vulnerable to SQL injection attacks.

2.2   Automatic Hardening by AutoRand

AutoRand automatically turns the code in (1) into code like

```
String query ="select<key> * from<key> users where<key> username='" +
    + username + "' and<key> password='" + password + "'";
ResultSet results = derandomizeAndExecuteQuery                        (5)
    (databaseConnection.createStatement(), query);
```

where <key> is a randomization key, i.e., a randomly chosen sequence of ASCII letters and numbers, e.g., di83e2371A. That is, all the SQL keywords that occur in string constants are randomized by appending <key>. The AutoRand run-time method derandomizeAndExecuteQuery tokenizes the query and checks each SQL keyword to ensure that it is suffixed by <key>. If the check succeeds, the query is deemed legitimate, all instances of <key> are removed, and the resulting query is executed normally by calling executeQuery. This check fails if an attacker injects a non-randomized keyword. For example, if username is "' or 1=1 --" and password is the empty string, the query

```
select<key> * from<key> users where<key> username=''
    or 1=1 --' and<key> password=''                                   (6)
```

fails the check because or and -- lack <key>. Since the attacker does not know the valid keywords for or and -- (i.e., does not know <key>), they are unable to create a successful attack.

AutoRand also automatically transforms other parts of the code to make keyword randomization transparent to non-SQL uses of the mutated strings. For instance, using `String.length()` to take the length of `query` in (5) should return the same value as `query` in (1)— the randomization key should not contribute to the count. Transparency is particularly important for output-related uses of the mutated strings, e.g., `String.out.println(query)`, because if the attacker were to see the randomization key in some output (e.g., error message) they would be able to inject correctly randomized keywords.

3   Technical Approach

AutoRand protects a Java application against SQL injection by statically transforming each class of the application, producing a hardened version of the application.

3.1   Correctness

In Java, strings are objects, whose contents are manipulated exclusively via a standard API, which consists of the classes `String`, `StringBuilder` and `String-Buffer`.[2] AutoRand intervenes in string method calls to ensure that keys are propagated (*propagation*) and do not affect the application (*transparency*)— other than protecting against SQL injection. AutoRand's transformation is correct if it maintains these properties.

- **Transparency:** A given AutoRand program state and (side-effect free) operation is *transparent* if running the operation in the state produces the same result as running the corresponding original operation in the derandomized state.
- **Propagation:** A given operation satisfies propagation if each keyword that is propagated from its inputs to its outputs is consistently randomized (i.e., the output keyword is randomized if and only if the corresponding input keyword was randomized).

Transparency guarantees that the original semantics of the program hold (except for the added SQL checks). Propagation ensures that randomized keywords in program constants or trusted inputs propagate through string manipulations to SQL statements. This ensures that they will parse correctly (in the absence of injection attacks). If a randomized keyword were not propagated correctly to an SQL statement the statement would not parse correctly and an exception would be incorrectly thrown (a false positive). A propagation error would *not* result in a false negative as the lack of a randomized key will always be treated as an error. There is no path by which an attacker can add the key to their keywords (other than by knowing the key).

---

[2] For simplicity, we use the term 'string' to refer to objects of all three classes.

Transparency. Abstractly, if op is an operation that takes a string S as input and yields a string as output, AutoRand's replacement operation op', in order to achieve transparency, must satisfy

$$op(S) = r^{-1}(op'(r(S))) \qquad (7)$$

where r randomizes strings and r^{-1} derandomizes strings.[3] The requirement (7) is easily adapted to operations that take multiple strings as input or yield non-strings (e.g. r^{-1} is a no-op for String.equals()). Derandomization r^{-1} removes all instances of the key, not only instances that follow SQL keywords, thus, string operations that modify keywords will not affect transparency.

Some string methods return values other than strings. The derandomization operation r^{-1} is a no-op for non-strings. Thus op' must return the same value as op (as required by equation (7)). Many of the non-string return values are indices into strings. These indices must reference the derandomized version of the string, not the randomized version. AutoRand's replacement operations must also accept index arguments that are with respect to the derandomized version of the string. These operations map any index arguments from the derandomized string to the corresponding index in the randomized string. For example, the following code adds some text to an SQL statement following the select keyword. The length of the select keyword is hard-coded.

```
StringBuffer sb = new StringBuffer(...);
int offset = sb.indexOf("select") + 6;                          (8)
sb.insert(offset, "field1, field2");
```

For this to work correctly on a randomized sb, the index must be translated to the corresponding index in the randomized buffer (after select<key>). Note that code similar to this exists in the real-world applications that we tested.

Propagation. Propagation is achieved if every randomized keyword in the input operands that is transferred to the result is also randomized in the result. For the purposes of SQL commands, keywords are a unit and only operations over a complete keyword (and not its individual characters) need to support propagation. Such sub-keyword operations may occur if the string is used for non-SQL purposes, but propagation is not required in such cases. As noted above, transparency is not affected by sub-keyword operations.

Abstractly, if op is an operation that takes a string S as input (where S may contain randomized keys) and yields a string as output, AutoRand's replacement operation op', in order to achieve propagation must satisfy

$$(K_r \in S) \wedge (K \in op(r^{-1}(S))) \iff K_r \in op'(S) \qquad (9)$$

---

[3] The requirement assumes that the key does not occur in S. The space of keys ensures a sufficiently small probability that the key occurs in the application code or data by happenstance.

where r^{-1} derandomizes strings, K_r is a randomized keyword and K is the corresponding keyword. A keyword in the output *corresponds* to a keyword in the input only if it is the same instance of the keyword (i.e., the characters that make up the keyword in the input were copied to the output).

3.2   String Randomization

AutoRand randomizes (each SQL keyword in) each string constant in the application code.

AutoRand randomizes each string constant by tokenizing it and then appending the randomization key to all the SQL keywords in the string. The string is left unmodified if no SQL keywords are found in it. The set of tokens that AutoRand regards as SQL keywords is easily configurable. The current default configuration protects against injection of standard SQL [11] as well as non-standard SQL extensions for popular databases. Since SQL keywords are case-insensitive, the AutoRand tokenizer is case-insensitive.

Each keyword is randomized by appending a randomization key consisting of 10 ASCII letters (upper case or lower case) or digits. For example, `select` could become `selecta2831jfy6`. To minimize the possibility that an attacker could generate the key by chance, we use a large space consisting of 62^{10} (i.e., over 800 quadrillion) possible keys. This corresponds to about 60 bits, which is small for cryptographic keys, whose threat model is offline brute force search. However, AutoRand's keys have a different threat model, namely an attacker attempting injections over the network, whose latency limits the rate at which keys can be tried. Nonetheless, AutoRand's key length is configurable and could be easily increased. Increasing the key by 10 characters increases the overhead (see Sect. 5.3) by only about 0.73 %.

3.3   SQL API Calls

Java applications access SQL databases via a standard Java API. The `java.sql.Statement` class provides methods to execute SQL statements passed as string arguments, e.g., `executeQuery()` in (1).

AutoRand wraps each call by the application to the methods of `Statement` and `Connection` that receive SQL statements and prepared statements as string arguments. Even though a prepared statement is not vulnerable to injections when the template is instantiated, the creation of the prepared statement itself is vulnerable to injection when the string (e.g., "`select * from users where username=? and password=?`") is assembled from parts that are not all trusted.

Each method wrapper first checks that all the keywords in the SQL string include the correct key. If any keyword does not have the key, the SQL string is deemed to result from an attack and the wrapper throws an exception.

If all the keywords have the correct key, the method wrapper removes every occurrence of the key and then calls the method of `Statement` or `Connection` with the resulting string.

3.4 String Manipulations

Just randomizing strings as described in Sect. 3.2 and wrapping SQL API calls as described in Sect. 3.3 would nullify SQL injection attacks but could disrupt the normal operation of the application. For instance, if `String.equals` were called on a program constant containing a keyword and an input containing the same keyword, it would incorrectly return `false`, changing the semantics of the application. Also, if a randomized string makes its way to an output that is visible to the attacker (e.g., `System.out.println(query)`), the attacker could learn the key and inject correctly randomized keywords. Thus, AutoRand implements further transformations to make keyword randomization transparent to the application (other than hardening the application against SQL injection), including any output that may be visible to the attacker.

When necessary, AutoRand intervenes in string method calls by replacing calls to string methods with calls to methods in the AutoRand string library.

The Java string methods fall into a few basic categories. AutoRand's approach for accomplishing transparency and propagation for each of those categories is described in the following subsections. The category, propagation, and transparency for each string method are shown in Fig. 2.

Observer Methods. Observer methods do not create or modify strings. They are handled by derandomizing each of the string arguments and then invoking the original method. Transparency is trivially accomplished as the original method is run on the derandomized arguments. There are no keyword propagation issues since strings are not created or modified.

For example, the implementation for `String.length` and `String.equals` are:

```
AutoRandLength (String s) {       AutoRandEquals (String s1, String s2) {
  return derand(s).length();        return derand(s1).equals(derand(s2));
}                                 }
```

Complete String Methods. Complete string methods operate on entire strings, and not on portions of them. Since the random keys are incorporated into the string itself, any operations that only involve complete strings will work correctly without modification. For example, `String.concat()` and `String-Buffer.append()` function correctly on randomized strings without modification.

Fortunately, these are amongst the most commonly used of the String functions, which is partially responsible for AutoRand's low overhead.

Partial String Methods. Partial string methods may operate on pieces of a string. The pieces are often specified by indices, but can also be specified by a string match (such as in `String.replace()`). For these methods, AutoRand

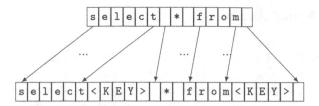

Fig. 1. Each character in the original (unrandomized) string is mapped to the corresponding character in the randomized string. There is no mapping to any of the characters in the randomization key. This ensures that no operation over mapped indices can create a partial key and that any operation over complete keywords will include the corresponding randomization key.

transfers the operation from the original (derandomized) string to the randomized string.

The three basic operators for partial strings are `substring`, `insert`, and `delete`. The location in the string is specified by one or more indices.

AutoRand creates an index map between the derandomized and randomized versions of the string (an example is shown in Fig. 1). This maps characters in the original (derandomized) string to the corresponding character in the randomized string. AutoRand implements `substring`, `insert`, and `delete` by looking up each index in the map and calling the original method on the randomized string using the mapped indices. This both propagates random keys and preserves transparency for each operation.

The `substring` method takes a substring from start (inclusive) to end (exclusive). Any substring that contains a keyword will include both the beginning character of the keyword and the character immediately after the keyword. Since the map of the character after the keyword will point after the randomization key, any substring that includes the keyword will also include its key. For example, consider `substring(9,13)` on the string in Fig. 1. This call would return the keyword `from` in the original string. After applying the index map this call is transformed into `substring(14,23)` on the randomized string. This will return `from<KEY>` in the randomized string, preserving the randomization key.

The `delete` method takes the same parameters as `substring` and works in the same fashion. For example, `delete(9,13)` would be transformed to `delete (14,23)` and would remove `from<KEY>` from the randomized string.

The `insert` method inserts its string argument before the specified index. The map ensures that inserts cannot occur between the keyword and its randomization key or in the middle of a randomization key, because there are no maps to those locations.

All other partial string methods can be built up from these core methods (substring, delete, and insert), and the observer and complete string methods. For example, the `String.replace(target,replacement)` can be implemented as

```
StringBuffer sb = new StringBuffer();
int start = 0;
int offset = this.indexOf(target);
while (offset != -1) {
  sb.append(this.substring(start,offset));
  sb.append(replacement);                        (10)
  start = offset + target.length();
  offset = this.indexOf(target,start);
}
sb.append(this.substring(start));
```

AutoRand re-implements each of the other non-core partial string methods in the same fashion.

Character Methods. Character methods convert (portions of) strings to their underlying characters, bytes, or code points (e.g., `toCharArray()`, `getChars()`, `getBytes()` and `charAt()`).

AutoRand derandomizes the string before making the conversion, preserving transparency. Since the result is not a string, random keys are not propagated (see Sect. 4 for more information)

Miscellaneous Methods. The `reverse()` method reverses the characters in a string. AutoRand derandomizes the string before making the conversion, preserving transparency. Propagation is not an issue as there are no single character keywords and thus keywords can not be transferred to the result. The `capacity()`, `ensureCapacity()`, and `trimToSize()` methods are not modified by AutoRand.

The `intern()` method returns a canonical representation for the string object. This is commonly used to conserve memory and also allows reference equality checks between interned strings. Since string constants are automatically interned and AutoRand modifies entries in the constant table, the randomized versions of constants are interned. This does not affect transparency unless reference equality is used to compare a constant with an interned input value. This kind of reference equality did not occur in any of the real-world programs used in the evaluation. Nonetheless, AutoRand could be extended to modify reference equalities (via the `if_acmp<cond>` bytecode) on strings to compare the (derandomized) contents of the strings if both sides of the equality test are interned.

3.5 External API Calls

Java strings can interact externally to the Java application through a number of Java system library calls. For example, writing to files/sockets, opening files, reading properties, reading environment variables, using reflection etc.

In these cases, the original strings should always be used. AutoRand accomplishes this by converting the application (and the system libraries themselves)

Category	Methods
Complete	\<init\>, append, appendCP, concat, copyValueOf, toString, valueOf
Observer	compareTo*, contains, contentEquals, endsWith, equals*, hashcode, indexOf, isEmpty, lastIndexOf, length, matches, offsetByCPs, regionMatches, startswith
Partial	delete*, format, insert, replace* setCharAt, setLength, split, subSequence, substring, toLowerCase, toUpperCase, trim
Character	charAt, codePoint*, getBytes, getChars, toCharArray
Misc	capacity, ensureCapacity, intern, reverse, trimToSize

Fig. 2. Synopsis of approach for each string method (in `String`, `StringBuffer`, and `StringBuilder`). Similar calls (indicated with *) are grouped together as are calls with the same name but different arguments. CodePoint is abbreviated as CP. *Category* is the type of call for AutoRand instrumentation purposes. See Sect. 3.4 for more information.

to call AutoRand's version of these routines. These routines derandomize their string arguments and then make the original call. This ensures that each external call acts correctly and that the random key is never visible to an attacker (since it is always removed before any external communications).

3.6   Standard Java Library

Strings are also manipulated within the standard Java library. For example, the `equals()`, `compareTo()` and `hashCode()` methods are called in the collection classes. Commonly used classes such as `Pattern` and `Matcher` call string methods and create new strings. AutoRand instruments the libraries in the same manner as it instruments the application. This ensures that any string manipulations within the libraries will correctly propagate random keys and ensures transparency over any strings containing random keys. The only differences are that constant strings within the standard libraries are not randomized (as they will not flow to application SQL commands).

AutoRand statically transforms the byte code of the standard Java libraries and creates a new version of the library. When an application hardened by AutoRand is run, it is run with the transformed version of the library.

3.7   Extensibility

AutoRand could be easily extended to randomize, besides SQL keywords, other kinds of keywords in strings, to provide protection against OS command injection, LDAP injection, XQuery/XPath injection, etc.

4   Threats to Validity

Our current AutoRand implementation is transparent with the following exceptions: (1) AutoRand performs the randomization checks at SQL API calls to detect SQL injection attacks. The lack of transparency at these API calls is one of the goals of AutoRand. (2) Intern calls may not be transparent with respect to reference equality. This is straightforward to implement but not currently implemented (see Sect. 3.4).

Our current AutoRand implementation satisfies propagation on all string operations over full keywords. However, there are some possible issues: (1) Converting strings to characters, bytes, or arrays thereof and back to strings. (2) Character-level manipulations that construct strings with SQL keywords (e.g., `"sel"` + `"ect"`). None of these occurred in any of the evaluation programs.

Because characters extracted from strings are manipulated as individual characters and not as strings, the randomization keys cannot be propagated for these methods. AutoRand thus derandomizes the string before making the conversion (preserving transparency). Fortunately, there is little reason to manipulate program constants in this fashion.

We evaluated this hypothesis experimentally by gathering information about how many times each character method is called in the evaluation programs on strings that contain randomization keys and the stack trace for each such call. We then examined each call to determine if it would pose a problem for propagation. Only strings that contain randomization keys are relevant to propagation.

The `getBytes()` method is called only in Ant and FTPS. In both cases it is used to prepare a string to be written to a stream. Strings that are written would be derandomized in any event (see Sect. 3.5) and are not an issue for propagation.

The `getChars()` and `toCharArray()` methods are called only by JMeter in a class that outputs XML (`PrettyPrintWriter`). Strings that are written out would be derandomized in any event (see Sect. 3.5) and are not an issue for propagation.

The `charAt()` method is called in 7 of the 8 evaluation applications. There were 12 unique call sites for `charAt()` on randomized strings in the seven applications. We examined each of these to determine how `charAt()` was being used and whether or not it was a problem for propagation. We found that these use cases for `charAt()` query the string for information, but do not use the resulting characters to build new strings. For example, the method `Selectorutils.tokenizePathAsArray` in Ant uses `charAt()` to look for slashes in the path. But the resultant array is built by normal string operations using the locations of the slashes as indices. Since AutoRand uses indices relative to the derandomized string, the offsets determined by querying `charAt()` are compatible.

The code point methods (e.g., `codePointAt()`) return full 32-bit character representations. Their usage would be similar to `charAt()` in programs that support the full Unicode set (and manipulate strings at the character level). These methods were not called in any of the evaluation applications.

None of the character methods were used to create new strings that are later used by the program. The examination of each use indicates that these do not present a propagation problem as they are commonly used. This validates our hypothesis that these calls are not used to manipulate strings but only to create specific output formats or to obtain information about the string. Propagation is not an issue in either case.

5 Experimental Evaluation

AutoRand has been experimentally evaluated using various Java programs.

5.1 Programs with Inserted Vulnerabilities

An independent test and evaluation (T&E) team hired by the government agency that is the sponsor of this research identified a set of Java programs, ranging in size up to 250 k lines of Java source, not including common third-party libraries:

- Ant (256 k LOC) —A build system.
- Barcode4J (28 k LOC)—A barcode generator.
- FindBugs (208 k LOC)—A bug finder.
- FTPS (40 k LOC)—An FTP server.
- HtmlCleaner (9 k LOC)—A reformatter of HTML files.
- JMeter (178 k LOC)—A performance measuring tool.
- PMD (110 k LOC)—A source code analyzer.
- SchemaSpy (16 k LOC)—A database inspecting tool.

The T&E team introduced SQL vulnerabilities into each program, and produced a set of malicious inputs to exercise the vulnerabilities. The T&E team also produced a set of benign inputs to exercise each program's standard functionality. They created 13 vulnerability variants to insert into the base programs. Each test case inserts one of the variants into the base program. The same variant can be applied to multiple locations in a base program. See Fig. 3 for details. As the figure shows, there are a total of 289 distinct test cases (base program + variant + injection location), 578 attack inputs, and 1444 benign inputs.

The malicious and benign inputs were sent to the program after hardening with AutoRand and the results observed to determine if the vulnerability was exploited in the case of malign inputs, and if functionality was preserved in the case of benign inputs. The inputs were also sent to the unaltered programs as a control. The AutoRand-hardened programs successfully blocked all of the attack inputs (i.e., injection attacks) and preserved functionality for all of the benign inputs.

The experiments were run using the Test and Evaluation Workbench (TEW) developed by the T&E team. The TEW works on an interconnected set of virtual machines where variant creation, compilation, and instrumentation are performed on one machine and execution of test cases performed on separate machine(s). The tests were performed on Debian 6.03 and the virtual machines were run on a 12 core machine using Xeon 3.47 Ghz processors. The TEW also includes support services such as the MySQL, PostgreSQL, SQLServer (Microsoft) and Hibernate database systems.

Test Program	Variant	Database	Cnt	Attack/ Benign inputs	Test Program	Variant	Database	Cnt	Attack/ Benign inputs
Ant	V01	MySQL	43	2/5	JMeter	V05	MySQL	1	2/5
Ant	V02	Postgres	1	2/5	JMeter	V08	SQLServer	2	2/5
Ant	V03	MySQL	9	2/5	JMeter	V10	SQLServer	1	2/5
Ant	V04	MySQL	1	2/5	JMeter	V11	SQLServer	1	2/5
FTPS	V01	MySQL	41	2/5	Barcode	V05	MySQL	1	2/5
FTPS	V03	MySQL	1	2/5	Barcode	V06	Postgres	55	2/5
FTPS	V04	MySQL	13	2/5	Barcode	V07	Postgres	1	2/5
FTPS	V05	MySQL	1	2/5	HtmlCleaner	V06	Postgres	44	2/5
PMD	V01	MySQL	11	2/5	FindBugs	V08	SQLServer	39	2/5
PMD	V12	MySQL	14	2/5	FindBugs	V09	SQLServer	6	2/5
PMD	V13	MySQL	1	2/5	FindBugs	V10	SQLServer	1	2/5
SchemaSpy	V02	Postgres	1	2/4					

Fig. 3. Injected vulnerability programs and variants. Each variant is injected into the base program at *Cnt* different locations creating *Cnt* versions of the program. The attack and benign inputs are then applied to each version. For example, in the first row, 43 versions of Ant are created with the V01 vulnerability code inserted in a different location in each. Then 2 attack inputs and 5 benign inputs are applied to each of the 43 versions of Ant. AutoRand detects each attack with no false positives or semantic changes to the program.

5.2 SQL Injection Test Programs

The same T&E team also wrote 17 small programs (see Fig. 4) for the purpose of testing systems like AutoRand that protect against SQL injection. Each program reads inputs and uses them in SQL queries. The programs work as expected with benign inputs but are subject to SQL injection with malicious inputs. The tests covered the MySQL, Hibernate, and PostgreSQL database engines, a variety of SQL query syntax, and the `Statement.execute()`, and `Connection.prepareStatement()` Java SQL API calls.

Several different types of attack inputs were used across the tests including:

- **String Tautology** - Closing the application's quote of a string input early and then adding a tautology. For example one attack input is: ' OR '1'='1. The resulting SQL is: ...`password=''` OR '1'='1'... which will always be true (thus evading the password check).
- **Adding Code** - After a valid string or numeric input, additional code is added.
- **Comment out code** - After a valid string or numeric input, comment characters are added that stop processing of any remaining characters in the command. This can be combined with *Adding Code* to execute arbitrary commands.

We hardened each program using AutoRand and executed the programs with each of their benign and attack inputs. The AutoRand-hardened programs

Test Program	Lines of code	Database	Attack/ Benign inputs	Test Program	Lines of code	Database	Attack/ Benign inputs
TC	1055	MySQL	3/1	TC-3073	198	Hibernate	2/2
TC-3008	1723	MySQL	1/2	TC-3078	192	Hibernate	1/3
TC-3010	1680	MySQL	1/2	TC-3104	197	Hibernate	1/3
TC-3014	1166	MySQL	1/2	TC-3105	199	Hibernate	1/3
TC-3015	1127	MySQL	3/1	TC-3106	194	Hibernate	1/3
TC-3016	1055	MySQL	1/1	TC-3166	1221	MySQL	2/1
TC-3017	1780	MySQL	1/2	TC-3174	1298	MySQL	1/1
TC-3044	1054	MySQL	3/1	TC-3177	370	MySQL	1/1
TC-3045	1730	Postgres	4/1	TC-3178	315	MySQL	1/1

Fig. 4. SQL injection tests written by the T&E team. Each test applies the benign and attack inputs to the same SQL statement. AutoRand detected each attack with no false positives.

Test Program	Variant	Runs	Overhead Percent	Test Program	Variant	Runs	Overhead Percent
Ant	V01	25	4.6	FTPS	V05	25	0.0
Ant	V02	25	0.5	FTPS	All	100	0.0
Ant	V03	25	2.2	HtmlCleaner	V06	25	6.8
Ant	V04	25	2.7	HtmlCleaner	All	25	6.8
Ant	All	100	2.5	JMeter	V05	25	2.7
Barcode	V05	25	3.5	JMeter	V08	25	0.3
Barcode	V06	25	3.4	JMeter	V10	25	0.3
Barcode	V07	25	17.2	JMeter	V11	25	0.4
Barcode	All	75	8.1	JMeter	All	100	0.9
FindBugs	V08	25	10.3	PMD	V01	25	6.1
FindBugs	V09	25	11.1	PMD	V12	25	7.2
FindBugs	V10	25	23.8	PMD	V13	25	8.6
FindBugs	All	75	15.1	PMD	All	75	7.3
FTPS	V01	25	0.0	SchemaSpy	V02	20	3.4
FTPS	V03	25	0.0	SchemaSpy	All	20	3.4
FTPS	V04	25	0.0	All	All	570	4.9

Fig. 5. Overhead for test programs. One example of each program/variant was run (native and instrumented) five times over each of its inputs.

successfully blocked every attack input while leaving behavior unchanged for every benign input.

5.3 Overhead

To measure the overhead incurred by randomization, we randomly chose one example test case from each program/variant combination (Fig. 3) for a total of 23 applications.[4] We ran each over each of its benign inputs five times and measured the total wall clock time. We repeated this process with the hardened version of each variant and compared the times. The average overhead ranged from 0 % for FTPS to 15.1 % for FindBugs with an average of 4.9 %. See Fig. 5.

We also measured server overhead (a common use case for SQL injection defenses). OpenCMS [12] is an open-source Java program (consisting of over 100k lines of code) for managing web sites. It runs as a web application in the Apache Software Foundation's Tomcat framework [13]. It uses a database to store web site content and configurations. SQL injection attacks might thus be possible by sending customized URLs to the OpenCMS web application.

To measure the overhead incurred by randomization, a script was developed to send 1,000 benign URLs to an OpenCMS installation and record the resulting HTML responses. (The URLs were captured while interacting with the installation to manage a web site.) The total time required to process all of the URLs was measured both before and after hardening of the OpenCMS code by AutoRand. The average overhead was 4.5 %. The recorded HTML responses were also compared to ensure that functionality was not altered.

The OpenCMS test was performed on a virtual machine running Ubuntu 12.04 on a 3.6 Ghz 4 core iMac with 32 GBytes of memory. Both the client and the server ran on the same machine using localhost with negligible network delays.

6 Related Work

6.1 Manual Prevention

The most common approach to preventing SQL injection attacks is defensive coding practices such as carefully validating all inputs and using parameterized query APIs [14, 15]. Unfortunately, as evidenced by the continuing prevalence of successful SQL attacks [5], these practices have not been sufficient to prevent attacks.

Defensive coding practices require trained developers that *always* follow the correct approach. A single shortcut can lead to a vulnerability. And they can be very expensive and time consuming to apply to legacy code. And they provide no protection without access to developers and source.

AutoRand, by contrast, allows code to be immediately protected without source code modifications or developer involvement.

6.2 Randomization

SQLRand [7] introduced a manual method to randomize SQL queries. To apply the method, a developer finds each string containing SQL keywords, determines whether or not that string is used to build an SQL command, runs the string

---

[4] The full test suite runs in a special environment and is difficult to instrument. The subset allowed for more manageable experiments.

through the SQLRand tool, and copies the result back into their program. SQL requests are checked by a database proxy. Requests that do not contain the correctly randomized keywords will result in an exception. SQLRand does not derandomize SQL keywords except in the proxy. Thus, if the modified strings are used for any other purpose, changes to program semantics may result (including accidental disclosure of the randomization key). SQLRand does not support strings that are used for multiple purposes (e.g., SQL and error messages).

AutoRand automatically transforms the program to randomize SQL keywords and ensure semantic correctness (e.g., string length, accidental disclosures, etc.). In addition, AutoRand does not require any additional network components (i.e., a proxy).

6.3 Dynamic Tainting

A popular technique for preventing SQL injection attacks is dynamic taint tracking [8,10,16–18]. Taint-tracking systems instrument applications with the ability to track the provenance of inputs and are thus able to determine if an SQL query contains any untrusted inputs. Unfortunately, most taint tracking systems have either (a) non-negligible performance overhead [8,10] or (b) reduce the scope of tracking they perform (i.e., they do not track character level information) that can lead to false positives and false negatives [16,17].

Chin et al. [10] implement a comprehensive taint tracking system (using character-level tainting), through modifications to the Java string library, that reports a modest overhead of about 15 %. Unfortunately, their performance evaluation numbers do not include any safety checks using the taint information. Safety checks typically contribute significantly to the overhead of taint tracking systems. Furthermore, their evaluation does not test the system on real-world applications; they focus on unit tests designed to test taint propagation. Their implementation requires changes to the string library that are only compatible with the IBM JVM and does not support common string related functions, such as regular expressions and `String.format()`.

WASP [8] is a taint tracking system that tracks trusted, rather than untrusted, data. WASP uses its MetaStrings library to mimic and extend the behavior of Java's standard string classes. It replaces strings allocated in the application with the MetaStrings equivalent. WASP does not, however, instrument the Java libraries (except to remove the `final` flag from the string classes). Strings allocated within the Java library will thus not include meta-data. Any operations within the library that creates a new string based on application strings (such as those in `Pattern`, `Matcher`, and `Formatter`) will not propagate taint. Also, the string classes contain methods (e.g., `format()` and `split()`) that are implemented using these classes. Unless MetaStrings re-implemented these without using the libraries these may suffer from the same propagation issues. Propagation failures in WASP can lead to false positives. In contrast, AutoRand propagates random keys through the Java libraries and has less overhead.

WASP could be extended to instrument the system libraries to avoid these issues, but one would expect its overhead to be significantly increased.

Diglossia [18] tracks taint in PHP by modifying the interpreter to create a shadow string that uses a mapped character set for trusted characters. It then parses the shadow string and the original string to ensure that tainted input doesn't change the parse tree. PHP interpreter based approaches are not directly applicable to Java as the complex Java JIT makes it significantly more difficult to efficiently modify the interpreter. AutoRand's bytecode transformation approach is more portable and maintainable.

6.4 Parse Tree Structure

Another technique for detecting SQL injection attacks is based on the observations that most attacks modify the SQL query structure (i.e., parse tree) as intended by the developer [9,19–21].

SQLGuard [19] and SQLCheck [20] are developer tools that can be used to statically define and dynamically check the integrity of SQL query structures. While successful at detecting a number of SQL inject attacks, they require manual modifications to the application. In contrast, AutoRand is fully automatic.

An alternative approach is to automatically learn query structure [9,21–23]. AMNESIA [22] and Halder et al. [23] use static analysis to create a model of query structure and a run-time system to detect structure violations. To scale its static analysis to real-world applications, AMNESIA is context- and flow-insensitive and thus susceptible to false-negatives and false-positives [21]. AutoRand is a dynamic technique and hence not susceptible to the imprecision introduced by static analysis.

CANDID [9,21] is a dynamic technique for extracting query structure. CANDID automatically transforms the application code to create a parallel, shadow data set for strings. Where the program assigns to a string variable, CANDID inserts code to assign to a shadow variable which will be used in the reference query. If the real variable is assigned a string constant, the shadow variable gets the same value. If the real variable receives a value from user input, the shadow variable gets a dummy value. String operations like concatenation are performed on both data sets in parallel. CANDID's published overhead is four times slower than AutoRand, most likely due to its added complexity.

6.5 Static Analysis

Several methods use static analysis to detect SQL injection attack vulnerabilities [24–26]. These systems identify unsanitized data flows from user input to SQL queries (i.e., they check whether every flow from input to query is subject to input validation). These techniques can verify that a sanitization technique is called on unsanitized flows but not whether the sanitization is correct, which can lead to false negatives. Given that static data-flow analysis must be conservative, these techniques, inescapably, also suffer from false positives.

7   Conclusion

SQL injection vulnerabilities comprise a prominent, serious, and ongoing source of security vulnerabilities. By delivering an automated, transparent, and efficient implementation of SQL keyword randomization, AutoRand provides one solution to this problem. Our results show that, on examples developed by an independent evaluation team, AutoRand, as designed, successfully blocked all SQL injection attacks and provided transparent execution for benign inputs, all with low overhead in large production Java applications.

Acknowledgements. We thank the MITRE Corporation test and evaluation team for creating an automatic and thorough testing apparatus. We thank Stephen Fitzpatrick and Eric McCarthy of Kestrel Institute for their contributions to the project. We thank Michael Gordon of Aarno Labs for comments that greatly improved the manuscript.

References

1. Common Weakness Enumeration (CWE) 89: Improper neutralization of special elements used in an SQL command ('SQL injection'). http://cwe.mitre.org
2. SANS Institute, MITRE, et al.: CWE/SANS Top 25 Most Dangerous Software Errors, September 2011. http://cwe.mitre.org/top25
3. OWASP Foundation: OWASP Top Ten Project, June 2013. https://www.owasp.org/index.php/Top_10_2013-Top_10
4. Clarke, J.: SQL Injection Attacks and Defenses, 2nd edn. Syngress, Massachusetts (2012)
5. Code Curmudgeon: SQL injection hall of shame. http://codecurmudgeon.com/wp/sql-injection-hall-of-shame/. Accessed 24 June 2014
6. Kc, G.S., Keromytis, A.D., Prevelakis, V.: Countering code-injection attacks with instruction-set randomization. In: CCS 2003, pp. 272–280 (2003)
7. Boyd, S.W., Keromytis, A.D.: SQLrand: preventing SQL injection attacks. In: Jakobsson, M., Yung, M., Zhou, J. (eds.) ACNS 2004. LNCS, vol. 3089, pp. 292–302. Springer, Heidelberg (2004)
8. Halfond, W.G.J., Orso, A., Manolios, P.: Using positive tainting and syntax-aware evaluation to counter SQL injection attacks. In: SIGSOFT 2006/FSE-14 (2006)
9. Bisht, P., Madhusudan, P., Venkatakrishnan, V.N.: Candid: dynamic candidate evaluations for automatic prevention of SQL injection attacks. ACM Trans. Inf. Syst. Secur. **13**(2), 14:1–14:39 (2010)
10. Chin, E., Wagner, D.: Efficient character-level taint tracking for Java. In: Proceedings of the 2009 ACM Workshop on Secure Web Services (2009)
11. ISO/IEC 9075:2011 - Information technology - Database languages - SQL
12. Alkacon Software: OpenCms, May 2012. http://www.opencms.org
13. Apache Foundation: Apache Tomcat, January 2012. http://tomcat.apache.org/
14. Veracode: SQL injection cheat sheet and tutorial. http://www.veracode.com/security/sql-injection. Accessed 1 August 2014
15. OWASP: SQL injection prevention cheat sheet. https://www.owasp.org/index.php/SQL_Injection_Prevention_Cheat_Sheet. Accessed 1 Aug 2014
16. Nguyen-Tuong, A., Guarnieri, S., Greene, D., Shirley, J., Evans, D.: Automatically hardening web applications using precise tainting (2005)

17. Pietraszek, T., Berghe, C.V.: Defending against injection attacks through context-sensitive string evaluation (2006)
18. Son, S., McKinley, K.S., Shmatikov, V.: Diglossia: detecting code injection attacks with precision and efficiency. In: CCS 2013, pp. 1181–1192 (2013)
19. Buehrer, G., Weide, B.W., Sivilotti, P.A.G.: Using parse tree validation to prevent SQL injection attacks. In: SEM 2005 (2005)
20. Su, Z., Wassermann, G.: The essence of command injection attacks in web applications. In: POPL 2006, pp. 372–382 (2006)
21. Bandhakavi, S., Bisht, P., Madhusudan, P., Venkatakrishnan, V.N.: Candid: preventing SQL injection attacks using dynamic candidate evaluations. In: CCS 2007 (2007)
22. Halfond, W.G.J., Orso, A.: Amnesia: analysis and monitoring for neutralizing SQL-injection attacks. In: ASE 2005, pp. 174–183 (2005)
23. Halder, R., Cortesi, A.: Obfuscation-based analysis of SQL injection attacks. In: ISCC 2010, pp. 931–938 (2010)
24. Jovanovic, N., Kruegel, C., Kirda, E.: Pixy: a static analysis tool for detecting web application vulnerabilities (short paper). In: SP 2006 (2006)
25. Livshits, V.B., Lam, M.S.: Finding security vulnerabilities in Java applications with static analysis. In: SSYM 2005, p. 18 (2005)
26. Fu, X., Lu, X., Peltsverger, B., Chen, S., Qian, K., Tao, L.: A static analysis framework for detecting SQL injection vulnerabilities. In: COMPSAC 2007 (2007)

AVRAND: A Software-Based Defense Against Code Reuse Attacks for AVR Embedded Devices

Sergio Pastrana[1]([✉]), Juan Tapiador[1], Guillermo Suarez-Tangil[2], and Pedro Peris-López[1]

[1] Department of Computer Science, University Carlos III de Madrid, Leganés, Spain
{spastran,jestevez,pperis}@inf.uc3m.es
[2] Information Security Group, Royal Holloway University of London, Egham, UK
guillermo.suarez-tangil@rhul.ac.uk

Abstract. Code reuse attacks are advanced exploitation techniques that constitute a serious threat for modern systems. They profit from a control flow hijacking vulnerability to maliciously execute one or more pieces of code from the targeted application. ASLR and Control Flow Integrity are two mechanisms commonly used to deter automated attacks based on code reuse. Unfortunately, none of these solutions are suitable for modified Harvard architectures such as AVR microcontrollers. In this work, we present a code reuse attack against embedded AVR devices that shows how an adversary can execute arbitrary code reused from the firmware and other external libraries. We then propose a software-based defense based on fine-grained random permutations of the code memory. Our solution is installed in the bootloader section of the embedded device and thus executes during every device reset. We also propose a self-obfuscation technique to hinder code-reuse attacks against the bootloader.

Keywords: Code reuse attacks · Return Oriented Programming · AVR · Internet-of-things · Embedded devices · Memory randomization

1 Introduction

The widespread adoption of communicating technologies such as smart or wearable devices enables users to interconnect their systems world-widely. The so-called Internet of Things (IoT) represents the integration of several computing and communications paradigms that facilitate the interaction between these devices. In this context, security and privacy play an important role as many of these devices incorporate sensors that could leak highly sensitive information (e.g., location, behavioral patterns, and audio and video of the device' surroundings). Moreover, embedded devices are frequently connected to the Internet, so they are valuable targets for malicious activities, such as botnets or spammers.

One common architecture for embedded devices is AVR[1], which is a modified Harvard architecture that physically separates the flash memory from the SRAM

---

[1] http://www.atmel.com/products/microcontrollers/avr/.

© Springer International Publishing Switzerland 2016
J. Caballero et al. (Eds.): DIMVA 2016, LNCS 9721, pp. 58–77, 2016.
DOI: 10.1007/978-3-319-40667-1_4

memory. While the former contains the executable binary, the latter stores the program data, heap, and stack. Flash memory can only be re-programmed from a special section called *bootloader*, and applications cannot be modified at runtime without flashing the entire memory. In addition, the number of times a memory can be flashed (namely cycles) is limited.

Memory corruption vulnerabilities have been widely explored as a strategy to hijack the execution control flow for a huge variety of systems, including embedded and mobile devices [6,12,15]. In the past, once the adversary gained control of the execution, the immediate next step was to directly jump into its own malicious payload, which was already injected in the exploit [8]. However, Data Execution Prevention (DEP) techniques turn code injection useless. AVR—together with other Harvard architectures—incorporate a type of hardware based DEP defense. This avoids the flash memory (where the executable code resides) being written from anywhere else except from the bootloader section, which also resides in the flash memory. Thus, the only means to exploit AVR devices is by reusing existing software from the flash memory [12,15].

Related Work. Code reuse attacks were first implemented by reusing different functions imported from various libraries (such as libc [27]). Well-known countermeasures such as Address Space Layout Randomization (ASLR) [5] modify the memory layout of the function libraries during the loading process to effectively hinder these return-to-lib attacks. However, modern code reuse attacks can arbitrarily perform certain operations to carefully chain different pieces of code (called gadgets) based on the Return Oriented Programming (ROP) paradigm [17,20]. In fact, code reuse attack are still feasible in ASLR-based defenses using ROP due to memory leakage vulnerabilities [24]. For example, the JIT-ROP attack in [23] disassembles pages obtained from the leaked address to build a gadget chain at runtime. The exploitation of memory leakages assumes that the adversary can use large payloads, and that she can exploit the vulnerability several times. However, these assumptions are not generally valid for AVR devices, and the threat model is different from other less constrained architectures such as ARM or x86.

Countermeasures against code reuse attacks have been widely explored recently [4,6,7,9,10,12,15,18,22]. Current defenses can be classified as follows:

1. Memory randomization [4,6,9,25] obfuscates the layout of the program binary. To overcome memory leakages, this technique relies on certain Execute-only-Memory (XoM) areas, which can neither be read nor written. These areas can be used to store trampolines to real, randomized areas of code. Many of these solutions rely on hardware-specific properties, such as Intel Extended Tables [9,25], which obviously are not applicable to AVR. A recent work by Braden et al. [6] performs a software-based XoM for ARM embedded devices. However, the authors also rely on a specific hardware component, namely the link register used in ARM, to prevent address disclosure.
2. Control Flow Integrity (CFI), which typically determines which are the valid targets for each control flow statement (e.g., jumps or returns), and prevents non-valid flows. CFI usually incurs an expensive overhead [18], which is not suitable for resource-constrained systems such as AVR.

Most of the attacks and defenses so far target either x86 or ARM architectures. In these cases, the adversarial model and the defense capabilities are radically different from those applicable to AVR. Current approaches aiming at hindering code reuse attacks in Harvard-based architectures rely on adding additional hardware [15] or modifying the existing one [13]. Such countermeasures introduce additional costs to these devices that cannot be overlooked. This is especially critical in scenarios where devices are expected to be inexpensive, as it usually happens with many IoT deployments. Furthermore, there are settings where the hardware is already given "as it is", such us in industrial environments [21], vehicular systems, and home automation projects [26], to name a few.

Contribution. In this work, we demonstrate code reuse attacks against AVR devices and provide a software-based defense named AVRAND. The novelty of our work lies in providing an inexpensive solution targeting endpoint users and distributions rather than manufacturers, vendors, or hardware architects. We argue that the capabilities of an attacker are much more limited when dealing with hardware constrained devices such as an Arduino. Based on this, we balance the trade-off between its capabilities and the level of protection implemented to provide a practical and robust countermeasure. To the best of our knowledge, this is the first work looking at this problem from this viewpoint that proposes a software-based defense for AVR-based devices. Our randomization engine is encoded in the bootloader section of the device and, thus, it is executed after every reboot. Moreover, since the bootloader itself is a potential target for code reuse attacks, AVRAND applies an obfuscation technique using an XOR-based self encryption function. To facilitate reproducibility of our results and foster research in AVR security, we provide functional prototypes of the attack and the proposed defense for an Arduino Yun device (Sect. 5), which is an emerging platform widely used in the IoT arena.

2   Background

In this section, we provide a brief background on the target systems studied in this work: the AVR architecture and the Arduino Yun, which is the platform used during our experimentation.

2.1   The AVR Architecture

AVR is a modified Harvard architecture implemented by Atmel in 1996. AVR is widely deployed in embedded devices due to its simplicity and low cost, and it is present in a variety of applications, including automotive systems [3], the toy industry, and home automation systems [26].

AVR devices store code and data in memories that are physically separated, i.e., the flash memory and the data or SRAM memory (see Fig. 1a). To allow self-programming, two special instructions are provided to load data from flash to SRAM memory (Load Program Memory, LPM), and to store data in the flash memory (Store Program Memory, SPM). The latter can only be invoked from

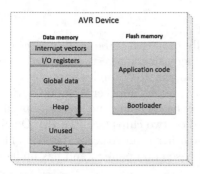

(a) Schematic view of AVR memories.   (b) Arduino Yun board.

Fig. 1. AVR and Arduino Yun boards.

a special memory region called the *bootloader*, and thus all the reprogramming code must reside in this region. The flash memory in AVR is structured in pages, which are addressed different than the SRAM. Actually, the program counter (PC) does not hold the actual address, but a page-based index. Specifically, the most significant bits of the PC are mapped to the page number, while the less significant bits are mapped to the offset within the page. As shown throughout this paper, AVRAND uses this property to manage the memory randomization efficiently. AVR has 3 special registers, called X, Y and Z, that are used for direct and indirect addressing and have added properties such as automatic increment (e.g., Y++) or fixed displacement (e.g., Y+k). These special registers are mapped with 8-bit general purpose registers (e.g., Y is the concatenation of r28 and r29).

The SRAM contains the program data, the heap and the stack, which are unique as AVR runs a single process at a time. A property of AVR is that the stack starts at the highest address and grows towards lower addresses (i.e., a *PUSH* instruction stores a new byte in the stack and decreases the stack pointer), while the heap grows towards higher addresses and can eventually collide with the stack. Additionally, the data memory also contains I/O registers such as the status register or the stack pointer. This implies that the stack pointer is directly mapped in program memory and can be read and write by load and store instructions, respectively.

Code running in embedded AVR devices may contain a huge amount of firmware and library functions required to integrate and operate different sensors, such as thermometers, motion sensors, cameras, etc. Since AVR does not provide dynamic loading of libraries, integrated libraries are statically linked at compilation time. AVR binaries follow the Hexadecimal Object File (HEX) format [16]. These binaries must be uploaded (flashed) to program memory using either an In-System Programming interface (ISP) or by communicating with the bootloader using a universal asynchronous receiver/transmitter (UART) [2].

2.2   Arduino Yun

Arduino[2] is an open-source platform originally proposed to be used in electronics and microcontroller projects. With the increasing interest in the IoT, the Arduino Yun has been designed specifically to run IoT applications, by combining both the low-level electronics originally present in other Arduino devices with higher level architectures running a Linux based operating system. Specifically, the Arduino Yun contains a board based on two chips (see Fig. 1b). One is the Atmel ATmega32u4 (AVR MCU) and the other is an Atheros AR9331. The Atheros processor holds a Linux distribution based on OpenWrt and has built-in Ethernet and WiFi support.

The AVR chip and the OpenWrt are connected through a *Bridge*, i.e., a logical component programmed in the OpenWrt which communicates with the AVR chip using a serial port. An Arduino Bridge library provides the required functionality to communicate applications running in the AVR chip with the OpenWrt, including a *Process* object that allows to run shell commands in the OpenWrt *shell* or a *HttpClientd* that allows to connect the AVR to internet. As shown in Sect. 3.3, the proposed exploit uses functions from the Bridge library to compromise the OpenWrt shell.

3   Code Reuse Attacks in AVR

In this section, we demonstrate code reuse attacks in AVR binaries using ROP and other similar exploiting techniques [27]. We first present the adversarial model assumed and then provide a general description of the attack. Finally, we describe the implementation of a prototype for Arduino Yun devices.

3.1   Assumptions and Adversarial Model

In this work, we consider the following assumptions and adversarial settings:

- The targeted embedded device is based on the AVR architecture and it is not tamper-proof. Thus, if physically accessible, the adversary can dump all the contents from the data and code memories at any time.
- The adversary cannot inject arbitrarily large payloads. We elaborate more on this limitation in Sect. 3.2. However, an adversary could inject relatively large payloads in memory by using software resets and multiple runs.
- The adversary could gain the control of the program flow by remotely exploiting a memory corruption vulnerability on the device, for example a stack or heap overflow.
- The program includes library functions that are useful for the adversary. For example, we assume that the program includes the *Bridge* lib that allows communication between the AVR and OpenWrt chips in Arduino Yun.

---

[2] https://www.arduino.cc.

3.2 Attack Overview

In this section we present a code reuse attack for AVR devices. Due to the limited capacity of the AVR memory, the adversary is not able to use large exploiting payloads, and thus she has to inject additional data into the SRAM. This is also used when a function library function is *called by reference*, i.e., when the arguments are passed as pointers to data memory. Contrarily to other architectures, function arguments in AVR are passed via registers whenever possible, and through the stack only when the arguments are larger than the length of the registers. An adversary may also be able to change any data from the SRAM memory. For example, Habibi et al. [15] proposed an attack that modifies the registers of an Unmaned Aerial Vehicle (UAV) gyroscope to control its flight.

Injecting Data into the SRAM. Injecting data into the SRAM is limited by the amount of memory available for the exploit. The main idea is to use a set of gadgets that, when chained together, could potentially store data into non-volatile areas of the SRAM memory [12,15]. We call this chain of gadgets *Store_data*. Ideally, the fewer the number of gadgets used the better, as each gadget may require to include its pointer in the exploit. During our experimentation, we have found a pair of gadgets that allow an adversary to build a payload that loads several values in memory recursively. We provide more details of these gadgets and how they are used in our prototype in Sect. 3.3.

Since the stack is located at the highest address of the SRAM memory, the space available to inject a payload after overflowing the stack is significantly limited. When a buffer is locally declared in a function, the return address is stored at a higher position of the memory allocated in the stack. This position may be close to the end of the SRAM address space (see Fig. 1a). Thus, the adversary is not able to send large attack payloads as it is usually done in ROP attacks against conventional architectures [23]. To partially overcome this issue and provide more space, the stack pointer can be moved to the beginning of the buffer as proposed in [15]. In this way, the buffer itself can be fully used to allocate the payload, and the size of the payload injected by the adversary intrinsically depends on the available buffer size. We call the gadgets that allow to move the stack *Stack_move*.

Given that the amount of injected data is limited, exploiting the same vulnerability multiple times could place the attacker in an advantageous position. However, exploiting a buffer overflow usually leaves the memory in a non-deterministic state and the attacker is usually forced to reset the device each time to maintain the device functional and/or resume its normal operation. To this end, existing works proposed to repair the stack right after the attack succeeds [14,15]. While this is useful to modify a few memory data bytes (such as the UAV gyroscope), repairing the stack does not provide the adversary with extra data space since the payload is always limited by the memory size—in fact, using the gadgets that repair the stack requires additional space in the payload. In this regard, Francillon and Castellucia [12] proposed to perform a software reset by directly jumping to the address $0x0000$ (i.e., the reset vector).

However, this approach is not suitable for modern AVR chips since it does not guarantee that the I/O registers are restored to their initial state[3]. In this work, we propose the use of a gadget, namely *Reset_chip*, that uses a *watchdog reset*, which is one of the reset sources used in AVR. More precisely, the gadget first establishes a watchdog timer and then jumps to an infinite loop. When the timer expires, the watchdog causes a software reset.

Figure 2 shows a schematic view of a generic data injection attack. When the vulnerable function is called, the return address is pushed on the stack. The attack starts by overwriting this address with the address of the *Stack_move* gadget (Step 1), which pops the new address and stores it in the memory address corresponding to the stack pointer (SP). From there on, the buffer constitutes the new stack (Step 2). Then, the address of the next gadget is popped from the stack, so the first bytes of the buffer must point to the *Store_data* gadget (Step 3) that stores the data at a given address (Step 4). As showed in Sect. 3.3, both the stored data and the SRAM memory addresses must be included in the payload. Finally, when the *Store_data* gadget returns (Step 5), the program jumps to the *Reset_chip* gadget (Step 6), which performs a clean software reset of the AVR chip. The adversary, while needed, may send a new payload to exploit the vulnerability and store additional data in consecutive addresses. In every reboot, the *.data* and *.bss* sections (i.e., data and heap) of the SRAM memory are cleared and reloaded, so if the adversary stores data in a memory area different from these (e.g., the region tagged as *unused* in Fig. 1a), then such data will persist across reboots.

Calling Library Functions. Once the required data are stored in memory, the adversary is ready to use library functions. The idea is to perform a similar approach to classical "return-to-lib" attacks [27]. Arguments are passed through registers, which can be easily loaded by using gadgets that pop values from the stack and stores them in registers. During our experimentation we have observed that these gadgets are frequent in many AVR binaries.

The adversary is now ready to call the library function using a chain of gadgets that performs the desired operation. First, she must load the arguments and prepare the required data (e.g., pointers to objects) using the data injection scheme explained above. Next, the program flow must jump to the desired function itself.

3.3   Attack Implementation in Arduino Yun

In this section, we describe and implement an attack that targets Arduino Yun devices, allowing an adversary to execute remote commands in the OpenWrt environment of these devices (i.e., bypassing the *Bridge* between the two chipsets). The attack comprises two phases: *injection* and *invocation*. First, it starts by injecting the command into SRAM memory as a *String* object, and then

---

[3] http://www.atmel.com/webdoc/AVRLibcReferenceManual/FAQ_1faq_softreset. html.

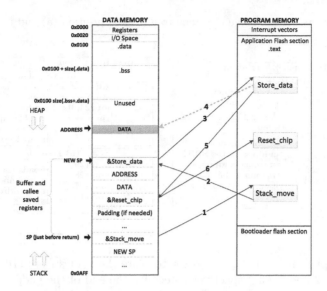

Fig. 2. Scheme of the data injection ROP attack.

forces the execution of the function *runShellCommand(String* cmd)* from the Bridge Library[4] by passing as argument the pointer to the injected object.

We assume that the adversary is able to exploit a memory corruption vulnerability and hijack the control flow. In this work, we have exploited a function (implemented ad-hoc for the prototype) that receives data from the serial port and stores it into a buffer, without checking its bounds. By sending crafted data, we are able to overwrite the return address of the function and take control of the program flow. We next explain the implementation details of the attack.

Command Injection into the SRAM. Table 1a shows a pair of gadgets that chained together move the stack pointer (SP) to a given address. The first gadget loads the new SP to registers r28 and r29, while the second gadget stores the SP in 0x3e and 0x3f, which are actually the positions mapping the SP. This is possible because AVR uses fixed positions of data memory to store I/O registers, including the SP. Gadgets used to move the stack are very frequent in AVR binaries, since they are used to save and restore the stack within the called functions.

To store the data in SRAM, we have found an optimal pair of gadgets (see Table 1b) that are included with the *String* library (imported by default in all Arduino programs). As these gadgets are consecutive in the code, they can be used recursively. In the first interaction, the gadget *Load_data* at address 0x2c00 loads data in registers r16 and r17, and the destination address in registers r28 an r29. As explained in Sect. 2.1, registers r28 and r29 are mapped to the register Y used for direct addressing. Here, the gadget *Store_data* showed in Table 1b uses

---

[4] https://www.arduino.cc/en/Reference/YunProcessConstructor.

Table 1. Gadgets used to move the stack to a desired position (a) and to inject data in SRAM (b).

Address	Instructions	Description
(a) Stack_mov_1		
0x0c84	pop r29 pop r28 ret	Loads the new stack pointer in registers r28 and r29
(a) Stack_mov_2		
0x39e4	in r0, 0x3f cli out 0x3e, r29 out 0x3f, r0 out 0x3d, r28 movw r28, r26 ret	Stores the new address in the SRAM memory addresses mapping the stack pointer (i.e. 0x3e and 0x3f)

Address	Instructions	Description
(b) Store_data		
0x2bf6	std Y+3, r17 std Y+2, r16 ldi r24, 0x01 rjmp .+2	Stores the values from r17 and r18 in addresses Y+3 and Y+4 (mapped to r29 and r28) and jumps to 0x2c00.
(b) Load_data		
0x2c00	pop r29 pop r28 pop r17 pop r16 ret	Loads the new values at r17 and r16 and new addresses at r28 and r29

the fixed displacement of the Y register to store the values from r16 and r17 in addresses Y+2 and Y+3 respectively. Because the end of the gadget *Store_data* directly jumps to the gadget *Load_data*, they can be used repetitively, as shown in Fig. 3.

To perform a software reset of the AVR chip, we use one of the reset sources provided by the AVR architecture, the *watchdog reset*, which establishes a time-out and resets the chip when it expires. Table 2a shows the gadgets used. A first gadget enables the watchdog and sets a timeout to 120 ms. This gadget is present in all Arduino programs since it belongs to one of its core libraries, CDC (the USB Connected Device Classes). The second gadget performs an infinite loop and is intended to wait until the timer expires. This gadget, which consists of just one instruction, is the last instruction of every Arduino program and represents the "stop-program" instruction that maintains the device in an *idle* state. By chaining these two gadgets, the chip automatically resets and the normal operation of the Arduino device is restored. Then, the adversary may send a new exploit to store more data, depending on what she wants to inject.

Command Invocation. In the previous section we have described how an adversary can store any data in the SRAM. Now, we show how she could use such data to execute commands in the OpenWrt of an Arduino Yun. Using the data injection process, the adversary writes in memory the raw sequence of characters of the command (e.g., "curl", as shown in Fig. 2). Then, a *String* object pointing to such sequence must be created. A *String* object has three components. First, a pointer to the sequence of characters (2 bytes); second, the length of the sequence (2 bytes); and, finally, its capacity (2 bytes).

To execute the inserted command, we call the function *runShellCommand* of the Bridge Library. This function takes as argument the address of the *String* object that represents the command, which is provided in registers. *Load_arguments* gadget, showed in Table 2b performs such loading. In many AVR binaries it is frequent to find pop instructions before a return, and thus

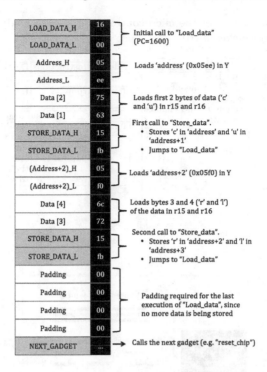

Fig. 3. Schematic view of a payload that inserts the command "curl" (0x63,0x75,0x72,0x6c) into a the address 0xef00 of SRAM memory using the gadgets from Table 1b.

it can be assumed that this gadget can be easily obtained. Finally, after the *Load_arguments* gadget is executed, the program should directly jump to the *runShellCommand* function which uses the Bridge between the two chips to execute the desired command in the OpenWrt.

4   Design and Overview of AVRAND

In order to defeat code reuse attacks, we propose AVRAND, a solution that randomizes the layout of the flash memory where the binary code resides and obfuscates the randomization engine. Since the core of AVRAND resides in the bootloader of the flash memory, it re-randomizes the complete program memory after every software reset, thus preventing attacks that exploit the vulnerability several times (e.g., brute force attacks) and requiring adversaries to use one-shot clean attacks (i.e., attacks that do not rely on software resets). Moreover, as we discuss in Sect. 6, AVRAND could be configured to defeat other exploitation techniques that do not require to reset the device.

AVRAND is composed by two main modules: *preprocessing* and *runtime*, as depicted in Fig. 4. First, the *preprocessing module* modifies the HEX file that is being uploaded into the AVR device so that it can be randomized. This module

Table 2. Gadgets used to reset the microcontroller (a) and to load the arguments to the function *runShellCommand* (b).

Address	Instructions	Description
	a) Reset_chip_1	
0x1c56	ldi r18, 0x0B	Sets the timeout
	ldi r24, 0x18	to 120 ms, disables
	ldi r25, 0x00	interrupts and enables
	in r0, 0x3f	the watchdog
	cli	
	wdr	
	sts 0x0060, r24	
	out 0x3f, r0	
	sts 0x0060, r18	
	ret	

Address	Instructions	Description
	a) Reset_chip_2	
0x3a0a	rjmp .-2	Relative jump to itself
		(i.e. infinitive loop)
	b) Load_arguments	
0x2b52	pop r25	Loads the arguments
	pop r24	into registers. Note that
	pop r23	some useless instructions
	pop r22	are omitted. Upon return
	...	the program should jump
	ret	to *runShellCommand*

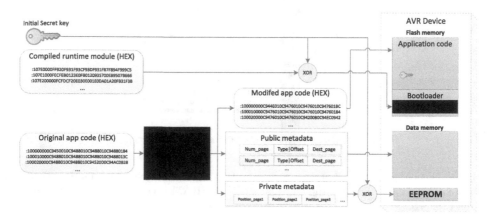

Fig. 4. AVRAND overview.

is executed once in an external computer, before uploading the binary to the device. Second, the *runtime module* is installed in the bootloader section of the device to perform the actual randomization of the flash memory after each device reset. Moreover, this module uses an obfuscation technique to prevent code reuse attacks on the bootloader, by applying XOR-based encryption.

Preprocessing Module. This module is executed once and prepares the code so that it can be randomized. First, it reads the original HEX file and gets a list of all the control-flow statements, including both absolute and relative pointers within the code (e.g., jumps and calls, conditional branches, etc.) and also indirect pointers that may be in the data section (e.g., C++ vtables). Using relative offsets is common in AVR binaries due to code-size optimization, but this is not compatible with a randomization approach since relative positions change from one layout to another. Thus, during the preprocessing module all the relative operations are replaced by their absolute versions (e.g., RJMP are substituted by JMP and RCALL by CALL instructions).

Since the flash memory in AVR is structured in pages, AVRAND performs randomization at a paged-grained level. However, in order to preserve the semantics of the entire code, pages are linked using JMP instructions. Thus, all control-flow statements in the code point to absolute positions and can be re-calculated at runtime during each randomization. Accordingly, the preprocessing module outputs a list of *public metadata* (i.e., we assume that an adversary may know this information) used to update the offsets during the randomization (see Sect. 5.1 for details). Furthermore, a list of initial page positions is also created to indicate the offsets of each page in the binary, which must be kept secret from adversaries and thus it is named *private metadata*.

The modified binary code is then flashed onto the flash memory and the *public metadata* in the SRAM, while the *private metadata* is encrypted with the XOR key and flashed in a non-readable memory area of the embedded device. For example, many AVR devices are equipped with an external EEPROM memory that is not directly addressable without special functions in the program binary, so it can be used to store the *private metadata*. Finally, the initial private key is stored in a fixed position of the flash memory. Note that during each randomization a new key is generated which overwrites the previous one.

Runtime Module. This module is installed in the bootloader section of the device and it performs the actual randomization of the memory layout each time the device is reset. First, it reads the current page positions (i.e., the offset of each page) from the *private metadata* to get the actual memory layout of the device, and decrypts it using the secret key. Second, it generates a map of random swaps indicating couples of pages randomly paired that must be exchanged. This map is used to update the current page positions in the *private metadata*. Furthermore, the offsets of every control-flow statement in the program memory are re-calculated and updated by using the new positions and looking at the *public metadata*. Finally, the entire memory is re-flashed, swapping all the pages that purely contain code. To do this, both pages are temporary stored in the SRAM and then they are re-written into each others' offsets of the flash memory. Note that a complete random permutation of the memory layout would require to store an entire copy of the binary in SRAM, which demands much more memory than keeping only two pages at a time in memory.

The entire flash memory is structured in pages, but certain pages cannot be shuffled during the randomization. These are pages that contain data (which are either before or after the code, never interleaved) and the first two pages which contains the interrupt vectors. Pages containing data remain in constant memory offsets. However, two pages may contain both data and code (i.e., one page before the program and one page after the program), and code in these pages may be used in a code reuse attack. In the worst case, each of these two pages will have a single byte of data and code in the bottom part of the section (i.e., $page\_size - 1$). Thus, the maximum size of code that remains constant during randomization is $2 * (page\_size - 1)$ (i.e., 254 bytes in the Atmega32u4 chip).

Each page contains 128 bytes of code, i.e., approximately 42 instructions. Thus, gaining knowledge of a single page does not position the attacker in a privileged situation since she may not find enough gadgets to perform a code-reuse attack. Moreover, the probability of guessing a page in AVRAND is $1/N_p$, where N_p is the number of swapped pages (which depends on the size of the program memory, as discussed below). This probability outperforms state-of-the-art solutions like Isomeron [10], which has a probability of 0.5 of being discovered at each gadget.

As stated before, the runtime module is compiled and uploaded into the bootloader section of the embedded system. Accordingly, this is the first piece of code being executed after every device reboot, which prevents code reuse attacks using software resets and reducing the chances for brute force attacks aiming to discover the memory layout. However, the bootloader itself could be the target of code reuse attacks (in our experiments, the bootloader contains around 4 KB of code) and thus it should be protected as well. AVRAND solves it by applying a simple obfuscation technique using an XOR based encryption. As such, most of the bootloader is stored encrypted. The runtime module uses a non-encrypted routine that is executed at the beginning to decrypt the bootloader and then jumps to its main function. Once the randomization is finished, and before jumping to the application section, a new random key is generated and used to re-encrypt the bootloader and the private data from the EEPROM.

5   Implementation

We have developed a freely available[5] prototype of AVRAND for the Atmel Atmega32u4 chip included in the Arduino Yun platform. In this section, we discuss its implementation details.

5.1   Preprocessing Module

We have implemented the preprocessing module in Python. It takes as input the HEX file of the original application and generates a modified HEX in such a way that it can be randomized at runtime by the bootloader. The initial list of control-flow statements is obtained from the assembly code, which is generated from the HEX file using the open source tools *avr-objcopy* and *avr-objdump* [19]. Control-flow statements may be one of the following: relative or absolute jumps (RJMP/JMP), relative or absolute calls (RCALL/CALL), conditional branches (BR), pointers to function prologues and epilogues (used by some functions to save registers in the stack), pointers to global variable constructors (CTORS) and C++ specific virtual pointers (vpointers). Also, a list of indivisible instruction sequences is obtained, in order to avoid placing jumps between them during the page linking. Examples of such non-breakable instructions are all the two-word instructions, or the CPSE instruction that compare two registers and jumps to PC+2 or PC+3 depending on the result.

---

[5] http://www.seg.inf.uc3m.es/~spastran/avrand/.

```
270: d9 f7      brne .-10; 0x268     270: 09 f4          brne .+2 ; 0x274
272: 24 e0      ldi r18, 0x04 ; 4    272: 02 c0          rjmp .+4 ; 0x278
                                     274: 0c 94 34 01    jmp 0x268 ;  0x268
                                     278: 24 e0          ldi r18, 0x04 ; 4
```

Fig. 5. Transformation of a relative conditional branch (left) to its absolute version (right).

Then, each instruction using relative offsets (i.e. RJMP and RCALL) is substituted by its corresponding absolute version (i.e., JMP and CALL). Changing relative by absolute versions adds 2 extra bytes. In case of conditional branches, we follow an approach similar to Oxymoron [4] to transform them into an absolute version, by adding a RJMP and a JMP instruction. This transformation is shown in Fig. 5. The whole BR/RJMP/JMP block is considered as an indivisible sequence in order to maintain its semantics. As it can be observed, each conditional branch modified adds 6 extra bytes to the binary code. Every time that the module inserts new code bytes, the offsets of the entire program are updated accordingly.

The next step is to link the pages using absolute JMP instructions, which are inserted in the bottom of each page, i.e., the last instruction of every page is a JMP to the first instruction of the next page. In this way, whenever a page changes its position during randomization, these linking pointers can be updated to point to the new address where the next page begins. The insertion of a JMP may occur between an indivisible sequence of instructions. If such situation is detected, the entire sequence is moved forward, to the beginning of the next page, by adding padding (i.e., NOP instructions).

Finally, the new HEX file is generated along with the *public metadata* and the *private metadata*. The *public metadata* provides the list of structures representing each control-flow statement. Concretely, each structure indicates the page where the statement is, the offset within the page, the type (i.e., CALL or JMP, prologue/epilogue function pointer, C++ vpointer or pointer to a global variable initialization routine), and the page pointed. Note that the offset within the page does not change in the randomization, and thus it is not necessary to store it since it can be obtained from the PC address, as explained in Sect. 2.1.

The binary code (HEX) and the *public metadata* are uploaded to the flash and data memories respectively, while the private metadata is encrypted (using an XOR-based encryption and a private key of 128 bytes) and uploaded to a memory region that is not directly observable by an adversary. During our experiments, we used the external EEPROM present in the Atmega32u4 chip of the Arduino Yun. In order to upload these contents to the device, we use the open source tool *avrdude* [11].

5.2 Runtime Module

The main purpose of the runtime module is to perform the randomization of the entire application after every device reset. Thus, it must be stored in the booloader section of the flash memory. However, the bootloader contains critical functions from the standard library, such as those for reading and writing the *private metadata*. In a scenario where the adversary can reuse any code from the flash section, this *private data* would be accessible by just jumping to the proper function in the bootloader.

To protect the bootloader, we introduce a self-encryption and self-decryption routines that obfuscate its contents. Thus, these are the only two routines that could be potentially used in code reuse attacks. In our prototype they both occupy less than 2 pages (i.e., 256 bytes), which prevents the use of a practical ROP attack against our system. Moreover, these non-encrypted pages can also be shuffled by the randomization engine to prevent attackers from pinpointing them. Indeed, as the adversary is forced to perform the attack in one-shot, then if she is able to decrypt the bootloader, when trying to use it or read the *private metadata*, the device may be reset, which modify the *private metadata*.

The runtime module can be divided into 3 main parts: an initialization routine, the bootloader itself, and the encryption/decryption routine. The first one holds the Interrupt vectors and some required initialization instructions, and jumps to the decryption routine. The second part, which is encrypted, contains the main functionality to setup the hardware and randomize the binary code. Finally, the last part encrypts again the bootloader and the private data, and jumps to the beginning of the application code.

The decryption process reads the key (stored at a fixed position of the flash memory). This key has the same length than the page size (i.e., 128 bytes). Then, it reads the encrypted bootloader page by page, performing the XOR to obtain the clear-text of the code, and rewrites the output in the same position. Then, it jumps to the beginning of the decrypted bootloader.

The bootloader starts by setting up the required hardware (e.g., to initialize the USB or the clock of the device). It then performs the actual randomization of the application binary. To do so, it first reads the *private metadata* and loads it into a temporary buffer of the SRAM memory (which is deleted once finished). Second, it creates a random list of pairs of pages (i.e., the random swap), that must be exchanged, and updates the *private data* by exchanging the page positions. We use the *rand* function implementation from `libc`, which uses a LFSR based random number generator. However, in order to get the random seed, we rely on a timing jitter produced after the variance introduced between the internal timer of the AVR chip and the oscillator used by the watchdog timer [1]. In this way, AVRAND produces truly random numbers in each execution of the randomization engine.

Once the random swap map is obtained, the bootloader processes one by one the pages from the bottom of the application section. Each page is temporarily stored in data memory, its control-flow statements are modified, and then it is stored again in the position indicated by the *private metadata*. Control-flow statements are updated by looking at the *public metadata* (i.e., where the pointer is, its type, and the page being pointed at) and the *private metadata* (i.e., the new position of the pointed page). In order to swap two pages, they are both stored in SRAM memory and then re-written in each other's previous position of the flash memory. Thus, the size of SRAM required during the randomization is *page_size*∗2. Finally, the new page positions (i.e. *private metadata*) is encrypted again, and written to the EEPROM memory. In order to prevent brute force attacks against the cryptosystem, the randomization engine generates a new XOR key each time. Figure 6 shows a schematic view of the memory layout of the application section before and after randomization.

Finally, when the randomization process is finished, the last step is to obfuscate the bootloader again using the XOR-based encryption routine and the newly generated key.

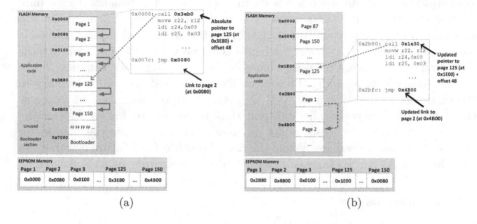

(a)   (b)

Fig. 6. Flash memory layout before (a) and after (b) randomization.

6   Discussion

AVRAND hampers code reuse attack by randomizing the application layout from the bootloader and by obfuscating the bootloader itself. We next provide a discussion of the suitability of our approach and the introduced overhead.

6.1   Suitability of AVRAND

AVRAND is designed specifically for AVR architectures. However, it could also be applied to other systems using a modified Harvard-based architecture, given that it is provided with a bootloader section that reprograms the flash memory. While the core idea of AVRAND (i.e., randomization of the memory layout) has been widely studied for other architectures such as x86 [5] or ARM [6], few works have addressed the problem in AVR. Moreover, our focus is on using a lightweight cryptographic routine, since AVR is designed for resource-constrained embedded devices. In our prototype we have used an XOR-based encryption and a linear PRNG, which fit well in the space given for the bootloader section (4 KB). Nevertheless, our architecture is designed to accept stronger cryptographic functions if enough resources are available (e.g., using AES or 3DES and the more robust MersenneTwister PRNG). Nonetheless, in addition to a greater performance overhead, the use of complex encryption would have an extra drawback in AVRAND: since the code used to encrypt and decrypt the bootloader can be used in code-reuse attacks, using encryption and decryption routines with larger code size increases the available code for attackers. As explained in Sect. 5.2, currently the XOR-based encryption only occupies 2 pages.

External hardware can also be applied to palliate code reuse attacks [13,15]. We emphasize that our approach is complementary, but it benefits from a pure software-based solution. This perfectly suits scenarios where cost-minimization strategies play an important role in the device design. Francillon and Castellucia mentioned different protection mechanisms to prevent code injection attacks [12], such as preventing software vulnerabilities or using stack canaries. These mechanisms aim at avoiding the control-flow hijack and are complementary to the randomization provided by AVRAND. Our solution assumes that somehow the control flow may be hijacked, and thus it intends to hinder code reuse. Additionally, when the sensor is not physically accessible, then the chances for and adversary also decrease. While this may be subject for future research, we consider that AVRAND takes a step forward in the security of AVR devices.

6.2   Limitations

During the design of AVRAND, we have assumed that the exploit size is restricted by the size of the SRAM memory. For example, as explained in Sect. 3.2, the stack size may not be large enough to store a complex payload, thus limiting stack-based exploitation and requiring the adversary to reset the device when injecting large payloads in memory. Additionally, some devices based on the TinyOS restrict the packet size to 28 bytes. However, this is not the case of other chips like the Atmega32u4. Accordingly, other exploitation techniques such as heap or integer overflows may provide the adversary with the ability to inject larger payloads.

In this work, we have considered that the memory should be re-randomized with every device reset. Indeed, it is reasonable that a reset may be produced because the device is under attack or some other abnormal activity. However, we are aware that a smart adversary may find techniques to attack the sensor without causing resets or a system crash (e.g., by cleaning the stack after the payload execution [14,15]). In any case, AVRAND could be configured to reset the device periodically, or only under certain conditions. Due to the limited number of write/erase cycles of the flash memory (e.g., 10,000 in the Atmega32u4 chip), this feature should be carefully adjusted to meet the security requirements while maximizing the lifetime of the chip, which in turn depends on the application scenario. For example, by periodically randomizing the device every 5 min, a device using the Atmega32u4 chip would last approximately 35 days.

Finally, it is important to understand that AVRAND is a countermeasure to code reuse attacks in AVR based chips. However, these chips may be directly connected to other sensors (e.g., wireless antennas or thermometers) or chips (e.g., the Atheros chip in the Arduino Yun). In this last case, the Atheros chip in the Arduino Yun has far more resources than the AVR to secure the device. Indeed, the installed OpenWrt OS has support for ASLR, DEP, and other security measures such as authenticating and encrypting communications (e.g., through SSH). If the adversary could gain access to the MIPS-based chip (for example, by performing a brute force attack against the SSH or exploiting a vulnerability in the Linux kernel), then the security gained by AVRAND would be useless. However, no matter how strong the security measures taken in the Atheros chip are, the exploitation of AVR opens a security hole, since both chips are connected through the Bridge library. This is where AVRAND is particularly helpful.

6.3   Overhead Incurred by AVRAND

We have tested the prototype of AVRAND in the Atmel atmega32u4 chip integrated within the Arduino Yun device, equipped with a 32 KB flash Memory (from which 4 KB corresponds with the bootloader section). Our evaluation indicates a noteworthy increase in the code size due to changes introduced by the preprocessing module. We have tested our prototype on the entire set of examples included in the Arduino IDE software. While all the tested programs fit in the flash memory, we have observed an average of 20 % of extra code on the modified binary. However, this overhead is related to a binary which has been compiled turning on the optimization flags of avr-gcc [19], that prioritizes the use of relative versions of control flow instructions. However, if these optimization flags were turned off, as done in MAVR [15], then the difference between initial code size and modified code size would be considerably smaller. Re-compiling all the libraries without an optimization requires having the source code of every library (which is certainly not possible in case of proprietary code), so we decided to transform the binary directly in our preprocessing module, thus providing a more general solution.

As for the time spent by the runtime module in the bootloader, results show that it requires an average of 1.7 s to randomize the code of our proof-of-concept program, which takes 18 KB of the flash memory. For example, a bootloader using the AVR 109 protocol [2] (that allows self-programming without external programmers) takes a minimum of 750 ms. Given the security provided by AVRAND, we consider that an overhead of 1 s is acceptable, especially since the bootloader is only executed under certain circumstances.

7   Conclusions

In this paper, we have presented a software-based defense against code reuse attacks for AVR systems—a modified Harvard architecture. These type of architectures are popular among embedded devices used in different contexts.

We focus on providing an inexpensive solution tailored for resourced constrained devices. Our system perfectly balances the trade-off between the attack surface exposed in this class of devices and the level of protection required to defeat code reuse attacks. Thus, we design an architecture based on a fine-grained randomization defense with self encryption that does not require additional hardware support. We have implemented a proof-of-concept for the Arduino Yun, an emerging open-source platform widely used in the IoT arena. Our prototype introduces a negligible overhead with respect to the normal operation of the Arduino. We evaluated the proposed scheme against a code reuse attack based on Return Oriented Programming that first exploits a buffer overflow to execute code from the Arduino libraries. Finally, to foster research in this area, we provide functional prototypes of the attack and the proposed defense.

Acknowledgments. We would like to thank our shepherd, Andrea Lanzi, for his assistance and the feedback provided during the reviewing process. This work was supported by the MINECO Grant TIN2013-46469-R (SPINY), the CAM Grant S2013/ICE-3095 (CIBERDINE) and the UK EPSRC Grant EP/L022710/1.

References

1. Anderson, W.: Entropy library documentation. Google Code Projects (2012)
2. Atmel, C.: Avr109: Self programming (2004). atmel.com/images/doc1644.pdf
3. Atmel, C.: Automotive compilation (2012). http://www.atmel.com/Images/atmel_autocompilation_vol9_oct2012.pdf
4. Backes, M., Nürnberger, S.: Oxymoron: making fine-grained memory randomization practical by allowing code sharing. In: USENIX Security Symposium (2014)
5. Bhatkar, S., DuVarney, D.C., Sekar, R.: Address obfuscation: an efficient approach to combat a broad range of memory error exploits. In: USENIX Security (2003)
6. Braden, K., Crane, S., Davi, L., Franz, M., Larsen, P., Liebchen, C., Sadeghi, A.R.: Leakage-resilient layout randomization for mobile devices. In: Network and Distributed Systems Security Symposium (NDSS) (2016)
7. Carlini, N., Wagner, D.: Rop is still dangerous: breaking modern defenses. In: USENIX Security Symposium (2014)
8. Cowan, C., Wagle, P., Pu, C., Beattie, S., Walpole, J.: Buffer overflows: attacks and defenses for the vulnerability of the decade. In: DARPA Information Survivability Conference and Exposition, 2000, DISCEX 2000, vol. 2, pp. 119–129. IEEE (2000)
9. Crane, S., Liebchen, C., Homescu, A., Davi, L., Larsen, P., Sadeghi, A.R., Brunthaler, S., Franz, M.: Readactor: practical code randomization resilient to memory disclosure. In: IEEE Symposium on Security and Privacy, S&P, vol. 15 (2015)
10. Davi, L., Liebchen, C., Sadeghi, A.R., Snow, K.Z., Monrose, F.: Isomeron: code randomization resilient to (just-in-time) return-oriented programming. In: Proceedings of the 22nd Network and Distributed Systems Security Symposium (NDSS) (2015)
11. Dean, B.S.: Avr downloader/uploader (2003). http://www.nongnu.org/avrdude/. Accessed Jan 2016
12. Francillon, A., Castelluccia, C.: Code injection attacks on harvard-architecture devices. In: Proceedings of the 15th ACM Conference on Computer and Communications Security, pp. 15–26. ACM (2008)

13. Francillon, A., Perito, D., Castelluccia, C.: Defending embedded systems against control flow attacks. In: Proceedings of the First ACM Workshop on Secure Execution of Untrusted Code, pp. 19–26. ACM (2009)
14. Gu, Q., Noorani, R.: Towards self-propagate mal-packets in sensor networks. In: Proceedings of the ACM Conference on Wireless Network Security, pp. 172–182. ACM (2008)
15. Habibi, J., Gupta, A., Carlsony, S., Panicker, A., Bertino, E.: MAVR: code reuse stealthy attacks and mitigation on unmanned aerial vehicles. In: Distributed Computing Systems (ICDCS), pp. 642–652. IEEE (2015)
16. Intel, C.: Hexadecimal object file format specification (1988)
17. Mohan, V., Hamlen, K.W.: Frankenstein: stitching malware from benign binaries. In: 6th USENIX Workshop on Offensive Technologies. USENIX (2012)
18. Mohan, V., Larsen, P., Brunthaler, S., Hamlen, K., Franz, M.: Opaque control-flow integrity. In: Network and Distributed Systems Security Symposium (NDSS) (2015)
19. GNU Project: Avr libc home page (1999). http://www.nongnu.org/avr-libc/. Accessed Jan 2016
20. Roemer, R., Buchanan, E., Shacham, H., Savage, S.: Return-oriented programming: systems, languages, and applications. ACM Trans. Inf. Syst. Secur. (TISSEC) **15**(1), 2 (2012)
21. Sadeghi, A.R., Wachsmann, C., Waidner, M.: Security and privacy challenges in industrial internet of things. In: Annual Design Automation Conference. ACM (2015)
22. Schuster, F., Tendyck, T., Pewny, J., Maaß, A., Steegmanns, M., Contag, M., Holz, T.: Evaluating the effectiveness of current Anti-ROP defenses. In: Stavrou, A., Bos, H., Portokalidis, G. (eds.) RAID 2014. LNCS, vol. 8688, pp. 88–108. Springer, Heidelberg (2014)
23. Snow, K.Z., Monrose, F., Davi, L., Dmitrienko, A., Liebchen, C., Sadeghi, A.R.: Just-in-time code reuse: on the effectiveness of fine-grained address space layout randomization. In: Security and Privacy (SP), pp. 574–588 (2013)
24. Szekeres, L., Payer, M., Wei, T., Song, D.: SoK: eternal war in memory. In: 2013 IEEE Symposium on Security and Privacy (SP), pp. 48–62. IEEE (2013)
25. Tang, A., Sethumadhavan, S., Stolfo, S.: Heisenbyte: thwarting memory disclosure attacks using destructive code reads. In: Proceedings of the 22nd ACM SIGSAC Conference on Computer and Communications Security, pp. 256–267. ACM (2015)
26. Trevennor, A.: Practical AVR Microcontrollers: Games, Gadgets, and Home Automation with the Microcontroller Used in the Arduino. Apress, USA (2012)
27. Wojtczuk, R.: The advanced return-into-lib (c) exploits: Pax case study. Phrack Magazine, vol. 0x0b, Issue 0x3a, Phile# 0x04 of 0x0e (2001)

Towards Vulnerability Discovery Using Staged Program Analysis

Bhargava Shastry[1]([⊠]), Fabian Yamaguchi[2], Konrad Rieck[2],
and Jean-Pierre Seifert[1]

[1] Security in Telecommunications, TU Berlin, Berlin, Germany
bshastry@sec.t-labs.tu-berlin.de
[2] Institute of System Security, TU Braunschweig, Braunschweig, Germany

Abstract. Eliminating vulnerabilities from low-level code is vital for securing software. Static analysis is a promising approach for discovering vulnerabilities since it can provide developers early feedback on the code they write. But, it presents multiple challenges not the least of which is understanding what makes a bug exploitable and conveying this information to the developer. In this paper, we present the design and implementation of a practical vulnerability assessment framework, called *Mélange*. Mélange performs data and control flow analysis to diagnose potential security bugs, and outputs well-formatted bug reports that help developers *understand* and *fix* security bugs. Based on the intuition that real-world vulnerabilities manifest themselves across multiple parts of a program, Mélange performs both local and global analyses in stages. To scale up to large programs, global analysis is demand-driven. Our prototype detects multiple vulnerability classes in C and $C++$ code including type confusion, and garbage memory reads. We have evaluated Mélange extensively. Our case studies show that Mélange scales up to large codebases such as Chromium, is easy-to-use, and most importantly, capable of discovering vulnerabilities in real-world code. Our findings indicate that static analysis is a viable reinforcement to the software testing tool set.

Keywords: Program analysis · Vulnerability assessment · LLVM

1 Introduction

Vulnerabilities in popularly used software are not only detrimental to end-user security but can also be hard to identify and fix. Today's highly inter-connected systems have escalated the damage inflicted upon users due to security compromises as well as the cost of fixing vulnerabilities. To address the threat landscape, software vendors have established mechanisms for software quality assurance and testing. A prevailing thought is that security bugs identified and fixed early impose lower costs than those identified during the testing phase or in the wild. Thus, vulnerability re-mediation—the process of identifying and fixing vulnerabilities—is being seen as part of the software development process rather than in isolation [28].

© Springer International Publishing Switzerland 2016
J. Caballero et al. (Eds.): DIMVA 2016, LNCS 9721, pp. 78–97, 2016.
DOI: 10.1007/978-3-319-40667-1_5

Program analysis provides a practical means to discover security bugs during software development. Prior approaches to vulnerability discovery using static code analysis have ranged from simple pattern-matching to context and path-sensitive data-flow analysis. For instance, ITS4 [42]—a vulnerability scanner for C/C++ programs—parses source code and looks up lexical tokens of interest against an existing vulnerability database. In our initial experiments, the pattern-matching approach employed by ITS4 produced a large number of warnings against modern C, and C++ codebases. On the contrary, security vulnerabilities are most often, subtle corner cases, and thus rare. The approach taken by ITS4 is well-suited for extremely fast analysis, but the high amount of manual effort required to validate warnings undermines the value of the tool itself.

On the other end of the spectrum, the Clang Static Analyzer [4] presents an analytically superior approach for defect discovery. Precise—context and path sensitive—analysis enables Clang SA to warn only when there is evidence of a bug in a feasible program path. While precise warnings reduce the burden of manual validation, we find that Clang SA's local inter-procedural analysis misses security bugs that span file boundaries. The omission of bugs that span file boundaries is significant especially for object-oriented code[1], where object implementation and object use are typically in different source files. A natural solution is to make analysis global. However, global analysis does not scale up to large programs.

In this paper, we find a middle ground. We present the design and implementation of Mélange, a vulnerability assessment tool for C and C++ programs, that performs both local and global analysis in stages to discover potential vulnerabilities spanning source files. Mélange has been implemented as an extension to the LLVM compiler infrastructure [32]. To keep analysis scalable, Mélange performs computationally expensive analyses locally (within a source file), while performing cheaper analyses globally (across the whole program). In addition, global analysis is demand-driven: It is performed to validate the outcome of local analyses. To provide good diagnostics, Mélange primarily analyzes source code. It outputs developer-friendly bug reports that point out the *exact* position in source code where potential vulnerabilities exist, why they are problematic, and how they can be remedied.

Results from our case studies validate our design decisions. We find that Mélange is capable of highlighting a handful of problematic corner cases, while scaling up to large programs like Chromium, and Firefox. Since Mélange is implemented as an extension to a widely used compiler toolchain (Clang/LLVM), it can be invoked as part of the build process. Moreover, our current implementation is fast enough to be incorporated into nightly builds[2] of two large codebases (MySQL, Chromium), and with further optimizations on the third (Firefox). In summary, we make the following contributions.

---

[1] All the major browsers including Chromium and Firefox are implemented in object-oriented code.

[2] Regular builds automatically initiated overnight on virtual machine clusters.

1. We present the design and implementation of Mélange, an extensible program analysis framework.
2. We demonstrate the utility of Mélange by employing it to detect multiple classes of vulnerabilities, including garbage reads and incorrectly typed data, that are known to be a common source of exploitable vulnerabilities.
3. We evaluate Mélange extensively. We benchmark Mélange against NIST's Juliet benchmark [36] for program analysis tools. Mélange has thus far detected multiple known vulnerabilities in the PHP interpreter, and Chromium codebases, and discovered a new defect in Firefox.

2 Background: Clang and LLVM

Mélange is anchored in the Clang/LLVM open-source compiler toolchain [13], an outcome of pioneering work by Lattner et al. [32]. In this section, we review components of this toolchain that are at the core of Mélange's design. While Clang/LLVM is a compiler at heart, it's utility is not limited to code generation/optimization. Different parts of the compiler front-end (Clang) and back-end (LLVM) are encapsulated into libraries that can be selectively used by client systems depending on their needs. Thus, the LLVM project lends itself well to multiple compiler-technology-driven use-cases, program analysis being one of them.

We build Mélange on top of the analysis infrastructure available within the LLVM project. This infrastructure mainly comprises the Clang Static Analyzer—a source code analyzer for *C*, C++, and *Objective-C* programs—and the LLVM analyzer/optimizer framework which permits analysis of LLVM Bitcode. In the following paragraphs, we describe each of these components briefly.

2.1 Clang Static Analyzer

The Clang Static Analyzer (Clang SA) is similar in spirit to *Metal/xgcc*, which its authors classify as a "Meta-level Compilation" (MC) framework [21,24]. The goal of an MC framework is to allow for modular extensions to the compiler that enable checking of domain-specific program properties. Abstractly viewed, an MC framework comprises a set of *checkers* (domain-specific analysis procedures) and a compilation system.

The division of labor envisioned by Hallem et al. [24] is that *checkers* only *encode* the property to check, leaving the mechanics of the actual checking to the compilation system. The compilation system facilitates checking by providing the necessary analysis infrastructure. Figure 1 shows how an MC framework is realized in Clang SA. Source files are parsed and subsequently passed on to the Data-Flow Analysis engine (*DFA* engine), which provides the analysis infrastructure required by checkers. Checkers encode the program property to be checked and produce bug reports if a violation is found. Bug reports are then reviewed by a human analyst.

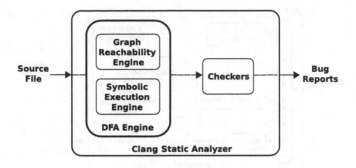

Fig. 1. Clang Static Analyzer overview

Data-Flow Analysis Engine. Clang SA performs *Context* and *Path* sensitive inter-procedural data-flow analysis. Context sensitivity means that the analysis preserves the calling context of function calls; path sensitivity means that the analysis explores paths forked by branch statements *independently*. Context sensitivity is realized in the *Graph Reachability Engine* which implements a namesake algorithm proposed by Reps et al. [37]. Path sensitivity is implemented in the *Symbolic Execution Engine*. The symbolic execution engine uses static Forward Symbolic Execution (FSE) [38] to explore program paths in a source file.

Checkers. Checkers implement domain-specific checks and issue bug reports. Clang SA contains a default suite of checkers that implement a variety of checks including unsafe API usage, and memory access errors. More importantly, the checker framework in Clang SA can be used by programmers to add custom checks. To facilitate customized checks, Clang SA exposes callbacks (as APIs) that *hook* into the DFA engine at pre-defined program locations. Clang SA and its checkers seen together, demonstrate the utility of meta-level compilation.

2.2   LLVM Pass Infrastructure

The LLVM pass infrastructure [13] provides a modular means to perform analyses and optimizations on an LLVM Intermediate Representation (IR) of a program. LLVM IR is a typed, yet source-language independent representation of a program that facilitates *uniform* analysis of whole-programs or whole-libraries.

Simply put, an LLVM Pass is an operation (procedure invocation) on a unit of LLVM IR code. The granularity of code operated on can vary from a *Function* to an entire program (*Module* in LLVM parlance). Passes may be run in sequence, allowing a successive *pass* to reuse information from (or work on a transformation carried out by) preceding *passes*. The LLVM pass framework provides APIs to tap into source-level meta-data in LLVM IR. This provides a means to bridge the syntactic gap between source-level and IR-level analyses. Source literals may be matched against LLVM IR meta-data programmatically. Mélange takes this approach to teach the LLVM pass what a source-level bug report means.

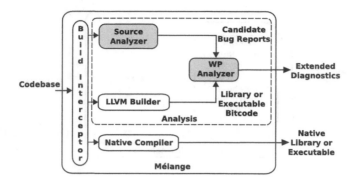

Fig. 2. Mélange overview

3   Mélange

Our primary goal is to develop an early warning system for security-critical software defects. We envision Mélange as a tool that assists a developer in identifying, and fixing potential security bugs *during* software development. Figure 2 provides an overview of our approach. Mélange comprises four high-level components: the build interceptor, the LLVM builder, the source analyzer, and the Whole-Program (WP) analyzer. We summarize the role of each component in analyzing a program. Subsequently, we describe them in greater detail.

1. *Build Interceptor.* The build interceptor is a program that interposes between the build program (e.g., *GNU-Make*) and the compilation system (e.g., Clang/LLVM). In Mélange, the build interceptor is responsible for *correctly* and *independently* invoking the program builders and the source analyzer. (Sect. 3.1)
2. *LLVM Builder.* The LLVM builder is a utility program that assists in generating LLVM Bitcode for C, C++, and Objective-C programs. It mirrors steps taken during native compilation onto LLVM Bitcode generation. (Sect. 3.1)
3. *Source Analyzer.* The source analyzer executes domain-specific checks on a source file and outputs candidate bug reports that diagnose a potential security bug. The source analyzer is invoked during the first stage of Mélange's analysis. We have implemented the source analyzer as a library of checkers that plug into a patched version of Clang SA. (Sect. 3.2)
4. *Whole-Program Analyzer.* The WP analyzer examines candidate bug reports (from Step 3), and either provides extended diagnostics for the report or classifies it as a false positive. The developer is shown only those reports that have extended diagnostics i.e., those not classified as a false positive by the WP analyzer. We have implemented the WP analyzer in multiple LLVM passes. (Sect. 3.3)

3.1   Analysis Utilities

Ease-of-deployment is one of the design goals of Mélange. We want software developers to use our analysis framework in their build environments seamlessly. The build interceptor and the LLVM builder are *analysis utilities* that help us achieve this goal. The build interceptor and the LLVM builder facilitate transparent analysis of codebases by *plugging in* Mélange's analyses to an existing build system. We describe them briefly in the following paragraphs.

Build Interceptor. Our approach to transparently analyze large software projects hinges on triggering analysis via the build command. We use an existing build interceptor, *scan-build* [12], from the Clang project. Scan-build is a command-line utility that intercepts build commands and invokes the source analyzer in tandem with the compiler. Since Mélange's WP analysis is targeted at program (LLVM) Bitcode, we instrument scan-build to not only invoke the source analyzer, but also the LLVM builder.

LLVM Builder. Generating LLVM Bitcode for program libraries and executables without modifying source code and/or build configuration is a daunting task. Fortunately, the *Whole-program LLVM* (WLLVM) [14], an existing open-source LLVM builder, solves this problem. WLLVM is a python-based utility that leverages a compiler for generating whole-program or whole-library LLVM Bitcode. It can be used as a drop-in replacement for a compiler i.e., pointing the builder (e.g., *GNU-Make*) to WLLVM is sufficient.

3.2   Source Analyzer

The source analyzer assists Mélange in searching for potential bugs in source code. We build a novel *event collection* system that helps detect both taint-style vulnerabilities as well as semantic defects. Our event collection system is implemented as a system of taints on C and C++ language constructs (*Declarations*). We call the underlying mechanism *Declaration Tainting* because taints in the proposed event collection system are associated with AST Declaration identifiers of C and C++ objects. Since declaration tainting is applied on AST constructs, it can be carried out in situations where local symbolic execution is not possible.

We write checkers to flag defects. Checkers have been developed as *clients* of the proposed event collection system. The division of labor between checkers and the event collection system mirrors the Meta-level Compilation concept: Checkers encode the policy for flagging defects, while the event collection system maintains the state required to perform checks. We have prototyped this system for flagging garbage (uninitialized) reads[3] of C++ objects, incorrect type casts in PHP interpreter codebase, and other Common Weakness Enumerations (see Sect. 4).

---

[3] The algorithm for flagging garbage reads is based on a variation of gen-kill sets [30].

We demonstrate the utility of the proposed system by using the code snippet shown in Listing 1.1 as a running example. Our aim is to detect uninitialized reads of class members in the example. The listing encompasses two source files, foo.cpp and main.cpp, and a header file foo.h. We maintain two sets in the event collection system: the Def set containing declaration identifiers for class members that have at least one definition, and the UseWithoutDef set containing identifiers for class members that are used (at least once) without a preceding definition. We maintain an instance of both sets for each function that we analyze in a translation unit i.e., for function F, Δ_F denotes the analysis summary of F that contains both sets. The checker decides how the event collection sets are populated. The logic for populating the Def and UseWithoutDef sets is simple. If a program statement in a given function defines a class member for the very first time, we add the class member identifier to the Def set of that function's analysis summary. If a program statement in a given function uses a class member that is absent from the Def set, we add the class member identifier to the UseWithoutDef set of that function's analysis summary.

```
1   // foo.h
2   class foo {
3   public:
4           int x;
5           foo() {}
6           bool isZero();
7   };
8
9   // foo.cpp
10  #include"foo.h"
11
12  bool foo::isZero() {
13    if (!x)
14      return true;
15  }
16
17  // main.cpp
18  #include "foo.h"
19
20  int main() {
21          foo f;
22          if (f.isZero())
23              return 0;
24          return 1;
25  }
```

Listing 1.1. Running example–The foo object does not initialize its class member foo::x. The call to isZero on Line 22 leads to a garbage read on Line 13.

In Listing 1.1, when function foo::isZero in file foo.cpp is being analyzed, the checker adds class member foo::x to the UseWithoutDef set of $\Delta_{foo::isZero}$

after analyzing the branch condition on Line 13. This is because the checker has not encountered a definition for `foo::x` in the present analysis context. Subsequently, analysis of the constructor function `foo::foo` does not yield any additions to either the Def or UseWithoutDef sets. So $\Delta_{foo::foo}$ is empty. Finally, the checker compares set memberships across analysis contexts. Since `foo::x` is marked as a use without a valid definition in $\Delta_{foo::isZero}$ and `foo::x` is not a member of the Def set in the constructor function's analysis summary ($\Delta_{foo::foo}$), the checker classifies the use of Line 13 as a candidate bug. The checker encodes the proof for the bug in the candidate bug report. Listing 1.2 shows how candidate bug reports are encoded. The bug report encodes the location and analysis stack corresponding to the potential garbage (uninitialized) read.

The proposed event collection approach has several benefits. First, by retrofitting simple declaration-based object tainting into Clang SA, we enable Checkers to perform analysis based on the proposed taint abstraction. Due to its general-purpose nature, the taint abstraction is useful for discovering other defect types such as null pointer dereferences. Second, the tainting APIs we expose are opt-in. They may be used by existing and/or new checkers. Third, our additions leverage high-precision analysis infrastructure already available in Clang SA. We have implemented the event collection system as a patch to the mainline version of Clang Static Analyzer. In the next paragraph, we describe how candidate bug reports are analyzed by our whole-program analyzer.

3.3 Whole-Program Analyzer

Whole-program analysis is demand-driven. Only candidate bug reports are analyzed. The analysis target is an LLVM Bitcode file of a library or executable. There are two aspects to WP analysis: Parsing of candidate bug reports to construct a query, and the analysis itself. We have written a simple python-based parser to parse candidate bug reports and construct queries. The analysis itself is implemented as a set of LLVM passes. The bug report parser encodes queries as preprocessor directives in a pass header file. A driver script is used to recompile, and run the pass against all candidate bug reports.

Our whole-program analysis routine is composed of a *CallGraph* analysis pass. We leverage an existing LLVM pass called the *Basic CallGraph* pass to build a whole-program call graph. Since the basic pass misses control flow at indirect call sites, we have implemented additional analyses to improve upon the precision of the basic callgraph. Foremost among our analyses is Class Hierarchy Analysis (CHA) [20]. CHA enables us to devirtualize those dynamically dispatched call sites where we are sure no delegation is possible. Unfortunately, CHA can only be undertaken in scenarios where no new class hierarchies are introduced. In scenarios where CHA is not applicable, we examine call instructions to resolve as many forms of indirect call sites as possible. Our prototype resolves aliases of global functions, function casts etc.

Once program call graph has been obtained, we perform a domain-specific WP analysis. For instance, to validate garbage reads, the pass inspects loads and store to the buggy program variable or object. In our running example

(Listing 1.1), loads and stores to the foo::x class member indicated in candidate bug report (Listing 1.2) are tracked by the WP garbage read pass. To this end, the program call graph is traversed to check if a load of foo::x does not have a matching store. If all loads have a matching store, the candidate bug report is classified as a false positive. Otherwise, program call-chains in which a load from foo::x does not have a matching store are displayed to the analyst in the whole-program bug report (Listing 1.2).

```
// Source-level bug report
// report-e6ed9c.html
...
Local Path to Bug: foo::x->_ZN3foo6isZeroEv

Annotated Source Code
foo.cpp:4:6: warning: Potentially uninitialized
    object field
  if (!x)
      ^

1 warning generated.

// Whole-program bug report
---------- report-e6ed9c.html ---------
[+] Parsing bug report report-e6ed9c.html
[+] Writing queries into LLVM pass header file
[+] Recompiling LLVM pass
[+] Running LLVM BugReportAnalyzer pass against
    main
------------------------------------------
Candidate callchain is:

foo::isZero()
main
----------------------
```

Listing 1.2. Candidate bug report (top) and whole-program bug report (bottom) for garbage read in the running example shown in Listing 1.1.

4   Evaluation

We have evaluated Mélange against both static analysis benchmarks and real-world code. To gauge Mélange's utility, we have also tested it against known defects and vulnerabilities. Our evaluation seeks to answer the following questions:

– What is the effort required to use Mélange in an existing build system? (Sect. 4.1)
– How does Mélange perform against static analysis benchmarks? (Sect. 4.2)
– How does Mélange fare against known security vulnerabilities? (Sect. 4.3)
– What is the analysis run-time and effectiveness of Mélange against large well-tested codebases? (Sect. 4.4)

4.1 Deployability

Ease-of-deployment is one of the design goals of Mélange. Build interposition allows us to analyze codebases as is, without modifying build configuration and/or source code. We have deployed Mélange in an Amazon `compute` instance where codebases with different build systems have been analyzed (see Sect. 4.4). Another benefit of build system integration is incremental analysis. Only the very first build of a codebase incurs the cost of end-to-end analysis; subsequent analyses are incremental. While incremental analysis can be used in conjunction with daily builds, full analysis can be coupled with nightly builds and initiated on virtual machine clusters.

4.2 NIST Benchmarks

We used static analysis benchmarks released under NIST's SAMATE project [35] for benchmarking Mélange's detection rates. In particular, the Juliet C/C++ test suite (version 1.2) [36] was used to measure true and false positive detection rates for defects spread across multiple categories. The Juliet suite comprises test sets for multiple defect types. Each test set contains test cases for a specific Common Weakness Enumeration (CWE) [41]. The CWE system assigns identifiers for common classes of software weaknesses that are known to lead to exploitable vulnerabilities. We implemented Mélange checkers and passes for the following CWE categories: *CWE457* (Garbage or uninitialized read), *CWE843* (Type confusion), *CWE194* (Unexpected Sign Extension), and *CWE195* (Signed to Unsigned Conversion Error). With the exception of CWE457, the listed CWEs have received scant attention from static analysis tools. For instance, type confusion (CWE843) is an emerging attack vector [33] for exploiting popular applications.

Figure 3 summarizes the True/False Positive Rates (TPRs/FPRs) for Clang SA and Mélange for the chosen CWE benchmarks. Currently, Clang SA only supports CWE457. Comparing reports from Clang SA and Mélange for the CWE457 test set, we find that the former errs on the side of precision (fewer false positives), while the latter errs on the side of caution (fewer false negatives). For the chosen CWE benchmarks, Mélange attains a true-positive rate between 57–88 %, and thus, it is capable of spotting over half of the bugs in the test suite.

Mélange's staggered analysis approach allows it to present both source file wide and program wide diagnostics (see Fig. 4). In contrast, Clang SA's diagnostics are restricted to a single source file. Often, the call stack information presented in Mélange's extended diagnostics has speeded up manual validation of bug reports.

4.3 Detection of Known Vulnerabilities

We tested five known type-confusion vulnerabilities in the PHP interpreter with Mélange. All of the tested flaws are taint-style vulnerabilities: An attacker-controlled input is passed to a security-sensitive function call that wrongly

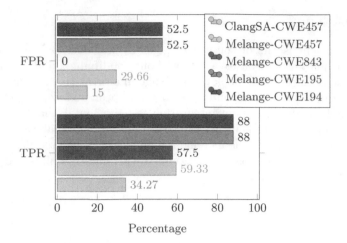

Fig. 3. Juliet test suite: True Positive Rate (TPR) and False Positive Rate (FPR) for Mélange, and Clang Static Analyzer. Clang SA supports CWE457 only. (Color figure online)

interprets the input's type. Ultimately all these vulnerabilities result in invalid memory accesses that can be leveraged by an attacker for arbitrary code execution or information disclosure. We wrote a checker for detecting multiple instances of this vulnerability type in the PHP interpreter codebase. For patched vulnerabilities, testing was carried out on unpatched versions of the codebase. Mélange successfully flagged all known vulnerabilities. The first five entries of Table 1 summarize Mélange's findings. Three of the five vulnerabilities have been assigned Common Vulnerabilities and Exposures (CVE) identifiers by the MITRE Corporation. Reporters of CVE-2014-3515, CVE-2015-4147, and PHP report ID 73245 have received bug bounties totaling $5500 by the Internet Bug Bounty Panel [7].

In addition, we ran our checker against a recent PHP release candidate (PHP 7.0 RC7) released on 12th November, 2015. Thus far, Mélange has drawn attention to PHP sub-systems where a similar vulnerability may exist. While we haven't been able to verify if these are exploitable, this exercise demonstrates Mélange's utility in bringing attention to multiple instances of a software flaw in a large codebase that is under active development.

4.4 Case Studies

To further investigate the practical utility of Mélange, we conducted case studies with three popular open-source projects, namely, Chromium, Firefox, and MySQL. We focused on detecting garbage reads only. In the following paragraphs, we present results from our case studies emphasizing analysis effectiveness, and analysis run-time.

Table 1. Detection summary of Mélange against production codebases. Mélange has confirmed known vulnerabilities and flagged a new defect in Firefox. Listed Chromium and Firefox bugs are not known to be exploitable. Chromium bug 411177 is classified as a Medium-Severity bug in Google's internal bug tracker.

Codebase	CVE ID (Rating)	Bug ID	Vulnerability	Known/New
PHP	CVE-2015-4147	69085 [9]	Type-confusion	Known
PHP	CVE-2015-4148	69085 [9]	Type-confusion	Known
PHP	CVE-2014-3515	67492 [8]	Type-confusion	Known
PHP	Unassigned	73245 [11]	Type-confusion	Known
PHP	Unassigned	69152 [10]	Type-confusion	Known
Chromium	(Medium-Severity)	411177 [2]	Garbage read	Known
Chromium	None	436035 [3]	Garbage read	Known
Firefox	None	1168091 [1]	Garbage read	New

Software Versions: Evaluation was carried out for Chromium version 38 (dated August 2014), for Firefox revision 244208 (May 2015), and for MySQL version 5.7.7 (April 2015).

Evaluation Setup: Analysis was performed in an Amazon compute instance running Ubuntu 14.04 and provisioned with 36 virtual (Intel Xeon E5-2666 v3) CPUs clocked at 2.6 GHz, 60 GB of RAM, and 100 GB of SSD-based storage.

Effectiveness

True Positives. Our prototype flagged 3 confirmed defects in Chromium, and Firefox, including a new defect in the latter (see bottom three entries of Table 1). Defects found by our prototype in MySQL codebase have been reported upstream and are being triaged. Figure 4 shows Mélange's bug report for a garbage read in the pdf library shipped with Chromium v38. The source-level bug report (Fig. 4a) shows the line of code that was buggy. WP analyzer's bug report (Fig. 4b) shows candidate call chains in the libpdf library in which the uninitialized read may manifest.

We have manually validated the veracity of all bug reports generated by Mélange through source code audits. For each bug report, we verified if the data-flow and control-flow information conveyed in the report tallied with program semantics. We classified only those defects that passed our audit as true positives. Additionally, for the Chromium true positives, we matched Mélange's findings with reports [2,3] generated by MemorySanitizer [40], a dynamic program analysis tool from Google. The new defect discovered in Firefox was reported upstream [1]. Our evaluation demonstrates that Mélange can complement dynamic program analysis tools in use today.

Bug Summary

File:	out_analyze/Debug/../../pdf/page_indicator.cc
Location:	line 94, column 19
Description:	Potentially uninitialized object field
Local Path to Bug:	chrome_pdf::PageIndicator::fade_out_timer_id_ →
	_ZN10chrome_pdf13PageIndicator12OnTimerFiredEj

Annotated Source Code

```
92   void PageIndicator::OnTimerFired(uint32 timer_id) {
93     FadingControl::OnTimerFired(timer_id);
94     if (timer_id == fade_out_timer_id_) {
```

            Potentially uninitialized object field

```
95       Fade(false, fade_timeout_);
96     }
97   }
```

(a) Source-level Bug Report

```
---------- page_indicator.cc.pass.html ----------
[+] Parsing bug report page_indicator.cc.pass.html
[+] Writing queries into LLVM pass header file
[+] Recompiling LLVM pass
[+] Selecting LLVM BC for analysis
[+] Target Found: libpdf.a
[+] Running LLVM BugReportAnalyzer pass
----------------------

Candidate callchain is:
chrome_pdf::PageIndicator::OnTimerFired(unsigned int)
chrome_pdf::Instance::OnControlTimerFired(int,
unsigned int const&, unsigned int)
```

(b) Whole-program Bug Report

Fig. 4. Mélange bug report for Chromium bug 411177.

False Positives. Broadly, we encounter two kinds of false positives; those that are due to imprecision in Mélange's data-flow analysis, and those due to imprecision in its control-flow analysis. In the following paragraphs, we describe one example of each kind of false positive.

Data-Flow Imprecision: Mélange's analyses for flagging garbage reads lack sophisticated alias analysis. For instance, initialization of C++ objects passed-by-reference is missed. Listing 1.3 shows a code snippet borrowed from the Firefox codebase that illustrates this category of false positives.

When `AltSvcMapping` object is constructed (see Line 2 of Listing 1.3), one of its class members `mHttps` is passed by reference to the callee function `SchemeIsHTTPS`. The callee function `SchemeIsHTTPS` initializes `mHttps` via its alias (`outIsHTTPS`). Mélange's garbage read checker misses the aliased store and incorrectly flags the use of class member `mHttps` on Line 8 as a candidate bug. Mélange's garbage read pass, on its part, tries to taint all functions that store to `mHttps`. Since the store to `mHttps` happens via an alias, the pass also misses the store and outputs a legitimate control-flow sequence in its WP bug report.

Control-Flow Imprecision: Mélange's WP analyzer misses control-flow information at indirect call sites e.g., virtual function invocations. Thus, class

Table 2. Mélange: analysis summary for large open-source projects. True positives for MySQL have been left out since we are awaiting confirmation from its developers.

Codebase	Build time	Analysis run-time*				Bug reports		
	N_t	SA_x	WPA_x	TA_x	$WPAvg_t$	Stage 1	Stage 2	True positive
Chromium	18 m 20 s	29.09	15.49	44.58	7.5 s	2686	12	2
Firefox	41 m 25 s	3.38	39.31	42.69	13 m 35 s	587	16	1
MySQL	8 m 15 s	9.26	21.24	30.50	2 m 26 s	2494	32	-

*All terms except $WPAvg$ are normalized to native compilation time.

members that are initialized in a call sequence comprising an indirect function call are not registered by Mélange's garbage read pass. While resolving all indirect call sites in large programs is impossible, we employ best-effort devirtualization techniques such as Rapid Type Analysis [16] to improve Mélange's control-flow precision.

```
1  AltSvcMapping::AltSvcMapping(...) {
2    if (NS_FAILED(SchemeIsHTTPS(originScheme, mHttps))) {
3      ...
4    }
5  }
6  void AltSvcMapping::GetConnectionInfo(...) {
7    // ci is an object on the stack
8    ci->SetInsecureScheme(!mHttps);
9    ...
10 }
11 static nsresult SchemeIsHTTPS(const nsACString &
        originScheme, bool &outIsHTTPS)
12 {
13   outIsHTTPS =
          originScheme.Equals(NS_LITERAL_CSTRING("https"));
14   ...
15 }
```

Listing 1.3. Code snippet involving an aliased definition that caused a false positive in Mélange.

The final three columns of Table 2 present a summary of Mélange's findings for Chromium, Firefox, and MySQL projects. We find that Mélange's two-stage analysis pipeline is very effective at filtering through a handful of bug reports that merit attention. In particular, Mélange's WP analyses filter out 99.6 %, 97.3 %, and 98.7 % source level bug reports in Chromium, Firefox, and MySQL respectively. Although Mélange's true positive rate is low in our case studies, the corner cases it has pointed out, notwithstanding the confirmed bugs it has flagged, is encouraging. Given that we evaluated Mélange against well-tested production code, the fact that it could point out three confirmed defects in the Chromium and Firefox codebases is a promising result. We plan to make our

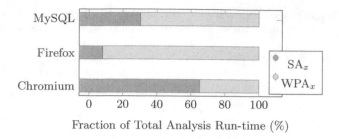

Fig. 5. For each codebase, its source and whole-program analysis run-times are shown as fractions (in %) of Mélange's total analysis run-time. (Color figure online)

tool production-ready by incorporating insights gained from our case studies. Next, we discuss Mélange's analysis run-time.

Analysis Run-Time. We completed end-to-analysis of Chromium, Firefox, and MySQL codebases—all of which have millions of lines of code—in under 48 h. Of these, MySQL, and Chromium were analyzed in a little over 4 h, and 13 h respectively. Table 2 summarizes Mélange's run-time for our case studies. We have presented the analysis run-time of a codebase relative (normalized) to its build time, N_t. For instance, a normalized analysis run-time of 30 for a codebase indicates that the time taken to analyze the codebase is 30**x** longer than its build time. All normalized run-times are denoted with the x subscript. Normalized source analysis time, WP analysis time, and total analysis time of Mélange are denoted as SA_x, WPA_x, and TA_x respectively. The term $WPAvg_t$ denotes the average time (not normalized) taken by Mélange's WP analyzer to analyze a single candidate bug report.

Figure 5 shows source and WP analysis run-times for a codebase as a fraction (in percentage terms) of Mélange's total analysis run-time. Owing to Chromium's modular build system, we could localize a source defect to a small-sized library. The average size of program analyzed for Chromium (1.8 MB) was much lower compared to MySQL (150 MB), and Firefox (1.1 GB). As a consequence, the WP analysis run-times for Firefox, and MySQL are relatively high. While our foremost priority while prototyping Mélange has been functional effectiveness, our implementation leaves significant room for optimizations that will help bring down Mélange's end-to-end analysis run-time.

4.5   Limitations

Approach Limitations. BBy design, Mélange requires two analysis procedures at different code abstractions for a given defect type. We depend on programmer-written analysis routines to scale out to multiple defect types. Two actualities lend credence to our approach: First, analysis infrastructure required to carry out extended analyses is already available and its use is well-documented. This has assisted us in prototyping Mélange for four different CWEs. Second, the complexity of analysis routines is many times lower than the program under analysis. Our analysis procedures span 2,598 lines of code in total, while our largest analysis target (Chromium) has over 14 million lines of C++ code.

While Mélange provides precise diagnostics for security bugs it has discovered, manual validation of bug reports is still required. Given that software routinely undergoes manual review during development, our tool does not introduce an additional requirement. Rather, Mélange's diagnostics bring attention to problematic corner cases in source code. The manual validation process of Mélange's bug reports may be streamlined by subsuming our tool under existing software development processes (e.g., nightly builds, continuous integration).

Implementation Limitations. Mélange's WP analysis is path and context insensitive. This makes Mélange's whole-program analyzer imprecise and prone to issuing false warnings. To counter imprecision, we can augment our WP analyzer with additional analyses. Specifically, more powerful alias analysis and aggressive devirtualization algorithms will help prune false positives further. One approach to counter existing imprecision is to employ a ranking mechanism for bug reports (e.g., Z-Ranking [31]).

5   Related Work

Program analysis research has garnered attention since the late 70s. Lint [29], a C program checker developed at Bell Labs in 1977, was one of the first program analysis tools to be developed. Lint's primary goal was to check "portability, style, and efficiency" of programs. Ever since, the demands from a program checker have grown as new programming paradigms have been invented and programs have increased in complexity. This has contributed to the development of many commercial [5,23,27], closed-source [19], free [6], and open source [4,15,17,18,22,26,39,40,43,44] tools. Broadly, these tools are based on *Model Checking* [17,26], *Theorem Proving* [6], *Static Program Analysis* [4,5,19,23,27,44], *Dynamic Analysis* [18,34,39,40], or are hybrid systems such as AEG [15]. In the following paragraphs, we comment on related work that is close in spirit to Mélange.

Program Instrumentation. Traditionally, memory access bugs have been found by fuzz testing (or fuzzing) instrumented programs. The instrumentation takes care of tracking the state of program memory and adds run-time checks before memory accesses are made. Instrumentation is done either during run time (as in Valgrind [34]), or at compile time (as in AddressSanitizer or ASan [39]). Compile-time instrumentation has been preferred lately due to the poor performance of tools that employ run-time instrumentation.

While sanitizer tools such as ASan, and MemorySanitizer (MSan) are expected to have a zero false positive rate, practical difficulties, such as uninstrumented code in an external library, lead to false positives in practice. Thus, even run-time tools do not eliminate the need for manual validation of bug reports. To guarantee absence of uninitialized memory, MSan needs to monitor each and every load from/store to memory. This all-or-nothing philosophy poses yet another problem. Uninstrumented code in pre-compiled libraries (such as the C++ standard library) used by the program will invariably lead to false program crashes. Until these false crashes are rectified—either by instrumenting the code where the crash happens or by asking the tool to suppress the warning—the sanitizer tool is rendered unusable. Thus, use of MSan impinges on instrumentation of each and every line of code that is directly or indirectly executed by the program or maintenance of a blacklist file that records known false positives. Unlike MSan, not having access to library source code only lowers Mélange's analysis accuracy, but does not impede analysis itself. Having said that, Mélange will benefit from a mechanism to suppress known false positives. Overall, we believe that dynamic tools are invaluable for vulnerability assessment, and that a tool such as ours can complement them well.

Symbolic Execution. Symbolic execution has been used to find bugs in programs, or to generate test cases with improved code coverage. KLEE [18], Clang SA [4], and AEG [15] use different flavors of forward symbolic execution for their own end. As the program (symbolically) executes, constraints on program paths (path predicates) are maintained. Satisfiability queries on path predicates are used to prune infeasible program paths. Unlike KLEE and AEG, symbolic execution in Clang SA is done locally and hences scales up to large codebases. Anecdotal evidence suggests that KLEE and AEG don't scale up to large programs [25]. To the best of our knowledge, KLEE has not been evaluated against even medium-sized codebases let alone large codebases such as Firefox and Chromium.

Static Analysis. Parfait [19] employs an analysis strategy that is similar in spirit to ours. It employs multiple stages of analysis, where each successive stage is more precise than the preceding stage. Parfait has been used for finding buffer overflows in C programs. In contrast, we have evaluated Mélange against multiple vulnerability classes. Mélange's effectiveness in detecting multiple CWEs validates the generality of its design. In addition, Mélange has fared well against multiple code paradigms: both legacy C programs and modern object-oriented code.

   Like Yamaguchi et al. [44], our goal is to empower developers in finding multiple instances of a known defect. However, the approach we take is different. Yamaguchi et al. [44], use structural traits in a program's *AST* representation to drive a Machine Learning (ML) phase. The ML phase *extrapolates* traits of known vulnerabilities in a codebase, obtaining matches that are similar in structure to the vulnerability. CQUAL [22], and CQual++ [43], are flow-insensitive data-flow analysis frameworks for C and C++ languages respectively. Oink performs whole-program data-flow analysis on the back of Elsa, a C++ parser, and Cqual++. Data-flow analysis is based on type qualifiers. Our approach has two advantages over Cqual++. We use a production compiler for parsing C++ code that has a much better success rate at parsing advanced C++ code than a custom parser such as Elsa. Second, our source-level analysis is both flow and path sensitive while, in CQual++, it is not.

Finally, Clang Static Analyzer borrows ideas from several publications including (but not limited to) [24,37]. Inter-procedural context-sensitive analysis in Clang SA is based on the graph reachability algorithm proposed by Reps et al. [37]. Clang SA is also similar in spirit to Metal/xgcc [24].

6 Conclusion

We have developed Mélange, a static analysis tool for helping fix security-critical defects in open-source software. Our tool is premised on the intuition that vulnerability search necessitates multi-pronged analysis. We anchor Mélange in the Clang/LLVM compiler toolchain, leveraging source analysis to build a corpus of defects, and whole-program analysis to filter the corpus. We have shown that our approach is capable of identifying defects and vulnerabilities in open-source projects, the largest of which—Chromium—spans over 14 million lines of code. We have also demonstrated that Mélange's analyses are viable by empirically evaluating its run-time in an EC2 instance.

Since Mélange is easy to deploy in existing software development environments, programmers can receive early feedback on the code they write. Furthermore, our analysis framework is extensible via compiler plug-ins. This enables programmers to use Mélange to implement domain-specific security checks. Thus, Mélange complements traditional software testing tools such as fuzzers. Ultimately, our aim is to use the proposed system to help fix vulnerabilities in open-source software at an early stage.

Acknowledgments. This work was supported by the following grants: 317888 (project NEMESYS), 10043385 (project Enzevalos), and RI 2468/1-1 (project DEVIL). Authors would like to thank colleagues at SecT and Daniel Defreez for valuable feedback on a draft of this paper, and Janis Danisevskis for discussions on the C++ standard and occasional code reviews.

References

1. Bugzilla@Mozilla, Bug 1168091. https://bugzilla.mozilla.org/show_bug.cgi?id=1168091
2. Chromium Issue Tracker, Issue 411177. https://code.google.com/p/chromium/issues/detail?id=411177
3. Chromium Issue Tracker, Issue 436035. https://code.google.com/p/chromium/issues/detail?id=436035
4. Clang Static Analyzer. http://clang-analyzer.llvm.org/. Accessed 25 Mar 2015
5. Coverity inc. http://www.coverity.com/
6. HAVOC. http://research.microsoft.com/en-us/projects/havoc/
7. PHP Bug Bounty Program. https://hackerone.com/php
8. PHP::Sec Bug, 67492. https://bugs.php.net/bug.php?id=67492
9. PHP::Sec Bug, 69085. https://bugs.php.net/bug.php?id=69085
10. PHP::Sec Bug, 69152. https://bugs.php.net/bug.php?id=69152

11. Report 73245: Type-confusion Vulnerability in SoapClient. https://hackerone. com/reports/73245
12. Scan-build. http://clang-analyzer.llvm.org/scan-build.html
13. The LLVM Compiler Infrastructure. http://llvm.org/
14. WLLVM: Whole-program LLVM. https://github.com/travitch/whole-program-llvm
15. Avgerinos, T., Cha, S.K., Hao, B.L.T., Brumley, D.: AEG: automatic exploit generation. In: NDSS, vol. 11, pp. 59–66 (2011)
16. Bacon, D.F., Sweeney, P.F.: Fast static analysis of c++ virtual function calls. In: Proceedings of the 11th ACM SIGPLAN Conference on Object-Oriented Programming, Systems, Languages, and Applications, OOPSLA 1996, pp. 324–341. ACM, New York (1996). http://doi.acm.org/10.1145/236337.236371
17. Ball, T., Rajamani, S.K.: The s lam project: debugging system software via static analysis. In: ACM SIGPLAN Notices, vol. 37, pp. 1–3. ACM (2002)
18. Cadar, C., Dunbar, D., Engler, D.R.: KLEE: unassisted and automatic generation of high-coverage tests for complex systems programs. In: OSDI, vol. 8, pp. 209–224 (2008)
19. Cifuentes, C., Scholz, B.: Parfait: designing a scalable bug checker. In: Proceedings of the 2008 Workshop on Static Analysis, pp. 4–11. ACM (2008)
20. Dean, J., Grove, D., Chambers, C.: Optimization of object-oriented programs using static class hierarchy analysis. In: Tokoro, M., Pareschi, R. (eds.) ECOOP 1995 Object-Oriented Programming. LNCS, vol. 952, pp. 77–101. Springer, Heidelberg (1995)
21. Engler, D., Chelf, B., Chou, A., Hallem, S.: Checking system rules using system-specific, programmer-written compiler extensions. In: Proceedings of the 4th Conference on Symposium on Operating System Design & Implementation, vol. 4, p. 1. USENIX Association (2000)
22. Foster, J.S., Johnson, R., Kodumal, J., Terauchi, T., Shankar, U., Talwar, K., Wagner, D., Aiken, A., Elsman, M., Harrelson, C.: CQUAL: a tool for adding type qualifiers to C (2003). https://www.cs.umd.edu/~jfoster/cqual/. Accessed 26 Mar 2015
23. GrammaTech: CodeSonar. http://www.grammatech.com/codesonar
24. Hallem, S., Chelf, B., Xie, Y., Engler, D.: A system and language for building system-specific, static analyses. In: Proceedings of the ACM SIGPLAN 2002 Conference on Programming Language Design and Implementation, PLDI 2002, pp. 69–82. ACM, New York (2002). http://doi.acm.org/10.1145/512529.512539
25. Heelan, S.: Vulnerability detection systems: think cyborg, not robot. IEEE Secur. Priv. 9(3), 74–77 (2011)
26. Henzinger, T.A., Jhala, R., Majumdar, R., Sutre, G.: Software verification with BLAST. In: Ball, T., Rajamani, S.K. (eds.) SPIN 2003. LNCS, vol. 2648, pp. 235–239. Springer, Heidelberg (2003)
27. Hewlett Packard: Fortify Static Code Analyzer. http://www8.hp.com/us/en/software-solutions/static-code-analysis-sast/
28. Howard, M., Lipner, S.: The Security Development Lifecycle. O'Reilly Media, Incorporated, Sebastopol (2009)
29. Johnson, S.: Lint, a C Program Checker. Bell Telephone Laboratories, Murray Hill (1977)
30. Knoop, J., Steffen, B.: Efficient and optimal bit vector data flow analyses: a uniform interprocedural framework. Inst. für Informatik und Praktische Mathematik (1993)

31. Kremenek, T., Engler, D.: Z-Ranking: using statistical analysis to counter the impact of static analysis approximations. In: Cousot, R. (ed.) SAS 2003. LNCS, vol. 2694, pp. 295–315. Springer, Heidelberg (2003). http://dl.acm.org/citation. cfm?id=1760267.1760289

32. Lattner, C., Adve, V.: Llvm: a compilation framework for lifelong program analysis & transformation. In: International Symposium on Code Generation and Optimization, 2004, CGO 2004, pp. 75–86. IEEE (2004)

33. Lee, B., Song, C., Kim, T., Lee, W.: Type casting verification: stopping an emerging attack vector. In: 24th USENIX Security Symposium (USENIX Security 15), Washington, D.C, August 2015, pp. 81–96. USENIX Association. https://www. usenix.org/conference/usenixsecurity15/technical-sessions/presentation/lee

34. Nethercote, N., Seward, J.: Valgrind: a framework for heavyweight dynamic binary instrumentation. In: ACM Sigplan Notices, vol. 42, pp. 89–100. ACM (2007)

35. NIST: SAMATE - Software Assurance Metrics And Tool Evaluation. http:// samate.nist.gov/Main_Page.html

36. NIST: Test Suites, Software Assurance Reference Dataset. http://samate.nist.gov/ SRD/testsuite.php

37. Reps, T., Horwitz, S., Sagiv, M.: Precise interprocedural dataflow analysis via graph reachability. In: Proceedings of the 22nd ACM SIGPLAN-SIGACT Symposium on Principles of Programming Languages, pp. 49–61. ACM (1995)

38. Schwartz, E.J., Avgerinos, T., Brumley, D.: All you ever wanted to know about dynamic taint analysis and forward symbolic execution (but might have been afraid to ask). In: 2010 IEEE Symposium on Security and Privacy (SP), pp. 317–331. IEEE (2010)

39. Serebryany, K., Bruening, D., Potapenko, A., Vyukov, D.: Addresssanitizer: a fast address sanity checker. In: Proceedings of the 2012 USENIX Conference on Annual Technical Conference, USENIX ATC 2012, Berkeley, CA, USA, p. 28. USENIX Association (2012). http://dl.acm.org/citation.cfm?id=2342821.2342849

40. Stepanov, E., Serebryany, K.: Memorysanitizer: fast detector of uninitialized memory use in c++. In: 2015 IEEE/ACM International Symposium on Code Generation and Optimization (CGO), pp. 46–55. IEEE (2015)

41. Tsipenyuk, K., Chess, B., McGraw, G.: Seven pernicious kingdoms: a taxonomy of software security errors. IEEE Secur. Priv. 3(6), 81–84 (2005)

42. Viega, J., Bloch, J., Kohno, Y., McGraw, G.: Its4: a static vulnerability scanner for c and c++ code. In: 2000 16th Annual Conference on Computer Security Applications, ACSAC 2000, pp. 257–267, December 2000

43. Wilkerson, D.: CQUAL++. https://daniel-wilkerson.appspot.com/oink/qual.html. Accessed 26 Mar 2015

44. Yamaguchi, F., Lottmann, M., Rieck, K.: Generalized vulnerability extrapolation using abstract syntax trees. In: Proceedings of the 28th Annual Computer Security Applications Conference, pp. 359–368. ACM (2012)

Malware Detection

Comprehensive Analysis and Detection
of Flash-Based Malware

Christian Wressnegger$^{(\boxtimes)}$, Fabian Yamaguchi, Daniel Arp, and Konrad Rieck

Institute of System Security, TU Braunschweig, Braunschweig, Germany
c.wressnegger@tu-braunschweig.de

Abstract. Adobe Flash is a popular platform for providing dynamic and multimedia content on web pages. Despite being declared dead for years, Flash is still deployed on millions of devices. Unfortunately, the Adobe Flash Player increasingly suffers from vulnerabilities, and attacks using Flash-based malware regularly put users at risk of being remotely attacked. As a remedy, we present GORDON, a method for the comprehensive analysis and detection of Flash-based malware. By analyzing Flash animations at different levels during the interpreter's loading and execution process, our method is able to spot attacks against the Flash Player as well as malicious functionality embedded in ActionScript code. To achieve this goal, GORDON combines a *structural analysis* of the container format with *guided execution* of the contained code, a novel analysis strategy that manipulates the control flow to maximize the coverage of indicative code regions. In an empirical evaluation with 26,600 Flash samples collected over 12 consecutive weeks, GORDON significantly outperforms related approaches when applied to samples shortly after their first occurrence in the wild, demonstrating its ability to provide timely protection for end users.

Keywords: Adobe flash · Malware · Classification

1 Introduction

Adobe Flash is a widespread platform for providing multimedia content on web pages—despite being declared dead for years and the recent standardization of HTML5. According to Adobe, the Flash Player is still deployed on over 500 million devices across different hardware platforms, covering a large fraction of all desktop systems [42]. Furthermore, a significant number of web sites employs Flash for advertising, video streaming and gaming, such that every *fourth* web site in the top 1,000 Alexa ranking still makes use of Flash-based content [22].

Unfortunately, the implementation of Flash is continuously suffering from security problems. During the last ten years over 690 different vulnerabilities have been discovered in the Adobe Flash Player [32]. In the year 2015 alone, 314 new vulnerabilities have been made public, 268 of which enable remote code execution and require a user to merely visit a web page to be infected. This growing attack surface provides a perfect ground for miscreants and has lead to a large variety of Flash-based malware in the wild.

© Springer International Publishing Switzerland 2016
J. Caballero et al. (Eds.): DIMVA 2016, LNCS 9721, pp. 101–121, 2016.
DOI: 10.1007/978-3-319-40667-1_6

Three factors render the Flash platform particularly attractive for attackers: First, the large number of vulnerabilities considerably increases the chances for compromising a wide range of systems. Second, the ability to execute Action-Script code as part of an attack allows to probe the target environment and carry out sophisticated exploit strategies. Finally, the Flash platform provides several means for obstructing the analysis of attacks—most notably the capability to execute downloaded or dynamically assembled code. As a result of such obfuscation, the analysis of Flash-based attacks is difficult and time-consuming. Often, signatures for virus scanners are only available with notable delay such that end users remain unprotected for a considerable period of time.

In this paper, we present GORDON, a method for the automatic analysis and detection of Flash-based malware. Our method combines a *structural analysis* of the Flash container format with *guided execution* of ActionScript code, a lightweight and pragmatic form of multi-path exploration. While related approaches orient analysis to normal execution [27,44,48] or external triggers [6,14,30], GORDON actively guides the analyzer towards interesting code regions to maximize the coverage thereof. This equips us with a comprehensive view on a sample, including downloaded and dynamically assembled code. By additionally inspecting the container format, we are able to construct a detection method capable of spotting malicious ActionScript code as well as exploits targeting the Flash Player directly.

To cope with the large diversity of Flash files in practice, GORDON implements support for all versions of Flash animations, including all versions of ActionScript code. To the best of our knowledge, we are the first to provide a generic method for the analysis and detection of Flash-based malware that enables a comprehensive view on the behavior and structure of a Flash animation across all versions. The efficacy of GORDON in practice is demonstrated in an evaluation with 26,600 Flash samples collected over a time of 12 consecutive weeks. GORDON detects 90 % of the malicious samples shortly after their appearance in the wild with a false-positive rate of at most 0.1 %. Consequently, our method provides an excellent starting point for fending off Flash-based malware more efficiently.

In summary we make the following contributions:

- **Guided code-execution.** We propose a lightweight and pragmatic approach for exploring ActionScript code in Flash-based malware that guides analysis towards large or otherwise characteristic code regions automatically.
- **Comprehensive analysis of Flash.** With the combination of a *structural analysis* of Flash containers and a *guided execution* of embedded code we provide a fine-grained view on samples across all versions of ActionScript code and Flash.
- **Effective detection of Flash-based attacks.** Based on this analysis, we develop a detection method that accurately identifies Flash-based exploits and malware shortly after their occurrence, providing a good starting point to bootstrap signature-based approaches.

The rest of the paper is structured as follows: In Sect. 2 we introduce GOR-DON, our method for the analysis and detection of Flash-based malware, followed by a detailed description of the employed structural analysis in Sect. 3, our guided code-execution in Sect. 4 and GORDON's detector in Sect. 5. Our evaluation is presented in Sect. 6. We discuss limitations and related work in Sect. 7 and Sect. 8, respectively. Section 9 concludes the paper.

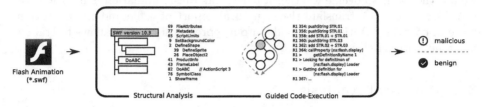

Fig. 1. Schematic depiction of the analysis and detection process of GORDON with a Flash-based malware as input, the two-step analysis of the profiler and the classification of our method's detector as output.

2 System Overview

The diverse nature of attacks based on Flash requires an analysis method to inspect these animations on different levels. To this end, we implement our method GORDON by integrating it into different processing stages of two Flash interpreters, thereby blending into existing loading and execution processes. This allows us to make use of data generated directly during execution, such as dynamically constructed code or downloaded files. We achieve this analysis using the following two-step procedure (see Fig. 1): First, we instrument the processing unit of the Flash interpreter in order to profile a malware's structure as well as the execution of contained code. Second, we combine these profiles into a common representation to power a classifier based on machine learning techniques, that allows to effectively discriminate malicious from benign Flash animations.

Profiling the Malware. GORDON's profiler is implemented on the basis of two popular and mature open-source implementations of the Flash platform that are complementary with respect to the versions they support: *Gnash* [20] and *Lightspark* [34]. While Gnash provides support for Flash up to version 9, Lightspark enables processing version 9 and higher. As a result, GORDON is able to analyze all currently relevant versions and file formats of Adobe Flash animations, including all versions of ActionScript code. The profiling implemented for both interpreters features two kinds of analyses, that in turn make use of data arising during an interpreter's regular loading and execution process [1]:

- First, the profiler of GORDON inspects the hierarchical composition of the Shockwave Flash (SWF) format. This can be done during the loading phase when the interpreter parses the file for further processing (Sect. 3).

– Second, the control flow of embedded ActionScript code is analyzed in order to determine *indicative regions*. By strategically changing the control flow at branches in the code, GORDON guides execution along paths covering as much indicative regions as possible (Sect. 4).

Detecting Flash-Based Malware. Based on the output of these different analyses, we are then able to decide whether a particular Flash animation is malicious or not. To this end we translate the structural report of a file and the execution trace of contained ActionScript code into a representation that allows to train a machine learning classifier (Sect. 5).

3   Structural Analysis

We begin our analysis by breaking down Flash animations into *tags*, the primary containers employed by the SWF file format [2] to store ActionScript code as well as data of various kinds, including audio, video, image and font data. Due to the large number of different types of tags Flash files expose a huge attack surface for memory corruption exploits. As a consequence, many exploits rely on very specific types and arrangements of tags to succeed, and thus, the sequence of tags alone can already serve as a strong indicator for malware.

For the structural analysis as employed by GORDON only tag identifiers and structural dependencies are of interest, contained data on the other hand is not considered. Consequently, GORDON does not need to know about the format of individual tags and hence can be applied to unknown tags, e.g., tags introduced in future versions. However, to further enhance the overall detection our method may be combined with approaches to specifically target data formats that can be included in a Flash animation's tags. Moreover, exploits often rely on corrupt or incomplete tags. To better account for these, we additionally include two specific tag identifiers that mark (a) *incomplete* tags, i.e. tags that are known to the interpreter, but could not be correctly parsed and (b) tags that contain *additional data* beyond their specified limits. The latter occurs, for instance, whenever the file contains data at the end that is not fully contained in its last tag.

```
69    FileAttributes
77    Metadata
 9    SetBackgroundColor
 2    DefineShape
      39    DefineSprite
      26    PlaceObject2
86    DefineSceneAndFrameLabelData
43    FrameLabel
87    DefineBinaryData    // Payload
87    DefineBinaryData    // Payload
82    DoABC               // ActionScript 3
76    SymbolClass
 1    ShowFrame
```

Fig. 2. Excerpt of the structural report for a LadyBoyle sample (See footnote 1).

As a result of this structural analysis, we obtain a sequence of container types including their nestings for each Flash file. Figure 2 shows the resulting container listing for a sample[1] of the LadyBoyle malware using `CVE-2015-323`.

In comparison to many other Flash animations, the content of this file is rather short. However, for this specific sample the presence of the `DefineBinaryData` and `DoABC` tags is crucial. The first contain the malware's payload as binary data, which in turn gets extracted by ActionScript 3 code embedded in the latter. These tags in combination comprise the malicious functionality of the sample. While in this particular case the structure alone is only an indicator for the malicious behavior, that needs to be backed up by an analysis of the embedded ActionScript code, other types of malware rely on corrupt tags that allow to distinctively distinguish these. Some containers, such as the `DefineShape` tag, allow to enclose an arbitrary number of other containers. We include these in the listing as children of the parent tag. Note that the `DefineShape` tag and its children are not present in the original sample and have been added for illustration purposes only.

For convenience, the structural report can also be represented as a sequential list of identifiers, where nested containers are indicated by brackets:

69 77 9 2 [39 26] 86 43 87 87 82 76 1

It is important to note, that this representation already encodes the complete hierarchy and relations of the tags to each other. This condensed form is particularly suitable for automated approaches that do not require a textual description of the tags. We revisit this topic when discussing the implementation of GORDON's detector in Sect. 5.

4   Guided Code-Execution

When analyzing a sample with GORDON we aim at observing as much indicative behavior of a Flash animation as possible—ideally the analysis covers all possible execution paths and corner cases. However, as extensively discussed in computer security literature in the past [e.g., 27, 30] this is not feasible due to the potentially exponential number of different paths, making it necessary to revert to approximations and heuristics in practice.

While related approaches orient analysis to normal execution [27, 44, 48] or external triggers [6, 14, 30], our method guides execution towards *indicative code regions*: Each branch is chosen such that the execution corresponds to the path that covers the most indicative ActionScript code not observed so far. In particular, we are interested in exploring paths containing security-related objects and functions as well as branches that contain more code than others. Figure 3 exemplarily shows the selected paths of two consecutive runs. During the first, GORDON's profiler guides execution towards the `loadMovie` function, which enables Flash animations using ActionScript 2 to dynamically load code in form of another SWF file. The second run then directs the interpreter along the path

---

[1] md5: `cac794adea27aa54f2e5ac3151050845`.

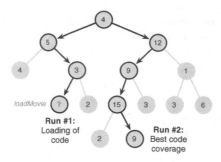

Fig. 3. Illustration of the path-selection strategy. Node labels correspond to the amount of bytecode instructions in each basic block. Black lines indicate chosen execution paths.

covering the most bytecode instructions. This strategy can hence be seen as a way to not only maximize code coverage locally (within the sample itself), but globally, including all code that is loaded dynamically.

This is made possible by inspecting the control flow of the ActionScript code contained in a Flash file with the aim of learning (a) how much code can be covered along a specific path and (b) where security-related objects and functions such as the aforementioned loadMovie are located. To this end, we first derive the control-flow graph (CFG) of the ActionScript bytecode in question and remove cycles induced by loops and recursive function calls (Sect. 4.1). Second, the resulting graph is annotated with locations of indicative functionality and the number of instructions contained in each branch, which in turn enables us to efficiently determine the overall code coverage of individual paths (Sect. 4.2). The results of this analysis is then used for the actual execution of the Flash animation, allowing GORDON to navigate through the code in a targeted way (Sect. 4.3).

4.1   Control-Flow Analysis

A control-flow graph (CFG) as shown in Fig. 4 contains basic code blocks as its nodes and directed edges for branches connecting them [see 3]. As part of the Adobe Flash Player's verification phase, the ActionScript VM already checks certain control flow properties when bytecode is loaded into the interpreter [1]. Our control-flow analysis can thus be thought of as a natural extension to the examinations conducted by Flash interpreters. We, however, make use of this information only as a starting point for the following analysis.

Upon the generation of a CFG, we are ready to find execution paths that maximize code coverage. To easily determine these paths, the graph needs to first undergo a few modifications. In particular, it is necessary to eliminate cycles that occur due to loop statements in the code. Once these cycles are removed we obtain an *acyclic control-flow graph (ACFG)* which allows us to efficiently determine the code size of complete paths in the graph. To this end, we rewrite all *back-edges* (edges pointing backwards with respect to the control flow) by

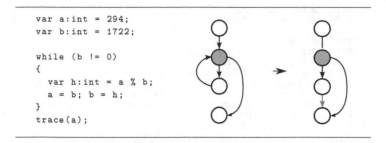

```
var a:int = 294;
var b:int = 1722;

while (b != 0)
{
    var h:int = a % b;
    a = b; b = h;
}
trace(a);
```

Fig. 4. An ActionScript 3 snippet, the corresponding control flow graph (CFG) and its acyclic transformation (ACFG). Dark nodes represent loop headers, bright nodes generic code blocks; newly inserted edges are shown in red. (Color figure online)

linking them to the first code block after the loop. Figure 4 demonstrates this for a simple while loop. All conventional loop, nested loops and their special cases such as *unnatural loops* can be efficiently resolved using the *dominance* relations of the individual nodes [see 3].

4.2 Annotating Control-Flow Edges

Once an ACFG has been generated, we annotate each of its edges with the number of bytecode instructions covered by the following code block. We artificially increase the weight of individual instructions, if they correspond to security-related objects and functions. For example, to pinpoint the dynamic loading of code, we set the weighting for calls to the `loadMovie` function (ActionScript 2) and the `Loader` object (ActionScript 3) to the maximum to ensure the analyzer targets these first. Both are frequently used by Flash-based malware to load code downloaded from the Internet or dynamically assembled at runtime. Similarly, it is possible to emphasize other security-related functions and objects in Action-Script, such as `readBytes` and `ByteArray` which are often used for obfuscated code.

Given the annotated graph, the search for the most indicative code regions can be rephrased as a *longest-path problem*. For arbitrary graphs determining the longest path is NP-hard. Fortunately, for *directed acyclic graphs* such as the ACFG extracted previously, this is possible [see 11, 38].

4.3 Path Exploration

With the annotated ACFG at hand, we can now guide the interpreter to execute security-related or large code regions by stopping at every conditional jump and choosing the branch corresponding to the path with the highest weight. In order to avoid executing indicative code unnecessarily often, we constantly update visited regions within the ACFG. Moreover, GORDON enables multiple executions based on the coverage analysis of previous runs. Hence, a different path is taken and different code regions are visited in each run, thereby challenging adversarial

```
R1 973:   pushString     "fla"
R1 975:   pushString     "sh.uti"
R1 977:   add            "fla" + "sh.uti"
R1 978:   pushString     "ls.Byt"
R1 980:   add            "flash.uti" + "ls.Byt"
R1 981:   pushString     "eArray"
R1 983:   add            "flash.utils.Byt" + "eArray"
R1 984:   callProperty [ns:flash.utils] getDefinitionByName 1
R1 >         Looking for definition of [ns:flash.utils] ByteArray
R1 >         Getting definition for [ns:flash.utils] ByteArray
R1 987:   getLex: [ns:] Class
```

Fig. 5. Excerpt of behavioral report (See footnote 2).

attempts to hide payload in paths not covered initially. As analysis output of the guided execution, we obtain all covered ActionScript instructions across multiple execution runs. Figure 5 shows a short excerpt of the instructions executed by a malware to facilitate the CVE-2015-03-313 exploit[2] in the first run (R1).

Instructions at offset 973 to 983 show how the malware obfuscates the usage of the ByteArray object at offset 984. This object is frequently used to construct malicious payloads at run-time. The complete listing shows how the encrypted payload is composed out of different parts, decrypted and finally loaded.

In the following we address certain implementation details of GORDON's guided code-execution with a special focus on the characteristics of Flash-based malware and potential adversarial attempts to avoid analysis.

Reducing Branch Candidates. Although GORDON is capable of pursuing all branches in ActionScript code, narrowing down the candidates speeds up the process and limits the possibility of breaking the semantics of a sample. Often, web-based attacks are tailored towards specific browser environments and thus only trigger malicious activity upon checking for the correct target environment [27,44]. The conditional jumps underlying these checks provide excellent candidates for our guided execution, as they usually lead to a malware sample's payload and are likely to be mutually exclusive, therefore reducing the risk of semantic side-effects.

To restrict our analysis to these conditional jumps, we implement a taint-tracking mechanism that propagates taint from environment-identifying data sources to conditional jumps. In the scope of Flash-based malware, such data typically originates from the System.capabilities and flash.system.Capabilities data structures available in ActionScript 2 and 3, respectively. To track the data flow across built-in functions, we conservatively taint the result whenever at least one of the input arguments is tainted. Note that for simplicity, we do not consider implicit data-flow and control dependencies in our implementation [see 8,31] but leave this for future work.

Countering Obfuscation. To account for dynamically loaded code, we additionally hook the interpreter's loading routines. All such code then passes through

---

[2] md5: 4f293f0bda8f851525f28466882125b7.

the same analysis steps as the host file, allowing to analyze files downloaded from the Internet as well as potentially encrypted code embedded in the Flash animation itself equally thoroughly. This scheme is applied recursively to ensure that all code is covered by our analysis.

Furthermore, GORDON implements an *adaptive timeout* mechanism rather than a fixed period of time as utilized in previous works [13,19,44]. In particular, we reset a 10s timer each time the sample attempts to load code, giving the sample time to react to this event. This may increase the analysis duration for certain files but significantly reduces the effort for those that do not load data or do not contain ActionScript code at all. On average a sample is executed for 12.6 s with a maximum duration of 3 min, reducing the analysis time by 93 % compared to a fixed timeout.

We also take precautions for the possibility that an execution path is not present in the statically extracted ACFG. In these rare cases, we switch to determining the size of the branch in an online manner: GORDON looks ahead in order to inspect the instructions right after the branching point and passively skips over instructions to determine the sizes of the branches. This analysis in principle is the same as performed earlier (Sect. 4.1) but applied to the newly discovered piece of bytecode only.

Lastly, we have observed an increase in the use of event-based programming in recent malware—presumably to circumvent automatic detection—and thus incorporate the automatic execution of such events into GORDON's profiler. Immediately after an event listener is added the specified function gets passed an appropriate dummy event object and is executed without waiting for the actual event to happen.

Updating the ACFG. Our method is designed to run a sample multiple times. To this end, we update the edge labels of the ACFG during execution to reflect the visited code and recompute the largest path in an online manner. Consequently, our method implements a lightweight variant of multi-path exploration that executes different code during each run. Since we decide on each condition at runtime and identical code regions (functions) may be referenced multiple times we not only cover the code of the single largest path in the graph but potentially a combination of a number of paths. This softens the definition of such a path as used in graph theory but makes a lot of sense for this application especially.

5   Learning-Based Detection

In order to demonstrate the expressiveness of our analysis, we implement a learning-based detector that is trained on known benign and malicious Flash animations. This approach spares us from manually constructing detection rules, yet it requires a comprehensive dataset for training (see Sect. 6.1). However, as most learning algorithms operate on vectorial data, we first need to map the analysis output of GORDON to a vector space.

Vector Space Embedding. To embed the structural and behavioral reports generated by GORDON in a vector space, we make use of classic *n-gram models*. These models have initially been proposed for natural language processing [9, 41] but are also used in computer security for analyzing sequential data [e.g., 24, 28, 33, 39, 47].

In particular, we extract *token n-grams* from both kinds of analysis outputs by moving a sliding window of length n over the tokens in the reports. While the compact output representation of GORDON's structural analysis already is in a format that can be used to extract such tokens, the reports generated by the guided code-execution need to be normalized first: We extract all instructions, including their names and parameters. Moreover, we replace values passed as parameters with their respective type, such as INT, FLOAT or STR. To avoid loosing relevant information we however preserve all names of operations, functions and objects. Finally, we tokenize the behavioral reports using white-space characters.

High-order n-grams compactly describe the content, implicitly reflect the structure of the reports and can be used for establishing a joint map to a vector space. To this end, we embed a Flash animation x in a binary vector space $\{0,1\}^{|S|}$ spanned by the set S of all observed n-grams in the analysis output. Each dimension in this vector space is associated with the presence of one n-gram $s \in S$. Formally, this mapping ϕ is given by

$$\phi : x \longmapsto \big(b(s,x)\big)_{s \in S}$$

where the function $b(s,x)$ returns 1 if the n-gram s is present in the analysis output of the file x and 0 otherwise.

Classification. Based on this vector space embedding, we apply a *linear Support Vector Machine* (SVM) for learning a classification between benign and malicious Flash animations. While several other learning algorithms could also be applied in this setting, we stick to linear SVMs for their excellent generalization capability and very low run-time complexity, which is linear in the number of objects and features [37].

In short, a linear SVM learns a hyperplane that separates two classes with maximum margin—in our setting corresponding to vectors of benign Flash animations and Flash-based malware. The orientation of the hyperplane is expressed as a normal vector w in the input space and thus an unknown sample can be classified using an inner product as follows

$$f(x) = \langle w, \phi(x) \rangle - t$$

where t is a threshold and $f(x)$ the orientation of $\phi(x)$ with respect to the hyperplane. That is, $f(x) > 0$ indicates malicious content in x and $f(x) \leq 0$ corresponds to benign content.

Due to the way the mapping of n-grams is defined, the vector $\phi(x)$ is sparse: Out of millions of possible token n-grams, only a limited subset is present in a particular sample x. These vectors can thus be compactly stored in memory.

Also, the inner product to determine the final score can be calculated in linear time in the number of n-grams in a sample

$$f(x) = \sum_{s \in S} w_s \, b(s, x) = \sum_{s \text{ in } x} w_s - t$$

We integrate this classifier into GORDON, such that it can be applied to either the analysis outputs individually or to the joint representation of both.

6   Evaluation

We proceed to empirically evaluate the capabilities of GORDON in different experiments. In particular, we study the effectiveness of the guided execution in terms of code covered (Sect. 6.2), compare the detection performance with related approaches (Sect. 6.3) and further demonstrate the effectivity of GOR-DON in a temporal evaluation (Sect. 6.4). Before presenting these experiments, we introduce our dataset of Flash-based malware and benign animations.

6.1   Dataset Composition

The dataset for our evaluation has been collected over a period of 12 consecutive weeks. In particular, we have been given access to submissions to the VirusTotal service, thereby receiving benign and malicious Flash files likewise. Since many web crawlers are directly tied to VirusTotal, the collected data reflects the current landscape of Flash usage to a large part.

We split our dataset into malicious and benign Flash animations based on the classification results provided by VirusTotal two months later: A sample is marked as malicious, if it is detected by at least 3 scanners and flagged as benign, if none of the 50 scanners hosted at VirusTotal detects the sample. Samples that do not satisfy one of the conditions are discarded. This procedure enables us to construct a reasonable estimate of the ground truth, since most virus scanners refine their signatures and thus improve their classification results over time. The resulting dataset comprises 1,923 malicious and 24,671 benign Flash animations, with about half the samples being of version 8 or below and the other half of more recent versions, therefore handled by the ActionScript VM version 1 and 2 respectively. A summary of the dataset is given in Table 1.

Table 1. Overview of the evaluation dataset

Classification	AVM1	AVM2	Total
Malicious	864	1,059	1,923
Benign	12,046	12,625	24,671
Total	12,910	13,684	26,594

To account for the point in time the samples have been observed in the wild, we group the samples in buckets according to the week of their submission to VirusTotal. Consequently, we obtain 12 sets containing benign and malicious Flash animations corresponding to the 12-week evaluation period. These temporal sets are used during the evaluation to construct temporarily disjoint datasets for training and testing to conduct our experiments in strict chronological order: For our experiments the performance is determined only on samples that have been submitted to VirusTotal after any sample in the training data. This ensures an experimental setup as close to reality as possible and demonstrates the approach's effectivity of providing timely protection.

6.2 Coverage Analysis

In our first experiment, we evaluate the effectiveness of the proposed guided code-execution strategy. To this end, we investigate the code coverage of malware samples in our 12 week dataset. We apply GORDON to the malware and inspect the output of the interpreter. Due to obfuscation techniques employed by malware, the amount of *statically* contained code of a Flash file often is not a reliable measure in this setting. Hence, we compare the number of executed instructions with respect to a regular execution of the samples. With the path-exploration strategy employed by GORDON, we manage to oberserve over 50 % more ActionScript code than during a naive execution, and unveil crucial information not provided otherwise. We mainly credit this leap in coverage to the recursive analysis of dynamically loaded code and code assembled at runtime.

6.3 Comparative Evaluation

We continue to evaluate the detection performance of GORDON, showing its ability to correctly classify Flash-based malware and specifically compare our method with FLASHDETECT [3] [44]. In particular, we evaluate the approaches on the complete set of 12 consecutive weeks, where we use *weeks 1–6* for training and *weeks 7–9* for validation to calibrate the parameters of the detectors. We then combine these two sets for final training and apply the detectors to *weeks 10–12* for testing the detection performance. Table 2 summarizes the results as the true-positive rates and the corresponding false-positives rates of the methods.

Table 2. Detection rates of FLASHDETECT and GORDON.

Method	FLASHDETECT[3]	GORDON-1%	GORDON-0.1%
False-postive rate	1 %	1 %	0.1 %
True-positive rate	26.5 %	95.2 %	90.0 %

---

[3] Versions not supported by FLASHDETECT (version 8 and below) have been excluded.

GORDON. As described in Sect. 5 GORDON's detector can be applied to either the analysis outputs individually or to the joint representation of both. The relation thereof is shown in Fig. 6(a) as a ROC curve with the detection performance as true-positive rate on the y-axis over the false-positive rate on the x-axis. To map the reports of GORDON's profiler to the vector space we make use of 4-grams. Each representation and the combination of both are plotted as different curves.

At a false-positive rate of 0.1 % the individual representations attain a detection rate of 60–65 %. The combination of both (GORDON-0.1%) increases the detection performance significantly and enables spotting 90.0 % of the Flash-based attacks. If the false-positive rate is increased to 1 %, our method even detects 95.2 % of the malicious samples in our dataset (GORDON-1%). Additionally we break down this results by CVE numbers. Figure 6(b) shows the detection performance as true-positive rate over the years of appearance of the particular vulnerabilities in our dataset. The average performance is slightly below the overall detection rate, indicating that we also detect malware that does not carry exploits itself, but facilitates a different attack or uses obfuscation to obscure the presence of an exploit. This perfectly demonstrates the capabilities of our approach: First, the complementary views on the behavior and structure of Flash animations provide a good basis for analyzing attacks and, second, this expressive representation can be effectively used for detecting malware in the wild.

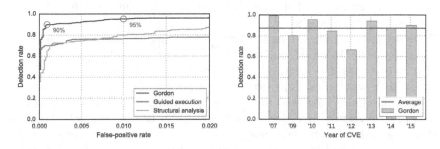

Fig. 6. Detection performance of GORDON as ROC curve and sorted by CVE numbers.

FLASHDETECT. For the related method FLASHDETECT we slightly modify the setting and exclude Flash animations of versions below 9 from the evaluation, as this detector is dedicated to the analysis of ActionScript 3 malware only. Nevertheless, FLASHDETECT only identifies 26.5 % of the malicious Flash samples at a false-positive rate of 1 %.

Although FLASHDETECT employs a heuristic for eliciting malicious behavior during the execution of a Flash animation, it misses 3 out of 4 attacks. We attribute this low performance to two issues: First, compared to our method the employed branch selection strategy is less effective and second, the method has been tailored towards specific types of attacks which are not prevalent anymore. GORDON in contrast does not rely on manually selected features, but models the underlying data using n-grams. Therefore it can better cope with the large diversity of today's malware. Due to the low performance of FLASHDETECT, we omit it from the ROC curve in Fig. 6(a).

AV Engines. We finally determine the detection performance of 50 virus scanners on the testing dataset. The 5 best scanners detect 82.3 %–93.5 % of the malicious samples. However, due to the very nature of signature-based approaches they provide detection with practically no false positives. If we parametrize GORDON to zero false positives only 47.2 % of the malware is detected. This clearly shows, that GORDON cannot compete with manually crafted signatures in the long run, but provides solid detection of Flash-based malware shortly after its first occurrence in the wild *without* the need for manual analysis.

As a consequence, we consider our method a valuable tool for improving the analysis of Flash-based malware in the short run and a way to provide traditional approaches with a good starting point in day-to-day business to efficiently craft signatures for AV products.

6.4   Temporal Evaluation

To demonstrate the use of GORDON as a fast, complementary detector, we study its performance over several weeks of operation. We again make use of 4-grams and 12 consecutive weeks of collected Flash data. This time we however apply the detector one week ahead of time, that is, we classify one week after the other, based on the previous weeks.

We start off with *week 1* as training, *week 2* as validation and *week 3* as first test dataset. Over the course of the experiment we shift the time frame forward by one week and likewise increase the training dataset. This can be seen as expanding a window over the experiment's period of time. Hence, GORDON's detector accumulates more and more data for training—just as a system operating in practice would. In order to optimally foster complementary approaches we choose a rather liberal false-positive rate of 1 %. Figure 7 shows the true-positive rates achieved by our method during 10 weeks of operation. GORDON starts off below its average performance and takes time till *week 5* to perform well, reaching detection rates between 80 % and 99 % for the remaining weeks. As our method makes use of machine learning techniques, the detector requires a certain amount of training data before it is fully operational and reaches its optimal performance. If parametrized to 0.1 % false positives, GORDON still reaches detection performances of 82 % on average.

Overall, this experiment shows GORDON's potential to improve on the detection performance shortly after a malware's appearance in the wild. We consider the number of false-positives—benign samples that need to be additionally analyzed without directly resulting in a malicious signature—as tolerable trade-off for the leap taken in short-term detection performance. In practice, one may start off with a rather strict configuration, accept a lower gain and scale up the interval according to available resources.

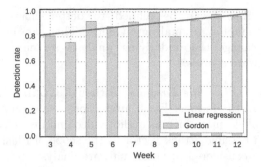

Fig. 7. GORDON's performance over 12 consecutive weeks. The red line illustrates the detector's progression over time, showing a clear uptrend towards its optimal performance. (Color figure online)

7   Limitations

The experiments discussed in the previous section demonstrate that our method provides an effective solution for the analysis and detection of Flash-based malware. Nonetheless, our approach has some limitations which are discussed in the following.

Breaking Code Semantics. With GORDON we make a trade-off between completeness and simplicity of analysis. By pragmatically forcing the execution of specific branches the analyzer avoids expensive computations at execution-time, but may—similar to previous approaches [27,48]—break semantics of underlying code. Our experiments however show that restricting GORDON to branches which depend on environment-identifying data (c.f. Sect. 4) reduces the impact of such inconsistencies and that the overall effectiveness of the detector is not influenced in a negative way. Note that, GORDON's path-exploration strategy of guiding analysis towards indicative code regions can also be used in combination with symbolic execution—an adaption worth exploring in future work.

Analysis-Aware Malware. Experience has shown that successful analysis systems have repeatedly been subject to dedicated evasion techniques of various types [10]. For GORDON two particular variations come to mind: First, a malware author may leverage differences in implementation of Lightspark and Gnash compared to the Adobe Flash Player. While this is true, the underlying concepts of GORDON can be easily transferred to any interpreter when used in production, possibly using instrumentation [21].

Second, malware might hide its payload in a seemingly irrelevant, low-weighted branch, veiled by branches containing more instructions—potentially across multiple stages. By maximizing the code coverage over multiple executions, GORDON systematically restricts the available space for hiding malicious code. The number of executions thereby is a parameter that allows to strike a balance between coverage and analysis time. Furthermore, the proposed weighting of the annotated ACFG can be refined to better characterize indicative code regions and adapted to malware trends. This can be deployed without the need to change the underlying analysis system and enhanced as analysis-aware malware evolves.

Dynamic Loading of Other File Formats. Although GORDON inspects dynamically loaded code in the form of Flash animations, we do not currently track and analyze other file formats such as audio, video and image containers. These have shown to be a possible attack vector in the scope of Flash malware in the past and have been considered in other malware analysis systems [19,44]. The detection of embedded malware, however, is a research field of its own and ranges from statically matching shellcode signatures to finding suspicious code in different file containers [4,39,40,50]. For GORDON, we thus consider the analysis of other file formats mainly an engineering effort of integrating other successful approaches.

Interaction with JavaScript and the DOM. Similarly to malware families that make use of ActionScript to set the grounds for exploiting a particular vulnerability in the browser, there also exist attack campaigns that utilize JavaScript for heap spraying, for instance, in order to exploit a vulnerability in the Flash Player. This cannot be handled with the current prototype of GORDON as we solely focus on the Flash part in this paper. Bringing together our method with systems that have proven effective for detecting JavaScript malware [e.g., 13,16,35] may close this gap elegantly.

Machine Learning for Malware Detection. Finally, as GORDON's detector is based on machine learning, it may be vulnerable to mimicry attacks [18,46,47]. For n-gram models, Fogla and Lee [17] show that generating a polymorphic blending attack is NP-hard, but can be approximated for low-order n-grams. While non-trivial in practice, such attacks could theoretically be conducted against GORDON. However, the use of high-order n-grams elevates complexity to a level where such attacks become impractical. In addition to mimicry, a powerful attacker may systematically introduce samples to shift the classification boundary to her advantage [5,23]. These attacks can have an effect on GORDON's detector, but require access to large portions of the training data to be effective. As a consequence, such attacks can be alleviated if data from different sources is mixed and subsequently sanitized [15].

8   Related Work

A large body of research has dealt with the detection and analysis of web-based attacks, yet Flash-based malware has received only little attention so far. In this section, we discuss work related to GORDON, focusing on two strains of research: (1) Flash-based malware and (2) multi-path exploration.

Note that the implementations of JavaScript and ActionScript interpreters are fundamentally different, making an application of detection approaches for malicious JavaScript *source-code* unlikely to operate on Flash-based malware available in *bytecode*. Consequently, we do not discuss approaches for malicious JavaScript code in this paper and refer the reader to a wide range of research [7, 13, 26, 27, 35]. Nonetheless, combining detection methods for malicious JavaScript and Flash can be of considerable value. Also, the work by Šrndić and Laskov [45] is of particular interest, since they have been the first to show the practicality of using hierarchical document structure for detection.

Flash-based Attacks and Malware. Only few works have studied means to fend off malware targeting the Adobe Flash platform [19, 44]. ODOSWIFF [19], focuses on detecting malicious ActionScript 2 Flash advertisements based on expert knowledge of prevalent attacks. In contrast to ODOSWIFF, our method employs machine learning to automatically produce a classifier based on benign and malicious Flash animations. FLASHDETECT [44], the successor of ODOSWIFF also makes use of machine learning techniques and, similar to GORDON, employs an instrumented interpreter to dump dynamically loaded code. However, FLASHDETECT only pursues one level of staged-execution, focuses solely on ActionScript 3 and employs a simple heuristic for subverting environmental checks that has proven insufficient for modern Flash-based malware. By contrast, GORDON aims at maximizing the coverage of indicative code regions independent of particular attacks, across multiple stages and versions. As a result, our method allows to uncover vitally more code than FLASHDETECT and thereby attains a better basis for detecting attacks. Furthermore, by not relying on hand-crafted features GORDON can better cope with the large diversity of today's malware.

Industry research has mainly focused on instrumenting Flash interpreters for analysis purposes. Wook Oh [49], for instance, presents methods to patch ActionScript bytecode to support function hooking, and more recently, Hirvonen [21] introduces an approach for instrumenting Flash based on the Intel Pin Platform. These systems complement GORDON and may be used to implement our method for other platforms.

Aside from Flash-based malware and therefore, orthogonal to GORDON several authors have inspected the malicious use of Flash's cross-domain capabilities [25], its vulnerability to XSS attacks [43] and the prevention of such [29].

Multi-path Exploration. Ideally an analysis covers all possible paths and corner case, which however is not feasible due to the potentially exponential number of different execution paths. Most notably in this context is the work by Moser et al. [30], who propose to narrow down analysis to paths influenced by input data such as network I/O, files or environment information. While this effectively decreases the number of paths to inspect it still exhaustively enumerates all paths of this subset under investigation. A second strain of research has considered symbolic execution for the analysis of program code and input generation [e.g., 12, 36]. Brumley et al. [6] combine dynamic binary instrumentation with symbolic execution to identify malware behavior triggered by external commands. Similarly, Crandall et al. [14] use symbolic execution to expose specific points in time where malicious behavior is triggered. Equally to the enumeration of paths, symbolic execution shares the problem of an exponential state space.

With Rozzle, Kolbitsch et al. [27] also make use of techniques from symbolic execution. However, instead of generating inputs, data in alternative branches is represented symbolically and, upon subsequent execution of both branches, merged. In doing so, Kolbitsch et al. except to break existing code due to the execution of infeasible paths. Based on the symbolic representation Rozzle likewise is subject to an exponential state space that is dealt with by limiting the depth of the symbolic trees used. Limbo [48] avoids this kind of state explosion and reverts to a more simple strategy of forcing branching conditions to monitor execution. Limbo however again exhaustively enumerates paths and thus does not address the underlying problem in the first place.

All these methods are either driven by the original execution path [27, 48] or focus on external triggers [6, 14, 30]. GORDON on the other hand, first identifies indicative code regions and guides the interpreter towards these, enabling a payload-centric analysis.

9   Conclusions

In light of an increasing number of vulnerabilities in Flash, there is an urgent need for tools that provide an effective analysis and detection of Flash-based malware. As a remedy, we present GORDON, a novel approach that combines a *structural analysis* of the Flash container format with *guided execution* of embedded ActionScript code—a lightweight and pragmatic form of multi-path exploration. Our evaluation on 26,600 Flash samples shows that GORDON is able to cover more code than observed with other approaches. Moreover, this increase of coverage exposes indicative patterns that enable GORDON's detector to identify 90–95 % of malware shortly after its appearance in the wild.

Our method can be used to bootstrap the current process of signature generation and point an analyst to novel malware samples. GORDON thereby provides a valuable step towards the timely protection of end users. Furthermore, the guided execution of code is a simple yet effective strategy for studying malicious code that might also be applicable in other branches of malware analysis, such as for JavaScript and x86 inspection.

Acknowledgments. The authors would like to thank Emiliano Martinez of Virus-Total for supporting the acquisition of malicious Flash files. Furthermore, we gratefully acknowledge funding from the German Federal Ministry of Education and Research (BMBF) under the projects APT-Sweeper (FKZ 16KIS0307) and INDI (FKZ 16KIS0154K) as well as the German Research Foundation (DFG) under project DEVIL (RI 2469/1-1).

References

1. Adobe Systems Incooperated: ActionScript virtual machine 2 (AVM2) overview. Technical report, Adobe System Incooperated (2007)

2. Adobe Systems Incooperated: SWF file format specification. Technical report, Adobe System Incooperated (2013)
3. Aho, A.V., Sethi, R., Ullman, J.D.: Compilers Principles, Techniques, and Tools, 2nd edn. Addison-Wesley, Reading (2006)
4. Baecher, P., Koetter, M.: libemu - x86 Shellcode Emulation (2008)
5. Biggio, B., Nelson, B., Laskov, P.: Poisoning attacks against support vector machines. In: Proceedings of International Conference on Machine Learning (ICML) (2012)
6. Brumley, D., Hartwig, C., Liang, Z., Newsome, J., Song, D., Yin, H.: Automatically identifying trigger-based behavior in malware. In: Lee, W., Wang, C., Dagon, D. (eds.) Botnet Detection, pp. 65–88. Springer, US (2008)
7. Canali, D., Cova, M., Vigna, G., Kruegel, C.: Prophiler: a fast filter for the large-scale detection of malicious web pages. In: Proceedings of the International World Wide Web Conference (WWW), pp. 197–206, April 2011
8. Cavallaro, L., Saxena, P., Sekar, R.: On the limits of information flow techniques for malware analysis and containment. In: Zamboni, D. (ed.) DIMVA 2008. LNCS, vol. 5137, pp. 143–163. Springer, Heidelberg (2008)
9. Cavnar, W., Trenkle, J.: N-gram-based text categorization. In: Proceedings of SDAIR, Las Vegas, pp. 161–175, NV, USA, April 1994
10. Chen, X., Andersen, J., Mao, Z.M., Bailey, M., Nazario, J.: Towards an understanding of anti-virtualization and anti-debugging behavior in modern malware. In: Proceedings of Conference on Dependable Systems and Networks (DSN), pp. 177–186 (2008)
11. Cormen, T.H., Leiserson, C.E., Rivest, R.L., Stein, C.: Introduction to Algorithms, 3rd edn. MIT Press, Cambridge (2009)
12. Cova, M., Felmetsger, V., Banks, G., Vigna, G.: Static detection of vulnerabilities in x86 executables. In: Proceedings of Annual Computer Security Applications Conference (ACSAC), pp. 269–278 (2006)
13. Cova, M., Kruegel, C., Vigna, G.: Detection and analysis of drive-by-download attacks and malicious JavaScript code. In: Proceedings of the International World Wide Web Conference (WWW), pp. 281–290 (2010)
14. Crandall, J.R., Wassermann, G., Oliveira, D.A.S., Su, Z., Wu, S.F., Chong, F.T.: Temporal search: detecting hidden malware timebombs with virtual machines. In: Proceedings of International Conference on Architectural Support for Programming Languages and Operating Systems, pp. 25–36 (2006)
15. Cretu, G., Stavrou, A., Locasto, M., Stolfo, S., Keromytis, A.: Casting out demons: Sanitizing training data for anomaly sensors. In: Proceedings of IEEE Symposium on Security and Privacy, pp. 81–95 (2008)
16. Curtsinger, C., Livshits, B., Zorn, B., Seifert, C.: Zozzle: fast and precise in-browser JavaScript malware detection. In: Proceedings of USENIX Security Symposium, pp. 33–48 (2011)
17. Fogla, P., Lee, W.: Evading network anomaly detection systems: formal reasoning and practical techniques. In: Proceedings of ACM Conference on Computer and Communications Security (CCS), pp. 59–68 (2006)
18. Fogla, P., Sharif, M., Perdisci, R., Kolesnikov, O., Lee, W.: Polymorphic blending attacks. In: Proceedings of USENIX Security Symposium, pp. 241–256 (2006)
19. Ford, S., Cova, M., Kruegel, C., Vigna, G.: Analyzing and detecting malicious flash advertisements. In: Proceedings of Annual Computer Security Applications Conference (ACSAC), pp. 363–372 (2009)
20. gnash. GNU Gnash. https://www.gnu.org/software/gnash. Accessed April 2016

21. Hirvonen, T.: Dynamic flash instrumentation for fun and profit. In: Proceedings of Black Hat USA (2014)
22. httparchive. http://www.httparchive.org. Accessed April 2016
23. Huang, L., Joseph, A.D., Nelson, B., Rubinstein, B.I.P., Tygar, J.D.: Adversarial machine learning. In: Proceedings of ACM Workshop on Artificial Intelligence and Security (AISEC), pp. 43–58 (2011)
24. Jang, J., Agrawal, A., Brumley, D.: ReDeBug: finding unpatched code clones in entire os distributions. In: Proceedings of IEEE Symposium on Security and Privacy, pp. 48–62 (2012)
25. Johns, M., Lekies, S.: Biting the hand that serves you: a closer look at client-side flash proxies for cross-domain requests. In: Holz, T., Bos, H. (eds.) DIMVA 2011. LNCS, vol. 6739, pp. 85–103. Springer, Heidelberg (2011)
26. Kapravelos, A., Shoshitaishvili, Y., Cova, M., Kruegel, C., Vigna, G.: Revolver: an automated approach to the detection of evasive web-based malware. In: Proceedings of USENIX Security Symposium, pp. 637–651, August 2013
27. Kolbitsch, C., Livshits, B., Zorn, B., Seifert, C.: Rozzle: de-cloaking internet malware. In: Proceedings of IEEE Symposium on Security and Privacy, pp. 443–457 (2012)
28. Laskov, P., Šrndić, N.: Static detection of malicious javascript-bearing PDF documents. In: Proceedings of Annual Computer Security Applications Conference (ACSAC), pp. 373–382 (2011)
29. Louw, M.T., Thotta, K., Venkatakrishnan, V.N.: AdJail: practical enforcement of confidentiality and integrity policies on web advertisments. In: Proceedings of USENIX Security Symposium, pp. 371–388 (2010)
30. Moser, A., Kruegel, C., Kirda, E.: Exploring multiple execution paths for malware analysis. In: Proceedings of IEEE Symposium on Security and Privacy, pp. 231–245 (2007)
31. Nair, S.K., Simpson, P.N.D., Crispo, B., Tanenbaum, A.S.: A virtual machine based information flow control system for policy enforcement. Electron. Notes Theor. Comput. Sci. (ENTCS) 197(1), 3–16 (2008)
32. Özkan, S.: CVE Details. http://www.cvedetails.com. Accessed April 2016
33. Perdisci, R., Ariu, D., Fogla, P., Giacinto, G., Lee, W.: McPAD: a multiple classifier system for accurate payload-based anomaly detection. Comput. Netw. 5(6), 864–881 (2009)
34. Pignotti, A.: Lightspark. https://github.com/lightspark. Accessed April 2016
35. Ratanaworabhan, P., Livshits, B., Zorn, B.: Nozzle: a defense against heapspraying code injection attacks. In: Proceedings of USENIX Security Symposium, pp. 169–186 (2009)
36. Saxena, P., Akhawe, D., Hanna, S., Mao, F., McCamant, S., Song, D.: A symbolic execution framework for javascript. In: Proceedings of IEEE Symposium on Security and Privacy, pp. 513–528 (2010)
37. Schölkopf, B., Smola, A.J.: Learning with Kernels. MIT Press, Cambridge (2002)
38. Sedgewick, R., Wayne, K.: Algorithms, 4th edn. Addison-Wesley, Boston (2011)
39. Shafiq, M.Z., Khayam, S.A., Farooq, M.: Embedded malware detection using markov n-grams. In: Zamboni, D. (ed.) DIMVA 2008. LNCS, vol. 5137, pp. 88–107. Springer, Heidelberg (2008)
40. Stolfo, S.J., Wang, K., Li, W.-J.: Towards stealthy malware detection. In: Christodorescu, M., Jha, S., Maughan, D., Song, D., Wang, C. (eds.) Malware Detection, pp. 231–249. Springer, USA (2007)
41. Suen, C.: N-gram statistics for natural language understanding, text processing. IEEE Trans. Pattern Anal. Mach. Intell. 1(2), 164–172 (1979)

42. Systems, A.: Adobe Flash runtimes: Statistics. http://www.adobe.com/products/flashruntimes/statistics.html. Accessed April 2016
43. van Acker, S., Nikiforakis, N., Desmet, L., Joosen, W., Piessens, F.: FlashOver: automated discovery of cross-site scripting vulnerabilities in rich internet applications. In: Proceedings of ACM Symposium on Information, Computer and Communications Security (ASIACCS) (2012)
44. Van Overveldt, T., Kruegel, C., Vigna, G.: FlashDetect: actionscript 3 malware detection. In: Balzarotti, D., Stolfo, S.J., Cova, M. (eds.) RAID 2012. LNCS, vol. 7462, pp. 274–293. Springer, Heidelberg (2012)
45. Šrndić, N., Laskov, P.: Detection of malicious PDF files based on hierarchical document structure. In: Proceedings of Network and Distributed System Security Symposium (NDSS) (2013)
46. Wagner, D., Soto, P.: Mimicry attacks on host based intrusion detection systems. In: Proceedings of ACM Conference on Computer and Communications Security (CCS), pp. 255–264 (2002)
47. Wang, K., Parekh, J.J., Stolfo, S.J.: Anagram: a content anomaly detector resistant to mimicry attack. In: Zamboni, D., Kruegel, C. (eds.) RAID 2006. LNCS, vol. 4219, pp. 226–248. Springer, Heidelberg (2006)
48. Wilhelm, J., Chiueh, T.: A forced sampled execution approach to kernel rootkit identification. In: Kruegel, C., Lippmann, R., Clark, A. (eds.) RAID 2007. LNCS, vol. 4637, pp. 219–235. Springer, Heidelberg (2007)
49. Wook Oh, J.: AVM inception - how we can use AVM instrumentation in a beneficial way. In: Shmoocon (2012)
50. Wressnegger, C., Boldewin, F., Rieck, K.: Deobfuscating embedded malware using probable-plaintext attacks. In: Stolfo, S.J., Stavrou, A., Wright, C.V. (eds.) RAID 2013. LNCS, vol. 8145, pp. 164–183. Springer, Heidelberg (2013)

Reviewer Integration and Performance Measurement for Malware Detection

Brad Miller[1]([✉]), Alex Kantchelian[2], Michael Carl Tschantz[3], Sadia Afroz[3], Rekha Bachwani[4], Riyaz Faizullabhoy[2], Ling Huang[5], Vaishaal Shankar[2], Tony Wu[2], George Yiu[6], Anthony D. Joseph[2], and J.D. Tygar[2]

[1] Google Inc., Mountain View, USA
bradmiller@google.com
[2] UC Berkeley, Berkeley, USA
{akant,riyazdf,vaishaal,tony.wu,adj,tygar}@cs.berkeley.edu
[3] International Computer Science Institute, Berkeley, USA
{mct,sadia}@icsi.berkeley.edu
[4] Netflix, Los Gatos, USA
rbachwani@netflix.com
[5] DataVisor, Mountain View, USA
ling.huang@datavisor.com
[6] Pinterest, San Francisco, USA
george@pinterest.com

Abstract. We present and evaluate a large-scale malware detection system integrating machine learning with expert reviewers, treating reviewers as a limited labeling resource. We demonstrate that even in small numbers, reviewers can vastly improve the system's ability to keep pace with evolving threats. We conduct our evaluation on a sample of Virus-Total submissions spanning 2.5 years and containing 1.1 million binaries with 778 GB of raw feature data. Without reviewer assistance, we achieve 72 % detection at a 0.5 % false positive rate, performing comparable to the best vendors on VirusTotal. Given a budget of 80 accurate reviews daily, we improve detection to 89 % and are able to detect 42 % of malicious binaries undetected upon initial submission to VirusTotal. Additionally, we identify a previously unnoticed temporal inconsistency in the labeling of training datasets. We compare the impact of training labels obtained at the same time training data is first seen with training labels obtained months later. We find that using training labels obtained well after samples appear, and thus unavailable in practice for current training data, inflates measured detection by almost 20 % points. We release our cluster-based implementation, as well as a list of all hashes in our evaluation and 3 % of our entire dataset.

1 Introduction

Malware constitutes an enormous arms race in which attackers evolve to evade detection and detection mechanisms react. A recent study found that only 66 %

B. Miller and G. Yiu—Primarily contributed while at UC Berkeley.
R. Bachwani—Primarily contributed while at Intel.

© Springer International Publishing Switzerland 2016
J. Caballero et al. (Eds.): DIMVA 2016, LNCS 9721, pp. 122–141, 2016.
DOI: 10.1007/978-3-319-40667-1_7

of malware was detected within 24 h, 72 % within one week, and 93 % within one month [9]. To evade detection, attackers produce a large number of different malware binaries, with McAfee receiving over 300,000 binaries daily [14].

Machine learning offers hope for timely detection at scale, but the setting of malware detection differs from common applications of machine learning. Unlike applications such as speech and text recognition where pronunciations and character shapes remain relatively constant over time, malware evolves as adversaries attempt to fool detectors. In effect, malware detection becomes an online process in which vendors must continually update detectors in response to new threats, requiring accurate labels for new data. Unfortunately, malware labeling poses unique challenges. Whereas reading is sufficient to label text, the deceptive and technical nature of malware requires expert analysis.

We present an approach to detection integrating machine learning and expert reviews to keep pace with new threats at scale. As expert labeling is expensive, we model the expert as capable of supplying labels for a limited selection of samples. We then combine the limited supply of expert reviewer labels with the broader supply of noisy labels produced by anti-virus scanners to train a detection model. We evaluate our approach using a sample of submissions to VirusTotal, a malware analysis and detection website [27]. The dataset includes a timestamp and anti-virus labels for each submission, capturing the emergence and prevalence of binaries, as well as label knowledge, over a 2.5 year period. We train new models weekly with a customized approach combining accurate reviewer labels and noisy anti-virus labels and evaluate each model over the coming week. To evaluate at scale, we simulate reviewer labels by revealing the results of automated scans taken at least 8 months after a sample first appears, providing opportunity for automated detectors to update and detect new threats.

We recognize that accurate training labels are not instantaneously available for all data, and therefore examine the impact of training label practices on performance measurement. Prior work has introduced *temporal sample consistency*, requiring that training binaries predate evaluation binaries [13]. We introduce *temporal label consistency*, imposing the requirement that training labels also predate evaluation binaries. Temporal label consistency restricts label quality relative to common practice, which collects labels well after binaries first appear and uses the same mature labels for both training and evaluation, leading to artificially inflated performance measurements.

Our work offers the following contributions:

- We present a detection system that integrates reviewers to increase detection from 72 % at 0.5 % false positive rate, comparable to the best vendors on VirusTotal, to 77 % and 89 % detection with a budget of 10 and 80 reviews daily on average. Additionally, our system detects 42 % of malicious binaries initially undetected by vendors in our evaluation.
- We demonstrate impact of temporally inconsistent labels on performance measurement, artificially inflating measured detection from 72 % to 91 % at a 0.5 % false positive rate.

– We publicly release[1] our implementation, 3 % of all data, and list of all 1.1 million unique binaries appearing over 2.5 years included in our evaluation.

Our evaluation also includes several additional experiments offering a more complete understanding of detection performance. Although our design includes both static and dynamic features, since VirusTotal detectors must operate statically we also compare our performance against VirusTotal using static features alone. Note that the restriction to static features actually disadvantages our approach, as VirusTotal detectors may operate against the arbitrary file and we restrict ourselves to static attributes available through VirusTotal. Our performance is slightly impacted, producing 84 % detection at 0.5 % false positive rate with 80 queries daily and still surpassing detectors on VirusTotal. We also explore the impact of inaccurate human labelers on the system's detection performance by adding random noise to the simulated expert labels. We find that our design is robust in the presence of imperfect labelers. Given reviewers with a 90 % true positive rate and a 5 % false positive rate our system still achieves 82 % detection at a 0.5 % false positive rate, as compared to 89 % detection using accurate reviewers.

We evaluate our contributions using VirusTotal data because each submission represents a request for analysis from a user, researcher or member of the security community. VirusTotal responds to requests by running dozens of antivirus products from the security industry, including large firms such as McAfee, Symantec and Kaspersky. As we evaluate our contributions on a dataset including submissions from researchers and the security industry, not a random sampling of files from end user machines, we envision our approach as improving the detection workflows within security firms which ultimately produce products for end users. We demonstrate that by investing a fraction of the engineering expertise of large security firms, we can vastly improve the ability to determine whether a binary is malicious.

In Sect. 2, we review prior work. Section 3 presents the design of our system, including feature extraction, machine learning and integration of the labeling expert, and Sect. 4 examines our dataset. Section 5 discusses our system implementation and then examines the impact of different performance measurement techniques and evaluates the performance of our detection system. Lastly, Sect. 6 concludes.

2   Prior Work

In this section we present the prior work most directly related to our own areas of contribution: reviewer integration to improve automated detection and performance measurement. Consistent with the focus of our work, we primarily discuss systems for malware detection rather than family classification or clustering. An extensive discussion of related work is available online [15].

---

[1] http://secml.cs.berkeley.edu/detection_platform/.

Since minimal prior work has explored reviewer integration, we begin by discussing systems that moderate access to any expensive labeling resource. Several works employ a *weak detector* design, which cheaply labels *some* instances as benign but requires an expensive confirmation to label *any* instance as malicious. Provos et al. and Canali et al. present weak detector systems for malicious URLs which moderate access to expensive analysis in a virtual machine [5,19]. Similarly, Chakradeo et al. present MAST, a system capable of detecting 95 % of Android malware at the cost of analyzing 13 % of non-malicious applications [6]. Karanth et al. prioritize JavaScript for manual review with the end goal of identifying new vulnerabilities [12]. In contrast with weak detectors, we view the expensive resource as an integrated component in a periodically retrained system, rather than the final step in a detection pipeline. Instead of attempting to pass the entire and exact set of malicious instances to the expensive resource for verification, we identify a smaller set of instances that improve automated detection and use scalable components to determine final instance labels.

In contrast to weak detector approaches, Nissim et al. present a system that integrates reviewers during retraining but focuses on increasing the raw number of malicious instances submitted to the reviewer rather than improving automated detection. Nissim et al. introduce two reviewer integration strategies and compare both to *uncertainty sampling*, a reviewer integration technique from machine learning [24]. Although each new strategy reviews more malicious samples, neither improves automated detection, instead producing lower true positive and higher false positive rates [16] or true positive rates within 1 % [17] of uncertainty sampling. The evaluation also lacks timestamped data and randomly divides samples into 10 artificial "days". Since there are no temporal effects in the sample ordering, it is not possible to accurately assess detector performance or reviewer workload when confronted with new attacks. In contrast, we demonstrate novel reviewer integration improving detection 17 % points over uncertainty sampling and conduct an evaluation with timestamped samples and labels spanning 2.5 years.

Sculley et al. present Google's approach to detecting adversarial advertisements, integrating human reviewers and automated detection [23]. Unfortunately, the presentation omits key details and the sensitive nature of the system prevents any code or data release. For example, the evaluation does not specify how many human reviewers are necessary, the added benefit from additional reviewers or the total number of queries to each reviewer. Likewise, the impact of reviewers errors and different integration strategies is also unspecified. We contribute an analysis of the marginal benefit from additional reviews, as well as the impacts of reviewer errors and different reviewer integration strategies. Additionally, we release all source code and sample data to facilitate future work.

We also examine prior work related to performance measurement. The most common performance measurement technique in malware detection is *cross-validation* (e.g., [4,8,21,26]). Cross-validation tends to inflate measured performance by partitioning training and evaluation data randomly, effectively guaranteeing that any attack seen in evaluation is also seen in training [11]. Kolter et al.

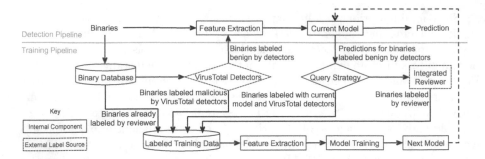

Fig. 1. The detection pipeline employs the current model to detect malware, and the training pipeline produces the next model for use in the detection pipeline. During each retraining period, the training pipeline reviews all available training data and selects binaries for submission to the integrated reviewer. Binaries labeled by the reviewer are combined with binaries labeled using the current model and anti-virus scan results to train the next model.

improve on cross-validation by using a separate training dataset which entirely predates any evaluation data [13]. Furthering this approach, Perdisci et al. and Srndic et al. conduct evaluations which use a single timestamped dataset divided chronologically into periods, using the first $n-1$ periods to detect content in period n [18,25]. While these works maintain temporal sample consistency, none present or systematically evaluate the impact of temporal label consistency.

Prior work approaching temporal label consistency has either evaluated a system in production, which would have no way to be temporally inconsistent, or a system that retrains on its own output. Rajab et al. evaluate a deployed PDF malware detector, which trains using presently available knowledge and is evaluated in retrospect after anti-virus labels have matured [20]. Schwenk et al. demonstrate the infeasibility of a JavaScript malware system which is iteratively retrained over time using its own output labels, but do not compare temporally consistent labels from an external source with labels from the future [22].

3   Detector Design

In this section we present our detector design, including feature extraction, machine learning and reviewer integration. Figure 1 presents an overview of our approach. When a binary arrives, the detection pipeline extracts the features, applies the current model to classify the binary as malicious or benign, and the training pipeline stores the binary in a database along with all other binaries seen to-date. During each retraining period, binaries not detected by scanners on VirusTotal are considered for submission to the integrated reviewer. Binaries confidently detected by the current model are included in training data with a malicious label, and the remaining purportedly benign binaries are submitted to the integrated reviewer as the review budget allows. The remaining un-submitted binaries are included in the training data as benign. At the end of the retraining period, the next model produced in the training pipeline replaces the current model and the process repeats.

We begin by examining the general techniques used for feature vectorization in Sect. 3.1, and then present the application of feature vectorization techniques to static and dynamic attributes of binaries in Sect. 3.2. Section 3.3 presents our approach to labeling training data, and Sect. 3.4 describes our approach to reviewer integration.

3.1 Approaches to Feature Vectorization

Many machine learning algorithms work best with numeric features, but not all attributes of binaries come in that format. We discuss four general techniques to convert static and dynamic attributes of binaries into numerical feature vectors. Which of the four techniques we can apply varies across attributes. For each technique, we discuss how we apply the technique to maximize robustness against evasion.

Categorical. The categorical mapping associates one dimension with each possible attribute value. For example, the `DeviceIoControl` API call may correspond to index i in feature vector x, where $x_i = 1$ if and only if the binary issues the `DeviceIOControl` API call. Since the absence of an attribute reveals information about a binary, we include a special *null index* to indicate that the value of the attribute is missing. For example, the file may not generate any network traffic, or may not be signed. Where possible, we structure our application of categorical feature extraction to constrain the attacker to remain within a limited set of values. For example, we apply subnet masks to IP addresses accessed by binaries to effectively shrink the IP space and associate access to similar IP addresses with the same feature index.

Ordinal. Ordinal attributes assume a specific value in an ordered range of possibilities, such as the size of a binary. To remain robust to moderate fluctuations as adversaries attempt to evade detection, we vectorize ordinal values using a binning scheme rather than associating each distinct quantity with a unique index. The binning scheme works as follows: for a given attribute value, we return the index of the bin which the value falls into, and set the corresponding dimension to 1. For attributes that vary widely, we use a non-linear scheme to prevent large values from overwhelming small values during training. For example, the number of written files v is discretized to a value i such that $3^i \leq v < 3^{i+1}$, where the exponential bins accommodate the large dynamic range of this quantity.

Free-Form String. Many important attributes appear as unbounded strings, such as the comments field of the signature check. Representing these attributes as categorical features could allow an attacker to evade detection by altering a single character in the attribute, causing the attribute to map into a different dimension. To increase robustness, we capture 3-grams of these strings, where each contiguous sequence of 3 characters represents a distinct 3-gram, and consider each of the 3-grams as a separate dimension. Since this approach is still sensitive to variations that alter 3-grams, we introduce an additional string simplification.

Table 1. Feature vectors reflect static and dynamic attributes of binaries. We apply categorical vectorization to all attributes, as well as *string, †ordinal and ‡sequential vectorization for selected attributes.

	Feature Name	Description	Example
Static	Binary Metadata*	Metadata from MAGIC and EXIFTOOL	`PECompact2 compressed`
	Digital Signing*	Certificate chain identity attributes	`Google Inc; Somoto Ltd`
	Heuristic Tools	TRID; Tools from ClamAV, Symantec	`InstallShield setup; DirectShow filter`
	Packer Detection	Packer or crypter used on binary	`UPX; NSIS; Armadillo`
	PE Properties*†	Section hashes, entropies; Resource list, types	`image/x-png; hash:eb0c7c289436...`
	Static Imports	Referenced library names and functions	`msvcrt.dll/ldiv; certcli.dll`
Dynamic	Dynamic Imports	Dynamically loaded libraries	`shell32.dll; dnsapi.dll`
	File Operations†	Number of operations; File paths accessed	`C:\WINDOWS\system32\mshtml.tlb`
	Mutex Operations*	Each created or opened mutex	`ShimCacheMutex; RasPbFile`
	Network Operations†	IPs accessed; HTTP requests; DNS requests	`66.150.14.*; b.liteflames.com`
	Processes	Created, injected or terminated process names	`python.exe; cmd.exe`
	Registry Operations	Registry key set or delete operations	`SET: ...\WindowsUpdate\AU\NoAutoUpdate`
	Windows API Calls‡	n-grams of Windows API calls	`DeviceIoControl	IsDebuggerPresent`

To reduce sensitivity to 3-gram variations, we define classes of equivalence between characters and replace each character by its canonical representative. For instance, the string 3PUe5f would be canonicalized to 0BAa0b, where upper and lowercase vowels are mapped to 'A' and 'a' respectively, upper and lowercase consonants are mapped to 'B' and 'b', and numerical characters to '0'. Likewise, the string 7SEi2d would also canonicalize to 0BAa0b. Occasionally, we sort the characters of the trigrams to further control for variation and better capture the morphology of the string. Mapping portable executable resource names, which sometimes exhibit long random-looking bytes sequences, is one application of this string simplification technique.

Sequential. The value of some attributes is a sequence of tokens where each token assumes a finite range of values. These sequential attributes are strongly related to free-form string attributes, although the individual tokens are not restricted to being individual characters. We use sequential feature extraction to capture API call information since there is a finite set of API calls and the calls occur in a specific order. As with free-form string features, we use an n-gram approach where each sequence of n adjacent tokens comprises an individual feature. Sequential vectorization can be vulnerable to evasion in situations where adversaries are able to introduce tokens which have no effect and separate meaningful tokens. To increase robustness, we apply n-gram vectorization with $n = 1$ and $n = 2$ as well as $n = 3$, decreasing the number of unique n-grams which the adversary is able to generate.

3.2   Attributes of Binaries

VirusTotal provides static and dynamic attributes for each binary. Whereas static attributes are obtained though analysis of the binary itself, dynamic attributes are obtained through execution in the Cuckoo sandbox [3]. Table 1 provides an overview of static attributes, dynamic attributes and associated vectorization techniques.

The static attributes available from VirusTotal consist of direct properties of the executable code itself, metadata associated with or derived from the executable and the results of heuristic tools applied to the executable. The attributes extracted directly from the code include any statically imported library functions and aspects of the portable executable format, such as resource language, section attributes (e.g. entropy) and resource attributes (e.g. type). The metadata associated with the code includes the output of the MAGIC and EXIFTOOL utilities, which infer properties such as the file type, and any digital signatures associated with the file. We collect the status of the verification, the identities of every entity in the certificate chain, comments, product name, description, copyright, internal name, and publisher from each digital signature. The heuristic tools applied to the executable include PEID [2] and utilities from ClamAV [1], and check for packing, network utilities or administrative utilities commonly associated with malware or potentially unwanted applications.

The dynamic attributes available from the Cuckoo sandbox capture interactions with the host operating system, disk and network resources. Interactions with the operating system include dynamic library imports, mutex activity and manipulation of other processes running on the system. Additionally, the Cuckoo sandbox provides an execution trace of all Windows API calls accessed by the binary, including the arguments, argument values and return values of any system call. The summary of disk activity includes file system and registry operations, capturing any persistent effects of the binary. We utilize both full and partial paths of file system operations as well as the types and number of operations to the file system during feature extraction; we also utilize the specific registry keys accessed or modified by the binary. Lastly, we extract features from the network activity of the binary, including HTTP and DNS traffic and IP addresses accessed via TCP and UDP.

3.3   Training Label Harmonization and Reviewer Query Strategy

During each retraining period, the training process must assign labels to all available training binaries. The process of assigning training labels harmonizes four distinct sources of information: scan results from anti-virus software, the current learned model, any prior reviews, and additional fresh reviews for a small number of binaries selected by the *query strategy* for review.

The labeling process begins with the anti-virus scan results and application of the current model, both of which prune the set of binaries which the query strategy will consider for submission to the integrated reviewer. Our application of anti-virus scan results leverages the intuition, which we confirm in Sect. 4, that anti-virus vendors bias detections towards false negatives rather than false positives. Correspondingly, we view consensus among anti-virus detectors that a binary is malicious as sufficient to label the binary malicious during training, but we do not label undetected binaries as benign without further analysis. We call this heuristic the *undetected* filter since only binaries which are not detected by the vendors remain as candidates for review.

Next, we apply our current detection model to all undetected binaries and assign a malicious label to any binaries which score above a threshold M. We refer to this heuristic as *auto-relabeling* since some undetected binaries are automatically relabeled, similar to the self-training concept from semi-supervised learning [7]. If the binary is both undetected by anti-virus vendors and cannot be auto-relabeled using our detector, we submit the binary to the query strategy.

From the binaries that could not be confidently labeled as malicious, the query strategy selects a subset for review to improve their training labels. The *uncertainty sampling* query strategy selects binaries that are closest to the decision boundary, intuiting that the model will benefit from knowing the labels of those binaries about which it is unsure [24]. Uncertainty sampling has experienced success in other application domains, such as text classification, and served as a baseline for comparison in prior work involving integrated manual review [16,17]. Designed for a case where the reviewer is the only source of labeling information, uncertainty sampling is unaware of how our two heuristics used the noisy labels from anti-virus scanners to filter the binaries for its consideration.

Consequently, we propose a new query strategy aware of our heuristics to increase the effectiveness of the integrated reviewer. Since the heuristics identify binaries likely to be malicious, we will label any binary not identified by them or selected for review as benign. Consequently, only reviews which label a binary malicious will impact the final training data labels. Accordingly, we develop the *maliciousness* query strategy, which selects binaries for review that received high scores from our detection model, but not high enough to be subject to auto-relabeling. More formally, the query strategy has a submission budget B, where B is determined as a fixed percentage of the total number of new training binaries during the retraining period. The maliciousness query strategy then submits the B remaining binaries with the greatest maliciousness scores less than the auto-relabeling threshold M to the integrated reviewer. The binaries in excess of B which are not submitted to the integrated reviewer are labeled benign. By selecting binaries likely to be malicious but would otherwise be labeled benign, maliciousness achieves a higher likelihood than uncertainty sampling that the review will effect a change in training labels.

3.4   Model Training and Integration of Reviewer Labels

After considering several forms of learning, including decision tree and nearest neighbor based approaches, we selected logistic regression as the basis for our malware detector. As a linear classifier, logistic regression assigns a weight to each feature and issues predictions as a linear function of the feature vector, resulting in a real valued quantity [10]. Scoring each binary as a real valued quantity enables us to create a tradeoff between true and false positive rates by adjusting the threshold at which binaries are labeled malicious. Linear classification scales well in prediction as the size of the model is a function of the dimensionality of the data and not the size of the training data, as happens with nearest neighbor techniques. Additionally, the clear relationship between weights and features allows analysts to easily understand what the detector is doing and why, which can be difficult with complex tree ensembles. Lastly, logistic regression scales well in training with many available implementations capable of accommodating high dimensional feature spaces and large amounts of training data.

We now discuss our training process integrating labels from the reviewer with noisy labels from anti-virus scanners and our own detector. Since the reviewer only labels a small minority of binaries, noisy labels from anti-virus vendors will overwhelm reviewer labels during training unless reviewer labels receive special treatment. We present the standard logistic regression training process below, and then describe the special treatment which we provide for reviewer labels. The logistic regression training process finds the weight vector $\mathbf{w}$ which minimizes the following loss function for labeled training set $\{(\mathbf{x}^1, y^1), \ldots, (\mathbf{x}^n, y^n)\}$ where $y^i \in \{-1, +1\}$ represents the label:

$$C_- * \sum_{i:y^i=-1} \ell(-\mathbf{w}^\mathsf{T}\mathbf{x}^i) \quad + \quad C_+ * \sum_{i:y^i=1} \ell(\mathbf{w}^\mathsf{T}\mathbf{x}^i) \quad + \quad \frac{1}{2}\|\mathbf{w}\|^2$$

$C_- > 0$ and $C_+ > 0$ are distinct hyper-parameters controlling for both regularization and class importance weighting and $\ell(x) = \log(1 + \exp(-x))$ is the logistic loss function. The first and second terms correspond to the misclassification losses for negative and positive instances, respectively, and the final term is a regularization term that discourages models with many large non-zero weights. To amplify the effect of reviewer labels, we assign a higher weight W during training to any binary labeled benign by the reviewer. We obtain superior results only weighting binaries that the reviewer labels benign since the maliciousness query strategy tends to select binaries for review which fall on the malicious side of the decision boundary. When a benign instance is classified as malicious during training, a particularly high weight is necessary to have a corrective effect on the model and force the instance to receive a benign classification.

4   Dataset and Evaluation Labeling Overview

We maintain that an evaluation dataset should include diverse binaries, reflect the emergence and prevalence of binaries over time, and record changes in the best available labeling knowledge for the binaries as time progresses. Our evaluation dataset, consisting of 1.1 million distinct binaries submitted to Virus-Total between January 2012 and June 2014, achieves these criteria. VirusTotal accepts submissions from end users, researchers and corporations, leading to a diverse sampling of binaries containing thousands of malware families and benign instances. To randomize interaction with daily and hourly batch submission jobs, VirusTotal supplied us with the hashes of binaries submitted during a randomized segment during each hour of our collection period, reflecting approximately 1 % of the total binaries during the collection period. We include each submission of each binary to accurately represent the prevalence and labeling knowledge of binaries over time. A more complete discussion of the dataset, including changes in vendor labels over time and analysis of our labeling methodology is available online [15].

Due to the regular distribution of the evaluation data over an extended period of time and the broad use of VirusTotal, the dataset includes a diverse sampling from many families of malware. Symantec, TrendMicro, Kaspersky and McAfee report 3,135, 46,374, 112,114 and 408,646 unique families for the dataset, respectively. The number of families reported varies due to differences in naming conventions between vendors. Although the exact number of families reported varies by vendor, each vendor agrees that the malware represents a broad sampling, with each vendor reporting less than 50 % of malware occurring in the most common 10 % of families.

As the dataset contains scan results form 80 different vendors, we employ a harmonization approach to create the *gold labels* which we use to characterize the dataset and evaluate detector performance. Since some vendors are only sporadically present in the data, we restrict our work to the 32 vendors present in at least 97 % of scan results to increase consistency in the set of vendors applied to each binary.[2] We observe that among binaries that receive multiple scans in our dataset, 29.6 % of binaries increase in number of detections as malware by at least 5 vendors from their first to last scan, and only 0.25 % of binaries decrease by 5 or more detections. This shift from benign to malicious labels confirms the intuition that vendors behave conservatively, preferring false negatives over false positives. Given vendors' demonstrated aversion to false positives, we set a detection threshold of 4 vendor detections as sufficient to label a binary as malicious, and request a rescan of any binary which received fewer than 10 detections at the most recent scan. We conduct rescans in February and March 2015, 8 months after the end of our data collection period, to allow time for vendor signature updates. We avoid rescanning binaries with 10 or more detections since decreases large enough to cross the four vendor detection threshold are unlikely. After rescanning, we assign a gold label to each binary in our dataset representing the best available understanding of whether the binary is malicious.

We reserve from January 2012 to December 2012, the first year of our data set, for obtaining an initial model and use the data from January 2013 to June 2014 to perform a complete rolling window evaluation of our detector. Figure 2a presents the occurrence of scans over time, indicating that scans consistently occur throughout the period during which we measure performance. Notice that scans do not occur evenly during the training period, with the first approximately 200 days containing fewer scans. The difference in available data occurs because fewer binaries have dynamic attributes available; the difference does not reflect an underlying phenomenon in submissions.

---

[2] In particular, we include the following vendors: AVG, Antiy-AVL, Avast, BitDefender, CAT-QuickHeal, ClamAV, Comodo, ESET-NOD32, Emsisoft, F-Prot, Fortinet, GData, Ikarus, Jiangmin, K7AntiVirus, Kaspersky, McAfee, McAfee-GW-Edition, Microsoft, Norman, Panda, SUPERAntiSpyware, Sophos, Symantec, TheHacker, TotalDefense, TrendMicro, TrendMicro-HouseCall, VBA32, VIPRE, ViRobot and nProtect.

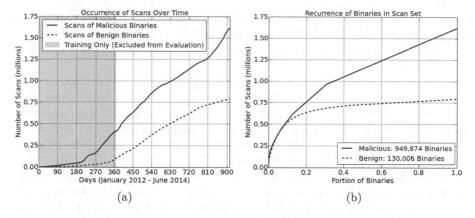

(a) (b)

Fig. 2. Data Overview. (a) and (b) Demonstrate that scans are well distributed across our evaluation period and distinct binaries, respectively. Note that relative scarcity of scans in the first 200 days reflects availability of necessary attributes in VirusTotal data, not underlying submission behavior.

In addition to being well distributed over time, scans are also well distributed across the different binaries in our dataset. Figure 2b depicts the impact of resubmissions on the dataset, with the horizontal axis ordering binaries from most commonly to least commonly submitted. We include re-submissions to ensure that the distribution of our evaluation data mirrors the distribution of actual data submitted to VirusTotal by incorporating the prevalence of each individual file, effectively balancing any effects of polymorphism in the dataset. Additionally, inclusion of rescan events in our analysis provides more timely labeling during evaluation.

5 Experimental Results and System Evaluation

In this section we briefly discuss our implementation, present experimental results and evaluate our detection system. Our presentation of experimental results demonstrates the impact of different performance measurement techniques on detection results. Our detection system evaluation demonstrates the potential for integrated review techniques to improve performance over current anti-virus vendors, as well as the impact of reviewer errors, marginal benefit of additional reviews and effects of different of reviewer integration strategies.

5.1 System Implementation

Since anti-virus vendors can receive in excess of 300,000 binaries daily [14], we design our detector with a focus on scalability. We implement our detection platform in five thousand lines of Python, which offers bindings for the numerical and infrastructure packages we require. We use Scikit Learn and Numpy for machine learning, and Apache Spark for distributed computation. Using a 40 core cluster with 600 GB of RAM, we were able to conduct feature vectorization, learning and prediction on our 778 GB dataset including 1.1 million unique binaries in 10 h.

To allow experimentation at scale, we simulate an integrated reviewer rather than employing an actual labeling expert. We model the analysis of the integrated reviewer by revealing the gold label associated with a binary. For experiments that consider an imperfect reviewer, we assign the simulated reviewer a true positive rate and a false positive rate, allowing the likelihood of the reviewer supplying the correct label to depend on the gold label for the sample. By conditioning the likelihood of a correct response on the gold label of a sample, we are able to more closely model the errors of an actual reviewer who may be highly likely to correctly identify a benign binary as benign, but less likely to correctly identify a malicious binary as malicious. We leave the comparison of this model to actual reviewer performance as future work.

Lastly, we describe our management of the system parameters discussed in Sect. 3, including a reviewer submission budget B, auto-relabeling confidence threshold M and learning parameters C_-, C_+ and W. Section 5.3 presents the effects of varying the submission budget B, with experiments conducted at 80 queries daily on average unless otherwise specified. The remaining parameters are tuned to maximize detection at false positive rates between .01 and .001 on a set of binaries obtained from an industry partner and excluded from our evaluation. We use the following values: $M = 1.25$, $C_- = 0.16$, $C_+ = .0048$ and $W = 10$.

5.2 Impact of Performance Measurement Techniques

The primary motivation for measuring the performance of a detection system in a research or development setting is to understand how the system would perform in a production setting. Accordingly, measurement techniques should seek to minimize the differences from production settings. In practice, knowledge of both binaries and labels changes over time as new binaries appear and malware detectors respond appropriately with updated labels. Performance measurement techniques that fail to recognize the emergence of binaries and label knowledge over time effectively utilize knowledge from the future, inflating the measured accuracy of the approach. For example, consider malware that evades detection but can be easily detected once the first instance is identified. Performance inflation occurs because inserting correctly labeled binaries into training data circumvents the difficult task of identifying the first instance of the malware.

We analyze three approaches to measuring the performance of malware detectors, each recognizing the emergence of binaries and labels over time to varying degrees. Cross-validation is a common approach for machine learning evaluations in situations where binaries are independent and identically distributed (i.i.d.). In the malware detection context the i.i.d. assumption does not hold since malware changes over time to evade detection. Cross-validation evaluations completely disregard time, dividing binaries randomly and applying evaluation

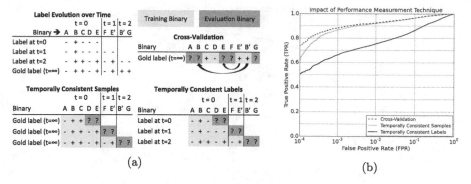

(a)   (b)

Fig. 3. Accurate performance measurement requires temporally consistent labels. (a) Illustrates three techniques. The upper left shows the evolution of labels over time for a series of binaries, with B' and E' denoting variants of previously submitted binaries B and E. Each remaining subfigure depicts the experiments a performance measurement technique would conduct given the example dataset. Rows correspond to successive retraining periods with specified training and evaluation data, binaries appear chronologically from left to right, and + and – denote malicious and benign labels, respectively. (b) Presents the effects of performance measurement technique on experimental results.

quality labels to all binaries. Evaluations maintaining temporally consistent samples recognize the ordering of binaries in time but not the emergence of labels over time, instead applying gold labels from future scan results to all binaries. Use of gold quality labels during training effectively assumes that accurate detection occurs instantly. Evaluations maintaining temporally consistent labels fully respect the progression of knowledge, ordering binaries in time and restricting the training process to binaries and labels available at the time of training. For measurements with both temporally consistent samples and labels, we divide data into periods and use the first $n - 1$ periods to detect content in period n. Unless otherwise specified we use a period length of one week. Figure 3a presents the specifics of each approach.

Our experiments demonstrate that measurement technique powerfully impacts performance results. Figure 3b presents the results of our analysis. Notice that cross-validation and temporally consistent samples perform similarly, inflating detection results 20 and 19 % points respectively over temporally consistent labeling at a 0.5 % false positive rate. Since reviewer integration effectively reduces the impact of temporally consistent labels by revealing future labels, we conduct these experiments without any reviewer queries. Note that our conclusions apply only to the setting of malware detection and not family classification, which presents a fundamentally different challenge as the set of known family labels may change over time.

Temporally consistent labeling requires that training labels predate evaluation binaries. Since VirusTotal scans each binary upon each submission our experiments are able to satisfy temporally consistent labeling requirements. However, since binaries are not necessarily rescanned at regular intervals, we are not

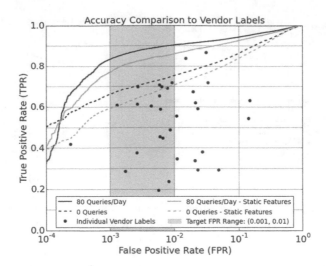

Fig. 4. Without reviewer integration our detector is competitive with VirusTotal detectors. With reviewer integration, detection improves beyond vendors on VirusTotal. We tune our system to maximize detection in the $(0.1\%, 1\%)$ false positive region, consequently decreasing detection at lower false positive rates.

able to guarantee that our labels are up to date. For example, consider a binary which receives benign scan results in week 1 and malicious scan results in week 10: the up-to-date training label in week 5 is unclear. To simulate the effects of more frequent rescanning, we conduct a second experiment in which we reveal the gold label for each binary once a fixed interval has passed since the binary's first submission. We find that without releasing gold labels temporally consistent evaluation results in 76 % detection at a 1 % false positive rate; releasing gold labels 4 weeks and 1 week after a binary appears increases detection to 80 % and 84 % respectively. Note that these figures represent an upper bound on the impact of frequent rescanning since malware may remain undetected much longer than 1 or 4 weeks. Considering that cross-validation and temporal sample consistency each achieve 92 % detection at a 1 % false positive rate, we see that even with regular rescanning, temporal label consistency impacts detection results.

5.3 Detection System Evaluation

In this section we evaluate our malware detection system and the impact of reviewer integration. We begin with the impact of the reviewer and performance relative to VirusTotal. Then, we examine parameters such as reviewer accuracy and retraining frequency. Lastly, we analyze impact of different types of features.

Impact of Integrated Reviewer. Given the breadth of our data and unique structure of our evaluation, the vendor detection results on VirusTotal provide the best performance comparison for our work. Based on the false positive rates of vendors, we tune our detector to maximize detection for false positive rates greater than 0.1 % and less than 1 %. Figure 4 compares our performance to vendor detectors provided on VirusTotal. Without involvement from the integrated reviewer our detector achieves 72 % detection at a 0.5 % false positive rate, performing comparably to the best vendor detectors. With support from the reviewer, we increase detection to 89 % at a 0.5 % false positive rate using 80 queries daily on average. Since we train a separate model during each weekly retraining period, the performance curve results from varying the same detection threshold across the results of each individual model.

VirusTotal invokes vendor detectors from the command line rather than in an execution environment, allowing detectors to arbitrarily examine the file but preventing observation of dynamic behavior. Since our analysis includes dynamic attributes, we also observe our performance when restricted to static attributes provided by VirusTotal. Note that this restriction places our detector at a strict disadvantage to vendors, who may access the binary itself and apply signatures derived from dynamic analysis. Figure 4 demonstrates that our performance decreases when restricted to static features but, with support from the integrated reviewer, surpasses vendors to achieve 84 % detection at a 0.5 % false positive rate.

Performance comparison must also consider the process of deriving gold labels, which introduces a circularity that artificially inflates vendor performance. Consider the case of a false positive: once a vendor has marked a binary as positive, the binary is more likely to receive a positive gold label, effectively decreasing the false positive rate of the vendor. An alternate approach would be to withhold a vendor's labels when evaluating that vendor, effectively creating a separate ground truth for each vendor. Although this approach more closely mirrors the evaluation of our own detector (which does not contribute to gold labels), in the interest of consistency we elect to use the same ground truth throughout the entire evaluation since efforts to correct any labeling bias only increase our performance differential.

In addition to offering superior detection performance aggregated across all data relative to vendor labels, our approach also experiences greater success detecting novel malware that is missed by detectors on VirusTotal. Of the 1.1 million samples included in our analysis, there are 6,873 samples which have a malicious gold label but are undetected by all vendors the first time the sample appears. Using 80 reviewer queries daily, our approach is able to detect 44 % and 32 % of these novel samples at 1 % and .1 % false positive rates, respectively. The ability of our approach to detect novel malware illustrates the value of machine learning for detecting successively evolving generations of malware.

To provide a corresponding analysis of false positives, we measure our performance on the 61,213 samples which have a benign gold label and are not detected as malware by any vendor the first time the sample appears. Of these 61,213 benign samples, our detector labels 2.0 % and 0.2 % as malicious when operating at 1 % and .1 % false positive rates over all data, respectively. The increased false positive rate on initial scans of benign samples is expected since the sample has not yet been included as training data.

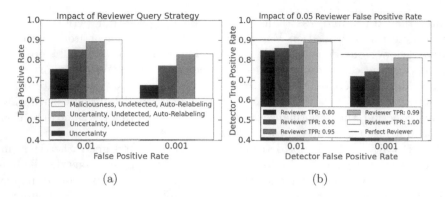

(a)   (b)

Fig. 5. (a) Presents the impact of each component in our customized query strategy. We improve detection over the uncertainty sampling approach from prior work. (b) Presents the performance of our detector for imperfect reviewers with the specified true and false positive rates. For example, given a reviewer with a 5 % false positive rate and 80 % true positive rate, our detector's true positive rate only decreases by 5 % at a 1 % false positive rate.

Reviewer Query Strategies. Our reviewer query strategy represents numerous advances over prior work. Figure 5a presents the impact of each of the three improvements we introduce and discussed in Sect. 3.3. For a fixed labeling budget $B = 80$, uncertainty sampling results in a detection rate 17 % points lower than the combination of our techniques at 0.1 % false positive rate.

Reviewer Accuracy. Our system also demonstrates strong results in the presence of an imperfect reviewer. Since malware creators may explicitly design malware to appear benign but benign software is less likely to appear malicious, we model the false positive and true positive rates of reviewers separately, reflecting a reviewer who is more likely to mistake malware for benign software than benign software for malware. Figure 5b presents detection rates for reviewers with a 5 % false positive rates and a range of true positive rates. For example, given a reviewer with a 5 % false positive rate and 80 % true positive rate, our detector's true positive rate only decreases by 5 % at a 1 % false positive rate.

Resource Parameterization. Beyond classifier parameters, detection performance is also influenced by operator resources including reviewer query budget and retraining frequency. We explore each of these parameters below.

As the allowed budget for queries to the reviewer increases, the detection performance increases since higher quality training labels are available. Figure 6a presents the detection increase from increased reviewer queries, with the benefit of 80 queries per day on average approaching the upper bound of having gold labels for all training data. The benefit of reviewer queries is non-linear, with the initial queries providing the greatest benefit, allowing operators to experience disproportionate benefit from a limited review budget.

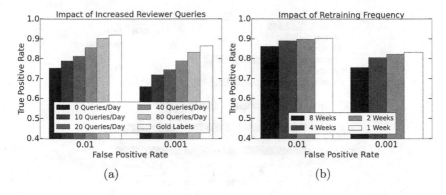

Fig. 6. (a) Presents performance for different reviewer query budgets, with significant return on minimal efforts and diminishing returns occurring around 80 queries/day. (b) Demonstrates that retraining more quickly improves detector performance.

Although our evaluation is large relative to academic work, an actual deployment would offer an even larger pool of possible training data. Since the utility of reviewer queries will vary with the size of the training data, increasing the amount of training data may increase reviewer queries required to reach full benefit. Fortunately, the training process may elect to use only a subset of the available training data. We demonstrate that 1.1 million binaries selected randomly from VirusTotal submissions is sufficient training data to outperform vendor labels for our evaluation data.

Lastly, we examine variations in the length of the re-training period governing how often models are updated. We conduct these experiments with 80 reviewer queries on average per day. Figure 6b presents the effect of variations in the retraining period. Notice that the benefit of frequent retraining begins to diminish around 2 weeks.

Detection Mechanics. Having analyzed detection accuracy and evaluation methodology, we now examine the features that our detector uses for classification. In the interest of understanding the dataset as a whole, we train a model over all data from all dates. Although we learn a linear model and can easily observe the weight of each feature, inspecting the weight vector alone is not enough to understand feature importance. A feature can be associated with a large weight but be essentially constant across the dataset, as may happen with strongly malicious features that are relatively rare in practice. Intuitively, such features have low discrimination power. Furthermore, we are interested in grouping low-level features together into high level concepts.

Thus, we use the following ranking method for sets of features. Let d be the total number of features, $\mathbf{w} \in \mathbb{R}^d$ be the weight vector and $\{\mathbf{x}^i\}$ be a given set of instances. The notation $\mathbf{x}^i_k$ designates the k-th coordinate of instance $\mathbf{x}^i$. We can compute the importance of a group $S \subset \{1, \ldots, d\}$ of features by quantifying the amount of score variation I_S they induce. Our ranking formula is:

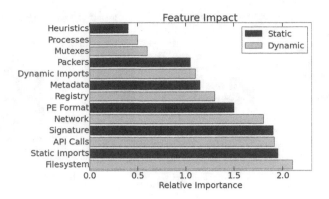

Fig. 7. Feature categories ranked by importance.

$$I_S = \sqrt{\mathrm{Var}_i \left[\sum_{k \in S} \mathbf{x}_k^i \mathbf{w}_k \right]}$$

Using this ranking method, Fig. 7 shows the global ranking of the features when grouped by their original measurements. The most important measurements are thus the file system operations, static imports, API call sequence and digital signature, while the least useful measurement is the heuristic tools. Further analysis including highly weighted features is available online [15].

6   Conclusion

In this paper, we explore the power of putting humans in the loop by integrating a simulated human labeling expert into a scalable malware detection system. We show it capable of handling over 1 million samples using a small cluster in hours while substantially outperforming commercial anti-virus providers both in terms of malware detection and false positive rates (as measured using VirusTotal). We explain why machine learning systems appear to perform very well in research settings and yet fail to perform reasonably in production settings by demonstrating the critical temporal factors of labeling, training, and evaluation that affect detection performance in real-world settings. In future work, we plan to expand our detection system to perform malware family labeling and detection of new malware families. Additionally, we may implement clustering or density based sampling techniques to further reduce the reviewer burden by eliminating any duplicate reviews.

References

1. ClamAV PUA, 14 November 2014. http://www.clamav.net/doc/pua.html
2. PEiD, 14 November 2014. http://woodmann.com/BobSoft/Pages/Programs/ PEiD

3. The Cuckoo Sandbox, 14 November 2014. http://www.cuckoosandbox.org
4. Arp, D., Spreitzenbarth, M., Hubner, M., Gascon, H., Rieck, K.: Drebin: effective and explainable detection of android malware in your pocket. In: NDSS (2014)
5. Canali, D., Cova, M., Vigna, G., Kruegel, C.: Prophiler: a fast filter for the large-scale detection of malicious web pages. In: WWW (2011)
6. Chakradeo, S., Reaves, B., Traynor, P., Enck, W.: Mast: triage for market-scale mobile malware analysis. In: ACM WiSec (2013)
7. Chapelle, O., Schlkopf, B., Zien, A.: Semi-Supervised Learning. The MIT Press, Cambridge (2010)
8. Curtsinger, C., Livshits, B., Zorn, B., Seifert, C.: Zozzle: fast and precise in-browser javascript malware detection. In: Usenix Security (2011)
9. Damballa: State of Infections Report: Q4 2014. Technical report, Damballa (2015)
10. Hastie, T., Tibshirani, R., Friedman, J.: The Elements of Statistical Learning. Springer, New York (2001)
11. Kantchelian, A., Afroz, S., Huang, L., Islam, A.C., Miller, B., Tschantz, M.C., Greenstadt, R., Joseph, A.D., Tygar, J.D.: Approaches to adversarial drift. In: ACM AISec (2013)
12. Karanth, S., Laxman, S., Naldurg, P., Venkatesan, R., Lambert, J., Shin, J.: ZDVUE: prioritization of javascript attacks to discover new vulnerabilities. In: ACM AISec (2011)
13. Kolter, J.Z., Maloof, M.A.: Learning to detect and classify malicious executables in the wild. J. Mach. Learn. Res. **7**, 2721–2744 (2006)
14. McAfee Labs: McAfee Labs Threats Report, August 2014
15. Miller, B.: Scalable Platform for Malicious Content Detection Integrating Machine Learning and Manual Review. Ph.D. thesis, UC Berkeley (2015)
16. Nissim, N., Cohen, A., Moskovitch, R., Shabtai, A., Edry, M., Bar-Ad, O., Elovici, Y.: ALPD: active learning framework for enhancing the detection of malicious pdf files. In: IEEE JISIC, September 2014
17. Nissim, N., Moskovitch, R., Rokach, L., Elovici, Y.: Novel active learning methods for enhanced pc malware detection in windows os. J. Expert Syst. Appl. **41**(13), 5843–5857 (2014)
18. Perdisci, R., Lee, W., Feamster, N.: Behavioral clustering of http-based malware and signature generation using malicious network traces. In: NSDI (2010)
19. Provos, N., Mavrommatis, P., Rajab, M.A., Monrose, F.: All your iframes point to us. In: USENIX Security (2008)
20. Rajab, M.A., Ballard, L., Lutz, N., Mavrommatis, P., Provos, N.: CAMP: content-agnostic malware protection. In: NDSS (2013)
21. Schultz, M.G., Eskin, E., Zadok, E., Stolfo, S.J.: Data mining methods for detection of new malicious executables. In: IEEE S&P (2001)
22. Schwenk, G., Bikadorov, A., Krueger, T., Rieck, K.: Autonomous learning for detection of javascript attacks: vision or reality? In: ACM AISec (2012)
23. Sculley, D., Otey, M.E., Pohl, M., Spitznagel, B., Hainsworth, J., Zhou, Y.: Detecting adversarial advertisements in the wild. In: KDD (2011)
24. Settles, B.: Active learning literature survey. Computer Sciences Technical report 1648, University of Wisconsin-Madison (2009)
25. Šrndic, N., Laskov, P.: Detection of malicious PDF files based on hierarchical document structure. In: NDSS (2013)
26. Stringhini, G., Kruegel, C., Vigna, G.: Shady paths: leveraging surfing crowds to detect malicious web pages. In: ACM CCS (2013)
27. VirusTotal. https://www.virustotal.com/. Accessed 30 Jul 2014

On the Lack of Consensus in Anti-Virus Decisions: Metrics and Insights on Building Ground Truths of Android Malware

Médéric Hurier[✉], Kevin Allix, Tegawendé F. Bissyandé, Jacques Klein, and Yves Le Traon

SnT, University of Luxembourg, Luxembourg City, Luxembourg
mederic.hurier@uni.lu

Abstract. There is generally a lack of consensus in Antivirus (AV) engines' decisions on a given sample. This challenges the building of authoritative ground-truth datasets. Instead, researchers and practitioners may rely on unvalidated approaches to build their ground truth, e.g., by considering decisions from a selected set of Antivirus vendors or by setting up a threshold number of positive detections before classifying a sample. Both approaches are biased as they implicitly either decide on ranking AV products, or they consider that all AV decisions have equal weights. In this paper, we extensively investigate the lack of agreement among AV engines. To that end, we propose a set of metrics that quantitatively describe the different dimensions of this lack of consensus. We show how our metrics can bring important insights by using the detection results of 66 AV products on 2 million Android apps as a case study. Our analysis focuses not only on AV binary decision but also on the notoriously hard problem of *labels* that AVs associate with suspicious files, and allows to highlight biases hidden in the collection of a malware ground truth—a foundation stone of any malware detection approach.

1 Introduction

Malware is ubiquitous across popular software ecosystems. In the realm of mobile world, researchers and practitioners have revealed that Android devices are increasingly targeted by attackers. According to a 2015 Symantec Mobile Threat report [1], among 6.3 million Android apps analyzed, over 1 million have been flagged as malicious by Symantec in 2014 and classified in 277 Android malware families. To stop the proliferation of these malware, device owners and market maintainers can no longer rely on the manual inspection of security analysts. Indeed, analysts require to know beforehand all patterns of malicious behaviors so as to spot them in new apps. Instead, the research and practice of malware detection are now leaning towards machine learning techniques where algorithms can learn themselves to discriminate between malicious and benign apps after having observed features in an a-priori labelled set. It is thus obvious that the performance of the detector is tightly dependent on the quality of the training dataset. Previous works have even shown that the accuracy of such detectors can

© Springer International Publishing Switzerland 2016
J. Caballero et al. (Eds.): DIMVA 2016, LNCS 9721, pp. 142–162, 2016.
DOI: 10.1007/978-3-319-40667-1_8

be degraded by orders of magnitude if the training data is faulty [2–6]. Following these findings, one can easily infer that it is also possible to artificially improve the performance of malware detectors by selecting a "ground truth" that splits around malware corner cases.

To build training datasets, Antivirus (AV) engines appear to be the most affordable means today. In particular, their use have become common thanks to online free services such as VirusTotal [7] that accepts the submission of any file for which it reports back the AV decisions from several vendors. Unfortunately, AV engines disagree regularly on samples. Their lack of consensus is actually observed in two dimensions: (1) their binary decisions on the maliciousness of a sample are often conflicting and (2) their labels are challenging to compare because of the lack of standard for naming malware samples.

To consolidate datasets as ground truth based on AV decisions, researchers often opt to use heuristics that they claim to be reasonable. For example, in the assessment of a state-of-the-art machine learning-based malware detection for Android [8], the authors have considered the reports from only 10 AV engines, selected based on their "popularity", dismissing all other reports. They further consider a sample to be malicious once two AV engines agree to say so. They claim that:

> "This procedure ensures that [their] data is (almost) correctly split into benign and malicious samples—even if one of the ten scanners falsely labels a benign application as malicious" [8, p. 7]

To gain some insights on the impact of such heuristics, we have built a dataset following these heuristics and another dataset following another common process in the literature [9], which considers all AV reports from VirusTotal and accepts a sample as malicious as long as any of the AV flags it as such. We compare the two datasets and find that the malware set in the first "ground truth" is reduced to only 6 % of the malware set of the second "ground truth" dataset.

An in-depth study of different heuristics parameters can further reveal discrepancies in the construction of ground truth datasets, and thus further question any comparison of detectors performance. Similarly, the lack of consensus in label naming prevents a proper assessment of the performance of detectors across malware families.

In a recent work, Kantchellian et al. [10] have proposed weighting techniques towards deriving better, authoritative, ground truth based on AV labels. Our work is an in-depth investigation to further motivate this line of research by highlighting different facets of the problem. To that end, we propose metrics for quantifying various dimensions of comparison for AV decisions and labels. These metrics typically investigate to what extent decisions of a given AV are exclusive w.r.t other AVs, or the degree of genericity at which AV vendors assign malware labels.

Contributions: We make the following contributions:

- We extensively overview the lack of consensus in AV engines' decisions and labels. Our work is a call for new approaches to building authoritative ground truth datasets, in particular for the ever-growing field of machine learning-based malware detection.

– Building on a large dataset of thousands Android apps, we provide insights on the practice of building ground truth datasets based on VirusTotal AV decisions.
– We define metrics for quantifying the consensus (or lack thereof) among AV products following various dimensions. Based on the values of these metrics for extreme cases, they can be leveraged as good indicators for assessing a ground truth dataset. We further expect these metrics to be used as important information when describing experimental datasets for machine learning-based malware detection[1].

Findings: Among the findings of this study, we note that:

– AVs that flag many apps as malicious (i.e. AVs that seem to favor high Malware Recall) are more consensual than AVs that flag relatively few samples (i.e. AVs that seem to favor high Precision).
– Labels assigned to samples present a high level of genericity.
– Selecting a subset of AVs to build a ground truth dataset may lead to more disagreement in detection labels.

The remainder of this paper is presented as follows. Section 2 overviews related work which either inspired our work, or attempted to address the problem that we aim at quantifying. Section 3 presents the datasets that we have used for our study as well as the use cases we focus on. Section 4 presents our metrics and show-cases their importance. We discuss the interpretation of the metrics and their limitations in Sect. 5 before giving concluding remarks in Sect. 6.

2   Related Work

Our study relates to various work in the literature which have been interested in the collection of ground truth, in the automation of malware detection and those that have experimented with AV labels.

2.1   Security Assessment Datasets

Ground truth datasets are essential in the realm of security analysis. Indeed, on the one hand, analysts rely on them to manually draw patterns of malicious behaviors and devise techniques to prevent their damages. On the other hand, automated learning systems heavily rely on them to systematically learn features of malware. Unfortunately, these datasets are seldom fully qualified by the research community [11,12]. This shortcoming is due to the rapid development of new malware [10] which forces the community to collect malware samples through generic techniques, which do not thoroughly validate the malicious behaviors [13].

---

[1] We make available a full open source implementation under the name STASE at https://github.com/freaxmind/STASE.

A number of researchers have lately warned that flaws in security datasets are frequent [11] and can lead to false assumptions or erroneous results [3,10,14]. In their study, Rossow et al. [11] have analyzed the methodology of 36 papers related to malware research. Most notably, they observed that a majority of papers failed to provide sufficient descriptions of experimental setups and that 50 % of experiments had training datasets with imbalanced family distributions. Related to this last point, Li et al. [14] raised a concern about such imbalances in clustering results. Using tools from a different domain (plagiarism detection), they were able to achieve results comparable to the state-of-the-art malware clustering algorithm at that time [15].

Nowadays, research in malware detection is often relying on AV engines to build ground truth datasets. Unfortunately, AVs often disagree, and AVs may even change their decision over time [16]. With our work, we aim to provide metrics that describe the underlying properties of experimental settings, focusing on ground truth collection, to transparently highlight biases and improve reproducibility.

2.2   Studies on Anti-Virus Decisions and Labels

Canto et al. [3] support that clear interpretations of malware alerts should be provided due to inconsistencies between antivirus engines. In view of these concerns, Rossow et al. [11] have also proposed a set of recommendations to design prudent experiments on malware. Kantchelian et al. [10] referred to Li et al. [14] study to point out that malware datasets obtained from a single source (e.g. antivirus vendors) could implicitly remove the most difficult cases. They thus propose supervised models to weight AV labels.

Another work related to malware experiments is AV-Meter by Mohaisen and Alrawi [5]. In their paper, the authors have described four metrics to assess the performance of antivirus scanners on a reference set of malwares. To our knowledge, this is the first attempt to formalize the comparison of security datasets. Their study also revealed that multiple antivirus are necessary to obtain complete and correct detections of malwares. Yet, AV-meter can not fully qualify datasets used in most common experiments. First, the metrics proposed by Mohaisen and Alrawi [5] are only applicable on ground-truth datasets where applications are known to expose malicious behaviors. In reality, this constraint can not be met due to the rising number of new malware samples which are created each year [10]. For instance, GData [17] experts identified more than 575 000 new malware samples between July and September 2015. This is an increase of 50 % compared to the same period in 2014. Consequently, their study relied on a small dataset of 12 000 samples in order to ensure the correctness of their labels. In comparison, Arp et al. [8] performed a recent experiment on more than 130 000 samples. Finally, only four metrics were proposed by the authors, which may not describe all the characteristics necessary to avoid potential biases as mentioned in [3,11,14].

2.3 Experiments in Android ML-based Malware Detection

Android malware has attracted a lot of attention from the research community [18–22], and a number of machine learning based approaches have been proposed recently [8,23,24]. State-of-the-art work, such as DREBIN [8] have even shown promising results. However, we observe that machine learning approaches have not been widely implemented in the malware detection industry. Sommer and Paxson [25] have presented multiple reasons which distinguish the security domain from other Computer Science areas, such as image recognition or natural language translation, where machine learning has been applied successfully. In previous work, we have shown how experimental scenarios can artificially improve the performance of detectors *in the lab* and make them unreliable on real-world settings [26,27].

Our work here is about providing metrics to help researchers characterize their datasets and highlight their potential biases, as was recommended by Rossow et al. [11] and Sommer and Paxson [25].

3 Preliminaries

3.1 Dataset of Android Apps and Antivirus

Our study leverages a large dataset of 2 117 825 Android applications and their analysis reports by 66 antivirus engines hosted by VirusTotal.

App Dataset: Our application samples have been obtained by crawling well-known app stores, including Google Play (70.33 % of the dataset), Anzhi (17.35 %) and AppChina (8.44 %), as well as via direct downloads (e.g., Genome - 0.06 %) [28].

AV Reports: The AV reports were collected from VirusTotal[2], an online platform that can test files against commercial antivirus engines[3]. For each app package file (APK) sent to VirusTotal, the platform returns, among other information, two pieces of information for each antivirus:

 – A binary flag (`True` = positive detection, `False` = negative detection)
 – A string label to identify the threat (e.g. `Trojan:AndroidOS/Ginger Master.A`)

Overall, we managed to obtain AV reports for 2 063 674 Android apps[4]. In this study we explore those reports and define metrics to quantify the characteristics of several *tentative ground truths*.

---

[2] https://www.virustotal.com.

[3] Since the goal of this study is not to evaluate the individual performance of antivirus engines, their names have been omitted and replaced by an unique number (ID).

[4] We could not obtain the results for 54 151 (2.56 %) applications because of a file size limit by VirusTotal.

3.2 Variations in Experimental Ground Truth Settings

When experimenting with machine learning-based malware detector, as it is nowadays common among security researchers, one of the very first steps is to build a ground truth, for training and also assessing the detector. The question is then how to derive a ground truth based on AV reports of the millions of apps in existence. In particular, we focus on which samples are considered as malicious and included in the malware set of the ground truth. Based on methods seen in the literature, we consider the following three settings for building a ground truth:

Baseline settings: In these settings, we consider a straightforward process often used [9, 26] where a sample is considered malicious as long as any AV reports it with a positive detection. Thus, our ground truth with the Baseline settings and based on our 2 million apps, contains 689 209 "malware" apps. These samples are reported by AVs with 119 156 distinct labels.

Genome settings: In a few papers of the literature, researchers use for ground truth smaller datasets constituted of manually compiled and "verified" malicious samples. We consider such a case and propose such settings where the malware set of the ground truth is the Genome [29] dataset containing 1 248 apps. AV reports on these apps have yielded 7 101 distinct labels.

Filtered settings: Finally we consider a refined process in the literature where authors attempt to produce a clean ground truth dataset using heuristics. We follow the process used in a recent state-of-the-art work [8]:

1. Use a set of 10 popular AV scanners[5].
2. Select apps detected by at least two AVs in this set.
3. Remove apps whose label from any AV include the keyword "adware".

With these settings the malware set of the ground truth include 44 615 apps associated with 20 308 distinct labels.

In the remainder of this paper, we use $\mathcal{D}_{genome}$, $\mathcal{D}_{base}$, and $\mathcal{D}_{filtered}$ to refer to the three ground truth datasets. We did not performed supplementary pre-processings besides the heuristics we mentioned in the previous paragraph to avoid potential biases in our study.

3.3 Notations and Definitions

Given a set of n AV engines $\mathcal{A} = \{a_1, a_2, \cdots, a_n\}$ and a set of m apps $\mathcal{P} = \{p_1, p_2, \cdots, p_m\}$, we collect the binary decisions and string labels in two $n \times m$ matrices denoted $\mathcal{B}$ and $\mathcal{L}$ respectively:

$$\mathcal{B} = \begin{array}{c} \\ p_1 \\ p_2 \\ \vdots \\ p_m \end{array} \begin{array}{c} \begin{array}{cccc} a_1 & a_2 & \dots & a_n \end{array} \\ \begin{pmatrix} b_{1,1} & b_{1,2} & \dots & b_{1,n} \\ b_{2,1} & b_{2,2} & \dots & b_{2,n} \\ \vdots & \vdots & \ddots & \vdots \\ b_{m,1} & b_{m,2} & \dots & b_{m,n} \end{pmatrix} \end{array} \quad \mathcal{L} = \begin{array}{c} \\ p_1 \\ p_2 \\ \vdots \\ p_m \end{array} \begin{array}{c} \begin{array}{cccc} a_1 & a_2 & \dots & a_n \end{array} \\ \begin{pmatrix} l_{1,1} & l_{1,2} & \dots & l_{1,n} \\ l_{2,1} & l_{2,2} & \dots & l_{2,n} \\ \vdots & \vdots & \ddots & \vdots \\ l_{m,1} & l_{m,2} & \dots & l_{m,n} \end{pmatrix} \end{array}$$

[5] AVs considered in [8]: AntiVir, AVG, Bit- Defender, ClamAV, ESET, F-Secure, Kaspersky, McAfee, Panda, Sophos.

where entry $b_{i,j}$ corresponds to the binary flag assigned by AV a_j to application p_i and entry $l_{i,j}$ corresponds to the string label assigned by AV a_j to application p_i. String label $l_{i,j}$ is $\emptyset$ (null or empty string) if the app p_i is not flagged by AV a_j. For any settings under study, a ground truth $\mathcal{D}$ will be characterized by both $\mathcal{B}$ and $\mathcal{L}$.

Let note $R_i = \{m_{i,1}, m_{i,2}, \cdots, m_{i,n}\}$ the ith row vector of a matrix M, and $C_j = \{m_{1,j}, m_{2,j}, \cdots, m_{m,j}\}$ the jth column. The label matrix $\mathcal{L}$ can also be vectorized as a column vector $\mathcal{L}' = (l_1, l_2, \cdots, l_k)$ which includes all distinct labels from matrix $\mathcal{L}$, excluding null values ($\emptyset$).

We also define six specific functions that will be reused through this paper:

- Let *positives* be the function which returns the number of positive detections from matrix $\mathcal{B}$, or the number of not null labels from matrix $\mathcal{L}$.
- Let *exclusives* be the function which returns the number of samples detected by only one AV in matrix $\mathcal{B}$.
- Let *distincts* be the function which returns the number of distinct labels (excluding $\emptyset$) in matrix $\mathcal{L}$.
- Let *freqmax* be the function which returns the number of occurrences of the most frequent label (excluding $\emptyset$) from matrix $\mathcal{L}$.
- Let *clusters* be the function which returns the number of applications which received a given label l_o with $l_o \in L'$.
- Let *Ouroboros* be the function which returns the minimum proportion of groups including 50 % elements of the dataset, normalized between 0 and 1 [30]. This function is used to quantify the uniformity of a list of frequencies, independently of the size of the list.

4   Definition of Metrics and Experiments

In this section we consider the two pieces of information, AV decision and AV label, and perform analyses that investigate various aspects of the inconsistencies that may be present among AV reports. We then propose metrics to quantify these aspects and allow for comparison between different ground truth datasets.

4.1   Analysis of AV Decisions

The primary role of an AV engine is to decide whether a given sample should be considered as malicious [13]. These decisions have important consequences in production environments since a positive detection will probably trigger an alert and an investigation to mitigate a potential threat. False positives would thus lead to a waste of resources, while False negatives can have dire consequences such as substantial losses. AV engines must then select an adequate trade-off between a deterring high number of false positives and a damaging high number of false negatives.

In this section, we analyze the characteristics of AV decisions and their discrepancies when different engines are compared against each other.

4.1.1   Equiponderance

The first concern in using a set of AV engines is to quantify their detection accuracies. If there are extreme differences, the collected "ground truth" may be polluted by decisions from a few engines. In the absence of a significant golden set to compute accuracies, one can estimate, to some extent, the differences among AVs by quantifying their detection rates (i.e., number of positive decisions).

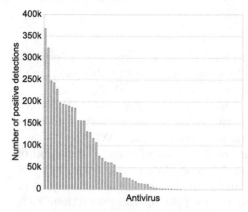

Fig. 1. AVs positive detections in $\mathcal{D}_{base}$

Figure 1 highlights the uneven distribution of positive detections per AV in the $\mathcal{D}_{base}$ baseline ground truth. The number of detected apps indeed ranges from 0 to 367 435. This raises the question of the confidence in a "ground truth" when malicious samples can be contributed by AVs from the head and tail of the distribution. Indeed, although we cannot assume that AV engines with high (or low) detection rates have better performances, because of their potential false positives (or false negatives), it is important to consider the detection rates of AVs for a given dataset to allow comparisons on a common ground. A corollary concern is then to characterize the ground truth to allow comparisons. To generalize and quantify this characteristic of ground truth datasets, we consider the following research question:

> *RQ1: Given a set of AVs and the ground truth that they produce together, Is the resulting ground truth dominated by only a few AVs, or do all AVs contribute the same amount of information?*

We answer this RQ with a single metric, *Equiponderance*, which measures how balanced—or how imbalanced—are the contributions of each AV. Considering our baseline settings with all AV engines, we infer that 9, i.e., 13.5 %, AVs provided as many positive detections as all the other AVs combined. The *Equiponderance* aims to capture this percentage in its output. Because maximum value for this percentage is 50 %[6], we weigh this percentage, by multiplying it by 2, to yield a metric between 0 and 1. We define the function *Ouroboros* [30] which computes this value and also returns the corresponding number of AVs, which we refer to as the Index of the *Equiponderance*.

$Equiponderance(\mathcal{B}) = Ouroboros(X)$ with $X = \{positives(C_j) : C_j \in \mathcal{B}, 1 \leq j \leq n\}$

- **Interpretation** – minimal proportion of antivirus that detected at least 50 % applications in the dataset. The metric value is weighted.
- **Minimum:** 0 – when a single antivirus made all the positive detections

---

[6] If one set of AVs leads to a percentage x over 50 %, then the other set relevant value is 100-x% < 50 %.

– **Maximum:** 1 – when the distribution of detection rates is perfectly even

When the *Equiponderance* is close to zero, the ground truth analyzed is dominated by the extreme cases: a large number of AV engines provide only a few positive detections, while only a few AVs engine provide most positive detections. In comparison with $\mathcal{D}_{base}$'s *Equiponderance* value of 0.27, $\mathcal{D}_{genome}$ and $\mathcal{D}_{filtered}$ present *Equiponderance* values of 0.48 and 0.59 respectively.

4.1.2   Exclusivity

Even in the case where several AVs would have the same number of detections, it does not imply any agreement of AVs. It is thus important to also quantify to what extent each AV tends to detect samples that no other AV detects.

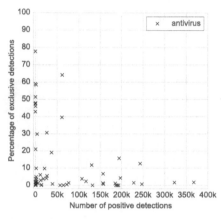

Fig. 2. Relation between positive and exclusive detections in $\mathcal{D}_{base}$

Figure 2 plots, for every AV product, the proportion of exclusive detections (i.e., samples no other AV detects) over the total number of positive detection of this AV. Five AVs provide a majority of exclusive detections while a large part of other AVs (45) provides less than 10 % such detections. For the 21 AVs that made the most positive detections, the proportion of exclusive detections remains below 16 %, while the highest ratios of exclusive detections are associated with AVs that made a (relatively) small number of positive detections. Figure 2 provides an important insight into Android malware detection by AVs: A very high absolute number of detections comes from adding more non-exclusive detections—not from detecting apps no other AV detects as could have been intuitively expected. The following research question aims at formally characterizing this bias in datasets:

> *RQ2: Given a set of AVs and the ground truth that they produce together, what is the proportion of samples that were included only due to one AV engine?*

To answer this RQ, we propose the *Exclusivity* metric, which measures the proportion of a tentative ground truth that is specific to a single detector.

$$Exclusivity(\mathcal{B}) = \frac{exclusives(\mathcal{B})}{m}$$

– **Interpretation** – proportion of applications detected by only one antivirus
– **Minimum:** 0 – when every sample has been detected by more than one AV
– **Maximum:** 1 – when every sample has been detected by only one antivirus

In $\mathcal{D}_{base}$, 31 % apps were detected exclusively by only one AV, leading to an *Exclusivity* value of 0.31. On the contrary, both $\mathcal{D}_{genome}$ and $\mathcal{D}_{filtered}$ do not include apps detected by only one AV and have an *Exclusivity* of 0.

4.1.3   Recognition

Because *Equiponderance* and *Exclusivity* alone are not sufficient to describe how experimental ground truth datasets are built, we investigate the impact of the threshold parameter that is often used in the literature of malware detection to consolidate the value of positive detections [8]. A threshold τ indicates that a sample is considered as a malware in the ground truth if and only if at least τ AV engines have reported positive detections on it. Unfortunately, to the best of our knowledge, there is no theory or golden rule behind the selection of τ. On one hand, it should be noted that samples rejected because of a threshold requirement may simply be either (a) new malware samples not yet recognized by all industry players, or (b) difficult cases of malware whose patterns are not easily spotted [10]. On the other hand, when a sample is detected by λ or γ AVs (where λ is close to τ and γ is much bigger than τ), the confidence of including the app in the malware set is not equivalent for both cases.

Figure 3 explores the variations in the numbers of apps included in the ground truth dataset $\mathcal{D}_{base}$ as malware when the threshold value for detection rates (i.e., threshold number τ of AVs assigning a positive detection a sample) changes. The number of apps detected by more than τ AVs is also provided for the different values of τ.

Both bar plots appear to be right-skewed, with far more samples detected by a small number of antivirus than by the majority of them. Thus, any threshold value applied to this dataset would remove a large portion of the potential

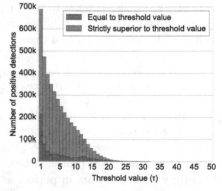

Fig. 3. Distribution of apps flagged by τ AVs in $\mathcal{D}_{base}$ (Color figure online)

malware set (and, in some settings, shift them into the benign set). To quantify this property of ground truth datasets, we investigate the following research question:

> *RQ3: Given the result of antivirus scans on ground-truth dataset, have applications been marginally or widely recognized to be malicious ?*

We answer this RQ with a single metric, *Recognition*, which simply computes the average number of positive detections that are assigned to a sample. In other words, it estimates the number of AVs agreeing on a given app.

$$Recognition(\mathcal{B}) = \frac{\sum_{i=1}^{m} X_i}{n \times m} \text{ with } X = \{positives(R_i) : R_i \in \mathcal{B}, 1 \leq i \leq m\}$$

- **Interpretation** – proportion of antivirus which provided a positive detection to an application, averaging on the entire dataset
- **Minimum:** 0 – when no detections were provided at all
- **Maximum:** 1 – when each AV have agreement to flag all apps

When a threshold is applied on an experimental dataset, the desired objective is often to increase the confidence by ensuring that malware samples are widely recognized to be malicious by existing antivirus engines. Although researchers often report the effect on the dataset size, they do not measure the level of confidence that was reached. As an example, the *Recognition* of $\mathcal{D}_{base}$ is 0.09: on average, 6 (9 %) AV engines provided positive detections per sample, suggesting a marginal recognition by AVs. The *Recognition* values for $\mathcal{D}_{filtered}$ and $\mathcal{D}_{genome}$ amounts to 0.36 and 0.48 respectively. These values characterize the datasets by estimating the extent to which AVs agree more to recognize samples from $\mathcal{D}_{filtered}$ as positive detections more widely than in $\mathcal{D}_{base}$. AVs recognize samples from $\mathcal{D}_{genome}$ even more widely.

4.1.4 Synchronicity

In complement to *Recognition* and *Exclusivity*, we investigate the scenarios where pairs of AV engines conflict in their detection decisions. Let us consider two AV engines U and V and the result of their detections on a fixed set of samples. For each sample, we can expect 4 cases:

	Detected by U	Not detected by U
Detected By V	(True, True)	(True, False)
Not detected by V	(False, True)	(False, False)

Even if the *Equiponderance* value of the dataset produced by AVs U and V amounts to 1, one cannot conclude on the distribution of those cases. The most extreme scenarios could be 50 % (True, True) and 50 % (False, False) or 50 % (True, False) and 50 % (False, True). For the first one, both AVs are in perfect synchrony while they are in perfect asynchrony in the second one.

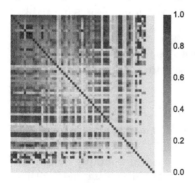

Figure 4 is a heatmap representation of the pairwise agreement among the 66 AV engines on our dataset. For simplicity, we have ordered the AV engines by their number of positive detections (the top row—left to right— and the left column—top to bottom—correspond to the same AVs). For each of the $\binom{66}{2}$ entries, we compute the *overlap* function [31]:

$$overlap(X, Y) = |X \cap Y| / min(|X|, |Y|)$$

Fig. 4. Overlap between pairs of AVs in $\mathcal{D}_{base}$

This function normalizes the pairwise comparison with the case of the AV presenting the smallest number of positive detections. From the heatmap, we can observe two patterns: (a) The number of cells where a full similarity is achieved is relatively small w.r.t the number of entries. Only 12 % of pairs of AVs achieved a pairwise similarity superior to 0.8, and only 1 % of pairs presented a perfect similarity. (b) There is no continuity from the right to the left (nor from the top to the bottom) of the map. This indicates that AVs with comparable number of positive detections do not necessarily detect the same samples. We aim to quantify this level of agreement through the following research question:

RQ4: Given a dataset of samples and a set of AVs, what is the likelihood for any pair of distinct AV engines to agree on a given sample?

We answer this RQ with the *Synchronicity* metric which measures the tendency of a set of AVs to provide positive detections at the same time as other antivirus in the set:

$$Synchronicity(\mathcal{B}) = \frac{\sum_{j=1}^{n} \sum_{j'=1}^{n} PairwiseSimilarity(C_j, C_{j'})}{n(n-1)} \text{ with } j \neq j', C_j \in \mathcal{B}, C_{j'} \in \mathcal{B}$$

- **Interpretation** – average pairwise similarity between pairs of AVs
- **Minimum:** 0 – when no sample is detected at the same time by more than one AV
- **Maximum:** 1 – when each sample is detected by every AV
- **Parameters**
  - *PairwiseSimilarity*: a binary distance function [31]
    * Overlap: based on positive detections and normalized (default)
    * Jaccard: based on positive detections, but not normalized
    * Rand: based on positive and negative detections

High values of *Synchronicity* should be expected for datasets where no uncertainty remains to recognize applications as either malicious or not malicious. $\mathcal{D}_{base}$ presents a *Synchronicity* of 0.32, which is lower than values for $\mathcal{D}_{genome}$ (0.41), and $\mathcal{D}_{filtered}$ (0.75). The gap between values for $\mathcal{D}_{genome}$ and $\mathcal{D}_{filtered}$ suggests the impact that a selection of Antivirus can have on artificially increasing the *Synchronicity* of the dataset.

4.2 Analysis of Malware Labels

Besides binary decisions on detection of maliciousness in a sample, AV engines also provide, in case of positive detection, a string label which indicates the type/family/behavior of the malware or simply identifies the malicious trait. These labels are thus expected to specify appropriately the threat in a meaningful and consistent way. Nevertheless, previous work have found that the disagreement of multiple AVs on labelling a sample malware challenges their practical use [2–5].

In this section, we further investigate the inconsistencies of malware labels and quantify different dimensions of disagreements in "ground truth" settings.

4.2.1   Uniformity

Figure 5 represents the distribution of the most frequently used labels on our $\mathcal{D}_{base}$ dataset. In total, the 689 209 samples detected by at least one AV were labeled with 119 156 distinct labels.

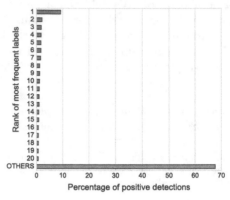

Fig. 5. Distribution of malware labels in $\mathcal{D}_{base}$

68 % of positive detections were associated with the most infrequent labels, i.e., outside the top 20 labels (grouped together under the 'OTHERS' label). The most frequent label, Android.Adware.Dowgin.I, is associated with 9 % of the positive detections. In a ground truth dataset, it is important to estimate the balance between different malicious traits, so as to ensure that the reported performance of an automated detector can generalize. We assess this property of ground truth by answering the following research question:

> *RQ5: Given a ground truth derived by leveraging a set of AVs, are the labels associated to samples evenly distributed?*

We answer this RQ with a single metric, *Uniformity*, which measures how balanced—or how imbalanced—are the clusters of samples associated to the different labels.

$$Uniformity(\mathcal{L}') = Ouroboros(X) \text{ with } X = \{clusters(l_k) : l_k \in \mathcal{L}', 1 \le k \le o\}$$

- **Interpretation** – minimal proportion of labels assigned to at least 50 % of total number of detected samples. The metric value is weighted
- **Minimum:** 0 – when each sample is assigned a unique label by each AV
- **Maximum:** 1 – when the same label is assigned to every sample by all AVs

The *Uniformity* metric is important as it may hint on whether some malware families are undersampled w.r.t others in the ground truth. In can thus help, to some extent, to quantify potential biases due to malware family imbalance. $\mathcal{D}_{base}$ exhibits a *Uniformity* value close to 0 (12×10^{-4}) with an index of 75: 75 labels occur as often in the distribution than the rest of labels (119 081), leading to an uneven distribution. We also found extreme values for both Filtered and Genome settings with *Uniformity* of 0.01 and 0.04 respectively. These values raise the question of malware families imbalance in most ground truth datasets. However, it is possible that some labels, although distinct, because of the lack of naming standard, actually represent the same malware type. We thus propose to further examine labels on other dimensions.

4.2.2 Genericity

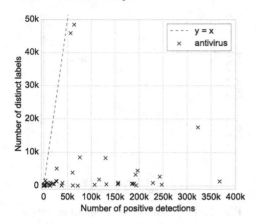

Fig. 6. Relation between distinct labels and positive detections per AV in $\mathcal{D}_{base}$

Once the distribution of labels has been extracted from the dataset, we can also measure how often labels are reused by antivirus. This property is an interesting behavior that Bureau and Harley highlighted [13]. If we consider the two extreme cases, AVs could either assign a different label to every sample (e.g. hash value), or a unique label to all samples. In both scenarios, labels would be of no value to group malware together [2].

In Fig. 6, we plot the number of detections against the number of distinct labels for each AV. While two AVs assign almost a different label for each detected sample (points close to the $y = x$ line), the majority of AVs have much fewer distinct labels than detected samples: they reuse labels amongst several samples. These two different behaviors might be explained by different levels of genericity of labels. For example, using very precise labels would make the sharing of labels among samples harder than in the case of very generic labels that could each be shared by several samples. To quantify this characteristic of labels produced by a set of AVs contributing to define a ground truth, we raise the following research question:

> *RQ6: Given a ground truth derived by leveraging a set of AVs, what is, on average for an AV, the degree of reuse of a label to characterize several samples?*

We propose the *genericity* metric to quantify this information:

$$Genericity(\mathcal{L}) = 1 - \frac{o - 1}{positives(\mathcal{L}) - 1} \text{ with } o \leftarrow \text{number of distinct labels}$$

- **Interpretation** – ratio between the number of distinct labels and the number of positive detections
- **Minimum: 0** – when every assigned label is unique
- **Maximum: 1** – when all labels are identical

Genericity assesses whether AVs assign precise labels or generic ones to samples. Although detectors with low *Genericity* would appear to be more precise in their naming, Bureau and Harley [13] support that such engines may not be the most appropriate w.r.t the exponential growth of malware variants. The *Genericity* $\mathcal{D}_{base}$ is 0.97, inline with our visual observation that there is far less distinct labels than positive detections. The *Genericity* values of $\mathcal{D}_{genome}$ and $\mathcal{D}_{filtered}$ are equal to 0.82 and 0.87 respectively.

4.2.3 Divergence

While *Uniformity* and *Genericity* can evaluate the overall distribution of labels that were assigned by AVs, they do not consider the question of agreement of AVs on each sample. Ideally, AVs should be consistent and provide labels similar to that of their peers. Even if this ideal case can not be achieved, the number of distinct labels per application should remain limited w.r.t the number of AVs agreeing to detect it.

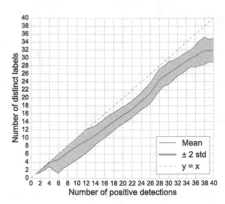

Fig. 7. Relation between distinct labels and positive detections per app in $\mathcal{D}_{base}$

For $\mathcal{D}_{base}$, Fig. 7 plots the relation between the number of positive detections of a sample and the average number of distinct labels associated to it. As a confidence margin, we also draw an area of two standard deviations centered on the mean. We note that the mean value for number of labels grows steadily with the number of detection, close to the maximum possible values represented by the dotted line. The Pearson correlation coefficient ρ between these variables evaluates to 0.98, indicating a strong correlation. Overall, the results suggest not only that there is a high number of different labels per application on our dataset, but also that this behavior is true for both small and high values of positive detections. The following research question investigates this characteristic of ground truth datasets:

> *RQ7: Given a set of AVs and the ground truth that they produce, to what extent do AVs provide for each sample a label that is inconsistent w.r.t. other AVs labels.*

We can quantify this factor with the following metric that measures the capacity of a set of antivirus to assign a high number of different labels per application.

$$Divergence(\mathcal{L}) = \frac{(\sum_{i=1}^{m} X_i) - n}{positives(\mathcal{L}) - n} \text{ with } X = \{distincts(R_i) : R_i \in \mathcal{L}, 1 \le i \le m\}$$

- **Interpretation:** – average proportion of distinct labels per application w.r.t the number of AVs providing positive detection flags
- **Minimum:** 0 – when AVs assign a single label to each application
- **Maximum:** 1 – when each AV assigns its own label to each application

Two conditions must be met in a ground truth dataset to reach a low *Divergence*: AVs must apply the same syntax consistently for each label, and they should refer to a common semantics when mapping labels with malicious behaviors/types. If label syntax is not consistent within the dataset, then the semantics cannot be assessed via the *Divergence* metric. It is, however, often possible to normalize labels through a basic preprocessing step.

The *Divergence* values of $\mathcal{D}_{base}$, $\mathcal{D}_{filtered}$ and $\mathcal{D}_{genome}$ are 0.77, 0.87 and 0.95 respectively. These results are counter-intuitive, since they suggest that more constrained settings create more disagreement among AVs in terms of labeling.

4.2.4   Consensuality

To complement the property highlighted by *Divergence*, we can look at the most frequent label assigned per application. Indeed, while the previous metric describes the number of distinct labels assigned per application, it does not measure the weight of each label, notably that of the most used label. Yet, to some extent, this label could be used to infer the family and the version of a malware, e.g., if it used by a significant portion of AVs to characterize a sample.

To visualize this information, still for $\mathcal{D}_{base}$, we create in Fig. 8 a plot similar to that of Fig. 7, looking now at the average number of occurrence of the Most Frequent Label (MFL) against the number of positive detections per application.

The correlation coefficient ρ between the two variables is 0.76, indicative of a correlation. Nevertheless, the relation is close to the potential minimum (x-axis). This is in line with our previous observations on $\mathcal{D}_{base}$ that the number of distinct labels per application was high. The plot further highlights that the most frequent label for an application is assigned simultaneously by one to six AVs (out of 66) on average. This finding suggests that, at least in $\mathcal{D}_{base}$, using the most frequent label to characterize the malicious sample is not a sound approximation. The following research question generalize the dimension of disagreement that we investigate:

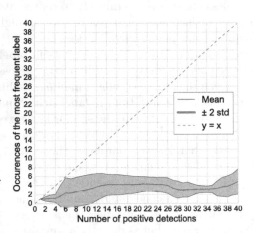

Fig. 8. Relation between MFL/τ and positive detections per app in $\mathcal{D}_{base}$

> *RQ8: Given a set AVs and the ground truth that they produce, to what extent can we rely on the most frequently assigned label for each detected sample as an authoritative label?*

We answer this RQ with the *Consensuality* metric:

$$Consensuality(\mathcal{L}) = \frac{(\sum_{i=1}^{m} X_i) - n}{positives(\mathcal{L}) - n} \text{ with } X = \{freqmax(R_i) : R_i \in \mathcal{L}, 1 \le i \le m\}$$

– **Interpretation** – average proportion of AVs that agree to assign the most frequent label. The frequency is computed per sample.

- **Minimum:** 0 – when each AV assigns to each detected sample its own label (i.e., unused by others on this sample)
- **Maximum:** 1 - when all AVs assign the same label to each sample. Different samples can have different labels however

A high *Consensuality* value highlights that the used AVs agree on most applications to assign a most frequent label. This metric is important for validating, to some extent, the opportunity to summarize multiple labels into a single one. In the $\mathcal{D}_{base}$ set, 79 % detection reports by AVs do not come with a label that, for each sample, corresponds to the most frequent label on the sample. The *Consensuality* value of the set evaluates to 0.21. In comparison, the *Consensuality* values for $\mathcal{D}_{filtered}$ and $\mathcal{D}_{genome}$ are 0.05 and 0.06 respectively.

4.2.5   Resemblance

Divergence and *Consensuality* values on $\mathcal{D}_{base}$ suggest that labels assigned to samples cannot be used directly to represent malware families. Indeed, the number of distinct labels per application is high (high *Divergence*), and the most frequent label per application does not occur often (low *Consensuality*). We further investigate these disagreements in labels to verify whether the differences between label strings are small or large across AVs. Indeed, in previous comparison, given the lack of standard naming, we have chosen to compute exact matching. Thus, minor variations in label strings may have widely influenced our metric values. We thus compute the similarity between label strings for each application and present the summary in Fig. 9. For each detected sample, we computed the Jaro-Winkler [32] similarity between pairwise combinations of labels provided by AVs. This distance metric builds on the same intuition as the edit-disance (i.e., Levenshtein distance), but is directly normalized between 0 and 1. A similarity value of 1 implies the identicality of strings while a value of 0 is indicative of high difference. We consider the minimum, mean and maximum of these similarity values and represent their distributions across all apps. The median of mean similarity values is around 0.6: on average labels only slightly resemble each other. The following research question highlights the consensus that we attempt to measure:

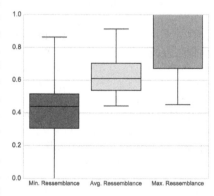

Fig. 9.   String similarity between labels per app in $\mathcal{D}_{base}$

> *RQ9: Given a set AVs and the ground truth that they produce, how resembling are the labels assigned by AVs for each detected sample?*

We answer this metric with the *Resemblance* metric which measures the average similarity between labels assigned by set of AVs to a given detected sample.

$$Ressemblance(\mathcal{L}) = \frac{1}{m} \sum_{i=1}^{m} \frac{\sum_{j=1}^{n'_i} \sum_{j'=1}^{n'_i} Jaro - Winkler(l_{i,j}, l_{i,j'})}{n'_i(n'_i - 1)}$$

with $j \neq j', l_{i,j} \neq \emptyset, l_{i,j'} \neq \emptyset, l_{i,j} \in \mathcal{B}, l_{i,j'} \in \mathcal{B}$ and $n'_i = positives(R_i), 2 \leq n'_i \leq n$

- **Interpretation** estimation of the global resemblance between labels for each app
- **Minimum** 0 when there is no similitude between labels of an application
- **Maximum** 1 when labels are identical per application

Resemblance assesses how labels assigned to a given application would be actually similar across the considered AVs. This metric, which is necessary when *Divergence* is high and *Consensuality* is low, can evaluate if the differences between label strings per application are small or large. $\mathcal{D}_{base}$, $\mathcal{D}_{filtered}$ and $\mathcal{D}_{genome}$ present *Resemblance* values of 0.63, 0.57 and 0.60 respectively. Combined with the *Divergence* metric values, we note that reducing the set of AVs has not yielded datasets where AVs agree more on the labels.

5   Discussions

5.1   Comparison of Ground-Truth Approaches

Table 1 summarizes the metric values for the three settings described in Sect. 3.3 that researchers may use to build ground truth datasets.

Table 1. Summary of Metrics for three common settings of Ground Truth constructions

	Equiponderance	Exclusivity	Recognition	Synchronicity	Uniformity	Genericity	Divergence	Consensuality	Resemblance
$\mathcal{D}_{base}$	0.27	0.31	0.09	0.32	0.001	0.97	0.77	0.21	0.63
$\mathcal{D}_{filtered}$	0.59	0	0.36	0.75	0.01	0.87	0.95	0.05	0.57
$\mathcal{D}_{genome}$	0.48	0	0.48	0.41	0.04	0.82	0.87	0.06	0.60

The higher values of *Recognition* and *Synchronicity* for $\mathcal{D}_{genome}$ and $\mathcal{D}_{filtered}$ in comparison with $\mathcal{D}_{base}$ suggest that these datasets were built with samples that are well known to be malicious in the industry. If we consider that higher *Recognition* and *Synchronicity* values provide guarantees for more reliable ground truth, then $\mathcal{D}_{genome}$ and $\mathcal{D}_{filtered}$ are better ground truth candidates than $\mathcal{D}_{base}$. Their lower value of *Genericity* also suggests that AV labels provided are more precise than that in $\mathcal{D}_{base}$. At the same time, higher values of *Equiponderance* and *Uniformity* imply that both AV detections and labels are more balanced across AVs.

Divergence and *Consensuality* values however suggest that the general agreement on AV labels has diminished in $\mathcal{D}_{genome}$ and $\mathcal{D}_{filtered}$ in comparison with $\mathcal{D}_{base}$. The *Exclusivity* value of 0 for $\mathcal{D}_{genome}$ and $\mathcal{D}_{filtered}$ further highlights that the constraints put on building those datasets may have eliminated corner cases of malware that only a few, if not 1, AV could have been able to spot.

We also note that $\mathcal{D}_{filtered}$ has a higher *Synchronicity* value than $\mathcal{D}_{genome}$, indicating that its settings lead to a selection of AVs which were more in agreement on their decision. In contrast, the *Divergence* values indicate that the proportion of distinct labels for each sample was higher in $\mathcal{D}_{filtered}$ than in $\mathcal{D}_{genome}$, suggesting that decisions in $\mathcal{D}_{genome}$ are easier to interpret for each sample. Nevertheless, the classification of samples in malware families would be more difficult because of the higher proportion of distinct labels to take into consideration.

5.2 Limitations and Future Work

The collection of metrics proposed in this paper is focused on the quantification of nine characteristics that we considered relevant based on our experience and the literature related to malware experiments [3,10,11,13]. Hence, we do not attempt to cover the full range of information that could be quantified from the output of AV scans. In addition, our analysis of antivirus reports has exposed a global lack of consensus that has been previously highlighted by other authors for other computing platforms [2,4,13,33]. Our work cannot be used to solve the challenge of naming inconsistencies directly. Instead, the metrics we presented can be used to evaluate ground truth datasets prior and posterior to their transformation by techniques proposed by other authors [6,10,34].

As future work, we will focus on surveying parameter values to yield ground truths that are suitable to practionners' constraints for consensus and reliability in accordance to their use cases.

6   Conclusion

We have investigated the lack of consensus in AV decisions and labels using the case study of Android samples. Based on different metrics, we assessed the discrepancies between three ground truth datasets, independently of their size, and question their reliability for evaluating the performance of a malware detector. The objective of our work was twofold: (1) to further motivate research on aggregating AV decisions results and improving the selection of AV labels; (2) to provide means to researchers to qualify their ground truth datasets, w.r.t AVs and their heuristics, so as to increase confidence in performance assessment, and take a step further to improve reproducibility of experimental settings, given the limited sharing of security data such as samples.

Acknowledgment. This work was supported by the Fonds National de la Recherche (FNR), Luxembourg, under the project AndroMap C13/IS/5921289.

References

1. Symantec: Symantec. istr 20 - internet security threat report, April 2015. http://know.symantec.com/LP=1123
2. Bailey, M., Oberheide, J., Andersen, J., Mao, Z.M., Jahanian, F., Nazario, J.: Automated classification and analysis of internet malware. In: Kruegel, C., Lippmann, R., Clark, A. (eds.) RAID 2007. LNCS, vol. 4637, pp. 178–197. Springer, Heidelberg (2007)

3. Canto, J., Sistemas, H., Dacier, M., Kirda, E., Leita, C.: Large scale malware collection: lessons learned. In: 27th International Symposium on Reliable Distributed Systems, vol. 52(1), pp. 35–44 (2008)
4. Maggi, F., Bellini, A., Salvaneschi, G., Zanero, S.: Finding non-trivial malware naming inconsistencies. In: Jajodia, S., Mazumdar, C. (eds.) ICISS 2011. LNCS, vol. 7093, pp. 144–159. Springer, Heidelberg (2011)
5. Mohaisen, A., Alrawi, O.: AV-Meter: an evaluation of antivirus scans and labels. In: Dietrich, S. (ed.) DIMVA 2014. LNCS, vol. 8550, pp. 112–131. Springer, Heidelberg (2014)
6. Perdisci, R., U, M.: Vamo: towards a fully automated malware clustering validity analysis. In: Annual Computer Security Applications Conference, pp. 329–338 (2012)
7. VirusTotal: VirusTotal about page. https://www.virustotal.com/en/about/
8. Arp, D., Spreitzenbarth, M., Malte, H., Gascon, H., Rieck, K.: Drebin: effective and explainable detection of android malware in your pocket. In: Symposium on Network and Distributed System Security (NDSS), pp. 23–26 (2014)
9. Yang, C., Xu, Z., Gu, G., Yegneswaran, V., Porras, P.: DroidMiner: automated mining and characterization of fine-grained malicious behaviors in android applications. In: Kutyłowski, M., Vaidya, J. (eds.) ICAIS 2014, Part I. LNCS, vol. 8712, pp. 163–182. Springer, Heidelberg (2014)
10. Kantchelian, A., Tschantz, M.C., Afroz, S., Miller, B., Shankar, V., Bachwani, R., Joseph, A.D., Tygar, J.D.: Better malware ground truth: techniques for weighting anti-virus vendor labels. In: AISec 2015, pp. 45–56. ACM (2015)
11. Rossow, C., Dietrich, C.J., Grier, C., Kreibich, C., Paxson, V., Pohlmann, N., Bos, H., Van Steen, M.: Prudent practices for designing malware experiments: Status quo and outlook. In: Proceedings of S&P, pp. 65–79 (2012)
12. Allix, K., Jérome, Q., Bissyandé, T.F., Klein, J., State, R., Le Traon, Y.: A forensic analysis of android malware-how is malware written and how it could be detected? In: COMPSAC 2014, pp. 384–393. IEEE (2014)
13. Bureau, P.M., Harley, D.: A dose by any other name. In: Virus Bulletin Conference, VB, vol. 8, pp. 224–231 (2008)
14. Li, P., Liu, L., Gao, D., Reiter, M.K.: On challenges in evaluating malware clustering. In: Jha, S., Sommer, R., Kreibich, C. (eds.) RAID 2010. LNCS, vol. 6307, pp. 238–255. Springer, Heidelberg (2010)
15. Bayer, U., Comparetti, P.M., Hlauschek, C., Kruegel, C., Kirda, E.: Scalable, behavior-based malware clustering. In: Proceedings of the 16th Annual Network and Distributed System Security Symposium (NDSS 2009) (1) (2009)
16. Gashi, I., Sobesto, B., Mason, S., Stankovic, V., Cukier, M.: A study of the relationship between antivirus regressions and label changes. In: ISSRE, November 2013
17. GData: Mobile malware report (Q3 2015). https://secure.gd/dl-en-mmwr201503
18. Enck, W., Ongtang, M., McDaniel, P.: On lightweight mobile phone application certification. In: Proceedings of the 16th ACM Conference on Computer and Communications Security - CCS 2009, pp. 235–245 (2009)
19. Enck, W., Octeau, D., McDaniel, P., Chaudhuri, S.: A study of android application security. In: Proceedings of the 20th USENIX Security, vol. 21 (2011)
20. Felt, A.P., Chin, E., Hanna, S., Song, D., Wagner, D.: Android permissions demystified. In: Proceedings of the 18th ACM Conference on Computer and Communications Security, CCS 2011, pp. 627–638. ACM, New York (2011)

21. Yan, L., Yin, H.: Droidscope: seamlessly reconstructing the os and dalvik semantic views for dynamic android malware analysis. In: Proceedings of the 21st USENIX Security Symposium, vol. 29 (2012)
22. Zhou, Y., Wang, Z., Zhou, W., Jiang, X.: Hey, you, get off of my market: detecting malicious apps in official and alternative android markets. In: Proceedings of the 19th Annual Network and Distributed System Security Symposium (2), pp. 5–8 (2012)
23. Barrera, D., Kayacik, H.G., van Oorschot, P.C., Somayaji, A.: A methodology for empirical analysis of permission-based securitymodels and its application to android. In: Proceedings of the 17th ACM CCS (1), pp. 73–84 (2010)
24. Peng, H., Gates, C., Sarma, B., Li, N., Qi, Y., Potharaju, R., Nita-Rotaru, C., Molloy, I.: Using probabilistic generative models for ranking risks of android apps. In: Proceedings of the 2012 ACM CCS, pp. 241–252. ACM (2012)
25. Sommer, R., Paxson, V.: Outside the closed world: on using machine learning for network intrusion detection. In: Proceedings of the 2010 IEEE S&P, pp. 305–316 (2010)
26. Allix, K., Bissyandé, T.F., Jérome, Q., Klein, J., State, R., Le Traon, Y.: Empirical assessment of machine learning-based malware detectors for android. Empirical Softw. Eng. **21**, 183–211 (2014)
27. Allix, K., Bissyandé, T.F., Klein, J., Le Traon, Y.: Are your training datasets yet relevant? In: Piessens, F., Caballero, J., Bielova, N. (eds.) ESSoS 2015. LNCS, vol. 8978, pp. 51–67. Springer, Heidelberg (2015)
28. Allix, K., Bissyandé, T.F., Klein, J., Le Traon, Y.: Androzoo: collecting millions of android apps for the research community. In: MSR 2016 (2016)
29. Zhou, Y., Jiang, X.: Dissecting android malware: characterization and evolution. In: Proceedings of the 2012 IEEE S&P, pp. 95–109. IEEE Computer Society (2012)
30. Hurier, M.: Definition of ouroboros. https://github.com/freaxmind/ouroboros
31. Pfitzner, D., Leibbrandt, R., Powers, D.: Characterization and evaluation of similarity measures for pairs of clusterings. Knowl. Inf. Syst. **19**(3), 361–394 (2009)
32. Cohen, W.W., Ravikumar, P., Fienberg, S.E.: A comparison of string metrics for matching names and records. In: KDD Workshop on Data Cleaning and Object Consolidation, vol. 3 (2003)
33. Harley, D.: The game of the name malware naming, shape shifters and sympathetic magic. In: CEET 3rd International Conference on Cybercrime Forensics Education & Training, San Diego, CA (2009)
34. Wang, T., Meng, S., Gao, W., Hu, X.: Rebuilding the tower of babel: towards cross-system malware information sharing. In: Proceedings of the 23rd ACM CIKM, pp. 1239–1248 (2014)

Evasion

Probfuscation: An Obfuscation Approach Using Probabilistic Control Flows

Andre Pawlowski$^{(\boxtimes)}$, Moritz Contag, and Thorsten Holz

Horst Görtz Institute for IT-Security (HGI), Ruhr-Universität Bochum,
Bochum, Germany
andre.pawlowski@rub.de

Abstract. Sensitive parts of a program, such as proprietary algorithms or licensing information, are often protected with the help of code obfuscation techniques. Many obfuscation schemes transform the control flow of the protected program. Typically, the control flow of obfuscated programs is deterministic, *i.e.*, recorded execution traces do not differ for multiple executions using the same input values. An adversary can take advantage of this behavior and create multiple traces to perform analyses on the target program in order to deobfuscate it.

In this paper, we introduce an obfuscation approach which yields *probabilistic control flow* within a given method. That is, for the same input values, multiple execution traces differ, whilst preserving semantics. This effectively renders analyses relying on multiple traces impractical. We have implemented a prototype and applied it to several different programs. Our experimental results show that our approach can be used to ensure divergent traces for the same input values and that it can significantly improve the resilience against dynamic analysis.

1 Introduction

Obfuscation (lat. *obfuscare* = darken) is the art of disguising a given system such that the analysis becomes harder. In the area of software engineering, obfuscation can be used on either the source code or binary level to obscure the code or data flow. Generally speaking, the goal is to hamper reverse engineering. Code obfuscation plays an important role in practice and such techniques are widely used. On the one hand, obfuscation techniques can be used to protect programs from reverse engineering or to at least increase the costs for such an analysis. Examples include protection systems for sensitive parts or proprietary algorithms of a given program, or digital rights management systems that contain licensing information. On the other hand, obfuscation is widely used by attackers to impede analysis of malicious software such that antivirus companies have a harder time to analyze new samples. As a result, many different kinds of obfuscation techniques were proposed in the last years (*e.g.*, [6,10,13,15]). Note that all obfuscation techniques have one constraint in common: the transformations used to obfuscate the program must ensure that the semantic meaning of the program is not changed.

© Springer International Publishing Switzerland 2016
J. Caballero et al. (Eds.): DIMVA 2016, LNCS 9721, pp. 165–185, 2016.
DOI: 10.1007/978-3-319-40667-1_9

Current state-of-the-art obfuscation techniques translate the target program's code into custom bytecode [17, 22]. This bytecode is generated specifically for the obfuscated program and an interpreter is embedded which handles execution of said bytecode. When analyzed statically, the translation to an unknown instruction set forces an analyst to examine the bytecode interpreter first, before actually reverse engineering the original algorithm. Because obfuscation schemes are often difficult to analyze statically, most deobfuscation approaches make use of dynamic analysis [7, 21, 25]. A drawback of current obfuscation techniques is the fact that the control flow does not differ for multiple program executions when using the same input values. Thus, it is easier for an analyst to monitor control flow, which exposes parts of the semantic of the target program. Note that state-of-the-art deobfuscation tools utilize a dynamic trace of the program to reconstruct an unobfuscated version of the program.

In this paper, we propose a novel obfuscation approach that tackles the aforementioned problem. Our obfuscation scheme is constructed in such a way that multiple traces of the same function with the same input values lead to different *observed* control flows, whilst preserving semantics. Our approach is inspired by the idea of Collberg et al. [5], which uses opaque predicates constructed using a specifically crafted graph data structure. However, their technique is based on a problem that is only difficult to tackle when the attacker is limited to static analysis. Hence, if an analyst employs dynamic analyses, she can easily determine the value of an opaque predicate which has been executed in the recorded trace. In an empirical evaluation, we show that our proposed obfuscation approach successfully introduces probabilism to the control flow of the target program. Thus, it thwarts dynamic analysis operating on multiple executions of the protected program significantly and does not focus solely on static analysis like other state-of-the-art obfuscation approaches [6, 13, 17, 22].

In summary, we make the following contributions:

- We present a novel obfuscation scheme that introduces probabilistic control flow, but still ensures that the code's semantics are preserved. Due the probabilistic nature of our scheme, it can withstand proposed deobfuscation approaches that rely on a trace-based analysis of several execution runs.
- We implemented a proof-of-concept obfuscation tool in the managed code programming language C# targeting .NET applications. The tool is freely available at https://github.com/RUB-SysSec/Probfuscator.
- We evaluate the prototype and demonstrate that probabilistic obfuscation is a viable obfuscation technique to protect sensitive parts of a given program.

2   Technical Background

The transformations applied by the obfuscation process aim to hide the program's semantics. If successful, the analysis and deobfuscation effort is considerably higher than feasible for an analyst. In the following, we refer to an analyst as *adversary* given that we study an obfuscation algorithm.

The main class of obfuscation schemes, as well as ours, target the control flow of the target program since it contains vital information about the general structure of a program and exposes high-level constructs such as loops or if-clauses. Doing so, these obfuscation schemes thwart attempts to statically analyze the target program. One building block used by said schemes is the construct of *opaque predicates* [5]. An opaque predicate is a boolean expression whose value is known at obfuscation time. However, its value is difficult to infer by an (automated) attacker. Collberg et al. introduce three types of opaque predicates which we will refer to as *true opaque predicates, false opaque predicates,* and *random opaque predicates,* whose expressions evaluate to the boolean values *true, false* or evaluate randomly to either, respectively [5]. In the following, we will denote by *(always) taken branch* the branch of an opaque predicate which is known to be always taken.

In case of a true opaque predicate, its taken branch will always be taken, as it corresponds to the predicate evaluating to true. Its other branch also has to point to meaningful code, though, and points to a block of *dead code*. From the obfuscator's point of view, it should be difficult to distinguish dead from live code. False opaque predicates operate analogously. Random opaque predicates differ in that their expression yields a random value and both branches may be taken. Consequently, the code blocks the branches point to have to be semantically equivalent for the obfuscation to be semantics-preserving. A resilient random opaque predicate aims to hide this fact by employing several transformations on the blocks to make comparison of their semantics harder.

Attacks against opaque predicates make use of *data flow analysis* and try to prove that the expression the predicate checks are in fact constant. More resilient opaque predicates hence build expressions involving *pointer aliases* by making use of the hardness of the *intraprocedural may-alias analysis problem* [20]. This problem states that it is generally undecidable if two given pointers into a complex data structure alias each other, *i.e.*, point to the same location in the structure. While algorithms that tackle the problem do exist, many of them are incapable of handling special cases like recursive or cyclic data structures [5].

3   Adversary Model

The goal of the adversary is to analyze and understand a protected algorithm inside the obfuscated method (*e.g.*, a serial key check algorithm or a proprietary algorithm embedded in the method). To this end, the adversary has to understand the effect of the input values on the program's observable behavior, among others. We assume an adversary that bases her deobfuscation attempts solely on dynamic analysis techniques, a common attacker model found in recent literature on attacks against obfuscation schemes [7,21,25].

The adversary is able to record multiple traces of the obfuscated method for any inputs as well as set breakpoints on specific points in the control flow. Note that deobfuscation with the help of static analysis is already tackled by obfuscation techniques proposed previously [1,5,20,23], which are orthogonal to our

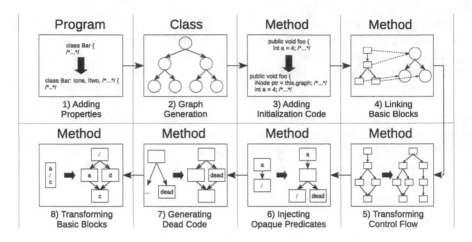

Fig. 1. Overview of the eight steps of the obfuscation process. On the top, it is noted which entity is targeted by the current obfuscation step.

approach. However, the adversary is subject to time constraints in her analysis. Given that modern programs change their protection implementations with the release of new versions (*e.g.*, anti-cheat systems, [14]) and recent deobfuscation approaches work solely on execution traces [7,21,25], we deem these assumptions reasonable.

4   Approach

Our approach makes use of an artificial graph, called *obfuscation graph*, whose nodes consist of objects of classes provided by the target program. Each protected method in the target program holds a pointer to the graph, linking both together. Each basic block of the protected method is linked to one or multiple nodes in the obfuscation graph. During the execution of the protected method, the pointer to the obfuscation graph is moved from node to node. The obfuscation only forwards the pointer to nodes linked to the basic blocks which are to be executed next. With the help of opaque predicates, the scheme ensures that tampering with the link most likely results in a crash of the program.

The obfuscation scheme consists of eight steps which are illustrated in Fig. 1 and shortly described in the following.

1. *Adding properties.* The scheme uses properties of the nodes in the obfuscation graph for opaque predicates. In order to increase the number of possible opaque predicates, additional properties are added to the nodes.
2. *Generating the obfuscation graph.* The obfuscator then builds the obfuscation graph with the help of the properties. It is then added to the class that contains the method that should be protected.
3. *Adding initialization code.* This step adds additional logic to initialize the obfuscation scheme for all methods that are to be protected.

4. *Linking basic blocks.* The basic blocks of the control flow graph (CFG) are linked to the nodes of the obfuscation graph. This connection is needed to ensure correct evaluation of the boolean expressions of the opaque predicates.
5. *Transforming control flow.* The CFG of the method is transformed with the help of the linked obfuscation graph in such a way that multiple paths through the CFG yield the same output.
6. *Injecting opaque predicates.* Opaque predicates are injected that only evaluate correctly if the pointer to the obfuscation graph points to the correct location during the execution.
7. *Generating dead code.* Dead basic blocks added during the insertion of opaque predicates are filled with artificially created code.
8. *Transforming basic blocks.* The basic blocks themselves are transformed to obfuscate the method's original code.

In the following, the eight steps are described in detail.

Adding Properties. In order to provide a diverse range of opaque predicates for the same node, the nodes should either have a large number of properties or a property which allows a wide range of different states. Note that all nodes in the obfuscation graph have to implement the *same* properties, which may be uncommon for a set of entities in non-obfuscated applications. Therefore, the obfuscator adds a set of random properties to all possible nodes of the obfuscation graph (*i.e.*, to all classes, as a node is an object of a class). However, the random properties use *different* states.

For our obfuscation approach, a *property* can be anything that can be added to all nodes of the obfuscation graph and can hold different *states*, so that boolean expressions for opaque predicates can be built. For example, common attributes or metadata of a class, like implemented interfaces, can be used. The state of an interface would be a boolean variable indicating whether the class implements the interface.

Generating the Obfuscation Graph. The obfuscation graph is embedded into the class that contains the method(s) that should be protected. If multiple methods of the same class should be protected, the same obfuscation graph can be used multiple times. The nodes of the graph consist of objects of different classes of the target program. Hence, every node is related to a specific class of the program and therefore has different states for the added properties. The graph is a tree-like graph structure where the leaf nodes have back-edges to the root of the "tree" (semi-cyclic structure).

The structure of the obfuscation graph allows traversal on multiple paths. The obfuscator chooses random paths through the obfuscation graph and declares them to be *vpaths* (as in *valid paths*). The number of vpaths is given by the user. An example for an obfuscation graph is shown in Fig. 2. Classes are randomly assigned to the nodes of the graph. The property states of the nodes on the vpaths are later used to build opaque predicates.

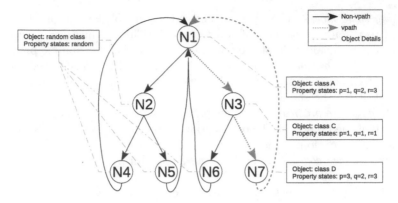

Fig. 2. An example obfuscation graph with one vpath printed as a dotted line. All classes for the nodes are picked randomly by the obfuscator. The classes and properties that are used for the nodes on the vpath are used to build opaque predicates.

The obfuscation graph is parametrized by its *depth* and *dimension*. The depth specifies the maximum length of a path whereas the dimension specifies the number of children of each node. These parameters can be chosen arbitrarily and determine the obfuscation graph's layout. An evaluation of the effect of chosen parameters is given in Sect. 6.1.

Adding Initialization Code. Because the opaque predicates use properties of the nodes on the vpaths, each method to protect needs a pointer into the obfuscation graph. In order to be consistent between executions, the pointer has to point to the same starting point each time. Therefore, in the beginning of the method, the pointer is reset to the root node of the graph. This pointer realizes the link between executed basic blocks and the nodes in the obfuscation graph.

Obviously, a single vpath can be easily monitored by an adversary using dynamic analysis. Thus, at least *two* distinct vpaths have to exist in the graph. Probabilistic control flow can then be ensured by letting the obfuscated method determine randomly at runtime which vpath is used. Therefore, a *vpath state* is added to each method which determines the vpath used in current transition. It is initialized randomly in the beginning of the method at runtime.

Linking Basic Blocks. The nodes on the vpaths are linked to basic blocks in the CFG. Detailed information about the links are used later in the obfuscation process to transform the control flow of the method and to build opaque predicates (*e.g.*, the properties used to construct the opaque predicates). This information is only needed during the obfuscation process. During execution of the method, only the states of the properties are used with the help of opaque predicates to position the pointer into the obfuscation graph. The detailed information is merely kept at obfuscation time.

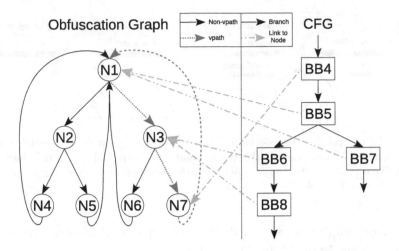

Fig. 3. An example relation between the *obfuscation graph* and the method's control flow. On the right side, a part of the control flow graph is shown. On the left side, the obfuscation graph is shown, where the vpath is printed as a dotted line. The relation between the nodes of the vpath and the basic blocks is printed using dash-dotted lines.

An example relation of the obfuscation graph and the CFG of the method to protect is shown in Fig. 3. The obfuscator links the first basic block of the CFG to the root node of the obfuscation graph (where the *first block* is the one executed first once the method is called). This is the initial position of the pointer into the graph, which is set by the initialization code added previously. The algorithm then iterates over all remaining basic blocks of the CFG and links each basic block to a node on the vpath of the obfuscation graph. During this process, the obfuscator checks for each basic block which node the preceding block is linked to. It then decides randomly to link the current processed basic block to the same node or to the next node on the vpath. This is done for each vpath the obfuscation graph possesses. Hence, each basic block has a link to one node of each vpath. The algorithm terminates when all basic blocks are linked to a node of the obfuscation graph.

Transforming Control Flow. The outgoing branches of each basic block are processed exactly once. In the following, we describe the control flow transformation process on the basis of the example shown in Fig. 4:

1. Each basic block has a link to one node in every vpath. The *vpath state* (introduced to the protected method while adding the initialization code) determines which of the vpaths is currently active during execution. In order to divert the control flow depending on the currently used vpath, logic must be added that switches the control flow accordingly. Hence, the obfuscator replaces the branch of basic block A to B with one branch for every

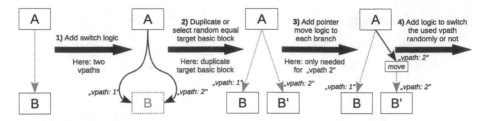

Fig. 4. The control flow transformation process operating on two consecutive basic blocks A and B. The target of the transformation is depicted by dotted lines. The caption "vpath: X" denotes the control flow path corresponding to the respective vpath in the obfuscation graph.

existing vpath (in this example there are two vpaths). At runtime, the branch corresponding to the vpath state is taken.

2. In order to avoid all of these new branches having the same target basic block, the obfuscator either duplicates the target basic block or randomly chooses a semantically equivalent basic block. The list of semantically equivalent basic blocks consists of the target basic block itself and all duplicates of this basic block. In this example, the basic block B is duplicated and the new basic block B' is executed when *vpath 2* is currently active.

3. The source basic block of a branch and the target basic block may be linked to different nodes on the vpath. Hence, the pointer into the obfuscation graph has to be moved from the node the source basic block is linked to to the node the target basic block is linked to (compare Fig. 3). As depicted in our example, basic block B is linked to the same node on *vpath 1* as basic block A, but basic block B' is not linked to the same node on *vpath 2* as A. Thus, a *move* block has to be inserted in between A and B'. Said block moves the pointer into the obfuscation graph to point to the node B' is linked to.

4. The current approach would not yield probabilistic control flow at all, as the *vpath state* is only set once in the initialization code of a method. Hence, for each outgoing branch of a basic block, logic may be added (determined during the obfuscation process) that may *switch* the vpath the method currently follows. The switching decision is made at runtime and at random. If switching occurs, the pointer into the graph has to be moved according to the chosen vpath.

Injecting Opaque Predicates. In this step of the obfuscation process, the obfuscator adds opaque predicates to the method that should be protected. For each basic block, the obfuscator randomly decides whether to inject an opaque predicate into the incoming branch. If an opaque predicate is injected, the obfuscator randomly decides to either create a true, false, or random opaque predicate. For the true and false opaque predicates, the never taken branch points to a newly created basic block that is marked as *dead*.

During the execution, the method's pointer into the obfuscation graph has to point to the exact node in the active vpath that is linked to the currently executed basic block. For each opaque predicate, the properties that are given by this node are used for its boolean expression. For example, with the obfuscation graph in Fig. 2, the obfuscator can build a true opaque predicate for a basic block that is linked to node $N1$ with the boolean expression $q == 2$. Note that this boolean expression is not unique to this node in the obfuscation graph, since it is also fulfilled by node $N7$ (and probably by other nodes that do not reside on the vpath). This design decision was made to ensure that an attacker is not able to distinctively connect the opaque predicate to a node in the obfuscation graph. Even if the focus of our approach lies on dynamic analysis, the obfuscation scheme should withstand a shallow static analysis.

Furthermore, true and false opaque predicates are deterministic and do not contribute to the probabilism of the control flow. But since the attacker is allowed to conduct a manual dynamic analysis and change the program state during the execution, it adds a tamper proofing mechanism: if the attacker changes the pointer to the obfuscation graph or the obfuscation graph itself in order to affect execution, one of the following opaque predicates would divert the control flow and with a high probability crash the program. This is an advantage over a solely use of random opaque predicates to create probabilistic control flow.

Generating Dead Code. Basic blocks marked as *dead* are filled with artificially generated code. During this process the obfuscator randomly chooses the terminating instruction (called *exit*) of the dead basic block. If the chosen exit is a branch, the target can either be an arbitrary (existing) basic block in the CFG or a new dead basic block. If the target is a new dead basic block, the process is repeated. Otherwise, if the target is an existing basic block, the interconnectivity of the method's CFG is increased.

Transforming Basic Blocks. The transformation of basic blocks is necessary because the algorithm duplicated basic blocks during the control flow transformation step. If no transformation was applied, a pattern matching of basic blocks could be sufficient to detect the always taken branch of an opaque predicate.

In order to make semantically equivalent blocks harder to detect, the obfuscator employs standard obfuscation techniques [4]. We focus on those affecting control flow (like splitting blocks or outsourcing the last instructions to a common block for a subset of blocks), but other techniques can be applied as well. This includes instruction re-ordering, replacement of instruction sequences with equal ones, or usage of opaque expressions.

5   Implementation

Our prototype obfuscator is written in C# and targets .NET programs. It uses the *CCI Metadata* libraries [11] in order to transform the target program. For now, the prototype of our obfuscation scheme operates on the bytecode of individual methods a user wishes to protect. In general, however, the approach is not limited to bytecode or methods only (or managed code programming languages). As mentioned in Sect. 4, the user chooses the method(s) he wants to protect. Note that typically only a very small number of methods in a given software project contain sensitive and valuable information that need to be protected.

All random numbers that are required during the obfuscation process are fetched from the same pseudo random number generator (PRNG). Hence, the seed of the PRNG can be used as a key for the obfuscation. This means the same seed used for the same target method results in the same obfuscated output.

The vpath through the obfuscation graph that is used for the current run is randomly determined during execution of the protected method. This randomness is used to implement non-deterministic control flow. We stress that these random numbers are created during the execution of the obfuscated method and not during the obfuscation process.

In our prototype implementation, the random number generator of the .NET *System* namespace is used. This implementation is sufficient for our proof-of-concept tool, but not for a real-world application. An attacker can potentially determine the points in the control flow which generates random numbers and replace them with fixed values. A detailed discussion about the random number generation during the execution of the obfuscated method is given in Sect. 7. More information about the actual implementation is available in a technical report [18]. The prototype implementation of our tool is freely available at https://github.com/RUB-SysSec/Probfuscator.

6   Evaluation

In this section, we evaluate the prototype of our proposed obfuscation technique. Since it is hard to evaluate obfuscation techniques in general, we evaluate it using the four aspects proposed by Collberg et al. [5]:

1. *Cost* gives a measurement of the time and space overhead that is induced by the obfuscation technique.
2. *Resilience* measures how well the protected program resists deobfuscation attempts.
3. *Potency* measures how complex the program has become after the obfuscation process.
4. *Stealth* measures how well the obfuscation blends into the original program.

Given that our obfuscation is parametrized, we evaluate the effect of the parameters on the obfuscation first. Afterwards, the four aspects cost, resilience, potency, and stealth are measured.

6.1   Obfuscator Parameters

The obfuscation graph is the only component of the obfuscation scheme that is memory dependent. Its size is mainly characterized by its *depth* and *dimension*.

Table 1. Size of the obfuscation graph and its dependency to the graph's depth and dimension.

Depth	Dim.	# Nodes	Depth	Dim.	# Nodes	Depth	Dim.	# Nodes
6	4	1,365	7	4	5,461	8	4	21,845
6	5	3,906	7	5	19,531	8	5	97,656
6	6	9,331	7	6	55,987	8	6	335,923

Table 2. Relation between the number of vpaths and the size of the obfuscated method.

vpaths	# Basic blocks	Growth factor	# Branches	Growth factor
4	2,520	504	3,059	611.8
5	5,963	1192.6	7,272	1454.4
6	15,418	3083.6	18,804	3760.8
7	26,215	5243	31,848	6369.6

Each node of the graph is represented by an object of a class in the target program and incurs an overhead dependent on the classes that are instantiated. Table 1 shows the size of the obfuscation graph for a range of parameters.

The length of the *vpath* is determined by the depth of the obfuscation graph. The number of vpaths affects the number of possible control flows of the method for the same input and thus influences the method's size as well. The effect of multiple possible control flows is further evaluated in Sect. 6.3. Table 2 shows the outcome of the obfuscation process for different numbers of vpaths for the same example method. The original method's CFG consists of five basic blocks and five edges. As evident from the table, the growth of the method's size proceeds exponentially.

While larger values for the parameters yield better protection levels, one has to weigh up the desired protection level with penalties in terms of size and speed. These penalties are evaluated in detail in Sect. 6.2.

6.2 Measuring Costs

In order to evaluate the cost of the obfuscation scheme on the program, we measure its performance, file size, and memory consumption during execution. These values are compared to the execution of the original, unobfuscated program. The tests were run on an Intel Core i7 870 CPU with 2.93 GHz using Windows 8.1 as operating system (OS). We set the number of *vpaths* through the obfuscation graph to six, the *depth* of the obfuscation graph to seven, and the *dimension* of the obfuscation graph to five. The chosen numbers provide a balance between the penalty introduced by the obfuscation scheme and the protection level that is provided, as described in Sect. 6.1. Since obfuscation introduces a performance overhead and is therefore usually only used to protect important parts of the program, we evaluate our approach only on the implementation of certain algorithms (representative of any intellectual property one wishes to protect). Because of its nested loop structure and variable input length, we deem the SHA-256 hash computation as best suited to represent a worst case for our obfuscation scheme in terms of performance penalties. The nested loop structure increases the effect of the probabilistic control flow and therefore slows down the computation. In the following, we describe this test case in detail. The evaluation of additional test cases can be found in our technical report [18].

Size. To quantify the impact of our obfuscation scheme on the file size, we measure the file size in bytes. In our setting, the size of the original binary is 12,288 bytes and the obfuscated binary has a file size of 7,666,688 bytes. This implies that the obfuscated binary is about 624 times larger than the original binary. This result is similar to the other test cases in the corresponding technical report [18]. Note that, as discussed in Sect. 6.1, the size of the obfuscated binary highly depends on the parameters chosen for the obfuscator. In order to ensure a variety of possible control flows, the obfuscator has to clone the basic blocks of the target method multiple times. Therefore, our obfuscation scheme also increases the size of the target method multiple times. We stress that the growth of the size is dependent on the target method and not on the entire program. A large program has the same growth as a small program if they implement the same method that is the target of the obfuscation.

Performance. The performance is measured by calculating the SHA-256 hash of a 10 MB file. In order to compensate for outliers, we repeat the calculation 1000 times and calculate the average time. We take two different timings. First, the time needed for the creation of an object of the obfuscated class, and second the time needed for the actual computation of the hash is measured. During the creation of the object itself, the obfuscation graph is built by the constructor of the class. The creation of the obfuscation graph impacts the overall performance depending on the parameters specified by the user. Therefore, we also have to take timings for the creation and not only for the actual computation. Timings are measured with a resolution of 1 ms.

The original binary takes less than 1 ms for object creation. The obfuscated binary takes 3,925 ms to create the object (and therefore to build the obfuscation graph). The calculation of the hash is performed in 785 ms by the original binary, whereas 5,658 ms are needed by the obfuscated binary. While the obfuscated SHA-256 algorithm takes around 7 times longer to perform the same calculation, we stress that this case constitutes a worst case scenario for our obfuscation scheme in terms of performance. The other tested algorithms in our technical report [18] need roughly the same time to create the object, but only need around 1.6 times longer to perform the same calculation. Again, these values are dependent on the parameters of the obfuscation graph. While parameters exists for which obfuscation graph creation consumes less time, the protection level for the obfuscated method is lowered as well. Additionally, algorithms that are usually protected with obfuscation in real-world applications are sparsely performed during the execution of a program. Therefore, we regard the introduced performance penalty as acceptable.

Memory. The only memory dependent component of the proposed obfuscation technique is the obfuscation graph. Hence, the memory consumption of the graph is measured after the object of the protected class is created in the program. The parameters yield an obfuscation graph with 19,531 nodes. The original program consumes 1,480 kB of memory after the object is created. The protected program needs 28,852 kB after the target object is allocated. Therefore, the obfuscation graph needs about 27,372 kB for the used parameters. This is similar to the memory consumption of the other test cases in our technical report [18]. Note that the memory required for one obfuscation graph is constant. Larger applications embedding the same obfuscation graph will face the same memory requirements.

6.3 Measuring Resilience

Resilience measures the resistance of the obfuscation scheme against deobfuscation attempts. Since we focus on thwarting dynamic analyses, we measure the resilience of our obfuscation scheme by quantifying the probabilistic control flow. Therefore, we trace the execution of an obfuscated method with the same input values and compare the similarity of these traces. To this end, we generate a graph from the traced basic blocks in the obfuscated method and compute the *graph-edit distance* between two execution traces using the algorithm proposed by Hu et al. [12]. The graph-edit distance yields the number of edits needed to transform one graph into another graph. Edits are node insertions/deletions and edge insertions/deletions.

We follow the proposal of Chan et al. [2] and normalize the graph-edit distance such that it computes a similarity score using the following formula:

$$\text{similarity}(G_1, G_2) = 1 - \left(\frac{\text{graph-edit distance}}{|G_1| + |G_2|} \right),$$

where the size of the graph G_i is given by the total number of nodes and edges and is denoted by $|G_i|$. The output of the similarity function is a value between 0.0 and 1.0. A result of 1.0 means that the two graphs are identical, whereas a result of 0.0 means they are completely different.

Results. As test case we use our running example, the SHA-256 hash computation. We generated 100 traces by executing the program 100 times in a row with the same input. Since the graph-edit distance calculation is NP-hard in general [26], we have to choose an input size that creates traces with graph dimensions that are still comparable. To this end, we used 100 bytes of random data. Since the SHA-256 hash computation operates on blocks of 512 bits, the algorithm runs through multiple iterations until it terminates. As obfuscation parameters we use the settings evaluated in Sect. 6.2.

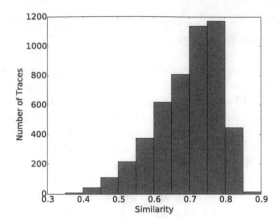

Fig. 5. The 4,950 similarity values of the traces displayed as a histogram. The bin size amounts to 0.05. The smallest similarity was 0.35 and the greatest 0.88. The majority of the values have a similarity of under 0.75.

In total, we calculated 4,950 graph comparisons (as graph comparison is commutative). The greatest similarity of two traces was 88.45 %. The smallest similarity was 35.29 %, while the average of all similarities is 69.65 %. An overview of the similarity between the traces is given in Fig. 5 as histogram. As can be seen, most of the similarity values are near the calculated average value in the range of 60 % to 75 %.

The smallest trace regarding the number of unique basic blocks visited 359 unique basic blocks and took 367 unique branches. The largest trace reached 1,183 unique basic blocks and took 1,255 unique branches. On average, 753 unique basic blocks were visited and 793 unique branches were taken by the traces. The number of all visited unique basic blocks and taken unique branches is given in Fig. 6. As evident from the figure, the number of visited unique basic blocks and taken unique branches correlate. If more unique basic blocks were executed, more unique branches were used. But still, the number of basic blocks and branches vary greatly between single executions. The size of the traces of our other test cases is provided in the corresponding technical report [18].

These results show that multiple executions for the same input values do not even once have the same execution path. This effectively hinders deobfuscation approaches working on multiple traces, such as state-of-the-art deobfuscation methods like the one proposed by Yadegari et al. [25]. In addition, a manual analysis using breakpoints is rendered unreliable in presence of the probabilistic control flow, as we explain in Sect. 7.

6.4   Measuring Potency

Potency measures how complex and confusing the program becomes after obfuscation. In order to evaluate the potency of our obfuscation scheme regarding

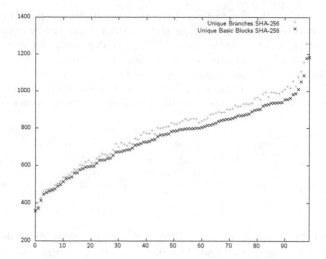

Fig. 6. The number of unique basic blocks and branches each trace used ordered by the number of reached basic blocks. The gray + dots depict the used unique branches and the black x dots show the visited unique basic blocks. On the x-axis the trace number is given. On the y-axis the number of unique basic blocks/unique branches are given.

dynamic analysis, we measure the differences between the original and an obfuscated control flow. Therefore, we recorded an execution trace for the original and obfuscated program with the same input. During the obfuscation process, all semantically equivalent basic blocks were labeled in order to recognize them in the obfuscated CFG. Note that this information is not available for an adversary trying to analyze the obfuscated method.

In order to quantify the *utilization* of the different semantically equivalent basic blocks we visited with respect to all available semantically equivalent basic blocks and the number of executions, we make the following case distinction:

$$\text{utilization} = \begin{cases} \frac{|diff|}{|exec|}, & \text{if } |exec| < |avail| \\ \frac{|diff|}{|avail|}, & otherwise \end{cases},$$

where $|exec|$ gives the number of times one of the semantically equivalent basic blocks were visited, $|avail|$ gives the number of available semantically equivalent basic blocks, and $|diff|$ gives the number of visited different semantically equivalent basic blocks. This way we can differentiate between cases where the total number of visited semantically equivalent basic blocks is lower than the available number of semantically equivalent basic blocks and vice versa. Consider for example a case where only one of the available semantically equivalent basic blocks is executed. If this is the case during multiple iterations of a loop, its utilization of the available semantically equivalent basic blocks is obviously not optimal because control flow visits only this available basic block multiple times. On the other hand, utilization is good if the code contains no loop and

Table 3. The results of the comparison of the obfuscated method trace with the trace of the original method for the same input (ID = ID for semantically equivalent basic blocks, $|avail|$ = number of available semantically equivalent basic blocks, $|exec|$ = total number of times one of the semantically equivalent basic blocks were visited, $|diff|$ = number of different semantically equivalent basic blocks executed, Util = utilization of the reached different semantically equivalent basic blocks with respect to available semantically equivalent basic blocks and the total number of executions in percent).

ID	0	1	2	3	4	5	6	7	8	9	10	11	12	13	14	15	16	Total
$|avail|$	9	43	40	30	35	24	22	20	29	18	22	31	25	22	43	23	33	469
$|exec|$	1	20	1	19	3	1	2	1	34	2	32	98	2	96	130	2	128	572
$|diff|$	1	10	1	8	3	1	2	1	15	1	10	4	1	4	24	2	20	108
Util	100	50	100	42.1	100	100	100	100	51.7	50	45.5	12.9	50	18.2	55.8	100	60.6	71

control flow visits only one of the semantically equivalent basic blocks during the execution only one single time. Therefore, we have to differentiate.

Results. As input data we used 100 bytes of random data and as obfuscation parameters we use the settings evaluated in Sect. 6.2. We recorded a trace by executing the obfuscated and original program with the same input. The resulting traces were compared with respect to their executed basic blocks.

The obfuscator cloned the basic blocks of the original method multiple times during the obfuscation process. Remember that the decision to clone a basic block is made randomly during the obfuscation process. The minimum number of semantically equivalent basic blocks in the obfuscated method amounts to 9 and the maximum number to 43. On average, the control flow has 27 different possibilities per basic block to exhibit the same behavior.

During the execution of the obfuscated method, the control flow has visited 572 relevant basic blocks that contribute to the calculation of the result. These basic blocks consist of the basic blocks of the original method and transformed copies of these original basic blocks. The utilization of the available semantically equivalent basic blocks ranges from 12.9 % to 100 %. In total, 71 % of the available semantically equivalent basic blocks were utilized during the execution of the obfuscated method. The results for our test case are shown in Table 3. All test cases in our technical report [18] have similar results.

The results show that an execution of the obfuscated method uses a variety of different but semantically equivalent basic blocks to compute its result. Hence, the number of basic blocks that are actually involved in the computation has been increased by our approach and with it the complexity of the control flow.

6.5   Measuring Stealth

Stealth measures the difficulty for an adversary to determine if the given method is obfuscated, *i.e.*, how well the obfuscated entity fits in legitimate code. Although stealth is not an objective of our approach, we evaluate it for the sake of completeness. Recently published obfuscation papers measure this aspect based on the distribution of instructions [3,19,24]. However, as Collberg et al. [5] describe it, stealth is a *context-sensitive* metric. Hence, instead of pursuing a static approach for evaluating stealth, we consider the *dynamic* behavior of the obfuscated program. This fits our general focus on dynamic analysis.

Given that our approach is by design supposed to yield different execution traces for the same input, *stealth* is inherently hard. An adversary only has to execute the program two times with the same input and compare the recorded execution traces. If they differ, the adversary can conclude that the program is most likely protected by our obfuscation approach.

7   Discussion

In the following, we discuss potential limitations of our approach.

Dynamic Analysis. Our approach aims to transform methods such that multiple traces of the same function using the same inputs differ, which implies that dynamic deobfuscation approaches are hampered [7,21]. Furthermore, this is done to thwart dynamic analyses operating on multiple executions (like [25]). For example, *manual* dynamic analysis of the obfuscated method is hindered by probabilistic control flow: an adversary observing the control flow at some fixed point during execution of the method cannot depend on the program reaching the exactly same point during a following run. Hence, pausing execution using breakpoints is rendered unreliable in presence of our obfuscation approach.

Single Trace Analysis. If an adversary knows that our obfuscation scheme is used, the best way to attack it is by resorting to work on a single execution trace. Since the goal of probabilistic control flow is to make dynamic analyses based on multiple traces harder, deobfuscation methods operating on only *one* trace are only affected if at least one loop is present. In this case, our scheme increases the size of the recorded trace because the obfuscator clones basic blocks in order to have multiple possible control flows to choose from. As shown in Sect. 6.4, the execution of multiple iterations of a loop results in different semantically equivalent basic blocks that are reached. Algorithms processing the recorded trace *dismiss* basic blocks that do not affect the outcome of the method [7,21, 25]. Since the visited semantically equivalent basic blocks of the probabilistic control flow affect the outcome of the method, they can not be dismissed. As a result, subsequent analysis of the recorded trace is more complicated due to our obfuscation scheme. As future work, we propose to integrate the use of the obfuscation graph into the calculations of the protected method. This way it gets harder to dismiss instructions based on their usage of the obfuscation graph.

Furthermore, deobfuscation methods operating on only one trace do not perform as good in terms of *code coverage* compared to those using multiple execution paths. This poses a problem for an adversary who wants to analyze multiple execution paths in an algorithmic manner in order to understand the obfuscated program better. Often, *multi-path exploration* techniques are considered when tackling this problem [21, 25]. This is where our approach proves useful: It introduces a variety of valid, but distinct control flows and adds probabilism. For the adversary, it is hard to distinguish whether a branch was taken due to probabilistic control flow or because the function was run with different input. In order to improve this aspect, we currently work on extending our approach by merging the semantics of multiple methods into one method. The semantic that is actually executed when the method is called is then determined with the help of the obfuscation graph and opaque predicates. Therefore, the same method can have multiple semantics and, depending on the vpath that is used, the correct semantic of the method is chosen.

Probabilistic Control Flow. An important component of our proposed approach is the obfuscation graph with its vpaths. The vpaths are used to select the current control flow through the obfuscated method and therefore to introduce probabilistic control flow. Which vpath is to be used is decided by a random value. In our prototype implementation, the used vpath is merely chosen using the PRNG as provided by the .NET *System* namespace. This implementation is obviously vulnerable, as the call to the PRNG could be replaced by the usage of fixed values. As a result, the probabilistic control flow is then merely reduced to a deterministic one.

A straightforward approach to make the random number generation more resilient is not to use any *external* PRNG. Instead, one could build a PRNG into the obfuscated method itself and replace the calls to the external PRNG with code sequences that generate random numbers. This way, the random number generation is harder to pinpoint by an adversary because the code that generates the random number is concealed by the code of the obfuscated method. The obfuscator is not limited to build only one PRNG into the obfuscated method but could inject multiple ones to make it even harder to find the code sequences that generate random numbers. Furthermore, the random number generation can be protected by additional layers of obfuscation like translating the obfuscated method to custom bytecode [1, 17, 22].

However, even this construct suffers from the problem that it needs an initial random seed to create different control flows every time it is executed. If an adversary is able to set this initial random seed to a fixed value, the PRNG in the obfuscated method generates the same sequence of random numbers every time the program is executed. Even if the user input influences the calculation of the random numbers, the program would only have different traces for different inputs (which still hampers analysis of the program with different inputs, but allows debugging of the function with the same input). This circumstance poses the greatest limitation of our current implementation of the proposed obfuscation scheme. However, due to their huge number, it is not easy in practice to detect every single state that is fetched by a program from the OS or to set every internal state of an OS every time to the exact same value in order to fix the seed. One approach to circumvent fixed OS states would be using non-deterministic sources like the intentional use of race conditions. For future work, we propose to develop methods to conceal the fetching of external states for the random number generation.

8 Related Work

The basic technique our approach is based on is presented in a paper by Collberg et al. [5]. They propose a method to create opaque constructs based on objects and pointer aliases. They also suggest a directed graph as concrete data type. However, their approach is mainly concerned with the creation of cheap, stealthy and resilient opaque constructs. We extend this approach and focus on the different paths we can insert into a target using their construct. This stems from the insight that while their technique efficiently makes static analysis harder, the traces obtained using dynamic analyses are very much the same. This, in turn, helps in determining the concrete value of an opaque predicate and might allow to partly reconstruct the control flow of the program.

Wang et al. describe a technique to obfuscate a target program using control flow transformations as well [23]. They transform a method's CFG in such a way that a new basic block in the beginning of the method decides which original basic block is executed next. These control flow decisions are made based on a state variable which gets updated after every basic block. Similar to the approach of Collberg et al., they transform the control flow analysis problem into a data flow analysis problem. However, their approach also merely aims to make static analysis of an obfuscated program harder.

More recent work focuses on deobfuscation of obfuscated programs [7,21,25]. All of them have in common that they are based on dynamic analysis. Traces of the program's execution are recorded and subsequently used to remove the applied obfuscation schemes. Approaches working on multiple traces in order to tackle the code coverage problem [16] of dynamic analysis are challenged by the probabilistic control flow introduced by our technique.

The recent work of Crane et al. also makes use of probabilistic control flow [8]. It enables them to thwart cache side-channel attacks. To this end, they clone program fragments and transform the clone in order to avoid making an exact copy. A stub is used to decide randomly if the clone or the original fragment is executed. Because an attacker has no knowledge about which was executed, it hampers cache side-channel attacks. Additionally, Davi et al. [9] use probabilistic control flow in combination with memory randomization in order to prevent conventional return-oriented programming (ROP) and JIT (just-in-time)-ROP attacks. To this end, they clone and diversify the code that is loaded into memory. Whenever a function is called, their system randomly decides if the original or cloned function is executed. Once the executed function returns, the system checks if execution shall continue at the normal or cloned version of the function caller by adding an offset to the return address. Therefore, an attacker is not able to precisely predict where execution will resume and cannot reliably perform an attack.

9   Conclusion

In this paper, we introduce a novel approach to obfuscate software, including, but not limited to, those written in managed code programming languages. The proposed scheme is based on a construct introduced by Collberg et al. [5]. However, instead of focusing on protecting the program against static analysis, we introduce a scheme achieving probabilistic control flow, aiming to make dynamic analysis harder. This is achieved by embedding an obfuscation graph containing multiple virtual paths. Based on these paths, opaque predicates are constructed and added to the target method. Consequently, control flow may take different paths exhibiting the same observable semantics.

We have implemented a prototype obfuscator for .NET applications and evaluated it using multiple programs. The experiments have shown that the obfuscated methods do not exhibit the same execution trace after executing it 100 times in a row with the same input. Inevitably, this comes with a significant performance and memory penalty. Resilience against dynamic analyses thus has to be weighed up with constraints on time and space. We are confident that the overhead is still acceptable to protect sensitive parts or proprietary algorithms of a given program. Since we believe our obfuscation approach provides a new strategy for tackling dynamic analysis and hence a building block for future research, we are making our obfuscation tool available to the research community.

References

1. Anckaert, B., Jakubowski, M., Venkatesan, R.: Proteus: virtualization for diversified tamper-resistance. In: Proceedings of the ACM Workshop on Digital Rights Management (2006)
2. Chan, P.P., Collberg, C.: A method to evaluate CFG comparison algorithms. In: International Conference on Quality Software (QSIC) (2014)
3. Chen, H., Yuan, L., Wu, X., Zang, B., Huang, B., Yew, P.C.: Control flow obfuscation with information flow tracking. In: Annual IEEE/ACM International Symposium on Microarchitecture (2009)
4. Collberg, C., Thomborson, C., Low, D.: A Taxonomy of Obfuscating Transformations. Technical report, Department of Computer Science, The University of Auckland, New Zealand (1997)
5. Collberg, C., Thomborson, C., Low, D.: Manufacturing cheap, resilient, and stealthy opaque constructs. In: ACM Symposium on Principles of Programming Languages (POPL) (1998)
6. Collberg, C.: The Tigress C Diversifier/Obfuscator. http://tigress.cs.arizona.edu
7. Coogan, K., Lu, G., Debray, S.: Deobfuscation of virtualization-obfuscated software: a semantics-based approach. In: ACM Conference on Computer and Communications Security (CCS) (2011)
8. Crane, S., Homescu, A., Brunthaler, S., Larsen, P., Franz, M.: Thwarting cache side-channel attacks through dynamic software diversity. In: Symposium on Network and Distributed System Security (NDSS) (2015)
9. Davi, L., Liebchen, C., Sadeghi, A.R., Snow, K.Z., Monrose, F.: Isomeron: code randomization resilient to (just-in-time) return-oriented programming. In: Symposium on Network and Distributed System Security (NDSS) (2015)

10. Fang, H., Wu, Y., Wang, S., Huang, Y.: Multi-stage binary code obfuscation using improved virtual machine. In: Lai, X., Zhou, J., Li, H. (eds.) ISC 2011. LNCS, vol. 7001, pp. 168–181. Springer, Heidelberg (2011)
11. Guy_Smith: Common Compiler Infrastructure: Metadata API. https:// ccimetadata.codeplex.com/
12. Hu, X., Chiueh, T.C., Shin, K.G.: Large-scale malware indexing using function-call graphs. In: ACM Conference on Computer and Communications Security (CCS) (2009)
13. Junod, P.: Obfuscator-LLVM. https://github.com/obfuscator-llvm/obfuscator/ wiki
14. Kushner, D.: Steamed: Valve Software Battles Video-game Cheaters. http:// spectrum.ieee.org/consumer-electronics/gaming/steamed-valve-software-battles-videogame-cheaters
15. Lee, B., Kim, Y., Kim, J.: binOb+: a framework for potent and stealthy binary obfuscation. In: ACM Symposium on Information, Computer and Communications Security (ASIACCS) (2010)
16. Moser, A., Kruegel, C., Kirda, E.: Exploring multiple execution paths for malware analysis. In: IEEE Symposium on Security and Privacy (S&P) (2007)
17. Oreans Technologies: Code Virtualizer: Total Obfuscation against Reverse Engineering. http://oreans.com/codevirtualizer.php
18. Pawlowski, A., Contag, M., Holz, T.: Probfuscation: An Obfuscation Approach using Probabilistic Control Flows. In: Technical Report TR-HGI-2016-002, Ruhr University Bochum (2016)
19. Popov, I.V., Debray, S.K., Andrews, G.R.: Binary obfuscation using signals. In: USENIX Security Symposium (2007)
20. Ramalingam, G.: The undecidability of aliasing. ACM Trans. Program. Lang. Syst. (TOPLAS) **16**(5), 1467–1471 (1994)
21. Sharif, M., Lanzi, A., Giffin, J., Lee, W.: Automatic reverse engineering of malware emulators. In: IEEE Symposium on Security and Privacy (S&P) (2009)
22. VMProtect Software: VMProtect: Software protection against reversing and cracking. http://vmpsoft.com/
23. Wang, C., Davidson, J., Hill, J., Knight, J.: Protection of software-based survivability mechanisms. In: International Conference on Dependable Systems and Networks, 2001, DSN 2001 (2001)
24. Wang, P., Wang, S., Ming, J., Jiang, Y., Wu, D.: Translingual obfuscation. In: IEEE European Symposium on Security and Privacy (Euro S&P) (2016)
25. Yadegari, B., Johannesmeyer, B., Whitely, B., Debray, S.: A generic approach to automatic deobfuscation of executable code. In: IEEE Symposium on Security and Privacy (S&P) (2015)
26. Zeng, Z., Tung, A.K., Wang, J., Feng, J., Zhou, L.: Comparing stars: on approximating graph edit distance. In: International Conference on Very Large Data Bases (VLDB) (2009)

RAMBO: Run-Time Packer Analysis with Multiple Branch Observation

Xabier Ugarte-Pedrero[1,2](✉), Davide Balzarotti[3], Igor Santos[1], and Pablo G. Bringas[1]

[1] University of Deusto, Bilbao, Spain
{xabier.ugarte,isantos,pablo.garcia.bringas}@deusto.es
[2] Cisco Talos Security Intelligence and Research Group, San Jose, USA
xabipedr@cisco.com
[3] Eurecom, Sophia Antipolis, France
davide.balzarotti@eurecom.fr

Abstract. Run-time packing is a technique employed by malware authors in order to conceal (e.g., encrypt) malicious code and recover it at run-time. In particular, some run-time packers only decrypt individual regions of code on demand, re-encrypting them again when they are not running. This technique is known as shifting decode frames and it can greatly complicate malware analysis. The first solution that comes to mind to analyze these samples is to apply multi-path exploration to trigger the unpacking of all the code regions. Unfortunately, multi-path exploration is known to have several limitations, such as its limited scalability for the analysis of real-world binaries. In this paper, we propose a set of domain-specific optimizations and heuristics to guide multi-path exploration and improve its efficiency and reliability for unpacking binaries protected with shifting decode frames.

Keywords: Malware · Unpacking · Multi-path exploration

1 Introduction

Malware authors employ a large variety of techniques to conceal their code and make reverse engineering and automatic detection more difficult. One of these techniques is packing, which consists in encoding or encrypting the code and data in the binary and revealing them only at run-time.

Packers have been widely studied by researchers and, as a result, many generic unpacking techniques have been proposed in the literature. In particular, researchers have addressed this problem from different perspectives: (i) by making the analysis platform resilient to anti-analysis techniques [1], (ii) by tracing the execution of the binary at different granularity levels [2,3], (iii) by adopting different heuristics to detect the original entry point of the binary [4], or by dumping the code at the appropriate moment [5], and (iv) by improving the efficiency of the unpacking process [6]. Although some of these approaches use static analysis techniques [7], the majority rely on the execution of the sample.

© Springer International Publishing Switzerland 2016
J. Caballero et al. (Eds.): DIMVA 2016, LNCS 9721, pp. 186–206, 2016.
DOI: 10.1007/978-3-319-40667-1_10

Nevertheless, there is a specific protection technique that takes advantage of an intrinsic limitation of dynamic analysis, i.e., the fact that it only explores a single execution path. *Shifting-decode-frames* or *partial code revelation* consists of unpacking the code on demand, just before its execution. These packers only reveal one code region at a time, decrypting only the code covered by a single execution path. In previous work [8], we classified this behavior at the highest level of complexity (with the exception of virtualization based packers). One of the most common and famous packers that employ this technique is Armadillo, which is widely used among malware writers.

These protection scheme is particularly effective in cases in which the sample employs anti-sandbox techniques to conditionally execute the payload, or when it is designed to communicate with external entities (e.g., a Command and Control Server). If the sample is executed inside an isolated environment or the server is unavailable, certain parts of its code will never be executed under a single-path dynamic execution engine. In both cases, a packer like Armadillo would not reveal the portions of the code that are not executed.

Therefore, the first solution that may come to mind to deal with these packers is to resort to some form of multi-path exploration. Several works [9–13] have studied multi-path exploration to improve coverage in dynamic analysis. While these works address some of the limitations of dynamic analysis, none of them has addressed the specific problems that may arise when adopting this technique for the generic unpacking of samples protected with shifting-decode-frames.

On the one hand, packers heavily rely on self-modifying code and obfuscated control flow, making very hard to automatically explore different execution paths. One of the major limitations of multi-path exploration is its computational overhead, making the approach almost infeasible for large-scale malware analysis. On the other hand, in our case we do not need to execute all possible paths, but only to guide the execution in a way to maximize the recovered code. Moreover, as the program does not need to continue once the code has been unpacked, the memory consistency is less of an issue in the unpacking problem. As a result, multi-path exploration of packed programs is still an open and interesting problem, that requires a new set of dedicated and custom techniques.

Peng et al. [13] proposed the application of a fully inconsistent multi-path exploration approach and applied their technique to improve the execution path coverage in malware, focusing in particular on environment sensitive malware. In this paper, however, we focus on the specific characteristics of the described packing technique. These particularities allow us to apply different optimizations and heuristics to multi-path exploration, improving the feasibility of this technique, especially for complex cases.

In particular, in this paper we want to answer two questions: *Is it possible to apply new optimizations to the classic multi-path exploration to efficiently uncover protected regions of code for packers using shifting-decode-frames? And is it possible to design new heuristics specific to the unpacking domain, that can guide the multi-path exploration and increase the recovery of the protected code?*

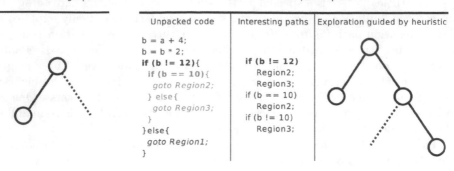

Fig. 1. General workflow of our approach.

Our main contributions are oriented to answer these questions: (i) we propose a set of optimizations for the application of multi-path exploration to binaries protected by shifting-decode-frames, (ii) we introduce a new heuristic that can guide multi-path exploration to unpack previously unseen regions of code and (iii) we evaluate this approach and present three different case studies.

2   Approach

Moser et al. [14] proposed for the first time the application of multi-path exploration for the analysis of environment-sensitive malware. This approach leveraged dynamic taint analysis, symbolic execution, and process snapshotting in order to explore multiple execution paths in depth-first order.

In order to evaluate our system, we implemented a modified version of multi-path exploration applying a set of domain specific optimizations that allow us to selectively explore certain *interesting* regions of code: which in our case is the code of the original program protected by the packer.

Our multi-path exploration engine is built on top of TEMU and Vine, the components of the Bitblaze [15] platform. TEMU allows to trace the execution of a binary, applying dynamic taint analysis, whereas Vine is an analysis engine based on Vine-IL, an intermediate language, that allows to design control-flow and data-flow analysis algorithms.

The general workflow of our solution is as follows (see Fig. 1). We first execute the sample in a single-path execution mode and extract different pieces of information. We analyze the packer structure and identify the regions of memory that contain the protected code, by applying the techniques developed in previous work [8]. In a second step, we extract the memory that was unpacked in this first run, and compute the control flow graph of the unpacked code in order to find interesting points in the code (i.e., control flow instructions that lead to the unpacking of new regions of code). This process provides us a list containing the control flow instructions that lead to new regions. We use this list as part of a heuristic to guide multi-path exploration. Finally, we apply our optimized multi-path exploration engine using this pre-computed information to prioritize paths that will likely drive to the unpacking of new regions. This two-step process is repeated until our system cannot recover any additional code.

This section is divided in three parts. First, we introduce our multi-path exploration approach, and describe several design decisions. Second, we describe a set of optimizations we developed over this model, and third, we present the heuristic that allows us to prioritize execution paths in this specific domain.

2.1   General Approach

Symbolic Execution. Symbolic execution allows to evaluate a program over a set of symbolic inputs instead of concrete values. A constraint solver can evaluate the symbolic expression that must be satisfied to follow a given path, providing an appropriate set of values for each input variable. The reader can refer to previous literature [14,16] for a better understanding of symbolic execution and its limitations.

Some symbolic execution engines [17,18] simplify symbolic expressions to enhance the efficiency of the computations of the constraint solver. Alternatively, other works [19,20] propose the use of weakest preconditions, a method that keeps the computational complexity and size of the formulas $O(n^2)$ [16]. We leveraged Vine, a tool that can compute the weakest precondition of an execution trace and to generate a query to the STP constraint solver.

Indirect memory accesses (i.e., memory access instructions in which the address itself is tainted and it depends on program input) are a recurrent problem in symbolic execution. When the program is evaluated symbolically, the address can contain any value constrained by the symbolic expression. This limitation is specially problematic for the symbolic execution of jump tables, a mechanism widely used by compilers to implement *switch* statements.

Some approaches let the constraint solver reason about the possible values, while other approaches perform alias analysis in order to determine the possible memory ranges pointed by the index [16]. In our case, we let Vine adopt the concrete value observed during the execution for every tainted memory index avoiding symbolic processing. Although this unsound assumption implies that some paths will never be executed, it simplifies the reasoning process involved in multi-path exploration. This limitation can be eventually mitigated in cases in which several paths in the program trigger the execution of a page or function, successfully triggering its unpacking routine.

System-Level Snapshots. In order to save the execution state at a given point (before a conditional jump is evaluated), we collect a system-snapshot. Previous approaches have proposed the use of process snapshots, a technique more efficient in terms of computational overhead and disk space. Nevertheless, making snapshots of the process state (memory and registers) involves many technical problems that are not easy to address. Processes running on the system generally use resources provided by the operating system like files, sockets, or the registry. Besides, the kernel of the operating system maintains many structures with information regarding the memory assignment, heaps, stacks, threads, and handles. While saving and recovering the memory and register state is not difficult to implement, it is hard to maintain the system consistency when the state of a process is restored. Moser et al. [14] proposed several methods to ensure that the process can continue running even if it is restored to a previous state (e.g., avoiding closing handles).

Since the optimization of process snapshots is beyond the scope of this study and stands as a research problem by itself, we adopt a system-snapshot approach that, in spite of sacrificing system efficiency, allows us to securely restart the execution of a program at any point maintaining the consistency of the whole system.

Taint Sources. We taint the output of the APIs that are most interesting for our goals, including network operations such as `connect`, `recv`, `gethostbyname` or `gethostbyaddr`, file operations such as `ReadFile` or `CreateFile`, command line argument related functions such as `__wgetmainargs` or `ReadConsoleInput`, and other functions typically used to query the system state like `GetSystemTime` or `Process32First`/`Process32Next`.

Target Code Selection. In *shifting-decode-frames*, we can distinguish two parts in the code. First, there must be a decryption routine that is usually highly obfuscated and armored with anti-analysis tricks. This routine is in charge of taking control when the execution of the protected code jumps from one region to another, decrypting the next region of code, and encrypting the previous one.

Our goal only requires to apply multi-path exploration to the protected code, avoiding the decryption and anti-analysis routines. In order to do this, we first need to determine the place where the original code is decrypted and executed. This problem has been widely studied in the past and researchers have proposed different heuristics. To this end, we implemented a framework based on a previous approach [8] to analyze the execution trace of the binary and divide the execution into layers. Our framework also incorporates several heuristics that can highlight the code sections that likely contain the original code. This information is also presented to the analyst who may select other regions to explore on demand, if necessary.

2.2   Domain Specific Optimizations

In this section we introduce six custom optimizations that simplify the multi-path exploration problem in the case of binary unpacking.

Inconsistent Multi-path Exploration. In some cases, traditional symbolic execution approaches cannot execute certain paths that, despite of being feasible, are difficult to solve for a constraint solver. For instance, a parser routine may access tables with a symbolic index. Reasoning about indirect symbolic memory accesses requires a complex processing such as alias analysis.

In these cases, when our constraint solver cannot provide a solution, we take an unsound assumption and query the constraint solver ignoring the path restrictions imposed by the previous instructions in the trace. This approach lets us explore the path by forcing a set of values consistent with the last tainted jump instruction, but potentially inconsistent with the previous path restrictions.

In our specific domain, maintaining the consistency of the system is only important in order to avoid system crashes until every protected region of code has been unpacked. While other domains may suffer from this unsound implementation (e.g., malware analysis may require to know under which circumstances a certain path is triggered), in our case this information is not relevant, as long as the system remains stable enough to unpack the different regions.

Partial Symbolic Execution. In order to reduce the size of the code to be explored symbolically, we restrict symbolic execution to the original malicious code (i.e., unpacking routines are explored in single-path execution mode). One may think that the unpacking code will never have conditional branches that depend on system input, but there are packers, like Armadillo, that apart from protecting the original code of the binary, apply licensing restrictions. Moreover, this packer fetches the system date using the GetSystemTime API function in kernel32.dll, and executes conditional jumps that depend on the information collected. Nevertheless, this code will not trigger the unpacking of new regions of code. Also, this code is generally highly obfuscated and does not follow standard calling conventions, making more difficult to correctly trace and symbolically process this code. For these reasons, we restrict multi-path exploration to the regions suspected to contain the code of the original application.

Local and Global Consistency. Another aspect to consider is the consistency of the symbolic execution engine. For example, the S2E project [18] allows to run programs at different consistency levels.

In order to minimize the computational overhead we apply a locally consistent multi-path exploration approach. This means that we respect the consistency within the regions that contain the original code of the binary, but we allow the variables in this region to adopt values that are inconsistent with the rest of the code (e.g., system libraries). For instance, a program may update a variable with a value coming from keyboard input after a scanf call. This function applies some restrictions to the input, as well as some parsing. As a result, the value adopted by the variable would be restricted by the (potentially complex code) present in the library. In order to avoid this complexity, we let the variable adopt any value creating a fresh symbolic variable for it.

First, we avoid tracing any taint-propagating instruction if it is executed outside the explored regions. In this way, when the execution trace is processed in the symbolic engine, only the instructions in the explored regions impose restrictions over the symbolic variables.

Second, the first time a new taint (that has been created outside the interesting regions of code), is propagated to our explored code, we create a completely new taint value for each of the memory bytes affected by this taint, in such a way that our system will consider those bytes as free variables.

Finally, whenever the program calls to a function outside the region delimited, if the arguments of the call are tainted then the result of the call can be consequently tainted. As we do not record the execution of such code, the taint propagation chain will be broken and our tool will be unable to provide a solution. Executing symbolically all the code present in these API functions can become computationally infeasible. For this reason, we avoid recording the execution of code outside the boundaries of our regions of interest. In order to allow Vine to process these traces with broken taint propagation, we create a new independent symbolic variable whenever necessary. In this case, again, we lose program consistency. Nevertheless, as we describe in Sect. 2.2, this inconsistency does not affect our approach but on the contrary, lets us explore as many paths as possible (triggering the execution and thus the unpacking of new regions of code).

State Explosion. One of the limitations that make multipath exploration infeasible to analyse large programs is the well-known state explosion problem [21]: when the number of state variables increases, the number of states grows exponentially. Many samples may have infinite program states, for example when unbounded loops are implemented in the explored code.

Unfortunately, constraint solvers are not suitable to reason about long execution traces. In our case, we configured our multi-path exploration engine to discard execution paths with a trace longer than a given threshold. This parametrization allows us to keep the analysis as simple as possible and computationally feasible.

Blocking API Calls. Our system uses a mechanism to bypass blocking API function calls. In some cases, the program gets blocked waiting for user input or certain events in the system. For this reason, when certain APIs such as the `read` or `recv` functions are called, instead of letting the program run, we restore the instruction pointer to the return address in the moment of the call. Also, we fill the output buffers and output values with fake data, and taint those buffers. This approach allows us to successfully run the samples that would otherwise need some network simulation or external interaction.

String Comparison Optimization. The last optimization implemented is related to string comparisons, an operation commonly performed by malware to parse commands (e.g., IRC or HTTP bots). These string comparisons are commonly implemented by means of system API calls such as `strcmp` and `strlen`.

Some functions can return different non-tainted constant values depending on the path followed during execution (that may depend on tainted conditional jumps). Nevertheless, since the code is outside the boundaries of the protected code, these paths will not be explored. For instance, an `strlen`-like function will have a character counter that is incremented for each non-null character found in the string. This counter is a non-tainted value, and our approach does not explore any alternative paths inside the function. As a result, the function will return a non-tainted constant value although the input parameter is tainted.

In order to deal with this limitation and to minimize the processing overhead in such string operations, we hooked 15 different string comparison functions in several DLLs in order to taint the return value of the function whenever a tainted value is provided as input parameter to it.

2.3   Heuristic to Guide the Multipath Exploration

One way to reduce the state space and thus the complexity of multipath exploration is to apply heuristics in order to determine which paths should be expanded first. We propose a heuristic based on the intuition that, for a packer protected using the shifting-decode-frames technique, a subset of its execution paths (i.e., one or several instructions in the program) can trigger the execution of a region (e.g., function or memory page). Therefore, in these cases, it is not necessary to explore all the possible paths in order to fully unpack all the content of a binary.

First, our system extracts all the executed code and unpacked memory regions from a single-path execution trace in order to recover as much code as possible. Then, it analyzes this code and determines the instructions that reference locations in the program that have not been unpacked yet. The system then constructs the call graph and control flow graph of the trace and finds the paths that lead to interesting instructions, and finally it provides this information as input to our multi-path exploration engine in order to prioritize the execution of certain paths that would trigger the unpacking of new regions of code. The next sections detail how this process is performed.

Dumping Unpacked Memory Regions. Our framework monitors memory writes and execution, and allows us to dump the unpacked and re-packed memory regions after each run. Once we obtain a complete memory dump, we filter it in order to keep only the regions susceptible of being explored in a multi-path fashion. In order to do this, we first indicate which regions we want to explore, and then we generate a filtered memory dump containing (i) the memory blocks that overlap those regions, and (ii) all the execution blocks traced for those regions.

Disassembly and Translation to Intermediate Language. In order to analyze the memory dumped by our tool, we implemented our custom disassembly engine to process the unpacked frames of code. This engine is based on the `binutils` disassembly interface and the `libdisasm` library.

First, for each execution block recorded during the analysis of the packer, we perform a linear sweep disassembly. Execution blocks do not contain any instruction that affects the control flow of the program and therefore a linear-sweep algorithm will always successfully extract the code for these blocks. Second, for each conditional jump pointing to blocks that were not executed, we disassemble the target blocks if they are located in memory already dumped. In this case, we follow a recursive-traversal algorithm in order to disassemble as many instructions as possible from the non-executed parts of the unpacked frames, following any jump, conditional jump or call instruction found. Finally, this code is translated to Vine Intermediate Language (Vine IL) for further processing.

Obtaining Interesting Points in the Code. Next, we build the Control Flow Graph for every function found in the disassembled code. We then process the result in order to find points in the code that may trigger the unpacking of other regions of code.

- **Control flow instructions.** Control flow instructions (jmp,call, and cjmp) alter the execution flow of the binary and therefore are susceptible of triggering the unpacking of new frames of code. First, if a non-conditional control flow instructions is executed, then the address pointed by the instruction will be executed next. In the case of cjmp instructions, it is possible to find cases in which only one of the branches is executed. Nevertheless, considering that we also disassemble non-executed instructions extracted from the unpacked memory frames, we can also find jump and call instructions that lead to regions of code not previously observed.
- **Direct memory addressing.** Instructions that access a memory address not previously unpacked can trigger the decryption of a new region.
- **Indirect function calls.** Indirect function calls constitute a problem in multi-path exploration. When the register containing the call address is tainted, we need to reason about all the possible values that it can adopt. In our case, we have simplified this problem by concretely evaluating the call address regardless of its taint value. In order to allow our system to explore different targets for the call, we consider these instructions as interesting points in the program. Our engine will try to explore all the different paths that drive the execution to this point, since they may write different values over the register or memory address used in the indirect call.
- **Constants.** Finally, we also analyze the constant values provided as immediate values in the code and check if they may reference a memory address contained in the original code. This approach allows us to consider potential register-indirect or memory-indirect addressing operations.

Finding Interesting Paths. Once we have identified the interesting points in the code, we can distinguish three different cases:

- Non-conditional instructions that were executed and triggered the unpacking of a region of code. Examples are direct memory addressing operations, constants, or unconditional jumps. We discard these points in the code since they are no longer interesting for guiding the execution.

- Conditional jumps in which only one of the possible branches was executed. In these cases, we notify our engine that the alternative branch is an interesting point that should be reached in the next iteration.
- We include any instruction that can potentially trigger the unpacking of a new region, if it is located at a memory address not executed before.

Finally, functions calls represent a special case that must be considered. For instance, there may be a case in which a fully unpacked function (that was executed) has unexplored paths that drive to new regions of code. There will be one or several points in the code that trigger a call to such function. Even if all these points were executed during previous runs, there are still unexplored paths in the function so we need to keep them in the list of interesting points. This can be applied recursively to all the inter-procedural calls we find in the code.

Once we have identified the list of interesting points in the code, we compute the paths that reach each of them. Whenever a loop in the CFG is detected, we consider two possible paths: one that enters the loop, and another one that does not satisfy the loop condition. We keep iterating the ancestor basic blocks until we reach the function entry point. The final result will be a sequence of *(cjmp, address)* pairs. For each conditional jump, we indicate the address that should be executed next in order to reach the interesting point in the code.

Eventually, there might be several different paths reaching interesting points in the code. Instead of simplifying the list, we keep all the possible paths because they might introduce different path restrictions during execution. In fact, many of the paths computed will not be feasible (i.e., there is no possible assignment for the variables in order to force the path). This feasibility will be tested by the constraint solver during multi-path exploration.

The output of our system is a complete list of the interesting points that can be reached for each of the two possible branches of each *cjmp*. This list is provided as input to the multi-path exploration engine to guide the execution to the interesting parts of the code.

Queries to the SMT Solver. Whenever a tainted conditional jump is executed, we check if it is present in the list of interesting conditional jumps computed in the previous phase. If the *cjmp* is present in the list, we inspect the number of interesting points that can be reached from each of its paths. Then, we query the SMT solver:

- If the two paths drive to interesting points.
- If only one of the paths leads to an interesting region, but it is not the path taken by default.

If the solver cannot provide a feasible solution, we query the solver again ignoring the path restrictions imposed by the execution trace. If there is a feasible set of values that can be forced in order to follow the alternative path, we create a snapshot and decide the next path to execute.

Path Selection Algorithm. In order to select the next path to execute, we iterate the execution tree in Breath First Search order. This approach allows us to incrementally expand all the paths in the execution tree. More specifically, we select the first path that meets the following conditions:

– The path has been forced less times than the rest of paths.
– If several paths have been forced the same number of times, we prioritize those that were solved by the SMT solver in a consistent manner.

This approach allows us to avoid the recursive exploration of loops, in cases in which there are other paths that will reach the same region more efficiently.

During exploration, we update the list of interesting paths whenever a new memory region is unpacked, removing all the entries that refer to the region.

Path Brute-Forcing. In order to avoid exploring repeatedly the same paths in cases in which there is a complex logic with loops, we limit the maximum number of times that a path can be forced. When we reach this limit, we query the list of conditional jumps we obtained from static analysis, and try to force the execution of conditional jumps that have never been tainted. Since the branch is not tainted, the SMT solver cannot be queried to compute a set of values to force the branch consistently. While this method to force the execution may result into an undetermined behavior or the instability of the process, there are cases in which this unsound approach lets the system reach other interesting regions of code. For instance, a command parsing routine may divide the input strings into tokens and have a complex parsing logic with plenty of loops. There may be cases in which a loop has to be repeated many times (i.e. loop condition is not tainted). If this loop includes tainted branches and a complex logic inside it, it would unnecessarily make the system expand the execution tree too many times. In these cases, when we reach a certain limit of expansions for each conditional jump, our approach forces the exit of the loop and continues execution. A similar case occurs when a loop variable is not tainted itself, but it is set to a constant value (that triggers the exit) when a specific path is followed. This path may only be triggered once we fully explore inner loops, growing the execution tree excessively. In this case our system will inconsistently force the path to reach this point before expanding further the tree. A different case may occur when the variable is updated using instructions that do not involve tainted values (e.g., inc, or add an immediate value). In this last case, our approach would force the exit of the loop even if the variable is never set with the correct value.

In conclusion, if a certain memory region can be reached from different execution paths, even if the constraint solver is not capable of providing a feasible set of values, our approach will reach the region if there is at least one path that can be forced in a consistent or inconsistent manner, always trying to maintain system consistency to avoid exceptions and system instability.

Also, in cases like page-granularity protection, we only need to trigger a subset of the paths in order to reach all the code pages, avoiding to explore the rest of paths and thus reducing the complexity of the problem.

3   Evaluation

In order to evaluate our approach, we implemented our engine on top of TEMU, totalling 7,500 C/C++, 1,300 Python and 500 OCaml lines of code.

In this section we present three different case studies corresponding to packers that protect samples at different granularity levels. On the one hand, *Backpack* is a packer proposed by Bilge et al. [22] that protects the binary with function-level granularity. On the other hand, Armadillo is a well-known commercial packer that allows to protect binaries with a page granularity.

3.1   Backpack

In order to test our approach against *Backpack*, we downloaded the source code of the Kaiten IRC bot, reported to be distributed using the *shellshock* bash vulnerability[1]. This sample connects to an IRC channel and receives commands to perform actions such as remote command execution or network flooding. Backpack is designed to protect the binary at compile time and it is implemented as an LLVM plugin to protect C programs. However, due to a limitation of the plugin, to successfully compile Kaiten using Backpack we had to modify the command dispatching routines of the malware to substitute function pointers with direct calls. Given the functionality of the malware, we configured our system to taint network input considering the `recv`, `connect`, `read`, `write` and `inetaddr` system API functions. Also, we parametrized our system to expand each tainted conditional jump a maximum of 8 times. Once this limit is reached, our system inconsistently forces the conditional jumps that were visited but not tainted.

Table 1 shows the results obtained for this experiment. The sample consists of 31 protected functions that implement a total of 22 different commands, triggered by IRC commands and private messages. The unpacking is performed iteratively. In the first iteration we run the malware without applying any multi-path exploration, revealing only 5 out of 31 functions.

Our heuristic engine reported 52 interesting points and 36 conditional jumps in the code. In the first multi-path iteration, 6 new functions were unpacked requiring a total of 167 snapshots. These functions correspond to the 6 different IRC commands implemented by the bot. One of these commands is `PRIVMSG`, that triggers the execution of a function that processes the rest of arguments to trigger different bot commands. Once this function was unpacked in the first multi-path iteration, our static analysis found 96 interesing points in the code and 110 conditional jumps that could drive the execution to functions not yet unpacked. In the last iteration, 27 functions were triggered requiring 525 snapshots. These results show that a concrete execution only reveals a little portion of the real contents of the binary. Also, the heuristic allows to discover new functions in the binary exploring a relatively low number of paths.

---

[1] http://blog.trendmicro.com/trendlabs-security-intelligence/shellshock-vulnerability-downloads-kaiten-source-code/. (Accessed: 2015-11-13).

Table 1. Results obtained for the Kaiten malware packed with backpack.

	Iteration 0	Iteration 1	Iteration 2	No heuristics
Functions unpacked	5/31	11/31	27/31	8/31
Interesting points	-	52	96	-
Cjmps	-	36	110	-
Snapshots	-	167	544	6015
Tainted-consistent cjmps	-	161	525	5888
Tainted-inconsistent cjmps	-	6	19	127
Untainted cjmps	-	0	40	-
Long traces discarded	-	6	0	-
Time	5 m	24 m	1.2 h	8 h

Table 1 also shows the number of tainted conditional jumps forced consistently and inconsistently. The number of inconsistently forced cjmps is very low in both cases. Our local-consistency based exploration algorithm and the rest of domain-specific optimizations allow us to tolerate certain inconsistencies with the rest of the system, improving the ability of the approach to force locally consistent paths. Nevertheless, there are still a few cases in which inconsistent assumptions allow to explore alternative paths that otherwise would be infeasible to explore.

We can also observe that our system recovered the code of almost all the protected functions. More specifically, the 22 main commands were revealed, and only 4 helper functions remained protected due to the early termination of the process. In the last multi-path exploration run, up to 40 untainted conditional jumps were forced inconsistently in order to trigger the unpacking of new functions. These cases correspond to non-tainted conditional jumps that were identified by our heuristic engine as points that could potentially lead to the unpacking of still protected regions of code. These inconsistencies caused the process to terminate when trying to access inexistent strings.

The last row shows the total time required in order to run the python and OCaml code in charge of postprocessing the execution traces, computing the heuristic, and the multi-path exploration itself. For this sample, the scripts related to the heuristic accounted for the 18 % of the total processing time.

The last column shows the results when only the domain specific optimizations were applied (no heuristics were used for path selection). In this case, we let the system run for a total of 8 h. In this time, the system explored up to 6,000 conditional branches, but was only able to recover 8 functions.

3.2 Armadillo

Armadillo is one of the most popular packers among malware writers. It allows to protect binaries with page granularity. This technique, also named *CopyMem-II*, consists of creating two separate processes. The first process attaches to the

second one as a debugger, capturing its exceptions. When this process starts
the execution at a region not present in memory, an exception is produced and
the debugger process takes control. This process makes sure that the exception
corresponds to a protected memory page, and then it decrypts the page and on
the memory of the debugged process, protecting again the previously executed
memory page so that it cannot be collected by an analyst. Following this scheme,
only one single page of memory is present in memory at any given time, making
extremely difficult for an analyst to recover the entire code of the malware.

We used Armadillo 8.0 to protect two different samples with several pages of
code and a complex internal logic. These samples belong to the SDBot and the
SpyBot malware families. These families of bots typically connect to IRC servers
and accept complex IRC commands. However, only the code of the requested
functionality is decrypted in memory. Moreover, these specific samples present
a very complex command parsing routine that triggers, at different points, code
in memory pages that cannot be reached in any other way. We selected these
samples in order to properly test our heuristics, and to demonstrate how our
optimizations allow to reduce the complexity of multi-path exploration allowing
to drive the execution towards the most interesting points in the execution tree,
recovering all the code pages efficiently.

In order to measure the complexity of these samples, we applied the IDA-
Metrics[2] plugin. The most complex function in SDBot has 417 branches and a
cyclomatic complexity of 321. Overall, it has 104 functions with a total cyclomatic complexity of 674. SpyBot, in contrast, has its command parsing routine
spread in 4 functions, and although the most complex function presents a cyclomatic complexity of 135, its overall complexity is 953, significantly higher than
SDBot.

Table 2 shows the results obtained for the SDBot sample protected by
Armadillo. The malware contains 7 pages of code, but a first concrete execution
only reveals code in the first and last pages, leaving a total of 5 protected pages.
To fully recover every page, we needed to run our engine in 3 iterations. Also,
for this sample, it is strictly necessary to trigger some specific paths inside the
command parsing routine in order to reach certain pages of code. This function
was reached in the first multi-path run, that revealed 2 more memory pages.
A second run revealed 2 more pages that were reached through the function,
and the last run reached the last memory page. We can observe that the number of interesting points (i.e. targets in the control flow graph that trigger the
unpacking of a previously unseen region) is always very low because only a few
paths linked the code in one page to code in the next. Although this means that
it is only possible to reach these pages by executing those points in the code,
it also means that our system only needs to focus on steering the execution
towards those points in the code, ignoring all other paths that are not related to
them. This brings a very large improvement over a classic multi-path execution
approach.

---

[2] https://github.com/MShudrak/IDAmetrics.

Table 2. Results obtained for the SDBot malware and Armadillo 8.0.

	Iter. 0	Iter. 1	Iter. 2	Iter. 3	No heuristics
Pages unpacked	2/7	4/7	6/7	7/7	4/7
Interesting points	-	3	2	7	-
Cjmps	-	65	162	264	-
Snapshots	-	14	366	367	3974
Tainted-consistent cjmps	-	13	295	296	3660
Tainted-inconsistent cjmps	-	1	71	71	314
Untainted cjmps	-	0	1	1	-
Long traces discarded	-	1	14	14	-
Time	30 m	2.2 h	2.8 h	3.2 h	8 h

Table 3. Results obtained for the SpyBot malware and Armadillo 8.0.

	Iteration 0	Iteration 1	Iteration 2	No heuristics
Pages unpacked	3/9	8/9	9/9	6/9
Interesting points	-	26	1	-
Cjmps	-	163	214	-
Snapshots	-	113	153	4466
Tainted-consistent cjmps	-	17	31	4096
Tainted-inconsistent cjmps	-	96	122	370
Untainted cjmps	-	17	34	-
Long traces discarded	-	9	34	-
Time	30 m	3 h	2.75 h	8 h

Despite the high number of conditional jumps reported in Table 2, we can observe that the number of snapshots remains low because our heuristics and optimizations allow to priorities the paths and to limit the depth of the execution tree in presence of loops. The number of inconsistent queries is lower than the number of consistent queries, as a result of the local consistency model described that allows tainted variables to adopt free symbolic values (i.e., not tied to global restrictions). We can also observe that our system only needed to force one untainted conditional jump in the second and third iterations, in order to force the exit of complex loops in the command parsing routine.

The last column shows the results for multi-path exploration without heuristics. Similarly to the previous experiment, we let the system run for 8 h and observed that although the number of expanded conditional jumps was much higher (3660 snapshots), only 4 pages were recovered.

Finally, Table 3 shows the results obtained for the SpyBot malware. In this case, the command parsing routine is spread in several functions that combined together present a more complex logic than SDBot and an higher number of untainted conditional jumps. This sample was unpacked in 2 multi-path exploration runs. In this case, the concrete execution revealed 3/9 code pages, the first multi-path exploration revealed 8 pages, and finally one last multi-path exploration reached the last page.

We can observe that the number of conditional jumps that can drive the execution to the interesting points is similar but there is a higher number of interesting points. Nevertheless, for this sample there was one single transition point to reach the last code page, located deep into the last command parsing routine of the bot. In this experiment, we can notice that the number of queries that the SMT solver was not able to solve is higher, resulting into more tainted and untainted conditional jumps forced inconsistently. Again, like in previous cases, when the system was run without heuristics, only 6 pages were recovered after 8 h, requiring a much higher number of snapshots. In this last case, the postprocessing scripts represented the 59 % of the processing time.

4   Discussion

In order to evaluate our approach we have presented three case studies corresponding to samples with complex routines, hundreds of conditional jumps depending on program input, and many string parsing loops. The results of our experiments show that, by adding several domain specific optimizations and heuristics, it is feasible to apply multi-path exploration to unpack complex binaries protected with shifting-decode-frames.

We selected three case studies in order to test our approach, using two different packers for protection. Although the number of tests is low, we selected representative samples with complex logic and different protection granularities. In fact, most of the packers reveal all the protected code at once and only few present this advanced protection mechanism. Beria applies the same approach as Armadillo, but presents a lower overall complexity. Unfortunately, it is not a common packer, and thus we found no interesting samples available.

We only tested one sample protected with Backpack because was developed for GNU/Linux and it requires the source code of the malware in order to apply the protection at compilation time. Given this restriction, we selected the most complex GNU/Linux malware source code we could compile with Backpack.

In the case of Armadillo, we needed to meet several requirements in order to properly test our approach and heuristics. First, we needed samples with complex routines depending on program input. These samples had to trigger the execution of new regions of code (not executed in a single concrete run), only after executing a fairly complex amount of code. Also, we selected samples that did not already present a custom packing routine. Otherwise, only that routine would be protected by Armadillo, greatly simplifying our job and not providing a challenge for our system. Similarly, we had to discard samples that decode and inject all their code into another process once the execution starts, as well as droppers, downloaders, and simple spyware due to their simplicity.

Our approach is based on whole system emulation, which has a number of well-known limitations. For instance, red-pills can be used to determine if the execution environment in which it runs is a virtual/emulated environment or a real machine. In fact, Paleari et al. [23] proposed a method to automatically discover and generate red-pills in system emulators. In particular, during this project we found two implementation errors in the Dynamic Binary Translation engine of QEMU that affected all its versions and impeded the correct emulation of the Armadillo packer. In this context, several publications and projects [3,24, 25] have reported the incapacity of emulators to correctly execute the Armadillo packer. We solved this issue and reported it to the QEMU developers.

Finally, although the samples evaluated in this study were not affected by the following techniques, complex packers may leverage them to hinder our approach.

- **Calling convention violation.** Malware can violate calling conventions in order to obfuscate the code. If these techniques are employed to obfuscate API function calls (e.g., stolen bytes), our tracing mechanisms could fail to locate string parsing functions, affecting some of our optimizations.
- **Alternative methods to redirect control-flow.** In order to evade multi-path exploration, malware samples may potentially use alternative methods to redirect the control flow: alternative combinations of instructions such as push + ret, indirect calls, call + pop + push + jmp, SEH or VEH based redirection, opaque predicates in branch instructions, or even obfuscating the computation of triggers [26].
- **Resource exhaustion.** Our techniques reduce the computing overhead of multi-path exploration. Nevertheless, creating memory snapshots and querying SMT solvers over long traces still requires significant computing resources. A packer may increase the complexity of the code affecting impacting the performance of multi-path exploration. A malware writer may design a complex CFG with a high number of loops and conditional jumps specifically crafted to increase the number of paths to explore with our heuristic.
- **Nanomites.** This technique consists in replacing conditional branch instructions by software interrupts (e.g. INT 3) that cause the execution to break. A parent process intercepts the exception and then overwrites the conditional jump. A more complicated example involves redirecting the execution of the child by evaluating its context (state of the EFLAGS register) and redirecting its execution to the appropriate address, without even replacing the interrupt instruction with the original instruction. This technique would break taint propagation and prevent us from successfully reconstructing the CFG.

5   Related Work

Manual unpacking requires a substantial reverse engineering effort. Consequently, many researchers have focused on generic unpacking in recent years. Both dynamic and static [7] approaches have been proposed, but due to the complexity of static approaches, most of the authors have focused on dynamic analysis, installing drivers in the system [6,27] or tracing the execution [3].

Some of these systems rely on heuristics or monitor coarse-grained events [27], while others monitor memory writes and memory execution at different granularity levels [3,6,28,29], compare the static and run-time version of the memory [2], perform statistical analysis [5], or measure the entropy variation [4].

Other approaches rely on hybrid static and dynamic analysis [30]. Virtualization based packers constitute a special category of protection techniques. Several authors have focused on unpacking these packers from different perspectives [31–33]. Nevertheless, these protection engines are a different challenge that require other techniques in order to recover the original code.

Transparent execution [1,34,35] is focused on dealing with malware capable of detecting the analysis environment and modifying its execution to evade detection. Nevertheless, these techniques do not explore the different execution paths that a binary may have. Bilge et al. [22] demonstrated that this limitation can be leveraged by an attacker in order to defeat unpackers that assume that all the code will be present in memory at some moment in time.

In order to improve the test coverage in malware analysis, Moser et al. [14] proposed a system to explore different execution paths based on taint analysis and symbolic execution. Our work is built on top of this research, adding a set of optimizations and heuristics to deal with a specific use-case.

Almost in parallel, Song et al. [15] developed a platform for binary analysis. This platform was used in many different follow-up works, including identification of trigger-based behaviour [10], reasoning about code paths in malware using mixed concrete and symbolic execution [11], or even triggering the unpacking routine of environment sensitive malware [12]. Another closely related project is S^2E [18], a platform that introduces the concept of selective symbolic execution (application of symbolic execution to only certain memory regions) and execution consistency models. Schwartz et al. [16] summarized the challenges and limitations that affect efficiency and feasibility of symbolic execution. Taint policies and the sanitization of tainted values have a direct impact on over-tainting and under-tainting errors. Indirect memory accesses with symbolic addresses, jump tables, or the size of the constraint systems are aspects that have no clear solution. Finally, X-Force [13] is a system capable of forcing execution paths inconsistently and recovering from execution errors by dynamically allocating memory and updating related pointers. More specifically, they focus on 3 different goals: (i) constructing the control flow graph of a binary, type reverse engineering, and discovering hidden behavior in malware. Our approaches share some concepts, such as forcing the execution inconsistently. However, their main contribution is a technique to recover from errors (which is not as important in our domain), while our contributions are a set of domain-specific optimizations, and a heuristic to drive the exploration. Also, we focus on applying multi-path exploration to unpacking samples with a complex command parsing logic, a problem that typically presents a high complexity. To this aim, our approach mixes consistent and inconsistent multi-path exploration to maximise system consistency in order to reach deep execution paths. Overall, our goal is not to improve multi-path exploration, but to show if and how this technique can be used for unpacking, and which customizations are required in order to improve its results. To sum up, all these approaches suffer from the well-known path explosion problem [21]. This limitation makes necessary to develop heuristics and optimizations in order to improve the feasibility of multi-path exploration, and this is the main contribution of our paper.

6 Conclusions

In previous sections we have described the domain-specific optimizations and heuristics that can be implemented over multi-path exploration to unpack shifting-decode-frames protectors. We have evaluated our approach over three different case studies covering Backpack, a function granularity based packer, and Armadillo, a well-known packer that protects binaries with a page-granularity. Our test cases cover different samples with complex command parsing logic.

Multi-path exploration has been addressed by several researchers but it is not generally used for real-scale malware analysis due to its technical complexity and its limitations. Our results show that it is possible to apply optimizations and heuristics to multi-path exploration in order to address specific problems such as the malware protection technique covered by this study.

Acknowledgements. We would like to thank the reviewers for their insightful comments and our shepherd Brendan Dolan-Gavitt for his assistance to improve the quality of this paper. This research was partially supported by the Basque Government under a pre-doctoral grant given to Xabier Ugarte-Pedrero.

References

1. Dinaburg, A., Royal, P., Sharif, M., Lee, W.: Ether: malware analysis via hardware virtualization extensions. In: Proceedings of the 15th ACM Conference on Computer and Communications Security, pp. 51–62. ACM (2008)
2. Royal, P., Halpin, M., Dagon, D., Edmonds, R., Lee, W.: Polyunpack: automating the hidden-code extraction of unpack-executing malware. In: Proceedings of the 22nd Annual Computer Security Applications Conference, pp. 289–300 (2006)
3. Kang, M., Poosankam, P., Yin, H.: Renovo: a hidden code extractor for packed executables. In: Proceedings of the 2007 ACM Workshop on Recurring Malcode, pp. 46–53 (2007)
4. Cesare, S., Xiang, Y.: Classification of malware using structured control flow. In: Proceedings of the Eighth Australasian Symposium on Parallel and Distributed Computing, vol. 107, pp. 61–70. Australian Computer Society, Inc. (2010)
5. Sharif, M., Yegneswaran, V., Saidi, H., Porras, P.A., Lee, W.: Eureka: a framework for enabling static malware analysis. In: Jajodia, S., Lopez, J. (eds.) ESORICS 2008. LNCS, vol. 5283, pp. 481–500. Springer, Heidelberg (2008)
6. Martignoni, L., Christodorescu, M., Jha, S.: Omniunpack: fast, generic, and safe unpacking of malware. In: Computer Security Applications Conference, 2007, ACSAC 2007, Twenty-Third Annual, pp. 431–441. IEEE (2007)

7. Coogan, K., Debray, S., Kaochar, T., Townsend, G.: Automatic static unpacking of malware binaries. In: 16th Working Conference on Reverse Engineering, 2009, pp. 167–176. IEEE (2009)
8. Ugarte-Pedrero, X., Balzarotti, D., Santos, I., Bringas, P.G.: [SoK] Deep packer inspection: a longitudinal study of the complexity of run-time packers. In: Proceedings of the IEEE Symposium on Security and Privacy. IEEE Computer Society, May 2015
9. Moser, A., Kruegel, C., Kirda, E.: Limits of static analysis for malware detection. In: Proceedings of the 23rd Annual Computer Security Applications Conference (ACSAC), pp. 421–430 (2007)
10. Brumley, D., Hartwig, C., Liang, Z., Newsome, J., Song, D., Yin, H.: Automatically identifying trigger-based behavior in malware. In: Lee, W., Wang, C., Dagon, D. (eds.) Botnet Detection, pp. 65–88. Springer, USA (2008)
11. Brumley, D., Hartwig, C., Kang, M.G., Liang, Z., Newsome, J., Poosankam, P., Song, D., Yin, H.: Bitscope: Automatically dissecting malicious binaries. School of Computer Science, Carnegie Mellon University, Technical report CMU-CS-07-133 (2007)
12. Jia, C., Wang, Z., Lu, K., Liu, X., Liu, X.: Directed hidden-code extractor for environment-sensitive malwares. Phys. Procedia **24**, 1621–1627 (2012)
13. Peng, F., Deng, Z., Zhang, X., Xu, D., Lin, Z., Su, Z.: X-force: force-executing binary programs for security applications. In: Proceedings of the 2014 USENIX Security Symposium, San Diego, CA (2014)
14. Moser, A., Kruegel, C., Kirda, E.: Exploring multiple execution paths for malware analysis. In: IEEE Symposium on Security and Privacy, 2007, pp. 231–245. IEEE (2007)
15. Song, D., et al.: BitBlaze: a new approach to computer security via binary analysis. In: Sekar, R., Pujari, A.K. (eds.) ICISS 2008. LNCS, vol. 5352, pp. 1–25. Springer, Heidelberg (2008)
16. Schwartz, E.J., Avgerinos, T., Brumley, D.: All you ever wanted to know about dynamic taint analysis and forward symbolic execution (but might have been afraid to ask). In: IEEE Symposium on Security and Privacy 2010, pp. 317–331. IEEE (2010)
17. Cadar, C., Dunbar, D., Engler, D.R.: Klee: unassisted and automatic generation of high-coverage tests for complex systems programs. In: Proceedings of the 8th USENIX Conference on Operating Systems Design and Implementation (OSDI), vol. 8, pp. 209–224 (2008)
18. Chipounov, V., Kuznetsov, V., Candea, G.: S2e: a platform for in-vivo multi-path analysis of software systems. ACM SIGARCH Comput. Archit. News **39**(1), 265–278 (2011)
19. Brumley, D., Wang, H., Jha, S., Song, D.: Creating vulnerability signatures using weakest preconditions. In: 20th IEEE Computer Security Foundations Symposium (CSF), pp. 311–325. IEEE (2007)
20. Leino, K.R.M.: Efficient weakest preconditions. Inf. Process. Lett. **93**(6), 281–288 (2005)
21. Clarke, E.M., Klieber, W., Nováček, M., Zuliani, P.: Model checking and the state explosion problem. In: Meyer, B., Nordio, M. (eds.) LASER 2011. LNCS, vol. 7682, pp. 1–30. Springer, Heidelberg (2012)
22. Bilge, L., Lanzi, A., Balzarotti, D.: Thwarting real-time dynamic unpacking. In: Proceedings of the 4th European Workshop on System Security, Article No. 5. ACM (2011)

23. Paleari, R., Martignoni, L., Roglia, G.F., Bruschi, D.: A fistful of red-pills: how to automatically generate procedures to detect cpu emulators. In: Proceedings of the USENIX Workshop on Offensive Technologies (WOOT), vol. 41, p. 86 (2009)

24. Deng, Z., Zhang, X., Xu, D.: Spider: stealthy binary program instrumentation and debugging via hardware virtualization. In: Proceedings of the 29th Annual Computer Security Applications Conference, pp. 289–298. ACM (2013)

25. Balzarotti, D., Cova, M., Karlberger, C., Kirda, E., Kruegel, C., Vigna, G.: Efficient detection of split personalities in malware. In: Network and Distributed System Security Symposium (NDSS) (2010)

26. Sharif, M.I., Lanzi, A., Giffin, J.T., Lee, W.: Impeding malware analysis using conditional code obfuscation. In: Network and Distributed System Security Symposium (NDSS) (2008)

27. Guo, F., Ferrie, P., Chiueh, T.C.: A study of the packer problem and its solutions. In: Lippmann, R., Kirda, E., Trachtenberg, A. (eds.) RAID 2008. LNCS, vol. 5230, pp. 98–115. Springer, Heidelberg (2008)

28. Stewart, J.: Ollybone: semi-automatic unpacking on ia-32. In: Proceedings of the 14th DEF CON Hacking Conference (2006)

29. Kim, H.C., Inoue, D., Eto, M., Takagi, Y., Nakao, K.: Toward generic unpacking techniques for malware analysis with quantification of code revelation. In: The 4th Joint Workshop on Information Security (2009)

30. Caballero, J., Johnson, N., McCamant, S., Song, D.: Binary code extraction and interface identification for security applications. In: Proceedings of the 17th Annual Network and Distributed System Security Symposium, ISOC, pp. 391–408 (2009)

31. Rolles, R.: Unpacking virtualization obfuscators. In: 3rd USENIX Workshop on Offensive Technologies (WOOT) (2009)

32. Sharif, M., Lanzi, A., Giffin, J., Lee, W.: Automatic reverse engineering of malware emulators. In: 30th IEEE Symposium on Security and Privacy, pp. 94–109. IEEE (2009)

33. Coogan, K., Lu, G., Debray, S.: Deobfuscation of virtualization-obfuscated software: a semantics-based approach. In: Proceedings of the 18th ACM Conference on Computer and Communications Security, pp. 275–284. ACM (2011)

34. Vasudevan, A., Yerraballi, R.: Cobra: fine-grained malware analysis using stealth localized-executions. In: IEEE Symposium on Security and Privacy, 15-pp (2006)

35. Kang, M.G., Yin, H., Hanna, S., McCamant, S., Song, D.: Emulating emulation-resistant malware. In: Proceedings of the 1st ACM Workshop on Virtual Machine Security, pp. 11–22. ACM (2009)

Detecting Hardware-Assisted Virtualization

Michael Brengel[✉], Michael Backes, and Christian Rossow

CISPA, Saarland University, Saarbrücken, Germany
mbrengel@mmci.uni-saarland.de

Abstract. Virtualization has become an indispensable technique for scaling up the analysis of malicious code, such as for malware analysis or shellcode detection systems. Frameworks like Ether, ShellOS and an ever-increasing number of commercially-operated malware sandboxes rely on hardware-assisted virtualization. A core technology is Intel's VT-x, which — compared to software-emulated virtulization — is believed to be stealthier, especially against evasive attackers that aim to detect virtualized systems to hide the malicious behavior of their code.

We propose and evaluate low-level timing-based mechanisms to detect hardware-virtualized systems. We build upon the observation that an adversary can invoke hypervisors and trigger context switches that are noticeable both in timing and in their side effects on caching. We have locally trained and then tested our detection methodology on a wide variety of systems, including 240 PlanetLab nodes, showing a high detection accuracy. As a real-world evaluation, we detected the virtualization technology of more than 30 malware sandboxes. Finally, we demonstrate how an adversary may even use these detections to evade multi-path exploration systems that aim to explore the full behavior of a program. Our results show that VT-x is not sufficiently stealthy for reliable analysis of malicious code.

1 Introduction

Malicious code continues to be a major security threat. The economics of cyber crime tempt attackers to improve their attacks in both quantity and quality. As such, analysts are confronted with a large number of sophisticated new attacks on a daily basis. This sheer volume of threats renders manual analysis impractical, which is why defenders seek to *automate* the analysis of potentially malicious code. In terms of automated analysis, defenders usually prefer *dynamic* over *static* analysis, since malware is usually heavily obfuscated [18,21,31]. While ideas exist to cope with this problem [4,11,12,25,27,28], in practice, a satisfying notion of static code analysis automation is still far from being established.

Dynamic analysis executes unknown programs in a controlled environment and monitors this execution to look for malicious behavior. The large number of dynamic malware analysis systems demonstrates their utility [6]. The security industry has also taken up the concept of malware sandboxes and one can choose from a variety of open-source and commercial systems, such as Cuckoo [19], Joe Sandbox, GFI Sandbox, VMRay or FireEye.

© Springer International Publishing Switzerland 2016
J. Caballero et al. (Eds.): DIMVA 2016, LNCS 9721, pp. 207–227, 2016.
DOI: 10.1007/978-3-319-40667-1_11

Realizing the benefits of dynamic analysis, attackers started to evade sand-boxes. Evasion enables an attacker to discover that the execution takes place in a controlled environment and to suppress any malicious behavior because of this insight. In its simplest form, evasion leverages the fact that most dynamic code analysis systems use some kind of virtualization solution and that these solutions usually come with artifacts such as specific device drivers or known hardware serial numbers, for example. By probing for those artifacts, the attacker can detect the analysis system and suppress any malicious behavior. Note that this approach relies on the assumption that virtualized code execution is equivalent to dynamic code analysis. While this is not generally true, e.g., due to cloud computing, typically attack targets can be assumed to operate on native systems. Virtual machine (VM) detection approaches are widely popular among attackers in the wild. Malware (e.g., the families Dyre, CryptoWall, Shifu, Kronos and Shylock) hide their actual behavior if they are executed in a VM.

When it comes to the choice of virtualization solution, defenders usually build upon hardware-assisted virtualization techniques such as Intel VT-x or AMD-V. Besides being faster due to hardware support, hardware-assisted virtualization also greatly reduces the number of artifacts, giving the attacker less room for simple evasion. Analysis systems such as Ether [5] and CXPInspector [30] use VT-x to analyze malware in a transparent manner. The authors of Ether have shown that malware that does not show behavior on other software-virtualized systems suddenly becomes active in their systems, which highlights the importance of hardware-assisted virtualization.

In this paper, we therefore aim at a more generic form of evasion. While an artifact indicates that the system might be virtualized, there is no semantic connection between the presence of an artifact and the concept of virtualization. Instead, we follow the intuition that virtualized guests operate more slowly than native systems. To this end, we propose three timing-based and assembly-level mechanisms to detect hardware-assisted virtualization *from user space*, i.e., without using privileged instructions. We first consider measuring the execution time of special x86 instructions, that cause a trap to the hypervisor, which will not occur during native execution. We then discuss how a hypervisor might try to hide the involved timing artifacts, and propose a second detection technique which exploits the Translation Lookaside Buffer (TLB) and which cannot be protected against in the same fashion. We leverage timing differences during accesses to pages whose address translations have been cached in the TLB, but whose cache entries a hypervisor has evicted due to the limited size of the TLB. We then consider the stealthiness of those two approaches. Given that the first two methods use special instructions excessively, we argue that those methods are not stealthy. Therefore, we propose a third method which is stealthier in that it limits the use of possibly suspicious instructions and resorts to a different timing source.

We evaluate our methods on a large variety of native and VT-x-based systems and show that the detection methods have a 99.4 % true positive rate on average. We then turn to a few practical use cases. First, we deploy our detection routine on 31 public malware sandboxes, all of which we can detect using the described methods. Second, we demonstrate that even a commercial sandbox with anti-evasion features falls for our caching-based detection mechanism. Finally, we show how an adversary may combine the detection results to evade multi-path exploration systems and demonstrate this with the use case of ShellOS [29], a VT-based shellcode detection framework.

2 Background

2.1 Hardware Virtualization

Most malware analysis systems that use hardware-assisted virtualization rely on Intel VT (or VT-x) as an underlying virtualization technique. With VT-x, the Virtual Machine Monitor (VMM, or *hypervisor*) can create and launch multiple virtual machines. Once the VM is running, the guest can return to the hypervisor; this is called a *VM Exit*. The guest can explicitly invoke the exit handler of the hypervisor, e.g., to establish communication between the host and the guest. After the hypervisor has performed the desired operations, control can be returned to the guest; this is called a *VM Entry*.

In addition to the *explicit* calls to the exit handler, the hypervisor also *implicitly* traps in certain occasions. We will use exactly these implicit traps as part of our timing side-channels, and thus briefly explain them in the following. For example, VM Exits are implicitly caused if the guest executes a sensitive instruction. This behavior is crucial, since it gives the hypervisor the chance to emulate important data structures and monitor the VM. Intel specifies all such VMM trap instructions in their manual. Since VM Exits are an inherent difference between virtualized and native executions, we use them as a way of detecting the presence of a VT-x hypervisor. While VT-x offers the possibility to disable traps for some instructions, Intel *enforces* VM Exits on a selected set of instructions in hardware. We also argue that in order to monitor the guest, the hypervisor has to use some kind of traps, which also gives additional space for evasion.

2.2 Translation Lookaside Buffer

One of the side effects of hypervisors that we will use targets the TLB, as outlined in the following. Modern operating systems use the concept of virtual memory to give each running process the impression of having a large contiguous space of memory, whereas in reality there is a mapping between virtual and physical memory in a non-contiguous manner. Resolving this mapping is called a *page walk*. Since a page walk can be costly, hardware developers introduced the TLB, which caches the mapping from virtual pages to physical pages. When a process accesses a virtual address v, it first checks if the virtual page of v is in the TLB. If it is, the physical address can be obtained from the TLB. Otherwise, the MMU needs to do a page walk and then caches the result in the TLB. Therefore, when accessing multiple addresses on the same page, it is likely that only the first access is slow relative to all subsequent accesses, as long as the TLB entry is not evicted in the meantime.

If we switch from a process p_1 to a process p_2 (context switch), the TLB will most likely contain invalid entries, since p_1 and p_2 have their own virtual memory and thus use different address space mappings. The simplest way to deal with this problem is to completely flush the TLB upon context switches. However, this strategy had severe performance penalties, as every VM Exit causes a context switch. To cope with this problem, Intel introduced a feature called VPID. With VPID enabled, the TLB entries are tagged with the ID of the virtual machine. As a consequence, when a virtual address is accessed, the MMU will only consider TLB entries which are tagged with the current VM's ID. Hence, there is no need to flush the TLB, resulting in better performance.

3   Threat Model

Throughout the remainder of this paper, we envision an adversary that has implemented an arbitrary program (e.g., malware) and tries to detect if this program is being executed in a virtualized environment. We aim to explore generic evasion attempts, i.e., those that (i) do not focus on particular analysis environments, but instead on inherent characteristics of such systems, (ii) an approach that is independent from the malicious payload that the adversary may aim to hide, and (iii) mechanisms that are not restricted to a certain operating system. All these requirements make our methods applicable to a wide set of programs, explicitly including typical malware targeting Windows or Linux.

Furthermore, we restrict ourselves to developing detection mechanisms that operate purely in user mode, i.e., unprivileged code that executes in ring 3. This assumption varies from existing approaches that aim to detect virtualization by using privileged instructions, such as reading the contents of the page tables or using nested virtualization. Approaches using privileged code (ring 0) are well known to be effective, but may raise suspicions to an analyst or even during auto-mated program analysis. In contrast, our assumption on user-mode execution is in line with the use case of in-the-wild malware, such as a myriad of banking trojans, droppers, clickbots, spambots, denial-of-service bots and even targeted malware—all of which typically run in user space. The most notable exceptions are malware families with a kernel-mode rootkit, which, however, could also use our proposed user-mode detection methods. For example, a user-space dropper could try to detect virtualization prior to installing further modules (such as kernel-mode rootkits), such that the second- or third-stage malware samples are not exposed to the analyst. In fact, this concept is common in the wild [15,26].

Finally, we assume that the actual target systems of an attacker, i.e., those that the attacker aims to infect, are *not* virtualized. While it is conceivable that an attacker may miss target systems that are indeed virtualized, widespread malware will still be successful in infecting the vast majority of native systems.

4   Timing-Based VT-x Detection

VT-x was invented with the goal to increase the performance as well as the transparency of virtualization. In this section, we aim to undermine that transparency by proposing three timing-based methods to detect virtualization.

4.1   Measuring Elapsed CPU Cycles

The first two proposed detection methods are based on a technique to accurately determine the execution time of machine code. To this end, we measure the number of CPU cycles that elapse when a piece of code is executed. To do so, we use the rdtsc instruction to read the CPU's time stamp counter (TSC), which is incremented every clock cycle. Upon execution of rdtsc, the edx register is loaded with the high-order 32 bits and eax holds the low-order 32 bits of the TSC. Reading the TSC before and after the machine code helps us to measure the number of cycles that have elapsed. We can thus execute rdtsc, save the TSC, execute the instructions to be measured, execute rdtsc again and subtract the saved TSC from the current TSC. To get more accurate results, we need to serialize the instruction stream to prevent out-of-order execution. We use the mfence instruction, which will serialize rdtsc with respect to load-from-memory *and* store-to-memory instructions.

This method over-approximates the execution time. This is a bias introduced by the measurement code, which also consumes CPU cycles. If necessary, to counteract this influence, we can measure the measuring overhead and subtract it from the measured time. To this end, we measure how long it takes to execute no code. We then subtract this overhead from subsequent measuring results to get a more realistic measurement of the actual clock cycles. We will use this technique for our implementation of a TLB-based VT detection that demands a higher measuring accuracy.

Finally, measurements may not be accurate due to context switches that occur during the measurement phase, in which another process would execute and implicitly increase the TSC. To tackle this problem, we repeatedly measure the same sequences of instructions, record the time of each execution, and then use the *minimum* of all measurements. Our assumption here is that at least one out of these many executions will not be clobbered by a context switch.

4.2   Method 1: Detecting VM Exit Overhead

Based on the timing measurements, we will now describe our first method to detect hardware virtualization. We follow the intuition that a VM Exit consumes CPU cycles. In particular, we leverage the fact that some CPU instructions provoke a VM Exit, which does *not* occur on native systems. The Intel manual specifies over 30 of such instructions, most of which are privileged and thus not usable in ring 3. Also, trapping of some instructions can be disabled during the VM setup phase. We will thus leverage cpuid, the only unprivileged instruction whose hypervisor traps cannot be disabled.

A naïve approach to detect VT-x would be to measure the execution time of a `cpuid` instruction and determine a threshold above which VT-x is detected. The threshold could be determined by comparing the execution time on native and virtualized systems. Whenever executing `cpuid` is below this threshold, the environment is believed to be native, and virtualized otherwise. However, this simple measurement suffers from the inaccuracy that the absolute execution time of instructions varies per CPU type, and it is thus not trivial to determine a reasonable absolute threshold. Instead, we follow the intuition that two different instructions execute similarly slower or faster on a different CPU model. We thus propose to compare the execution time of `cpuid` with the execution time of another instruction in terms of a ratio.

We proceed as follows: We measure both `cpuid` and a baseline instruction i times, compute the ratio and check if the ratio is larger than some threshold α. We chose `nop` as the baseline instruction, but found that other fast instructions are equally suitable (e.g., we experimented with `add`, `lea`, and `sub`). Given the short execution time of the baseline instruction, the measurement overhead dominates our measurements (as described in Sect. 4.1). Still, the execution time of `cpuid` is significantly higher than the baseline instruction. Thus, we decided not to deduct the overhead. To account for context switches, we compare these two minima and return true if the ratio r exceeds our threshold α, which will be determined in Sect. 5.

4.3   Method 2: Detecting TLB Evictions

The first method is susceptible to hypervisors that manipulate the TSC value. For example, upon each `cpuid` trap, the hypervisor can deduct the time that it spent in the exit handler from the value returned to `rdtsc`, which effectively evades our first detection method. We will now describe a second method, which does not fall for this evasion. Our second idea is again to detect whether the hypervisor was invoked, though this time by inspecting cache evictions in the TLB.

The idea behind our detection is to identify TLB entry evictions that were caused by VM Exits. The intuition is that the hypervisor needs to execute code and has to access data (e.g., the VM Exit reason), all of which requires memory translations. The CPU will cache these memory translations in the TLB. This inevitably changes the TLB, which we aim to detect. To this end, we allocate fresh memory pages and access them, e.g., using a read operation. This precaches the pages to the TLB. We then iterate twice over the pages and measure the time to access the pages. However, in the second iteration, prior to reading, we execute a `cpuid`. This will trigger a VM Exit, causing a context switch, evicting entries of the pre-filled TLB. In such a case, we can measure a notable difference in access times when revisiting the evicted page.

The details of the detection are as follows: After allocating n pages, we access all pages once to fill the TLB. We access a page by writing a 4-byte value to the start of the page. We then access all pages again i times, and for each iteration we record the maximum access time. Out of those maxima we then compute the minimum. The intuition behind this is that we want to find the minimum time that it took for the slowest of all n page accesses. Using the minimum also eliminates outliers. In addition, compared to similar measures like the median, computing the minimum has a relatively small assembly code size and a lower computational complexity. Then, we repeat this step, but execute cpuid before each memory access. To set up equivalent conditions, we also access each page once before entering the second outer loop. Finally, the ratio of both minima t_0 and t_1 is computed and compared against a threshold β. Again, we refer the reader to the evaluation for choosing the detection threshold.

A few implementation details require attention. First, after accessing a page, we use the clflush instruction to invalidate the corresponding cache lines from all levels of the processor cache. Doing so makes it more likely that timing discrepancies actually stem from the TLB (and not from other types of caches). Second, when we measure the page access time, we subtract the overhead of the measuring method. We do this since the difference in access time for TLB misses tends to be rather small and the influence of measurement overhead would thus be too high otherwise.

Finally, we need to know how many pages we should allocate. The difficulty here is that we have to prefill approximately as many pages as will fit in the TLB. On the one hand, we need enough pages to fill the TLB and to guarantee that the hypervisor evicts our TLB entries. On the other hand, choosing too many pages will itself cause TLB evictions in all loops, regardless of cpuid, and therefore undermine our detection. However, the exact number of pages is unpredictable and depends heavily on the TLB size and its page eviction strategy. To counter this problem, we will perform the detection multiple times with various page numbers and consider a system to be running VT-x if at least one detection finds a suspicious ratio. That is, we chose to run the algorithm for $n = 64, 128, \ldots, 4096$ pages, which covers typical TLB sizes.

4.4   Method 3: Stealth VM Exit Detection

The two aforementioned methods have the drawback that they make excessive use of two instructions (cpuid and rdtsc) that may not be as common in benign user-mode programs. This may raise suspicion in the analysis system, automatically flagging the program as malicious. Therefore, we advance the current state of research by studying *stealth* timing-based mechanisms, i.e., ones that do not use suspicious instructions. To this end, we (i) have to avoid excessive use of cpuid to trap the hypervisor, and (ii) require a reliable but less suspicious and non-modifiable source for timing information.

To invoke the hypervisor, we first inspected less suspicious alternatives to cpuid. However, the alternatives are either privileged or their VMM traps are optional. Thus, we explore detection methods that *conservatively* use cpuid. Note that cpuid is not suspicious *per se*. However, calling cpuid thousands of times—as done in our first two methods—may seem suspicious. As we will show, our discovered method will not trigger more than 3–4 cpuid calls on virtualized systems, which makes this behavior indistinguishable from benign usage.

Replacing the timing source (`rdtsc`) is trickier, as reliable and accurate timing sources are scarce and only accessible with privileged instructions. To measure the duration of a `cpuid` instruction, we therefore leverage parallel computation. Technically, we create a program which spawns a thread B in its main thread A. B continuously executes `cpuid` and increments a counter c after each execution. After spawning B, A performs a busy wait until it notices that B has started by examining c. After that, we wait a small amount of time by executing a short busy loop after which we can inspect c. We determine that the system is virtualized if the counter is smaller or equal than some threshold γ, following the intuition that more `cpuid` executions fit in the time window on a native system without context switches to they hypervisor. We will see in Sect. 5 that the number of `cpuid` instructions being executed will be fairly low for virtualized systems, which greatly contributes to the stealthiness of the detection.

5   Evaluation

5.1   Local Experiments

The accuracy of our VT-x detection methods greatly depends on reasonable detection thresholds. To determine the thresholds, we conducted the following experiment: We created a tool that measures the ratio of the execution time of `cpuid` to the execution time of `nop`. In addition, we measured the ratio of page accesses as described. To account for different TLB sizes and eviction strategies, we measured this ratio for $n = 64, 128, 256, \ldots, 4096$ pages, where we use the maximum of those ratios as the final ratio to on which base the detection. We measure the access time of `nop` and `cpuid` 1000 times and take the minimum, and the page accesses are measured 500 times for each page size. Finally, we also measure the number of times `cpuid` was executed during the busy loop of method 3. To create realistic conditions, we executed the tool 100 times each on ten native Windows/Linux systems. The systems used nine distinct CPUs. In addition, we executed the tool in 5 different Windows/Linux VMs using various hypervisors running on Windows, Mac OS and Linux.

Method 1: VM Exit Overhead (M1). Figure 1a shows the `cpuid`/`nop` ratio. The x-axis shows the hosts and the y-axis the distribution of the ratios in a boxplot. The boxes show the 25–75 % intervals, the whiskers indicate 10–90 % intervals. For nine out of the ten native hosts (n0–n9), the ratio is between 2 and 4. Host n4 is an outlier, with its ratio being constantly about 6.7. Hosts 11–15 represent VMs (v0–v4). The majority of the ratios of the VMs are significantly larger than the ratios of the native hosts. There is quite some variation among the different VMs. This can mainly be attributed to the hypervisor. For example, VMs 1 and 2 were running on the same physical machine; VM 1 was using VMware, whereas VM 2 was using VirtualBox. Given those results, we choose the threshold $\alpha = 9$ as indicated by the horizontal dashed line in the figure. Everything above this line indicates a VM, whereas everything below this line is

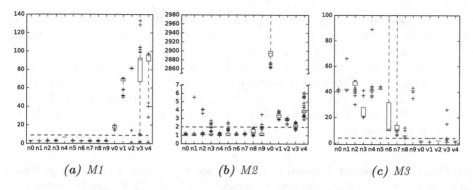

(a) M1   *(b) M2*   *(c) M3*

Fig. 1. Boxplots of the local experiments. Hosts n0–n9 are native; hosts v0–v4 are virtualized. The horizontal lines show the detection threshold that we derived from these local experiments: $\alpha = 9$ (left), $\beta = 2$ (center) and $\gamma = 4$ (right).

determined to be a native machine. We chose the threshold to tune the detection rates of the local experiment towards a low false positive rate: Out of the total of 1000 runs of the tool on the 10 native systems, we detect all systems as native systems, which gives us a true negative (TN) rate of 100 % and thus a false positive (FP) rate of 0 %. The executions on the VMs resulted in 17 ratios being below 9, which implies a true positive (TP) rate of 96.6 % and a false negative (FN) rate of 3.4 %. An adversary may adapt the detection thresholds depending on her goal. In particular, it is reasonable for an attacker to trade off false positives for false negatives, since losing a single victim is less critical than having the malware exposed in an analysis environment.

Method 2: TLB Eviction Overhead (M2). Figure 1b shows the computed ratios of the TLB-based measurements. As we can see, page accesses are more prone to variance than the previous measurements. This can be explained by the fact that the time window in which context switches would bias the measurement is significantly longer for the second method. While in the first method a context switch is only critical during the `cpuid` measurements, the second method assumes that the process is not interrupted during the entire measurement period, as otherwise the cached TLB entries would be overwritten (even on native systems). We will discuss how the system load may influence the measurements in Sect. 6. That being said, we see that for native hosts the median of the ratios is still about 1 and the majority of the ratios is in the range [0.9, 2].

Similar to the previous results, we can again see a clear difference between native and virtual machines, although the effect is smaller this time. This is caused by the fact that a TLB miss is rather cheap compared to a context switch caused by a VM Exit. VM v0 is an outlier, with the ratio being constantly larger than 2600. We suspect that this is caused by some VMware artifact, as the ratios of the other hypervisors are three orders of magnitude smaller. Using these results, we set the threshold $\beta = 2$ for M2. That is, out of the 1000 native runs we misclassify 17 runs, resulting in a TN rate of 98.3 % and thus a FP rate of 1.7 %. On the VMs, we detect 24 out of 500 runs as native, which results in a TP rate of 95.2 % and a FN rate of 4.8 %.

Finally, the attacker could combine both of the above methods and determine that a system is virtualized if at least one of the methods says so. By doing this, we would misclassify only 3 out of 500 virtualized executions, decreasing the FN rate to 0.6 %. Note that this would not change the FP rate, as only the TLB detection produced FPs.

Method 3: Counting Thread (M3). Finally, we evaluate our stealth method M3 separately from the non-stealth methods M1 and M2. Figure 1c shows the results of the thread counting measurements, where the y-axis indicates how often `cpuid` was executed. We can observe that the counter is much larger for the native hosts as the `cpuid` instruction is faster in that case. In contrast, the virtual hosts execute `cpuid` only a few times due to the significant overhead caused by the VM Exit. Using the gathered results, we determine the threshold $\gamma = 4$ as indicated by the horizontal line. Everything above this line is considered a native system and everything below it is detected as a virtualized system. This yields a TN rate of 99.9 % (n8 fails the test once) and a TP rate of 99.2 % (v3 fails this test 4 times).

5.2   Evasion Detection

Although the ratios of methods M1 and M2 work quite well in a normal setting, they may be biased if virtualized sandboxes hide timing artifacts to evade VM detection methods. For example, a hypervisor could trap `rdtsc` and set the TSC to a constant c before returning to the guest. The ratio for both M1 and M2 would then always be 1, which hides the hypervisor from our detection methods. To detect such anti-detection methods, we add sanity checks on top of our detection. In the following, we will describe four sanity checks, which we will use throughout the remainder of the evaluation for the `rdtsc`-based methods. The thresholds of these sanity checks were derived from the absolute values gathered from our local experiment in Sect. 5.1.

Measuring Overhead: First, we execute the measuring method without any instructions to get the measuring overhead. We will use these results to detect costly `rdtsc` traps. The measurements showed that `rdtsc` never takes more than 100 cycles to execute (including the overhead introduced by `mfence` and moving the TSC into a temporary register). To account for variance, we relax this threshold and say that the system is virtualized if executing `rdtsc` takes 500 or more cycles.

Execution Time of `cpuid`: Second, we inspect the absolute execution time of `cpuid` to get a lower bound in order to detect if a hypervisor returns suspiciously low values. Given the results of the measurements, we determine that a hypervisor tampers with the TSC if executing `cpuid` takes less than 20 cycles.

Execution Time of nop: Third, we verify if a hypervisor returns suspiciously high values for the execution time of a nop instruction. Given the results, we determine that a system is virtualized if executing a nop instruction takes 500 or more cycles.

TLB Delta: Fourth, the execution time overhead introduced by a TLB miss tends to be rather small compared to the time of a cached page access. The ratio is thus sometimes not sufficient to detect a hypervisor, especially if both values are rather large. To tackle this problem, we additionally inspect the absolute difference between t_0 and t_1 in M2. We say that a system is virtualized if $r \geq \beta$, or if $t_0 - t_1 \geq 150$, a carefully chosen threshold. We observed that only five runs resulted in a difference larger than 150. However, in those runs the ratio was above 2, which means that we will not change the results for the local experiments by including the TLB delta in the detection. Compared to the previous three thresholds, this one was chosen rather aggressively. We did this, since the previous parameters are used only to detect trivial anti-detection methods and for this purpose a conservatively chosen threshold is sufficient. However, in the case of TLB-based detection the window for optimization gets quite narrow, which is why we chose a more aggressive optimization. We refer to this optimized method as M2'.

5.3   PlanetLab

We then deployed our detection on a wider variety of systems. To this end, we identified 239 stable nodes in the PlanetLab [3] testbed. To check if a PlanetLab node is virtualized, we verified if the hypervisor bit returned by cpuid (with leaf 1) is set. Although a stealthy hypervisor does not have to set this bit, we find it unlikely that stealthy hypervisors are present in PlanetLab. We found that 233 of the 239 nodes are native and six are virtualized. On all hosts, we performed our detection methods 10000 times each, with $\alpha = 9$, $\beta = 2$, $\gamma = 4$ and $i = 1000$.

M1 We detected 232 out of the 233 non-virtualized nodes as native systems with 100 % confidence. On the remaining native node, 3 out of the 10000 runs misclassified the node as virtualized. Overall, this gives us a true negative rate of 99.99 %. All of the six virtualized nodes were correctly classified as virtualized with 100 % confidence, which gives us a true positive rate of 100 %.

M2 We detected the non-virtualized nodes as native systems with an overall true negative rate of 99.96 %. However, the detection rate for 7 out of those 232 nodes was below 99 % and as low as 73.1 % for one node. We suspect that this is due to high system load, since concurrent memory accesses cause TLB evictions, which does not favor M2. Out of the six virtualized nodes, we detected 3 nodes with 100 % confidence and failed to detect the remaining three virtualized nodes. We discovered that this is because our detection assumes a page size of 4 KiB, which was not true for the PlanetLab nodes in question as they are using the Page Size Extension feature of x86, which allows for pages larger than the traditional 4

KiB limit for performance reasons. This is not a restriction for an adversary in practice, since huge pages are not enabled by default in Windows user space. While huge pages are used by recent Windows kernels, enabling huge pages in user-space processes on Windows requires the "lock pages in memory" privilege.

M3 For M3, we had to use a different set of 185 stable nodes in the PlanetLab testbed, since the nodes of the first two methods were not available any longer when the experiments for the third method was conducted. Out of those nodes, 182 were native and 3 nodes were virtualized. We detected both the virtualized and the native systems with a confidence of 100 % giving us a true positive and a true negative rate of 100 % each.

5.4 Sandboxes

So far we have only tested our methods in a controlled environment. In the following, we will apply our detection methods in real-world use cases that are relevant in practice: malware sandboxes. We thus uploaded the detection tool (cf. Sect. 5.1) to 17 malware analysis services, such as VirusTotal and ThreatExpert. Despite the fact that bare-metal sandboxes have been proposed [13,14], we argue that most automated sandboxes are virtualized to cope with the masses of user submissions. We thus assume that a sandbox uses VT-x, provided that the reported CPU brand string indicates a processor model which supports hardware-assisted virtualization.

To collect the detection results, we configured the tool to send the results to a server under our control. In total, we received 76 measurement reports. We did not have any influence on how often our sample was run per sandbox. Some of the sandboxes repeatedly executed the same sample, i.e., increasing the number of reports. In total, 74 of 76 reports indicated a processor model which supports VT-x. The remaining two reports came from the same sandbox and showed the CPU brand string "Intel(R) Atom(TM) CPU D525 @ 1.80 GHz". For this sandbox, none of our detection methods indicated the presence of a hypervisor. We group the remaining reports based on the host names of the analysis systems, which clusters these 74 reports into 31 sandboxes. For a detailed overview of the results, see Fig. 2.

We observe that method 1 detects 89.19 % of the sandboxes. The improvements for method 2 increased the detection rate from 14.86 % to 60.81 %. By combining method 1 and method 2—that is, we detect a system if M1 or M2 detects it—we can detect 90.54 % of the sandboxes. By combining M1 with the improved version of M2, we can improve again and get a detection rate of 95.95 %. This shows that the proposed methods work well in a real-world setting.

A few sandboxes remain undetected, which is where the sanity checks help. The sanity checks themselves have a rather low detection rate of 18.92 %. Worst, the `cpuid` sanity check has a detection rate of 0 %. But the `nop` and `rdstc` measures alone are also not very helpful. However, recall that the sanity checks are mainly relevant for systems that tamper with the TSC to evade detection. When used in combination with the proposed two methods, they significantly

Sandbox	M1	M2	M2'	M1+M2	M1+M2'	RDTSC	CPUID	NOP	S	S+M1+M2'
s_0	5/5	2/5	3/5	5/5	5/5	0/5	0/5	0/5	0/5	5/5
s_1	10/10	2/10	5/10	10/10	10/10	0/10	0/10	0/10	0/10	10/10
s_2	4/4	0/4	4/4	4/4	4/4	0/4	0/4	0/4	0/4	4/4
s_3	2/2	0/2	0/2	2/2	2/2	0/2	0/2	0/2	0/2	2/2
s_4	1/1	0/1	1/1	1/1	1/1	0/1	0/1	0/1	0/1	1/1
s_5	1/3	0/3	0/3	1/3	1/3	0/3	0/3	3/3	3/3	3/3
s_6	1/1	0/1	1/1	1/1	1/1	0/1	0/1	0/1	0/1	1/1
s_7	3/3	1/3	1/3	3/3	3/3	0/3	0/3	0/3	0/3	3/3
s_8	1/1	0/1	0/1	1/1	1/1	0/1	0/1	1/1	1/1	1/1
s_9	3/3	0/3	2/3	3/3	3/3	0/3	0/3	0/3	0/3	3/3
s_{10}	6/6	0/6	3/6	6/6	6/6	0/6	0/6	0/6	0/6	6/6
s_{11}	1/1	0/1	1/1	1/1	1/1	0/1	0/1	0/1	0/1	1/1
s_{12}	1/1	1/1	1/1	1/1	1/1	0/1	0/1	0/1	0/1	1/1
$s_{13} \ldots s_{17}$	3/5	0/5	3/5	3/5	4/5	4/5	0/5	4/5	4/5	5/5
s_{18}	6/6	0/6	4/6	6/6	6/6	0/6	0/6	0/6	0/6	6/6
s_{19}	3/3	0/3	1/3	3/3	3/3	0/3	0/3	0/3	0/3	3/3
s_{20}	1/1	1/1	1/1	1/1	1/1	0/1	0/1	1/1	1/1	1/1
s_{21}	3/3	0/3	1/3	3/3	3/3	0/3	0/3	0/3	0/3	3/3
s_{22}	1/1	0/1	1/1	1/1	1/1	0/1	0/1	0/1	0/1	1/1
s_{23}	2/2	2/2	2/2	2/2	2/2	0/2	0/2	0/2	0/2	2/2
s_{24}	0/2	1/2	2/2	1/2	2/2	2/2	0/2	2/2	2/2	2/2
s_{25}, s_{26}	2/2	0/2	1/2	2/2	2/2	0/2	2/2	2/2	2/2	2/2
s_{27}	1/1	1/1	1/1	1/1	1/1	0/1	0/1	0/1	0/1	1/1
s_{28}	1/3	0/3	3/3	1/3	3/3	3/3	0/3	3/3	3/3	3/3
s_{29}	3/3	0/3	3/3	3/3	3/3	0/3	0/3	0/3	0/3	3/3
s_{30}	1/1	0/1	0/1	1/1	1/1	0/1	0/1	0/1	0/1	1/1
	66/74	11/74	45/74	67/74	71/74	9/74	0/74	14/74	14/74	74/74
	89.19%	14.86%	60.81%	90.54%	95.95%	12.16%	0.00%	18.92%	18.92%	100.00%

Fig. 2. Detection results per sandbox (1st major column) for both methods, the improved version of method 2 and their combinations (2nd major column), the sanity checks (3rd major column) and the overall combination (4th major column). Sandboxes $s_{13}, \ldots, s_{17}$ and s_{25}, s_{26} are aggregated due to similar hostnames

improve the detection rate. By combining the sanity checks with M1 and the improved version of method 2, we can detect all 74 hosts, resulting in a true positive rate of 100 %.

As the observed sandboxes are single-core VMs, there was no possibility to evaluate M3 using this dataset. Instead, we successfully detected these hosts as single-core systems using a simple load detection. In short, the load detection method leverages the fact that the OS cannot schedule two threads in parallel on single-core systems (or on systems with a high load). The load detection method thus schedules two threads in parallel and measures how many rescheduling events occur in a given time span. Rescheduling is an indicator for (i) high load or (ii) a single-core system. Although only allowing multi-core systems seems to restrictive at first, it is worth noting that this is also done by malware in practice to avoid sandboxes. For example, the popular banking trojan Dyre shows its real behavior only if executed on multi-core systems.

In conclusion, with high reliability, we could detect the virtualization in sandboxes using our timing-based methods. This demonstrates how a malware author may use similar techniques to hide the actual behavior of the malware.

5.5 Stealth Sandbox

Seeing our success in identifying sandboxes, we now test whether cutting-edge commercial sandboxes can evade our detection. We contacted a popular vendor that advertises their sandbox technology as being evasion-resistant. The sandbox is based on VT-x and implements a thin hypervisor. The vendor graciously allowed us to run our detection sample in their latest development version of the sandbox. We supplied the same tool to the system as for the other experiments.

In the first experiment, we managed to detect the presence of a hypervisor with M1 and M2'. We then interacted with the vendor and explained our detection methodologies. It turns out that their anti-evasion tricks mainly focused on removing system artifacts, and did not yet counter timing attacks. The vendor then implemented a countermeasure to tackle timing-based detection. Technically, the improved hypervisor measures its own execution time and then subtracts its overhead from the actual TSC. VT-x features the TSC_OFFSET parameter so that the hypervisor can adjust the TSC accordingly—an anti-evasion technique that was mentioned by Dinaburg et al. [5].

We then re-ran our experiment on the updated sandbox. This time, the timing-based detection failed to detect VT-x. In fact, the measured ratios in M1 looked quite similar to the ones measured on native systems, rendering M1 ineffective. However, M2' could still identify the virtualization. This is also intuitive, as the anti-evasion technique does not take into account overhead caused by caching. M2' does not measure the time spent in the hypervisor, but instead measures caching side effects of context switches.

Similar to the public sandboxes, the commercial sandbox can also be detected using M3 in combination with the load detection mechanism, as the sandbox operates on a single-core system. In fact, our load check is more reliable and cannot easily be fooled, unlike to existing methods such as reading the number of cores using the Windows PEB. Thus it presents a generic detection method for single-core systems.

5.6 ShellOS

```
push MAGIC
; is_vm := vm_detect()
if (not is_vm)
    pop edx
mov esi, [fs:edx+0x30-MAGIC]
...
```

Fig. 3. ShellOS evasion.

Finally, we turn to systems that aim to detect potential shellcode in arbitrary code. Snow et al. proposed ShellOS [29], a VT-x-based framework that deploys heuristics to detect shellcode. ShellOS uses a small kernel coupled with hardware-assisted virtualization by using the KVM hypervisor to detect and analyze shellcode.

To this end, ShellOS uses the heuristic proposed by Polychronakis et al. [23], monitoring and detecting accesses to the Windows PEB. We will evaluate whether we can combine our VT-x detection with an evasion for ShellOS. Our goal is to convert a shellcode that ShellOS flags as malicious to one that is not detected. The obvious idea in the form of if (vm) {benign} else {shellcode} will, however, not work, since ShellOS uses the concept of *execution chains*. ShellOS will execute the payload from each possible offset and will therefore flag the payload as malicious if it starts executing from the shellcode offset. To understand how an adversary may overcome this problem, recall that Windows shellcode usually starts by reading the PEB with an instruction like mov esi, [fs:edx+030] where edx is set to zero beforehand. The malicious behavior of all the following instructions depends on this first instruction, which in turn depends on the content of one register (edx in the example). Using this insight, we can evade ShellOS's execution chains with the idea illustrated in Fig. 3. We push some magic random number MAGIC > 0 on the stack, and only if the detection indicates the presence of a native system, we pop this magic number into edx. We then use this magic number in the calculation of the PEB in the first instruction of the shellcode. If ShellOS executes the code from any offset other than the actual start, the edx register will not contain the right value to correctly calculate the PEB offset. If ShellOS starts executing from the actual start, our detection will detect VT-x and the code will not be flagged as malicious, since the PEB will not be calculated correctly in this case either.

We injected the VM Exit-based detection method (M1) into the template in Fig. 3 with parameters $i = 20$ and $\alpha = 9$. We reduced the number of iterations to 20, since ShellOS imposes timeout limits on the payloads to be executed. We injected several shellcodes with our detection methods, but we intentionally left out the determining ratio check to provoke malicious behavior. All those shellcodes were flagged as malicious by ShellOS. After including the ratio check, ShellOS failed to detect the modified shellcodes, while the same payloads were properly executed on native systems.

We did the same for TLB-based detection (M2). Unfortunately, ShellOS responded with errors and the debug traces indicated that something went wrong. The ShellOS authors could not resolve the problem in the time available, which is why we cannot evaluate TLB-based detection for this use case. Since ShellOS does not support threading, we unfortunately could not evaluate M3 on ShellOS.

6   Discussion

In this section we discuss several aspects of our proposed methods, including countermeasures, limitations when facing target systems that are virtualized, other virtualization methods than VT-x and finally how an adversary can use our methods to defeat multi-path exploration techniques.

6.1   Countermeasures

Our detection methods are based on timing differences introduced by VM Exits. To evade detection, the hypervisor may tamper with the time-stamp counter (TSC) or avoid VM Exits. We first discuss techniques that aim to evade detection. In addition, we describe a technique for how our detection methods themselves can be detected at the hypervisor level.

Tampering with Timing Resources. In principle, the hypervisor has complete control of the timing resources. The hypervisor could disable `rdtsc` for use in ring 3, subtract the VM Exit overhead or try to return sane estimated values. Disabling the instruction is not a beneficial option, since the usage of `rdtsc` is not malicious *per se*. Subtracting the VM Exit overhead works for protecting against M1 as described in Sect. 5.5. It will, however, fail for the TLB based detection method M2, for reasons described in the same section. Estimating sane return values is not feasible in practice as it requires complete knowledge about the emulated hardware.

Not Trapping `cpuid`. Our detection methods rely on `cpuid` to trigger VM Exits. Disabling these exits by the hypervisor would thus evade detection. However, according to the Intel manuals, the VM Exit caused by `cpuid` cannot be disabled by the hypervisor. Therefore, a potential hardware-based solution could be to make traps to `cpuid` optional. But even then it would be likely that other timing biases remain, as hypervisors may need to trap on system calls or page faults to inspect host-based behavior.

Detecting Suspicious Timing-Based Evasion. Instead of evading our methods, the hypervisor can just try to *detect* them. This is useful for sandboxes that just aim to find suspicious programs, rather than exploring their behavioral profile. Our first two methods can be detected by the hypervisor due to the excessive use of `rdtsc` and `cpuid`. If encountered too often, the program is at least suspicious. However, this is no help to sandboxes that not only flag a program as malicious, but also aim to reveal program behavior. Finally, as we have shown, an attacker can even avoid excessive use of suspicious instructions by using counter-based as opposed to timing-based detection.

6.2   Virtualization on Target Systems

The main use case of our methods is attacks that aim to evade virtualized analysis systems, such as sandboxes or other types of code analysis systems (like ShelIOS). Such evasions are effective if we assume that the actual target systems (the victims) are *not* virtualized. However, research has suggested that virtualization will become more widespread in the future [2,9,32].

We argue that VM detection will still play an important role in the future. First, when looking at consumer devices, the degree of virtualization is negligible. Thus mass-targeting malware (such as ransomware, spambots, denial-of-service bots, or banking trojans) does not risk losing many potential victims by declining to run on VMs, while it can hide its behavior in virtualized sandboxes.

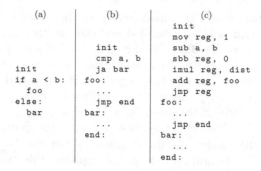

Fig. 4. Overcoming multiple execution paths.

In addition, even in targeted attacks, an adversary may be able to first spy on the exact environment, including the virtualization technology (if any), and then adapt her attack accordingly.

6.3   Multi-Path Exploration

Facing the problem of evasion, researchers proposed new techniques to analyze the hidden behavior of evasive malware. A generic approach to counter evasive behavior is exploring *multiple execution paths* (or multi-path exploration), as introduced by Moser et al. [17]. The idea is to explore all input-driven parts of the program to trigger behavior that may otherwise remain hidden. For instance, assume program (a) in Fig. 4, which first initializes, then does a check, and if the check succeeds, executes foo, or bar otherwise. Using multiple execution paths, we can explore all possible executions of the program, namely init→foo and init→bar, regardless of the values of a and b.

Kolbitsch et al. [16] proposed to identify and escape execution-stalling code during dynamic analysis. Their idea is to invert conditional branches once they are detected as such, e.g., turn a *greater-than* operation to a *less-or-equal*, with the goal to eventually explore all code regions. Related to this, Egele et al. [7] proposed *Blanket Execution*, a technique to cover all instructions within a function at least once during dynamic analysis [7]. In addition, the commercial sandbox vendor VMray has announced a technique to trigger dormant program functionality by inverting branch conditions, leveraging the history of recent branches in the Processor Tracing history of recent Intel CPUs[1]. All these techniques aim to explore the entire functionality of a program or its functions.

We can overcome these approaches by converting conditional branches to indirect jumps/calls. Doing so removes the outgoing edge of the source basic blocks, as the address of the target basic block is computed dynamically. For example, consider the assembly representation of program (a) in Fig. 4(b). Multi-path execution would identify the conditional jump ja bar as a control flow

---

[1] http://www.vmray.com/back-to-the-past-using-intels-processor-trace-for-enhanced-analysis/.

decision provided that a or b is considered interesting. As a consequence, both possible execution paths will be identified and executed regardless of the actual values of a and b. Now let dist be the distance between foo and bar and consider program (c). If a is smaller than b, then the sub a, b instruction will set the carry flag. Hence, the register reg will contain the address of foo and therefore the program will jump to foo. Conversely, if $a \geq b$, reg will hold the address of bar to which the program will jump. Programs (b) and (c) are thus semantically equivalent. However, in (c), one cannot identify the branching alternatives, since the conditional direct jump ja bar has been replaced with the unconditional direct jump jmp reg. By applying this transformation, an attacker can undermine multi-path execution to hide the malicious behavior of the program.

6.4   Non-Intel Virtualization

In this paper we have limited our analysis to Intel VT-x. We have shown that VT-x is the dominating virtualization technique used by sandboxes. In future work, we investigate whether our results are also applicable to other virtualization techniques, such as AMD-V. Due to the inherent timing artifacts introduced by the hypervisor, it is likely that the same concepts also apply to AMD-V. However, AMD-V enables the hypervisor to *disable* the cpuid trap, which is a notable difference between the two virtualization solutions. Therefore, AMD-V represents a stealthier alternative to VT-x. However, the presence of traps is inherent to the concept of sandbox monitoring, which likely introduces detection vectors other than cpuid traps.

7   Related Work

7.1   Virtualization Detection

In 2006, Ferrie [8] was one of the first to evaluate the transparency of software emulators, reduced privileged guests and hardware-assisted virtualization. Ferrie found bugs in the software emulators Hydra, Bochs and QEMU, which could be used to detect their presence. For reduced-privilege guests of the time, such as VMware, Virtual PC and Parallels, Ferrie found several artifacts. Ferrie concluded that reduced privilege guests cannot hide their presence, as their design does not allow them to intercept non-sensitive instructions, which will always imply detectable behavior.

Ferrie also mentioned timing-based attacks to detect hardware-assisted virtualization [8], such as measuring the overhead caused by VM Exits or considering a TLB-based attack. However, despite giving the general idea, he did not describe technical challenges, nor demonstrate or evaluate the methods. Research similar to Ferrie's work was conducted by Paleari et al. [20] in 2009 and by Raffetseder et al. [24] in 2007 to detect software emulators by exploiting implementation bugs. Raffetseder et al. additionally examined VT-x and observed that it is not possible to disable caching in a virtualized environment. We were inspired by these initial ideas, but are the first to go into detail and bring them to a realistic setting of user-mode code. In addition, we are the first to present a thorough evaluation of timing-based attacks to detect hardware-assisted virtualization in real-world use cases. Third, we also proposed a stealth method that is much harder to detect than existing approaches. Finally, we have demonstrated the risk that adversaries may combine the detection mechanisms to evade multi-path exploration systems.

In 2006, Rutkowska proposed a rootkit based on hardware-assisted virtualization called *Blue Pill*[2]. Blue Pill is a thin hypervisor which will virtualize the existing OS once started. By doing so, the hypervisor (and therefore the attacker) gains full control over the OS. Blue Pill can be detected in the same way any VM can be detected by using our methods. Garfinkel et al. [10] proposed a TLB-based solution without using timing resources to detect such rootkits by manipulating the page table entries. Manipulating those entries is, however, not possible in user mode and therefore outside of the range of our threat model where malware usually operates.

7.2 Sandboxes and Evasion

In addition to the discussed VM detection methods, others have documented the problem of evasive malware through real-world studies. Chen et al. [2] were the first to study the behavior of malware that tries to detect VMs. They ran 6900 different malware samples under different environments and noted that 4 % of the samples reduced their malicious behavior in the presence of a VM.

Balzarotti et al. [1] propose a system that records the system call trace of a program when it is executed on a non-virtualized reference system. This trace is then compared against the trace of the same program being executed on a virtualized system, revealing possibly split behavior of the malware. Lindorfer et al. [16] describe a similar system and additionally introduce techniques for distinguishing between spurious differences in behavior and actual environment-sensitive behavior to cope with false positives.

The phenomenon of environment-aware malware forced sandbox maintainers and researchers to develop more transparent systems which are harder to detect. Dinaburg et al. proposed Ether [5], a malware analysis system using hardware-assisted virtualization which aims at remaining transparent to malicious software. Ether tries to maintain a clear time-stamp counter, as discussed in Sect. 6. However, Ether is still prone to TLB-based detection methods, which the authors of Ether classify as "architectural limitations" of VT-x. Additionally, Pék et al. presented a detection method for Ether [22]. Their method builds upon the observation that between two `rdtsc` instructions, Ether tends to increase the TSC by only 1 as long as there are no trapping instructions in between. This is an implementation-specific artifact that is not necessarily shared by other sandboxes.

---

[2] http://theinvisiblethings.blogspot.com/2006/06/introducing-blue-pill.html.

To cope with the fundamental difficulties of creating a truly transparent hypervisor, Kirat et al. have suggested using bare-metal sandboxes [13,14]. Although bare-metal sandboxes can evade VM-based detection mechanisms, they are less scalable and harder to maintain than virtualized sandboxes. Alternatively, Moser et al. proposed multi-path exploration systems [17]. We have shown that adversaries can evade those systems and render them ineffective. The same holds for the brute force mechanism deployed by ShellOS [29], which simply aims to execute shellcode from every possible offset.

8   Conclusion

We have shown that hardware-assisted virtualization can be reliably detected by an adversary using timing-based measures. Unfortunately, not all of these methods can be detected as such, nor is there an effective and transparent way to evade all of them. This threatens important virtualized security infrastructures, such as malware sandboxes and state-of-the-art shellcode detection systems. Our attacks against multi-path exploration systems demonstrated that there is a need for further research to restore the guarantees that the full (possibly hidden) behavior of malicious code can be revealed with dynamic code analysis.

References

1. Balzarotti, D., Cova, M., Karlberger, C., Kruegel, C., Kirda, E., Vigna, G.: Efficient detection of split personalities in malware. In: Proceedings of NDSS (2010)
2. Chen, X., Andersen, J., Morley, M.Z., Bailey, M., Nazario, J.: Towards an understanding of anti-virtualization and anti-debugging behavior in modern malware. In: DSN (2008)
3. Chun, B., Culler, D., Roscoe, T., Bavier, A., Peterson, L., Wawrzoniak, M., Bowman, M.: PlanetLab: an overlay testbed for broad-coverage services. SIGC OMM Comput. Commun. Rev. 33(3), 3–12 (2003)
4. Coogan, K., Lu, G., Debray, S.: Deobfuscation of virtualization-obfuscated software: a semantics-based approach. In: Proceedings of the CCS (2011)
5. Dinaburg, A., Royal, P., Sharif, M., Lee, W.: Ether: malware analysis via hardware virtualization extensions. In: CCS (2008)
6. Egele, M., Scholte, T., Kirda, E., Kruegel, C.: A survey on automated dynamic malware-analysis techniques and tools. ACM Comput. Surv. 44(2), 6:1–6:42 (2012)
7. Egele, M., Woo, M., Chapman, P., Brumley, D.: Blanket execution: dynamic similarity testing for program binaries and components. In: USENIX Security (2014)
8. Ferrie, P.: Attacks on Virtual Machine Emulators. Technical report, Symantec (2006)
9. Franklin, J., Luk, M., McCune, J.M., Seshadri, A., Perrig, A., van Doorn, L.: Towards sound detection of virtual machines. In: Lee, W., Wang, C., Dagon, D. (eds.) Botnet Detection: Countering the Largest Security Threat, pp. 89–116. Springer, Heidelberg (2008)
10. Garfinkel, T., Adams, K., Warfield, A., Franklin, J.: Compatibility is not transparency: VMM detection myths and realities. In: Proceedings of USENIX HotOS (2007)

11. Kang, M.G., Poosankam, P., Yin, H.: Renovo: a hidden code extractor for packed executables. In: Proceedings of the 2007 ACM Workshop on Recurring Malcode (2007)
12. Kinder, J.: Towards static analysis of virtualization-obfuscated binaries. In: WCRE (2012)
13. Kirat, D., Vigna, G., Kruegel, C.: BareBox: efficient malware analysis on bare-metal. In: Proceedings of ACSAC (2011)
14. Kirat, D., Vigna, G., Kruegel, C.: Barecloud: bare-metal analysis-based evasive malware detection. In: Proceedings of the USENIX Security (2014)
15. Kwon, B.J., Mondal, J., Jang, J., Bilge, L., Dumitras, T.: The dropper effect: insights into malware distribution with downloader graph analytics. In: CCS (2015)
16. Lindorfer, M., Kolbitsch, C., Milani Comparetti, P.: Detecting environment-sensitive malware. In: Sommer, R., Balzarotti, D., Maier, G. (eds.) RAID 2011. LNCS, vol. 6961, pp. 338–357. Springer, Heidelberg (2011)
17. Moser, A., Kruegel, C., Kirda, E.: Exploring multiple execution paths for malware analysis. In: Proceedings of the S&P (2007)
18. Moser, A., Kruegel, C., Kirda, E.: Limits of static analysis for malware detection. In: Proceedings of ACSAC (2007)
19. Oktavianto, D., Muhardianto, I.: Cuckoo Malware Analysis. Packt Publishing, Birmingham (2013)
20. Paleari, R., Martignoni, L., Roglia, G.F., Bruschi, D.: A fistful of Red-pills: how to automatically generate procedures to detect CPU emulators. In: Usenix WOOT (2009)
21. Ugarte Pedrero, X., Balzarotti, D., Santos, I., Bringas, P.G.: SoK: deep packer inspection: a longitudinal study of the complexity of run-time packers. In: S&P (2015)
22. Pék, G., Bencsáth, B., Buttyán, L.: nEther: in-guest detection of out-of-the-guest malware analyzers. In: CCS (2011)
23. Polychronakis, M., Anagnostakis, K.G., Markatos, E.P.: Comprehensive shellcode detection using runtime heuristics. In: Proceedings of ACSAC (2010)
24. Raffetseder, T., Kruegel, C., Kirda, E.: Detecting system emulators. In: ICISC (2007)
25. Rolles, R.: Unpacking virtualization obfuscators. In: Usenix WOOT (2009)
26. Rossow, C., Dietrich, C., Bos, H.: Large-scale analysis of malware downloaders. In: Proceedings of DIMVA (2013)
27. Royal, P., Halpin, M., Dagon, D., Edmonds, R., Lee, W.: PolyUnpack: automating the hidden-code extraction of unpack-executing malware. In: CCS (2006)
28. Sharif, M., Lanzi, A., Giffin, J., Lee, W.: Automatic reverse engineering of malware emulators. In: Proceedings of the 2009 30th IEEE Symposium on Security and Privacy (2009)
29. Snow, K.Z., Krishnan, S., Monrose, F., Provos, N.: ShellOS: enabling fast detection and forensic analysis of code injection attacks. In: Proceedings of USENIX Security (2011)
30. Willems, C., Hund, R., Holz, T.: CXPInspector: Hypervisor-based, hardware-assisted system monitoring. Technical report, Horst Görtz Institute for IT Security (2012)
31. You, I., Yim, K.: Malware obfuscation techniques: a brief survey. In: Proceedings of BWCCA (2010)
32. Zhao, X., Borders, K., Prakash, A.: Virtual machine security systems. In: Advances in Computer Science and Engineering. Springer (2009)

Web Security

Financial Lower Bounds
of Online Advertising Abuse
A Four Year Case Study of the TDSS/TDL4 Botnet

Yizheng Chen[1]([⊠]), Panagiotis Kintis[1], Manos Antonakakis[2], Yacin Nadji[1],
David Dagon[1], Wenke Lee[1], and Michael Farrell[3]

[1] School of Computer Science, Georgia Institute of Technology, Atlanta, GA, USA
{yzchen,kintis,yacin}@gatech.edu, dagon@m.sudo.sh,
wenke.lee@cc.gatech.edu
[2] School of Electrical and Computer Engineering,
Georgia Institute of Technology, Atlanta, GA, USA
manos@gatech.edu
[3] Institute for Internet Security and Privacy,
Georgia Institute of Technology, Atlanta, GA, USA
michael.farrell@iisp.gatech.edu

Abstract. Online advertising is a complex on-line business, which has become the target of abuse. Recent charges filed from the United States Department of Justice against the operators of the DNSChanger botnet stated that the botnet operators stole approximately US $14 million [11,18] over two years. Using monetization tactics similar to DNSChanger, several large botnets (i.e., ZeroAccess and TDSS/TDL4) abuse the ad ecosystem at scale. In order to understand the depth of the financial abuse problem, we need methods that will enable us to passively study large botnets and estimate the lower bounds of their financial abuse. In this paper we present a system, A^2S, which is able to analyze one of the most complex, sophisticated, and long-lived botnets: TDSS/TDL4. Using passive datasets from a large Internet Service Provider in north America, we conservatively estimate lower bounds behind the financial abuse TDSS/TDL4 inflicted on the advertising ecosystem since 2010. Over its lifetime, less than 15 % of the botnet's victims caused *at least US$346 million* in damages to advertisers due to impression fraud. TDSS/TDL4 abuse translates to an average US$340 thousand loss per day to advertisers, which is three times the ZeroAccess botnet [27] and more than ten times the DNSChanger botnet [2] estimates of fraud.

1 Introduction

Many researchers have observed a shift in how botnets are monetized [33], away from traditional spam and bank fraud applications, towards advertising oriented abuse [5]. Large botnets such as Kelihos [25] and Asprox [1] have moved to monetization methods that abuse the online ad ecosystem. Unlike other types

© Springer International Publishing Switzerland 2016
J. Caballero et al. (Eds.): DIMVA 2016, LNCS 9721, pp. 231–254, 2016.
DOI: 10.1007/978-3-319-40667-1_12

of abuse, impression and click fraud are "low risk/high reward" for botmasters, given the inherent difficulty in attributing specific advertising events due to the complexity of the ad ecosystem [37].

To date, the evidence about the amount of ad-abuse attributed to modern botnets is sporadic, mainly because of measurement challenges. Studying the monetization components of botnets in a controlled environment (i.e., honeypots, dynamic malware analysis) requires researchers to *actively engage* in the abuse, which poses ethical challenges. In addition, dynamic malware analysis methods often fall short as botnets move their monetization components away from binaries [20, 36], and instead deliver them as separate, non-executable add-on modules. Such drawbacks point to the need for an efficient passive analysis system that can estimate the long-term *monetization campaign* separately from the traditional infection, command and control (C&C) and malware update methods.

To enable efficient, independent, and passive analysis of the long-term ad-abuse caused by botnets, we introduce a novel Ad-abuse Analysis System (A^2S). A^2S leverages spectral clustering methods on passive DNS datasets to identify the network infrastructure (domain names and IP addresses) the botnet under examination uses to perform ad-abuse. It also employs sinkhole datasets to estimate lower bounds of financial loss caused by the botnet's past DNS activities. This technique can estimate financial loss for any botnet where the monetization channel can be mapped to DNS requests. To demonstrate this we analyze a specific botnet's fiscal damage to the advertising world.

Using four years of network datasets, we use A^2S to estimate the scale of the ad-abuse potentially inflicted to advertisers from one of the most notorious botnets in history — TDSS/TDL4. Our conservative estimation shows that TDSS/TDL4 caused financial damage of *at least* US\$346 million, or US\$340 thousand per day. This estimate was made using less than 15 % of the botnet's population, which suggests that the global lower bound describing the financial damages towards the advertisers is likely to be higher.

While these numbers may appear large, they remain an underestimation of the true abuse due to the choices in our measurement methodology. We must emphasize that at every step of our analysis, we err on the side of being overly conservative, as we are interested in lower bounds. This will help us establish an as conservative of a lower bound as possible, using aggressive, empirically driven filtering and relying on the lowest possible estimates for constants used in our financial abuse calculation. We intentionally exclude highly likely TDSS/TDL4 domains in exchange for a safer lower bound estimate.

Our contributions in this paper include:

- An Ad-abuse Analysis System (A^2S) that enables researchers to independently and passively analyze the ad-abuse a botnet inflicts to advertisers. The goal of A^2S is to estimate lower bounds of the advertisers' financial loss caused by the botnet using data-driven approaches. With this knowledge, network operators, such as large ISPs, can design network policies to reduce both (1) the economic gains for adversaries that monetize ads and (2) the overall impact a botnet may have to the online ad ecosystem and the advertisers.

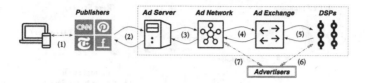

Fig. 1. An overview of the advertising ecosystem.

- We use A^2S to study the ad-abuse component of TDSS/TDL4, one of the most complex, sophisticated, and long-lived botnets in the history of the Internet. Using four years of network datasets from one of the largest Internet Service Providers (ISPs) in North America, we study: (1) the network infrastructure necessary to support the ad-abuse operation and (2) the financial model to estimate abuse inflicted by the botnet on advertisers. Our major findings include:
  - Online advertisers lost at least US$346 million to TDSS/TDL4. This amount is based solely on actions by less than 15 % of the botnet population. This translates to more than US$340 thousand per day on average, and the abuse was mostly accomplished by impression fraud. It is worth noting that daily abuse levels are three times of recent results reported for ZeroAccess botnet [27] and as large as ten times of the short-lived DNSChanger [2] botnet.
  - With respect to the infrastructure that supported this botnet operation, adversaries employed a similar level of network agility to achieve monetization as they do with traditional botnet C&C communication. *At least* 228 IP addresses and 863 domain names were used to support the entire ad-abuse operation over four years. The domain names are available at authors' homepages [3].

2   Background

2.1   The Ad Ecosystem

Figure 1 shows a conceptual view of the *overall* online advertising ecosystem. In general, when a user visits a website (Step (1)), a JavaScript or IFrame dynamically inserts ads. The HTTP session requesting an ad is called an "impression", and the content is sourced at Step (2) via an *ad server*. Ad servers typically work with an *ad network* to serve the impression (Step (3)) and log traffic source for payment. The ad networks are increasingly operated as free services to attract the "long tail" of content owners, but are otherwise monetized through CPM charges (*Cost Per Mille*, i.e., cost per 1,000 impressions) for undifferentiated impressions.

Publishers who source their ads from a search ad network can choose to *syndicate* the ads to other publishers. Search ad networks usually allow syndication in order to reach a wider audience who do not use their own search engines. Thus, there can be several redirections among publishers before Step (2) happens.

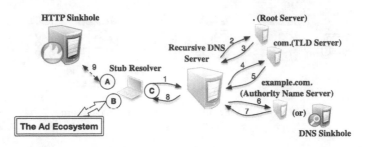

Fig. 2. A high level overview of DNS resolution (1–8), the sinkholing processes (A) and the points where ad-abuse can be observed (B and C).

Some advertisers work directly with the ad network (Step (7)). However, if a given impression cannot be fulfilled, it is sent to an *ad exchange* (Step (4)). The ad exchange provides market clearance for serving impressions, typically on an individual basis. Other advertisers work with demand-side platform providers (DSPs) to "broker" real-time bidding on impressions through ad exchanges (Step (5) and (6)). DSPs determine how much to bid, based on user-centric features such as IP addresses, cookies, referrers, etc. Instead of charging on CPM basis, they claim anywhere from 5 % to 60 % of the revenue spent by the advertiser.

If the displayed ad was clicked, the ad server logs which publisher the click comes from, and redirects the user to the advertiser's page. After the click, the advertiser is then charged based on CPC (*Cost Per Click*). The CPC for each click varies based on keywords, publisher popularity, user's profile, location, etc.

Entities in the ad ecosystem perform fraud detection independently. The technical details are not disclosed in public documents [13,17,34]. As a counter-measure for fraud, ad networks employ smart pricing to normalize CPC (Cost-Per-Click) for publishers based on relative conversion rates [13,14]. Examples of conversions include product news subscription, purchase activity, completing an online survey, etc. If click traffic from a publisher results in a low conversion rate compared to other publishers serving similar ads, the ad network may use smart pricing to reduce the CPC used to calculate payment to that publisher. The drawback of the smart pricing policy is that the conversion data are often considered sensitive information and therefore advertisers typically are not willing to share them with the ad networks. In practice, ad networks take many factors into account that would indicate the probability for a conversion [12]. Nevertheless, since the conversion data are limited, attackers have been able to get positive CPC values even after smart pricing discounts [36].

While smart pricing could reduce the levels of abuse from fraudulent clicks, this is not the case with fraudulent impressions. Only recently, Google and IAB announced the Ad "Viewability" standard in an effort to combat invalid impressions: at least 50 % of ad pixels need to be in view for a minimum of one second [8,15]. Advertisers can now choose whether to only bid on *viewable* impressions in the Real Time Bidding process.

2.2 Botnets and Sinkholes

In the Domain Name System (DNS) [23,24], domain names are composed of labels, separated by periods, which correspond to namespaces in a hierarchical tree structure. Each label is a node, and the root label (.) is root of the tree. The hierarchical concatenation of nodes creates a fully qualified domain name. A zone is a collection of nodes that constitute a subtree with *DNS authority servers* responsible for its content. Figure 2 illustrates a typical resolution process. It begins with a stub resolver issuing a domain name resolution request for a domain, `example.com`, to the local recursive DNS server (RDNS) (see step 1, Fig. 2). In the event that the RDNS does not have the resolution answer in its cache, it will begin an iterative process to discover it. The RDNS will iteratively "walk" the DNS hierarchy, starting from root server (steps 2 and 3), to the next level of effective top-level domain (TLD) server (steps 4 and 5), and down to the authority name server (ANS) for the requested zone (steps 6). Once the RDNS receives (step 7) the authoritative mapping between the requested domain names and its corresponding answer (e.g., IP address) from the authority, it forwards the answer back to the stub resolver (step 8).

After a command and control (C&C) domain for a botnet is resolved, the next step is a connection attempt (e.g., HTTP GET) from the stub to the C&C server. Network administrators and security researchers often take over such C&C domain names to change their DNS setting, effectively making them point to a new location. This is commonly known as "sinkholing" a domain name [6]. If `example.com` is sinkholed, the stub resolver will establish any future connections to the sinkhole (step 9, Fig. 2) rather the adversary's C&C server.

In addition to sinkholing a domain's A/AAAA record, one can also sinkhole the authority name server that serves it. For instance, `example.com` can be sinkholed by changing the ANS to a server under the control of the sinkholing party. Such an action would have the following result. during the DNS lookup chain in Fig. 2, after steps 1 to 5, the recursive DNS server will ask the new DNS sinkhole server controlled by the sinkholing party about the authoritative answer for the domain name. Sinkholing both the domain name and the ANS server is a common practice in the security community as it provides telemetry from both the DNS resolution and network communication planes of the threat being sinkholed.

Attackers often change C&C domains to avoid sinkholing. Domain name Generation Algorithms (DGAs) [4,36] can be used to rapidly update the C&C domains to remain agile against sinkholing efforts. A DGA can be implemented client-side in the malware sample itself, or server-side in the C&C server. Intuitively, client-side DGAs can be reverse engineered from the malware sample. Unfortunately, server-side DGAs are much more difficult to understand as reverse engineering requires obtaining the C&C server code, which is often heavily protected by the author. However, monitoring traffic from infected hosts guarantees the observation of C&C domain changes.

2.3   Observing Ad-abuse in Local Networks

To understand where and what an operator can monitor, we need to examine the typical life cycle of a host already infected with malware. First, the malware contacts the C&C server to get its commands. These vary from search engine syndication abuse to traditional impression and click fraud. Next, the malware will attempt to execute the commands by interacting with the ad ecosystem. Stealthy malware carries out these tasks by blending in with users' normal web browsing activities in order to evade detection from anti-abuse components within the ad ecosystem. Additionally, the malware often reports back to the botmaster various byproducts from the monetization activities (e.g., user's search history during the impression or click event) in order to maintain "bookkeeping" for the entire monetization campaign.

Typical egress monitoring functionality can be used to observe different aspects of ad-abuse. Administrators who can inspect the egress of their networks (points A, B and C in Fig. 2) are able to independently observe the interactions over DNS and the C&C protocol between the infected hosts, the ad ecosystem, and the ad-abuse infrastructure that supports the particular monetization campaign. From the network's point of view, this observation takes the form of DNS resolutions (i.e., for the domain facilitating ad-abuse from point C in Fig. 2) and any application-layer communications between local victims and the ad ecosystem (point B in Fig. 2). We select observation points A and C in Fig. 2, so we can mine sinkhole and DNS datasets. We should also note that HTTP connections can be observed for the sinkholed domain names (point A in Fig. 2). The communications to the sinkhole did not, at any point, reach the ad ecosystem. This means that our efforts to study the botnet did not contribute any additional abuse to the advertisers and other parts of the online advertising ecosystem.

3   Ad-abuse Analysis System

In this section we introduce the Ad-abuse Analysis System (A^2S, Fig. 3) that allows administrators to systematically analyze ad-abuse in their networks. The goal of the system is to provide a detailed analysis of the Internet infrastructure that supports ad-abuse. Such information helps administrators to *independently* (1) estimate the level of ad-abuse that victims in the local networks contributed to the entire ad ecosystem and (2) obtain a set of domain names and IPs that can be used for network policy actions. We begin by providing an overview of A^2S.

3.1   System Overview

The input of A^2S is ground truth obtained by either external threat reports or manual analysis of a particular threat (Step (1), Fig. 3). These are added to our knowledge base for two modules: the DNS Ad-abuse Rate Module (Step (2)) and the Spectral Expansion Module (Step (3)).

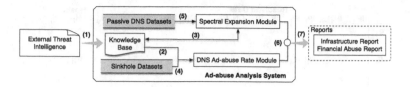

Fig. 3. Overview of the Ad-abuse analysis system (A^2S).

The **Passive DNS** and **Sinkhole** datasets are the input datasets for A^2S. At a high-level, the sinkhole dataset is used to identify the specifics of the command and control communication for monetization purposes and the passive DNS datasets are used to identify the botnet's full infrastructure, and estimate fraud costs at a larger scale. Collecting and handling these datasets are described in more detail in Sect. 4.

The **DNS Ad-abuse Rate Module** estimates how many ad-abuse events (i.e., C&C connections for impression or click fraud) are typically triggered after a single DNS resolution request for any ad-abuse domain (Step (4)). Multiple ad-abuse actions are often requested by each command received from the C&C server. This can be achieved by "taking-over" a small portion of such ad-abuse domain names for a period of time. Traditional sinkhole methods or commonly used walled garden policy techniques [21] at the recursive DNS level and perimeter egress points of a network can help administrators achieve this goal.

The **Spectral Expansion Module** identifies a set of domain names that have been used by the ad-abuse campaign *historically*. This can be done by combining ground truth from external threat intelligence with large passive DNS datasets (Step (5)). The passive DNS datasets enable the creation of graph between the botnet's victims and the Internet infrastructure that have been contacted by the local botnet victims. Using different sliding temporal windows, the spectral clustering of this graph enables operators to extend the ad-abuse domains to a larger set that is highly related to the ground truth. The module iteratively expands the set of ad-abuse domain names and improves our understanding behind the long-term ad-abuse operation (Step (3)). After expansion, the module sanitizes extended ad-abuse domains using historical WHOIS information in order to eliminate false positives.

The resulting output from both modules will be combined (Step (6)) to derive the final report (Step (7)), which includes all domain names and IP addresses that have been used to facilitate the ad-abuse campaign. The expanded set of ad-abuse domains and their historical DNS lookup volumes are used to approximate a lower bound of financial loss caused by the particular ad-abuse campaign against the ad ecosystem, and in particular the advertisers.

3.2 DNS Ad-abuse Rate Module

The DNS Ad-abuse Rate module quantifies the number of ad-abuse events that are performed after a single DNS request. In this case, the ad-abuse events are

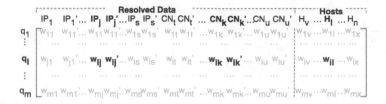

Fig. 4. Association matrix for domain, RDATA, and host.

the C&C connections issued for impression or click fraud. This allows accurate projection of DNS lookup volumes to the number of total ad-abuse events. To compute the rate, the module needs to analyze DNS queries and application-layer HTTP requests to sinkholed domains that are part of the ad-abuse campaign.

We define the "DNS Ad-abuse Rate" as $\zeta = y/x$, where x is the number of domain name resolution requests for the sinkholed domains and y is the number of application-layer communication attempts that reflect ad-abuse events. In other words, the module needs to observe x domain name resolution requests and y HTTP connections to the sinkhole, within a time window t, to safely assume a ζ level of ad-abuse happened with each historical ad-abuse domain lookup. Administrators can collect such sinkhole datasets either by acquiring a commercial sinkhole data feed or by independently taking over the ad-abuse domains, locally or globally.

Using ζ, the module can provide the system the ability to *pivot* from "short-term" sinkhole observations to "long-term" passive DNS observations. More specifically, we can project the DNS Ad-abuse Rate over many years of DNS traffic related to the ad-abuse operation using such passive DNS datasets. We now discuss how A^2S mines these datasets.

3.3   Spectral Expansion Module

The Spectral Expansion module uses local network traffic to reason about the domain names used for the ad-abuse operation, over a long time period. The module accurately identifies additional domains based on original ground truth knowledge of the ad-abuse operation, using a large passive DNS dataset. The module derives a larger set of ad-abuse domains, D_A, from the ground truth domains, $D_\$$ using spectral methods on DNS datasets from the local network. The spectral expansion algorithm iterates through the entire DNS query dataset. Each iteration walks over DNS data for a given day, with the ultimate goal of discovering new ad-abuse domains that will be added to the D_A set.

We conservatively assume that unknown ad-abuse domains were queried by a common group of infected hosts, or they pointed to the same Internet infrastructure that served the known ad-abuse domains over the same temporal window. Each day, we create a tripartite graph that "links" candidate domain names, their resolved IP addresses or Canonical Names (CNAMEs), and the network hosts that queried them. The association matrix representing such a graph can

---

Algorithm 1. Spectral Expansion Algorithm

Require:δ

1: $H \leftarrow \{h | \exists q \in D_A : h$ queried q on day $d_i\}$
2: $D \leftarrow \{q | \exists h \in H : h$ queried q on $d_i\}$
3: $Rdata \leftarrow \{ip | \exists q \in D : q$ resolved to ip historically$\} \cup \{cname | \exists q \in D : q$ resolved to $cname$ historically$\}$
4: Apply thresholds α and β to the sets of $Rdata$ and H, respectively, to remove noisy IPs and hosts.
5: $M \leftarrow$ relationship between D and $(Rdata, H)$. Normalize by IPs, CNAMEs and Hosts.
6: $S \leftarrow M \times M^T$
7: $U\Sigma V^* \leftarrow SVD(S)$
8: $clusters \leftarrow XMeans(U)$
9: $D_A \leftarrow$ Analyze $clusters$.
10: $i = i + \delta$, Go to line 1.

---

be seen in Fig. 4. Spectral decomposition of this matrix enables this module to group candidate domain names that either share common Internet infrastructure and/or local network hosts that queried them, via standard clustering methods. Then we analyze the clusters to add domain names to D_A. Domains are added if they have explicit relationships with already known ad-abuse Internet infrastructure or share common infected hosts.

Algorithm 1 formally describes the spectral expansion process. Each iteration of the algorithm processes the DNS resolutions of day, d_i, to update the ad-abuse domain set, D_A. The operator can set δ to determine how the algorithm iterates through time.

Next we discuss the steps in detail for one iteration. Initially we assume that $D_A = D_\$$. The first four steps prepare necessary data for assembling the association matrix between domains of interest and their resolved answers. In the **first step**, the algorithm identifies all internal network hosts (H) querying any known ad-abuse domain in D_A. In the **second step**, the algorithm narrows down potential unknown ad-abuse domains to all domains (D) queried by infected hosts (H). In the **third step**, we obtain all historical IP addresses and CNAMEs for domain names in D from the local passive DNS database, denoted as $Rdata$.

During the **fourth step**, the algorithm removes any "noisy IP addresses" from $Rdata$ and "noisy hosts" from H. IP addresses that are likely used for parking or sinkholing and hosts that are probably a large gateway or part of security research infrastructure can introduce noisy association between domains that do not reflect ad-abuse behavior. The algorithm excludes such "noisy" IPs and internal hosts by using two aggressive thresholds. Note that aggressively removing domains will not affect our lower-bound computation, it will only make our estimates safer.

The first threshold (α) denotes the number of related historical domain names for an IP address from typical network traffic on the local network. We exclude IPs with an unusually high number of domains. The second threshold (β) relates to the cardinality of set D queried by an infected host. In this case, if the number of domains queried by a host is over what we consider as typical for infected hosts in the local network, we exclude it from the set H. The way we reason and select the actual values of α and β will be discussed in Sect. 5.2.

In the **fifth step**, the algorithm builds an association matrix linking the domains in D with the IP addresses and CNAMEs in *Rdata* and the internal hosts in H that queried them (Fig. 4). The rows represent all the domains queried by infected hosts, and the columns reflect historically resolved IPs/CNAMEs and the hosts that queried the domains in the day. We compute two types of weights to assemble the matrix. The first weight reflects the DNS lookup properties from the domains in *Rdata*, with the respect of IPs and CNAMEs. Specifically, the weights w_{ij} and w'_{ij} reflect the timestamp for the first day (w_{ij}) and the last day (w'_{ij}) we observed domain name q_i resolving to IP_j. And the weights w_{ik} and w'_{ik} reflect the timestamp for the first and last day that domain name q_i resolved to CNAME CN_k. The second weight reflects a binary indicator of whether the particular domain name in *Rdata* was queried in day d_i by an internal host in H. Specifically, if host $host_l$ queried domain q_i on day d_i, the weight value w_{il} equals 1; otherwise, w_{il} equals 0. After the matrix has been assembled, the algorithm will normalize by row (for each q_i) the sum of "IP" values to one, the sum of "CNAME" values to one, and the sum of "Host" values to one.

In **step six** the algorithm transforms the association matrix $M_{m \times n}$ to its corresponding similarity matrix $S_{m \times m}$. This matrix represents how similar domain name q_i is to any other domain q_j. During the **seventh step**, the algorithm performs Singular Value Decomposition (SVD) on S, and obtains $U \Sigma V^* = SVD(S)$. The first twenty left-singular vectors are kept for **step eight**, which are clustered by XMeans [28].

Step nine analyzes the resulting clusters and finds new ad-abuse domain names. This cluster characterization process propagates the existing labels from ad-abuse domains in our knowledge base to unknown domains. The label propagation rules are based on IP infrastructure overlap and querying host overlap between domains. We discuss how we propagate labels based on cluster specific thresholds in Sect. 5.2. The known ad-abuse domain names set D_A is updated with the newly discovered domains.

The **tenth** and final step of the algorithm restarts the algorithm from the first step. Depending on the value δ set by the administrator, the algorithm determines the day to check next; for δ equals to 1, the algorithm proceeds to the next day, whereas -1 forces it to go backwards in time. This is very useful when the original ground truth resides in the center of time for our network observations. Taking advantage of the updated set D_A, the system can identify more ad-abuse domains. After reaching the last day of available data according to the iterating direction specified by δ, the algorithm stops.

Finally, the module sanitizes the derived D_A to exclude mistakenly characterized ad-abuse domains. We extract email addresses and name servers from WHOIS for domains in D_A, and compare these with known emails and name servers used for the domains in $D_\$$. If either email or name server matches, the newly discovered domain is kept in D_A. Otherwise, we exclude the domain for financial analysis. Thus, the derived D_A will be used to estimate conservative lower bounds of ad-abuse in the local network.

3.4 Reports on Ad-abuse and Financial Models

Outputs from the DNS Ad-abuse Rate and Spectral Expansion Modules are combined with further analysis of pDNS-DB to generate two reports. The first report describes the network infrastructure used to facilitate the ad-abuse, using historical IP addresses derived from the extended ad-abuse domains D_A. These domains, along with the DNS Ad-abuse Rate and the daily DNS lookup volumes, will help generate the second report that estimates the daily and overall financial impact of ad-abuse to the online advertising ecosystem.

Our financial model to calculate the lower bound of abuse M to the advertisers is:

$$M_{impression} = \sum_i \zeta * R_i * (p_{im} * \frac{\mu_{im}}{1000} * CPM) \tag{1}$$

For each day i, advertisers' loss is calculated based on the number of DNS requests R_i to $d \in D_A$ observed in the local network. $\zeta * R_i$ reflects the total number of ad-abuse HTTP connections for C&C purposes. We consider the connections in $\zeta * R_i$ that result into the p_{clk} component, which reflects the percentage of HTTP connections that corresponds to impression fraud communications. Since each connection may contain multiple impressions, μ_{im} represents the multiplicative factor necessary for the model to derive the total number of impressions. The number of thousand impressions multiplied by the CPM (cost-per-thousand impressions) allows us to calculate the financial loss from the fake impressions.

Using model $M_{impression}$ we assume that smart pricing policies were perfect across the entire ecosystem and no click fraud was successful at any point in the lifetime of the botnet operation, whereas the attackers were able to monetize fraudulent impressions from infected hosts. This assumption is realistic since detecting impression fraud has been extremely challenging to date [31,33].

4 Dataset Collection

To increase the situational awareness behind the problem of long-term ad abuse, we chose to analyze the ad-abuse component of the TDSS/TDL4 botnet, which uses a server-side DGA to generate its C&C domains. We describe the collected datasets in this section.

4.1 Sinkhole Datasets

We obtained sinkhole DNS and HTTP traces for the ad-abuse component of TDSS/TDL4 from two security companies. The datasets span over 10 months. All domain names that were sinkholed had a zero time-to-live (TTL) setting,

Table 1. Summary of datasets.

	Date range	Size	Records (millions)
DNS Sinkhole	8/1/2012–5/31/2013	6.9 G	565
HTTP Sinkhole	8/1/2012–5/31/2013	248.6 G	919
NXDOMAIN	6/27/2010–9/15/2014	133.5 G	13,557
pDNS-DB	1/1/2011–11/6/2014	17.9 T	10,209

which prevented caching at the recursive DNS server level, forcing it to contact the DNS sinkhole server for every lookup. Moreover, the HTTP sinkhole returned "HTTP 200 OK" answers back to the victims with no content. That is, the sinkhole administrator did not actively engage in ad-abuse (Table 1).

In order to quantify the DNS Ad-abuse Rate (Sect. 3.2), we need to understand the type of HTTP connections in the datasets. TDSS/TDL4 employs two C&C protocols to facilitate its ad-abuse operation. Both protocols were present in the HTTP datasets we obtained. The first protocol, "Protocol 1", is the primary mechanism through which the botnet performs impression fraud. This is achieved via an HTTP GET request to the active C&C, which will reply back with a set of advertisement URLs used for impression fraud. Among other information, Protocol 1 also reports the version of the malware behind the infection and a unique identifier for each victim, namely *bid*. All these observations are in-line with data collected and analyzed by other security researchers [26,29]. The second protocol, "Protocol 2", is used to report back information regarding search terms from the victim's browser, the publisher's website where ads have been *replaced* and *clicked on*, and the original ad that was replaced from the publisher's website. A semantically similar behavior of TDSS/TDL4 botnet is identified by Vacha et al. [10], where fraudulent clicks were only generated when a user engaged in real clicks. In order to protect infected users' privacy, the search terms were given to us in an aggregated form such that they cannot be mapped to the individual ID and the infected IP.

In total, we observed 565 million unique DNS resolution requests. 544 million were for Protocol 1 and 21 million were for Protocol 2 connections. This traffic was produced by 47,525 different recursive DNS servers (RDNS) around the world. Hosts with 66,669 unique identifiers (ID) contacted the HTTP sinkhole, using 615,926 different IP addresses. They made 343 million unique HTTP GET requests using properly formatted base64 encoded URLs. 919 million connections were recorded, only 0.87 % of which reflected Protocol 2 communication, while the rest 99.13 % reflected Protocol 1 connections. Thus, we assigned $p_{im} = 99.13\,\%$ for Eq. (1).

4.2 Passive DNS Datasets

We gathered two types of DNS datasets from a large US ISP that represents approximately 30 % of DNS traffic in the US. The first is the NXDOMAIN dataset, which covers over four years of DNS queries from clients of the ISP

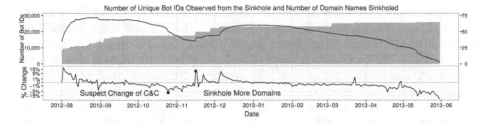

Fig. 5. Top: The line plot shows victim population of the botnet sample that contacted the sinkhole infrastructure, with y-axis on the left. The area plot shows the number of sinkholed domains with y-axis on the right. Bottom: Percent change.

for domains that did not resolve at the time of query. The second dataset we obtained is a historical passive DNS database (pDNS-DB), from the same ISP, containing DNS resource records (RR) [23,24] collected from 1/1/2011 to 11/5/2014.

The queries from the NXDOMAIN dataset are DNS answers with a return code of "NXDOMAIN". The dataset was collected below the recursive DNS servers, effectively capturing the queries from hosts to the recursive DNS servers. Throughout the four-year period, we gained access to 1,295 days of NXDOMAIN data (as the DNS query dataset) from the ISP sensors.

The pDNS-DB dataset contains over 10 billion RRs. Each RR provides resolved data and the daily lookup volume of a queried domain name. The pDNS-DB was collected from 24 geographically diverse ISP collection points in the United States.

5   Analysis and Measurements

In this section, we discuss how we compute the DNS Ad-abuse Rate, and how we propagate ad-abuse domains from ground truth $D_\$$ to the larger set D_A.

5.1   Computing the DNS Ad-abuse Rate

As a sanity check, we measure the average infection duration, the victim population, and the geographic distribution of sinkholed infections.

Figure 6a shows the cumulative distribution function of the *average infection duration* based on IP address and victim ID, a 40-byte long hexadecimal value that was tagged by TDSS/TDL4 malware as *bid* in Protocol 1 communications. The results show a relatively longer infection lifetime for the victims based on the unique identifier than using the victim's IP address. This is reasonable due to the complexity of network egress points, Network Address Translation (NAT) points, and DHCP churn rates [32], as other researchers have already noted.

Second, we measured the victim population coverage of the sinkhole traffic, using the number of unique daily IDs that contacted the sinkhole. Figure 5 illustrates how the number of daily victims changes over time and the percentage of change [16] for the botnet observed from the sinkhole data. In the first two months of the datasets, the number of infected IDs reached a maximum of almost 30,000. After a sudden 6.7 % drop in October, the number of IDs seen daily in our datasets decreased, until the middle of November 2012. The decrease indicates that the malware changed C&C domains from sinkholed domains to others. At that point the sinkhole administrators "refreshed" the sinkhole by adding six new domain names for the same botnet. This caused an increase in the number of IDs that were found in the sinkhole datasets. A large number of old IDs reappeared in the sinkhole data after the addition of these six new domains. This observation is expected, as the server side DGA churns through new domains and old infections catch up with the new sinkholed domain names. After a peak of almost 8.9 % increase at the end of 2012, the daily victim population remained around 23,000 until the middle of February 2013. Afterwards, the size decreased by a factor of almost 2 % daily.

Finally, we examined the geographic distribution of the infected population. As our passive DNS datasets were collected at a US ISP, we want to make sure that the sinkhole dataset contains a reasonable size of victims located in the US. We identified the corresponding CIDR and Autonomous System Number (ASN) for each victim IP address [22], and used historical data from Regional Internet Registries (RIR) to find the country codes for the identified ASNs. Almost half of the sinkhole traffic originates from victims in the US (46.77 %). In total, 174 countries were affected, however, only 15,802 infections resided in countries outside the top six countries (US, EU, DE, CA, FR, UK). These results show that TDSS/TDL4 traffic in our pDNS-DB dataset will allow us to study less than 15 % of the entire botnet. This is due to the fact that the passive DNS dataset is collected from an ISP in the United States, which represents 30 % of the overall DNS traffic in the US.

Computing the DNS Ad-abuse Rate ζ: Since our pDNS-DB dataset was obtained from a US ISP, we calculated the DNS Ad-abuse Rate ζ^{USISP} based on the sinkhole traffic that reflected victims in the particular ISP. This resulted in 9,664 unique victim IDs, 28,779,830 DNS connections, 154,634,443 HTTP Protocol 1 connections and 1,159,027 HTTP Protocol 2 connections over an observation window of 10 months. The mean for the entire ISP as $\zeta_{mean}^{USISP} = 27.62$. Which we used as the final DNS Ad-abuse Rate for our experiments. As discussed in Sect. 4.1, DNS caching will not bias our rate, since the sinkhole administrators had set a TTL equal to zero for the domains they sinkholed.

5.2   Spectral Analysis

We used Algorithm 1 described in Sect. 3.3 to derive ad-abuse domains set D_A starting from our limited ground truth $D_\$$. In this section we discuss the operational challenges we faced while running this algorithm.

Assembling the Association Matrix. Before we constructed the association matrix (see Fig. 4), we removed noisy IPs and internal hosts from the sets $Rdata$ and H.

Threshold (α) for Noisy IPs: Figure 6b shows the number of historical domain names per IP address, which were manually labeled from the TDSS/TDL4 ad-abuse domains in $D_\$$. We observed that under 40 % of confirmed TDSS/TDL4 C&C IPs historically have fewer than 1,000 domains pointing to them. The IPs having more historical domains are likely used for parking or sinkholing. We conducted a one-time manual analysis of a set of IP addresses around the limit of 1,000 related historical domains. The analysis revealed that considering IPs with more than 1,000 historical domains as noisy is an aggressive threshold. However, since we are estimating the lower-bound of TDSS/TDL4 ad-abuse operation, falsely removing IPs that were not used for parking or sinkholing will only help our lower bounds goal. That is, such an aggressive threshold will only remove links within the association matrix that would have allowed us to discover additional ad-abuse domains to be added to the set D_A.

Threshold (β) for Noisy Hosts: Figure 6c shows the cumulative distribution of the number of domains queried by infected hosts in a day. Note that the x-axis is in log scale and the y-axis starts at 90 %. The plot shows that only 0.7 % of infected hosts queried more than 1,000 domain names in a day. These hosts are likely gateways or research infrastructure that cannot link known and unknown ad-abuse domains reliably during the clustering process. Thus, we used the 1,000 mark as threshold. This means that any host that queried more than 1,000 domains in a day was instantly excluded. This should take care any network address translation (NAT) points and complex infrastructure within the ISP. Again, this is an aggressive threshold, which rather forces us to underestimate the infected hosts (and yield again closer to lower bounds).

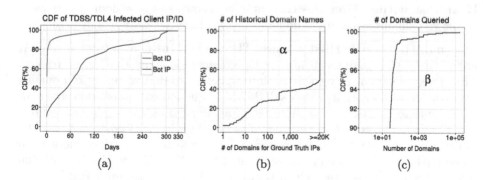

(a)   (b)   (c)

Fig. 6. a: Cumulative distribution function (CDF) for the infection duration based on the infection ID and IP address. b: CDF for number of related historical domain names per IP from initial ground truth ($D_\$$). c: CDF for the number of domains queried by internal hosts (H).

Table 2. Categories of newly detected ad-abuse domains with obfuscated email addresses.

	Detected	Labeled	Lookup Vol. (millions)
Shared Email Address			
email1@nhjhajsukk.cc	216	12	425
email2@aol.com	73	63	205
email3@dikloren.biz	65	9	144
email4@rocketmail.com	112	9	64
email5@kraniccky.com	6	3	57
email6@u7.eu	0	171	261
email7@gmx.com	0	20	28
Shared TDSS Name Server	6	-	4
No Active IP Address			
Sinkholed	64	9	
Two TDSS Parking Services	25	-	
Never Registered	268	-	
Non TDSS/TDL4	3	-	
Total	838	296	

Using these thresholds, we constructed the sparse matrix, performed Singular Value Decomposition, and extracted the first 20 left-singular vectors, which we used to cluster the domains in the matrix using XMeans [28].

Cluster Analysis. After clustering, we labeled ad-abuse domains based on IP infrastructure and infected hosts.

IP Infrastructure: From clusters containing known ad-abuse domains, we label unknown domains as ad-abuse domains if they share the same IP infrastructure.

Internal (Infected) Hosts: Since TDSS/TDL4 uses a server-side DGA, unknown C&C domains can also be nonexistent domains that never resolve. Therefore, we cannot rely solely on infrastructure to derive the set of domains D_A. Our intuition is that, if a NXDOMAIN is queried by a large percentage of known infected hosts, it is likely to be an ad-abuse domain. We use an aggressive filtering process to find such domains based on internal *host overlaps*. The internal *host overlap* was the percentage of the infected hosts that queried the domain names. We used an aggressive cutoff to on keep NXDOMAINs with the *strongest* 5 % host overlaps, which is in line with our lower-bound goal.

Correctness of Spectral Expansion Module. We bootstrapped the spectral expansion process with 296 TDSS/TDL4 domains recovered from various public resources. After operating Algorithm 1 2,590 times, going over every day of the NXDOMAIN dataset twice, we discovered 838 new TDSS/TDL4 domains. This means that the total number of TDSS/TDL4 domain names in the set D_A

was 1,134. Next, the sanitization process reduced D_A to 765 domains based on historical WHOIS (WHOWAS) information from DomainTools. These domains match known TDSS/TDL4 domain registration email addresses or name servers, as shown in Table 2. The lookup volume for these domains will be used for the financial analysis in Sect. 6.2.

We manually analyzed the rest of the domains, and found that only three domains were mistakenly added to the set D_A by the spectral expansion module, while the rest were related to ad-abuse. The category "No Active IP Address" in Table 2 contains domains that only resolved to known sinkholes, parking IPs, and domains that were never registered. "Sinkholed" represents domains sinkholed by researchers. "Two TDSS Parking Services" refers to domains pointed to the same two parking services used by known TDSS domains during the same time. Lastly, 268 of newly detected domains were never registered. However, based on the large host overlap of these domains with known TDSS domains and name string characteristics, we concluded that these domains were related to the TDSS/TDL4 botnet.

6 Ad-abuse Reports

This section discusses the two reports that summarize the network infrastructure properties behind the ad-abuse component of TDSS/TDL4 and our estimation around financial impact that the botnet brought to the advertisers over four years.

6.1 C&C Infrastructure

Using the 1,131 domains in set D_A, we analyzed the network infrastructure used by the ad-abuse component of the botnet. We separated IP addresses used by these domains into parking, sinkhole, and active categories. Besides well-known parking and sinkholing IPs, we consider IPs with more than 1,000 historical domains to be parking IPs because of the α threshold discussed in Sect. 5.2. All other IP addresses were considered to be *active*. Figure 7 shows the number of domains resolving into each category over the four year observation period. In total, *at least* 863 domains were registered and the botnet used 228 IP addresses. These IP addresses were used for two years and ten months, until 10/15/2013. These domains were mostly active before the middle of 2012. We should note that during July 2012, a number of researchers started sinkholing some of the TDSS/TDL4 domains. This perhaps forced the botmasters to change monetization tactics as security researchers were investigating the ad-abuse component.

The botnet used a variety of hosting infrastructures to facilitate the abuse. We obtained ASN information for 195 out of 228 total active IP addresses used by the ad-abuse C&C. They are under 49 different Autonomous System Numbers (ASN), 59 CIDRs and 24 countries. Table 3a shows the distribution of the servers around the globe, used by TDSS/TDL4 domains.

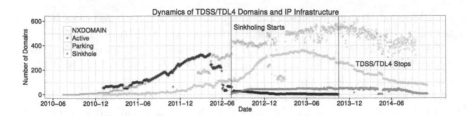

Fig. 7. Evolution of TDSS/TDL4 domains and their IP infrastructure. The number of active domain names daily increased from 2010, and reached the maximum (333) on 4/9/2012. None of the domains resolved to any active IP after 10/15/2013.

Fig. 8. Top: Daily advertisers' money loss caused by the ad-abuse component of TDSS/TDL4. Bottom: Cumulative financial loss for advertisers. Less than 15 % of the botnet population have been involved in ad fraud that cost at least US$346 million.

6.2 Financial Analysis

We used Eq. (1) to estimate the advertisers' financial loss. For our local network (the US ISP) we calculated the DNS Ad-abuse Rate to be $\zeta = 27.62$ (Sect. 5.1) and the percentage for impression fraud as $p_{im} = 99.13\%$ (Sect. 4.1). We calculated the daily number of DNS requests R_i to domains used for ad-abuse that resolved to *active* IP addresses. This is an *under-estimation* since we used aggressive thresholds to exclude potentially parked domains in our passive DNS traces (as we discussed in Sect. 5.2). This resulted in 1.2 billion DNS requests in total. μ_{im} denotes the number of ads returned by each Protocol 1 request (which relates to impression fraud activity). During our analysis, we identified instances where as many as 50 ads were returned from the C&C after each Protocol 1 request. We never saw fewer than 5 ads per request according to network traces of malware execution reported by [26]. Therefore, we used $\mu_{im} = 5$ for our lower bound estimate.

Throughout the lifetime of TDSS/TDL4, we estimate levels of ad-abuse on the order of at least US$346 million using Eq. (1). This lower bound is only based on the DNS datasets from the American ISP network to which we had access. Figure 8 shows the distribution of the financial loss caused by TDSS/TDL4 to advertisers. The daily financial loss is shown at the top of the figure, and the cumulative financial loss is at the bottom. We observed 1,018 days of active ad-abuse C&C DNS communications, caused by victims in the American ISP.

Table 3. a: The top 8 countries where C&C infrastructure has been identified. They count towards 71 % of the IP addresses. b: Financial break down approximation among the entities of the online ad ecosystem, in millions of dollars.

Country	IP Addresses	%
RU	42	18.42
US	34	14.91
LV	20	8.77
PT	19	8.33
DE	18	7.90
EU	17	7.46
NL	13	5.70
Other (17)	32	14.04
Unknown	33	14.47
Total	**228**	**100.00**

Stakeholders		Money (millions)
Advertisers' Capital		346.00
DSP	45%	155.70
Ad Exchange (inbound)	8%	27.68
Ad Exchange (outbound)	8%	27.68
Ad Networks	32%	110.72
Ad Server/Publisher (Affiliates)	**7%**	**24.22**

(b) Financial Break Down

This resulted to an average of US$340 thousand lost daily loss for advertisers. However, before the first sinkholed domain was registered on 7/11/2012, the daily estimate was on average US$616 thousand and peaked to US$1.97 million, on 1/7/2012. After the sinkholing action, the financial impact to the advertisers drastically decreased as the plateau of the bottom plot in Fig. 8 shows.

We strongly believe that other networks in the world were affected by this threat based on our sinkhole analysis described in Sect. 5.1. The victims in the *entire* ISP roughly accounted for 30 % of the total botnet population in the US. The infected hosts in the US were less than 50 % of the entire botnet population in the world. Thus, our lower bounds may only conservatively estimate loss caused by less than 15 % of the entire botnet population.

Cost for Operating the TDSS/TDL4 Infrastructure: The ad-abuse hosting infrastructure was located in 228 different IPs. Without knowing the hosting plans actually used by the botmasters, we have to consider an average cost plan for each service provider to approximate the cost of running the TDSS/TDL4 botnet. Using manual analysis, we conclude that the average minimum (i.e., the botmaster is using the least expensive plan) cost is approximately US $33.62 per month, whereas the average maximum cost is almost US $444 per month. We assume infrastructure is used around the clock. For IPs that we could not link to a particular AS, we assume a flat rate. This rate corresponds to the median of the observed prices around the world. Using this information, we conclude the cost to operate the TDSS/TDL4 C&C infrastructure to be between US $44,000 and US $260,000 over four years.

Potential Financial Reward for the Botnet Operators/Affiliates: While it is impossible to know for sure what the exact reward may have been, we tried to approximate the revenue that went to the affiliate TDSS/TDL4 entities. To derive the stakeholder and the break-down described in Table 3b we consulted the Chief Technology Officer (CTO) of a large Demand Service Platform company. According to his expert opinion, these are the most typical breakdowns to various entities in the ad ecosystem. As we can see from Table 3b, the potential financial reward for the affiliates is in the order of tens of millions of dollars.

The botmasters and affiliates are likely getting paid as publishers or traffic resellers. In this role, the estimated revenue is 7 % of money spent by advertisers, US$24.22 million. Our estimates are in-line with investigations from law enforcement on the amount stolen by fraudulent advertisement campaigns [11,18]. For example, law enforcement agencies recently estimated a minimum level of financial gains on the order of US $14 million dollars for the botmasters behind the DNSChanger botnet [35]. Note that DNSChanger was a significantly smaller botnet that operated over less than half the time period that TDSS/TDL4 was active.

7   Discussion

Our study aims to increase the situation awareness behind botnets that employ sophisticated techniques to abuse the online ad ecosystem and hopefully motivate further research in the space of ad-abuse. In this section we will discuss the most important challenges we faced while analyzing TDSS/TDL4.

7.1   Ground Truth Behind the Financial Loss

The botnets that interact with and monetize the ad ecosystem typically do not target a single entity (i.e., Google, Facebook, or Microsoft etc.). Due to the secrecy within the ecosystem, it is very hard to gather all the datasets from different entities necessary to verify whether the abuse levels we estimated are actually what the advertisers lost. For example, however unlikely it may be, we cannot exclude the possibility that some percentage of the impression fraud could have been detected and stopped by some entities in the ad ecosystem. Unfortunately, we cannot determine how much impression fraud, if any, was blocked, nor by whom. Thus, we had to rely on our own assumptions to estimate the lower bound. However, even in the scenario where one entity had perfect defenses, we cannot reliably assume it to be true for all the other entities in the ad ecosystem. While we contacted several entities in the ad ecosystem, they remain secretive about the methodology and tools that they use to detect fraud. Even if a small percentage (i.e., 30 %) of the reported fraudulent traffic evades detection, the losses are still significant.

7.2   Ground Truth Behind TDSS/TDL4

Our goal was to get ground truth around the way the TDSS/TDL4 botnet operates in the wild without contributing to online abuse. To that extent, we decided to gather the ground truth from external reports, and also from analyzing the sinkholing datasets of DGA domain names that supported the monetization module in TDSS/TDL4. Observation of DNS Ad-abuse Rate was made passively from actual infected hosts around the world. The TDSS/TDL4 victims were notified behind this sinkholing operation, and the sinkhole data were released to the operational community and several entities in the online ad ecosystem.

7.3   Smart Pricing Data for Impressions and Clicks

We assumed that perfect smart pricing for CPC was successfully used across the ad ecosystem, whereas all fraudulent impressions impacted the advertisers. However, attackers most likely can still profit from fraudulent clicks after smart pricing. For instance, recent work shows the actual CPC charged after smart pricing was between 10 to 30 cents for ZeroAccess [27]. Smart pricing is hard since not all conversion rates can be effectively measured. Not all conversion actions were logged and shared between advertisers and ad networks/exchanges. The fact that TDSS/TDL4 does both impression and click fraud implies that the monetization technique tried to avoid detection by generating positive click-through rates.

We chose to account for all the impressions since we do not have knowledge about how impression fraud was actually handled by the ad networks and ad exchanges. Although new standard of Ad Viewability has been announced and deployed to prevent advertisers from spending money on invalid ad impressions [8,15]. However, since there is almost no documentation about how impression fraud was dealt with by ad networks and ad exchanges when TDSS/TDL4 was active (before October 2013), it is not unreasonable to assume that a significant portion (if not all) of the impressions most likely went undetected.

8   Related Work

Operating a sinkhole is a safe, passive way to collect data regarding network connections between malware and the servers they try to contact. Malware needs to find a way to contact its Command and Control (C&C) server [7], which cannot always be done through P2P protocols, since network operators often block them. In the case of TDSS/TDL4, the malware uses P2P as an alternative communication method [30]. Data collected from a sinkhole operation can be used to measure the network behavior of a botnet. For example, [32] used sinkhole to uniquely identify infected hosts.

Studies on ad abuse often focus on the ad network's perspective [10,19]. Daswani et al. [9] showed how the value chain of ad-abuse operates online through the "Clickbot.A" botnet of 100,000 hosts. Springborn et al. [31] studied pay-per-view networks and described how millions of dollars are lost by fraudulent impressions annually. Moreover, Stone-Gross et al. [33], studied abuse from both a botnet's and ad network's point of view, showing the large amount of money the botnet can make. These works carefully focus on specific parts of the ad ecosystem, while ours characterizes overall abuse impact by using edge-based metrics.

The work most similar to ours is the recent ZeroAccess study [27] that estimated daily advertising losses caused by the botnet by analyzing one week of click fraud activities during a takedown against the ad-abuse component of ZeroAccess, mainly from the view of a single ad network. While the ZeroAccess study was novel, it did not help large network administrators independently measure the levels of ad-abuse originating from their network environments. Our system addresses these limitations from previous studies by studying the ad-abuse problem passively at the edge of the Internet over a multi-year time period.

9   Conclusion

This study aims to quantify the scale of online advertising abuse. To achieve this we present a novel system, Ad-abuse Analysis System (A^2S), able to conservatively estimate the long-term damage of the monetization component botnets use against the ad ecosystem. Using A^2S we studied one of the most notorious botnets that fraudulently monetized the ad ecosystem for four years: TDSS/TDL4. Using passive DNS and sinkhole observations, we were able to estimate TDSS/TDL4's lower bounds for its ad-abuse: no more than 15 % of botnet victims were responsible for at least US$346 million in financial loss to online advertisers since 2010. This includes a peak average daily loss of almost US $2 million at the height of the botnet's ad-abuse activity in early 2012. Overall, these figures reveal the extent of the abuse that botnets could bring to the advertisers over time, making ad-abuse a low risk and high reward monetization method for botmasters. The estimated lower bounds suggests the importance of additional research efforts in the ways botnets are being monetized.

Acknowledgements. The authors would like to thank Dr. Brett Stone-Gross and Dag Liodden for their comments and feedback. This material is based upon work supported in part by the US Department of Commerce under grant no. 2106DEK and Georgia Tech Research Institute (GTRI) IRAD grant no. 21043091. Any opinions, findings, and conclusions or recommendations expressed in this material are those of the authors and do not necessarily reflect the views of the US Department of Commerce nor GTRI.

References

1. Click-Fraud Attacks Being Used to Deliver More Sinister Threats. http://www.tripwire.com/state-of-security/security-data-protection/cyber-security/click-fraud-attacks-being-used-to-deliver-more-sinister-threats/
2. DNS Changer Remediation Study. https://www.m3aawg.org/sites/default/files/document/GeorgiaTech_DNSChanger_Study-2013-02-19.pdf
3. TDSS/TDL4 Domain Names. http://www.cc.gatech.edu/~ychen462/files/misc/tdssdomains.pdf
4. Antonakakis, M., Demar, J., Stevens, K., Dagon, D.: Unveiling the Network Criminal Infrastructure of TDSS/TDL4 DGAv14: A case study on a new TDSS/TDL4 variant. Technical report, Damballa Inc., Georgia Institute of Technology (GTISC) (2012)
5. Blizard, T., Livic, N.: Click-fraud monetizing malware: a survey and case study. In: 2012 7th International Conference on Malicious and Unwanted Software (MALWARE), pp. 67–72. IEEE (2012)
6. Bruneau, G.: DNS sinkhole (2010). http://www.sans.org/reading_room/whitepapers/dns/dns-sinkhole_33523

7. Bruneau, G., Wanner, R.: DNS Sinkhole. Technical report, SANS Institute InfoSec Reading Room, August 2010. http://www.sans.org/reading-room/whitepapers/dns/dns-sinkhole-33523

8. Bureau, I.A.: Viewability Has Arrived: What You Need To Know To See Through This Sea Change (2014). http://www.iab.net/iablog/2014/03/viewability-has-arrived-what-you-need-to-know-to-see-through-this-sea-change.html

9. Daswani, N., Stoppelman, M.: The anatomy of Clickbot.A. In: Proceedings of the First Conference on First Workshop on Hot Topics in Understanding Botnets, p. 11. USENIX Association (2007)

10. Dave, V., Guha, S., Zhang, Y.: Measuring and fingerprinting click-spam in ad networks. In: Proceedings of the ACM SIGCOMM 2012 Conference on Applications, Technologies, Architectures, and Protocols for Computer Communication, pp. 175–186. ACM (2012)

11. FBI New York Field Office: Defendant Charged In Massive Internet Fraud Scheme Extradited From Estonia Appeared In Manhattan Federal Court, April 2012. http://tinyurl.com/7mfrtqs

12. Google: About smart pricing. https://support.google.com/adwords/answer/2604607?hl=en

13. Google: Ad traffic quality resource center. http://www.google.com/ads/adtrafficquality/

14. Google: How Google uses conversion data. https://support.google.com/adwords/answer/93148?hl=en

15. Google: Just in time for the holidays – viewability across the google display network, December 2013. http://adwords.blogspot.co.uk/2013/12/just-in-time-for-holidays-viewability.html

16. Hyndman, R.J.: Transforming data with zeros (2010). http://robjhyndman.com/hyndsight/transformations/

17. Kelleher, T.: How Microsoft advertising helps protect advertisers from invalid traffic. http://advertise.bingads.microsoft.com/en-us/blog/26235/how-microsoft-advertising-helps-protect-advertisers-from-invalid-traffic

18. LawFuel(ed.): Massive Internet Fraud Nets Extradicted Estonian Defendant at Least $14 Million, October 2014. http://www.lawfuel.com/massive-internet-fraud-nets-extradicted-estonian-defendant-least-14-million

19. Li, Z., Zhang, K., Xie, Y., Yu, F., Wang, X.: Knowing your enemy: understanding and detecting malicious web advertising. In: Proceedings of the 2012 ACM Conference on Computer and Communications Security, pp. 674–686. ACM (2012)

20. Matrosov, A.: TDSS part 1 through 4 (2011). http://resources.infosecinstitute.com/tdss4-part-1/

21. Messaging Anti-Abuse Working Group and others: MAAWG Best Practices for the use of a Walled Garden, San Francisco, CA (2007)

22. Meyer, D., et al.: University of Oregon Route Views Project (2005)

23. Mockapetris, P.: Domain names - concepts and facilities (1987). http://www.ietf.org/rfc/rfc1034.txt

24. Mockapetris, P.: Domain names - implementation and specification (1987). http://www.ietf.org/rfc/rfc1035.txt

25. Neville, A.: Waledac reloaded: Trojan.rloader.b. (2013). http://www.symantec.com/connect/blogs/waledac-reloaded-trojanrloaderb

26. Parkour, M.: Collection of pcap files from malware analysis (2013). http://contagiodump.blogspot.com/2013/04/collection-of-pcap-files-from-malware.html

27. Pearce, P., Dave, V., Grier, C., Levchenko, K., Guha, S., McCoy, D., Paxson, V., Savage, S., Voelker, G.M.: Characterizing large-scale click fraud in zeroaccess. In: Proceedings of the 2014 ACM SIGSAC Conference on Computer and Communications Security, CCS 2014, NY, USA, pp. 141–152. ACM, New York (2014). http://doi.acm.org/10.1145/2660267.2660369

28. Pelleg, D., Moore, A.W.: X-means: extending k-means with efficient estimation of the number of clusters. In: Proceedings of the Seventeenth International Conference on Machine Learning, ICML 2000, Morgan Kaufmann Publishers Inc., San Francisco, CA, USA, pp. 727–734 (2000). http://dl.acm.org/citation.cfm?id=645529.657808

29. Rodionov, E., Matrosov, A.: The evolution of TDL: Conquering x64. ESET, June 2011

30. Rossow, C., Andriesse, D., Werner, T., Stone-Gross, B., Plohmann, D., Dietrich, C.J., Bos, H.: Sok: P2pwned-modeling and evaluating the resilience of peer-to-peer botnets. In: 2013 IEEE Symposium on Security and Privacy (SP), pp. 97–111. IEEE (2013)

31. Springborn, K., Barford, P.: Impression fraud in online advertising via pay-per-view networks. In: Proceedings of the 22nd USENIX Security Symposium (Washington, DC). Citeseer (2013)

32. Stone-Gross, B., Cova, M., Cavallaro, L., Gilbert, B., Szydlowski, M., Kemmerer, R., Kruegel, C., Vigna, G.: Your botnet is my botnet: analysis of a botnet takeover. In: Proceedings of the 16th ACM Conference on Computer and Communications Security, pp. 635–647. ACM (2009)

33. Stone-Gross, B., Stevens, R., Zarras, A., Kemmerer, R., Kruegel, C., Vigna, G.: Understanding fraudulent activities in online AD exchanges. In: Proceedings of the 2011 ACM SIGCOMM Conference on Internet Measurement Conference, pp. 279–294. ACM (2011)

34. Tuzhilin, A.: The lane's gifts v. google report. Official Google Blog: Findings on invalid clicks, posted, pp. 1–47 (2006)

35. United States District Court: Sealed Indictment, October 2011. http://www.wired.com/images_blogs/threatlevel/2011/11/Tsastsin-et-al.-Indictment.pdf

36. Wyke, J.: ZeroAccess (2012). http://sophosnews.files.wordpress.com/2012/04/zeroaccess2.pdf

37. Zhang, Q., Ristenpart, T., Savage, S., Voelker, G.M.: Got traffic?: an evaluation of click traffic providers. In: Proceedings of the 2011 Joint WICOW/AIRWeb Workshop on Web Quality, pp. 19–26. ACM (2011)

Google Dorks: Analysis, Creation, and New Defenses

Flavio Toffalini[1]([⊠]), Maurizio Abbà[2], Damiano Carra[1], and Davide Balzarotti[3]

[1] University of Verona, Verona, Italy
`flavio.toffalini@gmail.com, damiano.carra@univr.it`
[2] LastLine, London, UK
`mabba@lastline.com`
[3] Eurecom, Sophia-Antipolis, France
`davide.balzarotti@eurecom.fr`

Abstract. With the advent of Web 2.0, many users started to maintain personal web pages to show information about themselves, their businesses, or to run simple e-commerce applications. This transition has been facilitated by a large number of frameworks and applications that can be easily installed and customized. Unfortunately, attackers have taken advantage of the widespread use of these technologies – for example by crafting special search engines queries to fingerprint an application framework and automatically locate possible targets. This approach, usually called *Google Dorking*, is at the core of many automated exploitation bots.

In this paper we tackle this problem in three steps. We first perform a large-scale study of existing dorks, to understand their typology and the information attackers use to identify their target applications. We then propose a defense technique to render URL-based dorks ineffective. Finally we study the effectiveness of building dorks by using only combinations of generic words, and we propose a simple but effective way to protect web applications against this type of fingerprinting.

1 Introduction

In just few years from its first introduction, the Web rapidly evolved from a client-server system to deliver hypertext documents into a complex platform to run stateful, asynchronous, distributed applications. One of the main characteristics that contributed to the success of the Web is the fact that it was designed to help users to create their own content and maintain their own web pages.

This has been possible thanks to a set of tools and standard technologies that facilitate the development of web applications. These tools, often called *Web Application Frameworks*, range from general purpose solutions like Ruby on Rails, to specific applications like Wikis or Content Management Systems (CMS). Despite their undisputed impact, the widespread adoption of such technologies also introduced a number of security concerns. For example, a severe vulnerability identified in a given framework could be used to perform large-scale

© Springer International Publishing Switzerland 2016
J. Caballero et al. (Eds.): DIMVA 2016, LNCS 9721, pp. 255–275, 2016.
DOI: 10.1007/978-3-319-40667-1_13

attacks to compromise all the web applications developed with that technology. Therefore, from the attacker viewpoint, the information about the technology used to create a web application is extremely relevant.

In order to easily locate all the applications developed with a certain framework, attackers use so-called *Google Dork Queries* [1] (or simply *dorks*). Informally, a dork is a particular query string submitted to a search engine, crafted in a way to fingerprint not a particular piece of information (the typical goal of a search engine) but the core structure that a web site inherits from its underlying application framework. In the literature, different types of dorks have been used for different purposes, e.g., to automatically detect mis-configured web sites or to list online shopping sites that are built using a particular CMS.

The widespread adoption of frameworks on one side, and the ability to abuse search engines to fingerprint them on the other, had a very negative impact on web security. In fact, this combination lead to complete *automation*, with attackers running autonomous scout and exploitation bots, which scan the web for possible targets to attack with the corresponding exploit [2]. Therefore, we believe that a first important step towards securing web applications consists of breaking this automation. Researcher proposed software diversification [3] as a way to randomize applications and diversify the targets against possible attacks. However, automated diversification approaches require complex transformations to the application code, are not portable between different languages and technologies, often target only a particular class of vulnerabilities, and, to the best of our knowledge, have never been applied to web-based applications.

In this paper we present a different solution, in which a form of diversification is applied not to prevent the exploitation phase, but to prevent the attackers from fingerprinting vulnerable applications. We start our study by performing a systematic analysis of Google Dorks, to understand how they are created and which information they use to identify their targets. While other researchers have looked at the use of dorks in the wild [4], in this paper we study their characteristics and their effectiveness from the defendant viewpoint. We focus in particular on two classes of dorks, those based on portions of a website URL, and those based on a specific sequence of terms inside a web page. For the first class, we propose a general solutions – implemented in an Apache Module – in which we obfuscate the structure of the application showing to the search engine only the information that is relevant for content indexing. Our approach does not require any modification to the application, and it is designed to work together with existing search engine optimization techniques.

If we exclude the use of simple application banners, dorks based on generic word sequences are instead rarely used in practice. Therefore, as a first step we created a tool to measure if this type of dorks is feasible, and how accurate it is in fingerprinting popular CMSes. Our tests show that our technique is able to generate signatures with over 90 % accuracy. Therefore, we also discuss possible countermeasures to prevent attackers from building these dorks, and we propose a novel technique to remove the sensitive framework-related words from search engines results without removing them from the page and without affecting the usability of the application.

To conclude, this paper makes the following contributions:

- We present the first comprehensive study of the mechanisms used by dorks and we improve the literature classification in order to understand the main issues and develop the best defenses.
- We design and implement a tool to block dorks based on URL information without changing the Web application and without affecting the site ranking in the search engines.
- We study dorks based on combinations of common words, and we implement a tool to automatically create them and evaluate their effectiveness. Our experiments demonstrate that it is possible to build a dork using non-trivial information left by the Web application framework.
- We propose a simple but effective countermeasure to prevent dorks based on common words, without removing them from the page.

Thanks to our techniques, we show that there are no more information available for an attacker to identify a web application framework based on the queries and the results displayed by a search engine.

2   Background and Classification

The creation, deployment and maintenance of a website are complex tasks. In particular, if web developers employ modern CMSes, the set of files that compose a website contain much more information than the site content itself and such unintentional traces may be used to identify possible vulnerabilities that can be exploited by malicious users.

We identify two types of traces: (i) traces left by mistake that expose sensitive information on the Internet (e.g., due to misconfiguration of the used tool), and (ii) traces left by the Web Application Framework (WAF) in the core structure of the website. While the former type of traces is simple to detect and remove, the latter can be seen as a fingerprint of the WAF, which may not be easy to remove since it is part of the WAF itself.

There are many examples of traces left by mistake. For instance, log files related to the framework installation may be left in public directories (indexed by the search engines). Such log files may show important information related to the machine where the WAF is installed. The most common examples related to the fingerprint of a WAF are the application *banners*, such as "Powered by Wordpress", which contain the name of the tool used to create the website.

Google Dorks still lack a formal definition, but they are typically associated to queries that take advantage of advanced operators offered by search engines to retrieve a list of vulnerable systems or sensitive information. Unfortunately this common definition is vague (what type of sensitive information?) and inaccurate (e.g., not all dorks use advanced operators). Therefore, in this paper we adopt a more general definition of dorks: any query whose goal is to locate web sites using characteristics that are not based on the sites content but on their structure or type of resources. For example, a search query to locate all the e-commerce applications with a particular login form is a dork, while a query to locate e-commerce applications that sell Nike shoes is not.

Dorks often use advance operators (such as `inurl` to search in a URL) to look for specific content in the different parts of the target web sites. Below, we show two examples of dorks, where the attacker looks for an installation log (left by mistake) or for a banner string (used to fingerprint a certain framework):

```
inurl:"installer-log.txt" AND intext:"DUPLICATOR INSTALL-LOG"
intext:"Powered by Wordpress"
```

Note that all search engine operators can only be used to search keywords that are *visible* to the end users. Any information buried in the HTML code, but not visible, cannot be searched. This is important, since it is often possible to recognize the tool that produced a web page by looking at the HTML code, an operation that however cannot be done with a traditional search engine.

Since there are many different types of information that can be retrieved from a search engine, there are many types of dorks that can be created. In the following, we revise the classification used so far in the literature.

2.1   Existing Dorks Classification

Previous works (for a complete review, please refer to Sect. 6) divide dorks into different categories, typically following the classification proposed in the Google Hacking Database (GHDB) [5,6], which contains 14 categories. The criteria used to define these categories is the purpose of the dork, i.e., which type of information an attacker is trying to find. For instance, some of the categories are:

Advisories and Vulnerabilities: it contains dorks that are able to locate various vulnerable servers, which are product or version-specific.

Sensitive Directories: these dorks try to understand if some directories (with sensitive information) that should remain hidden, are made public.

Files Containing Passwords: these dorks try to locate files containing passwords.

Pages Containing Login Portals: it contains dorks to locate login pages for various services; if such pages are vulnerable, they can be the starting point to obtain other information about the system.

Error Messages: these dorks retrieve the pages or the files with errors messages that may contain some details about the system.

Different categories often rely on different techniques – such as the use of some advance operators or keywords – and target different parts of a website – such as its title, main body, files, or directories.

While this classification may provide some hints on the sensitive information a user should hide, the point of view is biased towards the attacker. From the defendant point of view, it would be useful to have a classification based on the techniques used to retrieve the information, so that it would be possible to check if a website is robust against such techniques (independently from the aim for which the technique is used). For this reason, in this paper we adopt a different classification based on the characteristics of the dorks.

2.2   Alternative Classification

We implemented a crawler to download all the entries in the GHDB [5,6] and a set of tools to normalize each dork and automatically classify it based on the information it uses[1].

We have identified three main categories, which are not necessarily disjoint and may be combined together in a single query:

URL Patterns: This category contains the dorks that use information present in the structure of the URL.

Extensions: It contains the dorks used to search files with a specific extension, typically to locate misconfigured pages.

Content-Based: These dorks use combination of words in the content of the page – both in the body, and in the title.

Since the content-based category is wide, we subsequently split such category into four sub-categories:

Application Banners: This category contains strings or sentences that identify the underlying WAF (e.g., *"Powered by Wordpress"*). These banners can be found in the body of the page (often in the foothold) or in the title.

Misconfiguration Strings: This category contains strings which correspond to sensitive information left accessible by mistake by human faults (such as database logs, string present in configuration files, or part of the default installation pages).

Errors Strings: Dorks in this category use special strings to locate unhandled errors, such as the ones returned when a server-side script is not able to read a file or it processes wrong parameters. Usually, besides the error, it is also possible to find on the page extra data about the server-side program, or other general information about the system.

Common Words: This class contains the dorks that do not fit in the other categories. They are based on combinations of common words that are not related to a particular application. For instance, these dorks may search for (*"insert"*, *"username"*, and *"help"*) to locate a particular login page.

Table 1 shows the number of dorks for each category. Since some of the dorks belongs to different categories, the sum of all categories is greater than the total number of entries. The classification shows that most of the dorks are based on banners and URL patterns. In particular, 89.5 % of the existing dorks use either a URL or a banner in their query.

Besides the absolute number of dorks, it is interesting to study the evolution of the dork categories over time. This is possible since the data from GHDB [6] contains the date in which the dork was added to the database. Figure 1 shows the percentage over time of the proposed dorks, grouped by category. It is interesting to note that banner-based dorks are less and less used in the wild, probably

---

[1] Not all dorks have been correctly classified automatically, so we manually inspected the results to ensure a correct classification.

Table 1. Number of dorks and relative percentage for the different categories. Since a dork may belong to different categories, the sum of the entries of all categories is greater than the total number of entries extracted from GHDB.

Category		Number	perc. (%)
URL pattern		2267	44
Extensions		318	6
Content-based	Banners	2760	54
	Misconfigurations	414	8
	Errors	71	1
	Common words	587	11
Total entries in GHDB [6]		5143	

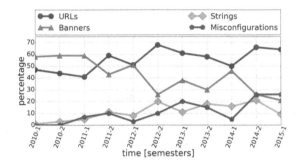

Fig. 1. Dorks evolution by category.

as a consequence of users removing those strings from their application. In fact, their popularity decreased from almost 60 % in 2010 to around 20 % in 2015 – leaving URL-based dorks to completely dominate the field.

2.3   Existing Defenses

Since the classification of the dorks has traditionally taken the attacker viewpoint, there are few works that provide practical information about possible defenses. Most of the them only suggests some best practices (e.g., remove all sensitive information), without describing any specific action. Unfortunately, some of these best practice are not compatible with Search Engine Optimizations (SEOs). SEOs are a set of techniques used to improve the webpage rank – e.g., by including relevant keywords in the URL, in the title, or in the page headers. When removing a content, one should avoid to affect such SEOs.

As previously noted, most of the dorks are based on banners and URL patterns, with mis-configuration strings at the third place. While this last category is a consequence of human faults, which are somehow easier to detect, the other dorks are all based on the fingerprint of the WAFs.

Banners are actually simple to remove, but the URL patterns are considerably more complex to handle. In fact, the URL structure is inherited from the underlying framework, and therefore one should modify the core structure of the WAF itself – a task too complex and error prone for the majority of the users. Finally, word-based dorks are even harder to handle because it is not obvious which innocuous words can be used to precisely identify a web application.

In both cases we need effective countermeasures that are able to neutralize such dorks. In the next sections, we show our solutions to these issues.

3 Defeating URL-Based Dorks

The URLs of a web application can contain two types of information. The first is part of the structure of the web application framework, such as the name of sub-directories, and the presence of default administration or login pages. The second is part of the website content, such as the title of an article or the name of a product (that can also be automatically generated by specific SEO optimization plugins). While the second part is what a search engine should capture and index, we argue that there is no reason for search engines to also maintain information about the first one.

The optimal solution to avoid this problem would be to apply a set of random transformations to the structure of the web application framework. However, the diversity and complexity of these frameworks would require to develop an ad-hoc solution for each of them. To avoid this problem, we implement the transformation as a filter in the web server. To be usable in practice, this approach needs to satisfy some constraints. In particular, we need a technique that:

1. It is independent from the programming language and the WAF used to develop the web site.
2. It is easily deployable on an existing web application, without the need to modify the source code.
3. It supports dynamically generated URLs, both on the server side and on the client side (e.g., through Javascript).
4. It can co-exist with SEO plugins or other URL-rewriting components.

The basic idea of our solution is to obfuscate (part of) the URLs using a random string generated at installation time. Note that the string needs to be random but it does not need to be secret, as its only role is to prevent an attacker for computing a single URL that matches all the applications of a give type accessible on the Web.

Our solution relies on two components: first, it uses standard SEO techniques to force search engines to only index obfuscated URLs, and then applies a filter installed in the web server to de-obfuscate the URLs in the incoming requests.

3.1 URL Obfuscation

The obfuscation works simply by XOR-ing part of the original URL with the random seed. Our technique can be used in two different ways: for selective-protection or for global protection. In the first mode, it obfuscates only particular pieces of URLs that are specified as regular expressions in a configuration file. This can be used to selectively protect against known dorks, for instance based on particular parameters or directory names.

When our solution is configured for global protection, it instead obfuscate all the URLs, except for possible substrings specified by regular expressions. This mode provides a better protection and simplifies the deployment. It can also co-exist with other SEO plugins, by simply white-listing the portions of URLs used by them (for example, all the URLs under /blog/posts/*). The advantage of this solution is that it can be used out-of-the-box to protect the vast majority of small websites based on popular CMSs. But it can also be used, by properly configuring the set of regular expressions, to protect more complex websites that have specific needs and non-standard URL schemes.

Finally, the user can choose to apply the obfuscation filter only to particular UserAgent strings. Since the goal is to prevent popular search engines from indexing the original URLs, the entire solution only needs to be applied to the requests coming from their crawlers. As we discuss in the next session, our technique works also if applied to all incoming requests, but this would incur a performance penalty for large websites. Therefore, by default our deployment only obfuscates the URLs provided to a configurable list of search engines[2].

3.2   Delivering Obfuscated URLs

In this section, we explain our strategy to show obfuscated URLs, and hide the original ones, in the results of search engines. The idea is to influence the behavior of the crawlers by using common SEO techniques.

Redirect 301. The Redirect 301 is a status code of the HTTP protocol used for permanent redirection. As the name suggests, it is used when a page changes its URL, in combination with a "Location" header to specify the new URL to follow. When the user-agent of a search engine sends a request for a cleartext URL, our filter returns a 301 error with a pointer to the obfuscated URL.

The advantage of this technique is that it relies on a standard error code which is supported by the all the search engines we tested. Another advantage of this approach is that the search engines move the current page rank over to the target of the redirection. Unfortunately, using the 301 technique alone is not sufficient to protect a page, as some search engines (Google for instance) would store in their database both the cleartext and the obfuscated URL.

Canonical URL Tag. The Canonical URL Tag is a meta-tag mainly used in the header of the HTML documents. It is also possible to use this tag as HTTP header to manage non-HTML documents, such as PDF files and images. Its main purpose is to tell search engines what is the real URL to show in their results.

For instance, consider two pages that show the same data, but generated with a different sorting parameter, as follow:

---

[2] Here we assume that search engines do not try to disguise their requests, as it is the case for all the popular ones we encountered in our study.

http://www.abc.com/order-list.php?orderby=data\&direct=asc
http://www.abc.com/order-list.php?orderby=cat\&direct=desc

In the example above, the information is the same but the two pages risk to be indexed as two different entries. The Canonical tag allows the site owner to show them as a single entry, improving the page rank. It is also important that there is only a single tag in the page, as if more tags are presents search engines would ignore them all.

Our filter parses the document, and it injects a Canonical URL Tag with the obfuscated URL. To avoid conflict with other Canonical URL Tags, we detect their presence and replace their value with the corresponding obfuscated version.

A drawback of this solution is that the Canonical URL Tag needs to contain a URL already present in the index of the search engine. If the URL is not indexed, the search engine ignores the tag. This is the reason why we use this technique in conjunction with the 301 redirection.

Site Map. The site map is an XML document that contains all the public links of a web site. The crawler uses this document to get the entire list of the URLs to visit. For instance, this document is used in blogs to inform the search engine about the existence of new entries, as for the search engine it is more efficient to poll a single document rather than crawling the entire site each time.

If a search engine tries to get a site map, our filter replaces all the URLs with their obfuscated versions. This is another technique to inform the crawler about the site structure and populate its cache with the obfuscated URLs.

Obfuscation Protocol. In this section, we show how the previous techniques are combined together to obtain our goal. Figure 2 shows the behavior of our tool when a crawler visits a protected web site. When the crawler requests a resource 'a' our tool intercepts the request and redirect it to the obfuscated URL O(a). The crawler then follows the redirect and requests the obfuscated resource. In this case, the system de-obfuscates the request, and then serves it according to the logic of the web site. When the application returns the result page, our filter adds the Canonical URL Tag following the rules described previously.

In Fig. 2, we also show how the tool behaves when normal users visit the web site. Typically, users would first request an obfuscated URL (as returned by a query to a search engine, for example). In this case, the request is de-obfuscated and forwarded to the web application as explained before. This action incurs a small penalty in the time required to serve the requests. However, once the user gets the page back, he can interact with the websites following links and/or forms that contain un-obfuscated URLs. In this case, the requests are served by the web server without any additional computation or delay.

Even if this approach might appear as a form of *cloaking*, the clocking definition requires an application to return different resources for a crawler and for other clients, as described in the guidelines of the major search engines [7–9]. Our technique only adds a meta-tag to the page, and does not modify the rest of the content and its keywords.

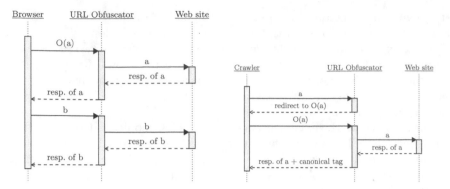

Fig. 2. On the left side: messages exchanged between a protected application ad a normal user. On the right side: messages exchanged between a protected application and a search engine crawler.

3.3 Implementation

Our approach is implemented as a module for the Apache web server. When a web site returns some content, Apache handles the data using the so-called *buckets* and *brigades*. Basically, a bucket is a generic container for any kind of data, such as a HTML page, a PDF document, or an image. In a bucket, data is simply organized in an array of bytes. A brigade is a linked list of buckets. The Apache APIs allow to split a bucket and re-link them to the corresponding brigade. Using this approach, it is possible to replace, remove, or append bytes to a resource, without re-allocating space. We use this technique to insert the Canonical URL Tag in the response, and to modify the site map. In addition, the APIs also permit to manage the header of the HTTP response, and our tool use this feature in order to add the Canonical URL Tag in the headers.

Since the Apache server typically hosts several modules simultaneously, we have configured our plugin to be the last, to ensure that the obfuscation is applied after any other URL transformation or rewriting step. Our obfuscation module is also designed to work in combination with the `deflate` module. In particular, it preserves the compression for normal users but it temporarily deactivate the module for requests performed by search engine bots. The reason is that a client can request a compressed resource, but in this case our module is not able to parse the compressed output to insert the Canonical Tag or to obfuscate the URLs in the site-map. Therefore, our solution removes the output compression from the search engine requests – but still allows compressed responses in all other cases.

Finally, to simplify the deployment of our module, we developed an installation tool that takes as input a web site to protect, generate the random seed, analyzes the site URL schema to create the list of exception URLs, and generate the corresponding snippet to insert into the Apache configuration file. This is sufficient to handle all simple CMS installations, but the user can customize the automatically generated configuration to accommodate more complex scenarios.

3.4 Experiments and Results

We tested our solution on Apache 2.4.10 running two popular CSMs: Joomla! 3.4, and Wordpress 4.2.5. We checked that our websites could be easily identified using dorks based on "`inurl:component/user`" and "`inurl:wp-content`".

We then protected the websites with our module and verified that a number of popular search engines (Google, Bing, AOL, Yandex, and Rambler) were only able to index the obfuscated URLs and therefore our web sites were no longer discoverable using URL-based dorks.

Finally, during our experiments we also traced the number of requests we received from search engines. Since the average number was 100 access per day, we believe that our solution does not have any measurable impact on the performance of the server or on the network traffic.

4 Word-Based Dorks

As we already observed in the Sect. 2, dorks based on application banners are rapidly decreasing in popularity, probably because users started removing these banners from their web applications. Therefore, it is reasonable to wonder if is also possible to create a precise fingerprint of an application by using only a set of generic and seemingly unrelated words.

This section is devoted to this topic. In the first part we show that it is indeed possible to automatically build word-based dorks for different content management systems. Such dorks may be extremely dangerous because the queries submitted to the search engines are difficult to detect as dorks (since they do not use any advanced operator or any string clearly related to the target CMS). In the second part, we discuss possible countermeasures for this type of dorks.

4.1 Dork Creation

Given a set of words used by a CMS, the search for the optimal combination that can be used as fingerprint has clearly an exponential complexity. Therefore, we need to adopt a set of heuristics to speed up the generation process. Before introducing our technique we need to identify the set of words to analyze, and the criteria used to evaluate such words.

Building Blocks. The first step to build a dork is to extract the set of words that may characterize the CMS. To this aim, we start from a vanilla installation of the target website framework, without any modification or personalization. From this clean instance, we remove the default *lorem ipsum* content, such as "Hello world" or "My first post". Then, using a custom crawler, our tool extracts all the visible words from all the pages of the web site, i.e., the words that are actually displayed by a browser and that are therefore indexed by search engines. After removing common stop words, usually discarded also by the search engines (e.g., *and, as, at, . . .*), our crawler groups the remaining words by page and also maintains a list with all the words encountered so far.

In order to build an automatic tool that creates word-based dorks for the different CMSes, we need two additional building blocks: (i) a set of APIs to interrogate a search engine, and (ii) an oracle that is able to understand if a website has been created with a specific CMS.

As for the APIs, we make use of the Bing APIs in order to submit a query to the Bing search engine. Clearly, any other search engine would be equivalent: we have chosen Bing since it has less restrictions in terms of the number of queries per day that a user can make. Given a query, Bing provides the total number of entries found for that query: this value represents the **coverage** of a query. Among these entries, our tool retrieve the first 1000 results. For each of these pages, we use the Wappalyzer-python library [10] to confirm whether the page is built using the target CMS. Wappalyzer looks at the HTML code of the page and tries to understand if there are traces left by a given CMS: this is fundamentally different from looking at the visible words, because to take a decision the tool needs to process the HTML content of the web page that is not indexed by the traditional search engines. Using this technique, we compute the **hit rank**, i.e., the number of results that are actually built with a given CMS divided by the number of results obtained by the query[3].

To build a dork, we need to evaluate its *precision* during the building process: the precision is a combination of the coverage and the hit rank, i.e., a good dork is the one that obtains the largest number of results with the highest accuracy.

Dork Generation. The basic idea used in our prototype is to build the dork step by step, adding one word at a time in a sort of gradient ascent algorithm. The first observation is that when a new word is added to an existing dork, its coverage can only decrease, but the hit rank may increase or decrease. As an example, in Fig. 3 we show the impact of adding a new word w_i while building a dork (in this case, the initial dork contained three words, with a hit rank equal to 30 %). For each word w_i we measure the new coverage and the new hit rank of the whole dork (three words with the addition of w_i), and we order the results according to the hit rank. As we can see, half of the new words decreases the hit rank, and therefore can be discarded from our process. Words that result in a higher hit rank usually considerably decrease the coverage – i.e., they return very few results. The goal is to find the best compromise, where we still retain a sufficiently high coverage while we increase the hit rank.

Our solution is to compute at each step the median coverage of all the candidate words for which the hit rank increases – shown in the figure as an horizontal dashed line at 16.6 M; we then choose the word that provides the highest hit rank *and* a coverage above the median – in this case, the word "posts".

The complete algorithm is shown in Algorithm 1. One of the inputs to the procedure is an initial set of words $\mathcal{D}$ for a given page, i.e., a basic dork to which new words should be added. Ideally we should start from an empty dork, and then we should evaluate the first word to add. However, since the coverage and the hit rank of a single word may be extremely variable, we decided to start

---

[3] For efficiency reasons, we compute the hit rank by visiting a random sample that covers 30 % of the first 1000 results.

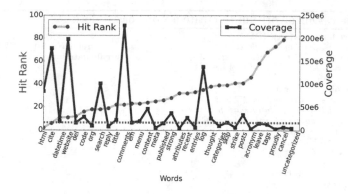

Fig. 3. Evolution of hit rank and coverage for a dork while adding different words.

from an initial dork of at least three words, so that to obtain meaningful values
for the coverage and the hit rank.

As initial dork, we have chosen the top three words with the highest coverage
(singularly) and that would provide a hit rank higher than 30 % (together).
While the choice of the initial point may seem critical, we have tested different
combinations of words obtaining similar results (in terms of final coverage and
hit rank). However, it is important to stress the fact that our goal is not to find
the best dork, but to find at least one that can be used to find websites created
with a specific CMS. In other words, our algorithm can return a local optimum
solution that changes depending on the initial point. However, any dork that
provides results in the same order of magnitude of other classes of dorks (such
as URL or banner-based) is satisfactory for our study.

The other input of the procedure is the set of words $\mathcal{V}$ that has been extracted
from the vanilla instance of the CMS, without the words used in the starting
dork, i.e., $\mathcal{V}' = \mathcal{V} \setminus \mathcal{D}$. Finally, we need to specify which CMS should be used to
compute the hit rank.

The algorithm keeps adding words to the dork until the final hit rank is
greater than or equal to 90 % or there are no more words to add. For each word
in $\mathcal{V}'$, it computes the new hit rank and the new coverage, and it stores the entry
in a table only if the word improves the hit rank (line 10).

If none of the words are able to improve the hit rank (line 14), the algorithm stops and returns the current dork. Otherwise, the algorithm computes
the median coverage which is used as a reference to obtain the best word. The
best word is the word with the highest hit rank among the ones with a coverage above the median. Finally, the best word is added to the dork and removed
from $\mathcal{V}'$.

Experiments and Results. In order to test our solution, we consider five well
known Web Application Frameworks: three general purpose CMSes (Wordpress,
Joomla!, and Drupal) and two E-Commerce CMSes (Magento and OpenCart).

Algorithm 1. Our algorithm to create a word-based dork

```
 1: procedure GETDORK(𝒟,𝒱',CMS)
 2:     url_list ← apiBing.search(𝒟)                          ▷ retrieve a list of URL given 𝒟
 3:     max_hr ← calcHitRank(url_list, CMS)              ▷ calculate hit rank from URL List
 4:     while max_hr < 90 % ∧ 𝒱' ≠ ∅ do
 5:         table ← empty()
 6:         for all w ∈ 𝒱' do
 7:             cov ← calcCoverage(𝒟 ∪ w)
 8:             url_list ← api_bing.search(𝒟 ∪ w)
 9:             hr ← calcHitRank(url_list, CMS)
10:             if hr > max_hr then
11:                 table ←_row (w, hr, cov)
12:             end if
13:         end for
14:         if table == ∅ then
15:             return 𝒟                                              ▷ final dork
16:         end if
17:         median ← calcMedian(table)
18:         (best_word, hr) ← getBestWord(table, median)
19:         𝒟 ← 𝒟 ∪ best_word
20:         max_hr ← hr
21:         𝒱' ← 𝒱' \ {best_word}
22:     end while
23:     return 𝒟                                                      ▷ final dork
24: end procedure
```

We run the tests on a machine with Ubuntu 15.10, Python 3.4, BeautifulSoup, and Wappalyzer-python.

For each CMS, we have created dorks starting from two different installations:

- **Vanilla**: we consider the basic out-of-the-box installation, with no changes to the default website obtained from the CMS;
- **Theme**: we add some personalization to the website, such as changing the basic graphical theme.

For two CMSes, Drupal and Opencart, the lists of words extracted with our crawler from the two installations (Vanilla and Theme) are the same, therefore the dorks obtained from the Vanilla and Theme installations are the same too.

We compare the results of the dorks created with our tool with the banner-based dorks. Table 2 shows, for each CMS, the hit rank and the coverage for the two dorks (derived from the Vanilla and Theme installations), as well as for the dork taken as a reference.

The results show that our dorks obtain a coverage with the same order of magnitude of the reference dork, with similar hit rank, i.e., they are as effective as banner-based dorks in finding targeted CMScs. It is interesting to note also that the differences between the Vanilla and the Theme dorks are small, suggesting that minor customizations of the website have little impact on our methodology.

Customized Websites. While a little customization have a small impact on the effectiveness of the dorks we created, it is interesting to understand if, instead, major modifications may make our methodology ineffective. In other words, we investigate if customization can compromise the fingerprint left by the CMS, and implicitly be a countermeasure to word-based dorks.

Table 2. Hit rank and coverage of the dorks created with our *GetDork* tool, compared with a reference banner-based dork. For each CMS, we consider the dorks derived from two installations, Vanilla and Theme.

	Vanilla	Theme	Reference	
Wordpress	93.8 %	74.1 %	96.7 %	hits
	47.1 M	22 M	83.6 M	cover
Joomla	87.8 %	75.6 %	88.7 %	hits
	7.24 M	1.44 M	3.73 M	cover
Drupal	82.7 %	82.7 %	99.7 %	hits
	7.87 M	7.87 M	3.27 M	cover
Magento	87.1 %	93.2 %	85.2 %	hits
	0.39 M	0.22 M	0.68 M	cover
OpenCart	89.1 %	89.1 %	99.8 %	hits
	0.59 M	0.59 M	1.42 M	cover

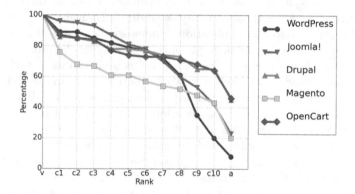

Fig. 4. Graph of common words for CMSs

To this aim, we selected and analyzed a set of popular websites built with known CMSes but largely customized, such as www.toyota.com, www.linux.com, and www.peugeot.com. For each CMS, we collected ten websites and extracted the list of words with our crawler. We then compared these lists with the corresponding lists extracted from the vanilla instances. Figure 4 shows the percentage of common words that each customized website has with the vanilla instance – for each CMS we have ordered the websites according to this percentage, therefore the x-axis shows the ranking, and not a specific website.

The point where the x-axis is labeled with "v" represents the vanilla instances, while the point "a" represents the intersection of all custom websites for that CMS with the vanilla instance. These points indicate the percentage of words that are common to all the websites, including the vanilla, and therefore represent the starting point for the creation of a dork. Except for Wordpress, most of the customized websites have high percentage of common words with the vanilla instance. Nevertheless, finding a common subset of words is not easy. We have actually tried to build a dork starting from the intersection of the sets of words of all the customized website and the vanilla instance, and we were successful only for Drupal and Opencart. This means that large customizations may be indeed a countermeasure for word-based dorks, but not for all CMSes. It is also important to note that such high customization is typical of a limited number of websites that are managed by large organizations, therefore the probability that such websites are vulnerable due to limited maintenance is not high.

4.2   Defense Against Word-Based Dorks

In the previous sections, we discuss an alternative method to create dorks using a combination of common words. While slightly less effective than banner-based dorks, we were able to achieve a relevant combination of hit rank and coverage, showing that this technique can be used by criminals to locate their victims.

To protect against this threat, we propose a simple solution in which we insert invisible characters into the application framework keywords. Luckily, in the Unicode standard there is a set of empty special characters that are not rendered in web browser. Thus, the appearance of the web sites does not change but a search engine would index the keywords including these invisible characters, preventing an attacker from finding these keywords in her queries. This technique also allows the obfuscation of the application banners without removing them.

Moreover, this technique does not influence the search engine optimization and ranking, because the obfuscated keywords are only part of the template, and not of the website content. In our prototype we use the *Invisible Separator* character with code "U+2063" in the Unicode standard. As the name suggests, it is a separator between two characters that does not take any physical space and it is used in mathematical applications to formally separate two indexes (e.g., ij). It is possible to insert this character in the HTML page using the code "⁣". For instance, an HTML code for a banner like "Powered by Wordpress" can be automatically modified to:

```
<div class="site-info">
    <a href="https://wordpress.org/">
        Power&#x2063;ed by Wor&#x2063;dpress
    </a>
</div>
```

The characters are ignored by search engines, effectively breaking each keyword in a random combination of sub-words. Obviously, this technique only works if a random number of invisible characters are placed at random locations inside each template keyword, so that each web application would have a different footprint. The highest combination that can be obtained using this technique is on the order of magnitude of $O(2^n)$, where n is the sum of entire characters of all the words that can be used to create a signature.

To test the effectiveness of this solution, we created a test web site containing two identical pages – one of which uses our system to obfuscate its content using the invisible separator character. We then performed queries on Google, Bing, AOL, and Rambler and we were able to confirm that all of them properly indexed the content of web site. However, while it was possible to find the website by searching for its cleartext content, we were not able to locate the obfuscated page by querying for its keywords.

5 Discussion

When a new vulnerability is disclosed, attackers rely on the ability to quickly locate possible targets. Nowadays, this is usually done by exploiting search engines with specially crafted queries called dorks. In Sect. 2.2 we showed that there are three main ways to fingerprint an application: using banner strings, using URL patterns, or using combination of words. The first type is easy to prevent, and in fact many popular websites are not identifiable in this way. This is also confirmed by our longitudinal study, which shows that the percentage of dorks belonging to this category is steadily decreasing over time.

In this paper we show that it is also possible to prevent the other two classes of dorks, without affecting the code or the rank of a web application. We believe this is a very important result, as it undermines one of the main pillar of automated web attacks. If criminals were unable to use dorks to locate their target, they would need to find workarounds that, however, either increase the cost or reduce the coverage of their operations.

The only way left to fingerprint an application is by looking at its HTML code. To do that, attacker needs to switch to special search engines that also index the raw content of each web pages. However, these tools (such as Mean-path [11]) have a much smaller coverage compared to traditional search engines, and typically require the user to pay a registration to get the complete list of results. Either way, this would slow down and reduce the number of attacks. Another possible venue for criminals would be to implement their own crawlers, using special tools that can automatically identify popular CMS and web application frameworks (such as Blind Elephant [12] and WhatWeb [13]). However, this requires a non negligible infrastructure and amount of time, so again it would considerably raise the bar – successfully preventing most of the attacks that are now compromising million of web sites.

6 Related Work

Google hacking has been the subject of several recent studies. Most of them discuss tricks and techniques to manually build dorks, and only few propose limited defenses, statistics, or classification schemes.

Moore and Clayton [14] studied the logs of compromised websites, and identified three classes of "evil queries": the ones looking for vulnerabilities, the ones looking for already compromised websites, and the ones looking for web shells.

SearchAudit [15] is a technique used to recognize malicious queries from the logs of a search engine. The study provides an interesting perspective on dorks that are used in the wild. In particular, the authors identify three classes of queries: to detect vulnerable web sites, to identify forums for spamming, and a special category used in Windows Live Messenger phishing attacks. While the first category is predominantly dominated by URL-based and banner-based dorks, the forum identification also included common strings such as "Be the first to comment this article". John et al., [16] then use SearchAudit to implement an adaptive Honeypot that changes its content in order to attract malicious users and to study their behaviors. The purpose of the study is to gain information about the attackers, and not to propose countermeasures.

Two books discuss Google Hacking: *"Google Hacking for Penetration Tester"* [1] and *"Hacking: The Next Generation"* [17]. Both of them show the techniques required to build dorks [18,19] using banner strings or URL patterns. These books adopt the same classification proposed by Johnny Long [5] and exploit-db.com [6]. As we already discussed in Sect. 2, this classification is focused on the goal of the dork (e.g., detect a vulnerable web sites, the presence of sensitive directories, or a mis-configuration error), while, in our work, we propose a classification based on the information that are used to build the fingerprint. Moreover, the defenses proposed in these books, as well as the ones proposed by Lancor [20], only discuss simple best practices – such as removing the name of the web application framework from the HTML footer.

Zhang et al., [4] study the type of vulnerabilities searched by the dorks (such as SQL-injection, XSS, or CSRF), and they compared them with the corresponding CVE. The authors also study the relation between dorks and advanced operators, but without considering the countermeasures as we do in this paper. Pelizzi et al. [21] propose a technique to create URL-based dorks to automatically look-up web sites affected by XSS vulnerabilities. Other works, such as Invernizzi et al. [22], and Zhang et al. [23], propose different techniques to create word dorks to identify malicious web sites. Their aim is to enlarge a database of compromised pages and not to find a fingerprint for a target web application framework. They create word dorks only with the common content of the infected pages without discussing how to improve the quality of the results.

Billing et al. [24] propose a tool to tests a list of provided dorks to find the ones that match a given web site. Similarly, several tools exist to audit a target site using public dorks databases, such as GooScan [25], Tracking Dog [26], or Diggity [27]. Sahito et al. [28] show how dorks can be used to retrieve private information from the Web (e.g., credit card numbers, private addresses, and telephone numbers). Similarly, Tath et al. [29,30] show how to use Google hacking in order to find hashed password, private keys or private information.

The literature also includes works not strictly related to dorks, but that deal with the problem of similarity of Web pages. For example, Soska et al. [31] show a correlation between attacked Web sites and future victims. The authors use comparison techniques (which include DOM features, common words, and URL patterns) in order to demonstrate that Web pages with similar features of compromised ones have high probability to be attacked too. Vasel et al. [32] use a database of compromised Web sites to calculate a risk-factor of future victims. They also seek common features of Web pages as Soska. Although their aims is different from ours, it could be intriguing to use their approach to improve our algorithm to create word-based dorks.

Finally, some studies discuss dorks as a propagation vector for malware. For example, Cho et al., [33] show a technique to retrieve C&C botnet servers using Google Hacking. Provos et al., [28] and Yu et al., [34] analyze a set of worms able to find other vulnerable machines using dorks. In these papers, the authors propose a system to block the malicious queries in order to stop the worm propagation.

7   Conclusion

In this paper we presented the first study about the creation, classification, and accuracy of different categories of Google dorks. We started by improving previous classifications by performing an analysis of a large database of dorks used in the wild. Our measurements showed that most of the dorks are based on URL patterns or banner strings, with the last category in constant declining. Therefore, we proposed a novel technique to randomize parts of the website URLs, in order to hide information that can be used as fingerprint of the underlying WAF. Our tool, implemented as a module for the Apache web server, does not require any modification to the sources of the WAF, and it does not decrease the rank of the web site.

We then showed how it is possible to combine common words in a CMS template to build a signature of a web application framework, with an accuracy and a coverage comparable to URL-based dorks. We implemented a tool to build these signatures and tested it on five popular CMS applications. Finally, we proposed a new technique to prevent this kind of dorks. The idea is inject invisible Unicode characters in the template keywords, which does alter the web site appearance or its usability.

References

1. Long, J., Skoudis, E.: Google Hacking for Penetration Testers. Syngress, Rockland (2005)
2. Provos, N., McClain, J., Wang, K.: Search worms. In: Proceedings of the 4th ACM Workshop on Recurring Malcode, pp. 1–8 (2006)
3. Christodorescu, M., Fredrikson, M., Jha, S., Giffin, J.: End-to-end software diversification of internet services. Moving Target Defense **54**, 117–130 (2011)
4. Zhang, J., Notani, J., Gu, G.: Characterizing Google hacking: a first large-scale quantitative study. In: Tian, J., et al. (eds.) SecureComm 2014. LNICST, vol. 152, pp. 602–622. Springer, Heidelberg (2015). doi:10.1007/978-3-319-23829-6_46
5. Johnny Google hacking database. http://johnny.ihackstuff.com/ghdb/
6. Exploit database. https://www.exploit-db.com/

7. Yandex cloacking condition. https://yandex.com/support/webmaster/yandex-indexing/webmaster-advice.xml
8. Baidu cloacking condition. http://baike.baidu.com/item/Cloaking
9. Google cloacking condition. https://support.google.com/webmasters/answer/663 55?hl=en
10. Wappalyzer-python. https://github.com/scrapinghub/wappalyzer-python
11. meanpath. https://meanpath.com/
12. Blind elephant. https://community.qualys.com/community/blindelephant
13. Whatweb. http://www.morningstarsecurity.com/research/whatweb
14. Moore, T., Clayton, R.: Evil searching: compromise and recompromise of internet hosts for phishing. In: Dingledine, R., Golle, P. (eds.) FC 2009. LNCS, vol. 5628, pp. 256–272. Springer, Heidelberg (2009)
15. John, J.P., Yu, F., Xie, Y., Abadi, M., Krishnamurthy, A.: Searching the searchers with searchaudit. In: Proceedings of the 19th USENIX Conference on Security, Berkeley, CA, USA, p. 9 (2010)
16. John, J.P., Yu, F., Xie, Y., Krishnamurthy, A., Abadi, M.: Heat-seeking honeypots: design and experience. In: Proceedings of WWW, pp. 207–216 (2011)
17. Michael, K.: Hacking: The Next Generation. Elsevier Advanced Technology, Oxford (2012)
18. Google advanced operators. https://support.google.com/websearch/answer/2466 433?hl=en
19. Bing advanced operators. https://msdn.microsoft.com/en-us/library/ff795667. aspx
20. Lancor, L., Workman, R.: Using Google hacking to enhance defense strategies. In: Proceedings of the 38th SIGCSE Technical Symposium on Computer Science Education, pp. 491–495 (2007)
21. Pelizzi, R., Tran, T., Saberi, A.: Large-scale, automatic XSS detection using Google dorks (2011)
22. Invernizzi, L., Comparetti, P.M., Benvenuti, S., Kruegel, C., Cova, M., Vigna, G.: Evilseed: a guided approach to finding malicious web pages. In: IEEE Symposium on Security and Privacy, pp. 428–442 (2012)
23. Zhang, J., Yang, C., Xu, Z., Gu, G.: PoisonAmplifier: a guided approach of discovering compromised websites through reversing search poisoning attacks. In: Balzarotti, D., Stolfo, S.J., Cova, M. (eds.) RAID 2012. LNCS, vol. 7462, pp. 230–253. Springer, Heidelberg (2012)
24. Billig, J., Danilchenko, Y., Frank, C.E.: Evaluation of Google hacking. In: Proceedings of the 5th Annual Conference on Information Security Curriculum Development, pp. 27–32. ACM (2008)
25. Gooscan. http://www.aldeid.com/wiki/Gooscan
26. Keßler, M., Lucks, S., Tatlı, E.I.: Tracking dog-a privacy tool against Google hacking. In: CoseC b-it, p. 8 (2007)
27. Pulp google hacking: the next generation search engine hacking arsenal
28. Sahito, F., Slany, W., Shahzad, S.: Search engines: the invader to our privacy - a survey. In: International Conference on Computer Sciences and Convergence Information Technology, pp. 640–646, November 2011
29. Tatlı, E.I.: Google hacking against privacy (2007)
30. Tatlı, E.I.: Google reveals cryptographic secrets. In: Kryptowochenende 2006-Workshop über Kryptographie Universität Mannheim, p. 33 (2006)
31. Soska, K., Christin, N.: Automatically detecting vulnerable websites before they turn malicious. In: Proceedings of USENIX Security, San Diego, CA, pp. 625–640 (2014)

32. Vasek, M., Moore, T.: Identifying risk factors for webserver compromise. In: Financial Cryptography and Data Security, pp. 326–345 (2014)
33. Cho, C.Y., Caballero, J., Grier, C., Paxson, V., Song, D.: Insights from the inside: a view of botnet management from infiltration. In: Proceedings of the USENIX Workshop on Large-Scale Exploits and Emergent Threats, San Jose, CA, April 2010
34. Yu, F., Xie, Y., Ke, Q.: Sbotminer: large scale search bot detection. In: ACM International Conference on Web Search and Data Mining, February 2010

Data Leaks

Flush+Flush: A Fast and Stealthy Cache Attack

Daniel Gruss[(✉)], Clémentine Maurice, Klaus Wagner, and Stefan Mangard

Graz University of Technology, Graz, Austria
daniel.gruss@iaik.tugraz.at

Abstract. Research on cache attacks has shown that CPU caches leak significant information. Proposed detection mechanisms assume that all cache attacks cause more cache hits and cache misses than benign applications and use hardware performance counters for detection.

In this article, we show that this assumption does not hold by developing a novel attack technique: the *Flush+Flush* attack. The *Flush+Flush* attack only relies on the execution time of the flush instruction, which depends on whether data is cached or not. *Flush+Flush* does not make any memory accesses, contrary to any other cache attack. Thus, it causes no cache misses at all and the number of cache hits is reduced to a minimum due to the constant cache flushes. Therefore, *Flush+Flush* attacks are stealthy, *i.e.*, the spy process cannot be detected based on cache hits and misses, or state-of-the-art detection mechanisms. The *Flush+Flush* attack runs in a higher frequency and thus is faster than any existing cache attack. With 496 KB/s in a cross-core covert channel it is 6.7 times faster than any previously published cache covert channel.

1 Introduction

The CPU cache is a microarchitectural element that reduces the memory access time of recently-used data. It is shared across cores in modern processors, and is thus a piece of hardware that has been extensively studied in terms of information leakage. Cache attacks include covert and cryptographic side channels, but caches have also been exploited in other types of attacks, such as bypassing kernel ASLR [14], detecting cryptographic libraries [17], or keystroke logging [10]. Hardware performance counters have been proposed recently as an OS-level detection mechanism for cache attacks and Rowhammer [5,13,31]. This countermeasure is based on the assumption that all cache attacks cause significantly more cache hits and cache misses than benign applications. While this assumption seems reasonable, it is unknown whether there are cache attacks that do not cause a significant number of cache hits and cache misses.

In this article, we present the *Flush+Flush* attack. *Flush+Flush* exploits the fact that the execution time of the `clflush` instruction is shorter if the data is not cached and higher if the data is cached. At the same time, the `clflush` instruction evicts the corresponding data from all cache levels. *Flush+Flush* exploits

---

C. Maurice—Part of the work was done while author was affiliated to Technicolor and Eurecom.

J. Caballero et al. (Eds.): DIMVA 2016, LNCS 9721, pp. 279–299, 2016.
DOI: 10.1007/978-3-319-40667-1_14

the same hardware and software properties as *Flush+Reload* [45]: it works on read-only shared memory, cross-core attack and in virtualized environments. In contrast to *Flush+Reload*, *Flush+Flush* does not make any memory accesses and thus does not cause any cache misses at all and only a minimal number of cache hits. This distinguishes *Flush+Flush* from any other cache attack. However, with both *Flush+Reload* and *Flush+Flush* the victim process experiences an increased number of cache misses.

We evaluate *Flush+Flush* both in terms of *performance* and *detectability* in three scenarios: a covert channel, a side-channel attack on user input, and a side-channel attack on AES with T-tables. We implement a detection mechanism that monitors cache references and cache misses of the last-level cache, similarly to state of the art [5,13,31]. We show that existing cache attacks as well as Rowhammer attacks can be detected using performance counters. However, we demonstrate that this countermeasure is non-effective against the *Flush+Flush* attack, as the fundamental assumption fails. The *Flush+Flush* attack is thus more stealthy than existing cache attacks, *i.e.*, a *Flush+Flush* spy process cannot be detected based on cache hits and cache misses. Thus, it cannot be detected by state-of-the-art detection mechanisms.

The *Flush+Flush* attack runs in a higher frequency and thus is faster than any existing cache attack in side-channel and covert channel scenarios. It achieves a cross-core transmission rate of 496 KB/s, which is 6.7 times faster than any previously published cache covert channel. The *Flush+Flush* attack does not trigger prefetches and thus allows to monitor multiple addresses within a 4 KB memory range in contrast to *Flush+Reload* that fails in these scenarios [10].

Our key contributions are:

– We detail a new cache attack technique that we call *Flush+Flush*. It relies only on the difference in timing of the `clflush` instruction between cached and non-cached memory accesses.
– We show that in contrast to all other attacks, *Flush+Flush* is stealthy, *i.e.*, it cannot be detected using hardware performance counters. We show that *Flush+Flush* also outperforms all existing cache attacks in terms of speed.

The remainder of this paper is organized as follows. Section 2 provides background information on CPU caches, shared memory, and cache attacks. Section 3 describes the *Flush+Flush* attack. Section 4 investigates how to leverage hardware performance counters to detect cache attacks. We compare the performance and detectability of *Flush+Flush* attacks compared to state-of-the-art attacks in three scenarios: a covert channel in Sect. 5, a side-channel attack on keystroke timings in Sect. 6, and on cryptographic algorithms in Sect. 7. Section 8 discusses implications and countermeasures. Section 9 discusses related work. Finally, we conclude in Sect. 10.

2 Background

2.1 CPU Caches

CPU caches hide the memory accesses latency to the slow physical memory by buffering frequently used data in a small and fast memory. Modern CPU architectures implement n-way set-associative caches, where the cache is divided into cache sets, and each cache set comprises several cache lines. A line is loaded in a set depending on its address, and each line can occupy any of the n ways.

On modern Intel processors, there are three cache levels. The L3 cache, also called last-level cache, is shared between all CPU cores. The L3 cache is inclusive, i.e., all data within the L1 and L2 caches is also present in the L3 cache. Due to these properties, executing code or accessing data on one core has immediate consequences even for the private caches of the other cores. This can be exploited in so called cache attacks. The last-level cache is divided into as many slices as cores, interconnected by a ring bus. Since the Sandy Bridge microarchitecture, each physical address is mapped to a slice by an undocumented so-called *complex-addressing* function, that has recently been reversed-engineered [27].

A cache replacement policy decides which cache line to replace when loading new data in a set. Typical replacement policies are least-recently used (LRU), variants of LRU and bimodal insertion policy where the CPU can switch between the two strategies to achieve optimal cache usage [33]. The unprivileged `clflush` instruction evicts a cache line from all the cache hierarchy. However, a program can also evict a cache line by accessing enough memory.

2.2 Shared Memory

Operating systems and hypervisors instrument shared memory to reduce the overall physical memory utilization and the TLB utilization. Shared libraries are loaded into physical memory only once and shared by all programs using them. Thus, multiple programs access the same physical pages mapped within their own virtual address space.

The operating system similarly optimizes mapping of files, forking a process, starting a process twice, or using `mmap` or `dlopen`. All cases result in a memory region shared with all other processes mapping the same file.

On personal computers, smartphones, private cloud systems and even in public clouds [1], another form of shared memory can be found, namely content-based page deduplication. The hypervisor or operating system scans the physical memory for byte-wise identical pages. Identical pages are remapped to the same physical page, while the other page is marked as free. This technique can lower the use of physical memory and TLB significantly. However, sharing memory between completely unrelated and possibly sandboxed processes, and between processes running in different virtual machines brings up security and privacy concerns.

2.3 Cache Attacks and Rowhammer

Cache attacks exploit timing differences caused by the lower latency of CPU caches compared to physical memory. Access-driven cache attacks are typically devised in two types: *Prime+Probe* [30,32,39] and *Flush+Reload* [11,45].

In *Prime+Probe* attacks, the attacker occupies a cache set and measures whenever a victim replaces a line in that cache set. Modern processors have a physically indexed last-level cache, use complex addressing, and undocumented replacement policies. Cross-VM side-channel attacks [16,24] and covert channels [28] that tackle these challenges have been presented in the last year. Oren et al. [29] showed that a *Prime+Probe* cache attack can be launched from within sandboxed JavaScript in a browser, allowing a remote attacker to eavesdrop on network traffic statistics or mouse movements through a website.

Flush+Reload is a two phase attack that works on a single cache line. First, it *flushes* a cache line using the clflush instruction, then it measures the time it takes to *reload* the data. Based on the time measurement, the attacker determines whether a targeted address has been reloaded by another process in the meantime. In contrast to *Prime+Probe*, *Flush+Reload* exploits the availability of shared memory and especially shared libraries between the attacker and the victim program. Applications of *Flush+Reload* have been shown to be reliable and powerful, mainly to attack cryptographic algorithms [12,17,18,48].

Rowhammer is not a typical cache attack but a DRAM vulnerability that causes random bit flips by repeatedly accessing a DRAM row [20]. It however shares some similarities with caches attacks since the accesses must bypass all levels of caches to reach DRAM and trigger bit flips. Attacks exploiting this vulnerability have already been demonstrated to gain root privileges and to evade a sandbox [36]. Rowhammer causes a significant number of cache hits and cache misses, that resemble a cache attack.

3   The *Flush+Flush* Attack

The *Flush+Flush* attack is a faster and stealthier alternative to existing cache attacks that also has fewer side effects on the cache. In contrast to other cache attacks, it does not perform any memory accesses. For this reason it causes no cache misses and only a minimal number of cache hits. Thus, proposed detection mechanisms based on hardware performance counters fail to detect the *Flush+Flush* attack. *Flush+Flush* exploits the same hardware and software properties as *Flush+Reload*. It runs across cores and in virtualized environments if read-only shared memory with the victim process can be acquired.

Our attack builds upon the observation that the clflush instruction can abort early in case of a cache miss. In case of a cache hit, it has to trigger eviction on all local caches. This timing difference can be exploited in form of a cache attack, but it can also be used to derive information on cache slices and CPU cores as each core can access its own cache slice faster than others.

The attack consists of only one phase, that is executed in an endless loop. It is the execution of the clflush instruction on a targeted shared memory line. The attacker measures the execution time of the clflush instruction. Based on the execution time, the attacker decides whether the memory line has been cached or not. As the attacker does not load the memory line into the cache, this reveals whether some other process has loaded it. At the same time, clflush evicts the memory line from the cache for the next loop round of the attack.

The measurement is done using the `rdtsc` instruction that provides a sub-nanosecond resolution timestamp. It also uses `mfence` instructions, as `clflush` is only ordered by `mfence`, but not by any other means.

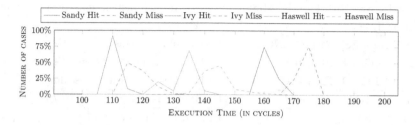

Fig. 1. Execution time of the `clflush` instruction on cached and uncached memory on different CPU architectures (Color figure online)

Figure 1 shows the execution time histogram of the `clflush` instruction for cached and non-cached memory lines, run on the three setups with different recent microarchitectures: a Sandy Bridge i5-2540M, an Ivy Bridge i5-3320M and a Haswell i7-4790. The timing difference of the peaks is 12 cycles on Sandy Bridge, 9 cycles on Ivy Bridge, and 12 cycles on Haswell. If the address maps to a remote core, another penalty of 3 cycles is added to the minimum execution time for cache hits. The difference is enough to be observed by an attacker. We discuss this timing difference and its implications in Sect. 9.1. In either case the execution time is less than the access time for both memory cached in the last-level cache and memory accesses that are not cached. Therefore, *Flush+Flush* is significantly faster than any other last-level cache attack.

The *Flush+Flush* attack inherently has a slightly lower accuracy than the *Flush+Reload* technique in some cases, due to the lower timing difference between a hit and a miss and because of a lower access time on average. Nevertheless, the same amount of information is extracted faster using the *Flush+Flush* attack due to the significantly lower execution time. Furthermore, the reload-step of the *Flush+Reload* attack can trigger the prefetcher and thus destroy measurements by fetching data into the cache. This is the case especially when monitoring more than one address within a physical page [10]. As the *Flush+Flush* attack never performs any memory accesses, this problem does not exist and the *Flush+Flush* attack achieves an even higher accuracy here. For the same reason, the *Flush+Flush* attack causes no cache misses and only a minimal number of cache hits. Thus, recently proposed detection mechanisms using cache references and cache misses fail to detect *Flush+Flush*.

4   Detecting Cache Attacks with Hardware Performance Counters

Cache attacks can lead to an increased number of cache hits or cache misses in the attacker process or in other processes. Thus, it may be possible to detect

Table 1. List of hardware performance events we use.

Name	Description
BPU_RA/_RM	Branch prediction unit read accesses/misses
BRANCH_INSTRUCTIONS/_MISSES	Retired branch instructions/mispredictions
BUS_CYCLES	Bus cycles
CACHE_MISSES/_REFERENCES	Last-level cache misses/references
UNC_CBO_CACHE_LOOKUP	C-Box events incl. `clflush` (all slices)
CPU_CYCLES/REF_CPU_CYCLES	CPU cycles with/without scaling
DTLB_RA/_RM/_WA/_WM	Data TLB read/write accesses/misses
INSTRUCTIONS	Retired instruction
ITLB_RA/_RM	Instruction TLB read/write accesses
L1D_RA/_RM/_WA/_WM	L1 data cache read/write accesses/misses
L1I_RM	L1 instruction cache read misses
LL_RA/_WA	Last-level cache read/write accesses

abnormal behavior on a system level. However, to stop or prevent an attack, it is necessary to identify the attacking process. Therefore, we consider an attack *stealthy* if the attacking spy process cannot be identified.

Hardware performance counters are special-purpose registers that are used to monitor special hardware-related events. Events that can be monitored include cache references and cache misses on the last-level cache. They are mostly used for performance analysis and fine tuning, but have been found to be suitable to detect Rowhammer and the *Flush+Reload* attack [5,13,31]. The focus of our work is to show that detection of existing attacks is straight-forward, but detection of the *Flush+Flush* attack using these performance counters is infeasible, due to the absence of cache misses and the minimal number of cache references.

We analyze the feasibility of such detection mechanisms using the Linux `perf_event_open` syscall interface that provides userspace access to a subset of all available performance counters on a per-process basis. The actual accesses to the model specific registers are performed in the kernel. The same information can be used by a system service to detect ongoing attacks. During our tests we ran the performance monitoring with system service privileges.

We analyzed all 23 hardware and cache performance events available with the Linux syscall interface on our system. Additionally, we analyzed the so called *uncore* [15] performance monitoring units and found one called C-Box that is influenced by cache hits, misses and `clflush` instructions directly. The `UNC_CBO_CACHE_LOOKUP` event of the C-Box allows monitoring a last-level cache lookups per cache slice, including by the `clflush` instruction. The C-Box monitoring units are not available through a generic interface but only through model specific registers. Table 1 lists all events we evaluated. We found that there are no other performance counters documented to monitor cache hits, misses or `clflush` instructions specifically. Furthermore, neither the hypervisor nor the operating system can intercept the `clflush` instruction or monitor the frequency of `clflush` instructions being executed using performance counters.

The number of performance events that can be monitored simultaneously is limited by hardware. On all our test systems it is possible to monitor up to 4 events simultaneously. Thus, any detection mechanism can only use 4 performance events simultaneously.

We evaluated the 24 performance counters for the following scenarios:

1. Idle: idle system,
2. Firefox: user scrolling down a chosen Twitter feed in Firefox,
3. OpenTTD: user playing a game
4. stress -m 1: loop reading and writing in dynamically allocated 256 MB arrays,
5. stress -c 1: loop doing a CPU computation with almost no memory,
6. stress -i 1: loop calling the I/O `sync()` function,
7. *Flush+Reload*: cache attack on the GTK library to spy on keystroke events,
8. Rowhammer: Rowhammer attack.

The first 3 scenarios are casual computer usage scenarios, the next 3 cause a benign high load situation and the last 2 perform an attack. A good detection mechanism classifies as benign the scenarios 1 to 6 and as attacks 7 and 8.

We use the instruction TLB (ITLB) performance counters (`ITLB_RA` + `ITLB_WA`) to normalize the performance counters to make cache attacks easier to detect, and prevent scenarios 2 and 3 from being detected as malicious. Indeed, the main loop that is used in the *Flush+Reload* and Rowhammer attacks causes a high number of last-level cache misses while executing only a small piece of code. Executing only a small piece of code causes a low pressure on the ITLB.

Table 2 shows a comparison of performance counters for the 8 scenarios tested over 135 s. These tests were performed in multiple separate runs as the performance monitoring unit can only monitor 4 events simultaneously. Not all cache events are suitable for detection. The `UNC_CBO_CACHE_LOOKUP` event that counts cache slice events including `clflush` operations shows very high values in case of `stress -i`. It would thus lead to false positives. Similarly, the `INSTRUCTIONS` event used by Chiappetta et al. [5] has a significantly higher value in case of `stress -c` than in the attack scenarios and would cause false positives in the case of benign CPU intensive activities. The `REF_CPU_CYCLES` is the unscaled total number of CPU cycles consumed by the process. Divided by the TLB events, it shows how small the executed loop is. The probability of false positive matches is high, for instance in the case of `stress -c`.

Thus, 4 out of 24 events allow detecting both *Flush+Reload* and Rowhammer without causing false positives for benign applications. The rationale behind these events is as follows:

1. `CACHE_MISSES` occur after data has been flushed from the last-level cache,
2. `CACHE_REFERENCES` occur when reaccessing memory,
3. `L1D_RM` occur because flushing from last-level cache also flushes from the lower cache levels,
4. `LL_RA` are a subset of the `CACHE_REFERENCES` counter, they occur when reaccessing memory,

Table 2. Comparison of performance counters normalized to the number of ITLB events in different cache attacks and normal scenarios over 135 s in separate runs.

Event/Test	Idle	Firefox	OTTD	stress -m	stress -c	stress -i	F+R	Rowhammer
BPU_RA	4.35	14.73	67.21	92.28	6109276.79	3.23	127443.28	23778.66
BPU_RM	0.36	0.32	1.87	0.00	12320.23	0.36	694.21	25.53
BRANCH_INST	4.35	14.62	74.73	92.62	6094264.03	3.23	127605.71	23834.59
BRANCH_MISS	0.36	0.31	2.06	0.00	12289.93	0.35	693.97	25.85
BUS_CYCLES	4.41	1.94	12.39	52.09	263816.26	6.2	30420.54	98406.44
CACHE_MISSES	0.09	0.15	2.35	58.53	0.06	1.92	693.67	13766.65
CACHE_REFER	0.4	0.98	6.84	61.05	0.31	2.28	693.92	13800.01
UNC_CBO_LOO	432.99	3.88	18.66	4166.71	0.31	343224.44	2149.72	50094.17
CPU_CYCLES	38.23	67.45	449.23	2651.60	9497363.56	237.62	1216701.51	3936969.93
DTLB_RA	5.11	19.19	123.68	31.78	6076031.42	3.04	47123.44	25459.36
DTLB_RM	0.07	0.09	1.67	0.05	0.05	0.04	0.05	0.03
DTLB_WA	1.7	11.18	54.88	30.97	3417764.10	1.13	22868.02	25163.03
DTLB_WM	0.01	0.01	0.03	2.5	0.01	0.01	0.01	0.16
INSTRUCTIONS	20.24	66.04	470.89	428.15	20224639.96	11.77	206014.72	132896.65
ITLB_RA	0.95	0.97	0.98	1.00	0.96	0.97	0.96	0.97
ITLB_RM	0.05	0.03	0.02	0.00	0.04	0.03	0.04	0.03
L1D_RA	5.11	18.3	128.75	31.53	6109271.97	3.01	47230.08	26173.65
L1D_RM	0.37	0.82	8.47	61.63	0.51	0.62	695.22	15630.85
L1D_WA	1.7	10.69	57.66	30.72	3436461.82	1.13	22919.77	25838.20
L1D_WM	0.12	0.19	1.5	30.57	0.16	0.44	0.23	10.01
L1I_RM	0.12	0.65	0.21	0.03	0.65	1.05	1.17	1.14
LL_RA	0.14	0.39	5.61	30.73	0.12	0.47	695.35	9067.77
LL_WA	0.01	0.02	0.74	30.3	0.01	0.01	0.02	4726.97
REF_CPU_CYC	157.70	69.69	445.89	1872.05	405922.02	223.08	1098534.32	3542570.00

Two of the events are redundant: L1D_RM is redundant with CACHE_MISSES, and LL_RA with CACHE_REFERENCES. We will thus focus on the CACHE_MISSES and CACHE_REFERENCES events as proposed in previous work [5,13,31].

We define that a process is considered malicious if more than k_m cache miss or k_r cache reference per ITLB event are observed. The attack is detected if

$$\frac{C_{\text{CACHE\_MISSES}}}{C_{\text{ITLB\_RA}} + C_{\text{ITLB\_WA}}} \geq k_m, \text{ or } \frac{C_{\text{CACHE\_REFERENCES}}}{C_{\text{ITLB\_RA}} + C_{\text{ITLB\_WA}}} \geq k_r,$$

with C the value of the corresponding performance counter. The operating system can choose the frequency in which to run the detection checks.

The thresholds for the cache reference and cache hit rate are determined based on a set of benign applications and malicious applications. It is chosen to have the maximum distance to the minimum value for any malicious application and the maximum value for any benign application. In our case this is $k_m = 2.35$ and $k_r = 2.34$. Based on these thresholds, we perform a classification of processes into malicious and benign processes. We tested this detection mechanism against various cache attacks and found that it is suitable to detect different *Flush+Reload*, *Prime+Probe* and Rowhammer attacks as malicious. However, the focus of our work is not the evaluation of detection mechanisms based on performance counters, but to show that such detection mechanisms cannot reliably detect the *Flush+Flush* attack due to the absence of cache misses and a minimal number of cache references.

In the following sections, we evaluate the performance and the detectability of *Flush+Flush* compared to the state-of-the-art cache attacks *Flush+Reload* and *Prime+Probe* in three scenarios: a covert channel, a side channel on user input and a side channel on AES with T-tables.

5 Covert Channel Comparison

In this section, we describe a generic low-error cache covert channel framework. In a covert channel, an attacker runs two unprivileged applications on the system under attack. The processes are cooperating to communicate with each other, even though they are not allowed to by the security policy. We show how the two processes can communicate using the *Flush+Flush*, *Flush+Reload*, and *Prime+Probe* technique. We compare the performance and the detectability of the three implementations. In the remainder of the paper, all the experiments are performed on a Haswell i7-4790 CPU.

5.1 A Low-Error Cache Covert Channel Framework

In order to perform meaningful experiments and obtain comparable and fair results, the experiments must be reproducible and tested in the same conditions. This includes the same hardware setup, and the same protocols. Indeed, we cannot compare covert channels from published work [24, 28] that have different capacities and error rates. Therefore, we build a framework to evaluate covert channels in a reproducible way. This framework is generic and can be implemented over any covert channel that allows bidirectional communication, by implementing the `send()` and `receive()` functions.

The central component of the framework is a simple transmission protocol. Data is transmitted in packets of N bytes, consisting of $N - 3$ bytes payload, a 1 byte sequence number and a CRC-16 checksum over the packet. The sequence number is used to distinguish consecutive packets. The sender retransmits packets until the receiver acknowledges it. Packets are acknowledged by the receiver if the checksum is valid.

Although errors are still possible in case of a false positive CRC-16 checksum match, the probability is low. We choose the parameters such that the effective error rate is below 5 %. The channel capacity measured with this protocol is comparable and reproducible. Furthermore, it is close to the effective capacity in a real-world scenario, because error-correction cannot be omitted. The number of transmitted bits is the minimum of bits sent and bits received. The transmission rate can be computed by dividing the number of transmitted bits by the runtime. The error rate is given by the number of all bit errors between the sent bits and received bits, divided by the number of transmitted bits.

5.2 Covert Channel Implementations

We first implemented the *Flush+Reload* covert channel. By accessing fixed memory locations in a shared library the a 1 is transmitted, whereas a 0 is transmitted by omitting the access. The receiver performs the actual *Flush+Reload* attack to determine whether a 1 or a 0 was transmitted. The bits retrieved are then parsed as a data frame according to the transmission protocol. The sender also monitors some memory locations using *Flush+Reload* for cache hits too, to receive packet acknowledgments.

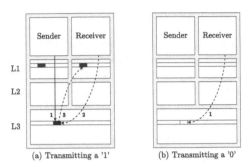

(a) Transmitting a '1'   (b) Transmitting a '0'

Fig. 2. Illustration of the *Flush+Flush* covert channel.

The second implementation is the *Flush+Flush* covert channel, illustrated by Fig. 2. It uses the same sender process as the *Flush+Reload* covert channel. To transmit a 1 (Fig. 2-a), the sender accesses the memory location, that is cached (step 1). This time, the receiver only flushes the shared line. As the line is present in the last-level cache by inclusiveness, it is flushed from this level (step 2). A bit also indicates that the line is present in the L1 cache, and thus must also be flushed from this level (step 3). To transmit a 0 (Fig. 2-b), the sender stays idle. The receiver flushes the line (step 1). As the line is not present in the last-level cache, it means that it is also not present in the lower levels, which results in a faster execution of the `clflush` instruction. Thus only the sender process performs memory accesses, while the receiver only flushes cache lines. To send acknowledgment bytes the receiver performs memory accesses and the sender runs a *Flush+Flush* attack.

The third implementation is the *Prime+Probe* covert channel. It uses the same attack technique as Liu et al. [24], Oren et al. [29], and Maurice et al. [28]. The sender transmits a 1 bit by priming a cache set. The receiver probes the same cache set. Again the receiver determines whether a 1 or a 0 was transmitted. We make two adjustments for convenience and to focus solely on the transmission part. First, we compute a static eviction set by using the complex addressing function [27] on physical addresses. This avoids the possibility of errors introduced by timing-based eviction set computation. Second, we map the shared library into our address space to determine the physical address to attack to make an agreement on the cache sets in sender and receiver. Yet, the shared library is never accessed and unmapped even before the *Prime+Probe* attack is started. We assume that the sender and receiver have agreed on the cache sets in a preprocessing step. This is practical even for a timing-based approach.

5.3   Performance Evaluation

Table 3 compares the capacity and the detectability of the three covert channels in different configurations. The *Flush+Flush* covert channel is the fastest of the three covert channels. With a packet size of 28 bytes the transmission rate is 496 KB/s. At the same time the effective error rate is only 0.84 %. The *Flush+Reload* covert channel also achieved a good performance at a packet size of 28 bytes. The transmission rate then is 298 KB/s and the error rate < 0.005 %. With a packet size of 4 bytes, the performance is lower in all three cases.

Table 3. Comparison of capacity and detectability of the three cache covert channels with different parameters. *Flush+Flush* and *Flush+Reload* use the same sender process.

Technique	Packet size	Capacity in KB/s	Error rate	Sender references	Sender misses	Sender stealth	Receiver references	Receiver misses	Receiver stealth
Flush+Flush	28	496	0.84 %	1809.26	96.66	✗	1.75	1.25	✓
Flush+Reload	28	298	0.00 %	526.14	56.09	✗	110.52	59.16	✗
Flush+Reload	5	132	0.01 %	6.19	3.20	✗	45.88	44.77	✗
Flush+Flush	5	95	0.56 %	425.99	418.27	✗	0.98	0.95	✓
Prime+Probe	5	67	0.36 %	48.96	31.81	✗	4.64	4.45	✗
Flush+Reload	4	54	0.00 %	0.86	0.84	✓	2.74	1.25	✗
Flush+Flush	4	52	1.00 %	0.06	0.05	✓	0.59	0.59	✓
Prime+Probe	4	34	0.04 %	55.57	32.66	✗	5.23	5.01	✗

A *Prime+Probe* covert channel with a 28-byte packet size is not realistic. First, to avoid triggering the hardware prefetcher we do not access more than one address per physical page. Second, for each eviction set we need 16 addresses. Thus we would require $28 B \cdot 4096 \cdot 16 = 14 GB$ of memory only for the eviction sets. For *Prime+Probe* we achieved the best results with a packet size of 5 bytes. With this configuration the transmission rate is 68 KB/s at an error rate of 0.14 %, compared to 132 KB/s using *Flush+Reload* and 95 KB/s using *Flush+Flush*.

The *Flush+Flush* transmission rate of 496 KB/s is significantly higher than any other state-of-the-art cache covert channels. It is 6.7 times as fast as the fastest cache covert channel to date [24] at a comparable error rate. Our covert channel based on *Flush+Reload* is also faster than previously published cache covert channels, but still much slower than the *Flush+Flush* covert channel. Compared to our *Prime+Probe* covert channel, *Flush+Flush* is 7.3 times faster.

5.4   Detectability

Table 3 shows the evaluation of the detectability for packet sizes that yielded the highest performance in one of the cases. *Flush+Reload* and *Flush+Flush* use the same sender process, the reference and miss count is mainly influenced by the number of retransmissions and executed program logic. *Flush+Reload*

Table 4. Comparison of performance counters normalized to the number of ITLB events for cache attacks on user input.

Technique	Cache references	Cache misses	Stealthy
Flush+Reload	5.140	5.138	✗
Flush+Flush	0.002	0.000	✓

is detected in all cases either because of its sender or its receiver, although its sender process with a 4-byte packet size stays below the detection threshold. The *Prime+Probe* attack is always well above the detection threshold and therefore always detected as malicious. All *Flush+Flush* receiver processes are classified as benign. However, only the sender process used for the *Flush+Flush* and the *Flush+Reload* covert channels with a 4-byte packet size is classified as benign.

The receiver process performs most of the actual cache attack. If it is sufficient to keep the receiver process stealthy, *Flush+Flush* clearly outperforms all other cache attacks. If the sender has to be stealthy as well, the sender process used by *Flush+Flush* and *Flush+Reload* performs better than the *Prime+Probe* sender process. However, due to the high number of cache hits it is difficult to keep the sender process below the detection threshold. An adversary could choose to reduce the transmission rate in order to be stealthier in either case.

6   Side-Channel Attack on User Input

Another cache attack that has been demonstrated recently using *Flush+Reload*, is eavesdropping on keystroke timings. We attack an address in the GTK library invoked when processing keystrokes. The attack is implemented as a program that constantly flushes the address, and derives when a keystroke occurred, based on memory access times or the execution time of the clflush instruction.

6.1   Performance Evaluation

We compare the three attacks *Flush+Flush*, *Flush+Reload*, and *Prime+Probe*, based on their performance in this side-channel attack scenario. During each test we simulate a user typing a 1000-character text into an editor. Each test takes 135 s. As expected, *Flush+Reload* has a very high accuracy of 96.1 %. This allows direct logging of keystroke timings. *Flush+Flush* performs notably well, with 74.7 % correctly detected keystrokes. However, this makes a practical attack much harder than with *Flush+Reload*. The attack with *Prime+Probe* yielded no meaningful results at all due to the high noise level. In case of *Flush+Reload* and *Flush+Flush* the accuracy can be increased significantly by attacking 3 addresses that are used during keystroke processing simultaneously. The decision whether a keystroke was observed is then based on these 3 addresses increasing the accuracy significantly. Using this technique reduces the error rate in case of *Flush+Reload* close to 100 % and above 92 % in case of *Flush+Flush*.

Fig. 3. Comparison of Cache Templates (address range of the first T-table) generated using *Flush+Reload* (left), *Flush+Flush* (middle), and *Prime+Probe* (right). In all cases $k_0 = $ 0x00.

6.2 Detectability

To evaluate the detectability we again monitored the cache references and cache misses events, and compared the three cache attacks with each other and with an idle system. Table 4 shows that *Flush+Reload* generates a high number of cache references, whereas *Flush+Flush* causes a negligible number of cache references. We omitted *Prime+Probe* in this table as it was not sufficiently accurate to perform the attack.

 Flush+Reload yields the highest accuracy in this side-channel attack, but it is easily detected. The accuracy of *Flush+Flush* can easily be increased to more than 92 % and it still is far from being detected. Thus, *Flush+Flush* is a viable and stealthy alternative to the *Flush+Reload* attack as it is not classified as malicious based on the cache references or cache misses performance counters.

7 Side-Channel Attack on AES with T-Tables

To round up our comparison with other cache attacks, we compare *Flush+Flush*, *Flush+Reload*, and *Prime+Probe* in a high frequency side-channel attack scenario. Finding new cache attacks is out of scope of our work. Instead, we try to perform a fair comparison between the different attack techniques by implementing a well known cache attack using the three techniques on a vulnerable implementation of a cryptographic algorithm. We attack the OpenSSL T-Table-based AES implementation that is known to be susceptible to cache attacks [2,30]. This AES implementation is disabled by default for security reasons, but still exists for the purpose of comparing new and existing side-channel attacks.

 The AES algorithm uses the T-tables to compute the ciphertext based on the secret key k and the plaintext p. During the first round, table accesses are made to entries $T_j[p_i \oplus k_i]$ with $i \equiv j \mod 4$ and $0 \leq i < 16$. Using a cache attack it is possible to derive values for $p_i \oplus k_i$ and thus, possible key-byte values k_i in case p_i is known.

7.1 Attack Implementation Using Flush+Flush

The implementation of the chosen-plaintext attack side-channel attacks for the three attack techniques is very similar. The attacker triggers an encryption,

Table 5. Number of encryptions to determine the upper 4 bits of a key byte.

Technique	Number of encryptions
Flush+Reload	250
Flush+Flush	350
Prime+Probe	4 800

Table 6. Comparison of the performance counters when performing 256 million encryptions with different cache attacks and without an attack.

Technique	Cache references	Cache misses	Execution time in s	References (norm.)	Misses (norm.)	Stealthy
Flush+Reload	$1\,024 \cdot 10^6$	19 284 602	215	2 513.43	47.33	✗
Prime+Probe	$4\,222 \cdot 10^6$	294 897 508	234	1 099.63	76.81	✗
Flush+Flush	$768 \cdot 10^6$	1 741	163	1.40	0.00	✓

choosing p_i while all p_j with $i \neq j$ are random. One cache line holds 16 T-Table entries. The cache attack is now performed on the first line of each T-Table. The attacker repeats the encryptions with new random plaintext bytes p_j until only one p_i remains to always cause a cache hit. The attacker learns that $p_i \oplus k_i \equiv_{\lceil 4 \rceil} 0$ and thus $k_i \equiv_{\lceil 4 \rceil} p_i$. After performing the attack for all 16 key bytes, the attacker has derived 64 bits of the secret key k. As we only want to compare the three attack techniques, we do not extend this attack to a full key recovery attack.

7.2   Performance Evaluation

Figure 3 shows a comparison of cache templates generated with *Flush+Reload*, *Flush+Flush*, and *Prime+Probe* using 1 000 000 encryptions to create a visible pattern in all three cases. Similar templates can be found in previous work [10,30, 37]. Table 5 shows how many encryptions are necessary to determine the upper 4 bits correctly. We performed encryptions until the correct guess for the upper 4 bits of key byte k_0 had a 5 % margin over all other key candidates. *Flush+Flush* requires around 1.4 times as many encryptions as *Flush+Reload*, but 13.7 times less than *Prime+Probe* to achieve the same accuracy.

Flush+Flush is the only attack that does not trigger the prefetcher. Thus, we can monitor multiple adjacent cache sets. By doing this we double the number of cache references, but increase the accuracy of the measurements so that 275 encryptions are sufficient to identify the correct key byte with a 5 % margin. That is only 1.1 times as many encryptions as *Flush+Reload* and 17.5 times less than *Prime+Probe*. Thus, *Flush+Flush* on multiple addresses is faster at deriving the same information as *Flush+Reload*.

7.3   Detectability

Table 6 shows a comparison of the performance counters for the three attacks over 256 million encryptions. The *Flush+Flush* attack took only 163 s whereas

Flush+Reload took 215 s and *Prime+Probe* 234 s for the identical attack. On a system level, it is possible to notice ongoing cache attacks on AES in all three cases due to the high number of cache misses caused by the AES encryption process. However, to stop or prevent the attack, it is necessary to detect the spy process. *Prime+Probe* exceeds the detection threshold by a factor of 468 and *Flush+Reload* exceeds the threshold by a factor of 1070. To stay below the detection threshold, slowing down the attack by at least the same factor would be necessary. In contrast, *Flush+Flush* is not detected based on our classifier and does not have to be slowed down to be stealthy.

8 Discussion

8.1 Using `clflush` to Detect Cores and Cache Slices

The *Flush+Flush* attack can be used to determine on which CPU core a process is running or to which cache slice an address maps. Indeed, a `clflush` on a remote cache slice takes longer than a `clflush` on a local cache slice, as shown in Fig. 4. This is due to the ring bus architecture connecting remote slices. Knowing the physical address of a memory access on a local slice, we can then use the complex addressing function [27] to determine on which core the process runs. However, this would require high privileges. Yet, it is possible to determine to which slice an address maps without knowing the physical address by performing a timing attack. This can be done by an unprivileged process, as pinning a thread to a CPU core requires no privileges.

This can be exploited to detect colocation on the same CPU, CPU core or hyperthreading core in restricted environments even if the `cpuid` instructions is virtualized. It is more difficult to determine which CPU core a thread runs on based on memory access timings because of the influence of lower level caches. Such an attack has also not been demonstrated yet. The information on the executing CPU core can be used to enhance cache attacks and other attacks such as the Rowhammer attack [9,20]. Running `clflush` on a local slice lowers the execution time of each Rowhammer loop round by a few cycles. The probability of bit flips increases as the execution time lowers, thus we can leverage the information whether an address maps to a local slice to improve this attack.

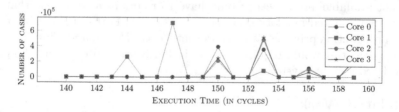

Fig. 4. Excerpt of the `clflush` histogram for an address in slice 1 on different cores. The lower execution time on core 1 shows that this address maps to slice 1.

A similar timing difference also occurs upon memory accesses that are served from the local or a remote slice respectively. The reason again is the direct connection to the local cache slice while remote cache slices are connected via a ring bus. However, as memory accesses will also be cached in lower level caches, it is more difficult to observe the timing difference without clflush. The clflush instruction directly manipulates the last-level cache, thus lower level caches cannot hide the timing difference.

While the operating system can restrict access on information such as the CPU core the process is running on and the physical address mapping to make efficient cache attacks harder, it cannot restrict access to the clflush instruction. Hence, the effect of such countermeasures is lower than expected.

8.2 Countermeasures

We suggest modifying the clflush instruction to counter the wide range of attacks that it can be used for. The difference in the execution time of clflush is 3 cycles depending on the cache slice and less than 12 cycles depending on whether it is a cache miss. In practice the clflush instruction is used only in rare situations and not in a high frequency. Thus, a hypothetical performance advantage cannot justify introducing these exploitable timing differences. We propose making clflush a constant-time instruction. This would prevent the *Flush+Flush* attack completely, as well as information leakage on cache slices and CPU cores.

Flush+Flush is the only cache attack that does not perform any memory accesses and thus causes no cache misses and only a minimal number of cache references. One theoretical way to detect our attack would be to monitor each load, e.g., by timing, and to stop when detecting too many misses. However, this solution is currently not practical, as a software-based solution that monitors each load would cause a significant performance degradation. A similar hardware-based solution called *informing loads* has been proposed by Kong et al. [21], however it needs a change in the instruction set. Without hardware modifications it would be possible to enable the rdtsc instruction only in privileged mode as can be done using seccomp on Linux [25] since 2008. Fogh [7] proposed to simulate the rdtsc in an interrupt handler, degrading the accuracy of measurements far enough to make cache attacks significantly harder.

Flush+Reload and *Flush+Flush* both require shared memory. If shared memory is not available, an attacker would have to resort to a technique that even works without shared memory such as *Prime+Probe*. Furthermore, making the clflush instruction privileged would prevent *Flush+Reload* and *Flush+Flush* as well. However, this would require changes in hardware and could not be implemented in commodity systems.

9   Related Work

9.1   Detecting and Preventing Cache Attacks

Zhang et al. [47] proposed HomeAlone, a system-level solution that uses a *Prime+Probe* covert channel to *detect* the presence of a foe co-resident virtual machine. The system monitors random cache sets so that friendly virtual machines can continue to operate if they change their workload, and that foe virtual machines are either detected or forced to be silent. Cache Template Attacks [10] can be used to detect attacks on shared libraries and binaries as a user. However, such a permanent scan increases the system load and can only detect attacks in a small address range within a reasonable response time.

Herath and Fogh [13] proposed to monitor cache misses to detect *Flush+Reload* attacks and Rowhammer. The system would slow down or halt all attacker processes. With the detection mechanism we implemented, we show that this technique is feasible for previous attacks but not for the *Flush+Flush* attack. Chiappetta et al. [5] proposed to build a trace of cache references and cache misses over the number of executed instructions to detect *Flush+Reload* attacks. They then proposed three methods to analyze this trace: a correlation-based method, and two other ones based on machine learning techniques. However, a learning phase is needed to detect malicious programs that are either from a set of known malicious programs or resemble a program from this set. They are thus are less likely to detect new or unknown cache attacks or Rowhammer attacks, in contrast to our ad-hoc detection mechanism. Payer [31] proposed a system called HexPADS to use cache references, cache misses, but also other events like page faults to detect cache attacks and Rowhammer at runtime.

Cache attacks can be *prevented* at three levels: at the hardware level, at the system level, and finally, at the application level. At the hardware level, several solutions have been proposed to prevent cache attacks, either by removing cache interferences, or randomizing them. The solutions include new secure cache designs [23,41,42] or altering the prefetcher policy [8]. However, hardware changes are not applicable to commodity systems. At the system level, page coloring provides cache isolation in software [19,34]. Zhang et al. [49] proposed a more relaxed isolation like repeated cache cleansing. These solutions cause performance issues, as they prevent optimal use of the cache. Application-level countermeasures seek to find the source of information leakage and patch it [4]. However, application-level countermeasures are bounded and cannot prevent cache attacks such as covert channels and Rowhammer. In contrast with prevention solutions that incur a loss of performance, using performance counters does not prevent attacks but rather detect them without overhead.

9.2   Usage of Hardware Performance Counters in Security

Hardware performance counters are made for performance monitoring, but security researchers found other applications. In defensive cases, performance counters allow detection of malware [6], integrity checking of programs [26], control flow integrity [44], and binary analysis [43]. In offensive scenarios, it has been used for side-channel attacks against AES [40] and RSA [3]. Performance counters have also been used by Maurice et al. [27] to reverse engineer the complex addressing function of the last-level cache of modern Intel CPUs.

9.3   Cache Covert Channels

Cache covert channels are a well-known problem, and have been studied relatively to the recent evolutions in microarchitecture. The two main types of access-driven attacks can be used to derive a covert channel. Covert channels using *Prime+Probe* have already been demonstrated in [24, 28]. *Flush+Reload* has been used for side-channels attacks [45], thus a covert channel can be derived easily. However, to the best of our knowledge, there was no study of the performance of such a covert channel.

In addition to building a covert channel with our new attack *Flush+Flush*, we re-implemented *Prime+Probe* and implemented *Flush+Reload*.[1] We thus provide an evaluation and a fair comparison between these different covert channels, in the same hardware setup and with the same protocol.

9.4   Side-Channel Attacks on User Inputs

Section 6 describes a side channel to eavesdrop on keystrokes. If an attacker has root access to a system, there are simple ways to implement a keylogger. Without root access, software-based side-channel attacks have already proven to be a reliable way to eavesdrop on user input. Attacks exploit the execution time [38], peaks in CPU and cache activity graphs [35], or system services [46]. Zhang et al. [46] showed that it is possible to derive key sequences from inter-keystroke timings obtained via `procfs`. Oren et al. [29] demonstrated that cache attacks in sandboxed JavaScript inside a browser can derive user activities, such as mouse movements. Gruss et al. [10] showed that auto-generated *Flush+Reload* attacks can be used to measure keystroke timings as well as identifying keys.

10   Conclusion

In this paper we presented *Flush+Flush*, a novel cache attack that, unlike any other, performs no memory accesses. Instead, it relies only on the execution time of the flush instruction to determine whether data is cached. *Flush+Flush* does not trigger prefetches and thus is applicable in more situations than other attacks. The *Flush+Flush* attack is faster than any existing cache attack. It achieves a transmission rate of 496 KB/s in a covert channel scenario, which is 6.7 times faster than any previous cache covert channel. As it performs no memory accesses, the attack causes no cache misses at all. For this reason, detection mechanisms based on performance counters to monitor cache activity fail, as their underlying assumption is incorrect.

While the *Flush+Flush* attack is significantly harder to detect than existing cache attacks, it can be prevented with small hardware modifications. Making the `clflush` instruction constant-time has no measurable impact on today's

---

[1] After public disclosure of the *Flush+Flush* attack on November 14, 2015, *Flush+Flush* has also been demonstrated on ARM-based mobile devices [22].

software and does not introduce any interface changes. Thus, it is an effective countermeasure that should be implemented.

Finally, the experiments led in this paper broaden the understanding of the internals of modern CPU caches. Beyond the adoption of detection mechanisms, the field of cache attacks benefits from these findings, both to discover new attacks and to be able to prevent them.

Acknowledgements. We would like to thank Mathias Payer, Anders Fogh, and our anonymous reviewers for their valuable comments and suggestions.

 Supported by the EU Horizon 2020 programme under GA No. 644052 (HECTOR), the EU FP7 programme under GA No. 610436 (MATTHEW), the Austrian Research Promotion Agency (FFG) and Styrian Business Promotion Agency (SFG) under GA No. 836628 (SeCoS), and Cryptacus COST Action IC1403.

References

1. Barresi, A., Razavi, K., Payer, M., Gross, T.R.: CAIN: silently breaking ASLR in the cloud. In: WOOT 2015 (2015)
2. Bernstein, D.J.: Cache-timing attacks on AES. Technical report, Department of Mathematics, Statistics, and Computer Science, University of Illinois at Chicago (2005)
3. Bhattacharya, S., Mukhopadhyay, D.: Who watches the watchmen?: Utilizing Performance Monitors for Compromising keys of RSA on Intel Platforms. Cryptology ePrint Archive, Report 2015/621 (2015)
4. Brickell, E., Graunke, G., Neve, M., Seifert, J.P.: Software mitigations to hedge AES against cache-based software side channel vulnerabilities. Cryptology ePrint Archive, Report 2006/052 (2006)
5. Chiappetta, M., Savas, E., Yilmaz, C.: Real time detection of cache-based side-channel attacks using hardware performance counters. Cryptology ePrint Archive, Report 2015/1034 (2015)
6. Demme, J., Maycock, M., Schmitz, J., Tang, A., Waksman, A., Sethumadhavan, S., Stolfo, S.: On the feasibility of online malware detection with performance counters. ACM SIGARCH Comput. Archit. News **41**(3), 559–570 (2013)
7. Fogh, A.: Cache side channel attacks (2015). http://dreamsofastone.blogspot.co.at/2015/09/cache-side-channel-attacks.html
8. Fuchs, A., Lee, R.B.: Disruptive prefetching: impact on side-channel attacks and cache designs. In: Proceedings of the 8th ACM International Systems and Storage Conference (SYSTOR 2015) (2015)
9. Gruss, D., Maurice, C., Mangard, S.: Rowhammer.js: a remote software-induced fault attack in javascript. In: DIMVA 2016 (2016)
10. Gruss, D., Spreitzer, R., Mangard, S.: Cache template attacks: automating attacks on inclusive last-level caches. In: USENIX Security Symposium (2015)
11. Gullasch, D., Bangerter, E., Krenn, S.: Cache games - Bringing access-based cache attacks on AES to practice. In: S&P 2011 (2011)
12. Gülmezoğlu, B., İnci, M.S., Irazoqui, G., Eisenbarth, T., Sunar, B.: A faster and more realistic Flush+Reload attack on AES. In: Mangard, S., Poschmann, A.Y. (eds.) COSADE 2015. LNCS, vol. 9064, pp. 111–126. Springer, Heidelberg (2015)

13. Herath, N., Fogh, A.: These are Not Your Grand Daddy's CPU Performance Counters - CPU Hardware Performance Counters for Security. Black Hat 2015 Briefings. https://www.blackhat.com/docs/us-15/materials/us-15-Herath-These-Are-Not-Your-Grand-Daddys-CPU-Performance-Counters-CPU-Hardware-Performance-Counters-For-Security.pdf
14. Hund, R., Willems, C., Holz, T.: Practical timing side channel attacks against kernel space ASLR. In: 2013 IEEE Symposium on Security and Privacy, pp. 191–205 (2013)
15. Intel: Intel® 64 and IA-32 Architectures Software Developer's Manual, vol. 3 (3A, 3B & 3C): System Programming Guide 253665 (2014)
16. Irazoqui, G., Eisenbarth, T., Sunar, B.: S$A: a shared cache attack that works across cores and defies VM sandboxing - and its application to AES. In: S&P 2015 (2015)
17. Irazoqui, G., Inci, M.S., Eisenbarth, T., Sunar, B.: Know thy neighbor: crypto library detection in cloud. In: Proceedings on Privacy Enhancing Technologies, vol. 1(1), pp. 25–40 (2015)
18. Irazoqui, G., Inci, M.S., Eisenbarth, T., Sunar, B.: Lucky 13 strikes back. In: AsiaCCS 2015 (2015)
19. Kim, T., Peinado, M., Mainar-Ruiz, G.: StealthMem: system-level protection against cache-based side channel attacks in the cloud. In: Proceedings of the 21st USENIX Security Symposium (2012)
20. Kim, Y., Daly, R., Kim, J., Fallin, C., Lee, J.H., Lee, D., Wilkerson, C., Lai, K., Mutlu, O.: Flipping bits in memory without accessing them: an experimental study of DRAM disturbance errors. In: Proceeding of the 41st Annual International Symposium on Computer Architecuture (ISCA 2014) (2014)
21. Kong, J., Acıiçmez, O., Seifert, J.P., Zhou, H.: Hardware-software integrated approaches to defend against software cache-based side channel attacks. In: Proceedings of the 15th International Symposium on High Performance Computer Architecture (HPCA 2009), pp. 393–404 (2009)
22. Lipp, M., Gruss, D., Spreitzer, R., Mangard, S.: Armageddon: Last-level cacheattacks on mobile devices. CoRR abs/1511.04897 (2015)
23. Liu, F., Lee, R.B.: Random fill cache architecture. In: IEEE/ACM International Symposium on Microarchitecture (MICRO 2014), pp. 203–215 (2014)
24. Liu, F., Yarom, Y., Ge, Q., Heiser, G., Lee, R.B.: Last-level cache side-channel attacks are practical. In: S&P 2015 (2015)
25. lwn.net: 2.6.26-rc1 short-form changelog, May 2008. https://lwn.net/Articles/280913/
26. Malone, C., Zahran, M., Karri, R.: Are hardware performance counters a cost effective way for integrity checking of programs. In: Proceedings of the Sixth ACM Workshop on Scalable Trusted Computing (2011)
27. Maurice, C., Le Scouarnec, N., Neumann, C., Heen, O., Francillon, A.: Reverse engineering intel complex addressing using performance counters. In: RAID (2015)
28. Maurice, C., Neumann, C., Heen, O., Francillon, A.: C5: cross-cores cache covert channel. In: Almgren, M., Gulisano, V., Maggi, F. (eds.) DIMVA 2015. LNCS, vol. 9148, pp. 46–64. Springer, Heidelberg (2015)
29. Oren, Y., Kemerlis, V.P., Sethumadhavan, S., Keromytis, A.D.: The spy in the sandbox: practical cache attacks in JavaScript and their implications. In: CCS 2015 (2015)
30. Osvik, D.A., Shamir, A., Tromer, E.: Cache attacks and countermeasures: the case of AES. In: Pointcheval, D. (ed.) CT-RSA 2006. LNCS, vol. 3860, pp. 1–20. Springer, Heidelberg (2006)

31. Payer, M.: HexPADS: a platform to detect "Stealth" attacks. In: Caballero, J., et al. (eds.) ESSoS 2016. LNCS, vol. 9639, pp. 138–154. Springer, Heidelberg (2016). doi:10.1007/978-3-319-30806-7_9
32. Percival, C.: Cache missing for fun and profit. In: Proceedings of BSDCan (2005)
33. Qureshi, M.K., Jaleel, A., Patt, Y.N., Steely, S.C., Emer, J.: Adaptive insertion policies for high performance caching. ACM SIGARCH Comput. Archit. News **35**(2), 381–391 (2007)
34. Raj, H., Nathuji, R., Singh, A., England, P.: Resource management for isolation enhanced cloud services. In: Proceedings of the 1st ACM Cloud Computing Security Workshop (CCSW 2009), pp. 77–84 (2009)
35. Ristenpart, T., Tromer, E., Shacham, H., Savage, S.: Hey, you, get off of my cloud: exploring information leakage in third-party compute clouds. In: CCS 2009 (2009)
36. Seaborn, M., Dullien, T.: Exploiting the DRAM rowhammer bug to gain kernel privileges. In: Black Hat (2015)
37. Spreitzer, R., Plos, T.: Cache-access pattern attack on disaligned AES T-tables. In: Prouff, E. (ed.) COSADE 2013. LNCS, vol. 7864, pp. 200–214. Springer, Heidelberg (2013)
38. Tannous, A., Trostle, J.T., Hassan, M., McLaughlin, S.E., Jaeger, T.: New side channels targeted at passwords. In: ACSAC, pp. 45–54 (2008)
39. Tromer, E., Osvik, D.A., Shamir, A.: Efficient cache attacks on AES, and countermeasures. J. Cryptology **23**(1), 37–71 (2010)
40. Uhsadel, L., Georges, A., Verbauwhede, I.: Exploiting hardware performance counters. In: 5th Workshop on Fault Diagnosis and Tolerance in Cryptography (FDTC 2008) (2008)
41. Wang, Z., Lee, R.B.: New cache designs for thwarting software cache-based side channel attacks. ACM SIGARCH Comput. Archit. News **35**(2), 494 (2007)
42. Wang, Z., Lee, R.B.: A novel cache architecture with enhanced performance and security. In: IEEE/ACM International Symposium on Microarchitecture (MICRO 2008), pp. 83–93 (2008)
43. Willems, C., Hund, R., Fobian, A., Felsch, D., Holz, T., Vasudevan, A.: Down to the bare metal: using processor features for binary analysis. In: ACSAC 2012 (2012)
44. Xia, Y., Liu, Y., Chen, H., Zang, B.: CFIMon: detecting violation of control flow integrity using performance counters. In: DSN 2012 (2012)
45. Yarom, Y., Falkner, K.: Flush+Reload: a high resolution, low noise, L3 cache side-channel attack. In: USENIX Security Symposium (2014)
46. Zhang, K., Wang, X.: Peeping tom in the neighborhood: keystroke eavesdropping on multi-user systems. In: USENIX Security Symposium (2009)
47. Zhang, Y., Juels, A., Oprea, A., Reiter, M.K.: HomeAlone: co-residency detection in the cloud via side-channel analysis. In: S&P 2011 (2011)
48. Zhang, Y., Juels, A., Reiter, M.K., Ristenpart, T.: Cross-tenant side-channel attacks in PaaS clouds. In: CCS 2014 (2014)
49. Zhang, Y., Reiter, M.: Düppel: retrofitting commodity operating systems to mitigate cache side channels in the cloud. In: CCS 2013 (2013)

Rowhammer.js: A Remote Software-Induced Fault Attack in JavaScript

Daniel Gruss[⊠], Clémentine Maurice, and Stefan Mangard

Graz University of Technology, Graz, Austria
daniel.gruss@iaik.tugraz.at

Abstract. A fundamental assumption in software security is that a memory location can only be modified by processes that may write to this memory location. However, a recent study has shown that parasitic effects in DRAM can change the content of a memory cell without accessing it, but by accessing other memory locations in a high frequency. This so-called Rowhammer bug occurs in most of today's memory modules and has fatal consequences for the security of all affected systems, e.g., privilege escalation attacks.

All studies and attacks related to Rowhammer so far rely on the availability of a cache flush instruction in order to cause accesses to DRAM modules at a sufficiently high frequency. We overcome this limitation by defeating complex cache replacement policies. We show that caches can be forced into fast cache eviction to trigger the Rowhammer bug with only regular memory accesses. This allows to trigger the Rowhammer bug in highly restricted and even scripting environments.

We demonstrate a fully automated attack that requires nothing but a website with JavaScript to trigger faults on remote hardware. Thereby we can gain unrestricted access to systems of website visitors. We show that the attack works on off-the-shelf systems. Existing countermeasures fail to protect against this new Rowhammer attack.

1 Introduction

Hardware-fault attacks have been a security threat since the first attacks in 1997 by Boneh et al. [10] and Biham et al. [9]. Fault attacks typically require physical access to the device to expose it to physical conditions which are outside the specification. This includes high or low temperature, radiation, as well as laser on dismantled microchips. However, software-induced hardware faults are also possible, if the device can be brought to the border or out of the specified operation conditions using software. Kim et al. [20] showed that frequently accessing specific memory locations can cause random bit flips in DRAM chips. 85 % of the DDR3 modules they examined are vulnerable. The number of bit flips varies from one module to another, *i.e.* some modules can be more vulnerable than others. More recently, DDR4 modules have been found to be vulnerable as well [32].

C. Maurice—Part of the work was done while author was affiliated to Technicolor and Eurecom.

© Springer International Publishing Switzerland 2016
J. Caballero et al. (Eds.): DIMVA 2016, LNCS 9721, pp. 300–321, 2016.
DOI: 10.1007/978-3-319-40667-1_15

Bit flips can be triggered by software by flushing a memory location from the cache and reloading it. Seaborn [36] demonstrated that an attacker can exploit such bit flips for privilege escalation. These exploits are written in native code and use special instructions to flush data from the cache.

We show that it is possible to trigger hardware faults by performing fast cache eviction on all architectures, if the DRAM modules are vulnerable. Compared to previous work, we do not use any specific instruction, but only regular memory accesses to evict data from the cache. The attack technique is thus generic and can be applied to any architecture, programming language and runtime environment that allows producing a fast stream of memory accesses. Therefore, proposed countermeasures such as removing the clflush instruction cannot prevent attacks. Even more severe, we show that on vulnerable modules, we can also perform remote JavaScript-based Rowhammer attacks.

Since an attack through a website can be performed on millions of victim machines simultaneously and stealthily, it poses an enormous security threat. Rowhammer.js is independent of the instruction set of the CPU. It is the first remote software-induced hardware-fault attack. As a proof of concept, we implemented a JavaScript version that as of today runs in all recent versions of Firefox and Google Chrome.

For a Rowhammer attack in JavaScript we perform the following steps:

1. Find 2 addresses in different rows
2. Evict and reload the 2 addresses in a high frequency
3. Search for an exploitable bit flip
4. Exploit the bit flip (e.g. manipulate page tables, remote code execution).

Steps 3 and 4 have already been solved in previous work [36], but step 1 and 2 remain open challenges.

The challenge in step 1 is to retrieve information on the physical addresses from JavaScript. It is strictly sandboxed and provides no possibility to retrieve virtual or physical addresses. To tackle this challenge, we determine parts of the physical addresses using large arrays that are allocated by operating systems on large pages. We thus do not exploit any weaknesses in JavaScript or the browser, but only OS-level optimizations.

The challenge in step 2 is to find fast cache eviction strategies to replace the clflush instruction. On older CPUs, simply accessing $n + 1$ addresses is sufficient to evict lines for an n-way cache [23,27]. On Intel CPUs produced in the last 4 years, i.e. post Sandy Bridge, the replacement policy has changed and is undocumented. Consequently, known eviction strategies have a low eviction rate or a high execution time, which is not suitable for Rowhammer attacks. To tackle this challenge, we present a novel generic method for finding cache eviction strategies that achieve the best performance in both timing and eviction rate by comprehensively exploring the parameter space. We present the best eviction strategies so far, outperforming previous ones on all recent Intel architectures. Based on this method, we build a two-phase online attack for remote systems with unknown hardware configuration.

Table 1. Experimental setups.

Platform	CPU	Architecture	RAM
Lenovo T420	i5-2540M	Sandy bridge	Corsair DDR3-1333 8 GB and Samsung DDR3-1600 4 GB (2×)
Lenovo x230	i5-3320M	Ivy bridge	Samsung DDR3-1600 4 GB (2×)
Asus H97-Pro	i7-4790	Haswell	Kingston DDR3-1600 8 GB
ASRock Z170 ITX	i7-6700K	Skylake	G.Skill DDR4-3200 8 GB (2×) and Crucial DDR4-2133 8 GB (2×)

We compare the different implementations of the Rowhammer attacks on a fixed set of configurations (see Table 1), some vulnerable in default settings, others at decreased refresh rates.

As of today, software countermeasures against Rowhammer native code attacks only target specific exploits, and, as we show, do not protect sufficiently against attacks from JavaScript. Hardware countermeasures are harder to deploy, since they do not affect legacy hardware including recent vulnerable DDR4 modules. BIOS updates can be used to solve the problem on commodity systems, however it is only a practical solution for very advanced users.

Summarizing, our key contributions are:

- We provide the first comprehensive exploration of the cache eviction parameter space on all recent Intel CPUs. This also benefits broader domains, e.g. cache attacks, cache-oblivious algorithms, cache replacement policies.
- We build a native code implementation of the Rowhammer attack that only uses memory accesses. The attack is successful on Sandy Bridge, Ivy Bridge, Haswell and Skylake, in various DDR3 and DDR4 configurations.
- We build a pure JavaScript Rowhammer implementation, showing that an attacker can trigger Rowhammer bit flips remotely, through a web browser.

The remainder of this paper is organized as follows. In Sect. 2, we provide background information on DRAM, the Rowhammer bug, CPU caches, and cache attacks. In Sect. 3, we describe a two-phase automated attack to trigger bit flips on unknown systems. In Sect. 4, we demonstrate the Rowhammer bug without `clflush` in native code and in JavaScript. In Sect. 5, we provide a discussion of our proof-of-concept exploit, limitations, and countermeasures. Finally, we discuss future work in Sect. 6 and provide conclusions in Sect. 7.

2   Background

2.1   DRAM

Modern memory systems have multiple *channels* of DRAM memory connected to the memory controller. A channel consists of multiple *Dual Inline Memory Modules* (*DIMMs*), that are the physical modules on the motherboard. Each

DIMM has one or two *ranks*, that are the sides of the physical module. Each rank is a collection of *chips*, that are further composed of *banks*. Accesses to different banks can be served concurrently. Each bank is an array of capacitor cells that are either in a charged or discharged state, representing a binary data value. The bank is represented as a collection of rows, typically 2^{14} to 2^{17}.

The charge from the cells is read into a *row buffer* on request and written back to the cells as soon as another row is requested. Thus, access to the DRAM is done in three steps: 1. opening a row, 2. accessing the data in the row buffer, 3. closing the row before opening a new row, writing data back to the cells.

DRAM is volatile memory and discharges over time. The *refresh interval* defines when the cell charge is read and restored to sustain the value. DDR3 and DDR4 specifications require refreshing all rows at least once within 64ms [1,20].

The selection of channel, rank, bank and row is based on physical address bits. The mapping for Intel CPUs has recently been reverse engineered [32,35].

2.2   The Rowhammer Bug

The increase of DRAM density has led to physically smaller cells, thus capable of storing smaller charges. As a result, cells have a lower noise margin, and cells can interact electrically with each other although they should be isolated. The so called *Rowhammer bug* consists in the corruption of data, not in rows that are directly accessed, but rather in rows nearby the accessed one.

DRAM and CPU manufacturers have known the Rowhammer bug since at least 2012 [5,6]. Hammering DRAM chips is a quality assurance tests applied to modules [3]. As refreshing DRAM cells consumes time, DRAM manufacturers optimize the refresh rate to the lowest rate that still works reliably.

The Rowhammer bug has recently been studied [16,20,29] and the majority of off-the-shelf DRAM modules has been found vulnerable to bit flips using the clflush instruction. The clflush instruction flushes data from the cache, forcing the CPU to serve the next memory access from DRAM. Their proof-of-concept implementation frequently accesses and flushes two memory locations in a loop, causing bit flips in a third memory location.

Seaborn implemented Rowhammer exploits [36] in native code with the clflush instruction: a privilege escalation on a Linux system caused by a bit flip in a page table and an escape from the Google Native Client sandbox caused by a bit flip in indirect jumps. As a countermeasure, the clflush instruction was removed from the set of allowed instructions in Google Chrome Native Client [36].

2.3   CPU Caches

A CPU cache is a small and fast memory inside the CPU hiding the latency of main memory by keeping copies of frequently used data. Modern Intel CPUs have three levels of cache, where L1 is the smallest and fastest cache and L3 the slowest and largest cache. The L3 cache is an inclusive cache, *i.e.* all data

Table 2. Complex addressing function from [24].

		Address Bit																									
		32	31	30	29	28	27	26	25	24	23	22	21	20	19	18	17	16	15	14	13	12	11	10	9	8	7	6
2 cores	o_0	⊕		⊕		⊕	⊕	⊕	⊕	⊕		⊕		⊕		⊕	⊕	⊕		⊕		⊕		⊕				⊕
4 cores	o_0	⊕		⊕		⊕	⊕	⊕	⊕	⊕		⊕		⊕		⊕	⊕	⊕		⊕		⊕		⊕	⊕			⊕
	o_1		⊕	⊕		⊕		⊕	⊕	⊕	⊕	⊕	⊕		⊕		⊕		⊕		⊕				⊕	⊕		

in L1 and L2 cache is also present in the L3 cache. It is divided into one slice per CPU core, but shared, *i.e.* cores can access all slices. The undocumented *complex addressing* function that maps physical addresses to slices was recently reverse engineered [18,24,40]. We used the results published by Maurice et al. [24], shown in Table 2. The table shows how address bits 6 to 32 are xor'd into one or two output bits o_0 and o_1. In case of a dual-core CPU, output bit o_0 determines to which of the two cache slices the physical address maps. In case of a quad-core CPU, output bits o_1 and o_0 determine the slice.

Caches are organized in sets of multiple lines. The mapping from physical addresses to sets is fixed. Addresses that map to the same set and slice are called *congruent*. To load a new line from memory, the *replacement policy* decides which line to evict. Intel has not disclosed the cache replacement policy of their CPUs. However, the replacement policies for some architectures have been reverse-engineered: Sandy Bridge has a pseudo-LRU replacement policy and Ivy Bridge a modification of the pseudo-LRU replacement policy [38]. Moreover, Ivy Bridge, Haswell and Skylake use adaptive cache replacement policies which only behave as pseudo-LRU in some situations [33]. These CPUs can switch the cache replacement policy frequently.

2.4 Cache Attacks and Cache Eviction

Cache side-channel attacks exploit timing differences between cache hits and cache misses. Practical attacks on cryptographic algorithms have been explored thoroughly [8,31]. There are two main types of cache attacks called Prime+Probe and Flush+Reload. The Prime+Probe attack has been introduced by Percival [31] and Osvik et al. [28]. It determines activities of a victim process by repeatedly measuring the duration to access once every address in a set of congruent addresses, *i.e.* a so-called eviction set. Prime+Probe on the last-level cache enables cross-core cache attacks such as cross-VM attacks without shared memory [19,23], covert channels [25] and attacks from within sandboxed JavaScript [27]. Oren et al. [27] and Liu et al. [23] compute the eviction set by adding addresses to the eviction set until eviction works. Flush+Reload has been introduced by Gullasch et al. [14] and Yarom and Falkner [39]. It exploits shared memory between attacker and victim and is very fine-grained. Cache lines are flushed with the `clflush` instruction or using cache eviction [13].

Evicting data from the cache is just as crucial to cache attacks as it is for the Rowhammer attack. Previous work either uses the `clflush` instruction or hand-crafted eviction loops. Hund et al. [17] showed that data can be evicted by filling a large memory buffer the size of the cache. However, this is very slow and thus not applicable to fine-grained cache attacks or Rowhammer attacks. Using the reverse-engineered complex addressing function solves the problem of finding addresses that are congruent in the cache, but it leaves the non-trivial problem of finding access sequences to achieve high eviction rates while maintaining a low execution time.

3   Cache Eviction Strategies

In this section, we describe how to find cache eviction strategies in a fully automated way for microarchitectures post Sandy Bridge. An *eviction strategy* accesses addresses from an eviction set in a specific access pattern and can ideally be used as a replacement for `clflush`. *Eviction set* is commonly defined as a set of congruent addresses. The access pattern defines in which order addresses from the eviction set are accessed, including multiple accesses per address.

An efficient eviction strategy can replace the `clflush` instruction in any cache attack and significantly improves cache attacks based on Prime+Probe, like JavaScript-based attacks [27] or cross-VM cache attacks [23]. It also allows to replace the `clflush` instruction in a Rowhammer attack (see Sect. 4).

The replacement policy of the CPU influences the size of the eviction set and the access pattern necessary to build an efficient eviction strategy. For a pseudo-LRU replacement policy, accessing as many congruent locations as the number of ways of the L3 cache (for instance 12 or 16) once, evicts the targeted address with a high probability. For adaptive cache replacement policies, an eviction strategy that is effective for one policy is likely to be ineffective for the other. Thus it is necessary to craft an eviction strategy that causes eviction for both policies and ideally does not introduce a significant timing overhead.

We distinguish between the following ways to generate an eviction strategy:

1. *Static eviction set and static access pattern*: uses information on cache slice function and physical addresses, and generates a pre-defined pattern in negligible time. Sections 3.2 and 3.3 describe new efficient eviction strategies computed this way.
2. *Dynamic eviction set and static access pattern*: computes the eviction set in an automated way, without any knowledge of the system, e.g. the number of cores. A good access pattern that matches the replacement policy of the targeted system is necessary for a successful attack. Section 3.3 describes this approach.
3. *Dynamic eviction set and dynamic access pattern*: automatically computes the eviction set and the access pattern based on randomness. This comes at the cost of performing a huge number of eviction tests, but it has the advantage to require almost no information on the system, and allows to

implement fully automated online attacks for unknown systems. Section 3.3 describes this approach.

4. *Static eviction set and dynamic access pattern*: uses a pre-defined eviction set, but a random pattern that is computed in an automated way. This is possible in theory, but it has no advantage over automatically testing static access patterns. We thus do not further investigate this approach.

We first describe a model to represent access patterns, given several parameters. To find a good eviction strategy for a given system, we define an offline and an online phase. In the offline phase, the attacker explores the parameter space to find the best eviction strategies for a set of controlled systems. The goal is to find a eviction strategy that matches the undocumented replacement policy the closest, including the possibility of policy switches. In the online phase, the attacker targets an unknown system, with no privileges.

3.1   Cache Eviction Strategy Model

The success of a cache eviction strategy is measured by testing whether the targeted memory address is not cached anymore over many experiments, *i.e.* average success rate. For such cases, we made the following three observations.

First, only cache hits and cache misses to addresses in the same cache set have a non-negligible influence on the cache, apart from cache maintenance and prefetching operations to the same cache set. We verified this by taking an eviction algorithm and randomly adding memory accesses that are not congruent. The eviction rate is the average success rate of the eviction function. It does not change by adding non-congruent accesses to an eviction strategy as long as the timing does not deviate. Thus, the eviction set only contains congruent addresses and the effectiveness of the eviction strategy depends on the *eviction set size*.

Second, addresses are indistinguishable with respect to the cache. Thus, we represent access patterns as sequences of address labels a_i, e.g. $a_1 a_2 a_3 \ldots$. Each address label is set to a different address and thus for each time frame the sequence defines which address to access. A pattern $a_1 a_2 a_3$ is equivalent to any pattern $a_k a_l a_m$ where $k \neq l \neq m$. If run in a loop, the number of *different memory addresses* has an influence on the effectiveness on the eviction strategy.

Third, repeated accesses to the same address are necessary to keep it in the cache, as replacement policies can prefer to evict recently added cache lines over older ones. Changing the eviction sequence from $a_1 a_2 \ldots a_{17}$ to $a_1 a_1 a_2 a_2 \ldots a_{17} a_{17}$ reduces the execution time by more than 33 % on Haswell, and increases the eviction rate significantly if executed repeatedly, as the cache remains filled with our eviction set. However, we observed a diminishing marginal utility for the number of accesses to the same address. For all addresses we observed that after a certain number of accesses, further accesses do not increase and can even decrease the eviction rate. Thus, we describe eviction strategies as a loop over an eviction set of size S, where only a subset of D addresses is *accessed per round*. A parameter L allows to make accesses *overlap* for repeated accesses.

```
1  for (s = 0; s <= S-D; s += L)
2    for (c = 0; c <= C; c += 1)
3      for (d = 0; d <= D; d += 1)
4        *a[s+d];
```

Listing 1. Eviction loop for pattern testing.

While testing all possible sequences even for very small sequence lengths is not possible in practical time (c.f., Stirling numbers of second kind as a good estimate), a systematic exploration of influential parameters is possible. In theory, better eviction strategies may lie outside of this reduced search space. However using this method, we found eviction strategies that allowed us to successfully trigger bit flips using eviction-based Rowhammer (see Sect. 4). To discuss and compare eviction strategies systematically, we use the following naming scheme in this paper to describe parametrized eviction strategies as depicted in Listing 1. The eviction strategy name has the form $\mathcal{P}\text{-}C\text{-}D\text{-}L\text{-}S$, with C, the number of accesses to each memory address per loop round, D, the number of different memory addresses accessed per loop round, L, the step size/increment of the loop (for overlapping accesses), and S, the eviction set size. For instance, LRU-eviction is $\mathcal{P}\text{-}1\text{-}1\text{-}1\text{-}S$ with an access sequence of $a_1a_2a_3\ldots a_S$.

3.2   Offline Phase

In the offline phase, the attacker has at his disposal a set of machines and tries to learn the eviction strategy that matches the replacement policy the closest for each machine. While it is not strictly a reverse engineering of the replacement policy, by knowing the best eviction strategy, the attacker gains knowledge on the systems. In this phase, the attacker has no time constraints.

We discuss the evaluation in detail for the Haswell platform with a single DIMM in single channel mode. We explored the parameter space up to degree 6 in the dimensions of C, D and L and 23 different eviction set sizes each, in order to find eviction strategies that are fast and effective enough to perform Rowhammer attacks. Including the equivalent eviction strategies we evaluated a total of 18293 eviction strategies on 3 of our test platforms. We tested each eviction strategy in 20 double-sided Rowhammer tests with 2 million hammering rounds (*i.e.* 80 million evictions per eviction strategy) and evaluated them using different evaluation criteria including eviction rate, runtime, number of cache hits and misses. The runtime was more than 6 days. The hammering was performed on a fixed set of physical addresses congruent to one specific cache set to allow for a fair comparison of the eviction strategies. Half of the evictions, *i.e.* 40 millions, were used to measure eviction rate, cache hits and cache misses. The other half was used to measure the average execution time per eviction. We verified that the sample size is high enough to get reproducible measurements.

The number of bit flips is not suitable for the evaluation of a single eviction strategy, but only to determine whether and how cache hits, cache misses, the execution time and the eviction rate influence the probability of a bit flip. Bit flips are reproducible in terms of the memory location, but the time and the number of memory accesses until a bit flip occurs again varies widely. In order to measure the average number of bit flips for a eviction strategy, we would have to test every eviction strategy for several hours instead of minutes. This would increase the test time per machine to several weeks, and even then, it would not yield reproducible results, as it has been observed that the DRAM cells get permanently damaged if hammered for a long time [20].

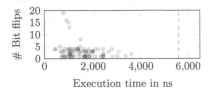

(a) Low execution time is better.

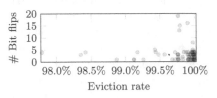

(b) High eviction rate is better. Average over all eviction strategies is 73.96%.

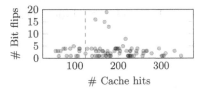

(c) Number of cache hits is not a good criteria for bit flips.

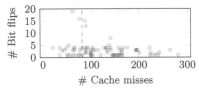

(d) Number of cache misses is not a good criteria for bit flips.

Fig. 1. Relation between the number of bit flips and average execution time, cache hits and cache misses per eviction and the eviction rate of the corresponding eviction strategy measured in 40 million samples. One point per eviction strategy that caused a bit flip, others are omitted. The darker the more points overlay. Average over all eviction strategies shown as dashed line. Good eviction strategies have high eviction rates and low execution times.

High execution times are too slow to trigger bit flips and low execution times are useless without a good eviction rate. The execution time of the eviction strategy is directly related to the number of memory accesses to the two victim addresses. Hence, it influences the probability of a bit flip directly. On our default configured Ivy Bridge notebook we observed bit flips even with execution times of $1.5\,\mu s$ per hammering round, that is approximately 21,500 accesses per address within the specified total refresh interval of 64ms. This maps to the average periodic refresh interval `tREFI` by dividing 64ms by 8192 [26]. Double-sided rowhammering using `clflush` takes only 60 ns on our Haswell test system, that is approximately 0.6 million accesses per address in 64 ms. Figure 1a shows how bit flips are correlated with the eviction execution time.

The eviction rate has to be very high to trigger bit flips. Figure 1b shows how many bit flips occurred at which eviction rate. We observe that 81 % of the bit flips occurred at an eviction rate of 99.75 % or higher and thus use this as a threshold for good eviction strategies on our Haswell system. Even though a bit flip may occur at lower eviction rates, the probability is significantly lower.

The eviction loop contributes to a high number of cache hits and cache misses, apart from the two addresses we want to hammer. We measure the number of cache hits and cache misses that occur during our test run using hardware performance counters through the Linux syscall interface perf_event_open. Cache hits have a negligible influence on the execution time and no effect on the DRAM. Cache misses increase the execution time and, if performed on a different row but in the same channel, rank and bank, additional DRAM accesses. However, Figs. 1c and 1d show that both cache hits and cache misses do not impact the number of bit flips significantly, as the average for all eviction strategies is in the range of the eviction strategies that triggered a bit flip.

Thus, we thus use the eviction rate as a criteria for good eviction strategies, and among those eviction strategies, we prefer those with a lower average execution time. This method requires no access to any system interfaces and can be implemented in any language and execution environment that allows to measure time and perform arbitrary memory accesses, such as JavaScript.

Table 3. The fastest 5 eviction strategies with an eviction rate above 99.75 % compared to clflush and LRU eviction on the Haswell test system.

C	D	L	S	Accesses	Hits	Misses	Time (ns)	Eviction
−	−	−	−	−	2	2	60	99.9999 %
5	2	2	18	90	34	4	179	99.9624 %
2	2	1	17	68	35	5	180	99.9820 %
2	1	1	17	34	47	5	191	99.8595 %
6	2	2	18	108	34	5	216	99.9365 %
1	1	1	17	17	96	13	307	74.4593 %
4	2	2	20	80	41	23	329	99.7800 %
1	1	1	20	20	187	78	934	99.8200 %

Table 3 shows a comparison of the fastest 5 of these eviction strategies with an eviction rate above 99.75 % (see Fig. 1b) and clflush based rowhammering as well as the fastest LRU ($\mathcal{P}$-1-1-1-20) eviction strategy that achieves the same eviction rate. The best two eviction strategies are $\mathcal{P}$-5- 2-2-18 and $\mathcal{P}$-2-2-1-17, both with an execution time around 180 ns.

Accessing each address in the eviction set only once (LRU eviction) is far from optimal for cache attacks and impractical for Rowhammer. Although counterintuitive, adding more accesses to the eviction loop will lower the overall execution time. We can observe this for instance by comparing the eviction strategies $\mathcal{P}$-1-1-1-20 and $\mathcal{P}$-4-2-2-20. While both access the same set of 20 addresses, the latter one performs 4 times as many memory accesses, yet its execution time is

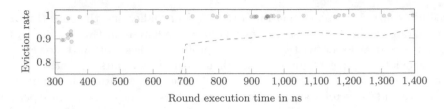

Fig. 2. Average execution time and eviction rate per eviction strategy on Ivy Bridge measured in 40 million samples per eviction strategy. One point per eviction strategy that caused a bit flip, others are omitted. The darker the more points overlay. Average over all eviction strategies shown as dashed line.

only one third. Comparing the best eviction strategy we found to LRU eviction as described in previous work, performs only as good if the set size is at least $S = 25$, increasing the average execution time 9 times higher than the one of the best eviction strategy we found. On the other hand, the eviction set size in previous work is typically specified as $S = 17$. For $\mathcal{P}$-1-1-1-17 we measured an eviction rate of 74.5 % and even then a 1.7 times higher execution time than with the best eviction strategy we found. This shows that the eviction strategies we found are a significant improvement over previously published eviction methods.

We performed the same evaluation for the other architectures. The distribution of bit flips on our Ivy Bridge test system relative to eviction rate and execution time is shown in Fig. 2. Most bit flips occurred at eviction rates above 99 %. The fastest 5 of these eviction strategies are shown in Table 4 in comparison with `clflush` and the fastest LRU ($\mathcal{P}$-1-1-1-15) eviction strategy.

Table 4. `clflush` and LRU eviction compared to the fastest 5 eviction strategies above 99 % eviction rate on the Ivy Bridge test system (left) and compared to the fastest 5 eviction strategies above 99.9 % eviction rate on the Skylake DDR4 test system (right).

C	D	L	S	Acc.	Hits	Misses	Time (ns)	Eviction	C	D	L	S	Acc.	Hits	Misses	Time (ns)	Eviction
-	-	-	-	-	2	2	40	100.000%	-	-	-	-	-	2	2	47	100.000%
4	5	5	20	80	43	35	327	99.514%	3	1	1	22	66	48	45	218	99.937%
1	1	1	13	13	52	33	333	72.145%	2	2	1	22	88	47	45	222	99.932%
3	1	1	17	51	46	41	341	99.081%	3	3	3	24	72	50	45	222	99.938%
4	5	5	17	68	45	37	345	99.604%	3	3	3	21	63	51	45	223	99.937%
3	1	1	19	57	50	47	369	99.267%	4	3	3	24	96	49	45	225	99.905%
3	2	2	18	54	48	43	376	99.412%	1	1	1	17	17	240	36	240	82.959%
1	1	1	15	15	97	84	632	99.085%	1	1	1	21	21	145	87	495	99.970%

According to our measurements the complex addressing function on Skylake is not the same as in Haswell, but it can be trivially derived from the reverse engineered 8-core function. We again found that LRU eviction performs much worse than the best eviction strategy we found as shown in Table 4.

3.3   Online Phase

In the online phase, the attacker targets an unknown system. In particular, microarchitecture and number of CPU cores are unknown to the attacker. The attacker has the knowledge gained from the offline phase at his disposal. However, he has no privilege on the victim's machine and no time to run the extensive search from the offline phase. The online phase consists in two attacks: an assumption-based attack, and a fall-back attack in case the first one does not work. In both cases the attack is based on a series of timing attacks and no access to specific system interfaces is necessary.

Assumption-Based Attack. The attacker first tests whether the targeted system resembles a system tested in the offline phase, by performing timing attacks. No access to syscalls or system interfaces is required for this step. The attacker defines a threshold eviction rate based on the results from the offline phase (for instance 99.75 %) and searches for eviction strategies above this threshold on the system under attack. By testing a set of eviction strategies from the offline phase, the attacker learns whether the architecture of the system under attack resembles an architecture from the offline phase. In this case the best eviction strategy for the system under attack is within the set of eviction strategies previously tested. The number of eviction strategies to test is as low as the number of targeted CPU architectures and thus it only takes a few seconds to compute.

```
0123 0123 0123 0123 1032 1032 1032 1032 2301 2301 2301 2301 3210 3210 3210 3210
1032 1032 1032 1032 0123 0123 0123 0123 3210 3210 3210 3210 2301 2301 2301 2301
2301 2301 2301 2301 3210 3210 3210 3210 0123 0123 0123 0123 1032 1032 1032 1032
3210 3210 3210 3210 2301 2301 2301 2301 1032 1032 1032 1032 0123 0123 0123 0123
```

Fig. 3. Slice patterns for 64-byte offsets on 4KB pages on a 4-core system. An attacker can derive which addresses map to the same cache slice. Substituting 2 by 0 and 3 by 1 gives the slice pattern for 2-core systems.

The eviction set can be computed in a static or dynamic way. Without any further assumptions we can run modified versions of the algorithms by Oren et al. [27] or Liu et al. [23]. Instead of the $\mathcal{P}$-1-1-1 access pattern they implement, we use one of the suspected eviction strategies to build a dynamic assumption-based algorithm. This improves the success rate of their algorithms on recent architectures. However, we make additional assumptions to reduce the execution time to a minimum and build a static assumption-based algorithm. One assumption is that large arrays are allocated on large pages, as has been observed before [11]. Based on this assumption we can use the complex addressing function from Table 2 to determine the slice patterns for 4KB and 2MB pages as shown in Fig. 3. These distinct patterns in the mapping from physical addresses to cache slices depend only on the number of cache slices and are the same for Intel CPUs since the Sandy Bridge architecture. The algorithm by Oren et al. [27] or Liu et al. [23] finds only addresses in the same cache slice and cache set. We use it to build an eviction set of 2MB-aligned congruent addresses in the same slice. Subsequent eviction set computations are performed statically based on the complex addressing function and the identified 2MB offsets.

Fall-Back Attack. If the assumption-based phase does not work on a system under attack, e.g. because the unknown system is none of the systems tested in the offline phase, the attacker runs a fall-back phase to find an eviction strategy that is sufficient to trigger a bit flip with Rowhammer.

Oren et al. [27] and Liu et al. [23] compute a dynamic eviction set with a static access pattern $\mathcal{P}$-1-1-1. We extend their algorithms to compute eviction strategies with dynamic eviction sets and dynamic access patterns. In the first step, we continuously add addresses to the eviction strategy multiple times to create eviction strategies with multiple accesses to the same address. We know that the eviction strategy is large enough as soon as we can clearly measure the eviction of the target physical address. In a second step, when the eviction rate is above the attacker chosen threshold, eviction addresses that do not lower the eviction rate are removed by replacing them with other addresses that are still in the eviction set. Thus, the number of memory accesses does not decrease, but the eviction set is minimized. This decreases the number of cache misses and thus the execution time. Finally, we randomly remove accesses that do not decrease the eviction rate and do not increase the execution time. This again decreases the number of unnecessary cache hits and thus the execution time.

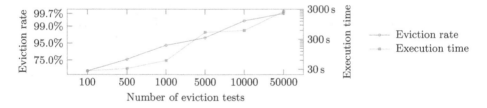

Fig. 4. The eviction rate and execution time of the dynamic eviction strategy when implementing the `cached(p)` function with n eviction tests.

The resulting eviction strategy can neither access less addresses nor can any duplicate accesses be removed without lowering the eviction rate. They thus perform similarly to statically computed eviction strategies. The result of the algorithm is a series of accesses that fulfill the eviction rate threshold chosen by the attacker and that has a low execution time on the system under attack. If the threshold was set high enough so that bit flips are likely to occur in practice, the eviction strategy found by the fall-back algorithm can be used for an attack.

The algorithm uses a function `cached(p)` that tries to evict a target address p using the current eviction strategy and set and decides whether p is cached or not based on the access time. The quality of the solution depends on the number of tests that are performed in this function. The function only returns true, if an eviction rate below the attacker defined threshold is measured. A higher number of tests increases the execution time and the accuracy of this binary decision. Figure 4 shows how the number of tests influences the eviction rate and the execution time of the resulting eviction strategy. If a high eviction rate is necessary, the execution time of the algorithm is can exceed 40 min. Thus, our algorithm can precompute a working eviction strategy once and subsequent eviction set computations are done with the fixed eviction strategy within seconds.

4   Implementation of Eviction-Based Rowhammer

We now perform Rowhammer attacks using the eviction strategies from Sect. 3 instead of `clflush` in different scenarios. First, we demonstrate that it is possible to trigger bit flips in the same conditions as in the existing attacks where an attacker is able to execute native code on the system under attack. We then show that given knowledge about the physical addresses, it is possible to trigger bit flips even from a remote website using JavaScript. In a third step, we show that the full Rowhammer attack is possible from a remote website using JavaScript without any additional information on the system.

4.1   Rowhammer in Native Code

We extended the `double_sided_rowhammer` program by Dullien [36] by using the best eviction strategy we have found. The two `clflush` instructions were first replaced by the eviction code described in Sect. 3.1, with parameters for a $\mathcal{P}$-2-2-1 eviction strategy. The eviction sets are either precomputed statically using the physical address mapping and the complex addressing function in Table 2, or using a dynamic eviction strategy computation algorithm.

This way, we were able to reproducibly flip bits on our Sandy Bridge and Ivy Bridge test machine using different eviction strategies when running with the Samsung DDR3 RAM and our Skylake test machine when running with the Crucial DDR4 RAM. The machines were operated in default configuration.

On our Haswell test machine we were not able to reproducibly flip bits with the default settings, not even with the `clflush` instruction. However, the BIOS configuration allows setting a custom refresh rate by setting the average periodic refresh interval `tREFI`. We had to increase the `tREFI` value from 6,549 to over 19,000 just to be able to trigger bit flips *with* the `clflush` instruction. The refresh interval is a typical parameter used by computer gaming enthusiasts and the overclocking community to increase system performance. However, while this might also be an interesting target group, we rather want to analyze the influence of the refresh interval on the applicability of the Rowhammer attack using cache eviction and the Rowhammer attack in JavaScript. Kim et al. [20] observed that the refresh interval directly influences the number of bit flips that occur and that below a module dependent `tREFI` value no bit flips occur. We will show that their observation also applies to Rowhammer with cache eviction and Rowhammer in JavaScript.

Lowering the refresh interval is not part of an actual attack. Existing work has already examined the prevalence of the Rowhammer and found that 85 % of the DDR3 modules examined are susceptible to Rowhammer bit flips [20]. Also in our case only the modules of the Haswell test system and the G.Skill DIMMs in the Skylake test system were not susceptible to Rowhammer bit flips at default settings, whereas it was possible to induce Rowhammer bit flips in the other three DIMMs at default settings. Thus, our results do not contradict previous estimates and we must assume that millions of systems are still vulnerable.

Rowhammer with eviction in native code revives the Google Native Client exploit [36] that allows privilege escalation in Google Chrome. The `clflush` instruction has been blacklisted to solve this vulnerability, however, this is ineffective and a sandbox escape is still possible, as we can trigger bit flips in Google Native Client based on eviction.

4.2 Rowhammer in JavaScript

Triggering the Rowhammer bug from JavaScript is more difficult as JavaScript has no concept of virtual addresses or pointers and no access to physical address mappings. We observed that large typed arrays in JavaScript in all recent Firefox and Google Chrome versions on Linux are allocated 1MB aligned and use anonymous 2MB pages when possible. The reason for this lies in the memory allocation mechanism implemented by the operating system. Any memory allocation in a comparable scripting language and environment will also result in the allocation of anonymous 2MB pages for large arrays.

By performing a timing attack similar to the one performed by Gruss et al. [11], we can determine the 2MB page frames in the browser. In this attack we iterate over an array and measure the access latency. The latency peaks during memory initialization are caused by the pagefaults that occur with the start of each new 2MB page, as shown in Fig. 5. This also works in recent browser versions with a reduced timer resolution as suggested by Oren et al. [27] and added to the HTML5 standard by the W3C [37]. Thus, we know the lowest 21 bits of the virtual and physical address by knowing the offset in the array.

As a first proof-of-concept we reproduced bit flips in JavaScript in Firefox by hammering the exact physical addresses as in native code. In order to do this we built a tool to translate physical to virtual addresses for another process.

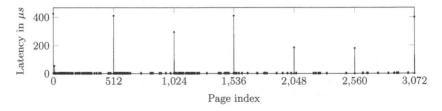

Fig. 5. Access latency of 4KB aligned addresses in a large array in JavaScript. Pagefaults cause the latency peaks at the start of the 2MB pages.

To compute the eviction sets we use the assumption-based algorithm from Sect. 3.2. We observed that simple memory accesses as in our native code implementation are not optimized out by the just-in-time-compiler.

The final JavaScript-based attack does not require any outside computation and thus, runs entirely without user interaction in the browser. It exploits the fact that large typed arrays are allocated on 2MB pages. Thus, we know that each 2MB region of our array is divided into 16 row offsets of size 128KB (depends on the lowest row index bit). We can now perform double-sided hammering in these 2MB regions to trigger a bit flip within the 2MB region or amplified single-sided hammering on the outer two rows of every 2MB pages to induce a bit flip in another physical 2MB region. The result is the first hardware-fault attack implemented in JavaScript on a remote website.

4.3 Attack Evaluation

As described by Kim et al. [20] not all addresses in a DRAM are equally susceptible to bit flips. Therefore, to provide a fair comparison of the different techniques, we measured the number of bit flips for a fixed address pair already known to be susceptible. Figure 6 shows how different refresh rates influence the number of bit flips for a fixed time interval in different setups. The system was under slight usage during the tests (browsing, typing in an editor, etc.). We see that the `clflush` instruction yields the highest number of bit flips. If the refresh interval was set to a value where bit flips can be triggered using `clflush`, they can be triggered using native code eviction as well. To trigger bit flips in JavaScript, a slightly higher refresh interval was necessary. Again, it depends on the particular DIMM whether the refresh interval is chosen correctly so that no bit flips occur.

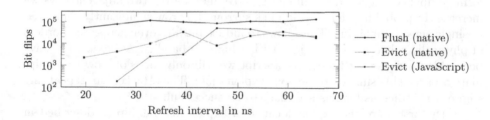

Fig. 6. Number of bit flips within 15 min on a fixed address pair for different values for the average periodic refresh interval `tREFI` on Haswell in three different setups. (Color figure online)

The probability for bit flips in JavaScript is slightly lower than in native code, as native code is slightly faster. However, if a machine is vulnerable to our native code implementation it is likely vulnerable using our JavaScript implementation as well. While these plots were obtained on the Haswell machine, we were also able to trigger bit flips on our Ivy Bridge laptop with default settings from

JavaScript. However, as the Laptop BIOSes did not allow to set the refresh interval tREFI directly, we could not obtain a comparable plot.

While DDR4 was assumed to have countermeasures against rowhammering, countermeasures are not part of the final DDR4 standard [1]. Using the Crucial DDR4 DIMMs we even were able to induce bit flips at default system settings and with the most recent BIOS version, after applying the functions reverse engineered by Pessl et al. [32]. On the G.Skill DDR4 DIMMs we could only induce bit flips at an increased refresh interval. Thus, even on these very recent and up-to-date systems Rowhammer countermeasures have not been implemented in hardware and those implemented in software are ineffective. Whether a system is vulnerable to Rowhammer-based attacks still crucially depends on the refresh interval chosen by DIMM.

5   Discussion and Related Work

5.1   Building an Exploit with Rowhammer.js

Existing exploits assume that a page table is mapped in a row between two rows occupied by the attacker. However, we observed that this situation rarely occurs in practice. The operating system prefers to use large pages to reduce the pressure on the TLB. To make the organization and changes to physical address mappings easier the operating system will also group small pages into the same organizational physical frames. Page tables are only allocated between two user pages in a near-out-of-memory situation. Thus, the exploits allocate almost all system memory to enforce such a situation [36]. However, swapping is enabled by default in all major operating systems and thus the system will be severely unresponsive due to swapping. In our proof-of-concept exploit, we perform "amplified single-sided hammering". By hammering two adjacent rows we increase the probability for a bit flip in a surrounding row significantly compared to single-sided hammering. This allows to induce bit flips even across the borders of physically coherent 2MB regions with a high probability. As we already have been able to trigger bit flips in JavaScript we will only focus on how to manipulate a page table similar to previous exploits [36]. The attacker can repeat any step of the attack as long as necessary to be successful.

In the first step, the exploit locates an exploitable bit flip as described in Sect. 4.2, $i.e.$ a bit flip in the $\frac{1}{3}$ of the page table bits that are used for physical addresses. An exploitable bit flip changes an address bit in a page table that is in an adjacent 2MB region. We have found such bit flips on our all our test machines. In the second step, the exploit script releases all pages but the two that have previously been hammered and the ones that are required for cache eviction. Thus, also the page that contained the bit flip is released. Allocating arrays requires the browser to reserve virtual memory regions and to map them to physical memory upon the first access. The attacker determines the largest array size that still triggers the allocation of a page table in a timing attack (see 4.2). The array size was 1MB on all our test systems. We only access and thus allocate one 4KB page per 1MB array and thus 2 user pages per page table.

The probability to place a group of page tables in the targeted 2MB region is $\approx \frac{1}{3}$. In the third step, the exploit script triggers the bit flip again and may find that its own memory mappings changed. With a chance of $\approx \frac{1}{3}$ the memory mapped is now one of the attackers page tables. The attacker can now change mapped addresses in that page table and if successful, has gained full access to the physical memory of the system. Our proof-of-concept works on recent Linux systems with all recent versions of Firefox and it does not require a near-out-of-memory situation. It does not work in Google Chrome due to the immediate allocation of all physical memory for an allocated 1MB array after a single access.

5.2 Limitations

In JavaScript we use 2MB pages to find congruent addresses and adjacent rows efficiently. If the operating system does not provide 2MB pages, we cannot perform double-sided or amplified single-sided hammering. However, the probability of a bit flip with single-sided hammering is significantly lower. Exploiting double-sided hammering with 2MB pages is not possible because we can then only induce bit flips in our own memory. Thus, an attack is only possible with amplified single-sided hammering to induce a bit flip in an adjacent row in an adjacent 2MB page. There is only a limited number of such rows in a system. Still the search for an exploitable bit flip can easily take several hours, especially as the probability of a bit flip in JavaScript is lower than in native code. Furthermore, if we cannot guess the best eviction strategy for the system, it will take up to an hour of precomputations to find a good eviction strategy. The victim has to stay on the website for the duration of the attack. While this was the case in our proof-of-concept attack it is less realistic for a real-world attack.

5.3 Countermeasures

The operating system allocates memory in large physical memory frames (often 2MB) for reasons of optimization. Page tables, kernel pages and user pages are not allocated in the same memory frame, unless the system is close to out-of-memory (*i.e.* allocating the last few kilobytes of physical memory). Thus, the most efficient Rowhammer attack (double-sided hammering) would not possible if the operating system memory allocator was less aggressive in near-out-of-memory situations. Preventing (amplified) single-sided hammering is more difficult, as hammering across the boundaries of a 2MB region is possible.

To fully close the attack vector for double-sided hammering, we also have to deal with read-only shared code and data, *i.e.* shared libraries. If the attacker hammers on a shared library, a fault can be induced in this library. Therefore, shared libraries should not be shared over processes that run at different privilege levels or under different users. As a consequence, the attacker would be unable to escape from a sandbox or gain access to a higher privilege level using `clflush` or eviction-based Rowhammer.

Kim et al. [20] proposed several countermeasures which should be implemented for new DRAM modules, including increasing the refresh rate. However, this would cause significant performance impacts. BIOS updates supplied so far only double the refresh rate, which is insufficient to prevent attacks on all DRAM modules. Moreover, many users to not update the BIOS unless it is unavoidable.

Pseudo Target Row Refresh (pTRR) and Target Row Refresh (TRR) are features that refresh neighboring rows when the number of accesses to one row exceeds a threshold. They have less overhead compared to double the refresh rate. Although TRR has been announced as implemented in all DDR4 modules it has been removed from the final DDR4 standard. Manufacturers can still choose to implement it in their devices, but if the memory controller does not support it, it has no effect.

Error-correcting code (ECC) memory is often mentioned as a countermeasure against Rowhammer attacks. However, recent work shows that it cannot reliably protect against Rowhammer attacks.cases [2, 21].

At the software level, one proposed countermeasure is the detection using hardware performance counters [4, 12, 15, 30]. The excessive number of cache references and cache hits allows to detect on-going attacks. However, this countermeasure can suffer from false positives, so it needs further evaluation before it can be brought to practice.

5.4   Related Work

The initial work by Kim et al. [20] and Seaborn's [36] root exploit made the scientific community aware of the security implications of a Rowhammer attack. However, to date, there have been very few other publications, focusing on different aspects than our work. Barbara Aichinger [1] analyzed Rowhammer faults in server systems where the problem exists in spite of ECC memory. She remarks that it will be difficult to fix the problem in the millions or even billions of DDR3 DRAMs in server systems. Rahmati et al. [34] have shown that bit flips can be used to identify a system based on the unique and repeatable error pattern that occurs at a significantly increased refresh interval. Our paper is the first to examine how to perform Rowhammer attacks based on cache eviction.[1] Our cache eviction techniques facilitated cache side-channel attacks on ARM CPUs [22]. Concurrent and independent work by Aweke et al. [4] has also demonstrated bit flips without `clflush` on a Sandy Bridge laptop. They focus on countermeasures, whereas we focus on attacking a wider range of architectures and environments.

6   Future Work

While we only investigated the possibility of a JavaScript Rowhammer attack in Firefox and Google Chrome on Linux, the attack exploits fundamental concepts that are inbuilt in the way hardware and operating system work. Whenever the operating system uses 4KB pages, page tables are required and at latest allocated when one of the 4KB pages belonging to this page table is accessed. Thus, the

---

[1] A draft of this paper was published online since July 24, 2015.

operating system cannot prevent that $\frac{1}{3}$ of memory is allocated for page tables. The same attack approach could be applied to hypervisors that allocate 4KB pages to virtual machines, even if they applies similar allocation mechanisms as the Linux kernel. While it might seem unreasonable and not realistic that hypervisors allocate 4KB pages, it in fact makes cross-VM page deduplication easier. According to Barresi et al. [7], page deduplication is in fact still widely used in public clouds. Our work opens the possibility for further investigation on whether page deduplication in fact is not only a problem for security and privacy of virtual machines, but a security problem for the hypervisor itself.

7   Conclusion

In this paper, we presented Rowhammer.js, an implementation of the Rowhammer attack using fast cache eviction to trigger the Rowhammer bug with only regular memory accesses. It is the first work to investigate eviction strategies to defeat complex cache replacement policies. This does not only enable to trigger Rowhammer in JavaScript, it also benefits research on cache attacks as it allows to perform attacks on recent and unknown CPUs fast and reliably. Our fully automated attack runs in JavaScript through a remote website and can gain unrestricted access to systems. The attack technique is independent of CPU microarchitecture, programming language and execution environment.

The majority of DDR3 modules are vulnerable and DDR4 modules can be vulnerable too. Thus, it is important to discover all Rowhammer attack vectors. Automated attacks through websites pose an enormous threat as they can be performed on millions of victim machines simultaneously.

Acknowledgments. We would like to thank our shepherd Stelios Sidiroglou-Douskos and our anonymous reviewers for their valuable comments and suggestions. We would also like to thank Mark Seaborn, Thomas Dullien, Yossi Oren, Yuval Yarom, Barbara Aichinger, Peter Pessl and Raphael Spreitzer for feedback and advice. Supported by the EU Horizon 2020 programme under GA No. 644052 (HECTOR), the EU FP7 programme under GA No. 610436 (MATTHEW), the Austrian Research Promotion Agency (FFG) and Styrian Business Promotion Agency (SFG) under GA No. 836628 (SeCoS), and Cryptacus COST Action IC1403.

References

1. Aichinger, B.: DDR memory errors caused by Row Hammer. In: HPEC 2015 (2015)
2. Aichinger, B.: Row Hammer Failures in DDR Memory. In: memcon 2015 (2015)
3. Al-Ars, Z.: DRAM fault analysis and test generation. TU Delft (2005)
4. Aweke, Z.B., Yitbarek, S.F., Qiao, R., Das, R., Hicks, M., Oren, Y., Austin, T.: ANVIL: Software-based protection against next-generation rowhammer attacks. In: ASLPOS 2016 (2016)
5. Bains, K., Halbert, J.: Row hammer monitoring based on stored row hammer threshold value (Jun 5 2014), US Patent App. 13/690,523

6. Bains, K., Halbert, J., Mozak, C., Schoenborn, T., Greenfield, Z.: Row hammer refresh command (Jan 2 2014), US Patent App. 13/539,415
7. Barresi, A., Razavi, K., Payer, M., Gross, T.R.: CAIN: silently breaking ASLR in the cloud. In: WOOT 2015 (2015)
8. Bernstein, D.J.: Cache-timing attacks on AES. Technical report, Department of Mathematics, Statistics, and Computer Science, University of Illinois at Chicago (2005)
9. Biham, E., Shamir, A.: Differential fault analysis of secret key cryptosystems. In: Kaliski Jr., B.S. (ed.) CRYPTO 1997. LNCS, vol. 1294, pp. 513–525. Springer, Heidelberg (1997)
10. Boneh, D., DeMillo, R.A., Lipton, R.J.: On the importance of checking cryptographic protocols for faults. In: Fumy, W. (ed.) EUROCRYPT 1997. LNCS, vol. 1233, pp. 37–51. Springer, Heidelberg (1997)
11. Gruss, D., Bidner, D., Mangard, S.: Practical memory deduplication attacks in sandboxed javascript. In: Pernul, G., et al. (eds.) ESORICS 2015. LNCS, vol. 9326, pp. 108–122. Springer, Heidelberg (2015). doi:10.1007/978-3-319-24174-6_6
12. Gruss, D., Maurice, C., Wagner, K., Mangard, S.: Flush+Flush: a fast and stealthy cache attack. In: DIMVA 2016 (2016)
13. Gruss, D., Spreitzer, R., Mangard, S.: Cache template attacks: automating attacks on inclusive last-level caches. In: USENIX Security 2015 (2015)
14. Gullasch, D., Bangerter, E., Krenn, S.: Cache games - bringing access-based cache attacks on AES to practice. In: S&P 2011 (2011)
15. Herath, N., Fogh, A.: These are Not Your Grand Daddys CPU Performance Counters - CPU Hardware Performance Counters for Security. Black Hat (2015)
16. Huang, R.F., Yang, H.Y., Chao, M.C.T., Lin, S.C.: Alternate hammering test for application-specific DRAMs and an industrial case study. In: DAC 2012 (2012)
17. Hund, R., Willems, C., Holz, T.: Practical timing side channel attacks against kernel space ASLR. In: S&P 2013 (2013)
18. Inci, M.S., Gulmezoglu, B., Irazoqui, G., Eisenbarth, T., Sunar, B.: Seriously, get off my cloud! Cross-VM RSA Key Recovery in a Public Cloud. Cryptology ePrint Archive, Report 2015/898, pp. 1–15 (2015)
19. Irazoqui, G., Eisenbarth, T., Sunar, B.: S$A: a shared cache attack that works across cores and defies VM sandboxing - and its application to AES. In: S&P 2015 (2015)
20. Kim, Y., Daly, R., Kim, J., Fallin, C., Lee, J.H., Lee, D., Wilkerson, C., Lai, K., Mutlu, O.: Flipping bits in memory without accessing them: an experimental study of DRAM disturbance errors. In: ISCA 2014 (2014)
21. Lanteigne, M.: How rowhammer could be used to exploit weakness weaknesses in computer hardware, March 2016. http://www.thirdio.com/rowhammer.pdf
22. Lipp, M., Gruss, D., Spreitzer, R., Mangard, S.: Armageddon: last-level cache attacks on mobile devices. CoRR abs/1511.04897 (2015)
23. Liu, F., Yarom, Y., Ge, Q., Heiser, G., Lee, R.B.: Last-level cache side-channel attacks are practical. In: S&P 2015 (2015)
24. Maurice, C., Le Scouarnec, N., Neumann, C., Heen, O., Francillon, A.: Reverse engineering intel last-level cache complex addressing using performance counters. In: RAID 2015 (2015)
25. Maurice, C., Neumann, C., Heen, O., Francillon, A.: C5: cross-cores cache covert channel. In: Almgren, M., Gulisano, V., Maggi, F. (eds.) DIMVA 2015. LNCS, vol. 9148, pp. 46–64. Springer, Heidelberg (2015)
26. Micron: Designing for 1Gb DDR SDRAM (2003). https://www.micron.com/~/media/documents/products/technical-note/dram/tn4609.pdf

27. Oren, Y., Kemerlis, V.P., Sethumadhavan, S., Keromytis, A.D.: The spy in the sandbox: practical cache attacks in javascript and their implications. In: CCS 2015 (2015)

28. Osvik, D.A., Shamir, A., Tromer, E.: Cache attacks and countermeasures: the case of AES. In: Pointcheval, D. (ed.) CT-RSA 2006. LNCS, vol. 3860, pp. 1–20. Springer, Heidelberg (2006)

29. Park, K., Baeg, S., Wen, S., Wong, R.: Active-precharge hammering on a row induced failure in DDR3 SDRAMs under 3x nm technology. In: IIRW 2014 (2014)

30. Payer, M.: HexPADS: a platform to detect "stealth" attacks. In: Caballero, J., et al. (eds.) ESSoS 2016. LNCS, vol. 9639, pp. 138–154. Springer, Heidelberg (2016). doi:10.1007/978-3-319-30806-7_9

31. Percival, C.: Cache missing for fun and profit. In: Proceedings of BSDCan (2005)

32. Pessl, P., Gruss, D., Maurice, C., Mangard, S.: Reverse engineering intel DRAM addressing and exploitation. CoRR abs/1511.08756 (2015)

33. Qureshi, M.K., Jaleel, A., Patt, Y.N., Steely, S.C., Emer, J.: Adaptive insertion policies for high performance caching. ACM SIGARCH Comput. Archit. News **35**(2), 381 (2007)

34. Rahmati, A., Hicks, M., Holcomb, D.E., Fu, K.: Probable cause: the deanonymizing effects of approximate DRAM. In: ISCA 2015 (2015)

35. Seaborn, M.: How physical addresses map to rows and banks in DRAM, May 2015. http://lackingrhoticity.blogspot.com/2015/05/how-physical-addresses-map-to-rows-and-banks.html. Accessed 20 July 2015

36. Seaborn, M., Dullien, T.: Exploiting the DRAM rowhammer bug to gain kernel privileges. In: Black Hat (2015)

37. W3C: High Resolution Time Level 2–W3C Working Draft 21, July 2015. http://www.w3.org/TR/2015/WD-hr-time-2-20150721/#privacy-security

38. Wong, H.: Intel Ivy Bridge Cache Replacement Policy. http://blog.stuffedcow.net/2013/01/ivb-cache-replacement/. Accessed 16 July 2015

39. Yarom, Y., Falkner, K.: FLUSH+RELOAD: a high resolution, low noise, L3 cache side-channel attack. In: USENIX Security 2014 (2014)

40. Yarom, Y., Ge, Q., Liu, F., Lee, R.B., Heiser, G.: Mapping the Intel Last-Level Cache. Cryptology ePrint Archive, Report 2015/905, pp. 1–12 (2015)

Detile: Fine-Grained Information Leak Detection in Script Engines

Robert Gawlik, Philipp Koppe[✉], Benjamin Kollenda, Andre Pawlowski, Behrad Garmany, and Thorsten Holz

Horst Görtz Institute for IT-Security (HGI),
Ruhr-Universität Bochum, Bochum, Germany
philipp.koppe@rub.de

Abstract. *Memory disclosure attacks* play an important role in the exploitation of memory corruption vulnerabilities. By analyzing recent research, we observe that bypasses of defensive solutions that enforce control-flow integrity or attempt to detect return-oriented programming require memory disclosure attacks as a fundamental first step. However, research lags behind in detecting such information leaks.

In this paper, we tackle this problem and present a system for fine-grained, automated detection of memory disclosure attacks against scripting engines. The basic insight is as follows: scripting languages, such as JavaScript in web browsers, are strictly sandboxed. They must not provide any insights about the memory layout in their contexts. In fact, *any* such information potentially represents an ongoing memory disclosure attack. Hence, to detect information leaks, our system creates a clone of the scripting engine process with a re-randomized memory layout. The clone is instrumented to be synchronized with the original process. Any inconsistency in the script contexts of both processes appears when a memory disclosure was conducted to leak information about the memory layout. Based on this detection approach, we have designed and implemented DETILE (detection of information leaks), a prototype for the JavaScript engine in Microsoft's Internet Explorer 10/11 on Windows 8.0/8.1. An empirical evaluation shows that our tool can successfully detect memory disclosure attacks even against this proprietary software.

1 Introduction

Over the last years, many different techniques were developed to prevent attacks that exploit spatial and temporal memory corruption vulnerabilities (see for example the survey by Szekeres et al. [52]). As a result, modern operating systems deploy a wide range of defense methods to impede a successful attack. For example, *Data Execution Prevention* (DEP) [38] marks data as non-executable and thus an attacker is prohibited from injecting data into a vulnerable application that is later on interpreted as code. Furthermore, *Address Space Layout Randomization* (ASLR) [43] randomizes the memory layout either once during the boot process or every time a process is started. Since the attacker lacks information about the exact memory layout, it is harder for her to predict where her shellcode or reusable code are located.

© Springer International Publishing Switzerland 2016
J. Caballero et al. (Eds.): DIMVA 2016, LNCS 9721, pp. 322–342, 2016.
DOI: 10.1007/978-3-319-40667-1_16

Besides these widely deployed techniques, many other defenses were proposed in the literature in the last years [52]. Most notably, the enforcement of *control flow integrity* (CFI) is a promising technique to prevent a whole class of memory corruption vulnerabilities [1]. The basic idea behind CFI is to verify that each control flow transfer leads to a valid target based on a control flow graph that is either statically pre-computed or dynamically generated. Several implementations of CFI with different design constraints, security goals, and performance overheads were published (e.g., [21,65,66]).

A general observation is that the first step in modern attacks is based on a *memory disclosure attack* (also referred to as *information leak*): the adversary finds a way to read a (raw) memory pointer to learn some information about the virtual address space of the vulnerable program. Generally speaking, the attacker can then de-randomize the address space based on this leaked pointer (thus bypassing ASLR), use ROP to bypass DEP, and finally execute shellcode of her choice. Modern exploits leverage information leaks as a fundamental primitive. Furthermore, recent CFI and ROP defense bypasses use memory disclosures as well. For example, Snow et al. introduced *Just-In-Time Code Reuse* attacks (JIT-ROP [48]) to bypass fine-grained ASLR implementations by repeatedly utilizing an information leak. *G-Free* [39], a compiler-based approach against any ROP attack, was recently circumvented by Athanasakis et al. [3]. Their technique requires successive information leaks to disclose enough needed information. Göktaş et al. demonstrated several bypasses of proposed ROP defenses and their exploit needs an information leak as a first step [27]. An information leak is also needed by Song et al., who showed that dynamic code generation is vulnerable to code injection attacks [49]. Similarly, *Counterfeit Object-oriented Programming* (COOP [44]) needs to disclose the location of *vtables* to mount a subsequent control-flow hijacking attack by reusing them. Disclosures are also utilized by *memory oracles* to weaken various defenses [24]. *All* of these offensive bypasses utilized an information leak as a first step and implemented the attack against a web browser.

Another general observation is that script engines in web browsers are commonly utilized by adversaries to abuse information leaks in practice. Browser vulnerabilities are prevalent and as the yearly *pwn2own* competition shows, researchers successfully use them to take control of the machine. Notably, most of these attacks are based on vulnerabilities that create an information leak utilizing the script engine.

In this paper, we take these observations into account and propose a technique for fine-grained, automated detection of memory disclosure attacks against script engines at runtime. Our approach is based on the insight that information leaks are leveraged by state-of-the-art exploits to learn the placement of modules—and thereby code sections—in the virtual address space in order to bypass ASLR. Any sandboxed script context is forbidden to contain memory information, i.e., no script variable is allowed to provide a memory pointer. As such, a viable approach to detect information leaks is to create a clone of the to be protected process with a re-randomized address space layout, which is

Table 1. Defenses and offensive approaches utilizing an information leak in browsers to weaken or bypass the specific defense. All mentioned attacks are mitigated by DETILE.

Protection flavor	Defense	Weakened/Bypassed by	Mitigated by DETILE
Address randomization	Fine-grained ASLR [29]	Just-In-Time Code Reuse [48]	✓
Code-reuse protection	RopGuard [23], KBouncer [41], ROPecker [12]	Size Does Matter [27], Anti-ROP Evaluation [45], COOP [44]	✓
Code-reuse protection	G-Free [39]	Browser JIT Defense Bypass [3], COOP [44]	✓
Coarse-grained CFI	CCFIR [65], BinCFI [66]	Stitching the Gadgets [18], Out of Control [26], COOP [44]	✓
Fine-grained CFI	IFCC [53], VTV [53]	Losing Control [13]	✓
Information-hiding	Oxymoron [4]	Vtable disclosure [19], Crash-Resistance [24], COOP [44]	✓
Information-hiding	CPI linear region [33]	Crash-Resistance [24]	✓
Execution randomization	Isomeron [19]	Crash-Resistance [24]	✓
Randomization/Information-hiding	Readactor [15]	Crash-Resistance [24], COOP [44]	✓

instrumented to be synchronized with the original process. An inconsistency in the script contexts of both processes can only occur when a memory disclosure vulnerability was exploited to gain information about the memory layout. In such a case, the two processes can be halted to prevent further execution of the malicious script. An overview of bypassed defenses by specific attacks which are mitigated by our approach is shown in Table 1.

We have implemented a prototype of our technique in a tool called DETILE (detection of information leaks). We extended Internet Explorer 10/11 (IE) on Windows 8.0/8.1 to create a synchronized clone of each tab and enforce the information leak checks. We chose this software mainly due to two reasons. First, IE is an attractive target for attackers as the large number of vulnerabilities indicates. Second, IE and Windows pose several interesting technical challenges since it is a proprietary binary system that we need to instrument and it lacks fine-grained ASLR. Evaluation results show that our prototype is able to re-randomize single processes without significant computational impact. Additionally, running IE with our re-randomization and information leak detection engine imposes a performance hit of ~17 % on average. Furthermore, empirical tests with real-world exploits also indicate that our approach is usable to unravel modern and unknown exploits which target browsers and utilize memory disclosures.

In summary, our main contributions in this paper are:

- We present a system to tackle the problem of information leaks, which are frequently used in practice by attackers as an exploit primitive. More specifically,

we propose a concept for fine-grained, automated detection of information leaks with per process re-randomization, dual process execution, and process synchronization. An extended version of this paper with more technical details is available as a technical report [25].
- We show that dual execution of highly complex, binary-only software such as Microsoft's Internet Explorer is possible without access to the source code, whereby two executing instances operate deterministic to each other.
- We implemented a prototype for IE 10/11 on Windows 8.0/8.1. We show that our tool can successfully detect several real-world exploits, while producing no alerts on highly complex, real-world websites.

2   Technical Background

In the following, we briefly introduce several concepts needed to understand the challenges we were confronted with when developing DETILE.

2.1   N-Variant Systems

N-Variant or *Multi-Execution* systems evolved from fault-tolerant environments to mitigation systems against security critical vulnerabilities [9,14,30,54]. Our concept of DETILE incorporates similar ideas like dual process execution and dual process synchronization. However, our approach is constructed specifically for scripting engines, and thus, is more fine-grained: While DETILE operates and synchronizes processes on the scripting interpreter's bytecode level, n-variant systems intercept only at the system call level. One drawback for these conventional systems is that they are prone to *Just-In-Time Code-Reuse* (JIT-ROP [48]) and *Counterfeit Object-oriented Programming* (COOP [44]) attacks, while DETILE is able to detect these (see Sects. 3.1 and 6 and for details).

2.2   Windows ASLR Internals

Address Space Layout Randomization (ASLR) is a well-known security mechanism that involves the randomization of stacks, heaps, and loaded images in the virtual address space. Its purpose is to leave an attacker with no knowledge about the virtual memory space in which code and data lives. Combined with DEP, ASLR makes remote system exploitation through memory corruption techniques a much harder task. While brute-force attacks against services that automatically restart are possible [6], such attacks are typically not viable in practice against web browsers.

In Windows, whenever an image is loaded into the virtual address space, a section object is created, which represents a section of memory. These objects are managed system-wide and can be shared among all processes. Once a DLL is loaded, its section object remains permanent as long as processes are referencing it. This concept has the benefit that relocation takes place once and whenever a process needs to load a DLL, its section object is reused and the view of the section is mapped into the virtual address space of the process, making the memory section visible. This way, physical memory is shared among all processes that load a specific DLL whose section object is already present. In particular, as long as the virtual address is not occupied, each image is loaded at the same virtual address among all running usermode processes.

2.3   WOW64 Subsystem Overview

64-bit operating systems are the systems of choice for today's users: 64-bit processors are widely used in practice, and hence Microsoft Windows 7 and later versions are usually running in the 64-bit version on typical desktop systems. However, most third-party applications are distributed in their 32-bit form. This is for example the case for Mozilla Firefox, and also for parts of Microsoft's Internet Explorer. As our framework should protect against widely attacked targets, it needs to support 32-bit and 64-bit processes. Therefore, the *Windows On Windows 64* (shortened as *WOW64*) emulation layer plays an important role, as it allows legacy 32-bit applications to run on modern 64-bit Windows systems.

Executing a user-mode 32-bit application instructs the kernel to create a WOW64 process. According to our observations, it creates the program's address space and maps the 64-bit and 32-bit *NT Layer DLL* (ntdll.dll) and the main executable into it. Even when a program may have been started in suspended mode, these three modules are already available. Afterwards, WOW64 layer DLLs are mapped, which mediate several necessary transitions between 64-bit and 32-bit at runtime [43]. Subsequent 32-bit DLLs are mapped into the address space via LdrLoadDll of the 32-bit ntdll.dll. The first of them is kernel32.dll. The loader assures that it is mapped to the same address in each WOW64 process system wide, using a unique address per reboot. It therefore compares its name to the hardcoded "KERNEL32.DLL" string in ntdll.dll upon loading. If the loader is not able to map it to its preferred base address, process initialization fails with a conflicting address error. As process based re-randomization plays a crucial role in our framework, this issue is handled such that each process contains its kernel32.dll at a different base address (see Sect. 4.1). After mapping kernel32.dll, all other needed 32-bit DLLs are mapped into the address space.

2.4   Internet Explorer Architecture

IE is developed as multi-process application [64]. That means, a 64-bit main frame process governs several 32-bit WOW64 tab processes, which are isolated from each other. The frame process runs with a medium integrity level and isolated tab processes run with low integrity levels. Hence, tab processes are restricted and forbidden to access all resources of processes with higher integrity levels [37]. This architecture implies that websites opened in new tabs can lead to the start of new tab processes. These have to incorporate our protection in order to protect IE as complete application against information leaks (see Sect. 4).

2.5   Scripting Engines

In the context of IE, mainly two scripting engines are relevant and we briefly introduce both.

Internet Explorer Chakra. With the release of Internet Explorer 9, a new JavaScript engine called *Chakra* was introduced. Since Internet Explorer 11, Chakra exports a documented API which enables developers to embed the engine into their own applications. However, IE still uses the undocumented internal COM interface. Nevertheless, some Chakra internals were learned from the official API. The engine supports just-in-time (JIT) compiling of JavaScript byte-code to speed up execution. Typed arrays like integer arrays are stored as native arrays in heap memory along with metadata to accelerate element access. Script code is translated to JS bytecode on demand in a function-wise manner to minimize memory footprint and avoid generating unused bytecode. The bytecode is interpreted within a loop, whereby undocumented *opcodes* govern the execution of native functions within a switch statement. Dependent on the opcode, the desired JavaScript functionality is achieved with native code.

ActionScript Virtual Machine (AVM). The *Adobe Flash* plugin for browsers and especially for IE is a widely attacked target. Scripts written in *ActionScript* are interpreted or JIT-compiled to native code by the AVM. There is much unofficial documentation about its internals [7,34]. Most importantly, it is possible to intercept *each* ActionScript method with available tools [28]. Thus, no matter whether bytecode is interpreted by the opcode handlers or JIT code is executed, we are able to instrument the AVM.

2.6   Adversarial Capabilities

Memory disclosure attacks are an increasingly used technique for the exploitation of software vulnerabilities [47,48,51]. In the presence of full ASLR, DEP, CFI, or ROP defenses, the attacker has no anchor to a memory address to jump to, even if in control of the instruction pointer. This is the moment where information leaks come into play: an attacker needs to read—in any way possible—a raw memory pointer in order to gain a foothold into the native virtual address space of the vulnerable program. As soon as the attacker can read process memory, she can learn the base addresses of loaded modules. Then, any code reuse primitives can be conducted to exploit a vulnerability in order to bypass DEP, ASLR, CFI [18] and ROP defenses [11,27]. Another possibility is to leak code directly in order to initiate an attack and bypass ASLR [48]. Other mitigations like Microsoft's Enhanced Mitigation Experience Toolkit (EMET) [36] cannot withstand capabilities of sophisticated attackers.

For applications with scripting capabilities, untrusted contexts are sandboxed (e.g., JavaScript in web browsers) and must not provide memory information. Thus, attackers use different vulnerabilities to leak memory information into that context [26,47,58]. We assume that the program we want to protect suffers from such a memory corruption vulnerability that allows the adversary to corrupt memory objects. In fact, a study shows that *any* type of memory error can be transformed into an information leak [52]. Furthermore, we assume that the attacker uses a scripting environment to leverage the obtained memory disclosure information at runtime for her malicious computations. This is consistent with modern exploits in academic research [11,18,26,27,45] as well as in-the-wild [46, 55,58–60]. Our goal is to protect script engines against such powerful, yet realistic adversaries.

3   System Overview

In the following, we explain our approach to tackle the challenge of detecting information leaks in script engines. Hence, we introduce the needed building blocks, namely per process re-randomization and dual process execution.

3.1   Main Concept

As described above, information leaks manifest themselves in the form of memory information inside a context which must not reveal such insights. In our case, this is any script context inside an application: high-level variables and content in a script must not contain memory pointers, which attackers could use to deduce image base addresses of loaded modules.

Unfortunately, a legitimate number and a memory pointer in data bytes received via a scripting function are indistinguishable. This leads us to the following assumption: a memory disclosure attack yields a memory pointer, which may be surrounded by legitimate data. The same targeted memory disclosure, when applied to a differently *randomized,* but otherwise *identical* process, will yield the same legitimate data, but a *different* memory pointer. Due to the varying base addresses of modules, different heap and stack addresses, a memory pointer will have a different address in the second process than in the first process. Thus, a master process and a cloned twin process—with different address space layout randomization—can be executed synchronized side-by-side and perform identical operations, e.g., execute a specific JavaScript function. In benign cases, the same data getting into the script context is equal for both processes. When comparing the received data of one process to the same data received in the second process, the only difference can arise because of a leaked memory pointer pointing to equal memory, but having a *different* address. In order to compare the data of the master and twin process, we have to instrument the interpreter loop of the script engine. We can instrument the `call` and `return` bytecodes to precisely check all outgoing data and therefore to detect an information leak.

Based on this principle, our prototype system launches the same script engine process twice with diverse memory layouts (see also Fig. 1). The script engines are coupled to run in sync which enables checking for information leaks. In spirit, this is similar to n-variant systems [9,14] and multi-execution based approaches [10,17,20]. However, our approach is more fine-grained since it checks

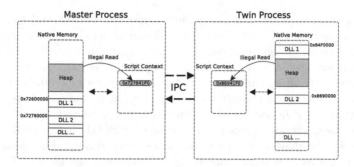

Fig. 1. Overview of our main information leak detection concept: The master process is synchronized with a re-randomized, but otherwise identical twin process. If a memory disclosure attack is conducted in the master, it appears as well in the twin. Due to the different randomization, the disclosure attack manifests itself in different data flowing into the script context and can be detected (0x727841F0 vs. 0x86941F0)

and synchronizes the processed data on the bytecode level of the script context and is capable of detecting the actual information leak, instead of merely detecting an artifact of a successful compromise (i.e., divergence in the control flow).

3.2   Per Process Re-randomization

To overcome the dilemma of modules having equal base addresses in different processes, we collect all base addresses of modules a process loads during its runtime. We refer to this first process, which is launched, as *master* process. A second process instance of the application known as the *twin* process is spawned. Upon its initialization, the base addresses gained from the master are occupied in the virtual address space of the twin. This forces the image loader to map the modules to other addresses than in the master process, as they are already allocated. We save us the time and trouble to re-randomize the stack and heap process-wise, as modern operating systems (e.g., Windows 8 on 64-bit) support it natively. Finally, we establish an *inter-process communication* (IPC) bridge between the master and twin process. This enables synchronized execution between them and comparison of data flows into their script contexts.

3.3   Dual Process Synchronization

After the re-randomization phase, both processes are ready to start execution at their identical entrypoints. After exchanging a handshake, both resume execution. In order to achieve comparable data for information leak checking, the executions of script interpreters in both processes have to be synchronized precisely. This is accomplished by intercepting an interpreter's native methods. Additionally, we install hooks inside the bytecode interpreter loop at positions where opcodes are interpreted and corresponding native functions are called. Thus, we perceive any high-level script method call at its binary level. The master drives execution and these hooks are the points where the master and twin process are synchronized via IPC. We check for information leaks by comparing binary data which returns as high-level data into the script context. All input data the master loads are stored in a cache and replayed to the twin process to ensure they operate on the same source (e.g., web pages a browser loads). Built-in script functions that potentially introduce entropy (e.g., `Math.random`, `Date.now`, and `window.screenX` in JavaScript) interfere with our deployed detection mechanism, since they generate values inside the script context that are different from each other in the master and twin processes, respectively. Additionally, they may induce a divergent script control flow. Both occurrences would be falsely detected as memory disclosure. Thus we also synchronize the entropy of both processes by copying the generated value from the master to the twin process. This way the twin process continues working on the same data as the master process and we are creating a co-deterministic script execution.

4   Implementation Details

Based on the concepts of per process re-randomization and dual process execution, we implemented a tool called DETILE for Windows 8.0 and 8.1 64-bit. The current prototype is able to re-randomize on a per process basis and instrument Internet Explorer 10 and 11 to run in dual process execution mode.

4.1   Duplication and Re-randomization

In order to re-randomize processes and load images at different base addresses, we developed a duplicator which creates a program's master process. It enumerates the master's initial loaded images with the help of the Windows API (`CreateToolHelp32Snapshot`) before the master starts execution. Then, the twin process is created in suspended mode, and a page is allocated in the twin at all addresses of previously gathered image bases. We then need to trick the Windows loader into mapping `kernel32.dll` at a different base in the twin. This is achieved by leveraging the DebugAPI and via manipulating parameters at calls of `RtlEqualUnicodeString` in the 32-bit loader in the `ntdll.dll`. This way, the loader believes that a *different* DLL than `kernel32.dll` is going to be initialized and allows the mapping to a different base. It is the first DLL which is loaded after the WOW64 subsystem. Thus, all subsequent libraries that are loaded and import functions from `kernel32.dll` have no problems to resolve their dependencies using the remapped `kernel32.dll`. The loader maps them to different addresses, as their preferred base addresses are reserved. Although the DebugAPI is used, all steps run in a fully automated way. As a next step, the DebugAPI is detached and the main image is remapped to a different address. As it is already mapped even in suspended processes, this has to be done specifically. Additionally, `LdrLoadDll` in the twin process is detoured to intercept new library loads and map incoming images to different addresses than in the master. Technical details about our remapping can be found in the technical report [25].

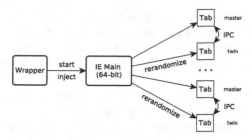

Fig. 2. DETILE running with Internet Explorer. A 64-bit duplicator library is injected into the main IE frame process to enable it creating and rerandomizing twin tab processes for each master tab process, by itself. The main IE frame also injects a 32-bit DLL into each tab process to allow synchronization, communication between master and twin, and information leak detection.

We were not able to re-randomize `ntdll.dll` because it is mapped into the virtual address space very early in the process creation procedure. Attempts to remap `ntdll.dll` later on did not succeed due to callbacks invoked by the kernel. The implications of a non re-randomized `ntdll.dll` are discussed in Sect. 7.

Note that this design works also with pure 64-bit processes. However, frequently attacked applications like tab processes of Internet Explorer are 32-bit and are running in the WOW64 subsystem. Hence, our framework has to protect them as well. The following explains how DETILE achieves this support.

While the above explained logic is sufficient to duplicate and re-randomize a single-process program, additional measures have to be taken in the case of multi-process architecture applications like Internet Explorer. Therefore, we developed a wrapper which starts the 64-bit main IE frame process and injects a 64-bit library, which we named duplicator library (see Fig. 2). This way, we modify the frame process, such that each time a tab process is started by the frame process, a second tab process is spawned. The first becomes the master, the second the twin. This is achieved via detouring and modifying the process creation of the IE frame. Additionally, our above explained re-randomization logic is incorporated into the duplicator library to allow the main IE frame process itself to re-randomize its spawned twins at creation time. To protect each new tab which is run by the IE frame, we ensure that each tab is run in a new process and gets a twin. To enable communication, synchronization, and detection of information leaks, the duplicator injects also a 32-bit library into the master and the twin upon their creation by the main IE frame process.

4.2 Synchronization

We designed our prototype to be contained in a DLL which is loaded into both target instances. To reliably intercept all script execution, we hook `LdrLoadDll` to initialize our synchronization as early as possible once the engine has been loaded. After determining the role (master or twin), the processes exchange a short handshake and wait for events from the interpreter instrumentation. While most of our work is focused on the scripting engine, we also instrument parts of `wininet.dll` to provide basic proxy functionality. The twin receives an exact copy of the web data sent to the master to ensure the same code is executed.

Entropy Normalization. The synchronization of script execution relies heavily on the identification of functions and objects introducing entropy into the script context. Values classified as entropy are overwritten in the twin with the value received from the master. This ensures that functions such as `Math.random` and `Date.now` return the exact same value, which is crucial for synchronous execution. While it is obvious for `Date.now`, it is not immediately clear for other methods. Therefore, *entropy inducing* methods are detected and filtered incrementally during runtime. Hence, if a detection has triggered but the cause was not an information leak, it is included into the list of entropy methods.

Rendezvous and Checking Points. Vital program points where master and twin are synchronized are bytecode handler functions. If a handler function returns data into the script context, it is first determined if the handler function is an entropy inducing function. However, the vast majority of function invocations and object accesses do not introduce entropy and are checked for equality between master and twin on the fly. If a difference is encountered that is not classified as entropy, we assume that an information leak occurred and take actions, namely logging the incident and terminating both processes.

4.3   Chakra Instrumentation

The Chakra JavaScript Engine contains a JIT compiler. It runs in a dedicated thread, identifies frequently executed (so called *hot*) functions and compiles them to native code. Our current implementation works on script interpreters, hence we disabled the JIT compiler. This is currently a prototype limitation whose solution we discuss in Sect. 7.

In order to synchronize execution and check for information leaks, we instrumented the main loop of the Chakra interpreter, which is located in the `Js::InterpreterStackFrame::Process` function. It is invoked recursively for each JavaScript call and iterates over the variable length bytecodes of the JavaScript function. The main loop contains a `switch` statement, which selects the corresponding handler for the currently interpreted bytecode. The handler then operates on the JavaScript context dependent on the operands and the current state. In the examined Chakra versions, we observed up to 648 unique bytecodes. Prior to the invocation of a bytecode handler, our instrumentation transfers the control flow to a small, highly optimized assembly stub, which decides whether the current bytecode is vital for our framework to handle.

We intercept all `call` and `return` as well as necessary `conversion` bytecodes in order to extract metadata such as JavaScript function arguments, return values, and conversion values. `Conversion` bytecodes handle dynamic type casting, native value to JavaScript object and JavaScript object to native value conversions. Additionally, we intercept engine functions that handle implicit type casts at native level, because they are invoked by other bytecode handlers as required and have no bytecode equivalents themselves. Furthermore, all interception sites support the manipulation of the outgoing native value or JavaScript object for the purpose of entropy elimination in the JavaScript context of the twin process.

4.4 AVM Instrumentation

Instrumentation of the AVM is based on prior work of F-Secure [28] and Microsoft [34]. We hook at the end of the native method `verifyOnCall` inside `verifyEnterGPR` to intercept ActionScript method calls and retrieve ActionScript method names. At these points, master and twin can be synchronized. Parameters flowing into an ActionScript method and return data flowing back into the ActionScript context can be dissected, too. They are also processed inside the method `verifyEnterGPR`. Based on their high level ActionScript types, the parameters and return data can be compared in the master and twin. This way, we can keep the master and twin in sync at method calls, check for information leaks and mediate entropy data from the master to the twin.

5 Evaluation

In the following, we present evaluation results for our prototype implementation of DETILE in the form of performance and memory usage benchmarks. The benchmarks were conducted on a system running Windows 8.0/8.1 that was equipped with a 4th generation Intel i7-4710MQ quad-core CPU and 8GB DDR3 RAM. Furthermore, we demonstrate how our prototype can successfully detect several kinds of real-world information leaks.

5.1 Re randomization of Process Modules

We evaluated our re-randomization engine according to its effectiveness, memory usage, and performance.

Effectiveness. We applied re-randomization to internal Windows applications and third-party applications, to verify that modules in the twin are based at different addresses than in the master. We therefore compared base addresses of all loaded images between the two processes and confirmed that all images in the twin process had a different base address than in the master, except `ntdll.dll`. See the discussion in Sect. 7 for details on the difficulties of remapping the 64-bit and 32-bit NT Layer DLLs. The extended version of this paper lists important Windows DLLs, re-randomized in different processes running *simultaneously* on a *single* user session [25].

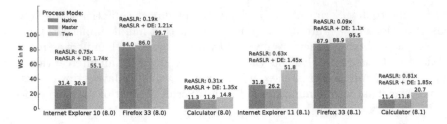

Fig. 3. Memory overhead of re-randomization and dual execution measured via working set (WS) consumption in megabytes (M): Native processes on Windows 8.0 and 8.1 are contrasted to their counterparts running in re-randomized dual execution mode (master and twin).

Physical Memory Usage. To inspect the memory overhead of our re-randomization scheme, we measured the working set characteristics for different master and re-randomized twin processes compared to native processes. Figure 3 shows the memory working sets of three applications. *ReASLR* denotes thereby the re-randomization within a single process. DE means that two processes are running, whereby the master's randomization is kept native while the twin is re-randomized. The applications besides IE are only included to measure the memory overhead and are not synchronized. We calculate the memory overhead of per process re-randomization (*ReASLR*) of a *single* process as follows:

$$Overhead(ReASLR) = \frac{WS(Twin)}{WS(Native)} - 1$$

Thus, the overall memory overhead based on working sets is 0.46 times. When running a program or process in per process re-randomization *and* dual process execution (*DE*), we have to include both master and twin into the memory overhead calculation. Therefore, the overhead is calculated by

$$Overhead(ReASLR + DE) = \frac{WS(Twin) + WS(Master)}{WS(Native)} - 1$$

Its overall value is 1.45 times. Note that memory working sets can highly vary during an application's runtime, and thus, are difficult to quantify. The measurements shown in Fig. 3 were performed after the application has finished startup, and was waiting for user input (i.e., it was idle and all modules were loaded and initialized). Due to additional twins for master processes, the overall additional memory is about one to two times per protected process. The technical report provides more details on the working set characteristics [25].

Re-randomization and Startup Time. When a program is started the first time after a reboot, the kernel needs to create section objects for image modules. Hence, the first start of a program always takes longer than subsequent starts of the same program. To measure the additional startup and module load times our

Table 2. Startup times in seconds and startup slowdowns of native 32-bit applications compared to their counterparts running with per process re-randomization and dual process execution on Windows 8.0 and Windows 8.1 (both 64-bit).

	Native (8.0)	ReASLR+DE (8.0)	Slowdown	Native (8.1)	ReASLR+DE (8.1)	Slowdown
IE tab spawn	0.9163 s	2.0710 s	1.3x	0.5194 s	1.3082 s	1.5x
Firefox	0.9624 s	1.8064 s	0.9x	1.3823 s	1.5441 s	0.1x
Calculator	0.3484 s	0.3610 s	0.0x	0.4391 s	0.6599 s	0.5x

Table 3. Native script execution of IE 11 on Windows 8.1 64-bit compared to the script execution of IE 11 instrumented with DETILE. Execution time is measured in milliseconds using the internal F12 developer tools provided by IE.

Website	google.com	facebook.com	youtube.com	yahoo.com	baidu.com	wikipedia.org	twitter.com	qq.com	taobao.com	linkedin.com	amazon.com	live.com	google.co.in	sina.com.cn	hao123.com
Native	425	774	1196	3674	1108	472	599	2405	645	439	958	254	483	3360	373
DETILE	482	961	1519	4722	1339	513	623	2724	824	517	1210	275	517	4269	379
Overhead	13.4%	24.1%	27%	28.5%	20.8%	8.6%	4%	13.2%	27.7%	17.7%	26.3%	8.2%	7%	27%	1.6%

protection introduces, we first run each program natively once to allow the kernel to create section objects of most natively used DLLs, and close it afterwards. We then start the program natively without protection and measure the time until it is idle and all of its initial modules are loaded. In the same way, we measure the time from process creation until both the master and twin process have their inital modules loaded. The startup comparison can be seen in Table 2. As expected, the startup times of applications protected with our approach are approximately doubled. This is caused by the fact that a twin process needs to be spawned for each master that should be protected.

5.2   Detection Engine

Next, we evaluate the impact of DETILE on the user experience and its effectiveness in detecting information leaks (Table 3).

Script Execution Time and Responsiveness. We used the 15 most visited websites worldwide [2] to test how the current prototype interferes with the normal usage of these pages. Besides the subjective impression while using the page, we utilized the F12 developer tools of Internet Explorer 11 to measure scripting execution time provided by the *UI Responsiveness* profiler tab. These tests were performed using Windows 8.1 64-bit and Internet Explorer 11. While we introduce a performance hit of around 17.0 % on average, the subjective user experience was not noticeably affected. This is due to IE's deferred parsing, which results in displaying content to the user before all computations have finished.

Information Leak Detection. We tested our approach on a pure memory disclosure vulnerability (CVE-2014-6355) which allows illegitimately reading data due to a JPEG parsing flaw in Microsoft's Windows graphics component [61].

It can be used to defeat ASLR by reading leaked stack information back to the attacker via the `toDataURL` method of a `canvas` object. We successfully detected this leak at the point of the call to `toDataURL` in the master and twin process. In the same way, detection was successful for an exploit for a similar bug (CVE-2015-0061 [62]).

To further verify our prototype, we evaluated it against an exploit for CVE-2011-1346, a vulnerability that was used in the pwn2own contest 2011 to bypass ASLR [63]. As this memory disclosure bug is specific for IE 8, we ported the vulnerability into IE 11. An uninitialized `index` attribute of a new HTML `option` element is used to leak information. Similarly, we successfully detected this exploitation attempt when the `index` attribute was accessed.

Additionally, we tested our prototype on another real-world vulnerability (CVE-2014-0322) that was used in targeted attacks [22]. It is a use-after-free error that can be utilized to increase an arbitrary bit, which is enough to create information leaks. DETILE triggered as a Vtable pointer was returned into the JavaScript context. Therefore, the information leak was detected successfully.

We also constructed a toy example in which our native code creates an information leak by overwriting the length field of an array. Additionally, the image base of `jscript9.dll` is written after the array data. In our tests, we reliably detected the out-of-bounds read of the image base and stopped the execution of the process. Exploit details are provided in the technical report [25].

False Positive Analysis. We analyzed the 100 top websites worldwide [2] to evaluate if our prototype can precisely handle real-world, complex websites and their JavaScript contexts without triggering false alarms. None of the tested websites did generate an alert, indicating that the prototype can accurately synchronize the master and twin process.

6   Related Work

In the following, we review work closely related to ours and discuss differences to our approach.

Randomization Techniques. Several approaches have been proposed to either improve address space layout randomization, randomize the data space, or randomize on single instruction level. For example, binary stirring [56] re-randomizes code pages at a high rate for a high performance cost. While it hinders attackers to *use* information leaks in code-reuse attacks, it does not impede their creation by itself. In contrast, our re-randomization scheme reuses the native operating system loader and is the base to allow information leak detection with dual process execution. Other solutions [32,40,40] are prone to JIT-ROP code-reuse attacks [48], which are based on information leaks. Address space layout permutation is an approach to scramble all data and functions of a binary [32]. Therefore, a given ELF binary has to be rewritten and randomization can be applied on each run. ORP [40] rewrites instructions of a given binary and reorders basic blocks. As discussed above, it is prone to information leak attacks, which we detect. Instruction set randomization [5,31] complicates code-reuse attacks as it encrypts code pages and decrypts it on the fly. However, in the presence of information leaks combined with key guessing [48,50,57] it can be circumvented. Instruction layout randomization (ILR) [29] randomizes the location of each instruction on each run, but no re-randomization occurs. Thus, the layout can be reconstructed with the help of an information leak. *Readactor* is a defensive system that aims to be resilient against just-in-time code-reuse attacks [15]. It hides code pointers behind execute-only trampolines and code itself is made execute-only, to prevent an attacker building a code-reuse payload just-in-time. However, it has been shown that it is vulnerable against an attack named *COOP*, which reuses virtual functions [44]. Unlike Readactor, DETILE prevents COOP, as this attack needs an information leak as first step. Crane et al. recently presented an enhanced version of Readactor, dubbed *Readactor++* [16], that also protects against whole function reuse attacks such as COOP. This is achieved through function pointer table randomization and insertion of booby traps. Consequently, an adversary can no longer obtain meaningful code locations that can be leveraged for code-reuse attacks. Readactor++ also does not detect or prevent the exploitation of memory disclosures, which poses a potential attack vector.

Multi-Execution Approaches. Most closely related to our research are *n-variant systems*, which run variants of the same program with diverse memory layout and instructions [14]. Similar work runs *program replicæ* synchronized at system calls to demonstrate the detection of memory exploits against the lightweight server `thttpd` on the Linux platform [9,30].

The major drawback of theses systems is the detection approach: if a memory error is abused, one of the variants eventually crashes, which indicates an attack. As information leaks *do not* constitute a memory error, they *do not* raise any exception-based signal. Thus, they remain undetected in these systems. One significant implication is that unlike DETILE, n-variant systems do not protect against just-in-time code-reuse attacks such as JIT-ROP [48]. Similarily, this is the case with COOP attacks in browsers [44]. N-variant systems prevent conventional ROP attacks [42,54] with multi process execution and disjunct virtual address spaces: An attacker supplied absolute address (e.g., obtained through a remote memory disclosure vulnerability) is guaranteed to be invalid in $n-1$ replicas. Hence, any system call utilizing this address will trigger a detection. However, JIT-ROP attacks may performs several memory disclosures and malicious computations without executing a system call inbetween, and thus, can evade traditional n-variant systems. COOP attacks may as well perform touring-complete computations on disclosed memory without executing a system call and evade these systems.

7 Discussion

In the following, we discuss potential shortcomings of our approach and the prototype, and also sketch how these shortcomings can be addressed in the future.

Further Information Leaks. Serna provided an in-depth overview of techniques that utilize information leaks for exploit development [47]. The techniques he discussed during the presentation utilize JavaScript code. As our prototype leverages the JavaScript engine of the browser itself, each information leak that is based on these techniques is detected. This implies that memory disclosure attacks that leverage other (scripting) contexts (e.g., VBScript) can potentially bypass our implementation. However, in practice exploits are typically triggered via JavaScript and thus our prototype can detect such attacks. Furthermore, due to the generic nature of our approach, our current prototype can be extended by instrumenting other scripting engines as well.

Prototype Limitations. In the unlikely event one of the functions we classified as entropy source, such as `Math.random` or `Date.now`, contain a memory disclosure bug, our approach can lead to an under-approximation of detected information leaks. In this specific case, the master confuses the leaked pointer with data from the entropy source and transfers it to the twin process. This is an undesirable state, because DETILE does not prevent the memory layout information to leak into the script context. However, the obtained pointer is only valid in the master process. An attempt to leverage the pointer to mount a code-reuse attack crashes the twin. As a consequence, DETILE halts the master process and prevents further damage.

The current prototype disables the JIT Engine as we protect the interpreter only. However, *dynamic binary instrumentation* (DBI [8,35]) frameworks allow to synchronize processes on the instruction or basic block level, and hence, make it possible to hook emitted JIT code to dispatch our assembly stub in order to synchronize and check within the JIT code.

Asynchronious JavaScript events are currently not synchronized. This is solvable with DBI frameworks as well: If an event triggers in the master process, we let the twin execute to the same point. Then DETILE sets up and triggers the same event in the twin process.

One additional shortcoming of our prototype implementation is the identical mapping of `ntdll.dll` in all processes. As this DLL is initialized already at startup, remapping it is a cumbersome operation. JavaScript, HTML, and other contexts in browsers normally do not interact directly with native `ntdll.dll` Windows structures, and thus internal JavaScript objects, do not contain direct memory references to it. Hence, attackers resort to disclose addresses from libraries other than `ntdll.dll` at first. On the contrary, there might be script engines which directly interact with `ntdll.dll`. Still, the issue is probably solvable with a driver loaded during boot time.

Another technical drawback is the application of re-randomization on every process on the OS, as DLL modules of each process would turn into non-shareable memory and increase physical memory consumption. This can be avoided by protecting only critical processes that represent a valid target for attacks.

Deployment. The current prototype is not meant to be a protection framework for end users of web browsers. It is intended to be deployed as a system for scanning web pages to discover unknown exploits which utilize information leaks. As ASLR needs to be circumvented as a first step of each modern exploit against web browsers, DETILE has the advantage to provide an early detection of the exploit process.

8 Conclusion

Over the last years, script engines were used to exploit vulnerable applications. Especially web browsers became an attractive target for a plethora of attacks. State-of-the-art vulnerability exploits, both in academic research [11,18,26,27, 45] and in-the-wild [46,55,58–60], rely on memory disclosure attacks.

In this work, we proposed a fine-grained, automated scheme to reliably detect such information leaks in script engines. It is based on the insight that information leaks result in a noticable difference in the script context of two synchronized processes with different randomization. We implemented a prototype of this idea for the proprietary browser IE to demonstrate that our approach is viable even on closed-source systems. An empirical evaluation demonstrates that we can reliably detect real-world attack vectors and that the approach induces a moderate performance overhead only (around 17 % overhead on average). While most research focused on mitigating specific types of vulnerabilities, we address the root cause behind modern attacks since most of them rely on information leaks as a first step. Our approach thus serves as another defense layer to complement defenses such as DEP and ASLR.

Acknowledgements. We would like to thank the anonymous reviewers for their valuable comments. This work was supported by the European Commission through the ERC Starting Grant No. 640110 (BASTION).

References

1. Abadi, M., Budiu, M., Erlingsson, U., Ligatti, J.: Control-flow integrity. In: ACM Conference on Computer and Communications Security (CCS) (2005)
2. Alexa. The top 500 sites on the web (2014). http://www.alexa.com/topsites
3. Athanasakis, M., Athanasopoulos, E., Polychronakis, M., Portokalidis, G., Ioannidis, S.: The devil is in the constants: bypassing defenses in browser JIT engines. In: Symposium on Network and Distributed System Security (NDSS) (2015)
4. Backes, M., Nürnberger, S.: Oxymoron: making fine-grained memory randomization practical byallowing code sharing. In: USENIX Security Symposium (2014)
5. Barrantes, E.G., Ackley, D.H., Palmer, T.S., Stefanovic, D., Zovi, D.D.: Randomized instruction set emulation to disrupt binary code injection attacks. In: AGM Conference on Computer and Communications Security (CCS) (2003)
6. Bittau, A., Belay, A., Mashtizadeh, A., Mazieres, D., Boneh, D.: Hacking blind. In: IEEE Symposium on Security and Privacy (2014)
7. Blazakis, D.: Interpreter Exploitation: Pointer Inference and JIT Spraying. BlackHat DC, USA (2010)

8. Bruening, D., Duesterwald, E., Amarasinghe, S.: Design and implementation of a dynamic optimization framework for windows. In: 4th ACM Workshop on Feedback-Directed and Dynamic Optimization (FDDO-4) (2001)

9. Bruschi, D., Cavallaro, L., Lanzi, A.: Diversified process replicæ for defeating memory error exploits. In: IEEE International Performance, Computing, and Communications Conference, 2007, IPCCC 2007 (2007)

10. Capizzi, R., Longo, A., Venkatakrishnan, V., Sistla, A.P.: Preventing information leaks through shadow executions. In: Annual Computer Security Applications Conference (ACSAC) (2008)

11. Carlini, N., Wagner, D.: ROP is still dangerous: breaking modern defenses. In: USENIX Security Symposium (2014)

12. Cheng, Y., Zhou, Z., Yu, M., Ding, X., Deng, R.H.: ROPecker: a generic and practical approach for defending against ROP attacks. In: Symposium on Network and Distributed System Security (NDSS) (2014)

13. Conti, M., Crane, S., Davi, L., Franz, M., Larsen, P., Negro, M., Liebchen, C., Qunaibit, M., Sadeghi, A.-R.: Losing control: on the effectiveness of control-flow integrity understack attacks. In: ACM Conference on Computer and Communications Security (CCS) (2015)

14. Cox, B., Evans, D., Filipi, A., Rowanhill, J., Hu, W., Davidson, J., Knight, J., Nguyen-Tuong, A., Hiser, J.: N.-variant Systems: a secretless framework for security through diversity. In: USENIX Security Symposium (2006)

15. Crane, S., Liebchen, C., Homescu, A., Davi, L., Larsen, P., Sadeghi, A.-R., Brunthaler, S., Franz, M.: Readactor: practical code randomization resilient to memory disclosure. In: IEEE Symposium on Security and Privacy (2015)

16. Crane, S., Volckaert, S., Schuster, F., Liebchen, C., Larsen, P., Davi, L., Sadeghi, A.-R., Holz, T., Sutter, B.D., Franz, M.: It's a TRAP: table randomization and protection against functionreuse attacks. In: ACM Conference on Computer and Communications Security (CCS) (2015)

17. Croft, J., Caesar, M.: Towards practical avoidance of information leakage in enterprise networks. In: HotSec (2011)

18. Davi, L., Lehmann, D., Sadeghi, A.-R., Monrose, F.: Stitching the gadgets: on the ineffectiveness of coarse-grainedcontrol-flow integrity protection. In: USENIX Security Symposium (2014)

19. Davi, L., Liebchen, C., Sadeghi, A.-R., Snow, K.Z., Monrose, F.: Isomeron: code randomization resilient to (just-in-time) return-oriented programming. In: Symposium on Network and Distributed System Security (NDSS) (2015)

20. Devriese, D., Piessens, F.: Noninterference through secure multi-execution. In: IEEE Symposium on Security and Privacy (2010)

21. Erlingsson, U., Abadi, M., Vrable, M., Budiu, M., Necula, G.C.: XFI: Software guards for system address spaces. In: Symposium on Operating Systems Design and Implementation (OSDI) (2006)

22. FireEye. Operation SnowMan (2014). http://www.fireeye.com/blog/technical/cyber-exploits/2014/02/operation-snowman-deputydog-actor-compromises-us-veterans-of-foreign-wars-website.html

23. Fratric, I.: Runtime Prevention of Return-Oriented Programming Attacks. http://ropguard.googlecode.com/svn-history/r2/trunk/doc/ropguard.pdf

24. Gawlik, R., Kollenda, B., Koppe, P., Garmany, B., Holz, T.: Enabling client-side crash-resistance to overcome diversification and information hiding. In: Symposium on Network and Distributed System Security (NDSS) (2016)

25. Gawlik, R., Koppe, P., Kollenda, B., Pawlowski, A., Garmany, B., Holz, T., Report, T.: Detile: Fine-Grained Information Leak Detection in Script Engines. Technical report, Ruhr-University Bochum (2016)
26. Göktaş, E., Athanasopoulos, E., Bos, H., Portokalidis, G.: Out of control: Overcoming control-flow integrity. In: IEEE Symposium on Security and Privacy (2014)
27. Göktaş, E., Athanasopoulos, E., Polychronakis, M., Bos, H., Portokalidis, G.: Size does matter: why using gadget-chain length to prevent code-reuseattacks is hard. In: USENIX Security Symposium (2014)
28. Hirvonen, T.: Dynamic flash instrumentation for fun and profit. Black Hat, USA (2014)
29. Hiser, J., Nguyen-Tuong, A., Co, M., Hall, M., Davidson, J.W.: ILR: Where'd my gadgets go? In: IEEE Symposium on Security and Privacy (2012)
30. Hosek, P., Cadar, C.: Varan the unbelievable: an efficient n-version execution framework. In: International Conference on Architectural Support for Programming Languages and Operating Systems (ASPLOS) (2015)
31. Kc, G.S., Keromytis, A.D., Prevelakis, V.: Countering code-injection attacks with instruction-set randomization. In: ACM Conference on Computer and Communications Security (CCS) (2003)
32. Kil, C., Jim, J., Bookholt, C., Xu, J., Ning, P.: Address space layout permutation (ASLP): towards fine-grained randomization of commodity software. In: Annual Computer Security Applications Conference (ACSAC) (2006)
33. Kuznetsov, V., Szekeres, L., Payer, M., Candea, G., Sekar, R., Song, D.: Code-pointer integrity. In: Symposium on Operating Systems Design and Implementation (OSDI) (2014)
34. Li, H.: Inside AVM. In: REcon (2012)
35. Luk, C.-K., Cohn, R., Muth, R., Patil, H., Klauser, A., Lowney, G., Wallace, S., Reddi, V.J., Hazelwood, K.: Pin: building customized program analysis tools with dynamic instrumentation. In: ACM Sigplan Notices (2005)
36. Microsoft. EMET 5.1 is available (2014). http://blogs.technet.com/b/srd/archive/2014/11/10/emet-5-1-is-available.asp
37. Microsoft. What is the Windows Integrity Mechanism? (2014). http://msdn.microsoft.com/en-us/library/bb625957.aspx
38. Molnar, I.: Exec Shield, new Linux security feature. News-Forge, May 2003
39. Onarlioglu, K., Bilge, L., Lanzi, A., Balzarotti, D., Kirda, E.: G-free: defeating return-oriented programming through gadget-lessbinaries. In: Annual Computer Security Applications Conference (ACSAC) (2010)
40. Pappas, V., Polychronakis, M., Keromytis, A.D.: Smashing the gadgets: hindering return-oriented programming usingin-place code randomization. In: IEEE Symposium on Security and Privacy (2012)
41. Pappas, V., Polychronakis, M., Keromytis, A.D.: Transparent ROP exploit mitigation using indirect branch tracing. In: USENIX Security Symposium (2013)
42. Prandini, M., Ramilli, M.: Return-oriented programming. In: IEEE Symposium on Security and Privacy (2012)
43. Russinovich, M., Solomon, D., Ionescu, A.: Windows Internals, Part 2. Microsoft Press, Redmond (2012)
44. Schuster, F., Tendyck, T., Liebchen, C., Davi, L., Sadeghi, A.-R., Holz, T.: Counterfeit object-oriented programming. In: IEEE Symposium on Security and Privacy (2015)

45. Schuster, F., Tendyck, T., Pewny, J., Maaß, A., Steegmanns, M., Contag, M., Holz, T.: Evaluating the effectiveness of current Anti-ROP defenses. In: Stavrou, A., Bos, H., Portokalidis, G. (eds.) RAID 2014. LNCS, vol. 8688, pp. 88–108. Springer, Heidelberg (2014)
46. Security, V.: Advanced Exploitation of Mozilla Firefox Use-after-free (MFSA2012-22) (2012). http://www.vupen.com/blog/20120625.Advanced_Exploitation_of_Mozilla_Firefox_UaF_CVE-2012-0469.php
47. Serna, F.J.: The info leak era on software exploitation. In: Black Hat USA (2012)
48. Snow, K.Z., Monrose, F., Davi, L., Dmitrienko, A., Liebchen, C., Sadeghi, A.-R.: Just-in-time code reuse: on the effectiveness of fine-grained addressspace layout randomization. In: IEEE Symposium on Security and Privacy (2013)
49. Song, C., Zhang, C., Wang, T., Lee, W., Melski, D.: Exploiting and protecting dynamic code generation. In: Symposium on Network and Distributed System Security (NDSS) (2015)
50. Sovarel, A.N., Evans, D., Paul, N.: Where's the FEEB? the effectiveness of instruction set randomization. In: USENIX Security Symposium (2005)
51. Strackx, R., Younan, Y., Philippaerts, P., Piessens, F., Lachmund, S., Walter, T.: Breaking the memory secrecy assumption. In: ACM European Workshop on System Security (EUROSEC) (2009)
52. Szekeres, L., Payer, M., Wei, T., Song, D.: SoK: eternal war in memory. In: IEEE Symposium on Security and Privacy (2013)
53. Tice, C., Roeder, T., Collingbourne, P., Checkoway, S., Erlingsson, Ú., Lozano, L., Pike, G.: Enforcing forward-edge control-flow integrity in gcc & llvm. In: USENIX Security Symposium (2014)
54. Volckaert, S., Coppens, B., De Sutter, B.: Cloning your gadgets: complete rop attack immunity with multi-variant execution. IEEE Trans. Dependable Secure Comput. (2015)
55. Vreugdenhil, P.: A browser is only as strong as its weakest byte - Part 2 (2012)
56. Wartell, R., Mohan, V., Hamlen, K.W., Lin, Z.: Binary stirring: self-randomizing instruction addresses of legacy x86 binary code. In: ACM Conference on Computer and Communications Security (CCS) (2012)
57. Weiss, Y., Barrantes, E.G.: Known/chosen key attacks against software instruction set randomization. In: ACM Conference on Computer and Communications Security (CCS) (2006)
58. Yan, T.: The art of leaks: the return of heap feng shui. In: CanSecWest (2014)
59. Yu, Y.: ROPs are for the 99 %. In: CanSecWest (2014)
60. Yu, Y.: Write Once, Pwn Anywhere. In: Black Hat USA (2014)
61. Zalewski, M.: Two more browser memory disclosure bugs (2014). http://lcamtuf.blogspot.de/2014/10/two-more-browser-memory-disclosure-bugs.html
62. Zalewski, M.: Bi-level TIFFs and the tale of the unexpectedly early patch (2015). http://lcamtuf.blogspot.de/2015/02/bi-level-tiffs-and-tale-of-unexpectedly.html
63. ZDI.CVE-2011-1346, (Pwn2Own) Microsoft Internet Explorer Uninitialized Variable Information Leak Vulnerability. http://www.zerodayinitiative.com/advisories/ZDI-11-198/
64. Zeigler, A.: IE8 and Loosely-Coupled IE (LCIE) (2008). http://blogs.msdn.com/b/ie/archive/2008/03/11/ie8-and-loosely-coupled-ie-lcie.aspx
65. Zhang, C., Wei, T., Chen, Z., Duan, L., Szekeres, L., McCamant, S., Song, D., Zou, W.: Practical control flow integrity & randomization for binary executables. In: IEEE Symposium on Security and Privacy (2013)
66. Zhang, M., Sekar, R.: BinCFI: control flow integrity for COTS binaries. In: USENIX Security Symposium (2013)

Understanding the Privacy Implications of ECS
(Extended Abstract)

Panagiotis Kintis[1]([envelope]), Yacin Nadji[1], David Dagon[1], Michael Farrell[2],
and Manos Antonakakis[3]

[1] School of Computer Science, Georgia Institute of Technology, Atlanta, GA, USA
{kintis,yacin}@gatech.edu, dagon@m.sudo.sh
[2] Institute for Internet Security and Privacy, Georgia Institute of Technology,
Atlanta, GA, USA
michael.farrell@iisp.gatech.edu
[3] School of Electrical and Computer Engineering, Georgia Institute of Technology,
Atlanta, GA, USA
manos@gatech.edu

Abstract. The edns-client-subnet (ECS) is a new extension for the
Domain Name System (DNS) that delivers a "faster Internet" with the
help of client-specific DNS answers. Under ECS, recursive DNS servers
(recursives) provide client network address information to upstream
authorities, permitting topologically localized answers for content delivery networks (CDNs). This optimization, however, comes with a privacy
penalty that has not yet been studied. Our analysis concludes that ECS
makes DNS communications less private: the potential for mass surveillance is greater, and stealthy, highly targeted DNS poisoning attacks
become possible.

Despite being an experimental extension, ECS is already deployed,
and users are expected to "opt out" on their own. Yet, there are no
available client-side tools to do so. We describe a configuration of an
experimental recursive tool to reduce the privacy leak from ECS queries
in order to immediately allow users to protect their privacy. We recom-
mend the protocol change from "opt out" to "opt in", given the experimental nature of the extension and its privacy implications.

1 Introduction

In 2011, an experimental Internet draft [5], suggesting some extensions to the
Domain Name System (DNS), was proposed to the Internet Engineering Task
Force (IETF). The proposed changes enable more efficient content delivery services, especially when edge devices make use of remote, open recursive servers.
These changes specifically call for the addition of the edns-client-subnet (ECS)
extension, and as part of this effort, an initiative for "a faster Internet" [17]
was announced to promote collaboration. The latest update of the ECS Internet draft, including the technical and implementation details, was published in
November 2014 [7].

© Springer International Publishing Switzerland 2016
J. Caballero et al. (Eds.): DIMVA 2016, LNCS 9721, pp. 343–353, 2016.
DOI: 10.1007/978-3-319-40667-1_17

ECS has seen increased adoption and delivered on its promise of a faster Internet for end users [21]. This improvement in performance, however, was achieved by changing the data shared between recursive DNS servers and authoritative DNS servers, which we will henceforth refer to as *recursives* and *authoritatives*. Historically, the authoritative only received (1) the fully qualified domain name and (2) the IP address of the recursive attempting to resolve the domain on behalf of the end user (located at the edge). The authoritative used the fully qualified domain name in order to provide an answer for the given DNS request. Optionally, the authoritative could provide an "optimized" answer based on the recursive's IP. In the past, this was a reasonable optimization because the recursive and client were more closely linked to each other. For example, the recursive was often provided by the client's Internet Service Provider (ISP). With the advent of large open recursives this is no longer a safe assumption.

By using ECS, the recursive can reveal a truncated portion of the client's IP address, such as the first three octets of the IP. This allows the authoritative to optimize answers for the client issuing the DNS request, rather than the client's recursive. This is particularly useful for content delivery networks (CDN). If a client uses a large open recursive, adding ECS provides better performance due to the improved localization in the authoritative's answers. Studies have shown that ECS not only decreases latency for end users but also has seen increased adoption worldwide [4], perhaps due to these benefits. While the performance improvements are clear, ECS allows anyone in the path between the authoritative and the recursive to surreptitiously read some bits of the client's IP address, which may raise privacy concerns.

Despite the IETF draft acknowledging that there might be privacy issues for clients using an ECS-speaking recursive, very little attention has been paid to identify and evaluate any possible privacy issues with the new extension. In fact, the IETF draft states that there should be a way for users to "opt out" of ECS. The draft also suggests that users should be able to specify how much of their IP address they wish to reveal to the remote authoritative. However, nearly **five years** after the ECS draft was proposed, there are still no client centric tools that empower users to control how much of their IP address is revealed. Thus, ECS is effectively opt-out in nature. In this study, we argue that ECS should be opt-in by default. As we discuss in detail, ECS could be "weaponized" for surveillance or targeted DNS poisoning attacks.

In summary, the study aims to increase the situational awareness around the use of ECS by making the following observations:

1. We describe the potential for novel surveillance and targeted cache poisoning attacks that are made possible by ECS. ECS adds an additional location where surveillance can be performed: between a client's recursive and the domain's authority. The targeted cache poisoning attack can selectively reroute users, down to the granularity of an IP address and be performed while making postmortem forensic analysis difficult.

2. We describe how to set up a custom version of Unbound to opt out of ECS that can be used by end users now who are concerned about their privacy. Prior to this, there was no way for users to opt out.

2   Background

In the following sections, we will discuss ECS and the fundamental technologies on which it relies. Since ECS is simply an extension on top of existing DNS infrastructure, we will start with a short discussion of DNS in Sect. 2.1. This will be followed by a more thorough discussion of the changes introduced by ECS in Sect. 2.2.

2.1   DNS Basics

The Domain Name System (DNS) [15] is a fundamental service that enables ease of use of the Internet. Its primary goal, is to translate human readable text (domain names) to IP addresses, like `example.com` to `93.184.216.34`. In order for this process to happen, a series of eight steps must take place. In step one a stub resolver or client (i.e. web browser, application, etc.), submits a DNS resolution request to a DNS recursive server, referred to as *recursive* from this point on. The recursive server will look for the domain name to IP address mapping in its cache memory; if found there, the latter will inform the stub of the IP address and the process will end. In the case where the IP address(es) is not available in the cache memory, the recursive will ask one of the 13 root servers for the IP address to which the domain name points, on behalf of the stub resolver (step two). The root server will reply with the IP address of the Top Level Domain server (or TLD) of the domain name for which it was queried (step three). During step four, the recursive will submit a query to that TLD for the domain server. The TLD will respond with the IP address of the Authoritative Server (referred to as *authoritative* from now on) and complete step five. Lastly, during steps six and seven, the recursive will communicate with the authoritative, asking for the IP address of the domain name and the latter will reply with it, in the simple case. Finally, step eight concludes the process, during which the recursive informs the stub resolver the IP address of the domain name it looked up.

This process can be divided in two communication phases: (1) the first one is between the stub resolver and the recursive, also known as *below the recursive*; and (2) the second is between the recursive and the servers queried in the DNS hierarchy, commonly referred to as *above the recursive*. The next section describes how the adoption of ECS affects the communication above the recursive.

2.2   Evolution of DNS with ECS

The previous section discussed the domain name resolution process. The adoption of ECS does not change that process, however, the information exchanged

between recursives and authoritatives does change. Prior to ECS, only communication below the recursive contained information about the client performing
a DNS query. Thus, any communication with the authoritative happened above
the recursive, and the authoritative received no information about the client
responsible for a particular request. ECS, embeds a truncated portion of the
client's IP address, referred to as the *source netmask*, into communication above
the recursive. According to the ECS RFC [7], the source netmask should be determined using the most detailed network information available to the recursive,
but by default, it will include the first three octets of a client's IP address. The
authoritative's reply will contain a *scope netmask* that may guide a recursive's
future choice of source netmask. The scope netmask indicates the authoritative's
desired source netmask length and should indicate the minimum source netmask
required to return an optimal answer, with respect to network performance.

These changes were prompted due to the introduction and growing use of
large, open recursives [10,11,16]. Traditionally, recursives were strongly tied to
a client's network, and therefore, they served as a reasonable proxy for a client's
location. Public recursives, however, need not be related to a client's network or
be in close geographic proximity to the client.

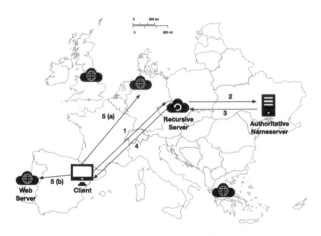

Fig. 1. The image shows the DNS resolution process. The last step of the resolution
request (5), is split in two cases. The first case shows how the resolution would take
place without using ECS, in step 5(a), whereas the second one shows the different reply
when utilizing the client subnet, in step 5(b).

Figure 1 shows an example of the problems that widespread use of public
recursives can cause and how ECS can help. In the figure, a client in Spain
connects to a public recursive in Czech Republic to resolve the domain name
for a web server. Steps (1) to (4) are part of every resolution process, when a
domain name is not stored in a recursive's cache, as described in Sect. 2.1. In this
particular case, when the authority notices the IP address of the recursive being

in Czech Republic, it will assume that the client is in the same geographical region and therefore reply with an IP address for the web service close to that. Provided that the web service is using a CDN or load balancing techniques to increase efficiency for both the provider and the client, this geographical assumption can actually be detrimental. As shown in step 5(a), the client will connect to a web server located in Germany, which is far less efficient than the one in Portugal. When ECS is used, the authority will be able to identify the geographic location of the client since the client's subnet is shared. Thus the authority will make an informed decision about the reply it will provide. In step 5(b), we can see that now the client is provided with an IP address of the web service located in Portugal and connects to that one instead.

3   Surveillance and Selective Cache Poisoning

Spurious ECS "speakers" enable Internet miscreants to potentially perform discreet and powerful surveillance and targeted cache poisoning attacks. The targeted poisoning can selectively reroute users, even down to the granularity of a specific IP address, to hosts under their control. It is important to note these attacks only require visibility of the path between a recursive and authoritative DNS server.

3.1   Surveillance

State sponsored surveillance has seen increased coverage in the press [9], with nation states using a myriad of techniques to monitor users. In light of such revelations, it is more important than ever to evaluate the privacy impact new technologies may have on the public – even if negative consequences are unintended. ECS provides another means for nation states or network operators to monitor individuals or groups on the Internet.

ECS simply makes surveillance easier. First, the introduction of ECS allows client information to be collected from a different vantage point: where an adversary is located between a client's recursive and the domain's authoritative. Second, since surveillance is done based on the domain name of the target server rather than its IP address, surveillance can be more fine-grained in instances where hosting is shared.

Prior to ECS, collecting DNS traffic above the recursive only revealed the IP address of the recursive; nothing was revealed about the user responsible for the original request. However, this is no longer true for ECS enabled domains. As discussed in Sect. 2.2, ECS allows a truncated version of the user's IP address to be embedded in a DNS request; this allows user-level surveillance to be approximated *above the recursive*, increasing the usefulness of DNS for surveillance of individual users on the Internet.

This change allows surveillance to be performed if the spying party is located in the path between the user's recursive and the authoritative of the domain name the user is querying (steps 2 and 3 in Fig. 1). This surveillance is less informative but more specific than IP-based surveillance that would occur between the user and the application server (steps 1 and 4 in Fig. 1). With ECS surveillance, only a portion of the user's IP address will be revealed, however, this will often allow the organization the user is connecting from to be identified. One benefit, however, is the specificity offered by performing surveillance on the server's domain name, rather than its IP address.

In a shared hosting environment, one IP address can host many distinct services separated by the domain name they use. For example, popular HTTP server software allows multiple websites to be hosted differentiated only by the domain name used to resolve the server's IP address. In instances where ECS enabled surveillance is performed, this can be catered specifically to the domain name used rather than the server's IP such that fewer packets have to be analyzed. For example, multiple blogs each using a distinct domain can resolve to one IP address. In the ECS surveillance case, monitoring a specific blog is easier. Furthermore, if used in concert with existing IP-based surveillance between the client and the server, an exact client IP match can be unified with more specific ECS enabled match by the server's domain name. Even more unsettling is the possibility of selective cache poisoning.

3.2   Selective Cache Poisoning

In the traditional context, a DNS Cache Poisoning attack, aims to insert false domain name to IP address mapping pairs in a recursive's cache memory. As explained in Sect. 2.1 the recursive server will store a response it receives from an authoritative for as long as it is instructed; this information is in the TTL field of the response. A fundamental problem in DNS is that the recursive cannot be sure that the response it received was actually from the authoritative or a rogue entity that submitted a response faster. To mitigate this problem randomization has been introduced in the DNS packets. This makes it harder for an adversary to correctly craft a packet that matches the response expected by the recursive. Countermeasures include the Transaction ID field, source port randomization [15] and 0×20 [8]. DNSSEC [2] is probably the best defense against cache poisoning, since the authoritative can use public/private key encryption to certify its identity to the recursive. It is worth noting that, besides DNSSEC, any other attempt to increase the packet entropy and make it harder for the attacker to succeed is only plaintext information within the packet itself. Anyone with access to the packet is able to construct a response, exactly as the authoritative would.

ECS information carried in the DNS packet when a resolution request takes place allows the authoritative to approximate with increased accuracy the geographic location of the entity that initiated the recursive procedure. This is also true for every other entity that is able to monitor the traffic between the recursive and the authoritative servers. For instance, a third party, can *tap the wire* and start collecting information about the clients performing resolution requests. Accessing the *question* packet means that any arbitrary response can be constructed, which will be accepted by the recursive server. Of course this is not something new and any network administrator between a recursive and an authoritative would be able to do it, but the consequence would have been to redirect all traffic around the world to a different IP address than the real one.

Using the client subnet within the ECS-enabled DNS packets, a network administrator could be motivated to change a response and make a recursive server "think" that a domain name points to a different IP address. In this case, a network administrator would do this if she wanted to impact a specific IP address, subnet or geographic location. The current implementation of ECS not only supports such behavior (it is in fact the reason ECS was created), but also understands the difference in caching for the affected subnet. For example, someone might be interested in manipulating only hosts in 10.0.0.0/24. Crafting a response for a resolution request that contains this subnet mask in the payload will force the recursive to cache this domain name to IP address mapping. This will happen for future client DNS lookup requests where the IP address is within that network. This network can be arbitrarily small, even targeting a specific IP address, i.e., 10.0.0.0/32. Every other client will be served with a different mapping pair. A truly stealthy adversary could set the time-to-live (TTL) of the DNS packet to zero to leave the minimum possible forensic trail.

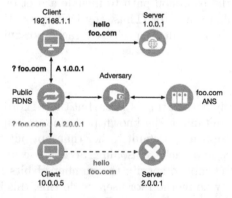

Fig. 2. An adversary monitoring the traffic between the recursive and the authoritative is able to selectively poison the cache of the recursive, even without ever capturing traffic from the clients initiating the requests.

Figure 2 shows how this scenario is possible to occur, when the adversary has access to the network traffic between the recursive and the authoritative server. The adversary will need to be able to process the incoming UDP DNS packets to the network and construct a reply faster than the authoritative. To prove the practicality of the attack, we used our ECS enabled domain name and targeted all IP addresses in a network we have machines located in (***.251.0.0/16). Using a simple network packet sniffer we were able to parse the DNS packets, extract the transaction ID, source port and requested domain fields, which are randomized by most recursive servers, and craft a custom response for requests with subnet masks within the aforementioned network. We used Google Public DNS (8.8.8.8) as the ECS-enabled recursive server, for the requests we submitted to be resolved for our clients. We have made a video[1] that demonstrates the feasibility of this attack, where a request is first sent from an IP address outside of the network and then another one with source IP address that matches our filters. The video shows the network topology on which the attack took place and is similar to Fig. 2. In the first case, the machine is not targeted and the poisoning attack does not occur. In the second case, however, the IP address is changed using a VPN service, making the filters trigger and the RDNS replies with the injected IP address 1.3.3.7. The output of both the packet sniffer that performs the injection and the *tcpdump* tool running on the authority is shown during the resolution requests.

Things can be more serious when one considers that the edns-client-subnet draft does not specify whether the DNS requests to the root and Top Level DNS (TLD) servers should carry the client's subnet mask or not. It explicitly states that the recursive servers *MAY* be configured to not send the ECS option to them, but it is not enough to ensure security. In a case where the recursive shares the exact same packet with the root and TLD servers, then the adversary does not need to be between the recursive and the authoritative exclusively. All an attacker needs is the recursion path to include a root or TLD server within the network she is able to monitor. Thus, any DNS query that the adversary is in position to identify can result to a selective cache poisoning attack.

4   Remedies

ECS enables potentially devastating attacks, but these shortcomings can be alleviated easily while maintaining the known performance improvements of ECS. First, ECS should be opt-in by default rather than opt-out to protect potential victims of surveillance and cache poisoning. Second, despite the fact that the RFC for ECS allows clients to specify the number of bits in their source netmask, there is currently no method for users to do this; this issue is exacerbated by the fact that ECS is already deployed. To this end, we provide instructions for configuring a personal recursive to specify a source netmask of 0 bits, effectively opting out of ECS entirely.

Opt-in vs. Opt-out. Many of the privacy issues that stem from ECS are due to the rapid deployment of ECS and the assumption that all users want to enable ECS by default. We argue that ECS should be disabled by default and users and networks should opt in to the service, rather than have it enabled by default and force users to opt out. In instances where performance is key, ECS is clearly beneficial, but ECS has the potential to be abused to infringe on users' privacy.

Tools to Opt Out. While the RFC suggests users can adjust the source netmask setting to cater to their privacy needs, this is not possible with standard tools.

---

[1] https://youtu.be/U1ehqjGwETc.

```
$ svn co http://unbound.nlnetlabs.nl/svn/branches/edns-subnet/
$ cd edns-subnet && ./configure --enable-subnet && make && make install
$ cat > /etc/unbound/unbound.conf <<EOF
server:
    verbosity: 1
    interface: ${INTERFACE}
    outgoing-interface: ${OUTBOUND_INTERFACE}
    use-caps-for-id: yes
    access-control: 127.0.0.0/8 allow # Allow local access only
    module-config: "subnetcache validator iterator"
    client-subnet-opcode: 8
    max-client-subnet-ipv6: 0
    max-client-subnet-ipv4: 0
forward-zone:
    name: "."
    forward-addr: ${RECURSIVE_IP_PRIMARY}
    forward-addr: ${RECURSIVE_IP_SECONDARY} # If needed
EOF
$ /usr/local/sbin/unbound -c /etc/unbound/unbound.conf
```

Fig. 3. Installation and configuration for Unbound recursive software to send scope-0 by default.

To assist privacy-conscious users we have provided instructions to compile and configure the ECS version of the Unbound recursive in Fig. 3. This configuration will forward connections to the recursive specified while sending scope-0.

5   Related Work

DNS is already known to be able to interfere with a user's privacy. Krishnan et al. [14] have shown how DNS prefetching can leak information regarding users' activity online, to a degree that information regarding web searches can be inferred by simply logging the resolution requests a web browser is making. Zhao et al. [22] performed a deep analysis on each step of a domain name resolution process, showing information that can be inferred from users' private data by only looking at public data. They also propose a simple range query scheme that can be used to protect the user. In the same context, Guha and Francis [12] describe an attack against the DNS by passively monitoring DNS-related traffic. This attack can provide a variety of information about a user that includes location, habits, and commute patterns. Lastly, an Internet Draft by Bortzmeyer [3] attempts to enumerate DNS-only attacks and their privacy implications. These are aggregated into six different categories, and the authors concluded their work with several security considerations on the matter. Some work has extended this to ECS, identifying cases where details of the infrastructure can be uncovered [21] identify more accurate geographic locations [6,18], but the implications for surveillance and poisoning have not been studied so far.

DNS cache poisoning attacks are well understood outside of the context of ECS. In [20], Stewart Joe describes two types of attacks and provides a brief history of the DNS cache poisoning evolution. In 2008, Kaminsky [13] demonstrated a new version that was able to cache poison DNS recursives much more efficiently and overcame all known countermeasures at the time. New controls and mitigation techniques were suggested and deployed: (1) Anax is a system able to identify poisoned records in the cache of a recursive resolver [1]; and (2) WSEC DNS [19] utilizes random subdomain strings for entropy WSEC DNS [19], utilizes random subdomain strings for entropy increase and poison resistance for the packets exchange between DNS servers. Lastly, 0×20 [8] proposed to randomize the case of the question a recursive submits to other DNS servers. This is effective since the protocol is case-insensitive, further increasing the number of attempts needed to successfully poison the cache of a recursive.

6 Conclusions

In this work we discussed ways that ECS can be used to help augment surveillance, and enable extremely targeted cache poisoning attacks against DNS. The latter is especially concerning. Even though ECS has not been officially standardized, it has seen increased adoption over the last several years. Therefore, the unintended consequences introduced by ECS represent *current* threats to Internet users and should be addressed sooner rather than later. To this end, we acknowledge the benefits that ECS provides, but we propose that it should be Opt-In instead of Opt-Out. We also propose a patch to the popular Unbound recursive DNS server that helps users opt-out of using ECS. However, in order to have broader impact, popular public recursives should provide their own mechanisms for disabling ECS, and they should make ECS usage opt-in only.

Acknowledgments. This material is based upon work supported in part by the US Department of Commerce under grant no. 2106DEK and Sandia National Laboratories grant no. 2106DMU. Any opinions, findings, and conclusions or recommendations expressed in this material are those of the authors and do not necessarily reflect the views of the US Department of Commerce nor Sandia National Laboratories.

References

1. Antonakakis, M., Dagon, D., Luo, X., Perdisci, R., Lee, W., Bellmor, J.: A centralized monitoring infrastructure for improving DNS security. In: Jha, S., Sommer, R., Kreibich, C. (eds.) RAID 2010. LNCS, vol. 6307, pp. 18–37. Springer, Heidelberg (2010)
2. Arends, R., Austein, R., Larson, M., Massey, D., Rose, S.: DNS Security Introduction and Requirements. RFC 4033 (Proposed Standard), March 2005. http://www.ietf.org/rfc/rfc4033.txt, updated by RFCs 6014, 6840
3. Bortzmeyer, S.: DNS Privacy Considerations, April 2014. https://tools.ietf.org/id/draft-bortzmeyer-dnsop-dns-privacy-02.txt
4. Calder, M., Fan, X., Hu, Z., Katz-Bassett, E., Heidemann, J., Govindan, R.: Mapping the expansion of Google's serving infrastructure. In: Proceedings of the 2013 Conference on Internet Measurement Conference, IMC 2013, pp. 313–326. ACM, New York (2013). http://doi.acm.org/10.1145/2504730.2504754
5. Contavalli, C., Gaast, W.V.D., Leach, S., Rodden, D.: Client Subnet in DNS Requests (draft-vandergaast-edns-client-subnet-00) (2011). https://www.ietf.org/archive/id/draft-vandergaast-edns-client-subnet-00.txt

6. Contavalli, C., Leach, S., Lewis, E., Gaast, W.V.D.: Client subnet in DNS requests (2013)
7. Contavalli, C., Leach, S., Lewis, E., Gaast, W.V.D.: Client Subnet in DNS Requests (draft-vandergaast-edns-client-subnet-02) (2014). https://datatracker. ietf.org/doc/draft-ietf-dnsop-edns-client-subnet/
8. Dagon, D., Antonakakis, M., Vixie, P., Jinmei, T., Lee, W.: Increased DNS forgery resistance through 0x20-bit encoding: security via leet queries. In: Proceedings of the 15th ACM Conference on Computer and Communications Security, pp. 211–222. ACM (2008)
9. Electronic Frontier Foundation: Mass Surveillance Technologies (2015). https:// www.eff.org/issues/mass-surveillance-technologies
10. Federrath, H., Fuchs, K.-P., Herrmann, D., Piosecny, C.: Privacy-preserving DNS: analysis of broadcast, range queries and mix-based protection methods. In: Atluri, V., Diaz, C. (eds.) ESORICS 2011. LNCS, vol. 6879, pp. 665–683. Springer, Heidelberg (2011)
11. Google: Introduction to Google Public DNS. https://developers.google.com/ speed/public-dns/docs/intro. Accessed 07 Apr 2015
12. Guha, S., Francis, P.: Identity trail: covert surveillance using DNS. In: Borisov, N., Golle, P. (eds.) PET 2007. LNCS, vol. 4776, pp. 153–166. Springer, Heidelberg (2007)
13. Kaminsky, D.: Black ops 2008: It's the end of the cache as we know it. Black Hat USA (2008)
14. Krishnan, S., Monrose, F.: DNS prefetching and its privacy implications: when good things go bad. In: Proceedings of the 3rd USENIX Conference on Large-scale Exploits and Emergent Threats: Botnets, Spyware, Worms, and More, p. 10. USENIX Association (2010)
15. Mockapetris, P.: Domain names - implementation and specification. RFC 1035 (INTERNET STANDARD), November 1987. http://www.ietf.org/rfc/rfc1035.txt
16. OpenDNS: The OpenDNS Global Network Delivers a Secure Connection Every Time, Everywhere (2010). http://info.opendns.com/rs/opendns/images/ TD-Umbrella-Delivery-Platform.pdf
17. OpenDNS: A Faster Internet (2011). http://www.afasterinternet.com
18. Otto, J.S., Sánchez, M.A., Rula, J.P., Bustamante, F.E.: Content delivery and the natural evolution of DNS: remote DNS trends, performance issues and alternative solutions. In: Proceedings of the 2012 ACM Conference on Internet Measurement Conference, pp. 523–536. ACM (2012)
19. Perdisci, R., Antonakakis, M., Luo, X., Lee, W.: WSEC DNS: protecting recursive DNS resolvers from poisoning attacks. In: IEEE/IFIP International Conference on Dependable Systems & Networks 2009, DSN 2009, pp. 3–12. IEEE (2009)
20. Stewart, J.: DNS cache poisoning-the next generation (2003)
21. Streibelt, F., Böttger, J., Chatzis, N., Smaragdakis, G., Feldmann, A.: Exploring EDNS-client-subnet adopters in your free time. In: Proceedings of the 2013 Conference on Internet Measurement Conference, pp. 305–312. ACM (2013)
22. Zhao, F., Hori, Y., Sakurai, K.: Analysis of privacy disclosure in DNS query. In: International Conference on Multimedia and Ubiquitous Engineering, 2007, MUE 2007, pp. 952–957. IEEE (2007)

Authentication

Analysing the Security of Google's Implementation of OpenID Connect

Wanpeng Li[✉] and Chris J. Mitchell

Information Security Group, Royal Holloway, University of London, Egham, UK
Wanpeng.Li.2013@live.rhul.ac.uk, C.Mitchell@rhul.ac.uk

Abstract. Many millions of users routinely use Google to log in to relying party (RP) websites supporting Google's OpenID Connect service. OpenID Connect builds an identity layer on top of the OAuth 2.0 protocol, which has itself been widely adopted to support identity management. OpenID Connect allows an RP to obtain authentication assurances regarding an end user. A number of authors have analysed OAuth 2.0 security, but whether OpenID Connect is secure in practice remains an open question. We report on a large-scale practical study of Google's implementation of OpenID Connect, involving forensic examination of 103 RP websites supporting it. Our study reveals widespread serious vulnerabilities of a number of types, many allowing an attacker to log in to an RP website as a victim user. These issues appear to be caused by a combination of Google's design of its OpenID Connect service and RP developers making design decisions sacrificing security for ease of implementation. We give practical recommendations for both RPs and OPs to help improve the security of real world OpenID Connect systems.

1   Introduction

In order to help alleviate the damage caused by identity attacks and simplify management of identities, a range of identity management systems, such as OAuth 2.0, Shibboleth, CardSpace and OpenID, have been put forward [1–3]. As a replacement for the well-established OpenID [3] scheme, OpenID Connect 1.0 [4] builds an identity layer on top of the OAuth 2.0 framework [2]. The OAuth 2.0 framework enables an RP to obtain profile information about the end user, but does not provide any means for the RP to obtain information about the authentication of the end user. In OpenID Connect, in addition to obtaining profile information about the end-user, RPs can obtain assurances about the end user's identity from an OpenID Provider (OP), which itself authenticates the user.

OpenID Connect involves interactions between four core parties:

1. the End User (U), who accesses on-line services of the RP;
2. the User Agent (UA), typically a web browser, that is employed by an end user to transmit requests to, and receive responses from, web servers;

© Springer International Publishing Switzerland 2016
J. Caballero et al. (Eds.): DIMVA 2016, LNCS 9721, pp. 357–376, 2016.
DOI: 10.1007/978-3-319-40667-1_18

3. the OpenID Provider (OP), e.g. Google, which provides methods to authenticate an end user and generates assertions regarding the authentication event and the attributes of the end user;
4. the Relying Party (RP), e.g. Wikihow, which provides protected on-line services and consumes the identity assertion generated by the OP in order to decide whether or not to grant access to the end user.

In summary, the end user employs a UA to access resources provided by the RP, which relies on the OP to provide authentic information about the user. Even though OpenID Connect was only finalised at the start of 2014, there are already more than half a billion OpenID Connect-based user accounts provided by Google [5], PayPal [6] and Microsoft [7]. This large user base has led very large numbers of RPs to integrate their services with OpenID Connect.

The security of OAuth 2.0, the foundation for OpenID Connect, has been analysed using formal methods [8–10]. Research focusing on implementations of OAuth 2.0 has also been conducted [11–15]. However, as a newly standardised protocol, it is not yet clear how secure practical implementations of OpenID Connect really are. Given the large scale use of Google's service, clarifying this issue is vitally important. To help answer the question, the operation of all one thousand sites from the GTMetrix Top 1000 Sites [16] providing services in English was examined. Of these sites, 103 were found to support the use of the Google's OpenID Connect service at the time of our survey (early 2015). All 103 of these websites were further examined for potential vulnerabilities, with results as reported below. All RPs and the Google OP site were treated as black boxes, and the HTTP traffic sent between RP and OP via the browser was carefully analysed. For every identified vulnerability, we implemented and tested an exploit to evaluate the possible attack surface.

Our study reveals serious vulnerabilities of a number of types, occurring in many of the examined sites; they either allow an attacker to log in to the RP as the victim user or enable compromise of potentially sensitive user information. Google has customised its implementation of OpenID Connect by combining SDKs, web APIs and sample code, and so the OpenID Connect specification only acts as a loose guide to what RPs actually implement. Further examination suggests that the identified vulnerabilities are mainly caused by Google's implementation of its *Hybrid Server-side Flow*, and by RP developers making design decisions sacrificing security for simplicity of implementation. Some of the attacks use cross-site scripting (XSS) [17–20] and cross site request forgeries (CSRFs) [21–26], well-established and widely exploited attack techniques.

OpenID Connect is used to protect millions of user accounts and sensitive user information stored at RPs and the Google OP server. Moreover, as of April 20th 2015, Google shut down its OpenID 2.0 [27] service; as a result a huge number of RPs have had to upgrade their Google sign-in service to use OpenID Connect. It is therefore vitally important that the issues we have identified are addressed urgently, and that Google considers issuing updated advice to all RPs using its service. In this connection we have notified all the RPs in whose

OpenID Connect service we have identified the most serious vulnerabilities, as well as Google itself. To summarise, we make the following contributions:

- We report on the first field study of the security properties of Google's implementation of OpenID Connect.
- We examined the security of all 103 of the RPs supporting the Google OpenID Connect service from the GTMetrix list of the Top 1000 Sites.
- We discovered a number of vulnerabilities which allow an attack to log in to the RP as a victim user, we reported our findings to the most serious affected websites and Google, and helped these RPs fix the identified problems.
- We propose practical improvements which can be adopted by OpenID Connect RPs and OPs that address the identified problems.

The paper is organised as follows. In Sect. 2 we review OpenID Connect. We describe our adversary model in Sect. 3. Section 4 describes the experiments we performed. Possible reasons for the identified vulnerabilities are discussed in Sect. 5. In Sect. 6 we propose mitigations for these vulnerabilities, we review related work in Sects. 7, and 8 concludes the paper.

2   OpenID Connect

As already noted, OpenID Connect 1.0 [4] builds an identity layer on the OAuth 2.0 protocol. The added functionality enables RPs to verify an end user identity by relying on an authentication process performed by an OpenID Provider (OP).

2.1   OpenID Connect Tokens

In order to enable an RP to verify the identity of an end user, OpenID Connect adds a new type of token to OAuth 2.0, namely the *id_token*. This complements the *access_token* and *code*, which are already part of OAuth 2.0. These three types of token are all issued by an OP, and have the following functions.

- A *code* is an opaque value which is bound to an identifier and a URL of the RP. Its main purpose in OpenID Connect is as a means of giving an RP authorisation to retrieve other tokens from the OP. In order to help minimise threats arising from its possible exposure, it has a limited validity period and is typically set to expire shortly after issue to the RP [2].
- An *access_token* is a credential used to authorise access to protected resources stored at a third party (e.g. the OP). Its value is an opaque string representing an authorization issued to the RP. It encodes the right for the RP to access data held by a specified third party with a specific scope and duration, granted by the end user and enforced by the RP and the OP.
- An *id_token* contains claims about the authentication of an end user by an OP together with any other claims requested by the RP. Claims that can be inserted into such a token include: the identity of the OP that issued it, the user's unique identifier at this OP, the identity of the intended recipient, the time at which it was issued, and its expiry time. It takes the form of a JSON Web Token [28] and is digitally signed by the OP.

Both an *access_token* [29] and an *id_token* [30] can be verified by making a call to the web API of the issuing OP.

2.2   Authentication Flows

OpenID Connect builds on user agent HTTP redirections. We suppose an end user wants to access RP services, which consumes OP-generated tokens. The RP generates an authorization request on behalf of the end user and sends it to the OP via the UA (typically a web browser). The OP provides ways to authenticate the end user, asks the end user to allow the RP to access the user attributes, and generates an authorization response which includes tokens of two types: *access_tokens* and *id_tokens*, where the latter contain claims about user authentication. The RP can use a received *access_token* to access end user's attributes using the OP-provided API, and after receiving an *id_token* the RP learns about the user authentication, as summarised in Fig. 1.

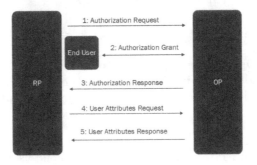

Fig. 1. OpenID connect protocol overview

OpenID Connect [4] supports four authentication flows [5], i.e. ways in which the system can operate, namely *Hybrid Server-side Flow* (or *Hybrid Flow*) [31], *Authorization Code Flow*, *Client-side Flow* (or *Implicit Flow*), and *Pure Server-side Flow*. We describe the first two, since they are most relevant here.

An RP must register with the OP before using Google OpenID Connect. During registration, the OP gathers security-critical information about the RP, including either the RP's redirect URI or its *origin*. The redirect URI is used in the *Authorization Code Flow*, and the user agent is redirected to it after step 5 of Sect. 2.2. The *origin* is used in the *Hybrid Server-side Flow* and *Client-side Flow*, and points to the RP's domain name. The OP issues the RP with a unique identifier (*client_id*) and a secret (*client_secret*), used to authenticate the RP when using the *Authorization Code Flow* or *Hybrid Server-side Flow*.

Hybrid Server-Side Flow. Google's OpenID Connect uses **postMessage** [32–35] to enable cross domain communication between an RP and Google's

OP. Normally, scripts on different pages can only access each other if the web pages that caused them to execute are at locations sharing the same protocol, port number and host. The **postMessage** method gives a way to securely pass messages across domains — see, for example, in Son and Shmatikov [35]. In the *Hybrid Server-side Flow* (see Fig. 2) and *Client-side Flow*, an RP JavaScript Client (RPJC) runs on the UA and listens for the postMessage event.

We now describe the *Hybrid Server-side Flow*, which is summarised in Fig. 2 where the numbers correspond to the numbered steps below.

1. U → UA → RPJC: The user clicks the Google button on the RP website, causing the UA to trigger the RPJC to generate an authorization request.
2. RPJC → UA → OP: The RP generates an OpenID Connect authorization request and sends it to the OP via the UA. This request includes *client_id*, an identifier the RP registered with the OP previously; *response_type=code token id_token*, requesting that a *code*, an *access_token* and an *id_token* be returned directly from Google; *redirect_uri=postmessage*, indicating **postMessage** is being used; *state*, used by the RP JavaScript Client to maintain state between the request and the callback (step 5 below); *origin*, a URL without a path appended; and the *scope* of the requested permission.
3. OP → UA: If the OP has already authenticated the user then this step and the next are skipped. If not, the OP returns a login form to collect authentication information (e.g. user account and password).
4. U → UA → OP: The user completes the login form and grants permission for the RP to access the attributes stored by the OP.
5. OP → UA: After receiving the permission grant, the OP generates an HTML document containing the authorization response and returns it to the UA. The authorization response contains the *code*, *access_token* and *id_token* generated by the OP; and *state* as sent in step 2.
6. UA → RPJC → RP: The UA executes the JavaScript inside the HTML document it received in the previous step. The JavaScript sends the authorization response using **postMessage** to the RPJC which is running on the UA and listening for the **postMessage** event. After the RPJC receives the authorization response it extracts the *code* and sends it back to the RP.
7. RP → OP: The RP produces an *access_token* request and sends it to the OP token endpoint directly (i.e. not via the UA). The request includes *grant_type=authorization_code*, indicating that the RP wants to use the *code* to retrieve an *access_token* from the OP; the *code* generated in step 5; *redirect_uri=postmessage*, indicating that **postMessage** has been used to get the *code*; and *client_secret*, the secret shared by the RP and OP.
8. OP → RP: The OP checks the *code*, *client_secret* and *redirect_uri* and, if correct, responds to the RP with *access_token* and *id_token*, the latter of which is the same as the *id_token* sent in step 5.
9. RP → OP: The RP verifies the *id_token*. If valid, the RP knows the user has been authenticated. If necessary it can make a web API call to retrieve user attributes from the OP, using the *access_token* as authorisation.

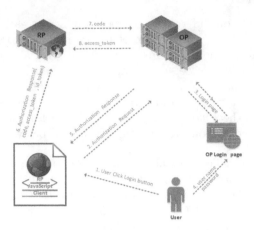

Fig. 2. Google's hybrid server-side flow

Authorization Code Flow. One advantage of this flow is that no tokens are available to the UA or any malicious application able to access the UA. If either of the tokens are compromised they could be used to access sensitive user data and/or successfully masquerade as the user. The OP must authenticate the RP before it issues the tokens, and hence use of the *Authorization Code Flow* requires that an RP shares a secret with the OP. The flow involves the OP returning an authorization *code*, typically a short-lived opaque string, to the RP, which uses it to obtain the *id_token* and *access_token* directly from the OP's *access_token* endpoint, i.e. not via the UA. The main steps are as follows.

1. U → RP: The user clicks a button on the RP website, as displayed by the UA, causing the UA to send an HTTP or HTTPS request to the RP.
2. RP → UA → OP: The RP generates and sends an OpenID Connect authorization request to the OP via the UA, including *client_id*, previously registered by the RP with the OP; *response_type=code*, indicating use of *Authorization Code Flow*; *redirect_uri*, to which the OP will redirect the UA after granting access; *state*, used by the RP to maintain state between request and callback (step 5 below); and the *scope* of the requested permission.
3. OP → UA: If the OP has already authenticated the user then this step and the next are skipped. If not, the OP returns a login form to collect user authentication data.
4. U → UA → OP: The user completes the login form and grants permission for the RP to access the attributes stored by the OP.
5. OP → UA: After using the information provided in the login form to authenticate the user, the OP generates an authorization response and sends it back to the UA. The authorization response contains *code*, the authorization code generated by the OP; and *state*, the value sent in step 2.
6. UA → RP: The UA redirects the response received in Step 5 to the RP.
7. RP → OP: The RP produces an *access_token* request and sends it to the OP token endpoint directly (i.e. not via the UA). The request includes

grant_type=code, indicating the RP wants to use the *code* to retrieve an *access_token*; the *code* sent in step 5; the *redirect_uri*; and *client_secret*, the secret shared by the RP and OP.

8. OP → RP: The OP checks the *code*, *client_secret* and *redirect_uri* and if all are correct responds to the RP with an *access_token* and *id_token*.

9. RP → OP: The RP verifies the *id_token*. If valid, the RP now knows that the user has been authenticated. If necessary it can also make a call to the OP's web API, using the *access_token* for authorisation, to retrieve user attributes.

3 Adversary Model

In our assessment of the security of Google's OpenID Connect service, and of RPs using the service, we consider two adversary scenarios.

- **A Web Attacker** can share malicious links or post comments containing malicious content (e.g. stylesheets or images) on a benign website; and/or exploit vulnerabilities in an RP website. Malicious content forged by a web attack might trigger the UA to send HTTP(S) requests to an RP and OP using GET or POST methods, or execute attacker JavaScripts. For example, a web attacker could operate an RP website to collect *access_tokens*.

- **A Passive Network Attacker** can intercept unencrypted data sent between an RP and a UA (e.g. by monitoring an open Wi-Fi network).

Conducting a security analysis of commercially deployed OpenID Connect SSO systems requires various challenges to be addressed. These include lack of detailed specifications for the SSO systems, undocumented RP and OP source code, and the complexity of APIs and/or SDK libraries in deployed SSO systems. The methodology we used is similar to that of Wang et al. [14] and Sun and Beznosov [13], i.e. we treated the RPs and OP as black boxes and analysed the BRMs produced during authorization. Since we used a black-box approach, there may be vulnerabilities and implementation flaws we did not uncover.

4 A Security Study

We used Fiddler[1] to capture BRMs sent between RPs and the OP; we also developed a Python program to parse the BRMs to simplify analysis and avoid mistakes arising from manual inspections. All experiments were performed using accounts set up specially for the purpose, i.e. at no time was any user's account accessed without permission. Of the 103 RPs supporting Google OpenID Connect that we examined, 69 (67%) adopt the *Authorization Code Flow*, 33 (32%) use the *Hybrid Server-side Flow*, and just 1 adopted the *Client-side Flow*.

---

[1] http://www.telerik.com/fiddler.

4.1   Studying the Security of the Hybrid Server-Side Flow

As described in Sect. 2.2, Google's OpenID Connect API uses **postMessage** to deliver the authorization response from the OP to an RP. When the RPJC running on the user's browser receives the authorization response from the OP, it extracts the *code* from the authorization response and then submits the *code* back to the RP's OpenID Connect sign-in endpoint.

Authentication by Google ID. As stated above, the RPJC running on the UA submits the *code* it receives from the Google OP back to the RP's Google sign-in endpoint (see step 6 in Sect. 2.2). The RP is meant to use the *code* to retrieve the *access_token* and *id_token* from the OP. However, we observed that 18 % of the RPs using the Hybrid Server-side Flow (i.e. 6 of 33) simply submit the user's Google ID to the RP's Google sign-in endpoint; of these, two submit the user's Google ID without appending a *code*, and one submits the user's Google ID with an *access_token*. This led us to suspect that such RPs might be basing their verification of user identity solely on the Google ID, and not using the *code* as intended. If so, then a web attacker knowing a user's Google ID could use it to log in to the user's RP account. We tested this, and found that 9 % of the RPs using the Hybrid Server-side Flow (i.e. 3 of 33) have this vulnerability.

Learning a user's Google ID can be relatively simple, as a user's Google+ post URL reveals it. An attacker can use the Google+ *search for people* function to find a victim user to attack, and can then visit the chosen user's Google+ page to learn the ID. For example, https://plus.google.com/u/0/115722834054889887046/posts is the Google+ post URL for a Gmail account, for which the ID is 115722834054889887046.

We reported our findings to the three affected websites, and recommendations were also provided to enable the RP developers to fix the problem (see also Subsect. 6.3).

Using the Wrong Token. An *access_token* is a bearer token, so anyone can use it to get access to the associated user attributes stored by Google. By contrast, the *id_token* is designed for use in providing assurances about user authentication. However, in practice, some RPs use an *access_token* to obtain user authentication assurances without verifying it (i.e. making a web API call to the OP token information endpoint [29]). In such a case, any party with a user's *access_token* can impersonate that user to the RP simply by submitting it. This is a particular threat for a malicious RP, which can routinely obtain *access_tokens* from the Google OP. In other words, any RP using Google OpenID Connect can log in as a victim user to any RPs using an *access_token* to authenticate the user without verifying it. Unfortunately, we found that 58 % of RPs using the *Hybrid Server-side Flow* (i.e. 19 of 33) submit an *access_token* back to their Google sign-in endpoint (see step 6 in Sect. 2.2) and 45 % (i.e. 15 of these 19) use the *access_token* to authenticate the user; of these 15 RPs, only two RPs verify the *access_token* before using it to retrieve user attributes. As a result, 39 % of the RPs (i.e. 13 of 33) we examined are vulnerable to this impersonation attack.

We tested the above attack using Burp Suite[2] by submitting an *access_token* obtained from a randomly chosen RP using the *Hybrid Server-side Flow* to the target RP's Google sign-in endpoint. If the attack succeeds, we are able to log in to the target RP as the victim user. As noted above, as many as 39 % of the RPs using the *Hybrid Server-side Flow* are vulnerable to this attack. Some of the vulnerable RPs (i.e. 3 out of 13) require additional evidence of the user to be submitted with the *access_token*, in the form of the Google ID or the user's email address. However, an attacker with an *access_token* can readily use it to get the user's Google ID or email address from Google, and so such additional steps do not prevent the attack.

Intercepting an *access_token*. As stated above, 58 % of RPs using the *Hybrid Server-side Flow* require the submission of an *access_token* back to their Google sign-in endpoint (see step 6 in Sect. 2.2). If the RPJC running on the UA sends an *access_token* back to its Google sign-in endpoint without SSL protection, a passive network attacker is able to intercept it (see Sect. 3). According to the OAuth 2.0 specification [36], an *access_token* should never be sent unencrypted between the user browser and the RP. However, we found that 12 % of RPs using the *Hybrid Server-side Flow* (i.e. 4 out of 33) send the *access_token* unprotected. A sniffer written in Python was implemented to test this.

We also observed that one additional site, namely TheFreeDictionary[3] does use SSL to protect the transfer of the *code* to its Google sign-in endpoint. However, the *access_token* is subsequently stored in a cookie, and when the cookie is sent from the browser back to TheFreeDictionary the link is not SSL-protected. That is, the *access_token* is observable by a passive eavesdropper.

Privacy Issues. When a user chooses to use OpenID Connect to log in to an RP website, the user attributes (e.g. email address, name) that the RP retrieves from the OP should never be revealed to parties other than the RP. SSL connections should be established to protect user information transmitted between the browser and the RP or OP.

However, as explored below, user information leakage might happen if:

- the RPJC running on the user's browser sends user information, the *id_token* or the *access_token* back to its Google sign-in endpoint without SSL protection (see step 6 in Sect. 2.2);
- the RP Google sign-in endpoint sends the user information directly to the user's browser without SSL protection; or
- the RP uses SSL to protect the link to the Google sign-in endpoint, but changes to http when sending user information back to the UA.

As described in Sect. 4.1, a passive eavesdropper can intercept the *access_token* for 12 % of the RPs that use the Hybrid Server-side Flow (i.e. 4

---

[2] http://portswigger.net/burp/.
[3] http://www.thefreedictionary.com.

of 33), and can then use it to retrieve potentially sensitive user information, e.g. including Google ID and email address. As stated in Sect. 2.1, the *id_token* is a JSON web token in which the user email address and Google ID are encoded in cleartext; so anyone obtaining the token can immediately obtain the information within. One of the four RPs referred to above sends an *id_token* in addition to the *access_token* to its Google sign-in endpoint, and thus a passive web attacker can retrieve the token's user information without requesting it from Google. We also found that one RP did not enable SSL to protect its Google sign-in endpoint, and returned user information directly to the UA. Another RP sends user information back to its Google sign-in endpoint without SSL protection. Yet another RP uses SSL to protect the link to the Google sign-in endpoint, but changes to HTTP when sending user information back to the UA. As a result, user privacy cannot be guaranteed for 21 % of the RPs we examined (i.e. 7 out of 33). As noted above, a sniffer in Python was implemented to demonstrate the feasibility of the attack.

Session Swapping. As discussed earlier, the RPJC running on the UA sends the user's OpenID tokens (i.e. a *code*, an *access_token*, an *id_token*, and/or the user's Google ID) back to its Google sign-in endpoint (see step 6 in Sect. 2.2). The OpenID Specification [4] recommends a *state* value should be appended when the RPJC sends the tokens back, and that this *state* value should be bound to the session. If the RPJC fails to send *state*, an attacker can execute a session swapping attack [13, 21, 37] as follows.

1. The attacker logs in to the RP website using his/her own account (step 4 in Sect. 2.2), and intercepts the Google-generated tokens (step 5 in Sect. 2.2).
2. The attacker constructs a request to the RP's Google sign-in endpoint, including the attacker's own tokens.
3. The attacker inserts the request in an HTML document (e.g. in the **src** attribute of a **img** or **iframe** tag) made available via an HTTP server.
4. The victim user is now, by some means, induced to visit the website offering the attacker's page. The HTML can be constructed in such a way (described in detail below) that the victim's UA will automatically use GET or POST to send the attacker-constructed request to the RP; as a result the user session on the RP website will be bound to the attacker's account.

We observed that 42 % of the RPJCs using *Hybrid Server-side Flow* (i.e. 14 of 33) use POST to submit the tokens back to the RP's server without an accompanying *state*. Use of a static **img** or **iframe** tag to perform an attack of the above type does not work against these RPs, as the browser will automatically use GET to retrieve the img and iframe data. In order to use POST to submit those tokens, we created a special HTML page to conduct the attack. We used JavaScript to create an iframe with a unique name in the browser. We then constructed a form inside the iframe whose action points to the RP's Google sign-in endpoint, put the attacker's tokens into the form input, and configured the HTML to submit the form whenever the HTML is loaded by a browser.

To deploy the attack, the constructed HTML page is made available via a web server. If a victim's UA visits the page, the JavaScript inside the HTML automatically submits the attacker's tokens to the RP using POST; as a result the victim user's session at the RP is bound to the attacker's, i.e. a session-swapping attack has been performed. An attacker could use such an attack to collect sensitive user information, e.g. if the victim user updates his credit card information on the RP website, this information will be written to the attacker's account.

Sadly, we found that 73 % of RPs using *Hybrid Server-side Flow* (i.e. 24 of 33) are vulnerable. Of these 24 RPs, eight (i.e. 24 % of this category) submit a *code* to their Google sign-in endpoint; as *code* is a one-time value, the attacker must update it within the attack HTML every time the page is retrieved by a victim. For the other 48 % of vulnerable RPs (i.e. 16 of 33), an *access_token* or the user's Google ID is submitted back to the Google sign-in endpoint, in which case the attacker does not need to update the attack page HTML as frequently.

4.2   Studying the Security of the Authorization Code Flow

We first observe that Google's OAuth 2.0 *Authorization Code Flow* implementation [38] has similar steps to those in Subsect. 2.2. The token endpoint provided as part of Google's implementation of OAuth 2.0 (as checked on April 22, 2015) returns an *id_token* to the RP. That is, without knowing details of the RP's internals, we cannot tell whether an RP is using OpenID Connect or OAuth 2.0. We therefore cover all cases where Google returns a *code* to the RP's Google sign-in endpoint under our discussion of the OpenID Connect *Authorization Code Flow*, even though some of the RPs may actually be using OAuth 2.0. However, this makes no difference to our security analysis.

Around 67 % of the RPs we examined (i.e. 69 of 103) use *Authorization Code Flow*. Unlike the *Hybrid Server-side Flow*, Google's implementation of *Authorization Code Flow* uses HTTP status code redirect techniques (using code 302) to deliver the authorization response to the RP's Google sign-in endpoint.

Intercepting an *access_token*. In the *Authorization Code Flow*, a *code* is returned by Google to the RP's Google sign-in endpoint (see step 6 in Sect. 2.2). No tokens are transmitted during the authorization procedure. After the RP receives the *code*, it can use it to retrieve an *access_token* from Google (steps 7/8 in Subsect. 2.2); it can then use the *access_token* to retrieve user attributes from Google (step 9 in Subsect. 2.2). The RP then logs the user in to its website.

If an RP does not use SSL to protect communications with its Google sign-in endpoint, a passive web attacker may be able to intercept the *code*. A passive web attacker cannot use the *code* to retrieve an *access_token* from Google, as it will not know the RP's *client_secret* (shared by the RP and Google). However, we observed that, of the RPs using the *Authorization Code Flow*, 6 % of their Google sign-in endpoints (i.e. 4 out of 69) return an *access_token* to the user's browser instead of binding the user to the RP's session. As these RPs do not use

SSL to protect the transfer of the *access_token*, a passive web attacker is able to obtain the user's *access_token* returned from the RP's Google sign-in endpoint.

Stealing an *access_token* via Cross-site Scripting. Google's 'automatic authorization granting' feature [13] generates an authorization response automatically if a user has a session with Google and previously granted permission for the RP concerned. Using this feature, an attacker might be able to steal a user *access_token* by exploiting an XSS vulnerability in the RP or UA.

To test the feasibility of such an attack, an exploit written in JavaScript was implemented. The exploit takes advantage of a recently revealed vulnerability in Android's built-in browser [39] which allows an attacker to conduct a universal XSS attack [17–20]. The exploit uses a browser **window.open** event to send a forged authorization request to Google's authorization server, within which *response_type=code* (see step 2 in Sect. 2.2) is changed to *response_type=code token id_token*. If the user is logged in to his or her Google account and has previously granted permission for this RP, Google automatically generates an authorization response without the involvement of the user; this response is appended as a URI fragment (#) to the redirect URI (see step 5 in Sect. 2.2) and is sent back to the RP (see step 6 in Sect. 2.2). As the RP Google sign-in endpoint does not expect an URI fragment, a predefined error page will be generated by the RP (e.g. a '404 not found' or 'Failed connection' error). The exploiting JavaScript can now extract the authorization response from the URL of the error page and send it to its opener window, where the **window.open** event is triggered. The opener window then sends the *access_token* to the attacker's server.

Unfortunately, we found that all the RPs using *Authorization Code Flow* are vulnerable to this attack. The vulnerability affects all Android versions up to 4.4, which as of April 6, 2015 still accounted for 53.2 % of Android devices[4].

Privacy Issues. Unlike the *Hybrid Server-side Flow*, only a *code* is submitted back to the RP's Google sign-in endpoint (see step 6 in Sect. 2.2). No user information (e.g. a Google ID or *id_token*) is transmitted during authorisation. However, user information might still leak if the RP Google sign-in endpoint sends the user data directly to the UA without SSL.

We found that 16 % of RPs using the *Authorization Code Flow* (i.e. 11 of 69) return user information to the browser directly without SSL protection. Thus a passive web attacker is able to intercept potentially sensitive user information, e.g. if the user is using an open Wi-Fi network (see Sect. 3).

Session Swapping. If an RP using *Authorization Code Flow* does not enable anti-CSRF measures (e.g. by appending a *state* bound to the browser session to the tokens) to protect its Google sign-in endpoint, a web attacker can launch

---

[4] https://developer.android.com/about/dashboards/index.html?
utm_source=suzunone.

a session swapping attack, as described in Subsect. 4.1 for *Hybrid Server-side Flow*.

Unlike the session swapping attack in Subsect. 4.1, in the *Authorization Code Flow* only the GET method is used to submit the *code* back to the RP's Google sign-in endpoint. This means that the attacker can simply insert the forged request in the **src** attribute of a **img** or **iframe** tag of an HTML document. When the victim user visits the malicious HTML, the browser will automatically send the request to the RP's Google sign-in endpoint using the GET method.

We found that 35 % of the RPs using the *Authorization Code Flow* (i.e. 24 of 69) are vulnerable to this attack. However, as *code* is a one time value, the attacker must update it every time the attack page is visited by a victim. Thus such an attack is not as harmful as session swapping in the *Hybrid Server-side Flow*, where an *access_token* which can be used multiple times is submitted back to the RP's Google sign-in endpoint.

Forcing a Login Using a CSRF Attack. A CSRF login attack operates in the context of an ongoing interaction between a target UA (running on behalf of a target user) and a target RP. A malicious website somehow causes the target UA to initiate an OpenID Connect authorization request to the OP. Because of Google's 'automatic authorization granting' feature, receiving such a request can cause the Google OP to generate an authorization response, which is delivered to the RP without involvement by the user. If the target user is logged in to Google, the UA will send cookies containing the target user's Google OP-generated tokens, along with the attacker-supplied authorization request, to the OP. The OP will process the malicious authorization request as if initiated by the target user, and will generate and send an authorization response to the RP. The target UA could be made to send the spurious request in various ways; for example, a visited malicious site could use the HTML **img** tag's **src** attribute to specify the URL of a malicious request, causing the UA to silently use a GET method to send the request.

We found that 35 % of the RPs using *Authorization Code Flow* (i.e. 24 of 69) are vulnerable to such an attack. One consequence is that an attacker can cause a victim user to log in to the RP, as long as the user has previously logged in to Google. This could damage the user experience of the RP website, as the victim user might dislike such a potentially annoying 'automatic login' feature.

5   Security Concerns over Google's Implementation of OpenID Connect

In the *Hybrid Server-side Flow*, any authorization request generated by an RPJC using Google's OpenID Connect API will always include *response_type=code token id_token*; as a result, the authorization response returned by Google to the RPJC always contains a *code*, *access_token* and *id_token*. Unfortunately, this feature is the source of many security threats to the system. First, as the *access_token* and *id_token* are directly transferred to the UA, this means that these tokens are potentially revealed to the user agent and any applications which might be able to access the user agent. Second, it gives RP developers a choice — that is, they can choose which token will be submitted back to the RP server by the RPJC. We found that 67 % (i.e. 22 out of 33) of RPs using the *Hybrid Server-side Flow* design their RPJC to submit an *access_token* or a user's Google ID back to the RP's Google sign-in endpoint, and this leads to most of the attacks described in Sect. 4.1.

5.1 Giving RPs the Ability to Customise the Hybrid-Server-side Flow

According to the OpenID Connect specification [4], a *code* must be returned by the OP to the RP's Google sign-in endpoint (see step 6 in the *Hybrid Server-side Flow*). However, as described above, in Google's implementation of the Hybrid Server-side Flow, a *code*, *access_token* and *id_token* are always returned by Google to the RPJC running on the user's browser. Unlike the *Authorization Code Flow*, where only a *code* is returned to the RP's Google sign-in endpoint (see step 6 in Sect. 2.2) and no RPJC exists, this gives RPs the ability to customise their *Hybrid Server-side Flow*. In fact our experiments have shown that as many as 67 % of RPs (i.e. 22 out of 33) customise their implementation of the *Hybrid Server-side Flow* by submitting an *access_token* or a user's Google ID back to the RP's Google sign-in endpoint. Among these RPs, 73 % (16 out of 22) are vulnerable to the first two attacks (namely **Authentication by Google ID** which allows an attacker to log in to the RP as any victim user and **Using the Wrong Token** which allows an attacker to impersonate the victim user using an *access_token* generated for another RP) described in Sect. 4.1. Moreover, as the *code*, *access_token* and *id_token* are returned by Google inside a HTML document, these values are also revealed to the user agent and hence to any applications (e.g. browser plug-ins), which might be able to access the user agent. If the plug-in or user agent has vulnerabilities which could allow an attacker to access these values, the attacker can steal the user's *access_token*; for example a malicious plug-in which has the right to read the content of HTML pages could obtain the *access_token*.

5.2 No CSRF Countermeasures in the Hybrid-Server-side Flow

In Google's implementation of the *Hybrid Server-side Flow*, the authorization request generated by the RPJC includes a *state* value which is designed to prevent CSRF attacks [21, 23–25]. However, we found that the *state* value extracted by the RPJC is actually a null value; this means that Google itself fails to deliver the *state* value to the RPJC, and hence the *state* value cannot be used to mitigate the threat of a CSRF attack. We also observed that one of the RPs using the *Authorization Code Flow* sends a null *state* value back to its Google sign-in endpoint. As the *state* value generated by the RPJC is not bound to the RP's session and cannot be extracted by the RPJC, another *state* value which is bound to the session needs to be implemented to protect the RP's Google sign-in endpoint against a CSRF attack.

In addition, checking the Google OpenID Connect sample code [40] reveals that Google has not included a *state* value in its example of an RPJC-generated AJAX request, used to send data back to the RP [31] (see step 6 in *Hybrid Server-side Flow*). The lack of a *state* parameter in the sample code and the complexity of implementing anti-CSRF measures helps to explain why 73 % of the RPs using the *Hybrid Server-side Flow* are vulnerable to this attack.

5.3 Automatic Authorization Granting

The 'automatic authorization granting' feature of Google's OpenID Connect significantly enhances the user experience and system performance. Without this, users would have to click an "OK" button in a popup window whenever they wished to log in to an RP, in order to grant authorisation. However, it can also be harmful, since it may allow an attacker to steal an *access_token* (see Sect. 4.2) and force a user log in to the RP (see Sect. 4.2).

We also found that, in the *Hybrid Server-side Flow*, iframes are used to manage the session [33] between the RPJC and the OP. Suppose a user, who has previously both granted permission for the RP and logged in to his or her Google account, visits the RP login page which contains an iframe pointing to the authorization request. Because of the 'automatic authorization granting' feature, the browser can use the GET method to retrieve the authorization response from Google without involvement by the user. The UA and any applications (e.g. plug-ins) which can access the UA are able to extract the authorization response, which might expose the *Hybrid Server-side Flow* to new attacks.

6 Recommendations

OpenID Connect has been deployed by many RPs and OPs, and increasing numbers of RPs supporting the Google service will likely implement it now Google has shut down its OpenID service. We found serious vulnerabilities in existing deployments of OpenID Connect, and there is a significant danger that these vulnerabilities will be replicated in the future. Below we make a number of recommendations designed to address the identified vulnerabilities. These recommendations primarily apply to RPs using the Google service and to the Google OP itself, but some may have broader applicability. These recommendations are intended both to try to address the problems that exist in current systems, and to help ensure that future systems are built more robustly.

6.1 Recommendations for RPs

When using OpenID Connect, especially the *Hybrid Server-side Flow*, RP developers are responsible for designing the RPJC action on receiving an authorization response from the Google OP. As a result, system security for the RP largely depends on its developers. We have the following recommendations for RPs.

- **Do not customise the Hybrid Server-side Flow:** One reason OpenID Connect is vulnerable to the attacks in Sect. 4.1 is that some RPs customise the *Hybrid Server-side Flow*. In particular, instead of submitting a *code* back to its Google sign-in endpoint, the RPJC running in the UA submits an *access_token* or Google ID, which is then used by the RP to authenticate the user. Such a customised *Hybrid Server-side Flow* might improve user experience and RP website efficiency, but this is at the cost of opening serious vulnerabilities. RPs must implement the OpenID Connect *Hybrid Server-side Flow* strictly conforming to the OpenID Connect Specification.
- **Deploy countermeasures against CSRF attacks:** One reason the OpenID Connect systems we investigated are vulnerable to CSRF and session swapping attacks is that the RPs have not implemented any of the well-known countermeasures. In order to prevent CSRF attacks, Google recommends that RPs include the *state* parameter in the OpenID Connect authorization request and response, and RPs should follow this recommendation.
- **Do not use a constant or predictable *state* value:** Some RPs include a fixed *state* value in the OpenID Connect authorization request. If the *state* value is fixed, it cannot be uniquely bound to the browser session, thereby allowing an attacker to successfully forge a response, since the RP cannot distinguish between a legitimate response produced by a valid user and a forged response produced by an attacker. Hence, in such a case, the inclusion of the *state* value does not protect against CSRF attacks. Thus RPs must generate a non-guessable *state* value which should be bound to the browser session so that the *state* value can used to verify the validity of the response.

6.2   Recommendations for OPs

In an OpenID Connect SSO system, the OP designs the process and provides the API for RPs. An RP supporting a particular OP must therefore comply with the requirements of that OP, and so OPs play a critical role in the system. We have the following recommendations for OPs (and in particular for Google).

- **Remove the *token* from the authorization request in the Hybrid Server Flow:** In the *Hybrid Server-side Flow*, the *token* in the authorization request causes Google to return an *access_token* to the RPJC. This allows RPJCs to submit an *access_token* back to their Google sign-in endpoints, as was the case for 58 % of the RPs using the *Hybrid Server-side Flow* that we investigated. This practice gives rise to a range of possible impersonation attacks. Sending the *access_token* also creates further risks, since if the RP does not enable SSL to protect its Google sign-in endpoint, a passive network attacker could steal it. This would not only enable a malicious RP to impersonate a user to those RPs which submit an *access_token* to the Google sign-in endpoint, but also allow the possibility of other misuses of this token, e.g. to compromise sensitive user data.
- **Add a *state* value to the sample code:** OPs typically provide sample code to help RP developers make their website interact appropriately with

the OP. As we discovered, Google does not include a *state* value in its sample code for the *Hybrid Server-side Flow*. It seems reasonable to speculate that this is the main reason why 73 % of the RP-OP interactions we analysed (see Sect. 4.1) are vulnerable to session swapping attacks. However, for cases where a *state* value is included in Google's sample code, this number fell to 35 % (see Sect. 4.2).

– **Allow the RP to specify the *state* value in the Hybrid Server Flow:** The *state* value in the authorization request of the *Hybrid Server-side Flow* is automatically handled by the Google OpenID Connect API. However, the RPJC cannot extract the *state* as it is null. As the *state* value is not bound to the browser session, it does not protect the RP against CSRF attacks. It would probably be better to let the RP handle the *state* rather than the Google API. Google should also check the source code of its postmessage.js script to ensure that *state* can be extracted by the RPJC.

6.3   Notifying Affected Parties

Given their seriousness, we reported the **Authentication by Google ID** issues directly to the affected parties in Feb. 2015 and also gave advice to help fix the problems. As of 16/11/15, one had fixed the problem, one ignored our warning, and the third terminated support for Google SSO. On 17/4/15 we notified Google of all the issues described here. Google acknowledged the problem in Sect. 5.2 and notified their OpenID Connect group. However, as of 16/11/15 we are not aware of any other steps taken by Google.

7   Related Work

OAuth 2.0 has been analysed using formal methods. Pai et al. [9] confirmed a security issue described in the OAuth 2.0 Thread Model [8] using the Alloy Framework [41]. Chari et al. analysed OAuth 2.0 in the Universal Composability Security framework [42] and showed that OAuth 2.0 is secure if all the communications links are SSL-protected. Frostig and Slack [10] discovered a cross site request forgery attack in the Implicit Grant flow of OAuth 2.0, using the Murphi framework [43]. Bansal et al. [44] analysed the security of OAuth 2.0 using the WebSpi [45] and ProVerif models [46]. However, all this work is based on abstract models, and so delicate implementation details are ignored.

Meanwhile, the security properties of real-world OAuth 2.0 implementations have also been examined. Wang et al. [14] examined deployed SSO systems, focussing on a logic flaw present in many such systems, including OpenID. In parallel, Sun and Beznosov [13] also studied deployed systems of OAuth 2.0. Li and Mitchell [12] examined the security of deployed OAuth 2.0 systems providing services in Chinese. In parallel, Zhou and Evans [15] conducted a large scale study of the security of Facebook's OAuth 2.0 implementation. Chen et al. [11], and Shehab and Mohsen [47] have looked at the security of OAuth 2.0 implementations on mobile platforms. However, unlike OAuth, very little research has been conducted on OpenID Connect security, except for the recent work of Mladenov et al. [48] who looked at the security of the OpenID Connect Discovery and Dynamic Registration extensions.

8 Concluding Remarks

We have reported on the first field study of the security properties of Google's implementation of OpenID Connect. We examined the security of all 103 of the RPs that implement support for the Google OpenID Connect service from the GTMetrix list of the Top 1000 Sites. Our study reveals widespread serious vulnerabilities of a number of types, many allowing an attacker to log in to an RP website as a victim user. We give practical recommendations for both RPs and OPs to help improve the security of real world OpenID Connect systems.

References

1. Chappell, D.: Introducing windows cardspace (2006). http://msdn.microsoft.com/en-us/library/aa480189.aspx
2. Hardt, D.: The OAuth 2.0 authorization framework (2012). http://tools.ietf.org/html/rfc6749
3. Recordon, D., Fitzpatrick, B.: OpenID Authentication 2.0 – Final (2007). http://openid.net/specs/openid-authentication-2_0.html
4. Sakimura, N., Bradley, J., Jones, M., de Medeiros, B., Chuck, M.: OpenID Connect Core 1.0 (2014). http://openid.net/specs/openid-connect-core-1_0.html
5. Google Inc.: Google OpenID Connect 1.0 (2015). https://developers.google.com/accounts/docs/OpenIDConnect
6. PayPal Holdings Inc.: PayPal OpenID Connect 1.0 (2014). https://developer.paypal.com/docs/integration/direct/identity/log-in-with-paypal/
7. Microsoft Inc.: Microsoft OpenID Connect (2014). https://msdn.microsoft.com/en-us/library/azure/dn645541.aspx
8. Lodderstedt, T., McGloin, M., Hunt, P.: OAuth 2.0 Threat Model and Security Considerations (2013). http://tools.ietf.org/html/rfc6749
9. Pai, S., Sharma, Y., Kumar, S., Pai, R.M., Singh, S.: Formal verification of OAuth 2.0 using alloy framework. In: Proceedings of the International Conference on Communication Systems and Network Technologies (CSNT), 2011, pp. 655–659. IEEE (2011)
10. Slack, Q., Frostig, R.: Murphi Analysis of OAuth 2.0 Implicit Grant Flow (2011). http://www.stanford.edu/class/cs259/WWW11/
11. Chen, E.Y., Pei, Y., Chen, S., Tian, Y., Kotcher, R., Tague, P.: Oauth demystified for mobile application developers. In: Ahn, G., Yung, M., Li, N. (eds.) Proceedings of the 2014 ACM SIGSAC Conference on Computer and Communications Security, Scottsdale, AZ, USA, 3–7 November 2014, pp. 892–903. ACM (2014)
12. Li, W., Mitchell, C.J.: Security issues in OAuth 2.0 SSO implementations. In: Chow, S.S.M., Camenisch, J., Hui, L.C.K., Yiu, S.M. (eds.) ISC 2014. LNCS, vol. 8783, pp. 529–541. Springer, Heidelberg (2014)
13. Sun, S.T., Beznosov, K.: The devil is in the (implementation) details: an empirical analysis of OAuth SSO systems. In: Yu, T., Danezis, G., Gligor, V.D. (eds.) The ACM Conference on Computer and Communications Security, CCS 2012, Raleigh, NC, USA, 16–18 October 2012, pp. 378–390. ACM (2012)

14. Wang, R., Chen, S., Wang, X.: Signing me onto your accounts through facebook and google: a traffic-guided security study of commercially deployed single-sign-on web services. In: IEEE Symposium on Security and Privacy, SP 2012, San Francisco, California, USA, 21–23 May 2012, pp. 365–379. IEEE Computer Society (2012)
15. Zhou, Y., Evans, D.: SSOScan: automated testing of web applications for single Sign-On vulnerabilities. In: Fu, K., Jung, J. (eds.) Proceedings of the 23rd USENIX Security Symposium, San Diego, CA, USA, 20–22 August 2014, pp. 495–510. USENIX Association (2014)
16. GTmetrix: GTmetrix Top 1000 Sites (2015). http://gtmetrix.com/top1000.html
17. Nadji, Y., Saxena, P., Song, D.: Document structure integrity: a robust basis for cross-site scripting defense. In: Proceedings of the Network and Distributed System Security Symposium, NDSS 2009, San Diego, California, USA, 8th February–11th February 2009. The Internet Society (2009)
18. Vogt, P., Nentwich, F., Jovanovic, N., Kirda, E., Krügel, C., Vigna, G.: Cross site scripting prevention with dynamic data tainting and static analysis. In: Proceedings of the Network and Distributed System Security Symposium, NDSS 2007, San Diego, California, USA, 28th February–2nd March 2007. The Internet Society (2007)
19. Wassermann, G., Su, Z.: Static detection of cross-site scripting vulnerabilities. In: Schäfer, W., Dwyer, M.B., Gruhn, V. (eds.) 30th International Conference on Software Engineering (ICSE 2008), Leipzig, Germany, 10–18 May 2008, pp. 171–180. ACM (2008)
20. Kirda, E., Krügel, C., Vigna, G., Jovanovic, N.: Noxes: a client-side solution for mitigating cross-site scripting attacks. In: Haddad, H. (ed.) Proceedings of the 2006 ACM Symposium on Applied Computing (SAC), Dijon, France, 23–27 April 2006, pp. 330–337. ACM (2006)
21. Barth, A., Jackson, C., Mitchell, J.C.: Robust defenses for cross-site request forgery. In: Ning, P., Syverson, P.F., Jha, S. (eds.) Proceedings of the 2008 ACM Conference on Computer and Communications Security, CCS 2008, Alexandria, Virginia, USA, 27–31 October 2008, pp. 75–88. ACM (2008)
22. De Ryck, P., Desmet, L., Joosen, W., Piessens, F.: Automatic and precise client-side protection against CSRF attacks. In: Atluri, V., Diaz, C. (eds.) ESORICS 2011. LNCS, vol. 6879, pp. 100–116. Springer, Heidelberg (2011)
23. Jovanovic, N., Kirda, E., Kruegel, C.: Preventing cross site request forgery attacks. In: Second International Conference on Security and Privacy in Communication Networks and the Workshops, SecureComm 2006, Baltimore, MD, 28 August 2006–1 September 2006, pp. 1–10. IEEE (2006)
24. Mao, Z., Li, N., Molloy, I.: Defeating cross-site request forgery attacks with browser-enforced authenticity protection. In: Dingledine, R., Golle, P. (eds.) FC 2009. LNCS, vol. 5628, pp. 238–255. Springer, Heidelberg (2009)
25. Zeller, W., Felten, E.W.: Cross-Site Request Forgeries: Exploitation and Prevention. Princeton University, Bericht (2008)
26. Shernan, E., Carter, H., Tian, D., Traynor, P., Butler, K.: More guidelines than rules: CSRF vulnerabilities from noncompliant OAuth 2.0 implementations. In: Almgren, M., Gulisano, V., Maggi, F. (eds.) DIMVA 2015. LNCS, vol. 9148, pp. 239–260. Springer, Heidelberg (2015)
27. Google Inc.: Google OpenID 2.0 (2015). https://developers.google.com/accounts/docs/OpenID
28. Jones, M., Sakimura, N., Bradley, J.: JSON Web Token (JWT) (2014). http://tools.ietf.org/html/draft-ietf-oauth-json-web-token-21

29. Google Inc.: Google OAuth 2.0 Client-side (2015). https://developers.google.com/identity/protocols/OAuth2UserAgent?hl=es
30. Bray, T.: Verify ID Tokens (2015). https://www.tbray.org/ongoing/When/201x/2013/04/04/ID-Tokens
31. Google Inc.: Google OpenID Connect Server-side Flow (2015). https://developers.google.com/+/web/signin/server-side-flow
32. W3C: HTML5 Web Messaging (2012). http://www.w3.org/TR/2012/WD-webmessaging-20120313/
33. de Medeiros, B., Agarwal, N., Sakimura, N., Bradley, J., Jones, M.B.: OpenID Connect Session Management (2014). http://openid.net/specs/openid-connect-session-1_0.html
34. Barth, A., Jackson, C., Mitchell, J.C.: Securing frame communication in browsers. Commun. ACM **52**, 83–91 (2009)
35. Son, S., Shmatikov, V.: The postman always rings twice: attacking and defending postmessage in HTML5 websites. In: 20th Annual Network and Distributed System Security Symposium, NDSS 2013, San Diego, California, USA, 24–27 February 2013. The Internet Society (2013)
36. Jones, M., Hardt, D. (eds.): The OAuth 2.0 Authorization Framework: Bearer Token Usage (2012). https://tools.ietf.org/html/rfc6750
37. van Delft, B., Oostdijk, M.: A security analysis of OpenID. In: de Leeuw, E., Fischer-Hübner, S., Fritsch, L. (eds.) IDMAN 2010. IFIP AICT, vol. 343, pp. 73–84. Springer, Heidelberg (2010)
38. Google Inc.: OAuth 2.0 Authorization Code Flow (2015). https://developers.google.com/identity/protocols/OAuth2WebServer
39. Baloch, R.: Android Browser Same Origin Policy Bypass (2014). http://www.rafayhackingarticles.net/2014/08/android-browser-same-origin-policy.html
40. Google Inc.: Google OpenID Connect Hybrid Server-side Flow (2014). https://developers.google.com/+/web/signin/
41. Jackson, D.: Alloy 4.1 (2010). http://alloy.mit.edu/community/
42. Chari, S., Jutla, C.S., Roy, A.: Universally composable security analysis of OAuth v2.0. IACR Cryptology ePrint Archive 2011 526 (2011)
43. Dill, D.L.: The murphi verification system. In: Alur, R., Henzinger, T.A. (eds.) CAV 1996. LNCS, vol. 1102, pp. 390–393. Springer, Heidelberg (1996)
44. Bansal, C., Bhargavan, K., Delignat-Lavaud, A., Maffeis, S.: Discovering concrete attacks on website authorization by formal analysis. J. Comput. Secur. **22**, 601–657 (2014)
45. Bansal, C., Bhargavan, K., Maffeis, S.: WebSpi and web application models (2011). http://prosecco.gforge.inria.fr/webspi/CSF/
46. Blanchet, B., Smyth, B.: (ProVerif: Cryptographic protocol verifier in the formal model) http://prosecco.gforge.inria.fr/personal/bblanche/proverif/
47. Shehab, M., Mohsen, F.: Securing OAuth implementations in smart phones. In: Bertino, E., Sandhu, R.S., Park, J. (eds.) Fourth ACM Conference on Data and Application Security and Privacy, CODASPY 2014, San Antonio, TX, USA, 03–05 March 2014, pp. 167–170. ACM (2014)
48. Mladenov, V., Mainka, C., Krautwald, J., Feldmann, F., Schwenk, J.: On the security of modern Single Sign-On protocols: OpenID Connect 1.0. CoRR abs/1508.04324 (2015)

Leveraging Sensor Fingerprinting for Mobile Device Authentication

Thomas Hupperich$^{(\boxtimes)}$, Henry Hosseini, and Thorsten Holz

Horst Görtz Institute for IT-Security (HGI), Ruhr-Universität Bochum,
Bochum, Germany
{thomas.hupperich,henry.hosseini,thorsten.holz}@rub.de

Abstract. Device fingerprinting is a technique for identification and recognition of clients and widely used in practice for Web tracking and fraud prevention. While common systems depend on software attributes, sensor-based fingerprinting relies on hardware imperfections and thus opens up new possibilities for device authentication. Recent work focusses on accelerometers as easily accessible sensors of modern mobile devices. However, it has remained unclear if device recognition via sensor-based fingerprinting is feasible under real-world conditions.

In this paper, we analyze the effectiveness of a specialized feature set for sensor-based device fingerprinting and compare the results to feature-less fingerprinting techniques based on raw measurements. Furthermore, we evaluate other sensor types—like gravity and magnetic field sensors—as well as combinations of different sensors concerning their suitability for the purpose of device authentication. We demonstrate that combinations of different sensors yield precise device fingerprints when evaluating the approach on a real-world data set consisting of empirical measurement results obtained from almost 5,000 devices.

Keywords: Device fingerprinting · Sensor fingerprinting · Device authentication

1 Introduction

Many providers of modern Web services aim to recognize the device a user accesses their services from. An emerging functionality is the detection whether a user has changed the device, e. g., owns a new smartphone. The main target of this is authentication of a user's hardware to detect malicious activity like account theft: If a user logs in from a device never used before, this might be a hint that the login credentials have been stolen and are abused for malicious purposes. If a user logs in from an authenticated device which is known to be the user's device, it is probably a legitimate login. Google+ already implements such a detection: If a group member performs a login from a device never seen before and this login is deemed suspicious, a security alert is raised resulting in an email to the group's administrator. Facebook keeps track of its users' devices and aims to associate all systems belonging to a single user. Hence, detecting

© Springer International Publishing Switzerland 2016
J. Caballero et al. (Eds.): DIMVA 2016, LNCS 9721, pp. 377–396, 2016.
DOI: 10.1007/978-3-319-40667-1_19

whether a login is performed either from a known or a new device is essential for fraud detection and account theft. Authenticating a device—and consequently binding an action to a specific device—can be an important step to achieve this security goal.

For this purpose, often the browser is fingerprinted at login time. *Fingerprinting* describes the process of obtaining a set of characteristic attributes from a system and assembling them to features which can be used to recognized or identify unique systems among all others. This technique usually complements cookie-based recognition which has been state of the art for many years. In the course of browser fingerprinting, software attributes like user-agent and installed plugins are leveraged [1,10,18,23]. Previous research found that software-based device fingerprinting performs reasonably well for highly customized commodity systems like desktop computers, mainly since the configurations of these devices vary significantly [8,26]. In contrast, mobile devices like smartphones and tablets are highly standardized. Still, it is possible to gather characteristic attributes of such systems and even about its user using Web technologies only [15]. However, device fingerprinting is strongly dependent on software attributes.

For device authentication, the fingerprint should be as immutable as possible and thus it should be hardware-based. As cookies may be deleted and software can be changed, device authentication should not rely on these factors. A hardware-based fingerprint should stay the same if a users decides to use another browser or even installs a different operating system. A devices' sensors seem to be suitable for this purpose and offer essential advantages:

1. Sensors are easily accessible: accelerometers and gyroscope data can be obtained even via JavaScript without special permissions needed.
2. Sensors yield measurable hardware imperfections which can be leveraged for fingerprinting a device.
3. These imperfections are immune to most software changes.

Due to their manufacturing processes, hardware sensors exhibit imperfections which cause minimal yet measurable deviations between every single sensor [5]. Hence, several sensors provide distinguishable measurements for the same events, making them a suitable source for device fingerprinting. Dey et al. proposed a system called ACCELPRINT introducing a thorough feature set setting new standards for accelerometer fingerprinting [7]. However, mobile devices typically contain several sensors and an open challenge is to figure out which sensor (or combination of sensors) yields the best device fingerprint in practice. Furthermore, the performance of such sensor-based device fingerprinting techniques was only analyzed in lab settings so far, thus it remains unclear if these techniques could actually be applied in practice, e. g., for device authentication.

In this paper, we address these open research gaps and focus on two different aspects of sensor-based fingerprinting: First, we evaluate the features proposed by ACCELPRINT on a data set containing almost 5,000 devices. This data set includes more than eight million accelerometer events collected by an app we developed and enables us to review the performance of such an approach in real-world conditions: While the mathematical features introduced by Dey et al.

enable device recognition based on accelerometer data under scientific/ideal circumstances in a lab, our goal is to shed light on how precise sensor-based fingerprinting can be in the real world and what limitations such an approach yields in practice. We also compare the recognition precision of the introduced features and the raw measurement data to determine whether there is a realistic need for these features. Second, we study other sensors available on modern devices (e. g., gyroscope and magnetic field sensors) and assess how device fingerprinting techniques can be improved by leveraging this information. We extend current research by investigating how the seven most common sensor types can be used for fingerprinting devices on a hardware level and empirically verify our proposed approach. Our analysis is based on five different machine learning algorithms and three data preparation processes in order to perform a comprehensive feasibility study. We evaluate the precision at which a unique device and a device model can be recognized.

In summary, we make the following contributions:

- We examine the performance and necessity of the state-of-the-art feature set for accelerometer fingerprinting on a large, real-world data set.
- We investigate how other kinds of sensors available on modern devices can extend hardware-based fingerprinting for the goal of device authentication.
- We show how sensor data from several sensors can be combined to achieve a better device recognition precision.

2 Sensor-Based Device Authentication

In contrast to *user authentication* which aims to prove a user's identity, we target to confirm a specific device (e. g., a unique smartphone) with *device authentication*. The overall goal is to bind an action performed by a user to a specific system (device) which is used to perform this action. Hence, if a device is authenticated, one can be sure that a specific user action was performed using exactly this device.

Use cases include online banking, handling of suspicious logins, and password reset requests. If a user of an online platform has forgotten his password and requests a new one, he usually has to answer a security question. Instead of proving his identity with the knowledge of the answer, he could authenticate his device which would make this an authentication by possession. This also applies for suspicious logins: large Web service providers keep track of the devices which are used to access their services and consequently check if a user performs a login from a known or a never-seen-before system. If a login attempt seems suspicious, a user could authenticate his device to prove his identity. Another use case is online banking: In Europe and in several countries around the world, online banking transactions—no matter if Web-based or app-based—need to be confirmed via a transaction number (TAN). Additionally to this established method, device authentication could be performed for crucial actions like transactions above a certain amount or voiding a lost credit card. This way, the bank can be sure from which device this action was performed.

In a practical attack, an attacker may get hold of an original SIM card or a replacement card of a victim's phone number and abuse it (e. g., for app-based banking as the phone number is commonly used as identifier). Implementing a hardware-based mechanism for device authentication may remedy this fault: Binding transactions to hardware—in this case a user's mobile device—enables the detection of such fraud attempts as the service provider is capable to recognize that the attacker's action is not performed on the user's device. With hardware-based device authentication, SIM card theft and spoofing may be detected before a crucial action can be carried out by an attacker.

In any case, the hardware of the device to be authenticated needs to be *fingerprinted* as relying on software fingerprints may not be robust enough for this purpose. We differentiate between two types of use cases:

1. Web context: The provider operates an online platform and fingerprint techniques are restricted to Web technologies like HTML5 and JavaScript.
2. App context: The provider has deployed an app for using the service. As such an application may possess more permissions than a browser, it is able to access more of the device's resources (namely its sensors) for fingerprinting.

Although device authentication is not user authentication, it may be used as a second factor for user authentication as it constitutes that a specific user *owns* a specific device. This can be used as second factor, e.g. besides a *knowledge*-based authentication like passwords.

2.1   Device Registration

In order to use a device's sensor fingerprint for authentication, it needs to be registered first. The provider obtains the fingerprint belonging to a device which is to be registered and stores it in the fingerprint database.

During this registration process, the device needs to stay still for some seconds. In this time, the sensors' manufacturing imperfections are measured resulting in the device's sensor fingerprint. These specific measuring errors are an inherence factor of the device. In contrast to knowledge and ownership/possession factors of authentication, one could refer to these hardware peculiarities as "biometrics of hardware", thus to be considered as authentication by inherence.

The registration procedure is crucial and needs to be secured against adversaries. An attacker could try to register a device for a targeted user account as legitimate user device and consequently authorize banking transactions or perform successful logins or password resets. Therefore, the registration of a new device must only be possible after a successful user authentication, e. g., login at a provider's website. For example, a user may login to his online banking account and register a new device which needs to be confirmed via email. Only when such a second channel is used, the registration process can be performed, so that an attacker is not able to register a device without the user's knowledge and confirmation. Hence, the registration should be on-demand only.

Additionally, for banking scenarios the device registration could be confirmed by a device-independent TAN method to avoid malicious registrations.

2.2 Device Authentication

Once the registration is done, a provider is able to distinguish and recognize devices based on their sensor fingerprints. In practice, this additional authentication could be performed to authorize crucial transactions in online banking (e. g., transactions above a certain threshold) or password resets at online platforms. It could also be used to verify a login attempt which is considered suspicious by common methods to clarify whether it is a legitimate login or a possible attack.

In any of these cases, a user would have to let the phone lay still for a few seconds, e. g., by laying it on a table. Previous work has proven that sensor imperfections can be measured in a duration of less than 30 s [7]. During this time, the device's sensors are fingerprinted again by measuring their hardware imperfections. The fingerprint can then be checked against previously registered devices by the provider, resulting either in a match which represents a legitimate user action or a reject possibly indicating illicit behavior. Figure 1 illustrates this procedure.

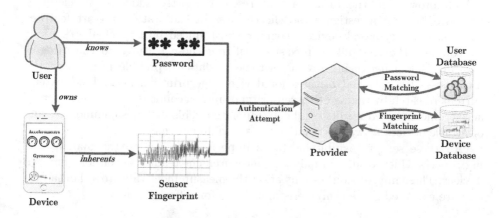

Fig. 1. Sensor-based device authentication for user authentication

In practice, if a device cannot be recognized exactly, instead of failing the authentication immediately there could be a fallback solution: The unique device may not be determined but at least the device model could be recognized from the sensor data. So, instead of being sure that a user performs an action from a specific device, at least information about the device type and model are available as enrichment for other fingerprint mechanisms. We included this scenario in our experiments as well.

As the sensor data is transferred to the provider during authentication, an attacker could try to replay a specific device fingerprint instead of her own to perform a successful authentication without the previously registered device.

However, obtaining the victim's sensor fingerprint or even mimic the devices' sensors' peculiarity is hard to achieve in practice given that the sensor imperfections are hard to replicate. An attacker would either have to possess a special mobile device to intercept its sensor readings by manipulating system drivers or she has to setup a computer to simulate the targeted mobile device exactly. Consequently, if any other fingerprinting or system check is assembled by the provider, this has to be deceived as well, resulting in an increased effort for such a mimicry attack. Furthermore, sensor-based device authentication is an enhancement to other mechanisms and designed as reinforced user authentication. An attacker would still need to obtain user credentials or break other user authentication methods to successfully perform an attack.

3   Fingerprinting Sensors

Modern mobile devices contain a multitude of hardware sensors like accelerometers, gyroscopes and sensors for rotation, magnetic fields and gravity. Accelerometer and gyroscope sensor readings are usually accessible via JavaScript and therefore useful for Web-based fingerprinting and tracking. Although other sensors are accessible via native applications and may be accessible from within a Web browser in the future, recent research mostly addresses accelerometers [5,6,14]. We investigate the effectiveness of the state-of-the-art features for accelerometer-based device recognition introduced by Dey et al. [7]. First, we compare the recognition precision utilizing these features to the recognition precision when using raw accelerometer data to provide insights on the usefulness of specialized features for device fingerprinting. Second, we extend current research by taking other sensor types into account to determine whether accelerometer-based results can be extrapolated. This includes common sensors of mobile devices as well as combinations of different sensors' data.

All these sensors exhibit hardware imperfections due to the manufacturing process which results in quivering measurement readings even for unmoved devices. These imprecisions usually affect the measurement value to a thousandth and are expected to be characteristic features for different sensors.

3.1   Data Set

The first step of our analysis is the preparation of a comprehensive data set of sensor measurements collected from a diverse set of mobile devices. We developed a sensor benchmarking app designed to collect raw sensor readings of accelerometers and other sensors from mobile devices in two stages: First, the user is instructed to put the mobile device on a flat table and leave it still to gather clean measurements for calibration. Second, the user is asked to turn the device in different directions, so we can collect readings when an actual interaction is happening. During both of these stages, the time window of each measurement is 2 s at the highest possible sampling frequency available, just like proposed by Dey et al. [7]. The app is available for Android and Blackberry phones and was distributed via the vendors' app stores. We made sure that users of the app were aware of the fact that they participated in a scientific study and that we collected information about the sensors in their mobile device. We did not store any personally identifiable information. Note that a user of the app is instructed to follow the two phases, but a user might not follow these instructions and thus the collected data might contain outliers or even wrong measurement readings. Therefore, significant movements have been detected as outliers and filtered out for our analyses. Minor movements may be included and represent real-world settings for device authentication as a user may have to authenticate her device being on the go.

We collected 41,610 benchmarks consisting of 58,280,607 raw measurement events in total from 7 different types of sensors and from nearly 5,000 devices. Every *event* yields a value for x, y and z axes coordinates as well as a timestamp to specify when the event was measured. A *benchmark* consists of all events which occurred within a 10 s time slot. Depending on the sensor type and model, there are different numbers of events per benchmark. The precise numbers of events, benchmarks, and devices per sensor are shown in Table 1. Although data from other sensors (e. g., proximity sensors) was collected by the app, only a minority of devices possess such sensors: Only a few benchmarks for these sensor types could be obtained and hence the data might not be substantive enough to make a claim about the recognition precision in general. For this reason, we take only those sensors into account having representative benchmark data available.

As different devices happen to integrate sensors manufactured by the same vendor, we show in Table 2 the number of different sensors in our data set. Taken from our representative data set, we see that there are many different vendors for general purpose accelerometers (275), but only a few for gravity sensors or linear acceleration sensors (each 37).

There is a unique identifier within the data set for every single device such that we can recognize specific devices as a ground truth. Furthermore, we store an identifier for every device model (e. g., "Google Nexus 5"). These two identifiers enable us to group the sensor measurement data by device model as well as by single devices. Hence, we are able to determine the effectiveness of fingerprinting features for recognizing device types (e. g., are hardware imperfections of iPhone 6 devices significantly different compared to hardware imperfections of Nexus 5 devices?) and for recognizing single devices (e. g., is it possible to tell one Nokia Lumia 930 apart from another?). In the following, we use the term *ModelID* to describe the identifier used to group data by device model and the term *DeviceID* for the identifier used to group data by single devices. For every sensor type in the data set, we group the data once per *DeviceID* and once per *ModelID*. For both groups, we compute the features described in Sect. 3.2 from the raw sensor readings obtained by our app. This builds up four data sets in total:

1. Raw sensor measurements grouped by *DeviceID* called $R_{DeviceID}$.
2. Feature set grouped by *DeviceID* defined as $F_{DeviceID}$.
3. Raw sensor measurements grouped by *ModelID* named $R_{ModelID}$.
4. Feature set grouped by *ModelID* which we define as $F_{ModelID}$.

Table 1. Numbers of events, benchmarks and devices per sensor type

Sensor type	Events	Benchmarks	Devices
Acceleration	8,005,352	7,004	4,179
Magnetic field	2,855,199	5,230	3,676
Orientation	8,047,497	6,228	4,963
Gyroscope	12,578,437	6,342	4,698
Gravity	9,061,253	5,726	4,374
Linear acceleration	8,687,132	5,556	4,297
Rotation vector	9,045,737	5,524	4,401

Table 2. Number of different sensor hardware models by sensor type

Sensor type	No. of sensor models
Acceleration	275
Magnetic field	179
Orientation	147
Gyroscope	100
Rotation vector	43
Gravity	37
Linear acceleration	37

3.2   Feature Set

As the second step of our analysis, we extract state-of-the-art features described below, originally proposed by Dey et al. [7], from the raw data records. We analyze if such features can be leveraged for other sensors as well and thus briefly introduce the feature set in the following.

Preliminary, we calculate the Root Sum Square (RSS) of the x, y, and z axes. Then, we extract the time domain features utilizing NumPy [33] and SciPy [17] libraries. In order to extract the frequency domain features, we have to transfer the raw sensor readings from time domain into frequency domain. For this purpose, we interpolated the RSS data. We applied a cubic spline interpolation as it addresses the accuracy of the minimal hardware deviations in our data set. For having less than 4 samples per measurement or lack of sensor readings from all three axes, 183 measurements had to be omitted during the interpolation phase. This might happen on hardware failure, broken sensors, or faulty drivers. After completing this task, we utilize the Fast Fourier Transformation (FFT) to transfer the interpolated measurements into the frequency domain. The frequency domain features are extracted from the transformed data. Finally, we vectorize the data to obtain sensor fingerprints utilizing the following features:

Time Domain Features. *Mean* is described as the result of dividing the sum of measurements to the number of samples in a specified time window: $\bar{x} = \frac{1}{N} \sum_{i=1}^{N} x(i)$.

Standard Deviation describes how much the measurements deviate from the mean of all measurements in a specified time window. This feature provides the ability to consider noisy signals in our tests [32]: $\sigma = \sqrt{\frac{1}{N-1} \sum_{i=1}^{N} (x(i) - \bar{x})^2}$.

Average Deviation provides the mean of the deviations of all samples in a specified time frame. By definition, only the absolute value of amplitudes are considered [32]: $D_{\bar{x}} = \frac{1}{N} \sum_{i=1}^{N} |x(i) - \bar{x}|$.

Skewness measures the (lack of) symmetry of a distribution in a specified time frame. If the data set is symmetric, it looks even on the left and right side of the mean. Skewness can be positive or negative if the data set is more distributed to the left or right, respectively. The skewness of symmetric data is near zero [29]: $\gamma = \frac{1}{N}\sum_{i=1}^{N}(\frac{(x(i)-\bar{x})}{\sigma})^3$.

Kurtosis states how much the data points are distributed near or far from the mean, i.e., whether a peak of data points exists near the mean or not. The ideal kurtosis is three according to our formula [29]: $\beta = \frac{1}{N}\sum_{i=1}^{N}(\frac{x(i)-\bar{x}}{\sigma})^4 - 3$.

Root Mean Square (RMS) Amplitude measures the mean of all amplitudes over time. In order to calculate this feature, first all amplitudes are squared, so that both negative and positive values become positive. After calculating the mean of these values, they are scaled back to the right size by calculating the square root: $A = \sqrt{\frac{1}{N}\sum_{i=1}^{N}(x(i))^2}$ The RMS amplitude is normally equal to 70.7 % of the peak amplitude [11].

Lowest Value is the smallest amount among the measurements in a specified time window: $L = Min(x(i))|_{i=1\,to\,N}$.

Highest Value is the greatest value among the measurements in a specified time window: $H = Max(x(i))|_{i=1\,to\,N}$.

Frequency Domain Features. *Spectral Standard Deviation* shows the spread of the frequencies in a spectrum relative to its mean along the frequency axis [13, 28]: $\sigma_s = \sqrt{\frac{\sum_{i=1}^{N}(y_f(i))^2 * y_m(i)}{\sum_{i=1}^{N} y_m(i)}}$.

Spectral Centroid can be considered as the middle point of the amplitude spectrum [3]: $\zeta_s = \frac{\sum_{i=1}^{N} y_f(i)y_m(i)}{\sum_{i=1}^{N} y_m(i)}$.

Spectral Skewness measures the symmetry of the distribution of the spectral magnitude values relative to their mean [19, 22, 30]: $\gamma_s = \frac{\sum_{i=1}^{N}(y_m(i)-\zeta_s)^3 * y_m(i)}{\sigma_s^3}$.

Spectral Kurtosis determines if the distribution of the spectral magnitude values contains non-Gaussian components [34]: $\beta_s = \frac{\sum_{i=1}^{N}(y_m(i)-\zeta_s)^4 * y_m(i)}{\sigma_s^4 - 3}$.

Spectral Crest measures the peakiness of a spectrum and is inversely proportional to the flatness feature [36]: $CR_s = \frac{(Max(y_m(i))|_{i=1\,to\,N}}{\zeta_s}$.

Irregularity-K measures the degree of variation of successive peaks in a spectrum. Irregularity-K refers to the definition of Krimphoff et al. [21] where irregularity is the sum of the amplitude minus the mean of the preceding, same and next amplitude: $IK_s = \sum_{i=2}^{N-1}\left|y_m(i) - \frac{y_m(i-1)+y_m(i)+y_m(i+1)}{3}\right|$.

Irregularity-J measures the same as irregularity-K, but refers to the definition of Jensen [16] where irregularity is defined as the sum of squaring the differences in amplitude between adjoining partials [35]: $IJ_s = \frac{\sum_{i=1}^{N-1}(y_m(i)-y_m(i+1))^2}{\sum_{i=1}^{N-1}(y_m(i))^2}$.

Smoothness measures the degree of differences between adjacent amplitudes [24, 27]: $S_s = \sum_{i=2}^{N-1} |20.log(y_m(i)) - \frac{(20.log(y_m(i-1)) + 20.log(y_m(i)) + 20.log(y_m(i+1)))}{3}$.

Flatness measures the flatness of a spectrum and is inversely proportional to the spectral crest. The differences between spectral crest and flatness are in the less required computational power for spectral crest, but more accurate results in spectral flatness since not normalized signals have less influence on the result [9]: $F_s = \frac{\sqrt[N]{(\prod_{i=1}^{N} y_m(i))}}{\frac{1}{N}\sum_{i=1}^{N} y_m(i)}$.

3.3   Classifier

In the third step of our analysis, we apply five field-tested classification algorithms to all data sets described in Sect. 3.1. We chose algorithms from different machine learning categories to address the model selection problem. Note that our scenario for device or model recognition does not pose a typical classification problem, as every device and model which needs to be "classified" has been seen during the training phase. This circumstance is more likely related to matching problems. We evaluate the following five classification and ensemble methods in our experiments:

- **k-NN**: The k-Nearest-Neighbor classifier is a basic ML algorithm. We chose $k = 1$ as this correlates with the fact that we want to achieve a matching.
- **SVM**: As Support Vector Machines are designed to handle numeric values, they are naturally suitable for processing our data set.
- **Bagging Tree**: This classifier has been used originally by Dey et al. [7]. In order to evaluate the effectiveness on the basis of real-world data, we must evaluate this classifier as well.
- **Random Forest**: The Random Forest classifier combines the merits of Bagging Tree and a random selection of features. This method remedies tendencies of overfitting.
- **Extra Trees**: Extra Trees is an averaging ensemble method known for a high prediction accuracy. The drawback is that it usually grows bigger than Random Forests, especially on large data like our sensor measurements.

In every test, we split the existing data into a training set and a test set. The training set is used for cross validating the classifiers' parameters before creating a model and testing the test set. In the research of Guyon [12] and Amari et al. [2], the ratio of the test set to the training set is proposed to be inversely proportional to the square root of the number of features if the number of features is greater than one. For the 17 features described above, this means:

$$\frac{1}{\sqrt{\#features}} = \frac{1}{\sqrt{17}} \approx 0.243$$

Hence, we use a split of 75 % of the data for training and 25 % for testing.

Please note that we did not use the same machine learning classification models for recognition of device manufacturing models and for recognition of single devices. We conducted these experiments separately and trained classification models for the specific tasks. To perform a comprehensive analysis, we prepared each data set in three different ways for every experiment and applied the classifiers to the data (i) as-is, (ii) normalized and (iii) scaled.

Finally, we determine the maximum recognition precision of all *raw* classifications and *features* classification for each data set in order to clarify whether classification of models and devices can be performed better on raw data or the introduced features. Every test—from splitting the data set into training set and test set up to classification—has been performed three times and the mean of these repetitions is represented to mitigate "lucky strikes", which may occur when a data set is split randomly.

3.4   Formalization

In the following, we work with the four data sets $R_{ModelID}$, $F_{ModelID}$, $R_{DeviceID}$, and $F_{DeviceID}$ described in Sect. 3.1. Consequently, R represents all raw sensor measurements and F represents the features calculated on the basis of R. Hence, the feature set is derived as a function from raw sensor events: $F = f(R)$.

The function f includes the steps for feature extraction described in Sect. 3.2 including calculations of Root Sum Square, interpolation and Fast Fourier Transformation. Consequently, F includes all features from time domain *and* frequency domain. Please keep in mind that every data set is split into a training subset and a test subset for subsequent machine learning procedures.

Every data record of these data sets consists of a data vector and a class attribute. The data vector D includes all attributes which are used for recognition by machine learning. For data vectors of the raw sensor measurements data sets, the single values are plain readings of the dimensions x, y and z provided by the sensors directly: $D_R = r_1, r_2, ..., r_n, n \in \mathbb{N}$. Consequently, for data vectors of the examined feature sets, every value represents a feature: $D_F = f_1, f_2, ..., f_n, n \in \mathbb{N}$. The class attribute c is derived from the chosen identifier which is either the *ModelID* or the *DeviceID*.

In order to calculate the recognition precision, we define a *match* as true positive. A match will be achieved if a data vector of a test set is related to a data vector with the same class c of the corresponding training set by the machine learning algorithm. A correct *reject* expresses a true negative, meaning that a non-trained device is not matched accidentally to a trained device. If a device which has been in the training set gets rejected while testing, it is a false negative while a non-trained device which is matched with a device from the training set poses a false positive.

Finally, we are able to define the recognition precision P for specific data sets and feature sets as

$$P_{S,M_{id}} = ML(Set_{Training}, Set_{Test}),$$

where S is a sensor type, $M \in \{R, F\}$, $id \in \{ModelID, DeviceID\}$, ML is the chosen machine learning algorithm and *trainingset* and *testset* are subsets corresponding to S and id. For instance, the recognition precision achieved by a Bagging Tree classifier (BT) for the data set of features grouped by $DeviceID$ and based on gravity sensor data will be

$$P_{Gravity,F_{DeviceID}} = BT(train_{F_{DeviceID}}, test_{F_{DeviceID}}).$$

4 Evaluation

We conducted recognition experiments for every sensor type with each data set utilizing each classifier seeking for the best precision to use for device authentication. Hence, we present only the results of the best performing classifiers for each experiment. More specifically, for each sensor type and each data set we applied the algorithms described in Sect. 3.3, but for comparison we take the maximum recognition rate of all classifiers into account. Furthermore, we repeated every test with the data set three times using it (i) as-is, (ii) scaled and (iii) normalized to ensure to have the best preprocessing for every test. Again, we describe only the best results of all preprocessing methods in the following to compare the results of the best performing fingerprinting processes. A comparison of non-best performing classifiers and preprocessing methods would be possible but does not support our aim to find the best method for hardware-based fingerprinting for the purpose of device authentication.

In order to determine the effectiveness of state-of-the-art features over raw data for sensor fingerprinting, we carried out several tests in two phases: First, we ran comparison tests for every single sensor listed in Table 1. The goal of these tests is to compare the recognition precision between utilizing the raw sensor data and the extracted features for fingerprints for each sensor. Second, we combined the data from different sensors to multi-sensor tests and applied the described methods to clarify the recognition precision when taking several sensors into account. We determined five combinations to be of interest due to results from previous experiments:

1. *Accelerometers* including sensors for measuring acceleration and linear acceleration. Recognizing this data precisely has been the explicit purpose of the fingerprint features.
2. *Accelerometers & Gyroscope* extends the combination by gyroscope sensor readings. Usually, if a device embeds accelerometers, a gyroscope is built-in.
3. *All Available Sensors* includes data from all sensors listed in Table 2.
4. *No Accelerometers* takes only sensors into account that do not measure acceleration. This is the "inverse scenario" of 1.
5. *No Accelerometers & Gyroscope* is the "inverse scenario" of 2 and excludes acceleration sensors as well as gyroscope measurements.

In the following, we present the results of the single sensor tests as well as the combination tests.

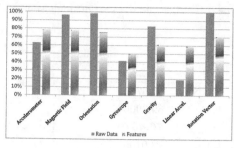

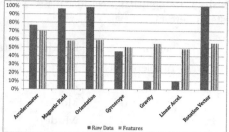

Fig. 2. Recognition precisions per sensor for device recognition

Fig. 3. Recognition precisions per sensor for model recognition

4.1 Single Sensor Tests

Our experiments confirm the overall result by Dey et al. [7]: The presented features provide the best precision for recognizing single devices on the basis of general purpose accelerometer data. Nevertheless, the precision of this case is about 78 %, leaving room for improvement. Our results indicate that for linear accelerometer sensors as well as for gyroscope data, the proposed feature set provides a better recognition rate than using the raw sensor readings. But the corresponding precision rates of about 49 % and 59 % are not suitable for device authentication in practice. Hence, device authentication methods should not rely on accelerometers and gyroscopes only.

For all other sensors, the utilization of features leads to a lower precision compared to the raw sensor measurements. The highest recognition precision could be achieved with plain sensor measurements and more different sensor types lead to a better precision. Thus, device authentication does not need to be based on a mathematical feature set but is feasible using raw sensor data as well. Table 3 summarizes the results of all single-sensor recognition experiments.

It is tempting to suspect a connection between a high device recognition precision and the number of different sensor hardware models shown in Table 2. Nevertheless, we could not show a significance to substantiate this assumption: Linear accelerometers and rotation sensors both have low model diversity and while the first are not suitable for device recognition showing a maximum precision of about 59 %, the second show an outstanding precision for recognizing single devices of almost 100 %. These differences are visualized in Fig. 2.

As shown in Fig. 3, the precision based on accelerometers, magnetic field sensors, orientation sensors and rotation sensors is significantly lower compared to when raw measurement events are used when it comes to model recognition. Concurrently, using raw data for model recognition fails for data from gyroscopes, gravity sensors and linear accelerometers. Using the feature set performs better for these sensors, but still the recognition precision does not exceed 55 % and cannot be considered for a reliable model recognition in a practical setting. In summary, recognizing device models by only one sensor type does not require the use of features and can be done on the basis of raw sensor data for four of seven

Table 3. Recognition precisions per sensor type, identifier and data set of single-sensor tests in percent

Sensor	Identifier	Data	Classifier	Average precision
Acceleration	**Device**	**F**	**ET**	**78.2300**
	Device	R	k-NN	62.6781
	Model	F	ET	69.3900
	Model	**R**	**BT**	**76.4570**
Magnetic field	Device	F	ET	78.0100
	Device	**R**	**RF**	**96.3808**
	Model	F	ET	57.9100
	Model	**R**	**ET**	**96.4232**
Orientation	Device	F	ET	75.2400
	Device	**R**	**k-NN**	**98.2033**
	Model	F	ET	58.7400
	Model	**R**	**k-NN**	**98.1090**
Gyroscope	**Device**	**F**	**BT**	**49.4400**
	Device	R	k-NN	41.4460
	Model	**F**	**BT**	**50.5000**
	Model	R	k-NN	45.1595
Gravity	Device	F	ET	60.9500
	Device	**R**	**k-NN**	**82.9912**
	Model	**F**	**ET**	**54.7200**
	Model	R	k-NN	9.9967
Lin. acceleration	**Device**	**F**	**BT**	**58.9200**
	Device	R	k-NN	18.8124
	Model	**F**	**BT**	**48.3500**
	Model	R	k-NN	10.1388
Rotation vector	Device	F	ET	70.7200
	Device	**R**	**k-NN**	**99.8063**
	Model	F	ET	55.5700
	Model	**R**	**k-NN**	**99.8216**

R = raw data, F = features, k-NN = k-NearestNeighbor, BT = BaggingTree, ET = ExtraTrees, RF = RandomForest; showing only best performing classifiers; bold rows show maximum precision rate

sensor types, while the other three sensor types cannot be used to distinguish between device models at all.

In summary, the state-of-the-art feature set for accelerometer fingerprinting serves its purpose and is a reasonable way for device recognition based on accelerometers and gyroscope data. However, it is not suitable to distinguish devices based on data from other sensor types. Furthermore, using raw

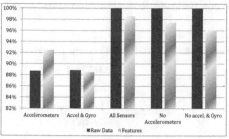 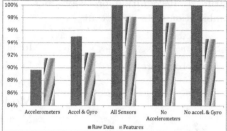

Fig. 4. Recognition precisions per combination for model recognition

Fig. 5. Recognition precisions per combination for model recognition

measurements of these other sensor types enables an even higher recognition precision. The use of accelerometer-based fingerprinting utilizing mathematical features for device authentication is questionable as fingerprinting based on other sensors performs significantly better.

4.2 Multi Sensor Tests

While the use of single sensors does not seem to provide a reliable method for device or model recognition—and thus for device authentication—precision rates increase generally when sensor types are combined.

The first combination includes both types of accelerometers. In this case, using the feature set for device recognition performs well and achieves a precision of about 92 %. For every other case we tested, the utilization of features did not exceed the precision achieved by the use of raw measurements. Especially when accelerometers are left out (cases four and five), the recognition based on raw data is more effective. In total, there is no precision result lower than 88.5 %, while the maximum of 99.99 % can be achieved by using raw data of all sensors except accelerometers. Table 4 shows the results for all combination test.

Consequently, using raw measurements of sensors for magnetic field, orientation, gravity, rotation and gyroscope is most effective for fingerprinting mobile devices. These sensors, which are common in modern devices, improve sensor-based fingerprinting significantly and can be used as a basis for reliable device fingerprinting in practice. Figure 4 shows the achieved maximum precisions of each sensor combination described above.

This finding is also valid for model recognition: Again, for accelerometers the feature set yields the best precision, but in all other combinations, features are not necessary to achieve recognition rates of up to 99.995 %. Figure 5 shows the results of the combination tests per model.

4.3 Discussion

While we found the feature set to be most precise for device recognition on the basis of accelerometer data, best recognition rates for devices and models can

Table 4. Recognition precisions per sensor combination, identifier and data set of combination tests in percent

Sensors	Identifier	Data	Classifier	Average precision
Accelerometers	**Device**	**F**	**BT**	**92.4782**
	Device	R	BT	88.6941
	Model	**F**	**ET**	**91.5432**
	Model	R	BT	89.6469
Accelerometers gyroscope	Device	F	ET	88.5019
	Device	**R**	**BT**	**88.8444**
	Model	F	ET	92.3950
	Model	**R**	**RF**	**95.0076**
All available sensors	Device	F	ET	98.6026
	Device	**R**	**ET**	**99.9806**
	Model	F	ET	98.1615
	Model	**R**	**RF**	**99.9950**
No accelerometers	Device	F	RF	97.2484
	Device	**R**	**ET**	**99.9922**
	Model	F	ET	97.4589
	Model	**R**	**ET**	**99.9821**
No accelerometers &no gyroscope	Device	F	RF	94.6407
	Device	**R**	**RF**	**99.9848**
	Model	F	RF	96.0450
	Model	**R**	**ET**	**99.9671**

R = raw data, F = features, k-NN = k-NearestNeighbor, BT = BaggingTree, ET = Extra-Trees, RF = RandomForest; showing only best performing classifiers; bold rows show maximum precision rate

be achieved by sensor combinations without accelerometers applied to raw measurements. Taking common sensors together, recognition precisions of 99.98 % up to 99.995 % can be achieved without needing to consider complex features. Our experiments indicate that combining the data of different sensors leads to a more effective fingerprinting than the application of the proposed features.

The feature set is suitable for the case of recognizing single devices by accelerometer data, but not reliable in any other case. Furthermore, given a large quantity of real-world data, the same results can be achieved without these features using the same or comparable machine learning techniques. For other sensor types, using raw sensor data is more effective, esp. for recognition of single devices. However, both data types yield disadvantages: On the one hand, calculating features needs computational power but also condenses the data. On the other hand, storing all events' raw measurements requires more storage capacities but no mathematical calculations need to be made. Ultimately, single devices as well as device models can be recognized best when combining the measurement data of several sensors.

For the purpose of device authentication, sensor fingerprinting is a valid method: High recognition rates can be achieved under realistic conditions in a real-world data set. While previous research mostly focusses on accelerometers and gyroscopes as these are accessible via the Web, we found other sensor types' hardware imperfections to be more characteristic making them even more important in this context. As sensor-based hardware fingerprinting opens up the possibility to distinguish unique devices at very high precision, it does not seem to be necessary to have a fallback solution like device model recognition at all.

Additional to the adversarial scenarios described in Sect. 2, it may be possible to randomize sensor measurements in order to prevent a recognition of a specific device. However, tampering sensor readings with random data requires a customization of the device's software like its browser when sensors are queried by websites or even the operating system when apps access the sensors for fingerprinting. Furthermore, tampering sensor readings raises a problem in practice: Sensors are used for specific reasons and adding randomness to their measurements may be helpful to evade fingerprinting their hardware imperfections but may also result in unwanted behavior of functionalities which rely on sensors. For instance, if a websites accesses a device's accelerometers or gyroscope and their data is randomized or tampered by the device first, the website's functionality and hence the user experience may be affected. Ultimately, as the goal is to authenticate a device and randomization is only capable of preventing a recognition, the more relevant attack would be the imitation of a specific device.

For such a mimic attack, an attacker would need to fake her own sensor data and replace it by the target device's sensor data. As described in Sect. 2.2, an attacker has to solve some challenges to perform this attack while having little chances of success. Although such an attack is difficult to carry out in practice, we will investigate this scenario in future work.

As more and more sensors are embedded in modern mobile devices, examining more sensor types for the purpose of hardware-based device fingerprinting will be the subject of future work. The availability of other sensors may lead to even better recognition results.

5 Related Work

Dey et al. [7] proposed mathematical features based on accelerometer readings for fingerprinting mobile devices. Their work illustrates the possibility to identify devices by conducting a series of training and test set scenarios on 107 different stand-alone chips, smartphones, and tablets under laboratory conditions. While their work focuses on accelerometers only, we also inspected other sensor types like magnetic field or rotation vector sensors. The usefulness of the feature set could be verified for accelerometers on a large real-world dataset of nearly 5,000 devices. We have also shown that fingerprinting mobile devices is more precise when taking other available sensor data into account. Furthermore, our results indicate that machine learning algorithms can be applied on the raw measurement events and specific features used for pre-processing the raw measurements do not yield better results.

Several studies focus on real-world accelerometer data for recognizing movement or behavior. For instance, it has been shown that steps of a walking or running person can be detected clearly with the help of a smartphone's accelerometers [31]. Dargie and Denko studied the behavior of accelerometers during similar movements and placed accelerometers on moving humans and cars [6]. They conclude that the extracted frequency domain features remain generally more robust than time domain features. In our study, we applied sensor readings gathered from both resting and moving devices and included features of time domain as well as frequency domain.

A study by He utilized machine learning techniques to recognize human activities by accelerometer and gyroscope data [14]. Three feature sets were applied including 561, 50 and 20 features to distinguish between six different human activities. While this work aims to detect activities, our experiments do not consider the current movement as artefact, but aim to identify devices (and group devices by model) on the basis of real-world sensor data.

A non sensor-based method for hardware fingerprinting has been introduced by Moon et al. [25] as well as Kohno et al. [20]. The identification of devices is achieved by measuring *clock skews*. While the common idea is the recognition of devices by hardware differences, these studies focus on time differences and do not consider any of a device's sensors.

Bates et al. explored mobile device model recognition and showed that manufacturer models can be distinguished by USB data with an accuracy of 97 % [4]. Notwithstanding, our experiments have shown that an even higher accuracy can be achieved by sensor-based hardware fingerprinting.

6   Conclusion

In this paper, we performed a detailed assessment of the effectiveness of sensor-based fingerprinting. We compared the benefit of using a well-defined feature set including attributes from time domain as well as frequency domain to using raw sensor data as input. We utilized five different machine learning techniques together with three data preparation processes and compared the precision at which a single device or a device model can be recognized on the basis of its hardware. To base our work upon real-world conditions, we gathered sensor data of almost 5,000 mobile devices. As a part of our work, we implemented the signal feature extraction process described by Dey et al. [7].

While we found the proposed feature set suitable for accelerometer-based recognition of single devices we have shown that it lacks precision for other sensor types. For non-accelerometer sensors the use of raw sensor readings as a basis for hardware fingerprinting results in a higher recognition precision. Furthermore, combining different sensor types leads to an even better precision and a higher robustness. We find that accelerometer measurements combined with other sensor data yield real-world recognition precisions of 99.98 % up to 99.995 %. In general, taking other common sensor types into account for fingerprinting results in a better precision than utilizing the previously proposed feature set.

Given these findings, hardware-based device fingerprinting with sensor data is feasible and a valid method for device authentication. However, device authentication methods should not rely on accelerometers and gyroscopes only but on combinations of different sensor types. For these, the calculation of features means computational effort without improving device recognition. Ultimately, using raw measurements of different sensor types is the most accurate way to instrument sensor-based hardware fingerprinting for device authentication. Implementing such an authentication mechanism may help handling suspicious login attempts, password resets, and even remedy SIM spoofing.

References

1. Acar, G., Juarez, M., Nikiforakis, N., Diaz, C., Gürses, S., Piessens, F., Preneel, B.: FPDetective: dusting the web for fingerprinters. In: ACM Conference on Computer and Communications Security (CCS) (2013)
2. Amari, S.I., Murata, N., Muller, K.R., Finke, M., Yang, H.H.: Asymptotic statistical theory of overtraining and cross-validation. IEEE Trans. Neural Netw. 8(5), 985–996 (1997)
3. Bader, R.: Nonlinearities and Synchronization in Musical Acoustics and Music Psychology. Current Research in Systematic Musicology. Springer, Heidelberg (2013)
4. Bates, A., Leonard, R., Pruse, H., Butler, K., Lowd, D.: Leveraging USB to establish host identity using commodity devices. In: Proceedings of the Network and Distributed System Security Symposium (NDSS) (2014)
5. Bojinov, H., Michalevsky, Y., Nakibly, G., Boneh, D.: Mobile Device Identification via Sensor Fingerprinting. arxiv preprint arXiv:1408.1416. (2014)
6. Dargie, W., Denko, M.K.: Analysis of error-agnostic time-and frequency-domain features extracted from measurements of 3-D accelerometer sensors. IEEE Syst. J. 4(1), 26–33 (2010)
7. Dey, S., Roy, N., Xu, W., Choudhury, R.R., Nelakuditi, S.: AccelPrint: imperfections of accelerometers make smartphones trackable. In: Proceedings of the Network and Distributed System Security Symposium (NDSS) (2014)
8. Eckersley, P.: How unique is your web browser? In: Atallah, M.J., Hopper, N.J. (eds.) PETS 2010. LNCS, vol. 6205, pp. 1–18. Springer, Heidelberg (2010)
9. Eisenberg, G.: Identifikation und Klassifikation von Musikinstrumentenklängen in monophoner und polyphoner Musik. Cuvillier (2008)
10. Eubank, C., Melara, M., Perez-botero, D., Narayanan, A.: Shining the floodlights on mobile web tracking - a privacy survey. In: Web 2.0 Security & Privacy Conference (W2SP) (2013)
11. Gelfand, S.: Essentials of Audiology. Thieme, Stuttgart (2011)
12. Guyon, I.: A scaling law for the validation-set training-set size ratio. In: AT & T Bell Laboratories (1997)
13. Hardcastle, W., Laver, J., Gibbon, F.: The Handbook of Phonetic Sciences. Blackwell Handbooks in Linguistics, Wiley (2012)
14. He, H.: Human Activity Recognition on Smartphones Using Various Classifiers (2013)
15. Hupperich, T., Maiorca, D., Kührer, M., Holz, T., Giacinto, G.: On the robustness of mobile device fingerprinting. In: Annual Computer Security Applications Conference (ACSAC) (2015)

16. Jensen, K.: Timbre models of musical sounds. Ph.D. thesis, Department of Computer Science, University of Copenhagen (1999)
17. Jones, E., Oliphant, T., Peterson, P., et al.: SciPy: open source scientific tools for Python (2001), 26 April 2016. http://scipy.org
18. Kamkar, S.: Evercookie - never forget (2010). http://samy.pl/evercookie/. Accessed June 2015
19. Klapuri, A., Davy, M.: Signal Processing Methods for Music Transcription. Springer, Heidelberg (2007)
20. Kohno, T., Broido, A., Claffy, K.C.: Remote physical device fingerprinting. IEEE Trans. Dependable Secure Comput. **2**(2), 93–108 (2005)
21. Krimphoff, J., McAdams, S., Winsberg, S.: Caractérisation du timbre des sons complexes. ii. Analyses acoustiques et quantification psychophysique. Le. J. Phys. IV **4**, 625–628 (1994)
22. Lerch, A.: An Introduction to Audio Content Analysis: Applications in Signal Processing and Music Informatics. Wiley, New York (2012)
23. Liang, B., You, W., Liu, L., Shi, W., Heiderich, M.: Scriptless timing attacks on web browser privacy. In: Annual IEEE/IFIP International Conference on Dependable Systems and Networks (DSN) (2014)
24. Mcadams, S.: Perspectives on the contribution of timbre to musical structure. Comput. Music J. **23**(3), 85–102 (1999)
25. Moon, S.B., Skelly, P., Towsley, D.: Estimation and removal of clock skew from network delay measurements. In: Proceedings of the IEEE, INFOCOM 1999, Eighteenth Annual Joint Conference of the IEEE Computer and Communications Societies, vol. 1, pp. 227–234. IEEE (1999)
26. Nikiforakis, N., Kapravelos, A., Joosen, W., Kruegel, C., Piessens, F., Vigna, G.: Cookieless monster: exploring the ecosystem of web-based device fingerprinting. In: IEEE Symposium on Security and Privacy (2013)
27. Park, T.H.: Salient feature extraction of musical instrument signals. Ph.D. thesis, DARTMOUTH COLLEGE Hanover, New Hampshire (2000)
28. Peeters, G., Giordano, B.L., Susini, P., Misdariis, N., McAdams, S.: The timbre toolbox: extracting audio descriptors from musical signals. J. Acoust. Soc. Am. **130**(5), 2902–2916 (2011)
29. Sanei, S., Chambers, J.: EEG Signal Processing. Wiley, New York (2013)
30. Satapathy, S., Udgata, S., Biswal, B.: Advances in intelligent systems and computing. In: Proceedings of the International Conference on Frontiers of Intelligent Computing: Theory and Applications (FICTA) 2013. Springer (2013)
31. Sinofsky, S.: Supporting sensors in Windows 8 (2012), 6 May 2016. http://blogs.msdn.com/b/b8/archive/2012/01/24/supporting-sensors-in-windows-8.aspx
32. Smith, S.W.: Digital Signal Processing: a Practical Guide for Engineers and Scientists. Newnes, Oxford (2003)
33. Van Der Walt, S., Colbert, S.C., Varoquaux, G.: The NumPy array: a structure for efficient numerical computation. Comput. Sci. Eng. **13**(2), 22–30 (2011)
34. Wang, J., Yen, G., Polycarpou, M.: Advances in Neural Networks ISNN 2012. 9th International Symposium on Neural Networks, ISNN 2012, Shenyang, China, July 11-14, 2012. Proceedings, Part II. Springer, Heidelberg (2012)
35. Yang, Y., Chen, H.: Music Emotion Recognition. Multimedia Computing, Communication and Intelligence. CRC Press, Boca Raton (2011)
36. Zelkowitz, M.: Advances in Computers: Improving the Web. Elsevier Science, San Diego (2010)

Malware Classification

MtNet: A Multi-Task Neural Network for Dynamic Malware Classification

Wenyi Huang[1] and Jack W. Stokes[2]([⊠])

[1] Information Sciences and Technology, Pennsylvania State University,
University Park, PA 16802, USA
wzh112@ist.psu.edu
[2] Microsoft Research, One Microsoft Way, Redmond, WA 98052, USA
jstokes@microsoft.com

Abstract. In this paper, we propose a new multi-task, deep learning architecture for malware classification for the binary (i.e. malware versus benign) malware classification task. All models are trained with data extracted from dynamic analysis of malicious and benign files. For the first time, we see improvements using multiple layers in a deep neural network architecture for malware classification. The system is trained on 4.5 million files and tested on a holdout test set of 2 million files which is the largest study to date. To achieve a binary classification error rate of 0.358 %, the objective functions for the binary classification task and malware family classification task are combined in the multi-task architecture. In addition, we propose a standard (i.e. non multi-task) malware family classification architecture which also achieves a malware family classification error rate of 2.94 %.

1 Introduction

PandaLabs recently reported that 27 % of all of malware detected by their antivirus engine was first encountered in 2015 [16]. Malware authors continue to accelerate the automation of malware production using techniques such as polymorphism at an alarming rate. Clearly, automated detection employing highly accurate malware classifiers is the only option to combat this problem long term.

Recently, deep learning has led to significant improvements in diverse areas including object recognition in images [14] and speech recognition [8]. Broadly speaking, deep learning is a branch of machine learning which includes algorithms that learn a distributed feature representation of a training set using a neural network architecture composed of multiple non-linear hidden layers. For supervised deep learning algorithms where the training set includes labels, a deep learning classifier such as a deep neural network (DNN) can be trained to predict the label of unseen examples. DNNs are typically considered to be neural networks composed of two or more hidden layers while a neural network with a single hidden layer is known as a shallow neural network. Given the impressive vision and speech results, it is important that malware researchers explore

© Springer International Publishing Switzerland 2016
J. Caballero et al. (Eds.): DIMVA 2016, LNCS 9721, pp. 399–418, 2016.
DOI: 10.1007/978-3-319-40667-1_20

different deep learning models to hopefully discover improved architectures for detecting malware.

Given the potential repercussions of installing malware on a corporate or personal computer, there have been many proposed solutions for automated malware classification [10]. Recently, researchers have been attempting to use deep learning models to improve malware classification. In 2013, Dahl et al. [7] first studied deep learning for malware classification in the context of dynamic analysis, and their best single neural network architecture has an error rate of 0.49 %. Their architecture consists of a random projection layer to reduce the high dimensional (179 thousand) sparse binary input feature vector to a 4000 dimensional dense feature vector suitable for training a neural network. The authors found that adding a second and third hidden layer to the neural network did not improve the overall accuracy compared to a shallow architecture. Pascanu et al. [20] recently proposed a two component, dynamic analysis system for malware classification including a lower-level recurrent model, which learns a feature representation for API events, and a higher-level, potentially deep, classifier which uses the output of the recurrent model as features. The authors proposed eight different recurrent models, based on variants of either a recurrent neural network or an echo state network, and some of these models did learn a better representation for the input sequence compared to a bag of words model or a collection of trigrams. Similar to [7], the authors found that adding additional layers to the classifier again did not improve the overall accuracy presumably due to the small training set size of 65 thousand samples. Saxe and Berlin [21] proposed a static malware analysis classification system which consists of a two hidden layer DNN where the features are derived from the structure, including elements from the header, of a Windows portable execution (PE) file. However in this paper, the authors do not compare the results for their DNN with a shallow neural network or a DNN with more than two layers so we do not know if deep learning improves their classification rate.

While deep learning has achieved state-of-the-art classification results in speech recognition and visual object recognition, no one has been able to demonstrate any gains for deep learning applied to malware classification. In this paper, we propose *MtNet*, a new deep learning malware classification architecture which shows for the first time that deep learning offers a modest improvement compared to a shallow neural architecture. To achieve these results, *MtNet* includes several improvements over Dahl's architecture. Multi-task learning encourages the hidden layers to learn a more generalized representation at lower levels in the neural architecture. Our architecture also employees rectified linear unit (ReLU) activation functions and dropout for the hidden layers. ReLU activations and dropout were also used in [20,21], but the effects of these components were not analyzed. In our work, we study the contributions of these components and show that ReLU activation functions cut the number of epochs needed for training a binary malware classifier in half while dropout leads to significant reductions in the test error rate. When trained and tested on a dataset consisting of 6.5 million files these modifications allow *MtNet* to achieve a binary malware error rate of 0.358 % and family error rate of 2.94 % beating the previous best architectures by 26.17 % and 19.21 %, respectively. Contributions of our work include:

1. We propose and implement a novel multi-task neural network malware classification architecture. This architecture leads to modest gains for deep learning with a detection threshold of 0.5 where a file is predicted to be malware if the probability that file is malicious exceeds the probability that it is benign.
2. We conduct a deep learning study on an extremely large dataset trained with 4.5 million files and test the model with an additional 2 million files.
3. We demonstrate that dropout significantly reduces the error rate for both shallow and deep neural architectures.
4. We show that rectified linear activation functions allow a binary neural network model to be trained in half the number epochs compared to sigmoid activation functions which were used in previous work.

2 Deep Learning

To better understand deep learning, we next provide background on several key concepts. Figure 1 depicts a typical deep neural network architecture. A DNN usually consists of an input layer followed by several hidden layers and an output layer. The input layer consumes an input feature vector representing the object to be classified. The output layer is responsible for producing the class probability vector associated with the input vector. In total, the deep neural network predicts the class for the input vector.

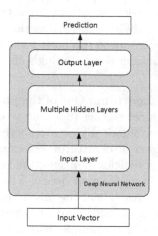

Fig. 1. A standard feed forward, deep learning architecture.

Hidden Units and Activation Functions: The basic component in a neural network is the hidden unit. A hidden unit takes an n-dimensional feature vector

$\mathbf{x} = [x_1, x_2, \cdots, x_n]$ from the input vector or the lower-level hidden units, and outputs a numerical output $y_j = f(\sum_{i=1}^{n} w_{ji}x_i + b_j)$ to the hidden units in higher layers or the output layer. For hidden unit j, y_j is the output, b_j is the bias term, while w_{ji} are the elements of a layer's weight matrix. The function $f(\cdot)$ is often referred to as the activation function which determines the hidden unit's output. The activation function introduces non-linearities to the neural network model. Otherwise, the network remains a linear transformation of its input signals.

Hidden Layers: A group of m hidden units forms a hidden layer which outputs a feature vector $\mathbf{y} = [y_1, y_2, \cdots, y_m]$. Each hidden layer takes the previous layer's output vector as the input feature vector and calculates a new feature vector for the layer above it:

$$\mathbf{y}_n = f\left(\mathbf{W_n}\mathbf{y}_{n-1} + \mathbf{b}_n\right) \tag{1}$$

where $\mathbf{y}_n$, $\mathbf{W_n}$, and $\mathbf{b}_n$ are the output feature vector, the weight matrix, and the bias of the nth layer. Proceeding from the input layer at the bottom of the DNN in Fig. 1, each subsequent higher hidden layer learns a more complex and abstract feature representation which captures higher-level structure. The underlying idea of adding multiple layers is that these layers correspond to improved levels of abstraction or composition of the observed data.

Input and Output Layers: The lowest level of a deep neural network which receives the original feature vector is known as the input layer. The original feature vector is passed to the hidden layers from bottom to top and is transformed into a fixed-dimensional vector that the final layer can process. The final layer, which interacts with and presents the processed data, is called the output layer. The behaviour of the output layer depends on the problem we are solving. For example, in a classification task, the output layer transforms the last hidden layer's activation into a probability distribution that estimates the input sample's class. So far we have introduced the most basic components and concepts in deep learning. Next we consider deep learning's ability to improve the model's feature representation.

Feature Representation Learning: One of the promises of deep neural networks is that the model reduces the need for feature engineering. Instead, deep learning provides a way to automatically extract more complex, higher-level features derived from simple lower-level features. For example, in the case of object recognition of transportation vehicles in images, the lowest-level input layer consumes the raw pixel information from an image. The first hidden layer usually learns a set of edge-like features. Then, the second layer learns to combine the lower-level features from the first hidden layer to produce a slightly richer set of features. In our image recognition example, features extracted at higher levels might represent different types of components from the vehicles such as a door, wing, tire or handle bars. Finally, the output layer fine tunes the final classification based on the object labels allowing the system to distinguish between a car, an airplane, a motorcycle, and so on.

3   *MtNet* System

Figure 2 depicts the high-level overview for training the *MtNet* system and evaluating unknown files with the trained model. The top row provides the steps required for identifying the selected features and training the *MtNet* model, while the bottom row indicates the process for evaluating an unknown file given a set of selected features and the trained *MtNet* model. For training, raw data is extracted from labeled files during dynamic analysis by a modified version of a production anti-malware engine. Unlike in-depth emulation executed on a fully capable virtual machine (VM) such as Anubis [4], the anti-malware engine used in this study only provides lightweight emulation of the operating system and tries to coax the file into execution. Since anti-malware engines are designed to quickly scan unknown files for viruses, many more files can be evaluated with this method than using full VMs. Once the raw data has been collected from the labeled files for the training set, feature selection training is performed to produce the final sparse binary features (*File Extracted Features*) required for training *MtNet*. Next, the *MtNet* model is trained for two tasks including binary classification which predicts whether an unknown file is malicious or benign and 100-class family classification which predicts if the file belongs to one of 98 important families, a generic malware class, or the benign class. In our data, analysts provide labels for tens of thousands of individual malware families. However, they selected 98 families for the family classifier based on their severity and prevalence of infection. Files in the long tail belonging to the remaining families are assigned to the generic "Malware" class. All legitimate files belong to the "Benign" class. After training, the *Selected Features* are then used to restrict the features extracted by emulating unknown files and these *File Extracted Features* can then be evaluated by the trained *MtNet* model. The *MtNet* binary prediction score is used to automatically classify the unknown file as either malicious or benign. Likewise the family classifier attempts to assign a specific family label to the unknown file. We next consider some of these steps in more detail.

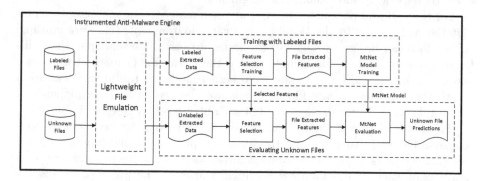

Fig. 2. High-level overview of *MtNet* training and unknown file evaluation.

Dataset: We were provided a large corpus of labeled, raw data by analysts from the Microsoft Corporation which was extracted from 6.5 million files. We believe this is the largest dataset used in a published malware classification study. Among this data collection, 2.85 million examples were extracted from malicious files and 3.65 million from benign files. The set of malicious files contained 1.3 million belonging to the 98 malware families and 1.55 million from the generic malware class. We randomly selected 4.5 million examples for training and 2.0 million for a hold out test set. All of the samples were scanned with a single combination of the anti-malware engine software and signature set. This dataset allows us to measure the performance of our system without introducing noise from varying anti-malware engine and signature set updates. Malicious files are labeled by professional analysts and anti-malware engine detections. The benign file collection is used in a production environment to prevent false positives by the anti-malware engine and was obtained either directly from legitimate companies or downloaded from verified web sites.

Features: Much research in the area of malware classification has focussed on improved feature generation. The underlying strategy is that malware experts handcraft potentially complex features using domain knowledge which hopefully leads to better overall classification performance. Deep learning takes the opposite approach and instead tries to learn the distributed feature representation from the raw input data. Just as in object recognition which learns from the raw pixels, we use low-level features extracted from dynamic analysis of the file as input for training.

For each executable file which is emulated by the anti-malware engine, two sets of raw information are extracted: a sequence of application programming interface (API) call events plus their parameters and a sequence of null-terminated objects recovered from system memory during emulation. A large percentage of malicious files are packed. During the unpacking process, null-terminated objects are often written to system memory by the malware. We find that the majority of the null-terminated objects are indeed unpacked strings but a few correspond to individual code fragments.

For the API and parameter stream, we use a many-to-one mapping to represent the API events. In the Windows software environment, there are multiple APIs which can be used to achieve the same objective. For example, three different ways to create a file include calling the CreateFile() method from user mode, the ZwCreateFile() method from kernel mode, or the fopen() call from C. All three of these create file API calls are mapped to a single higher-level CreateFile event. In total, there are 114 such high-level API events in our data.

Three sets of sparse binary features are derived from the two data sources. A sparse binary feature is set if the feature is present in the data; we do not use feature counts in *MtNet* to prevent missed detections due to attackers polymorphically varying the number of critical features. The presence or absence of the null-terminated objects are used directly as one of the feature sets. Two additional feature sets are derived from the API and parameter stream. The first feature set is derived from each unique combination of high-level API event and one individual input parameter setting. As a result, several sparse binary features are generated from each API call. The second feature set consists of trigrams of API events. An API trigram event feature is generated by the unique combination of three consecutive API events. A trigram feature provides a small amount of context for each central API call.

Feature Selection: The combined feature set consisting of null-terminated tokens, API event plus parameter value, and API trigrams contains millions of potential features. In order to reduce the input space so that it can be classified by a deep neural network, we perform feature selection using mutual information [17] to generate features that best characterize each class. The output of the feature selection process is a ranked set of 50,000 features which is input to the *MtNet* system. The 50,000 features are initially selected during training. Later, these features are applied when evaluating an unknown file.

4   Multi-Task Neural Malware Classification

Figure 3 depicts the architecture of the proposed deep, multi-task malware classification model. We seek to use the features described in the previous section to identify whether unknown files are malicious or benign. We also want to classify the malicious files into different malware families with 100 classes.

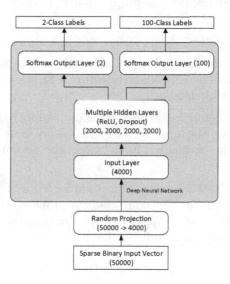

Fig. 3. Proposed deep model for multi-task learning.

4.1   Random Projections

After feature selection, the dimension of the input feature vector is reduced to 50,000. However, training a neural network with such a large input dimension is still computationally prohibitive. To overcome this problem, this original input feature vector must be projected to a lower dimensional subspace which then serves as the input vector to the neural network. Dahl et al. [7] experimented with principal component analysis (PCA) but were only able to project the original data down to 500 dimensions due to its $\mathcal{O}(N^3)$ computational requirements. Therefore to further reduce the data size to a suitable dimension for the neural network's input layer, we use the random projection technique [15] which is also used in [7]. The core idea of random projections, which has been shown to work well in practice [15], is that a sparse matrix that is randomly initialized can be used to project the original input feature vector to the reduced dimension subspace. The sparse random projection matrix R is initialized with 1 and -1 as

$$Pr(R_{i,j} = 1) = Pr(R_{i,j} = -1) = \frac{1}{2\sqrt{d}} \tag{2}$$

where d is the size of the original input feature vector. For $MtNet$, the dense, projected feature space of the random projection is reduced to 4,000 as in [7]. With $d = 50,000$ in our model, R is highly sparse and includes 0.22% of its values set to 1 and another 0.22% of its values set to -1. The remaining 99.56% of the values in the sparse, random project matrix have an implied value of 0.

4.2   Deep Neural Network

We next train a deep feed-forward neural network from the projected features for malware classification. The network architecture is identical to that described in Sect. 2 with the following details.

Normalized Input: Before inputting the feature vectors to the deep neural network, we first normalize the input vector so that every dimension has zero mean and unit variance. The normalized input makes the network training converge faster.

ReLU: The sigmoid activation function, used in [7], and the tanh activation function typically exhibit the vanishing gradient problem which makes the deep neural networks hard to train [9]. To overcome this problem, we use the rectified linear unit (ReLU) activation function for each layer. The ReLU function is defined as:

$$f(\gamma) = max(0, \gamma) \tag{3}$$

for any input value γ. It not only solves the vanishing gradient problem but also accelerates the convergence of stochastic gradient descent compared to the sigmoid and tanh activation functions.

Dropout: Dropout [24] is a regularization technique proposed for training deep neural networks. The core idea is that when updating a hidden layer, the algorithm randomly chooses not to update (i.e. "dropout") a subset of the hidden units. The intuition for dropout is that when randomly zeroing out hidden units in a layer, the network is forced to learn several independent representations of the patterns with identical input and output. In our model, we use dropout for all hidden layers of the neural network.

Loss function: The deep neural network learns different feature representations at each layer. The output layer implemented with the softmax function is used to output the categorical probability distribution. In our case for binary classification, the output is two dimensional representing malware and benign, while for the family classification task, the output size is 100 representing the different malware families, the generic malware class, and the benign files. To fine tune the deep model, we use the cross entropy loss function to quantify the quality of the neural network's classification results. The cross entropy loss is defined as

$$L_C(\theta(\mathbf{x})) = -\sum_{c \in C} g_c(\mathbf{x}) \log \theta_c(\mathbf{x}) \tag{4}$$

where $\mathbf{x}$ is the input feature vector, c is the class, C is the collection of classes to predict, $\theta(\mathbf{x})$ is the probability distribution output by the deep neural network, and g is the ground truth distribution.

Multi-Task Learning: In order to improve the generalization of the deep model, we train both the 2-class classification output and the 100-class classification output together with the same neural network. The multi-task model shares the same feature learning in the hidden layers, while the two top-level output softmax layers project these learned features into 2- or 100-dimensional vectors to calculate the probability distribution for each task. We define the multi-task loss function to be a weighted sum of each of the individual loss functions,

$$L_M(\theta(\mathbf{x})) = \alpha_1 L_2(\theta(\mathbf{x})) + \alpha_2 L_{100}(\theta(\mathbf{x})) \tag{5}$$

where the multi-task weights are α_1 and α_2, and $\alpha_1 + \alpha_2 = 1.0$. The two tasks are trained simultaneously with mini-batch stochastic gradient descent and back-propagation, and the gradients at each layer are updated with respect to the weight of each task.

5   Experimental Results

In this section, we evaluate the performance of our multi-task *MtNet* model, along with several baseline models, and seek to answer several questions about malware classification with deep learning including the following. *Does adding additional hidden layers in a deep neural network improve binary and family classification? Do larger datasets allow deep learning to help improve malware classification accuracy? How do the various deep learning components affect the classification accuracy? Can we improve detection rates at extremely low false positive rates?*

We implemented all models in this section, including the baseline system proposed in [7], using the computational neural toolkit (CNTK)[1]. The sparse, binary feature vectors for each file are extracted as described in Sect. 4. For all neural network models, we fix the input layer size to 4,000 and the hidden layer size to 2,000 for all layers. We choose the input layer size to match [7], whereas the hidden layer size is chosen by hyper-parameter tuning. The mini-batch size for stochastic gradient descent (SGD) is set to 300 samples, and the initial learning rate for mini-batch SGD is initialized to 0.01. The momentum of the gradient update is set to 0.9 to avoid getting trapped in a local minimum. We dynamically adjust the learning rate during training. If the loss does not drop after the current epoch, we reload the previous epoch's model, halve the current learning rate, and retrain the model for this epoch. After each epoch, the entire dataset is shuffled so that the data samples in each mini-batch are randomly selected. We train each model until convergence but no more than 200 epochs. Each model is trained and tested on a single NVIDIA Tesla K40 GPU. To evaluate the *MtNet* model, we report the test error rate which is defined as the ratio of misclassification in the entire test dataset. During test, an unknown file is predicted to belong to each class represented in the softmax layer. For binary classification, a file is predicted to malicious if $P(c = malware|\mathbf{x}) \geq P(c = benign|\mathbf{x})$ which corresponds to a detection threshold of 0.5 in Tables 1 and 3. In addition we also plot the receiver operating characteristic (ROC) curves of different models.

5.1 Comparison of the Baseline and Single-Task Baseline Models

Before investigating the performance of the multi-task *MtNet* model in the next section, we first evaluate the test error rates for a hold out test set on two baseline architectures for both binary and malware family classification. Tables 1 and 2, respectively, summarize the results of our best single-task deep models compared with the baseline method proposed in [7]. For reference, the second column presents the test error rates in [7] for up to three hidden layers originally evaluated using their implementation and dataset. The third column presents the results from our re-implementation of their architecture in CNTK and trained and tested with our new dataset. The number of epochs required for training to converge is listed in column 4. It should be noted that our CNTK implementation of Dahl's previously proposed models is independent and provides confirmation of their earlier results. In the final two columns, we present the results for the single task baseline versions of the *MtNet* model depicted in Fig. 3 trained and tested with our dataset. For example, the single-task baseline model for binary classification, whose results are found in Table 1, only includes the top left softmax output layer. Similarly the single-task malware family classification model, whose results are listed in Table 2, only uses the righthand softmax output layer. Both of these baseline models employ rectified linear units and dropout.

Comparing the results for Dahl's model in [7] with our implementation of their model for binary classification in Table 1, we see that the best performing baseline model in our implementation uses three hidden layers compared to one in the original study. Several factors changed between these two experiments. The training and test set sizes were essentially doubled, the number of features and families both decreased, and the underlying implementation was completely changed. In addition, only family-based models were trained in [7], and the binary classification results were computed based on whether or not the predicted family was malicious or benign. In this study, the 2-class models were trained with the true binary labels. It is interesting that the lowest test error rates for the two implementations are essentially identical (i.e. 0.49 % for their implementation and 0.4845 % for ours). In addition to the hidden layer size, this single-task version of *MtNet* differs from [7] in two aspects: the sigmoid activation function is replaced with the rectified linear activation function and dropout is included. For both binary and family classification, our single-task models significantly improve the baseline classification results by 23.98 % and 19.21 %, respectively. These results indicate that switching to the ReLU activation function and adding dropout help the deep model to learn a better feature representation of the file for classification. In both tables, we also show the number of epochs needed to reach convergence. We found that although adding dropout to the hidden layers generally increases the number of required training epochs, ReLU accelerates the convergence of the mini-batch stochastic gradient descent process for binary classification. Compared to sigmoid activation functions, rectified linear activation functions significantly reduce the number of iterations required for training a binary classifier.

Table 1. Comparison of two implementations of the baseline model versus our best single-task baseline model on 2-class binary classification.

Layers	Baseline model (Original results [7])	Baseline model (Our data)		Single task model (Our data)	
	Test error(%)	Test error(%)	Epoch	Test error(%)	Epoch
1	0.49	0.5906	190	0.3711	64
2	0.50	0.4882	186	0.3702	82
3	0.51	0.4845	200	0.3686	77
4		0.4934	200	**0.3683**	81

5.2   Multi-Task Results

Table 3 compares the test error rates for the multi-task models with their single-task counterparts. Using hyper-parameter tuning, we set the weights for the binary classification task to $\alpha_1 = 0.8$ and for the family classification task to $\alpha_2 = 0.2$. We observe that for binary classification, classifiers trained with the multi-task models consistently improve the error rate. However, the multi-task, family classification models perform worse than the single-task variants. Compared to the baseline results shown in Tables 1 and 2, we observe that both classifiers obtain significant improvements. While the family test error rate remains at

Table 2. Comparison of two implementations of the baseline model versus our best single-task baseline model on 100-class family classification.

Layers	Baseline model (Original results [7])	Baseline model (Our data)		Single task model (Our data)	
	Test error(%)	Test error(%)	Epoch	Test error(%)	Epoch
1	9.53	3.633	152	**2.935**	124
2	9.55	3.652	70	2.983	130
3	9.74	3.715	96	2.982	122
4		3.795	96	2.970	146

2.935 % with a 19.21 % improvement compared to the baseline result, the multi-task binary test error rate drops further to 0.3577 % with a relative improvement of 26.17 %.

Table 3. Test error rates for multi-task training vs. single-task training on 2-class and 100-class classification.

Layers	2-Class Test error(%)		100-Class Test error(%)	
	Multi-task	Single-task	Multi-task	Single-task
1	0.3657	0.3711	2.935	**2.935**
2	**0.3577**	0.3702	3.025	2.983
3	0.3618	0.3686	3.026	2.982
4	0.3655	0.3683	3.070	2.970

In Fig. 4, we compare the ROC curves at very low false positive rates with $\alpha_1 = 0.8$ and $\alpha_2 = 0.2$. Although we do see some improvement in Table 3 for binary classification by adding additional layers, the 1- and 2-layer networks offer comparable performance for very low false positive rates.

In Fig. 5, we compare the ROC curves for binary classification for the single-task model with two different $MtNet$ models using $\alpha_1 = 0.8$ and $\alpha_1 = 0.9$. All models have a single hidden layer. This figure indicates that the multi-task $MtNet$ model outperforms the single-task model at very low false positive rates; including the family classification task helps regularize the neural network model to learn better feature abstractions for binary classification.

5.3 Model Parameter Contributions

We perform hyper-parameter tuning on two additional parameters in $MtNet$, the dropout rate and the multi-task mixing weight, and measure their contribution to the $MtNet$ model test error.

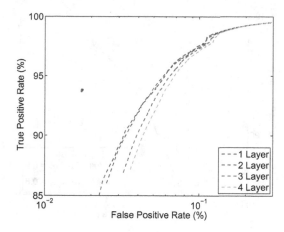

Fig. 4. ROC curves for the best performing multi-task *MtNet* at very low false positive rates. (Color figure online)

Dropout Rate: Figures 6 and 7, respectively, show the test error rates for binary and family classification with different dropout settings. It is clear that dropout is the main contributor to the improvement in classification accuracy in both cases. The best dropout setting for binary classification is 0.25, where *MtNet* is able to learn a better feature representation with more hidden layers. Although the 0.25 dropout rate also improves the family classification test error rate significantly, adding more hidden layers fails to learn better feature representations for this task.

Multi-Task Weight: We next vary the multi-task weight corresponding to binary classification task α_1, in (5), and measure its impact on *MtNet's* binary classification error rate in Fig. 8 and family classification error rate in Fig. 9. From Fig. 8, we observe that as α_1 increases, the test error decreases until $\alpha_1 = 0.8$ for all models. Whereas in Fig. 9, we observe that the error rate of the family classification models generally increases as α_1 increases. Note that setting $\alpha_1 = 1$, in the multi-task model, is equivalent to the single-task binary classification model, and setting $\alpha_1 = 0$ corresponds to the single-task family classification model. These two figures show that multi-task learning favors the task with the larger weight. In summary when $\alpha_1 = 0.8$, multi-task modelling significantly improves the binary classification result with the help of the family class labels.

5.4 Dataset Size and Deep Learning

Based on the published results, we believe this is the largest malware classification experiment run to date. We essentially doubled the number of training and test samples compared to [7]. However compared to the results reported in [7], our CNTK implementation of the baseline model shows similar test error rates. In addition, although we found modest gains by increasing the number of layers

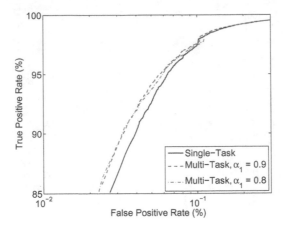

Fig. 5. ROC curves for binary classification by multi-task *MtNet* model versus single-task model for different binary classification task weights α_1. (Color figure online)

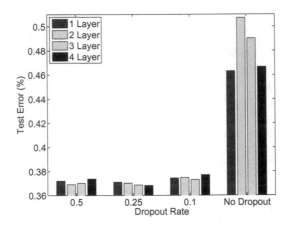

Fig. 6. *MtNet* test error rates for binary classification with different dropout rates of 0.5, 0.25, 0.1 and without dropout. (Color figure online)

in *MtNet* in the case of 2-class binary classification, we did not find significant improvements using deep learning compared to other domains such as object and speech recognition. As a result, we do not believe that adding even more samples to our training set will enable deep learning to offer significant performance increases for the dynamic analysis features investigated in this study.

5.5 Training and Testing Efficiency

An important aspect of training large-scale neural network architectures is the training and testing efficiency. Table 4 presents the time required to train and test the large-scale *MtNet* multi-task, deep neural networks for up to four layers.

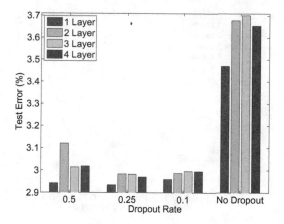

Fig. 7. *MtNet* test error rates for family classification with different dropout rates of 0.5, 0.25, 0.1 and without dropout. (Color figure online)

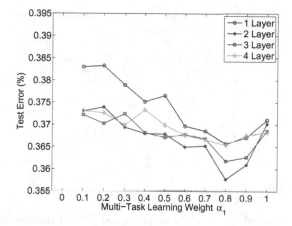

Fig. 8. *MtNet* test error rates for 2-class classification with different values of the multi-task learning weight α_1. (Color figure online)

These times are listed in (hours:minutes). The reason that the training times are similar for the 3 and 4 layer networks is because the 3 layer network trained for 181 epochs before the early stopping criterion halted training while the 4 layer network only required 144 epochs. The most time consuming aspect of training and testing the system is the extraction of the data which required approximately 2 weeks on a single computer.

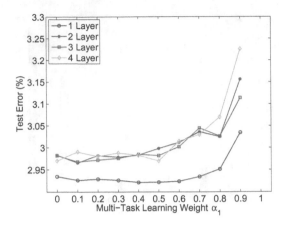

Fig. 9. *MtNet* test error rates for 100-class classification with different values of the multi-task learning weight α_1. (Color figure online)

Table 4. Training and test times required in (hours:minutes) for evaluating up to four layers in the *MtNet* DNN malware classifier.

Layers	Training time	Test time
1	06:58	01:34
2	12:34	02:09
3	18:08	02:41
4	18:12	02:32

6   Discussions

We now discuss several aspects of our proposed *MtNet* multi-task, neural classification system and then consider how attackers may attempt to evade its detection.

Achieving improvements using deep learning for malware classification is extremely challenging. The primary issue is that the classification accuracy for a neural network architecture with millions of files is already so good that it is difficult for additional layers to offer significant performance increases. For example, the best accuracy from the previous large-scale malware classification study [7] for a single neural network with one hidden layer is 99.51 %. Figure 4 indicates that the ROC curves for this dataset are beginning to approach the ideal classifier. Although we do find some gains in Tables 1, 2 and 3, there is not much room for significant improvement in the binary classification results by including additional hidden layers. In contrast, the detection error rates for object recognition and speech recognition were much higher prior to the significant improvements using deep learning. However, this study confirms that using other types of algorithmic techniques from the deep learning literature, such as dropout and rectified linear unit activation functions, can further improve the test error rate of a neural network malware classifier.

Even though it is somewhat disappointing that we cannot obtain significant improvements in malware classification using deep learning, this result has a major benefit. Shallow networks can evaluate unknown files more quickly because the computational complexity for each hidden layer is $\mathcal{O}(H^2)$ where H is the size of the hidden layer. As a result, we can scan more files with a shallow neural network than with a DNN.

All of the samples were analyzed at the same time with the same version of the anti-malware engine. Thus we expect the performance to be worse when analyzing new samples in a production setting where the anti-malware engine and its signatures are updated frequently.

As with many other malware detection systems, *MtNet* is susceptible to attacks and can be evaded. *MtNet* relies on dynamic analysis of a PE file. As such, the well known anti-emulation attack where the malware detects that it is being emulated and halts any malicious activity [3] will prevent *MtNet* from detecting the malicious file. In addition, *MtNet* is also vulnerable to the recently reported attack for deep neural networks proposed by Papernot, et al. [19]. In this attack, the authors construct adversarial samples and demonstrate that all ten digits in the MNIST database can be altered in such a way as to confuse a DNN classifier thereby producing any other digit. This attack is based upon computing the forward derivative of the DNN evaluated at the proposed initial input sample. Given this attack, the *MtNet* classifier should not be run on the client computer where the parameters of the DNN can be recovered by reverse engineering. However assuming a secure machine learning infrastructure with no intrusions, *MtNet* can still be run on the backend to evaluate unknown files.

7   Related Work

Previous research most closely related to the *MtNet* system broadly falls into two main areas, deep learning and automated malware classification.

Neural networks have been explored for over three decades. Deep learning has recently become popular in many areas such as computer vision [14] and speech recognition [8]. Training deep models was not practical until the recent growth of computational power and large datasets. Newly proposed techniques such as dropout [24], and rectified linear units [18] solved several problems such as over-fitting and the vanishing gradient problem. The multi-task learning approach [6] has recently gained popularity among deep learning models. It usually leads to a better primary task model when training simultaneously with other related tasks. Multi-task learning has been adapted in several applications such as text recognition [11] and speech recognition [23].

Given the problems associated with stolen credentials and data exfiltration, malware classification has been an active research area since 1994. Idika and Mathur [10] present a good overview of malware classification. Kephart et al. [12] were the first to use neural networks for malware classification. Later important malware classification studies include the works by Schultz et al. [22] and Kolter et al. [13]. Random projections were first proposed for malware classification by Atkinson [2].

A few researchers have started to explore deep learning architectures for malware classification. Dahl et al. [7] proposed a simple feed-forward neural network with random projections [15] to learn from a selected feature set extracted from the executable files. Dahl's shallow neural architecture is the current best performing malware classification model in terms of binary and family classification accuracy, but the deep models fail to improve the classification accuracy in their study. Our proposed model is closely related to Dahl's architecture [7]. We utilize multi-task learning and recent deep learning techniques which allow our deep model to outperform their model. Benchea and Gavrilut [5] combine a Restricted Boltmann Machine (RBM) with a One-Sided Perceptron for detecting malware. Their study is quite large consisting of over 1.2 million files although only 31,507 are malicious. An RBM is an unsupervised method for learning a stochastic neural network. It learns one set of weights from an input layer to a single hidden layer. Dahl et al. [7] found that pre-training their neural network classifier with an RBM slightly degraded the performance. Recurrent neural networks and echo state networks have been used to analyze executable files to identify malware [20]. However, recurrent models are computationally expensive when trained with many files and long sequences. Finally, a static analysis-based DNN was proposed by Saxe and Berlin [21].

8   Conclusions

In this paper, we propose and implement several different binary and family malware classifier architectures. The best binary classifier employs multi-task learning for the binary and family malware classification tasks. In particular, multi-task learning improves the classification results for extremely low false positive rates under 0.07 %. The best performing two-class, binary classification architecture in Table 3 uses two hidden layers and multi-task learning while a shallow, multi-task network performs best for family classification. These results are achieved using rectified linear unit activation functions and dropout. Including dropout is the key to the majority of the accuracy improvement compared to Dahl's architecture, and rectified linear units reduce the number of epochs required for training by almost half. Given these results, we believe that training neural network architectures with millions of files offers the best overall performance for malware classification.

Acknowledgements. The authors would like to thank Mady Marinescu with helping in the data collection. We also thank our shepherd Juan Tapiador and the anonymous reviewers for their very valuable feedback.

References

1. Agarwal, A., Akchurin, E., Basoglu, C., Chen, G., Cyphers, S., Droppo, J., Eversole, A., Guenter, B., Hillebrand, M., Hoens, R., Huang, X., Huang, Z., Ivanov, V., Kamenev, A., Kranen, P., Kuchaiev, O., Manousek, W., May, A., Mitra, B., Nano, O., Navarro, G., Orlov, A., Padmilac, M., Parthasarathi, H., Peng, B., Reznichenko, A., Seide, F., Seltzer, M.L., Slaney, M., Stolcke, A., Wang, Y., Wang, H., Yao, K., Yu, D., Zhang, Y., Zweig, G.: An introduction to computational networks and the computational network toolkit. Technical report MSR-TR-2014-112. https://github.com/Microsoft/CNTK
2. Atkison, T.: Applying randomized projection to aid prediction algorithms in detecting high-dimensional rogue application. In: Proceedings of the Annual Southeast Regional Conference (ACMSE) (2009)
3. Balzarotti, D., Cova, M., Karlberger, C., Kruegel, C., Kirda, E., Vigna, G.: Efficient detection of split personalities in malware. In: Proceedings of the Network and Distributed System Security Symposium (NDSS) (2010)
4. Bayer, U., Kruegel, C., Kirda, E.: TTAnalyze: A tool for analyzing malware. In: Proceedings of 15th Annual Conference of the European Institute for Computer Antivirus Research (EICAR) (2006)
5. Benchea, R., Gavriluţ, D.T.: Combining restricted boltzmann machine and one side perceptron for malware detection. In: Hernandez, N., Jäschke, R., Croitoru, M. (eds.) ICCS 2014. LNCS, vol. 8577, pp. 93–103. Springer, Heidelberg (2014)
6. Caruana, R.: Multitask learning. Mach. Learn. **28**(1), 41–75 (1997)
7. Dahl, G.E., Stokes, J.W., Deng, L., Yu, D.: Large-scale malware classification using random projections and neural networks. In: Proceedings of the IEEE International Conference on Acoustics, Speech and Signal Processing (ICASSP), pp. 3422–3426. IEEE (2013)
8. Hinton, G., Deng, L., Yu, D., rahman Mohamed, A., Jaitly, N., Senior, A., Vanhoucke, V., Nguyen, P., Sainath, T., Dahl, G., Kingsbury, B.: Deep neural networks for acoustic modeling in speech recognition. In: IEEE Signal Processing Magazine, vol. 29, pp. 82–97 (2012)
9. Hochreiter, S., Bengio, Y., Frasconi, P., Schmidhuber, J.: Gradient flow in recurrent nets: the difficulty of learning long-term dependencies. In: Kolen, J.F., Kremer, S.C. (eds.) A Field Guide to Dynamical Recurrent Neural Networks. IEEE Press, Wiley-IEEE Press (2001)
10. Idika, N., Mathur, A.P.: A survey of malware detection techniques. Technical report, Purdue University. http://www.eecs.umich.edu/techreports/cse/2007/CSE-TR-530-07.pdf
11. Jaderberg, M., Vedaldi, A., Zisserman, A.: Deep features for text spotting. In: Fleet, D., Pajdla, T., Schiele, B., Tuytelaars, T. (eds.) ECCV 2014, Part IV. LNCS, vol. 8692, pp. 512–528. Springer, Heidelberg (2014)
12. Kephart, J.O.: A biologically inspired immune system for computers. In: Proceedings of the Fourth International Workshop on the Synthesis and Simulation of Living Systems, pp. 130–139. MIT Press (1994)
13. Kolter, J., Maloof, M.: Learning to detect and classify malicious executables in the wild. J. Mach. Learn. Res. (JMLR) **7**, 2721–2744 (2006)
14. Krizhevsky, A., Sutskever, I., Hinton, G.E.: Imagenet classification with deep convolutional neural networks. In: Advances in neural information processing systems, pp. 1097–1105 (2012)

15. Li, P., Hastie, T.J., Church, K.W.: Very sparse random projections. In: Proceedings of the ACM SIGKDD International Conference on Knowledge Discovery and Data Mining (ICDM), pp. 287–296 (2006)
16. Lopez, M.: 27% of all recorded malware appeared in 2015 (2016). http://www.pandasecurity.com/mediacenter/press-releases/all-recorded-malware-appeared-in-2015/
17. Manning, C.D., Raghavan, P., Schutze, H.: An Introduction to Information Retrieval. Cambridge University Press, New York (2009)
18. Nair, V., Hinton, G.E.: Rectified linear units improve restricted boltzmann machines. In: Proceedings of the International Conference on Machine Learning (ICML), pp. 807–814 (2010)
19. Papernot, N., McDaniel, P., Jha, S., Fredrikson, M., Celik, Z.B., Swamix, A.: The limitations of deep learning in adversarial systems. In: IEEE European Symposium on Security and Privacy (2016)
20. Pascanu, R., Stokes, J.W., Sanossian, H., Marinescu, M., Thomas, A.: Malware classification with recurrent networks. In: Proceeding of the IEEE International Conference on Acoustics, Speech and Signal Processing (ICASSP), pp. 1916–1920. IEEE (2015)
21. Saxe, J., Berlin, K.: Deep neural network based malware detection using two dimensional binary program features. arXiv preprint (2015). arXiv:1508.03096v2
22. Schultz, M., Eskin, E., Zadok, E., Stolfo, S.: Data mining methods of detection of new malicious executables. In: Proceedings of the 2001 IEEE Symposium on Security and Privacy (SP), pp. 38–49. IEEE Press, New York (2001)
23. Seltzer, M.L., Droppo, J.: Multi-task learning in deep neural networks for improved phoneme recognition. In: Proceedings of IEEE International Conference on Acoustics, Speech and Signal Processing (ICASSP). IEEE (2013)
24. Srivastava, N., Hinton, G., Krizhevsky, A., Sutskever, I., Salakhutdinov, R.: Dropout: a simple way to prevent neural networks from overfitting. J. Mach. Learn. Res. **15**(1), 1929–1958 (2014). http://dl.acm.org/citation.cfm?id=2627435.2670313

Adaptive Semantics-Aware Malware Classification

Bojan Kolosnjaji$^{(\boxtimes)}$, Apostolis Zarras, Tamas Lengyel, George Webster, and Claudia Eckert

Technical University of Munich, Munich, Germany
{kolosnjaji,zarras,tklengyel,webstergd,eckert}@sec.in.tum.de

Abstract. Automatic malware classification is an essential improvement over the widely-deployed detection procedures using manual signatures or heuristics. Although there exists an abundance of methods for collecting static and behavioral malware data, there is a lack of adequate tools for analysis based on these collected features. Machine learning is a statistical solution to the automatic classification of malware variants based on heterogeneous information gathered by investigating malware code and behavioral traces. However, the recent increase in variety of malware instances requires further development of effective and scalable automation for malware classification and analysis processes.

In this paper, we investigate the topic modeling approaches as semantics-aware solutions to the classification of malware based on logs from dynamic malware analysis. We combine results of static and dynamic analysis to increase the reliability of inferred class labels. We utilize a semi-supervised learning architecture to make use of unlabeled data in classification. Using a nonparametric machine learning approach to topic modeling we design and implement a scalable solution while maintaining advantages of semantics-aware analysis. The outcomes of our experiments reveal that our approach brings a new and improved solution to the reoccurring problems in malware classification and analysis.

1 Introduction

Malware has evolved over the years to the point where it generates a global threat for our digital lives. Nowadays, the amount of malware that arises every day has increased exponentially. Security companies currently need to analyze hundreds of thousands of malicious samples on a daily basis, which directly affects their performance. In some cases, this number can be larger than one million distinct files per day [34]. Meanwhile, malware classification is becoming increasingly critical as new malware instances integrate sophisticated techniques to deceive the signature-based detectors and operate under the radar for longer period. This fact, along with the rapid increase in the number of malware samples, presents a very real challenge that cannot be met by manual reverse engineering efforts or by generating static signatures. Specifically, while it is relatively easy

© Springer International Publishing Switzerland 2016
J. Caballero et al. (Eds.): DIMVA 2016, LNCS 9721, pp. 419–439, 2016.
DOI: 10.1007/978-3-319-40667-1_21

for antivirus and other security companies to obtain large numbers of malicious samples, it requires significant effort to successfully classify them.

To address this problem, researchers proposed statistical machine learning methods that can enable analysts to focus on new and previously unseen attacks by classifying malware as being part of a larger family [29]. These methods leverage gathered static and behavioral malware data to generate statistically confident knowledge. Towards this direction, Schultz et al. [29] used statistical methods to detect malicious executables based on n-grams of instructions. Rieck et al. [27], on the other hand, utilized behavioral features of malware for both detection and classification, and proved the superiority of this approach against the traditional signature-based methods. This performance improvement is explained with the inherent advantages of statistical methods in capturing the variety of malware samples.

Nevertheless, statistical malware classification systems are not without their own problems. Foremost, there is a scarcity of reliable labels for fully supervised malware classification systems. Malware analysts could potentially retrieve antivirus results and use them to label malware samples. Although this approach seems ideal, unfortunately, many times it is difficult to provide confident labels this way. Antivirus companies offer malware signatures, which are mostly used in the academic community for testing the malware classification systems. However, we have observed by manual inspection of antivirus results that the reliability of those signatures is not always high. Every antivirus program has its own system of labeling malware, and although sometimes the signatures match between different antivirus programs, very often they are different or even contradictory. Furthermore, there is a limited public information about the process by which companies assign these signatures and how accurate these signatures are. Yet another problem is the very high data dimensionality when the execution logs contain whole system behaviors [6]. Finally, the malware analysis tools provide different features of malware with respect to static and dynamic analysis [1–3,19]. Using multiple tools ensures that all the information is considered, yet, there exist only few efforts that try to join this information [4]. This problem is non-trivial because data retrieved from the analysis tools is heterogeneous, which means that different machine learning models might be optimal for different data. For example, dynamic malware analysis results have a sequential nature, while metadata from static analysis, such as code entropy or size of code sections, do not always have such interdependencies.

The number and variety of malware samples that need to be processed has surpassed the ability of the classical approaches that analyze the static and behavioral characteristics of malicious samples and create signatures. Automation of detection and classification procedures that take into account the aforementioned approaches is becoming less effective when dealing with large amount of data, let alone extracting useful knowledge about malware. Since the problem is essentially the automatic analysis of high amounts of noisy data, statistical machine learning methods constitute a superior approach. These methods, however, need to be adapted to online setting, where a high influx of samples imposes a necessity for retraining of machine learning models in order to maintain accurate label predictions.

In this paper, we evaluate and improve the use of statistical topic modeling with respect to the curse of dimensionality of long execution sequences. Further, combined with semi-supervised learning methods of exploiting unlabeled samples, we effectively overcome the problem of the lack of labeled data. Finally, we show how the use of data obtained from static and dynamic analysis increases the reliability of the classification results, demonstrating that data heterogeneity can in fact boost confidence in classification. In essence, we use a nonparametric machine learning approach, where parameter set is not set up in advance, but depends on the training data. Nonparametric approach is, to the best of our knowledge, novel in malware classification problems. This enables a more stable approach, where semantic interpretation is automatically updated on arrival of new malware samples. Our evaluation reveals that our model achieves over 90 % precision and recall in classification for most of the tested malware families, while it retains stability in classification performance and retraining speed.

In summary, we make the following main contributions:

- We create a semi-supervised malware classification system that unifies views of static and dynamic malware analysis.
- We perform an automatic extraction of semantic behavioral features from the results of dynamic malware analysis.
- We design and evaluate a nonparametric model that is adaptive in a setting of online training.

2   Background

The key concepts from the area of machine learning that constitute the lifeblood of our approach are *topic modeling*, *semi-supervised learning*, and *nonparametric learning*. In this section, we briefly introduce the aforementioned concepts.

2.1   Topic Modeling

As behavioral malware execution data is a sequence of tokens taken from a predefined dictionary, it closely resembles text documents by structure. Therefore, methods of information retrieval designed for extracting latent properties of text can be of great importance. In machine learning, data is very often organized in long sequences. Most explored examples of this kind of data are audio and video recordings, genetic sequences, and text documents. For instance, it has been determined that very often news articles belong to a smaller set of latent topics such as *Basketball, Tour De France, Hollywood, FBI Investigation*, etc. [22]. On a higher level, topics could be *sports, culture*, and *finance*. Furthermore, words in text documents belong to these topics with certain probability, where one word can be attributed with multiple different topics as well. If topics are semantically interpretable, created model also has a semantic meaning. This text modeling problem and vocabulary can be translated to problems with other types of data.

Topic modeling methods are mostly constructed as generative methods: they are not designed just for classification but also for generation of data based on the probability distributions inferred from the model. In essence, the topics are constructed in such a way that the training documents can be generated with high probability using just the topics inferred from the model. Given a reasonable assumption that our documents can be confidently described by a smaller set of topics, we can determine these topics and their distribution by training a topic model. We do not need to know the topics in advance, as they can be inferred from the data (i.e., from the documents and the words contained in them).

Overall, topic modeling is a method to statistically explain a large set of documents using a small set of clusters (topics), based on frequency of different words in these documents. Note that it counts the words independently without a specific interest of their sequences inside the documents. This approach has been often called *bag-of-words* and it greatly simplifies document analysis.

One of the most adequate random processes used for topic modeling is the *Dirichlet* process. This is a suitable model especially for datasets where only few latent topics can describe a large set of documents. The notion of latent topics was popularized with the development of *Latent Dirichlet Allocation* (LDA) method [7]. In this method the topic structure is sampled from a Dirichlet distribution as prior, which gives more flexibility in training the generative model. Although there exist related methods of topic modeling [10], LDA is the most used regarding document information retrieval because of its flexibility and modular structure. This method has been further adapted to discriminative learning, i.e., classification [25]. In its standard form, LDA uses a bag-of-words assumption, which means that it does not capture the sequential nature of the document: it only counts words independently.

2.2   Semi-supervised Learning

The lack of proper labeling has already been defined as an important problem in malware research [5]. Consequently, one would benefit from a method that offers maximum utilization of a minimal number of highly confident labels. This setting is known in machine learning as semi-supervised learning and is halfway between supervised and unsupervised algorithms. While supervised learning is a paradigm that encompasses machine learning methods where the training data is labeled and the purpose of the algorithm is to optimize the classification of data on the test dataset, unsupervised learning discovers the underlying structure in the data such as locating clusters in the dataset. We use unsupervised learning when we do not have information about labels in the time of training. Since in semi-supervised setting we do have labeled data, but it is scarce, we combine the advantages of two separate methods to overcome this limitation. More specifically, in semi-supervised learning we leverage the property of data that it forms natural clusters. Even if we only have a small number of labeled data that identifies the clusters that exist in the dataset, we can propagate these labels in the neighborhood of the labeled data, by considering the clusters detected in the dataset.

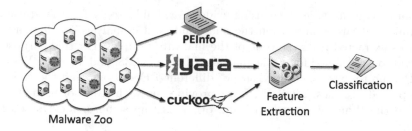

Fig. 1. Malware classification architecture.

2.3   Nonparametric Learning

In many scenarios the parameter set of machine learning models cannot be always defined in advance. This is also the case with malware classification, as high influx of malware samples imposes a need to adapt the model incrementally. This can be done using a nonparametric approach, where parameter set grows with the size of the dataset. Since this growth of the parameter set increases complexity of the model, additional effort is needed to stabilize the classifier. We utilize an improved approach in order to maintain this stability.

3   Methodology

We propose a classification scheme aimed at solving the problems indicated in the introductory sections. In particular, we want to be able to discover semantic features of malware classes, maintain an adaptive topic model, and maximize the utilization of a semi-labeled dataset from heterogeneous data sources. To do so, we first emphasize on extracting semantic features from high-dimensional and noisy data. Second, we optimize the classification mechanism under the setting where low number of labeled samples is available. To this end, we join results of static and dynamic malware analysis to unify these different views on properties of malware samples. Finally, we design an architecture that is adaptive in the online training setting. In summary, our malware classification architecture complies with the scheme displayed on Fig. 1.

3.1   Experimental Environment

To perform data extraction against malware samples we employ a *malware zoo*, in which we can execute malicious samples while monitoring their behavior. The zoo back-end infrastructure is composed of a custom version of CRITs [33] that utilizes large scale analysis concepts proposed by Hanif et al. [15]. Specifically, our modifications use custom CRITs Services to extract API call information from Cuckoo [1] and execute the requested work in a distributed fashion. The malware samples were collected over multiple months from three primary sources: Virus Share [28], Maltrieve [21], and private collections. We chose these sources to provide a large and diverse volume of samples for evaluation.

Data acquisition is done using widely available tools for the static and dynamic malware analysis. On the one hand, static analysis provides us with features extracted from the code of the malware samples. For this purpose, we use two sources aimed for static analysis: PEInfo [33,38] and Yara [3]. We leverage PEInfo to extract entropy, size of different PE sections, and the collection of imported libraries. Similarly, Yara provides us with a list of used function calls to the Windows kernel API and other custom signatures extracted from the code.

On the other hand, dynamic analysis enables us to gather reliable behavioral data without the need for deobfuscation. There exist various tools that enable tracing the execution of malware and gather logs of execution sequences [1,19]. We select the Cuckoo Sandbox, which provides a controlled environment for executing malware. During the execution of malware samples we record calls to the kernel API that we later use to characterize malware activity. For each sample we obtain a sequence of API calls, which is preprocessed by removing subsequences where one API call is repeated multiple times in a row. We cut these subsequences by using only one kernel API call instance as representative in the resulting sequence. In multiple samples we have noticed the repetition of one API call; for example, when malware repeatedly tries to open a file.

In addition, we leverage VirusTotal [2] by extracting antivirus signatures from its web service, for each malware sample we use. Users can upload MD5 hashes of malware executables to VirusTotal and retrieve results from multiple antivirus engines through the VirusTotal API. These engines are signature-based and compare the submitted hash to the data in their own database. By using the VirusTotal services we access malware analysis results and signatures, out of which we are mostly interested in retrieving ground truth labels for our classification. In a lack of other label sources, we use antivirus signatures in label construction for training and testing our classification scheme. Since antivirus programs use customized strategies for signature generation, we need to find a way to extract one numerical training label per unique sample using the diverse antivirus signatures. We use signature clustering to achieve this goal.

3.2 Signature Clustering

To get more confident training and testing labels, we perform a selection process that uses a simplified version of signature clustering method introduced in VAMO [23]. Specifically, we create signature vectors for every malware sample that contains signatures given by different antivirus engines. We use boolean features to generate these vectors, where each feature reveals presence or absence of a certain antivirus signature. Our assumption is that the malware samples of the same family will have the same or similar boolean feature vector. Next, we use a variant of *cosine distance* as a measure of difference among signature vectors for our clustering process. We cluster the samples using DBSCAN [12], as we do not know their number in advance. Finally, we select ten clusters with the highest number of members as classes for classification. This way we cover most of our labeled dataset. Since the classes assigned to our malware resemble the families defined by antivirus engines, we use the terms *class* and *family* interchangeably.

3.3 Feature Selection

Static analysis tools provide us with a high number of features. In detail, we retrieve 23,060 features from PEInfo and 3805 features from Yara extracted from the malware binary files. Using a high number of features makes the classification problem ill-posed and therefore we choose to utilize feature selection methods to obtain an optimal feature set. We use *univariate feature selection* approach and perform a χ^2 test for all training samples. This way we can extract the features that are most relevant to our classification problem and reduce the computational effort needed for the training process. For our purpose we achieve best results by selecting 10,000 features for PEInfo and 1000 features for Yara.

3.4 Topic Modeling Algorithms

To extract features from the kernel API call sequences we utilize the topic modeling approach, which includes a well-developed set of methods already heavily used for automatic information retrieval from text and image data.

General Approach. As we already mentioned, topic modeling is a method based on the fact that a collection of tokens (words) from documents can be grouped to a limited set of topics. More specifically, we apply topic modeling to process data from dynamic malware analysis, as we consider that a list of API calls can be divided into a smaller number of latent activities. In our case, documents are malware execution logs and words are elements of malware execution sequences—calls to the Windows Kernel API. Additionally, topics are groups of these elements that constitute an elementary operation, for instance, registry access and modification, file manipulation, process creation and invocation.

This analogy justifies the attempt to adapt the topic modelling approach for the malware classification problem. The general topic modeling scheme can be represented with the following formulas:

$$G \sim DP(\alpha, H) \tag{1}$$

$$\theta_i \mid G \sim G \tag{2}$$

$$x_{j,i} \mid \theta_i \sim F(\theta_i) \tag{3}$$

where parameter G (a Dirichlet distribution) controls the topics and generates the parameter θ_i. Words ($x_{j,i}$) are generated based on this parameter. Dirichlet process is actually a distribution of distributions. The draws from Dirichlet processes are probability distributions, which are inferred for the next parameter in the chain. This parameter controls the word distribution for single topics. Topic modeling based on a Dirichlet process enables us to define a generative model, where each document is a mixture of a small number of topics.

It is important to note that topics are not known in advance, but are inferred by the topic modeling methods. This enables us to uncover previously unknown semantics from the malware execution logs. Parameters are approximately determined using variational inference and Markov Chain Monte Carlo methods [35], as exact inference is not tractable. This also enables fast retraining in case of need for online update of the model. Figure 2 contains a graphical model used for topic inference, where the directed edges show the process of word generation.

Topic models can be essential for classification performance, as important latent structure is inferred and noise canceling is implicitly executed by extracting the important topics. However, even more crucial is the possibility of semantic interpretation. Although malware analysts are able to get a rich set of information from the dynamic malware analysis tools, this information needs to be further analyzed and significant expert knowledge is required to extract the important information out of the logs retrieved from these tools. Thus, it would be extremely useful to automate this procedure and to extract relevant data about the malware activity.

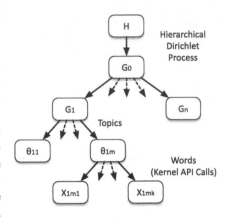

Fig. 2. Graphical model for our Hierarchical Dirichlet Process.

This would enable analysts to achieve their goals faster and with statistically confident results. Therefore, we develop a more efficient alternative to the cumbersome deterministic manual analysis procedure. Even if the topics do not have an obvious semantic meaning, comparing the topic structure among different malware families can enhance the classification process and provide new knowledge about the dataset in use.

Previous work demonstrated the utility of topic modeling for extracting semantics out of kernel API call logs by using LDA, where topic parameters are drawn out of the Dirichlet distribution [7]. Furthermore, this method was adapted from a bag-of-words method to a new scheme that takes account of sequential data ordering [39]. However, this approach is not scalable on large sets of malware and online learning, and is sensitive to noisy sequences. It also requires a predefined number of topics, which would need to be manually updated by the malware analyst as new data is acquired. In case of an organization that maintains its own malware dataset and receives a high amount of submissions on a daily basis, this kind of setting may not be satisfactory.

Hierarchical Dirichlet Processes. Given the limitations of LDA, we take a different approach, using methods that bring the required improvement to online learning. More precisely, we utilize an adaptive method called *Hierarchical Dirichlet Process* (HDP) [32]. In this method the topic distributions are also determined by Dirichlet processes, yet there exist different processes for each document. These processes, however, are not independent. They are drawn from a prior Dirichlet process, which depends on parameters that control the growth of topics and their distribution as the dataset grows in time:

$$G_0 \sim DP(\alpha_0, H) \tag{4}$$

$$G_j \mid G_0 \sim DP(\alpha_j, G_0) \tag{5}$$

where Dirichlet processes G_j are conditioned by the prior G_0.

Overall, the general setting of the topic modeling remains the same: documents belong to multiple topics and words depend on topic distributions. HDP is an instance of nonparametric machine learning methods. As a difference from parametric methods, like LDA, nonparametric methods are used when we want the parameter set to change with the dataset. HDP introduces a more flexible approach, which is also more computationally demanding. Actually, this is the case with all the nonparametric machine learning methods. Nevertheless, there exist modifications that trade the accuracy of the method for performance in an online setting [36]. We use these modifications to create a scalable approach with respect to the computational demand. Our implementation is based on the *GenSim* library [26], developed for the estimation of text document similarity.

3.5   Semi-supervised Malware Classification

Accurate malware classification is often difficult due to lack of confident label sources. We can find proper signatures only for a small subset of malware samples, even by utilizing services such as VirusTotal. To deal with the scarceness of labeled data, we use semi-supervised learning, where we influence the usual malware clustering procedure with high-confidence labels. Figure 3 displays our semi-supervised classification scheme. Our system unifies advantages of topic modeling and semi-supervised learning. To this end, data retrieved from static and

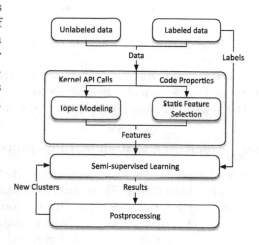

Fig. 3. Semi-supervised learning scheme.

dynamic analysis tools are run through feature extraction and forwarded to the classification stage.

To achieve an effective semi-supervised learning model, we take two separate approaches to classify the static and dynamic analysis results. For results retrieved from static analysis we use label propagation. This method uses labeled data and density-based clustering to propagate the given labels through the dataset. The propagation of labels is conditioned by the similarity structure between data samples. In particular, we use a regularized variant of label propagation, to take account of the possible noise in labeling [42].

For dynamic analysis results we use another alternative. In a semi-supervised setting we can use unlabeled data for initial pretraining of topic models before using the actual labeled data. To discriminate between classes of malware, we make use of a *maximum-a-posteriori* (MAP) approach. This approach is used in machine learning very often when estimating distributions and parameters of a model. As a result, when classifying, we assign the class label to the data that is inferred with a highest probability.

We create a topic model for every existing class, based on the available logs of API calls. For each new log we evaluate the likelihood that its API call sequence would be generated from each topic model ($P(D = x \mid y = c_i)$). We also estimate independent prior probability of a certain class ($P(y = c_i)$) by simply calculating the share of certain class in the labeled dataset. Using the MAP approach, we evaluate the conditional probability of a certain sample belonging to the class i:

$$P(y = c_i \mid D = x) = \frac{P(D = x \mid y = c_i)P(y = c_i)}{\sum_i P(D = x \mid y = c_i)P(y = c_i)} \tag{6}$$

After computing the conditional probabilities for all classes, we find the most probable class by maximization:

$$CLASS(x) = \underset{i}{\mathrm{argmax}}(P(y = c_i \mid D = x)) \tag{7}$$

Malware sample is classified to the class to which it belongs with the highest probability.

Once the separate classification procedures finish for the outputs of available static and dynamic malware analysis tools, we forward the classification results to the aggregation and postprocessing stage.

3.6 Result Aggregation and Postprocessing

Our semi-supervised learning method returns probabilities of malware belonging to the predefined classes. These probabilities are results of separate classification using our three data sources (i.e., PEInfo, Yara, and Cuckoo). We combine these results to get a reliable class probability estimation. In machine learning-based classification it is often beneficial to combine multiple data sources and different classifiers to reduce model overfitting and use advantages of different methods in one system [18]. This approach is called *ensemble learning*. Multiple methods of various sophistication exist for combining different classifiers. We argue that, since we do not have a large set of classifiers, there is no need for complicated ensemble learning approaches. In case of a larger number of data sources, an approach such as mixture of experts can be used, however, we did not notice any advantage of this approach in our case. For our experiments we use median and average of probability values, and majority voting of class assignments resulting from the three data sources. By aggregating the classification results, we get a more robust classifier. In fact, we combine the advantages of the static and dynamic analysis, to get a better classification performance. The combination of multiple views on data makes our results more reliable.

During the online classification procedure our system can detect the appearance of a new cluster. This can happen in one of the following cases: (*i*) new data has been put in the learning algorithm that contains a previously unknown label, or (*ii*) there is a new region of high local density that is detected during the execution of the learning algorithm. With the postprocessing algorithm, it is determined if the new sample can be confidently assigned to one of the existing classes, or a new class needs to be defined. Introduction of new classes can be done automatically by tuning the machine learning model, and in addition the new labels can be approved by a malware analyst. If we do not expect the new classes to appear very often, we can assign this job to the analyst, who can give a reliable estimation and help avoid possible mistakes in labeling. If indeed a new cluster is confirmed, the algorithm must be retrained in order to include this new fact into the machine learning model.

4   Evaluation

In this section we evaluate our approach. The extracted results prove advantages of topic models, semi-supervised methods, and combining results of static and dynamic malware analysis into a unified classification procedure.

For this purpose, we took ten recurring malware families from our labeled dataset of 2000 malware samples. The class titles were directly extracted from VirusTotal, where we manually chose signatures from multiple antivirus programs that were most prominent in our dataset. In addition to the labeled samples, we had 15,000 samples that we used as unlabeled, as the results of VirusTotal did not provide us with signatures for them. We then divided the dataset into training and test sets using a

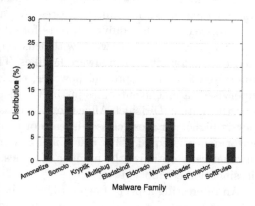

Fig. 4. Samples distribution by family.

variant of three-fold cross-validation. More precisely, the dataset is divided randomly in three parts, where two parts are used for training and the last part for evaluation. This division and accuracy experiment were repeated ten times and we took the average of the results. The distribution of samples in our dataset is mostly uniform, except for one significantly bigger and three smaller families (see Fig. 4). However, we take this into account in cross-validation when determining the training and test set, as well as during the evaluation of our approach.

Table 1. Accuracy evaluation of LDA for different number of topics.

Family	LDA for a different number of topics						HDP
	1(%)	5(%)	10(%)	20(%)	40(%)	80(%)	
Amonetize	0.0	0.0	10.0	100.0	100.0	100.0	100.0
Somoto	0.0	0.0	0.1	30.3	20.4	30.0	99.8
Kryptik	0.0	18.0	30.0	70.0	60.0	30.5	91.5
Multiplug	0.0	57.4	80.0	30.0	40.0	69.4	80.0
Bladabindi	0.0	1.7	5.7	4.0	7.0	10.3	93.0
Eldorado	0.0	0.0	0.0	0.0	0.0	0.0	54.4
Morstar	0.0	0.0	0.0	0.0	0.0	0.0	100.0
Preloader	0.0	0.0	7.5	71.0	50.0	60.0	100.0
SProtector	100.0	100.0	100.0	100.0	100.0	100.0	100.0
SoftPulse	0.0	4.2	4.1	6.7	5.0	6.9	86.2

4.1 Topic Models

Using the training set, we created a topic model for each class using HDP. We computed the statistical likelihood of drawing each particular sample from the model. Based on this likelihood we classified the samples using the already described MAP approach. Next, we executed ten cross-validation tests with a random division into training and test set and averaged the obtained results. We also executed the equivalent tests for LDA with different number of topics in order to compare our work with this approach. Table 1 displays the averaged results for different malware families. These results are obtained using the supervised learning approach, however, the distribution is similar in the semi-supervised case. The outcomes justify the use of Hierarchical Dirichlet Processes over the Latent Dirichlet Allocation. More specifically, the classification accuracy is higher for most classes in case of using HDP, and in the worst case the performance is equal. This result along with the property that the HDP can automatically optimize the number of topics, gives us an adaptive and accurate classification component.

An interesting aspect of using LDA is that depending on the malware family we want to detect, we should apply different number of topics. Although the overall results reveal a significant advantage when using a higher number of topics on average, the correlation is not clear for all the families we tested. An example of this is Multiplug which exhibits better detection accuracy by selecting just ten topics, while Amonetize offers better accuracy when selecting 20 or more topics. Unfortunately, we could not detect any samples that belong to Eldorado and Morstar families using LDA. One possible reason is that we did not find the optimal number of topics for these samples.

In our experiments we noticed that the topics that were results of our topic modeling experiment often have an obvious semantic meaning. This makes our

Table 2. Overview of main semantically relevant topics.

Registry manipulation	Memory management	File manipulation	Process handling
NtWriteFile	VirtualAllocEx	NtReadFile	OpenProcess
RegOpenKeyExW	VirtualQueryEx	NtWriteFile	ReadProcessMemory
RegCloseKey	VirtualQuery	NtDelayExecution	WriteProcessMemory
RegEnumValueW	VirtualFreeEx	LdrGetProcedureAddress	CloseHandle
RegQueryValueExW	VirtualFree	NtSetInformationFile	LocalAlloc
LdrGetProcedureAddress	LdrGetProcedureAddress	NtCreateFile	LocalFree
RegOpenKeyExA		NtQueryDirectoryFile	

Table 3. Comparative accuracy test using results from static and dynamic malware analysis data, separately and combined.

Family	[Cuckoo + HDP](%)	[Yara + LP](%)	[PEInfo + LP](%)	Average(%)	Median(%)	Majority(%)
Amonetize	100.0	99.6	100.0	100.0	100.0	100.0
Somoto	99.0	100.0	51.0	100.0	100.0	100.0
Kryptik	100.0	100.0	100.0	100.0	100.0	100.0
Multiplug	99.2	100.0	100.0	100.0	100.0	100.0
Bladabindi	93.2	96.6	100.0	96.6	96.6	99.0
Eldorado	56.6	80.2	83.0	84.9	86.8	81.0
Morstar	100.0	40.0	100.0	40.0	100.0	100.0
Preloader	100.0	100.0	100.0	100.0	100.0	100.0
SProtector	100.0	100.0	100.0	100.0	100.0	100.0
SoftPulse	86.1	88.8	0.0	88.8	88.8	77.8
Average	93.4	90.5	83.4	91.0	97.2	95.8

classification approach semantics-aware. Some examples of semantically meaningful topics are presented in Table 2. It is worth to mention that some kernel API calls belong to different topics simultaneously, which is a useful property of topic models, since activities represented by topics can consist of overlapping sets of operations.

4.2 Static and Dynamic Analysis Combination

Table 3 illustrates a comparison of classification accuracy of our three data sources, determined by executing cross-validation with these sources separately, using a semi-supervised procedure. More specifically, we combined on the one hand the Cuckoo sandbox with HDP, and on the other hand Yara and PEInfo with label propagation. It is evident from the results that even in cases with a small number of labeled samples we can achieve a sufficient accuracy. Furthermore, we notice that each separate data source is significant for the overall performance, as none of the data sources gives maximal classification accuracy for all classes. The maximal accuracy is, however, achieved when combining the three data sources. All the methods of combining results give a high accuracy for most of the families, with slight advantage for median and majority voting. These results justify our motivation for combining multiple data sources in order to get a better performance.

4.3   Comparing Supervised and Semi-supervised Learning

We gathered results from semi-supervised and fully supervised learning. Table 4 shows the comparison of results of both approaches, when taking median class probability from all available data sources as classification criterion. The two colons for semi-supervised learning represent two separate experiments that we executed in order to evaluate the advantages and disadvantages of a partially labeled sample set.

The first experiment for supervised and semi-supervised methods is done using the same set of labeled examples, with the difference that in the semi-supervised case two thirds of the labeled data are used as unlabeled. We can notice that despite of using only a small number of labeled examples, we can get an adequate performance in classification. This performance is provided by our label propagation procedure, where we used the local density around the labeled points to propagate the class affiliation through the affinity matrix.

For the second experiment we used the samples for which we do not have antivirus labels as unlabeled samples and attempt to improve the classification performance. This approach shows that in most classes we can obtain a marginal improvement in the classification performance, as the unlabeled data helps in inferring the high density regions in the dataset.

Finally, we compared our classification performance with the results from related papers. Our results on average represent a significant improvement with respect to the related work in terms of average accuracy.

4.4   Open World vs. Closed World

We measured the performance of our closed world experiment to an open world situation, where not all classes are known in advance. We did this by executing the cross-validation test, always leaving out one class from the training set. In the test phase, we classified the samples that belonged to one of the training classes with probability higher than 50 % into the appropriate training class. We put the samples which did not belong to any classes with such a high probability into the "outlier" class. Our hypothesis is that the "outlier" samples will be the ones belonging to the class that is missing from the training set. This method was previously used by Rieck et al. [27], where the drop in accuracy in the open world was around 20 %. Our experiments showed that in our case, for most of the families, the performance dropped by 10 % or less. However, our system could not reliably detect the family *Eldorado* in the open setting, as the performance drop was over 40 %. This may be due to the comparatively shorter system call sequences, which makes the discrimination against other classes more difficult.

Table 4. Performance experiment with fully supervised and semi-supervised classification models regarding the accuracy, precision, and recall.

Family	Supervised(%)			Semi-supervised(%)					
				1st Experiment			2nd Experiment		
	ACC	PR	RC	ACC	PR	RC	ACC	PR	RC
Amonetize	100.0	100.0	100.0	100.0	88.3	100.0	100.0	98.4	100.0
Somoto	100.0	100.0	100.0	93.6	72.2	93.3	100.0	96.8	100.0
Kryptik	100.0	100.0	100.0	100.0	86.4	100.0	100.0	100.0	100.0
Multiplug	100.0	100.0	100.0	100.0	100.0	100.0	100.0	100.0	100.0
Bladabindi	99.4	98.1	96.0	83.5	95.4	82.9	96.6	95.8	96.6
Eldorado	75.6	26.3	86.0	31.4	98.1	31.6	86.8	98.9	86.8
Morstar	100.0	98.5	100.0	99.2	97.5	99.2	100.0	99.0	100.0
Preloader	100.0	100.0	100.0	57.1	100.0	55.4	100.0	100.0	100.0
SProtector	100.0	100.0	100.0	100.0	100.0	100.0	100.0	100.0	100.0
SoftPulse	64.4	75.4	87.0	49.5	51.1	50.8	88.9	86.5	88.9
Average	93.9	89.8	96.9	81.4	88.9	81.3	**97.2**	**97.5**	**97.2**
Rieck et al. [27]	**88.0**	-	-	-	-	-	-	-	-
Dahl et al. [9]	**90.5**	-	-	-	-	-	-	-	-

4.5   Time of Training

In our last experiment we wanted to measure the time of training of our approach. Therefore, we executed various number of samples and measured the time frame in which the training was complete. Figure 5 illustrates the distribution of the time it takes to retrain the topic models on arrival of new data points. It is noticeable that training time growth is linear, which is acceptable in online setting, considering that usually computational complexity of

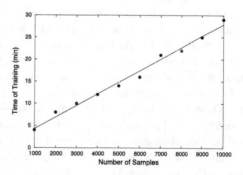

Fig. 5. Time of training.

topic models grows not only with the number of documents, but also with the number of topics [7].

4.6   Summary of Findings

The outcomes of our experiments reveal that our methodology is adaptive, as our topic model can deal with varying number of topics and with this outperforms the standard LDA approach. Additionally, we show the semantic awareness of our method by displaying topics retrieved from system call sequences. Furthermore, we justify our approach by showing performance advantages of semi-supervised learning and joining static and dynamic analysis results. Finally, we compare the performance of our approach to previous works and show improvement in classification accuracy. Overall, our approach can assist analysts by offering them a more accurate malware classification.

5   Discussion

The experiments provide an insight into the performance of the methods used in our classification system. Our classification accuracy experiment on topic models shows a comparison of HDP and LDA, where HDP outperforms LDA in most classes. Nevertheless, it is also noticeable that the overall accuracy varies between different classes. For most of the classes the accuracy is high, yet there exist outliers. An explanation for this would be the overall limited reliability of the ground truth labels based on the antivirus signatures and lack of possibility of explicit evaluation of label confidence. The results could be more reliable if a more trustworthy source of labels was available. For instance, it would be useful to initially perform unsupervised learning with unknown number of clusters and in addition enhance the results with custom labeling using the analyst domain knowledge. As a difference from work done by Xiao and Stibor [40], we use the sequence of kernel API calls as a bag-of-words (i.e., we ignore the information about order between the calls). This gives flexibility to our model, however, it may reduce accuracy. A further study is needed to experimentally compare these two approaches. Aside from the obtained accuracy of our classification, we are able to add another feature to our approach. This feature is the ability to extract semantics out of kernel API logs using inferred topics of Hierarchical Dirichlet Processes. Although a minority of the extracted topics has such an obvious semantic interpretation as in the presented examples, it can be very useful for a malware analyst to have such an insight.

In our evaluation, we compared results of static and dynamic malware analysis. While both static and dynamic analysis data were very useful for malware classification, the combination of the two methods proves to be the best of both worlds. Unfortunately, we had two data sources for static analysis data and only one source of dynamic analysis results. Therefore, the utilization of more data sources that provide additional data related to the program execution path, such as Drakvuf [19], would enhance the inference capability of our method.

Finally, we evaluated precision and recall of our classification and compared it with related work. Overall our system achieves a significant improvement over the previously published work in terms of classification performance, while retaining semantic model interpretation.

6   Related Work

This section contains the description of the research efforts that precede our work. These efforts are mostly divided into research dedicated to (*i*) application of machine learning methods in malware analysis and (*ii*) designing systems to support the malware analysis process. Therefore we explain the evolution and current state of those two groups of methods separately. Furthermore, we explain how the methodology used in our approach takes into account the related papers and builds a new approach upon this work.

6.1   Machine Learning Methods for Malware Detection

Machine learning has been used in multiple research efforts as a malware detection and classification method. Various features that characterize program behavior have been used as input data for the machine learning-based procedures: system calls [37], registry accesses [16], and network packets [31]. These event sequences are analyzed using unsupervised (e.g., clustering), semi-supervised, or supervised learning (classification) methods. Static program code features have also been deployed for malware classification [29]. The classification methods can be further divided into one-class anomaly detection [16], binary classification [24], and multiclass learning [27]. One-class classification is used in case that we want to create a model for normal behavior (benign samples) and detect malware as a deviation from that model. In binary classification we optimize the classification boundary between benign and malicious samples. Multiclass classification methods are able to differentiate between different— previously known and defined—classes of malware instead or in addition to differentiating between benign and malicious samples.

Researchers that perform malware detection, usually maintain a sample set from different malware families with their static and behavioral patterns, and use them as a baseline to properly classify the suspicious applications. For instance, in the case of sequential data, automatic methods for extraction of relevant features can be used to cope with the possibly noisy and high-dimensional data. An example of this is given by recent application of statistical topic modeling approaches to the classification of system call sequences [40]. This approach could be extended by taking system call arguments as additional information and including memory allocation patterns and other traceable operations [39]. Support vector machines with string kernels represent an another novel methodology, where a standard classification scheme is augmented to work robustly with system call sequences of variable length [24]. However, most of these approaches only consider malware detection, and do not focus on classifying malware samples into families. Another example of sequential data is the network traffic. Towards this direction, the network traffic produced by the analyzed samples can be classified by taking into account the frequency and length of different types of packets or generating n-gram features out of packet payloads. As a matter of fact, researchers have already proposed various approaches to model the network data and design anomaly detection procedures for network infrastructures with purpose of network security [13, 20, 30, 41].

Previous works have considered many potential solutions for semantics-aware malware classification and analysis, including topic modeling. However, they have not dealt with the typical setting in malware analysis systems where a high number of samples is acquired online and models must be updated to give an accurate result. Therefore their methodology is only adequate in a scenario of offline malware analysis.

6.2 Big Data Malware Analysis Systems

Since security companies get overwhelmed with hundreds of thousands of malware samples on a daily basis, the problem of malware classification can be defined as a *Big Data* problem. Recently, there have been many efforts to create Big Data platforms for malware analysis. Examples of such systems are BinaryPig [14], Polonium [8], BitShred [17], and WINE [11]. BinaryPig is a system for distributed processing of data obtained by static malware analysis, leveraging the recent advances in tools for Big Data domain. It uses Hadoop File System, MapReduce, and ElasticSearch as building blocks for scalable processing of static analysis data. Polonium is an another system for large-scale mining of malware. It leverages graph mining approaches to build a reputation-based system to identify malware among terabytes of anonymously submitted suspicious files. BitShred, on the other hand, is an attempt to design and build a scalable malware analysis system. It focuses on increasing efficiency of similarity analysis with feature hashing and uses similarity information for clustering. Finally, WINE is an approach that leverages Big Data and creates a scalable reputation-based security intelligence system, which also includes intrusion detection for network-based attacks.

These systems use machine learning-based technology and represent advances in scalability of malware detection and feature extraction. However, they do not emphasize on the development of statistical methods and do not consider semantic interpretability of the statistical models. Machine learning models very often need tuning and the absence of semantics can make such efforts extremely difficult for malware analysts. It is very important for analysts to be able to interpret the model in order to focus their efforts properly. In our approach, we do not only consider advanced topic modeling methodology for semantics-aware modeling, but we also take into account the scenario that a high influx of malware induces changes in the dataset and requires adaptation of the classification model. We automate this adaptation in order to maintain topic modeling feature extraction, using the nonparametric modeling methodology. Furthermore, our approach joins results of static and dynamic malware analysis and acknowledges the case where labeled examples are scarce.

7 Conclusion

In this paper, we presented an improved semi-supervised malware classification approach that joins the results from static and dynamic malware analysis to give an optimal classification performance. It uses separate algorithms for classification of static and dynamic analysis results: static analysis results are classified using a semi-supervised label propagation procedure, while the results from dynamic malware analysis are preprocessed by statistical topic modeling, which uncovers the latent semantically interpretable topics that capture the important properties of malware families. The method used for topic modeling is flexible and offers automatic adjustment of the topic set in case of online learning. Overall, our nonparametric approach creates an adaptive online system for malware classification that outperforms previous approaches.

Acknowledgments. The research was supported by the German Federal Ministry of Education and Research under grant 16KIS0328 (IUNO) and by the Bavarian State Ministry of Education, Science and the Arts as part of the FORSEC research association.

References

1. The Cuckoo Sandbox. https://www.cuckoosandbox.org/
2. VirusTotal. http://www.virustotal.com
3. Alvarez, V.M.: Yara. http://plusvic.github.io/yara/
4. Anderson, B., Storlie, C., Lane, T.: Improving malware classification: bridging the static/dynamic gap. In: Workshop on Security and Artificial Intelligence (AISec) (2012)
5. Bailey, M., Oberheide, J., Andersen, J., Mao, Z.M., Jahanian, F., Nazario, J.: Automated classification and analysis of internet malware. In: Kruegel, C., Lippmann, R., Clark, A. (eds.) RAID 2007. LNCS, vol. 4637, pp. 178–197. Springer, Heidelberg (2007)
6. Bayer, U., Comparetti, P.M., Hlauschek, C., Kruegel, C., Kirda, E.: Scalable, behavior-based malware clustering. In: ISOC Network and Distributed System Security Symposium (NDSS) (2009)
7. Blei, D.M., Ng, A.Y., Jordan, M.I.: Latent Dirichlet allocation. J. Mach. Learn. Res. **3**, 993–1022 (2003)
8. Chau, D.H., Nachenberg, C., Wilhelm, J., Wright, A., Faloutsos, C.: Polonium: tera-scale graph mining and inference for malware detection. In: SIAM International Conference on Data Mining (SDM) (2011)
9. Dahl, G.E., Stokes, J.W., Deng, L., Yu, D.: Large-scale malware classification using random projections and neural networks. In: IEEE International Conference on Acoustics, Speech and Signal Processing (ICASSP) (2013)
10. Dumais, S.T.: Latent semantic analysis. Ann. Rev. Inf. Sci. Technol. **38**(1), 188–230 (2004)
11. Dumitras, T., Shou, D.: Toward a standard benchmark for computer security research: the Worldwide Intelligence Network Environment (WINE). In: Workshop on Building Analysis Datasets and Gathering Experience Returns for Security (BADGERS) (2011)
12. Ester, M., Kriegel, H.-P., Sander, J., Xu, X.: A density-based algorithm for discovering clusters in large spatial databases with noise. In: Kdd (1996)
13. Garcia-Teodoro, P., Diaz-Verdejo, J., Maciá-Fernández, G., Vázquez, E.: Anomaly-based network intrusion detection: techniques, systems and challenges. Comput. Secur. **28**(1), 18–28 (2009)
14. Hanif, Z., Calhoun, T., Trost, J.: Binarypig: Scalable Static Binary Analysis Over Hadoop. Black Hat, USA (2013)

15. Hanif, Z., Lengyel, T.K., Webster, G.D.: Internet-Scale File Analysis. Black Hat, USA (2015)
16. Heller, K., Svore, K., Keromytis, A.D., Stolfo, S.: One class support vector machines for detecting anomalous windows registry accesses. In: Workshop on Data Mining for Computer Security (DMSEC) (2003)
17. Jang, J., Brumley, D., Venkataraman, S.: Bitshred: feature hashing malware for scalable triage and semantic analysis. In: Conference on Computer and Communications Security (CCS) (2011)
18. Kuncheva, L.I.: Combining Pattern Classifiers: Methods and Algorithms. Wiley, New York (2004)
19. Lengyel, T.K., Maresca, S., Payne, B.D., Webster, G.D., Vogl, S., Kiayias, A.: Scalability, fidelity and stealth in the Drakvuf dynamic malware analysis system. In: Annual Computer Security Applications Conference (ACSAC) (2014)
20. Leung, K., Leckie, C.: Unsupervised anomaly detection in network intrusion detection using clusters. In: Australasian Conference on Computer Science (2005)
21. Maxwell, K.: Maltrieve. https://github.com/krmaxwell/maltrieve
22. Newman, D., Chemudugunta, C., Smyth, P., Steyvers, M.: Analyzing entities and topics in news articles using statistical topic models. In: Mehrotra, S., Zeng, D.D., Chen, H., Thuraisingham, B., Wang, F.-Y. (eds.) ISI 2006. LNCS, vol. 3975, pp. 93–104. Springer, Heidelberg (2006)
23. Perdisci, R., U, M.C.: VAMO: towards a fully automated malware clustering validity analysis. In: Annual Computer Security Applications Conference (ACSAC) (2012)
24. Pfoh, J., Schneider, C., Eckert, C.: Leveraging string kernels for malware detection. In: Lopez, J., Huang, X., Sandhu, R. (eds.) NSS 2013. LNCS, vol. 7873, pp. 206–219. Springer, Heidelberg (2013)
25. Ramage, D., Hall, D., Nallapati, R., Manning, C.D.: Labeled LDA: a supervised topic model for credit attribution in multi-labeled corpora. In: Conference on Empirical Methods in Natural Language Processing (2009)
26. Řehůřek, R., Sojka, P.: Software framework for topic modelling with large corpora. In: Workshop on New Challenges for NLP Frameworks (2010)
27. Rieck, K., Holz, T., Willems, C., Düssel, P., Laskov, P.: Learning and classification of malware behavior. In: Zamboni, D. (ed.) DIMVA 2008. LNCS, vol. 5137, pp. 108–125. Springer, Heidelberg (2008)
28. Roberts, J.-M.: Virus Share. https://virusshare.com/
29. Schultz, M.G., Eskin, E., Zadok, F., Stolfo, S.J.: Data mining methods for detection of new malicious executables. In: Symposium on Security and Privacy (2001)
30. Stringhini, G., Egele, M., Zarras, A., Holz, T., Kruegel, C., Vigna, G.: B@bel: leveraging email delivery for spam mitigation. In: USENIX Security Symposium (2012)
31. Tegeler, F., Fu, X., Vigna, G., Kruegel, C.: Botfinder: finding bots in network traffic without deep packet inspection. In: International Conference on Emerging Networking Experiments and Technologies (CoNEXT) (2012)
32. Teh, Y.W., Jordan, M.I., Beal, M.J., Blei, D.M.: Hierarchical Dirichlet processes. J. Am. Stat. Assoc. **101**(476), 1566–1581 (2006)
33. The MITRE Corporation. CRITS. https://crits.github.io/
34. VirusTotal. File Statistics. https://www.virustotal.com/en/statistics/
35. Wainwright, M.J., Jordan, M.I.: Graphical models, exponential families, and variational inference. Found. Trends Mach. Learn. **1**, 1–305 (2008)

36. Wang, C., Paisley, J.W., Blei, D.M.: Online variational inference for the hierarchical Dirichlet process. In: International Conference on Artificial Intelligence and Statistics (2011)
37. Warrender, C., Forrest, S., Pearlmutter, B.: Detecting intrusions using system calls: alternative data models. In: Symposium on Security and Privacy (1999)
38. Wicherski, G.: Pehash: a novel approach to fast malware clustering. In: USENIX Workshop on Large-Scale Exploits and Emergent Threats (LEET) (2009)
39. Xiao, H., Eckert, C.: Efficient online sequence prediction with side information. In: IEEE International Conference on Data Mining (ICDM) (2013)
40. Xiao, H., Stibor, T.: A supervised topic transition model for detecting malicious system call sequences. In: Workshop on Knowledge Discovery, Modeling and Simulation (2011)
41. Zarras, A., Papadogiannakis, A., Gawlik, R., Holz, T.: Automated generation of models for fast and precise detection of HTTP-based malware. In: Annual Conference on Privacy, Security and Trust (PST) (2014)
42. Zhou, D., Bousquet, O., Lal, T.N., Weston, J., Schölkopf, B.: Learning with local and global consistency. Adv. Neural Inf. Process. Syst. **16**(16), 321–328 (2004)

Author Index

Printed in the United States
By Bookmasters